THE CONSTITUTION OF MALAYSIA
ITS DEVELOPMENT: 1957—1977

THE CONSTITUTION OF MALAYSIA

ITS DEVELOPMENT: 1957–1977

Edited by

TUN MOHAMED SUFFIAN
Lord President of the Federal Court of Malaysia

H. P. LEE
Lecturer in Law, Monash University, Melbourne

F. A. TRINDADE
Associate Professor, Faculty of Law
Monash University, Melbourne

1978

KUALA LUMPUR
OXFORD UNIVERSITY PRESS
OXFORD NEW YORK MELBOURNE
1978

Oxford University Press
OXFORD LONDON GLASGOW
NEW YORK TORONTO MELBOURNE WELLINGTON
KUALA LUMPUR SINGAPORE JAKARTA HONG KONG TOKYO
DELHI BOMBAY CALCUTTA MADRAS KARACHI
IBADAN NAIROBI DAR ES SALAAM CAPE TOWN
● *Oxford University Press 1978*

ISBN 0 19 580406 6 (*boards*)
ISBN 0 19 580405 8 (*limp*)

The Publishers wish to thank the Lee Foundation
for a generous grant which has been used
to subsidize the paperback edition

*Printed in Singapore by Dainippon Tien Wah (Pte) Ltd.
Published by Oxford University Press, 3, Jalan 13/3,
Petaling Jaya, Selangor, Malaysia*

✎ TUN MOHAMED SUFFIAN
Lord President of the Federal Court, Malaysia

Foreword

THIS book records developments during the first twenty years of the life of the Malayan—since 1963 Malaysian—Constitution in its various aspects. The idea of compiling this book was conceived—of all places—in the Law Faculty of Monash University, Melbourne, Australia, by Professor Francis Trindade and H. P. Lee, whose love is constitutional law. Trindade had lectured on Malaysian and Singapore constitutional law at the University of Singapore, and Lee, a native of Penang, won his LL.M. at the University of Malaya after having obtained his LL.B. at the University of Singapore. Living in far-away Australia they see more sharply than those living in Malaysia that our constitutional developments during the first two decades merit examination and study.

The question has been asked why review constitutional developments during the first twenty years—why not during the first twenty-five or fifty years? I suppose the answer is that we co-editors happen to be around now. It is hoped that others after us will produce a similar book reviewing our constitutional developments during the first twenty-five or fifty years of this newly independent country—for by then it is not likely that all three of us will have much steam left even if we are still around.

In 1976 when I was an official guest in the United States together with three jurists from Asia to take part in celebrating the Bicentenary of American Independence, and to speak at various universities and other learned institutions on the influence of the sparsely-worded American Constitution on constitutions in Asia, I often thought then how lucky Malaysia would have been if our Constitution could last fifty years, let alone 200 years—seeing that (a) our Constitution makers were not content with merely stating general principles but instead wrote in a lot of detailed provisions which old-time draftsmen would have left to the ordinary law, and (b) the carefully drafted constitutions of some thirty new Commonwealth countries had in these revolutionary times been torn up by as many colonels and generals.

Well, certainly so far Malaysians who value continuity and stability have been lucky and the Malaysian Constitution, despite many amendments, is still recognizable by its makers, and for that we should be grateful to our leaders. They are not brilliant theorists but mostly experienced ex-civil servants and sensible down-to-earth persons (some of them lawyers) who know that they cannot please all the people all the time, that there are constraints which even the best intentions in the world have to reckon with, and that government, like politics, is the art of the possible. They have a firm grasp of the realities of the country, have to get the people to understand the limits of choice and to recognize that political leaders and voters must together adapt, adjust, amend, and accommodate to changing realities within the agreed constitutional framework.

The essays in this volume have been written by two kinds of contributors:

1. Academics who teach law, who have time to read, digest, absorb, and think, and who have the expertise to teach theories and concepts to fire young law students with an interest in constitutional law, which is quite a daunting task. When a student myself I found constitutional law a very dull subject—compared for instance with criminal law which is full of drama; and it was only when I worked in the Attorney-General's department and had to refer to the Constitution almost every other day that for me constitutional law became alive;

2. The other kind of contributors to this volume consists of officials in the public service who actually operate the Constitution and who have the responsibility to see that it works and works well in practice—quite a delicate task in a multi-racial Federation of States at different stages of development, a Federation with many divergent interests pulling in different directions.

It will be seen that their essays contain nuggets of inside information of great interest. The fact that the essays herein have been written by these two kinds of contributors will, it is hoped, enhance the value of this volume and widen its appeal—not only in universities and in the legal profession and amongst law students, but also amongst past, present, and future ministers and other politicians, amongst civil servants, and even amongst other members of the public who follow and wish to understand the news that they read in their daily papers.

A British Prime Minister has said that a week is a long time in politics. Twenty years is a very long time indeed in the politics of a newly independent country. Within that period Malaysia has seen rapid advances in many areas made possible by political stability. This stability has been made possible by a workable and living Constitution. If during the next two decades Malaysians of all races and ranks continue to exhibit the same spirit of goodwill and tolerance, the same degree of common sense, keeping under control racial, religious, and linguistic fanaticism, as in the past twenty years, many of us would have good reason to be optimistic about the future.

Lord President's Chambers,   TUN MOHAMED SUFFIAN
Federal Court,
Kuala Lumpur,
18 January 1978

Contents

Foreword by the Lord President of the Federal
   Court of Malaysia   v
Preface   xi
Notes on Contributors   xiii
Table of Cases   xv
Table of Statutes   xx

1. AN OVERVIEW OF CONSTITUTIONAL
   CHANGES IN MALAYSIA:1957-1977
   R. H. Hickling   1

2. FUNDAMENTAL LIBERTIES IN THE
   CONSTITUTION OF THE FEDERATION
   OF MALAYSIA
   H. E. Groves   27

3. THE POSITION OF ISLAM IN THE
   CONSTITUTION OF MALAYSIA
   Ahmad Ibrahim   41

4. THE CITIZENSHIP LAWS OF MALAYSIA
   Visu Sinnadurai   69

5. THE CONSTITUTIONAL POSITION OF THE
   YANG DI-PERTUAN AGONG
   F. A. Trindade   101

6. MINISTERIAL RESPONSIBILITY IN
   MALAYSIA
   M. C. Puthucheary   123

7. THE MALAYSIAN PARLIAMENT
Nik Abdul Rashid   136

8. FEDERALISM IN MALAYSIA—CHANGES
IN THE FIRST TWENTY YEARS
Tan Sri Datuk Mohd. Salleh bin Abas   163

9. PROBLEMS OF HARMONIZING THE LAWS
IN THE MALAYSIAN FEDERATION
Tan Sri D. B. W. Good   192

10. DEVELOPMENTS IN THE LAW
CONCERNING ELECTIONS IN MALAYSIA
Yaacob Hussain Merican   208

11. THE JUDICIARY—DURING THE FIRST
TWENTY YEARS OF INDEPENDENCE
Tun Mohamed Suffian   231

12. THE PUBLIC SERVICE AND PUBLIC
SERVANTS IN MALAYSIA
V. S. Winslow   263

13. FINANCIAL PROVISIONS OF THE
MALAYSIAN CONSTITUTION AND THEIR
OPERATION IN PRACTICE
Tan Sri Dato' Abdullah bin Ayub   304

14. EMERGENCY POWERS IN MALAYSIA
S. Jayakumar   328

15. THE PROCESS OF CONSTITUTIONAL
CHANGE IN MALAYSIA
H. P. Lee   369

Index   413

Preface

IT is not necessary to find an excuse for publishing a volume of essays on the Malaysian Constitution. There is not an abundance of legal literature on the subject and a volume of essays which examines the development of the Constitution over the last twenty years will, we are sure, be welcomed by all those involved or interested in the constitutional law of Malaysia.

In one sense, the Constitution has stood the test of time; the Constitution of the Federation of Malaya which came into existence on 31 August 1957 still provides the basic framework of the present-day Malaysian Constitution. In another sense however the Constitution could be said to have been much changed. Constantly changing economic, political and social circumstances have been reflected in the various amendments to the Constitution and it would be foolish to pretend that the document of 1957 is in no way different from the document of 1977. Nevertheless as Tun Suffian has pointed out in his Foreword, the changes have been wrought within the existing constitutional and legal framework and revolutionary situations have been avoided. This volume, in its various essays, looks at those changes and each contributor was asked to consider the development of the Constitution during the course of the last twenty years.

The contributors to this volume have all at one time or another written on various aspects of the Malaysian Constitution. Several of them are intimately associated with its operation in practice. All were invited to contribute to this volume by the editors and we are grateful to them for their prompt and scholarly response.

The essays deal with developments between 31 August 1957 and 31 August 1977 but in a few instances, editorial licence has permitted the extension of that period to take into account more recent developments of some significance.

And now to our many debts. We are particularly grateful to Tun Suffian who not only encouraged us to bring this volume to fruition but who also as joint editor with us took on more than his fair share of editorial responsibility for the volume. He has also been kind enough to write the Foreword. To the Faculty of Law, Monash University we record our thanks for assistance in various ways. To the Lee Foundation in Malaysia we express our appreciation for a generous donation which will enable students to purchase this book at a considerably reduced price.

Faculty of Law,   F. A. TRINDADE
Monash University,   H. P. LEE
Melbourne,
April 1978

Notes on Contributors

TAN SRI DATUK HAJI MOHD. SALLEH b. ABAS
Solicitor-General of Malaysia. Author of *Prinsip Perlembagaan dan Pemerentahan Malaysia*.

TAN SRI DATO' ABDULLAH b. AYUB
Secretary-General, Ministry of Finance, Malaysia. Author of *Cara Pemerintahan Tanah Melayu*.

TAN SRI D. B. W. GOOD
Chairman, Advisory Board, Malaysia. Former Judge of the High Court, Malaya and of the Court of Appeal, Malaya, and formerly Law Revision Commissioner of Malaysia.

H. E. GROVES
Dean of Law, North Carolina Central University, Durham, North Carolina, U.S.A. Formerly Dean, Faculty of Law, University of Singapore. Author of *The Constitution of Malaysia* (1964). Joint author of *The Constitution of Malaysia* (1967).

R. H. HICKLING
Lecturer in Law, School of Oriental and African Studies, London. Formerly Visiting Professor of Law, University of Singapore. Formerly Law Revision Commissioner of Malaysia. Editor of *Malaysian Constitutional Documents* and author of *An Introduction to the Federal Constitution*.

AHMAD IBRAHIM
Professor and Dean, Faculty of Law, University of Malaya, Malaysia. Author of *Towards a History of Law in Malaysia and Singapore*, *The Distribution of Estates According to Shafii Law*, etc.

S. JAYAKUMAR
Associate Professor and Dean, Faculty of Law, University of Singapore. Author of *Constitutional Law Cases from Malaysia and Singapore*, etc.

H. P. LEE
Lecturer in Constitutional Law, Monash University, Melbourne, Australia.

DR. YAACOB HUSSAIN MERICAN
Advocate and Solicitor, High Court of Malaya, Malaysia.

DR. M. C. PUTHUCHEARY
Associate Professor, Faculty of Economics and Administration, University of Malaya, Malaysia.

NIK ABDUL RASHID
Associate Professor and Vice-Dean, Faculty of Law, University of Malaya, Malaysia.

VISU SINNADURAI
Associate Professor, Faculty of Law, University of Malaya, Malaysia.

TUN MOHAMED SUFFIAN
Lord President of the Federal Court of Malaysia. Author of *An Introduction to the Constitution of Malaysia*, etc.

F. A. TRINDADE
Associate Professor, Faculty of Law, Monash University, Melbourne, Australia. Formerly Lecturer in Constitutional Law, University of Singapore.

V. S. WINSLOW
Senior Lecturer in Constitutional Law, University of Singapore.

Table of Cases

Abdul Rahman Talib v. *Seenivasagam & Anor.* [1965] 31
M.L.J. 142; [1966] 2 M.L.J. 66 134
Ah Thian v. *Government of Malaysia* [1976] 2 M.L.J. 112 260
Ainan v. *Syed Abubakar* [1939] M.L.J. 209 65
Akar v. *Attorney-General of Sierra Leone* [1969] 3 All E.R.
384 412
Amalgamated Union of Public Employees v. *Permanent Secretary*
(Health) [1965] 2 M.L.J. 209 .... 281, 287, 302
Aminah v. *Superintendent of Prisons, Pengkalan Chepa, Kelantan*
[1968] 1 M.L.J. 92 .... 17, 26, 39
Anchom binte Lampong v. *Public Prosecutor* [1940] M.L.J. 22 ..... 44, 66
Anisminic v. *Foreign Compensation Commission* [1969] 2 A.C.
147 .... 287, 355
Arumugam Pillai v. *Govt. of Malaysia* [1975] 2 M.L.J. 29 ...... 35, 39
Asma Jilani v. *Government of Punjab* P.L.D. 1972 S.C. 139 ...... 63, 64
Assa Singh v. *Mentri Besar, Johore* [1969] 2 M.L.J. 30 .. 17, 26, 40, 249
Attorney-General, Singapore v. *Ling How Doong* [1969] 1
M.L.J. 154 .... 290, 302
Augustine v. *Commissioner of Police* [1964] 30 M.L.J. 438 161
Australian Communist Party v. *The Commonwealth* [1951] 83
C.L.R. 1 344
B. v. *Comptroller of Inland Revenue* [1974] 2 M.L.J. 110 40
Bakar bin Ahmad v. *Public Prosecutor* (1969, Unreported) 39
Bhagat Singh & Ors. v. *The King Emperor* [1931] L.R. 58
I.A. 169 337
C.B. Reilly v. *R.* [1934] A.C. 176 .... 301, 302
Chia Khin Sze v. *Mentri Besar, State of Selangor* [1958]
M.L.J. 105 16
Chik Kwan v. *The British Resident, Selangor* (1931–2)
F.M.S.L.R. 271; [1932] 1 M.L.J. 99 72

Comptroller-General of Inland Revenue v. N.P. [1973] 1
M.L.J. 165 31
Datuk James Wong Kim Min v. Minister of Home Affairs,
Malaysia & Ors. [1976] 2 M.L.J. 245 191
Dhingra v. Union of India [1958] S.C.R. 828 301
Doresamy v. Public Services Commission [1971] 2 M.L.J. 127 291
Enderby Town Football Club Ltd. v. The Football Association
Ltd. [1971] 1 All E.R. 215 303
Eng Keock Cheng v. Public Prosecutor [1966] 1 M.L.J. 18, 19, 36,
40, 151, 340
Errington v. Minister of Health [1935] 1 K.B. 249 302
Fan Yew Teng v. Public Prosecutor [1975] 2 M.L.J. 235 .... 40, 343
Fan Yew Teng v. Setia Usaha, Dewan Ra'ayat & Ors. [1975]
2 M.L.J. 41 222
Francis v. Municipal Councillors of Kuala Lumpur [1962]
M.L.J. 407 302
Gnanasundram v. Government of Malaysia [1971] 1 M.L.J.
208 302
Government of Malaysia v. Government of the State of Kelantan
[1968] 1 M.L.J. 129 249
Government of Malaysia v. Iznan bin Osman [1975]
2 M.L.J. 61 .... 294, 295, 296, 303
Government of Malaysia v. Lionel [1974]
1 M.L.J. 3 .... 18, 26, 280, 286, 301, 302
Government of Malaysia v. Mahan Singh [1975]
2 M.L.J. 155 .... 276, 279, 280, 283, 284, 301, 341
Government of Malaysia v. Rosalind Oh Lee Pek Inn [1973] 1
M.L.J. 22 281
Government of Malaysia & Anor. v. Selangor Pilot Association
[1977] 1 M.L.J. 133 34
Government of Malaysia v. Zainal bin Hashim [1977] 2
M.L.J. 254 .... 224, 225, 296, 410
Government of the State of Kelantan v. The Government of the
Federation of Malaya and Tunku Abdul Rahman Putra Al-Haj
[1963] M.L.J. 355 .... .25, 171, 191, 373, 376
Haji Ariffin v. Government of Pahang [1969]
1 M.L.J. 6, 10 .... 18, 276, 277, 278, 280, 284, 300, 302
Haji Wan Othman & Ors. v. Government of the Federation of
Malaya [1965] 2 M.L.J. 31 .... 276, 280, 301
I. C. Golak Nath & Ors. v. State of Punjab & Ors. [1967] 2
S.C.R. 762 .... 391, 411
Indira Nehru Gandhi v. Raj Narain A.I.R. 1975 S.C. 2299 411
Iznan bin Osman v. Government of Malaysia [1977] 2 M.L.J.
1 (P.C.) 387
Jacob v. Attorney-General [1970] 2 M.L.J. 133 ... 277, 287, 290, 294, 302
Johnson Tan Han Seng v. Public Prosecutor [1977] 2 M.L.J.
66 .... 340, 342, 348

Karam Singh v. *Mentri Hal Ehwal Dalam Negeri, Malaysia*
[1969] 2 M.L.J. 129, 136 .... 18, 26, 35, 351, 352, 355, 356
Kathiravalupillai v. *Government of Malaysia* [1976] 2 M.L.J.
114 303
Koh Yin Chye v. *Leong Kee Nyean* [1961] 2 M.L.J. 67 222
Kung Aik v. *Public Prosecutor* [1970] 2 M.L.J. 174 40
Lai Tai v. *The Collector of Land Revenue* [1960] M.L.J. 82 40
Land Acquisition by the State of Selangor, In Re, [1950] M.L.J.
152 260
Lee Mau Seng v. *Minister for Home Affairs, Singapore & Anor.*
[1971] 2 M.L.J. 137 .... 331, 332, 334, 353
Liew Shin Lai v. *Minister for Home Affairs* [1970] 2 M.L.J.
7 92
Lim Lian Geok v. *Minister of the Interior, Federation of Malaya*
[1964] M.L.J. 158 87
Lim Sing Hiaw v. *Public Prosecutor* [1965] 1 M.L.J. 85 40
Liversidge v. *Anderson* [1942] A.C. 206 337
Loh Kooi Choon v. *Government of Malaysia* [1977] 2 M.L.J.
187 .... 223, 387, 388, 390
Madhavan Nair v. *Government of Malaysia* [1975] 2 M.L.J.
286 .... 116, 119, 336, 339, 345
Madhavan Nair & Anor. v. *Public Prosecutor* [1975] 2 M.L.J.
264 40
Mah Kah Yew v. *Public Prosecutor* [1971] 1 M.L.J. 1 258
Mak Sik Kwong v. *Minister of Home Affairs, Malaysia* [1975]
2 M.L.J. 168 .... 89, 90, 92
Mak Sik Kwong v. *Minister of Home Affairs, Malaysia (No. 2)*
[1975] 2 M.L.J. 175 92
Melan bin Abdullah & Anor. v. *Public Prosecutor* [1971] 2
M.L.J. 281 343
Minister of Home Affairs v. *Chu Choon Yong & Anor.* [1977]
2 M.L.J. 20 40
Mohamed Sidin v. *Public Prosecutor* [1967] 1 M.L.J. 106 40
Mundell v. *Mellor* [1929] S.S.L.R. 152 291
Munusamy v. *Public Services Commission* [1967] 1 M.L.J. 199 .. 283, 301
Munusamy v. *Subramaniam & Ors.* [1969] 2 M.L.J. 108 .... 30, 31
Myriam v. *Ariff* [1971] 1 M.L.J. 265 65
Najar Singh v. *Government of Malaysia & Anor.* [1974] 1
M.L.J. 138 .... 290, 303
Niaz Ahmad Khan v. *Sind* P.L.J. 1977 Kar. 338 68
Nusrat Bhutto v. *Chief of Army Staff and Federation of Pakistan*
P.L.J. 1978 S.C. 47 68
Ong Yew Teck, Re [1960] M.L.J. 67 352
Ooi Ah Phua v. *Officer-in-Charge, Criminal Investigations,*
Kedah/Perlis [1975] 2 M.L.J. 198 39
Osman & Anor. v. *Public Prosecutor* [1968] 2 M.L.J. 137 .... 40, 152, 340,
341

P.E. Long @ Jimmy & Ors., Re [1976] 2 M.L.J. 133 ....352, 354
Pett v. *Greyhound Racing Association, Ltd.* [1968] 2 All E.R.
    545 302
Phang Moh Shin v. *Commissioner of Police & Ors.* [1967] 2
    M.L.J. 186 .... 290, 302
Philip Hoalim Jr. & Anor. v. *State Commissioner, Penang*
    [1974] 2 M.L.J. 100 40
Pillai v. *State of Kedah* 6 F.M.S.L.R. 160 276
Ponnambalam, G.G., In Re, [1969] 2 M.L.J. 263 39
Powell v. *Apollo Candle Co.* (1885) 10 A.C. 282 162
Public Prosecutor v. *Adnan bin Khamis* [1972] 1 M.L.J. 274 258
Public Prosecutor v. *Anthony Wee Boon Chye* [1965] 1 M.L.J.
    189 .... 18, 26
Public Prosecutor v. *Datuk Harun bin Haji Idris* [1977] 1
    M.L.J. 14 254
Public Prosecutor v. *Joseph Chin Saiko* [1972] 2 M.L.J. 129 258
Public Prosecutor v. *Khong Teng Khen & Anor.* [1976] 2
    M.L.J. 166 .... 152, 341, 342, 344, 365
Public Prosecutor v. *Mills* [1977] 1 M.L.J. 4 258
Public Prosecutor v. *Musa* [1970] 1 M.L.J. 101 .... 40, 356
Public Prosecutor v. *Ooi Kee Saik & Ors.* [1971] 2 M.L.J.
    108 .... 40, 337, 340, 343, 344, 364
Public Prosecutor v. *Ramasami* [1970] 2 M.L.J. 71 99
Public Prosecutor v. *Tengku Mahmood Iskandar & Anor.*
    [1973] 1 M.L.J. 128 32
R. v. *Burah* (1883) 9 A.C. 117 162
R. v. *Governor of Brixton Prison* [1962] 2 Q.B. 243 337
Rajion bin Haji Sulaiman v. *Government of Kelantan* [1976] 1
    M.L.J. 118 282
Ratnavale v. *The Government of the Federation of Malaya*
    [1963] M.L.J. 393 285
Reynolds v. *United States* 98 U.S. 155, 25 L.Ed. 244 (1878) 37
Ridge v. *Baldwin* (1964) A.C. 40 275
Sajjan Singh v. *State of Rajasthan* [1965] 1 S.C.R. 933 411
Sambasivam v. *Public Services Commission* [1970] 1 M.L.J. 61 302
Selangor Pilot Association (1946) v. *Government of Malaysia &*
    Anor. [1975] 2 M.L.J. 66 19
Shankari Prasad v. *Union of India* [1952] S.C.R. 89 411
Sithambaran v. *Attorney-General* [1972] 2 M.L.J. 175 .... 291, 302
Soon Chi Hiang, In Re, [1969] 1 M.L.J. 218 92
Soon Kok Leong v. *Minister of the Interior, Malaysia* [1968] 2
    M.L.J. 88 92
State v. *Zia-ur-Rahman* P.L.D. 1973 S.C. 49 .... 62, 64
State of Bombay v. *Atma Ram* A.I.R. 1951 S.C. 157 355
Stephen Kalong Ningkan v. *Government of Malaysia*
    [1968] 2 M.L.J. 238 (P.C.) 7, 25, 116, 121, 336, 337, 346
    [1968] 1 M.L.J. 119 (F.C.) 116, 121, 335, 336, 337,
                                                338, 346, 364, 365

Stephen Kalong Ningkan v. *Tun Abang Haji Openg and Tawi
Sli* [1966] 2 M.L.J. 187 .... 116, 121, 222
Stephen Kalong Ningkan v. *Tun Abang Haji Openg and Tawi
Sli (No. 2)* [1967] 1 M.L.J. 46 .... 107, 108, 116, 121,
260, 336, 337, 338
Surinder Singh Kanda v. *The Federation of Malaya* [1962]
M.L.J. 169 .... 15, 26, 288, 293, 294, 303
Syarikat Banita Sdn. Bhd. v. *Government of State of Sabah*
[1977] 2 M.L.J. 217 260
Tan Boon Liat & Ors., Re Application of, [1976] 2 M.L.J. 83 353
[1977] 2 M.L.J. 18 367
Tan Boon Liat @ Allen & Anor., et al., Re v. *Mentri Hal
Ehwal Dalam Negeri & Ors.* [1977] 2 M.L.J. 108 ... 40, 354, 356, 367
Tengku Mariam v. *Commissioner for Religious Affairs,
Trengganu* [1970] 1 M.L.J. 222 65
Terrell v. *Secretary of State* [1953] 2 Q.B. 482 .... 232, 277, 301
Thambipillai v. *The Government of Malaysia* [1969] 2 M.L.J.
206 .... 280, 283, 302
The King Emperor v. *Benoari Lal Sharma* [1945] A.C. 14 ...... 337, 338
University of Ceylon v. *Fernando* [1960] 1 All E.R. 631 .... 302, 303
Wee Toon Lip & Ors. v. *The Minister for Home Affairs,
Singapore & Anor.* [1972] 2 M.L.J. 46 353
Wong Ah Fook v. *State of Johore* [1937] M.L.J. 128 43
Wong Keng Sam & Ors. v. *Pritam Singh Brar* [1968] 2
M.L.J. 158 302
Yeap Hock Seng @ Ah Seng v. *Minister for Home Affairs,
Malaysia & Ors.* [1975] 2 M.L.J. 279 ...... 40, 352, 353, 356, 368
Yong Joo Lin & Others v. *Fung Poi Fong* [1941]
M.L.J. 63 57

Table of Statutes

Arms Act 1960 s. 30 244
British Nationality Act 1948 .... 72, 74, 180
Capitation Grant Act 1977 (Act A392) 400
Civil Law Act 1956 65
Civil Law Act 1953 s. 3 151
Companies Act 1965 186
Constitution (Amendment) Act 1960 (No. 10 of 1960) ... 276, 330, 334,
                                                         350, 393
Constitution (Amendment) Act 1962 (No. 14 of 1962) .. 79, 384, 394
Constitution (Amendment) Act 1963 (No. 25 of 1963) 384, 395
Constitution (Amendment) Act 1964 (No. 19 of 1964) 396
Constitution (Amendment) Act 1966 (No. 59 of 1966) 396
Constitution (Amendment) Act 1968 (No. 27 of 1968) 397
Constitution (Amendment) Act 1969 (Act No. A1) 397
Constitution (Amendment) Act 1971 (Act No. A30) ... 12, 177, 370,
                                                    379, 380, 381, 382, 398
Constitution (Amendment) (No. 2) Act 1971 (Act No.
  A31) 398
Constitution (Amendment) Act 1973 (Act No. A193) 399
Constitution (Amendment) (No. 2) Act 1973 (Act A206) 102, 216, 399
Constitution (Amendment) Act 1976 (Act A354) 29, 32, 36,
                                         85, 102, 254, 255, 274, 296,
                                         297, 350, 386, 387, 388, 390, 399
Constitution (Amendment) Act 1976 (Act A354) s. 10 105
Constitution (Amendment) Act 1976 (Act A354) s. 12 ..... 108, 109
Constitution (Amendment) Act 1976 (Act A354) s. 31(b) 252
Constitution (Amendment) Act 1976 (Act A354) s. 35 253
Constitution (Amendment) (No. 2) Act 1976 (Act No. A335) 399
Constitution and Malaysia (Amendment) Act 1965 (No.
  31 of 1965) 396

Constitution and Malaysia (Singapore Amendment) Act
1965 (Act 53) 177, 385, 396
Constitution of India (First Amendment) Act 1951 391
Constitution of India (Fourth Amendment) Act 1955 391
Constitution of India (Seventeenth Amendment) Act 1964 391
Courts (Amendment) Act A33 1971 .... 243, 244, 245
Courts of Judicature Act 1964 (Act 7 of 1964) 198, 247, 255
Courts of Judicature Act 1964 s. 48 17
Courts of Judicature Act 1964 s. 74 247
Dental Act 1971 198
Education Act 1961 198
Elections Act 1958 218
Election Act 1963 209
Elections (Amendment) Act 1965 210
Election Offences Act 1954 215
Election Offences (Amendment) Act 1961 209
Election Offences (Amendment) Act 1964 210
Elections (Registration of Electors) Regulations 1971 210
Emergency (Federal Constitution and Constitution of
Sarawak) Act 1966 (Act 68 of 1966) 334, 385, 389, 397
Emergency Powers (Kelantan) 1977 (Act 192) 347, 348
Employment (Restriction) Act (No. 36 of 1968) 93
Evidence Act 56 255
Evidence Ordinance (now the Evidence Act) s. 112 65
Federal Constitution:
Article 4(2)(a) 33
Article 5(1) 28, 30
Article 5(3) 31, 32
Article 5(4) 32
Article 5(5) 32
Article 6(2) 28
Article 7(1) 32
Article 7(2) 32
Article 8(1) 32
Article 8(2) 51
Article 8(5) 28
Article 8(5)(a) 33
Article 9(2) 29
Article 10(2) 29
Article 11 51
Article 11(4) 29, 51
Article 12 52
Article 12(2) 29
Article 13(1) 29, 30
Article 13(2) 34
Article 15 77
Article 15(2) 77

Article 15A 77
Article 16 78
Article 24 84
Article 25 .... 85, 86
Article 27 86
Article 32(1) 107
Article 35(1) 103
Article 42(1) 114
Article 44 150
Article 53 148
Article 66 150
Article 116 212
Article 119 209
Article 131(1) 246
Article 131(4) 246
Article 132 112
Article 149 35
Article 150 .... 30, 35, 115, 116, 151
Article 151 36
Article 153 29
Article 153(1) 114
Article 159 150
Article 171 212
Firearms (Increased Penalty) Act 1971 244
Houses of Parliament (Privileges and Powers) Ordinance
   1953 155
Immigration Act No. 27 of 1963 .... 94, 197
Immigration Ordinance No. 12 of 1959 94
Incorporation (State Legislatures Competency) Act 1962 181
Incorporation (State Legislative Competency)
   (Amendment) Act 1976 191
Internal Security Act 1960 353
Interpretation Act 1965 294
Johore Constitution of 1895:
   Article VII 43
   Article LVIII 43
Legal Profession Act 1976 (Act 166) 184, 198, 256
Local Government Elections Act 1960 209
Malaysia Act (Act 26 of 1963) 102, 175, 194, 195, 202,
                           209, 273, 334, 350, 374, 384, 395
Malaysia Act (Act 26 of 1963) s. 74(2) 202
Malaysia Act (Act 26 of 1963) s. 88 258
Medical Act 1971 198
Members of the Administration and Members of
   Parliament (Pensions and Gratuities) Act 1971 155
Muslim Courts (Criminal Jurisdiction) Act 1965 59
Naturalisation Act 1867 (Straits Settlements) 69

Parliament (Members Remuneration) Act 1960 154
Parliamentary Services Act 1953 155
Petroleum Development Act 1974 173
President of the Senate (Remuneration) Act 1960 154
Probate and Administration Act (Act 97) 59
Public Authorities (Control of Borrowing) Act 1961 186
Revision of Laws Act 1968 200
Revision of Laws Act 1969 206
Sedition Act 1948 .... 12, 33, 220, 383
Small Estates (Distribution) Act (Act 98) 59
Societies Act 1966 226
Speaker (Remuneration) Act 1960 154
Subordinate Courts Act (Act 92) 198, 250

❧ R. H. HICKLING

1. An Overview of Constitutional Changes in Malaysia: 1957-1977

INTRODUCTORY

OF all acts of the human intellect, those related to our efforts to construct a political system reconciling mankind's conflicting desires for freedom and order have, perhaps, the greatest nobility. To organize the accumulation of popular power in the hands of a select group of representatives of the people, and then to distribute that power in a manner productive of the least injustice to society, is one of the most difficult tasks known to the politician and the lawyer. The trail of torn-up constitutions grows. Even in such comparatively sophisticated countries as Thailand and Pakistan, efforts to create and develop parliamentary democracy seem doomed to disaster; and amidst the strains and stresses of developing economies periodically shaken by the booms and depressions created by the appetites of the western world, it is no mean achievement to have maintained for twenty years a law-making institution representative of the will of the people.

Such was the aim of the chief architect of the Malaysian Constitution, Tunku Abdul Rahman: and it is a tribute to his vision, and to the genius of the Malaysian people, that in spite of the shocks and disasters of the past two decades parliamentary democracy still counts for something in Malaysia. Debate and consensus continue to be accepted as the means whereby reasonable men may attain to a harmonious resolution of their differences of opinion. To have held on to that concept is, in all the circumstances, remarkable.

Now to stand upon a peak and to look back upon the past twenty years of the history of a nation is an awesome task. For the historian of the future it will be easier, for he will be able to see events in a truer perspective; the winds of time will have winnowed the wheat of truth and blown away the chaff of gossip, bias, and prejudice. To one of my generation, many of the major figures of Malaysian politics are well-known: some, indeed, were friends. So, judgment is not for me. The assessment I can make is a subjective one: and any comments upon the Constitution must be assessed in the light of one or two brutal facts.

According to the *Mid-Term Review of the Second Malaysia Plan 1971-1975*,[1] in 1970 the average monthly income of a Malay household was 179 dollars; that of an Indian household 310 dollars; and that of a Chinese household, 387 dollars. Such figures are not, of course, necessarily an index to prosperity, for the Malay household is usually one in a country area, where the cost of living is cheaper than in the towns. Yet the disparity of income must be a cause for concern and is, indeed, a basic reason for the evolution of the New Economic Policy, a policy designed to correct such imbalances. It is, too, the essential reason for the existence of that much-debated provision, Article 153 of the Constitution, and for the emergence of the word *bumiputra* into the politics of Malaysia. Economic advance is the contemporary criterion of success for the laws and constitution of Malaysia and, to the distress of the lawyer dedicated to the preservation of liberty, politics has an increasingly Marxist aspect, and one that may in the end be reflected in judicial attitudes. To preserve individual liberties in the face of economic pressures is not easy, and to do so we must hold on to certain basic truths.

THE ORIGINAL CONCEPTS

So, in order to assess the degree to which the Constitution has assisted in economic and social advance, let us first consider the ideas behind the Constitution, the ideas upon which it is based. Today, these seem clear enough: yet twenty years ago they had an air of novelty. After all, the word *constitution* had not been popularly used to describe the Malayan Union Order in Council of 1946 or, indeed, the Federation of Malaya Agreement of 1948. The concept of constitutional government in Malaya was, even then, of comparatively recent origin, extending back over only a few generations: generations that had experienced accelerating political change.

In reviewing the Constitution of today, therefore, it is essential to remember its origin and nature. There is no proud preamble, declaratory of the will of the people; no constituent assembly hammered it out with the strange sorts of paradox to be found in the Indian Constitution; nor did any formal referendum set a popular seal upon its simple but lengthy text.

No, it was a different sort of product, and bears the strengths and weaknesses of its origin. Evolutionary in its character, it grew out of the mishaps of the past: out of the confused constitutional structure of the old Straits Settlements and the Malay states, the strengths and weaknesses of the advisory treaties, the disasters of the Japanese occupation, the peremptory nature of the Malayan Union and the various compromises of the Federation of Malaya Agreement. At each step the emphasis was more on the authoritarian and the utilitarian, than upon the democratic and the cosmetic. Other framers of constitutions tended to be carried away on tides of populist euphoria: not so, those who worked out the principles of the Malaysian Constitution.

Taking as their pattern the Constitution of India, they addressed themselves to its text in realist and pragmatic terms. That Constitution has of course its own long history in the government of India: but, in 1957, there was a body of Indian case law in being sufficient to disclose the weaknesses in the structure of that constitution. In particular, the powers of the courts in relation to the interpretation of fundamental liberties had become manifest, with the courts acting not only as the guardians, but as the interpreters of the Constitution, assuming powers that even the legislators themselves were denied.

From this situation, the contrivance of skilled constitutional lawyers, many tragedies followed, and their sequence is not yet done. Too blind a faith in the skill and competence of others, too little regard for the unique nature of Malaysian society itself, and the Constitution of 1957 would not have endured for a decade. To its consideration came two bodies of lawyers and politicians, first the Reid Commission itself, and then the group of Malaysian and British lawyers and politicians who amended and adapted the Reid draft and provided the constitution of an independent federation.

Much is owed to the wisdom of the men of this latter group, notably to Tunku Abdul Rahman, justly to be named *bapa kemerdekaan*. His personality did much to inform and influence the pattern of the new Constitution: and it is his most lasting monument. Reflecting as it did the aspiration of the people, it was drafted in not too rigid a style. The rules of law, like a *baju*, should not be too tight in their fitting: and he and his colleagues appreciated the character of the political body of which the Constitution is, as it were, the outer garment.

Yet, what were the ideas, traditions, and principles on which the original compact was founded: and how were these adapted to the needs of Malaya?

To deal with such questions fully is outside the scope of this chapter, but we can at least essay an attempt at an outline answer. A study of Malayan history confirms the evolutionary nature of the Constitution. In a political sense it is the product of the Federation Agreement of 1948—an agreement representing a major break with the imposed solution of the Malayan Union Order in Council of 1948—and its consensual nature is readily apparent. The creature of compromise, it reflected the political aspirations of those who were party to the agreements of 1948 and 1957: British and Malayan politicians, and the Malay Rulers. Consensus was its base.

Now we know that at least since 1937,[2] and indeed from a much earlier date, the evolution of Malayan jurisprudence was shaped by the common law. British civil servants, at first administrators, later judges, brought with them concepts of the English common law: the principles of extracting a *ratio decidendi* from a case and using it to further the development of the law through the doctrine of precedent, and the construction of a hierarchy of courts. All this is so familiar to us as to be taken for granted, although the manner in which political precedent is used to shape convention is not, perhaps, so well appreciated.

Coupled with the concept of the common law is another principle which, equally familiar, was somehow taken for granted: the principle of parliamentary supremacy. That no Parliament can bind a successor: this, too, is well enough known, and now offers a problem to the English lawyers involved in the law of the European Community. The supremacy of the courts and of the legislature, each in their own sphere, was accepted by the English common law lawyer without demur: at least until, say, 1972,[3] and certainly during the period in which the principles of the Constitution of 1957 were being evolved.

For the Malayan lawyer, too, these principles were valid enough. Trained in an Inn of Court, in the polite, inward-looking school of the English bar, he absorbed the same concepts and applied the same principles. To what extent the tenets of Islam might colour his approach to law remained a question for the future. Familiar with the language and ideas of the common law, like his English counterpart he inhabited a world in which the rule of law as conceived by Dicey was alive, as an active influence. Parliament and the judges between them offered the certainty of ordered government, developing upon a law of England 'stripped of technicality and local peculiarities, shortened, simplified, made intelligible and precise'.[4]

These words, descriptive of the Indian Penal Code, offer an objective of the common law lawyer at work in Malaya prior to Independence. And the philosophy covers all; a studied refinement and adaptation of English principles, in so far as these were apt to the circumstances of the inhabitants and consistent with the local concept of justice and equity: such was the aim, consciously or unconsciously applied. The grim, utilitarian equity of the abortive Malayan Union having been swept away in 1948, peace, order, and good government, in accordance with the principles of the common law, became the agreed aim of all parties to the compact.

So, when in 1956 the time came to seek a constitution for an independent Federation of Malaya, the terms of reference of the Reid Constitutional Commission laid strong emphasis upon a federal form of constitution 'based on Parliamentary democracy': and that key phrase invoked, again, the concept not only of Parliamentary democracy, but also that of Parliamentary supremacy.

Yet those who selected the members of the Reid Commission were mindful of the need to seek the advice of those familiar with the problems of federal government, and appointed as members distinguished men from the United Kingdom, Australia, India, and Pakistan.[5] The men so appointed were rich in experience: yet not even they could, perhaps, have been expected to emphasize what they, as federalists, knew well enough, but what those trained and gaining their experience within the confines of an English common law system could not know: that, as Wheare so succinctly puts it,[6] '[It] must follow that constitutions which are federal are also supreme and, in the original sense of the term as Bryce used it, "rigid" '.

Ah, the astute observer may say, what about Article 4—did that not declare the supremacy of the Constitution? True enough, so it did, and so it does: yet can we, even now, twenty years later, affirm that this provision has been truly understood? To the federalist, the Article seems superfluous, to the parliamentarian, a piece of nonsense: this is one of the ironies of Malaysian constitutional history, yet it is one that needs occasional mention, for to misunderstand Article 4 is to misunderstand the whole document. The doctrine of constitutional supremacy has taken a long time to take root in Malaysia: but we can, I think, affirm that the tree is now reasonably secure and, short of a landslide or earthquake, it will continue to grow.

LEGISLATIVE INTERVENTION

In general, I think it true to state that there was no fundamental disagreement among the majority of citizens over the basic principles of the Constitution: and these have remained. Whether such lack of disagreement illustrated agreement, indifference, or ignorance is a nice question. Constitutions, after all, come and go, but the land, sea, and rivers remain; for the humble citizen, be he fisherman, padi cultivator, or market gardener, the distribution of power inherent in the document is sometimes irrelevant, for flood and drought, famine and plenty, operate in accordance with other and more eternal principles; even for the rubber tapper and tin miner, the powerful forces of international supply and demand may be regarded as of greater consequence than those of law and order.

Nevertheless, in looking at the amendments made to the Constitution by the lawmakers over the past twenty years, we can see them as, essentially, reactions to an existing reality. Sometimes they have been dictated by proved or anticipated weaknesses in the Constitution itself, sometimes by pressure of political events. Without analysing in detail all the various amendments that have been made since 1957—a task admirably accomplished by H. P. Lee[7]—I think that the most significant amendments to the Constitution have been reactions to political events. That this should be so, that the Constitution could be amended to restore the harmony prejudiced by such events, is a tribute to those who framed the document, and to those who have, as legislators, been entrusted with the power of amendment. The Malaysian politician, too, tends to react to events, rather than to anticipate them: and this attitude, while it may sometimes lead to difficulties, seems to be wiser than that of the anxious politician elsewhere, who tends to over-react and thereby sow the seeds of future disorder.

> The less a leader does and says
> The happier his people
> The more a leader struts and brags
> The sorrier his·people.

So says Lao Tzu,[8] offering a political insight into Taoist philosophy: one, I think, understood by the Malaysian politician, who aspires to wisdom, not cleverness.

The following events, then, I would list as significant: and if, here, I compound the event and the reaction, this is because it is difficult, in short space, to disentangle each from the other. The items mentioned here have an air of the subjective, admittedly: but major events have left their mark on the text of the Constitution, and what is commonly subjective might be said to approach to reality.

The first major event reflected in the contemporary Constitution is the winding-up of the state of emergency that began in 1948. In 1960 the emergency ended: but in fact, the opportunity was then taken to strengthen the powers of the executive in countering subversion and dealing with a state of emergency.

On such an occasion it might have been supposed that the law on preventive detention could be repealed. As the draftsman of the Internal Security Bill, I put this view to the Minister in charge of the

Bill, the late Tun Razak. 'But put yourself in my position,' he sensibly asked, 'would you release every detainee, now?' The question illustrates the reality, and indeed the responsibility, of power: and if the price of the ending of the emergency was the Internal Security Act, then I believe it was worth paying. The powers conferred by the Act of 1960 were not, initially at least, abused, nor was the Act in its origin designed to afford a weapon against political opponents, other than those dedicated to violence as a means of persuasion.

Yet a few more significant changes took place in 1960, apart from the enlargement of Article 149 (in order to cover the non-violent aspects of subversion) and the amendment of Article 151 (under which, originally, a detainee had to be released after three months' detention, unless the advisory board on detainees considered that there was sufficient cause for his detention). The twelve-month limit on any anti-subversion law was abolished; and the positive approval of each House of Parliament to action taken in relation to an emergency, under Article 150, within two months of such action, was no longer required.

The net result of the amendments of 1960,[9] was, therefore, that the executive was equipped with wider emergency powers, subject to lesser parliamentary control, than those contemplated in 1957: when, of course, a state of emergency was already in existence. Further, it is now accepted that, as Lord MacDermott explained in 1968, 'the word "emergency" as used in Article 150(1) cannot be confined to the unlawful use or threat of force in any of its manifestations'. Article 150 can be, and I think has been on two occasions used for political ends.

It is arguable that such wide powers are desirable for, as we may note from the experience of other countries, a constitution that fails to confer on the executive the plenitude of powers it requires to maintain law and order will be swept aside *in toto*, with an imposition of martial law flowing from a gun-barrel, not a ballot-box. Even so, it is all too easy to erode the barriers of liberty: just as no man becomes wicked overnight, so does freedom itself not vanish in an instant. Vigilance is necessary all the time, and the nature of the amendments made in 1960 imposes a heavier responsibility upon members of Parliament than that under which they laboured prior to that date.

In 1962 there came[10] a small but significant alteration to the citizenship law. Citizenship is of course a matter of importance, for some fundamental liberties—such as freedom of expression—are (perhaps curiously, but so it is) confined to citizens. Under the original Constitution every person born within the Federation on or after Merdeka Day was, subject to certain exceptions, a citizen by operation of law. In 1962 the principle of *jus soli* was eroded: and a person born in the Federation will not be a citizen unless one of his parents is at the time of birth either a citizen of, or permanently resident in Malaysia. To what extent this provision deprives anyone of a citizenship to which he was entitled before its enactment is difficult to assess: but the provision itself must operate to impose a certain sense of insecurity that is unlikely to work to the public benefit. It serves to cut down a simple principle, and one serving to counter the insidious doctrine of the *jus sanguinis*, which may or may not (the position in relation to the Chinese nationality laws of 1909 and 1929 remains obscure) affect many Malaysian Chinese. Exactly what prompted the dilution of the *jus soli* is not clear: but of its importance to the integration of Malaysian society there can, I believe, be no doubt.

A major event then followed, for on 27 May 1961 Tunku Abdul Rahman, in an address to the Foreign Correspondents' Association of South-East Asia, put forward the concept of Malaysia: a concept which, as the months wore on, gathered momentum, and finally—at the eleventh hour—fell under attack, in perhaps the one and only direct attack so far made upon the Constitution.

That attack should not have been unexpected. Apart from the common law principles upon which the Constitution was based, apart from the separation of legislative, judicial, and executive authority to which the Constitution made more than a token nod, and apart from the preservation of the prerogatives of the Malay Rulers, there was a fundamental principle of equality running throughout the whole document. Privilege was eschewed, in the sense that all member states, founder members of the independent federation created in 1957, shared common rights and responsibilities. No state, whether rich, powerful and developed like Perak, Selangor, or Johore, or less rich, less well-developed like Perlis, Kelantan, Trengganu or Pahang, had established a claim to special privilege. The only difference in the status of the member states lay in that dictated by their origins as Malay State or Crown Colony: Penang and Malacca maintained the office of Governor, and in their domestic affairs retained some of the aspects of the old, classical form of Crown Colony government.

Yet these were and are minor anomalies, little different, say, from the status of Yang di-Pertuan Besar as compared with that of Sultan. All the founder states of the federation of 1957 shared, in substance and in fact, a common status. Indeed, that common status might be said to have been of the essence of the original compact: and out of that concept of equality grew the unique office of Yang di-Pertuan Agong, of a Supreme Head of State elected by that discreet but powerful body, the Conference of Rulers.

Now, in the early 1960s, the notion of a greater federation was revived, and with that revival came the constitutional discussions and ingenious horse-trading associated with political compromise and evolution. For Singapore, the preservation of autonomy in the sphere of education, labour, and health was of paramount importance: and as soon as the principle of equality was about to be breached, the new member states of Sarawak and Sabah were, inevitably, not slow to seek a greater degree of autonomy than that to which they would have been entitled as states on a par with the founder members of the federation.

Nor was this all. Once the concept of equal status among member states was broken, other equally basic concepts fell into hazard. Citizenship itself, the basic brick on which the nation itself was built, became a political pawn: and once this had occurred, the idea of freedom of travel and equal opportunities for employment throughout the federation also lost their virtue.

It may be overstating the case to suggest that the events of 1963 did irreparable damage to the original federal concept of equality: but I do not think so. A reinforcement of Malay rights—which during the previous five or six years had been withering away as the Reid Commission might have suspected they would—took place against a background of general unequal treatment. Out of harmony, disharmony grew, as the events of the next decade were to illustrate.

It was left to the David of Kelantan to do battle against the Goliath of the Federation when, on the very eve of Malaysia, Thomson C.J. was called upon to adjudicate upon Kelantan's objection to its formation.[11] As we all know, the Government of Kelantan, fighting the case of all states of the federation although apparently supported by not one, argued that the Malaysia Agreement and the Malaysia Act were 'null and void, or alternatively not binding on the state of Kelantan'. Thomson C.J. briefly summarized the grounds of the State's objections:

They are that the Malaysia Act will in effect abolish the Federation of Malaya, that this is contrary to the 1957 Agreement, that in any event the proposed changes require the consent of each of the constituent states, including Kelantan, and this has not been obtained, that the Ruler of the State of Kelantan should have been a party, which he was not, to the Malaysia Agreement, that apart from anything else there is a constitutional convention that the Rulers of the individual States should be consulted regarding any substantial changes in the Constitution, and that in any event the Federal Parliament has no power to legislate for the State of

Kelantan in respect of any matter regarding which the State has its own legislation.

The issue was momentous, and one can but sympathize with the Chief Justice in having it thrust upon him so urgently. In a phrase now famous among students of constitutional law, he affirmed that 'the Constitution is primarily to be interpreted within its own four walls and not in the light of analogies drawn from other countries such as Great Britain, the United States of America or Australia'. Resting himself upon the Constitution itself, he noted that the 'real question' was 'whether Parliament or the Executive Government' had 'trespassed in any way the limits placed on their powers by the Constitution'. If the words were inelegant, the thinking was clear enough: and after a review of Articles 2, 75, 76, 160, and 159 the Chief Justice commented on Parliament's powers in passing the Malaysia Act by observing,

> In doing these things I cannot see that Parliament went in any way beyond its powers or that it did anything so fundamentally revolutionary as to require fulfilment of a condition which the Constitution itself does not prescribe, that is to say a condition to the effect that the State of Kelantan or any other State should be consulted.

Kelantan was therefore unsuccessful, and Malaysia was duly born as a kind of hybrid federation, or perhaps a confederation, which has enjoyed—if that is the word—an uneasy decade. Much of that uneasiness may perhaps be traced to the breach of the concept of equality on which the original compact of federation was founded.

The Government of Kelantan did, however, succeed in opening for a moment a door upon a new world of constitutional interpretation. There have not been wanting those who have been alarmed by the Chief Justice's vision of 'fundamentally revolutionary' reforms, and some stern remarks have been made upon this apparent denial of the letter of the Constitution. Yet the learned Chief Justice might here be said to have been speaking *obiter*, in adumbrating a test of radical amendment that may yet have to be invoked.

For the spirit of Kelantan is not, I believe, dead. Indeed, the events of the past decade suggest that it is alive and well, and not only in Kota Bharu. In India the courts have been compelled to retreat from an inviolability of fundamental rights: but the retreat is to a new citadel, from which another battle may be fought. In the meantime, may this observer offer a silent salute to the Government of Kelantan for its courage in asserting that a constitution is more than mere words, and that custom and convention can often supply the spirit which the letter may lack.

The next major event to shape the evolution of the Constitution lay in the troubles of that Black Tuesday, 13 May 1969. The happenings of that day are a blot on the history of Malaysia. The periods of progress to Independence, of the transition of power, and of the evolution of an independent national spirit: all these phases in the history of the people had been, by and large, peaceful in character. To the English colonialist, the Malay, whether a Ruler, a padi-farmer, or a fisherman, was always a gentleman, a man to whom good manners were of paramount importance; to be polite to an enemy is the sign of a civilized man, who then discovers that the soul of courtesy is friendship. It is easy to hate those one does not know, difficult to hate those one knows and understands: and in the attainment of understanding the rituals of ceremony, the habits of courtesy, are important.

Yet communities do not readily break down their barriers, and naturally desire to keep their cultural identities intact. To retain the life of those cultures and at the same time to assimilate one race within the boundaries of another is one of the major problems of modern politics; few countries now lack racial tension in some degree or other: and few legal formulae can offer *mantras* against disaster.

That there has been, and is, an economic imbalance between the Malays and others has been all too well known. While that economic imbalance was redressed in the shape of political power, the situation was tolerable. Then, given the evolution of citizenship and the attainment of democratic rights, the balance of society began to change, and many observers saw that the poor Malay might yet become more poor. Out of such anxiety was Article 153 born.

Now it is axiomatic that privilege creates envy, and that envy is the parent of hate and violence. The concept of special rights for the Malays and natives of Borneo must of necessity tend to raise some resentment in the minds of the poor and deprived of other communities: and there is no doubt that an unscrupulous politician can exploit that resentment for his own advantage. Exactly how to prevent this situation arising is a problem to tax the wisest of statesmen; whether it has been solved in Malaysia any more than in, say, Sri Lanka, remains to be seen.

The violence that erupted in Kuala Lumpur on 13 May 1969 almost—I suspect—led to the breakdown of the Constitution. The measures then taken merit the study of the constitutional lawyer: for the whole of the legislative structure of the Constitution was virtually suspended, and the whole of the executive authority of the Yang di-Pertuan Agong delegated to one man, the Director of Operations. Much therefore depended upon the personality of that man: and it was Malaysia's good fortune that in Tun Razak a decisive politician well versed in the arts of law and government was available. Under his guidance Malaysia was nursed back to constitutional, democratic government.

To restore constitutional government was no easy matter. That the principles of Article 153 could not be abandoned was clear: there could be no surrender of that dearly-won provision—yet how could its inviolability be secured? The problem seemed intractable, and was tackled in two ways, one legislative, the other non-legislative. Let us consider each, in turn.

At the legislative level came the Constitution (Amendment) Act of 1971: some thought, a desperate remedy for a desperate situation. As an emergency measure the Sedition Act of 1948—a measure based on provisions of the English common law whose abolition is now recommended by the Law Commission—has been amended in order to make it seditious to question any matter, right, status, position, privilege, sovereignty, or prerogative established or protected by the citizenship provisions of the Constitution, together with those Articles dealing with the national language, the reservation of quotas in respect of services, permits, etc. for Malays and natives of the Borneo States, and the Rulers' prerogatives. That sanctity was, and is now, protected by an amendment to Article 10.

That in itself was bad enough. The amending Act went even further, so that it became (and remains) a crime for even a member of the Dewan Ra'ayat, acting in accordance with normal parliamentary procedure, to address the House in such a manner as to question the existence of these protected subjects. The Speaker cannot permit the question to be raised; no secret session can admit it; not even on a substantive motion in the House can the existence of Article 153 be challenged. In this wise is Article 153 so entrenched in the Constitution that it has become impossible of discussion, except in relation to its implementation.

Whether this gag upon discussion will work to a tolerance and acceptance of Article 153 remains to be seen. Fires long suppressed can, as coalminers know, erupt with sudden and devastating fury. To any champion of parliamentary privilege—a privilege that represents a deep, traditional wisdom—the prohibition within Parliament itself appears potentially dangerous. Parliament should be the forum of the people, where all their hopes and fears can be aired—indeed, the act of expression is itself a valuable safety-valve to frustration.

The amendment of 1971 was, therefore, the negative solution to the problems posed by Article 153. A positive solution, of an original nature, was and is provided by the *Rukunegara*, a document that could well exercise a profound influence upon the interpretation and evolution of the Constitution. As a consequence of the national emergency following the troubles of 13 May, a National Operations Council and, in 1970, a National Consultative Council, were established, as instruments of national discussion and reconciliation. Out of these bodies grew a document known as the *Rukunegara*, consisting of a declaration of objectives and beliefs, coupled with a commentary thereon. Expressed in broad terms, the *Rukunegara* offers a certain basic philosophy, aimed at the evolution of a democratic Malaysian nation and emphasizing the need to adhere to the rule of law. In some respects, therefore, it offers a summary of principles within the Constitution itself, and is a reaffirmation of these, in a dramatic form. It is, as Syed Hussein Alatas says,[12] 'a miniature charter for a single country. Like the U.N. Charter it indicates an agreement on fundamentals upheld by different political systems, parties and ideologies. Though its formulation is simple, the *Rukunegara* is intended to function like the mariner's chart in a troubled sea.' These fundamentals may well become important, in relation to questions of the interpretation of the Constitution, as time goes by, and by their philosophy create a new climate of opinion in which the revised principles of the Constitution can grow in peace.

At the electoral level, one of the more ominous developments—and one developing as a kind of counterpoint to the theme of Article 153—has been the evolution of the Thirteenth Schedule to the Constitution. This Schedule, added in 1962, sets out the principles for the delimitation of constituencies for the election of members to the House of Representatives and the Legislative Assemblies of the States. Originally Articles 113 to 117 laid down certain clear-cut principles, as follows:

a. constituencies should be allocated in such a manner that there would be no 'undue disparity' between the population quota of the State and the electoral quota of the Federation: the 'population quota' being ascertained by dividing the number of the population by the number of constituencies, and the 'electoral quota' by dividing the number of electors by the number of constituencies;

b. each State should be divided into single-member constituencies in such a manner that each constituency contained a number of electors as close to the electoral quota of the State as might be, after making 'due allowance for the distribution of the different communities and for differences in density of population and the means of communication': the permitted variation not, however, to exceed 15 per cent;

c. delimitation of constituencies in accordance with the provisions of the Constitution was entrusted to an independent Election Commission.

In 1962 a radical change took place, with the insertion into the Constitution of what is now the Thirteenth Schedule. The principles of delimitation were replaced by new ones under which a rural constituency might contain as little as one-half of the electors of an urban constituency; and the power of delimitation was transferred from the Election Commission to a bare majority of the total number of members of the House of Representatives.

These amendments effected a major change in the nature of representative government in the Federation. In one respect they constituted an indirect buttress to the provisions of Article 153, for (to make a sweeping generalization) Malays might be said to predominate in rural areas, and non-Malays in the conurbations in the west of the peninsula. However, the proportion of representation of the States in the House of Representatives has also been affected by political events. At first consisting of 104 members (a simple halving of each of the constituencies for the last general election before *merdeka*), the creation of Malaysia brought in a further 16 members from Sabah, 24 members from Sarawak, and 15 members from Singapore: making a total of 159 elected members. The disparity in the relative representation of the new States is all too obvious, and can only be justified on the grounds of political expediency and the fact that the new States were not admitted upon the same terms as those of the founder members of the original Federation. Singapore, in particular, came off badly, even if the fact that, say, labour, education, and medicine and health remained within its legislative competence.

With Singapore's departure the total number of elected members of course fell; in 1973 a readjustment of State representation took place, following upon the carving out of the State of Selangor of the Federal Territory: that territory returning 5 members, and the States a total of 149 members, 2 from Perlis, 4 from Malacca, 6 from Negri Sembilan, 7 from Trengganu, 8 from Pahang, 9 from Penang, 11 from Selangor, 12 from Kelantan, 13 from Kedah, 16 each from Johore and Sabah, 21 from Perak, and 24 from Sarawak.

As one with a soft spot for Sarawak, I am gratified by its eminence at the head of the electoral table: but I ask myself whether in fact it is deserved. Indeed, the distribution of seats among the States— which, as vigorously pointed out by 'I.S.A.' in the *Journal of Malaysian and Comparative Law*, 'cannot be altered unless two-thirds of the total membership of *each* House of Parliament agrees to a constitutional amendment'[13]—introduces a rare flavour of expediency into a document notable, in its inception, for a lucid and equitable exposition aimed at furthering the principle of equality so carefully expressed in Article 8, and originally entrusted for its execution to the hands of a commission as independent as the judiciary.

JUDICIAL ATTITUDES

Turning from the legislators' reactions to the events of the past twenty years, let us now take a look at the reactions of the judges: bearing always in mind that the law-making functions of the judiciary differ in one major respect from those of the legislators. The judge, after all, views a problem in the isolation of its application to the individual parties before him; of necessity, he takes the role of arbitrator upon issues carefully argued in accordance with prescribed rules of procedure and evidence. To this extent, therefore, he is fettered by the constraints of adjectival law: constraints not often recognized by critics of the judges and the judicial system. We often find among academic lawyers and (in England) trade unionists, a facile, Marxist criticism of judges, as men representing and protecting a variety of vested interests in society. There is, of course, some colour of justification for such a view: but it represents so partial and prejudiced a view of the role and function of the judge as to be not only meaningless, but positively dangerous. It is all too easy—and indeed, it is all too often done. A researcher will analyse the cases of a particular judge, throw away all those in which the judge has decided in favour, say, of the individual (and many of these cases are of course never reported) and then indulge in a criticism of the judge, on the basis of his having found for the Government in some case or other. Found for the Government: as if this were some sort of judicial crime deserving of contumely and abuse.

Here I will endeavour to avoid such an attitude: although this is not as easy as it may seem. One of the difficulties in assessing the virtues of any judicial system is that, for the most part, issues are outlined in terms of black and white, of right or wrong. Judgment for one party suggests that the other party was wholly in error; a successful appeal implies that the trial judge, too, was utterly mistaken; and advice from the Privy Council may put an end to the stately dance, by consigning the appellate court to the ignominy its critics have demanded. The clear-cut outcome of our adversary methods of trial can be misleading.

Now the composition of the Malaysian bench has altered over the past two decades. When I look at the *Malayan Law Journal* for 1958 I see that out of eleven judges, eight (including two acting appointments) were expatriates; by 1970 all were, if not *bumiputras*, Malaysian sons of the soil—and when, O when may we expect the first woman judge? To make the latter comment is, of course, to open the door to the operation of Article 153, and to an assessment of the number of Malay judges, as distinct from non-Malay judges: but in my view none of these distinctions has any significance. A judge is a judge is a judge, as Gertrude Stein might have said. Taking a trawl through the Malaysian law reports of the last twenty years, I doubt whether in any case we could assert that this judge or that was an English, Scots, Malay, Chinese, or Indian lawyer, on the basis of his judgment. In other words, delete his name as author of the judgment, and you will be unable to identify the ethnic origin of the judge. O, you might well be able to assert from his actual style: from his liking for Lord Denning's prose: or from his passion for polysyllabic profundities, that it is Judge X who is speaking rather than Judge Y or Z: but these are the product of normal, personal idiosyncrasies, of the kind that give life and colour to the courts and, indeed, the law reports. They are not, and never have been, and I hope never will be, founded in ethnic attitudes or communal aspirations.

Now it is not difficult to see one trend, in the course of judicial interpretation of the Constitution over the past twenty years. The change from a judicial understanding of a constitution lacking in supremacy—of the kind familiar to the English common law lawyer—to that of a constitution embodying the supreme law of the State, has been effected: but not with the abruptness that a perusal of Article 4 of the Constitution itself might suggest.

This change is perhaps best manifest in the application of Article 5 of the Constitution. The first case that arose under this Article was, of course, that of *Chia Khin Sze* v. *Mentri Besar, State of Selangor*.[14] In that case Sutherland Ag. J. had to determine whether Article 5 applied to the provisions of the Restricted Residence Enactment of Selangor, so that a person arrested under that Enactment was entitled to be defended by a legal practitioner. The judge here was, it seems, misled by the text of Article 4(1), which invalidates any law, passed after Merdeka Day, which is inconsistent with the Constitution: the presumption here being that any law passed before Merdeka Day might be valid, even if inconsistent with the Constitution. The application of Article 162(6) was not, it seems, argued.

On this hazardous rock of Article 4(1) the application foundered. The judgment was criticized, and in my view rightly: yet it does not, perhaps, deserve much of the criticism levelled against it. For the wording of the Constitution was not as clear as all that: we have only to continue in our researches, to encounter the rare entertainment posed by *Surinder Singh Kanda's* case.[15] In that case, we may remember, Inspector Kanda was dismissed from the Royal Federation of Malaya Police Force by the Commissioner of Police: and the question was, did the Commissioner possess the power of appointment and dismissal—a power vested, 'subject to the provisions of any existing law', in the Police Service Commission.

The manner in which the Privy Council extricated themselves

from the difficulties of construing Article 144(1) was ingenious. It seems clear (at least, it seemed clear to this observer, in 1957) that those who drafted and adopted the new Constitution did not wish to create any major upheavals in the day-to-day administration of government affairs.[16] They wished to ensure the inviolability of existing laws, and their gradual adaptation to the circumstances of the new Constitution.

Such, at least, was the trend of thought in 1957 and 1958. Of the supremacy of the Constitution itself we were assured: but we knew, well enough, that we could not hope to adapt to it the whole corpus of existing law by express modifications made under Article 162. We adopted a 'blanket' form of modification to hold the line, as it were; then drew up a table of priorities, listing all those laws which required express modification as a matter of urgency; and then we hoped that common sense and the practical expertise of administrators and judges would resolve the rest.

It is against this background that the above judgments of Sutherland J. and (in the Court of Appeal) Thomson C.J. and Hill J.A. must be assessed: and even now, I am not so sure that the principle of the complete supremacy of the Constitution over all laws, whether pre- or post-*merdeka*, is as obvious as all that. Of the construction of Article 144(1), Lord Denning himself observed that 'Their Lordships realize that it is a difficult point ...'. So it was, and so it is. It was not until ten years later, that Wan Suleiman J. could[17] cite Article 162(6) with the confidence born of a knowledge of the Privy Council's views in the case of Inspector Kanda, and register a reasoned dissent from the case of *Chia Khin Sze*.

A further, and probably final result of this sequence of cases lay in the case of *Assa Singh*,[18] a reference to the Federal Court under section 48 of the Courts of Judicature Act 1964: a case virtually involving the question of whether such legislation as that relating to restricted residence was 'contrary to the provisions of the Constitution and void'. Here, the Federal Court not only affirmed the validity of the provisions of a pre-*merdeka* law, the Restricted Residence Enactment, accepting it as a law relating to public security and, as such, one permitting restrictions on movement and residence, but grafted onto the Enactment (as Wan Suleiman J. had adumbrated) clauses (3) and (4) of Article 5: an amiable exercise, since there was here no conflict to be resolved.

In the realm of the public service we have, in the course of the past two decades, observed a kind of tussle between the lawmakers and the judiciary: a tussle beginning, I think, with the case of Inspector Kanda. Part X of the Constitution has proved a fruitful field for litigation, an interesting area for constitutional amendment. In 1960 the principle that civil servants hold office 'during the pleasure' of the Yang di-Pertuan Agong or (in the case of State Officers) of the Ruler of the State, was added to Article 132, and accepted with a certain amount of relief by the judiciary. The provision, as Suffian F.J. (as he then was) stated in *Haji Ariffin* v. *Government of Pahang*,[19] 'only reaffirms the previous common law rule that a member of the public service of the State held office during the pleasure of the Ruler': but, like a few other manifestations of the prerogatives of the common law, it is all the clearer for being spelled out in the letter of the Constitution.

In determining cases affecting the public service the judges have enjoyed the dubious benefit of Indian case law on provisions of the Indian Constitution. The same judge has observed[20] that 'judgments of the Indian Supreme Court are of great persuasive value here, particularly on the Constitution because to a great extent the Indian Constitution was the model for our own Constitution'. Another Lord President had noted[21] that 'although not binding on us, any judgment of the Supreme Court of India must always be regarded as of very great persuasive value', and a Chief Justice in the same case[22] observed a decision of the Supreme Court of India as warranting 'the greatest respect and consideration': a sentiment not, perhaps, completely shared by another Chief Justice in a later case,[23] when observing that 'English courts take a more realistic view of things, while Indian judges, for whom I have the highest respect, impress me as indefatigable idealists seeking valiantly to reconcile the irreconcilable whenever good conscience is pricked by an abuse of executive powers'.

Even so, the movement of the judiciary in matters of employment has been, it seems, towards a recognition of the importance of contract. In the realm of English labour law status is—unfortunately, as it seems to some of us—more important than agreement. A man may make a contract with an employer, to find it varied by a trade union the following day: a state of affairs explaining much of the confusion and decay of modern Britain. No such decline is manifest in the robust attitude of the Malaysian judiciary, whose courts now recognize the subtle distinction between the dismissal of a public servant and the determination of his contract of service.[24]

While (possibly spurred on by the *Kanda* case) there has been a reasonable amount of legislation on those provisions of the Constitution dealing with the public service, there has been a curious lack of any judicial discussion or interpretation of what is perhaps the most critical article in the Constitution, Article 153. That Article is not, after all, such a generous boon to the *bumiputra* as many suppose: for it seeks, to the best of its intent, to balance the interests of all races in Malaysia in as equitable a manner as conditions may admit. The Article is the legacy, indeed, a continuation of a policy dating from as far back as 1913, when 'concern was felt (by the administration itself and by the Malay rulers) that the Malay, succumbing to the lure of high prices, might divest himself entirely of his patrimony',[25] and the Federal Council passed the Malay Reservations Enactment: but no doubt the policy dates back to an earlier time, when political and economic relationships between Britain and the Malay Rulers first developed, and large-scale immigration began.

For Article 153 affords the machinery for ensuring that, as far as is possible, the special position of the Malays shall not work to the prejudice of others. Whether the safeguards in the Article can be enforced effectively is perhaps another matter: in relation to which, the provisions of the Evidence Act, and the ability of government to refuse to withhold information in certain cases, are relevant. It would be of great advantage if any directions issued under the Article were laid on the table of the Dewan Negara and the Dewan Ra'ayat. Even so, the action for a declaratory judgment could possibly be used, to ensure that there is no abuse of the powers contained in the Article, and it is perhaps a matter of surprise that it has not been the subject of action. I appreciate that the brutally realistic Chinese may see little or no advantage in litigation: but there are more litigious, non-Malay communities. Article 153 deserves to be studied and used, not abused.

Looking at the corpus of the hundred or so reported cases on the Constitution, it is difficult to assess their relative significance. Some of them, like the *Kelantan* and the *Ningkan* cases, have passed into the realm of comparative constitutional law, and have an impact in many jurisdictions beyond Malaysia. Again, such cases as that of the *Selangor Pilot Association (1946)* v. *Government of Malaysia and Anor*[26] have, although subsequently over-ruled by the Privy Council (with Lord Salmon dissenting), illustrated the independence of the Malaysian judiciary, and its insistence on following an impartial construction of the Constitution, and not necessarily any government arguments thereon. One or two cases, such as that of *Eng Keock Cheng* v. *Public Prosecutor*,[27] in which the Chief Justice of Borneo suggested that Article 150 confers power on Parliament 'to legislate on any subject and to any effect, even if inconsistencies with articles of the Constitution ... are involved. This necessarily includes authority to delegate part of that power to legislate to some other authority, notwithstanding the existence of a written Constitution', cause one a little concern, as opening the door to a possible subversion of the basic principles of the Constitution: but, as against that tendency, the *Rukunegara* and the diffusion of the principles on which it is based may create a climate of opinion in which such usurpation is impossible. At present we can, I believe, be grateful for the vigilance of the judges, some of whom have been in the forefront of protest over any threat to the normal principles of the rule of law. The reader will, no doubt, in later pages of this volume be able to assess for himself the position and attitudes of the judiciary. From an outsider's point of view, I think that the country is well-served by skilful and articulate judges, whose judgments are, in general, a pleasure to read.

For it can be affirmed with confidence that the Malaysian bench has produced a fair share of writers of elegant prose. To those of us who have had occasion to dip into the dark and turbulent waters of the Indian law reports, the judgments of most Malaysian judges are as clear and refreshing as a woodland spring. Rare indeed is it to find a judgment so confused that it is not readily comprehensible: and, while I can appreciate the skill of the learned editors of the *Malayan Law Journal*, the clarity of both Malaysian and Singaporean judgments deserves a special word of praise. The Constitution would not have remained in being without a competent judiciary: but to the interpretation of the Constitution the Malaysian judges have brought not only common sense, but skilful pens.

After all, it is not easy to write a clear, legal judgment. To sit on the bench and listen to the opposing arguments of parties at variance with each other, and both usually well served by competent counsel; to sift, analyse, and finally decide the merits of a case; and then to couch that process of analysis and decision in simple, unambiguous English is no mean task: indeed, it calls for a far greater degree of skill than that required of the critic or editorial writer. That the condition of Malaysian law is in such a healthy state is in no small measure due to the succinct eloquence of the Malaysian bench: and long may it continue!

One reason for this state of affairs may lie in the common law tradition itself. Frequently there is citation of the better-known common law judges; and Lord Denning himself has been a powerful influence indeed, both directly (in such a case as that of *Surinder Singh Kanda*) and, indirectly, in the prose style of his judgments in the Court of Appeal. Echoes of his style are to be found often enough in the judgments of the Malaysian bench: and these have brought a Stevensonian simplicity of style to erudite, constitutional issues, to the advantage of all concerned.

Of course, the Malaysian judges have been spared many of the burdens of their Indian contemporaries. The latter, made responsible for distinguishing, say, the reasonable from the unreasonable restriction, have often found themselves embroiled in issues taking them on a collision course with politicians: to the public disadvantage. Fashionable as it now is to deride the activities of Mrs. Gandhi, the fact remains that if those who framed the Indian Constitution had put less of a burden upon the judiciary, and more of a burden on the lawmakers, that Republic might have been spared many crises, much misery. In drafting a constitution, it is essential to ascertain the true nature of the judicial function, and not to overload the judges with duties outside their proper sphere of competence: and in assessing that sphere of competence the nature of the judicial process itself, and the limitations within which it operates, must be clearly appreciated.

TO THE FUTURE

We may see, in the development of the Malaysian Constitution over the past twenty years, powerful forces at work, and strenuous efforts made to channel and preserve these forces within the rule of law. The pressures are powerful, and Article 153 makes them manifest at both the legal and political level. Twenty years is not long in the life of a people, in the development of a nation: and there is no doubt that the worst unfairnesses of the law are to be preferred to the excesses of lawlessness and anarchy. The balance of power between the Malay and non-Malay peoples that is embodied in the Constitution is a precarious thing: but it is to be treasured, and reform can come only through the operation of law itself, if violence and conflict are to be avoided.

On the one occasion when it was put abruptly to the test, in 1969, the strength of the Constitution was made manifest, with Tun Razak becoming a virtual, if reluctant dictator. 'Life itself is full of problems', says the Introduction to the *Rukunegara*, philosophically: and no constitution ever devised can solve them. Even so, the Constitution contained within itself the machinery for instant action, without a loss of the whole. Not for Malaysia the usurpation of the Constitution by means of, say, a proclamation from the Yang di-Pertuan Agong, declaring martial law: an event that could well have happened and (*pace* Pakistan in 1958 or 1977) set an unfortunate precedent for the future.

For, in the 1969 crisis, the emergency powers contained within the Constitution were used. True, some fundamental liberties went into eclipse: this, sad to say, is the inevitable result of emergency conditions. Yet the Constitution could—and, I suspect, lawfully—have been brushed aside, possibly never to return, as a result of those trying days when, for a few weeks, violence and fear hung in the air of Kuala Lumpur.

The drive to constitutionalism and the desire for strict legality were maintained, therefore, even at a time when discontinuity, novelty and radical action could perhaps have been justified. The deceptive ease with which, from a legal point of view, the emergency was tackled and overcome, may of course offer a precedent for the future: when the next Director of Operations may be less of a parliamentarian than the late Tun Razak. This is something on which one can only speculate. The candles illuminating the future fade into the darkness and burn but fitfully, and we can discern little for certain.

Yet we can, I believe, take comfort from the lessons of the past. Constitutional government and parliamentary democracy have, in Malaysia, proved to have a strength few would have guessed, twenty years ago. The ideas within the Constitution itself, the spirit of the laws: these have, it seems, been understood and absorbed by the vast majority of those in authority. For this the teachers and lecturers in the schools and universities may take credit: but most credit is attached, perhaps, to those leaders of Malaysian politics of all races and creeds, who have set a pattern for the future. Mistakes have been made, many injustices must be set to right and the lot of the ordinary man, be he Malay, Chinese, Indian or Tamil, must be improved: but that spirit of tolerance of which the Constitution is a manifestation must be maintained.

That the economic condition of the Malay people in particular requires improvement, there can be no doubt. In an address to an UMNO Youth Seminar in 1962[28] Ungku A. Aziz noted that '[T]he economic condition of the Malays, I mean those living in the villages, have really worsened ... the main question is how to raise the level of income of the rural people. There are two ways to do this: firstly, abolish exploitation and secondly, increase the productivity of the farmers.' However, as Dr. Mahathir bin Mohamed pointed out in 1970,[29]

... suddenly, it has dawned upon the Malay that he cannot even call Malaya his land. There is no more *Tanah Melayu*—the Land of the Malays. He is now a different person, a Malaysian, but a Malay Malaysian whose authority in Malaya—his land—is now not only shared with others, but shared unequally. And as if this is not enough, he is being asked to give up more and more of his share of influence.

From one aspect the problem can be seen in purely economic terms and it may well be that the long-term solution can only be along the lines of economic parity. Yet the issue seems to be, in psychological terms, one of identity. To create a nation requires the evolution of a common identity: one often forged by strife and disaster. In other circumstances *konfrontasi* and the disputes over Sabah and Limbang might have been expected to accelerate the development of such an identity; while, in another way, the existence of Article 153 may be said to hinder it.

As noted, Article 153 has so far remained outside the area of constitutional litigation, in spite of the fact that, if carefully studied, it offers some scope for manoeuvre for those non-*bumiputras* who may consider themselves victims of injustice. Of course, litigation is often an expensive luxury; perhaps no legal aid is readily available in the area of Article 153, perhaps it is thought best to leave its operation to administrative agencies alone. Even so, it offers a means of progress and justice; as its existence cannot be questioned, let its implementation at least fall for such judicial review as may be necessary. In such a way may the common bond of citizenship develop.

In May 1957, almost on the eve of Independence, the *China Press*, in an editorial,[30] observed that

The question of special rights for a particular community may be excusable at the start of the building of a nation, but if the period of 'special rights' is not restricted, or the scope of special rights is not clearly defined, then endless disputes ... will arise later on. For the granting of special rights, whether right or wrong, has in fact caused those with special rights and those without them to be in opposite positions, a cause which may breed mutual mistrust and aversion among the people.

Writing in 1965, K. J. Ratnam noted that 'this uneasiness, quite widespread as the 1957 Constitution was being drawn up, has persisted to the present day, largely because the Malay community has itself continued to remain divided in its views'.[31] The divisions in the Malay community were then seen by Ratnam as consisting of those 'willing to agree that the Malays need to be given special privileges until such time as they are capable of competing without any help', and those who tended 'to denounce the whole idea of special Malay rights as contrary to democratic principles'.

The issue initially resolved itself into one of the duration of special rights: for the Reid Commission was required to provide for the 'safeguarding of the special position of the Malays and the legitimate interests of the other communities'. History had virtually dictated a protection of Malay rights; British presence in Malaya was lawful only under treaties with the Malay Rulers; the influx of non-Malays arose with the development of the tin and rubber industries; and it was only when immigrant labour ceased to be immigrant and began to regard Malaya as home, that tension was to arise.

In this history there are no culprits. Just as a Greek tragedy acquires its power from the sense of doomed inevitability that possesses and surrounds its protagonists, so the influx of immigrants brought not only a general prosperity, but a popular hazard. There were plenty who could read the signs: but, on the tide of rising expectations of better living standards, there was reason to hope that the threatened disasters might not befall.

In these circumstances it was asking much of the makers of a constitution, to draft a formula capable of warding off the anger and frustration of those who saw themselves as less privileged than others. Modern politics takes economic advancement as its primary objective: a bitter, painful fact of contemporary life. In the Malaysian Constitution this objective is obscured by the political powers, rights, and duties that are necessary to such advancement: and to the man in the street, the Constitution is therefore almost an irrelevance. In so far as it protects him in his contemporary situation and gives a nebulous, hopeful aura to his aspirations, it has a kind of shadowy significance: but such of its ideas and concepts as come across to him in the course of his daily life are so vague and tenuous as to be almost meaningless.

That there should be a term to Article 153 I have no doubt, but when and how its duration can be determined is a matter solely for the Malaysian people. With the amending legislation of 1971 the Article appeared to be entrenched, a permanent feature of the Constitution whose existence could never be questioned. Fortunately, with the passage of but a few years, a wise, more realistic attitude is manifest. In his weekly news commentary in *The Star*, on 9 May 1977[32] Tunku Abdul Rahman, the very *bapa kemerdekaan*, said 'There is much talk about bumiputras [sons of the soil and primarily the Malays] today that it appears in the minds of the other (races) that they are being turned into second-class citizens in the country.' Such a situation infringes the principle of equality on which the Constitution is based: so here, in the Tunku's words, is a hope of progress; and in the rising generation, too, one detects signs of an appreciation that it is in the economic circumstances and objectives of society that political principles originate. Just as culture, in the sense of music, literature, and art, is the product of surplus time and wealth, so does the philosophy of politics grow out of the fulfilment of man's needs for food, shelter, and clothing.

In one respect the policy of an inevitably close association with the Republic of Indonesia requires great care, for an adoption of the anti-Chinese policies manifest in Indonesia from the late 1950s onwards would be likely to cause great difficulties. To make it illegal to use Chinese characters on shop signs, to speak Chinese, to celebrate Chinese festivals, or to have a Chinese name are measures exhibiting too great a haste to ensure assimilation. All the same, experience asserts that the Chinese are a law-abiding people. 'In Bangkok', Dennis Bloodworth has written, 'their new readiness to be assimilated is demonstrated by the fact that few Chinese under twenty-five years old speak Chinese or have Chinese names any more. At least fifteen Thais in every hundred have Chinese blood in their veins, on the other hand, and they include the King and most of the Cabinet.'[33] It is as Dr. Mahathir has said,

> For equality to come about it is necessary that these strikingly contrasting races [the Malays and the Chinese] adjust to each other. Laws cannot do this. Only understanding, time and good will can. And understanding and good will can only come about in time if the meaning of racial equality is understood by all concerned.[34]

Adjustment can come with the evolution of the principle of equality on which the Constitution is based.

So far the politicians of Malaysia have in general eschewed appeals to those powerful forces of pride, selfishness, and violence which masquerade under the name of nationalism. Long may they continue to do so: but the task is unlikely to get any easier over the next twenty years. Wisdom and skill will be required of everyone in authority if bloodshed, chaos, anarchy, and partition are not to come about. The nation walks on a razor's edge.

In this situation the concepts of the rule of law and the impartiality of the Bench are essential for the preservation of internal peace. Insurgency in Malaysia has been contained so far, because the majority of people see law and order as constituting a reasonable framework for economic advancement, progress, and reform. Yet the frustration of youth, the bitterness of envy, and worst of all, the loss of hope, can all too easily change the situation. In such a situation the guardians of the Constitution must respond, in advance, to the challenges of the future, if constitutional government is to survive to the millenium.

1. At p. 9.

2. With the promulgation of the Civil Law Enactment of the Federated Malay States.

3. When the European Communities Act was enacted.

4. The words of Whitley Stokes, *The Anglo-Indian Codes*, Vol. 1, p. 71, cited in Eric Stokes, *The English Utilitarians in India*, p. 226.

5. An effort to obtain a Canadian lawyer for the Commission failed.

6. *Modern Constitutions*, p. 30.

7. 'Constitutional Amendments in Malaysia' (1976) 18 Mal. L.R. 59-124.

8. *The Way of Life*, translated by Witter Bynner, stanza 58.

9. See *Stephen Kalong Ningkan* v. *Government of Malaysia* [1968] 2 M.L.J. 238.

10. Act 14 of 1962.

11. *The Government of the State of Kelantan v. The Government of the Federation of Malaya and Tunku Abdul Rahman Putra Al-Haj* [1963] M.L.J. 355.

12. 'The Rukunegara and the Return to Democracy in Malaysia', *Pacific Community*, 2 (July 1971). Quoted in *Southeast Asia, Documents of Political Development and Change*, ed. by Roger M. Smith, Cornell, 1974, p. 299.

13. (1974) J.M.C.L. at p. 135.

14. [1958] M.L.J. 105.

15. *Surinder Singh Kanda* v. *The Government of the Federation of Malaya* [1962] M.L.J. 169 (Privy Council).

16. I remember the problem posed in relation to the disciplining in 1958 of a railway driver whose engine ran out of steam halfway between Kuala Lumpur and Singapore: a matter no longer for prompt action by the General Manager, but for the protracted rituals of the Railway Service Commission.

17. In *Aminah v. Superintendent of Prison, Pengkalan Chepa, Kelantan* [1968] 1 M.L.J. 92.

18. *Assa Singh v. Mentri Besar, Johore* [1968] 2 M.L.J. 30 (Federal Court, Malaysia).

19. [1969] 1 M.L.J. 6.

20. *Karam Singh* v. *Mentri Hal Ehwal Dalam Negeri, Malaysia* [1969] 2 M.L.J. 129.

21. *Public Prosecutor* v. *Anthony Wee Boon Chye and Anor.* [1965] 1 M.L.J. 189.

22. Wylie C.J. (Borneo), ibid.

23. Ong C.J. Malaya, in *Karam Singh*'s case (*ubi, supra.*).

24. *Government of Malaysia* v. *Lionel* [1974] 1 M.L.J. 3, where the Privy Council restored the judgment of the trial judge.

25. Roff, *The Origins of Malay Nationalism*, University of Malaya Press, 1967, p. 123.

26. [1975] 2 M.L.J. 66.

27. [1966] 1 M.L.J. 18.

28. Cited in *Southeast Asia, Documents of Political Development and Change*, edited by Roger M. Smith, Cornell, 1974, p. 285.

29. *The Malay Dilemma*, Asia Pacific Press, 1970, p. 121.

30. Quoted in Ratnam, *Communalism and the Political Process in Malaya*, University of Malaya Press, 1965, p. 116.

31. Ibid.

32. Quoted in *Far Eastern Economic Review*, 10 June 1977, p. 24.

33. *An Eye for the Dragon*, Farrar, Straus and Giroux, New York, 1970, p. 333.

34. Op. cit., p. 97.

※ HARRY E. GROVES

2. Fundamental Liberties in the Constitution of the Federation of Malaysia

INTRODUCTION

IN 1959, when I first wrote on this subject,[1] little was available for examination beyond the text of the Constitution and some legislative history. Scholars had not yet written extensively on the document; and, most importantly, courts had only just begun to interpret it and apply its provisions. In the last two decades not only have the Fundamental Liberties provisions of the basic charter been amended, but a substantial body of literature, both case and commentary, has begun to surround them.

While the concept of what liberties are fundamental may, of course, vary with each society which chooses to define them, legal systems grounded in English law tend, as one might suppose, at least to list many of the same subjects under the general rubric of Fundamental Liberties, or one of its cognates.[2]

In the Constitution of the Federation of Malaysia nine 'liberties' or rights, are included as fundamental. These are: (1) Liberty of the person,[3] (2) Freedom from slavery and forced labour,[4] (3) Protection against retrospective criminal laws and repeated trials,[5] (4) Equality,[6] (5) Prohibition against banishment and freedom of movement,[7] (6) Freedom of speech, assembly, and association,[8] (7) Freedom of religion,[9] (8) Rights in respect of education,[10] and (9) Rights of property.[11]

An examination of the text of each Article suggests that the makers of the Constitution regarded some liberties as more fundamental than others. The Fundamental Liberties can be placed in two distinct categories: (1) Those that are absolute in the terms of the constitutional provision, and (2) Those that are limited by the terms of the constitutional grant itself.

The following Fundamental Liberties appear, in the language of the constitutional provision of which they are a part, to be absolute: (a) Freedom from slavery,[12] (b) Protection against retrospective criminal laws and repeated trials,[13] (c) Prohibition against banishment of citizens,[14] (d) Freedom to profess and practise a religion, (e) Freedom from special, but not general, taxation to support a religion other than one's own, (f) Freedom of a religious group to manage its own religious affairs and to establish and maintain institutions for religious or charitable purposes,[15] (g) Right not to receive instruction in or to take part in any ceremony or act of worship of a religion other than one's own,[16] and (h) Freedom from the compulsory acquisition or use of one's property without adequate compensation.[17]

All of the other Fundamental Liberties are qualified, by language in the Article which recognizes the right, of some body, usually Parliament, to limit, in some fashion, the extent of the grant.

Article 5(1) provides, 'No person shall be deprived of his life or personal liberty save in accordance with law'. One is thus obliged to learn what the scope of the term 'law' is in this phrase and what 'in accordance with law' means.

Article 6(2) provides, 'All forms of forced labour are prohibited, but Parliament may by law provide for compulsory service for national purposes'. The crucial term here may be 'national purposes'. What are they? Under what circumstances may they be declared? Clause (3) contains the not unusual exception from the definition of forced labour of work incidental to the serving of a sentence of imprisonment imposed by a court of law. A clause (4), added by the Constitution (Amendment) Act 1976, binds employees of one public authority to the transfer to another, provided any written law transfers all or any of the functions of the first public authority to the second.

Article 8(5) extensively qualifies the concept of equality by excepting (a) any provision regulating personal law; (b) any provision or practice restricting office or employment connected with the affairs of any religion, or of an institution managed by a group professing any religion, to persons of that religion; (c) any provision for the protection, wellbeing or advancement of the aboriginal peoples of the Malay Peninsula (including the reservation of land) or the reservation to aborigines of a reasonable proportion of suitable positions in the public service; (d) any provision prescribing residence in a State or part of a State as a qualification for election or appointment to any authority having jurisdiction only in that State or part, or for voting in such an election; (e) any provision of a Constitution of a State, being or corresponding to a provision in force immediately before Merdeka Day; and (f) any provision restricting enlistment in the Malay Regiment to Malays.

Article 9(2) places freedom of movement within the complete discretion of Parliament. Moreover Article 4(2)(a)[18] relieves Parliament of even the requirement of drafting niceties in laws it enacts limiting freedom of movement or the right to reside in any part of the Federation.

Article 10(2) places freedom of speech, association, and assembly within the complete discretion of Parliament, and, as in the case of Article 9, Article 4(2)(b)[19] relieves Parliament of the necessity of care in drafting and protects Parliament from any impugning of its motives.

Article 11(4) permits State law and in respect of the Federal Territory, federal law to control or restrict the propagation of any religious doctrine or belief among persons professing the Muslim religion. Otherwise the right to propagate religious doctrine appears to be absolute. Clause (5) states, 'This Article does not authorize any act contrary to any general law relating to public order, public health or morality'.[20]

Article 12(2) as amended by the Constitution (Amendment) Act 1976 (Act A354) provides,

Every religious group has the right to establish and maintain institutions for the education of children in its own religion, and there shall be no discrimination on the ground only of religion in any law relating to such institutions or in the administration of any such law; but it shall be lawful for the Federation or a State to establish or maintain or assist in establishing or maintaining Islamic institutions or provide or assist in providing instruction in the religion of Islam and incur such expenditure as may be necessary for the purpose.

Article 13(1) provides, 'No person shall be deprived of property save in accordance with law'.

Although Article 153[21] appears in Part XII of the Constitution, called 'General and Miscellaneous', Part II, 'Fundamental Liberties', must be read together with Article 153, because the latter significantly qualifies the provisions on Equality, by virtue of the special status accorded Malays and natives of the Borneo States in the public service, scholarships, exhibitions, and other similar educational or training privileges or special facilities, and in permits or licences for the operation of trades and businesses.

Part XI, 'Special Powers Against Subversion, and Emergency Powers', permits, by Article 149, the suspension of Articles 5, 9, and 10, and perhaps of others of the Fundamental Liberties, since it validates any legislation otherwise outside the legislative power of Parliament, provided Parliament follows the drafting formula of Article 149.[22]

Article 150, which provides for the Proclamation of Emergency, permits Parliament, as well as the Yang di-Pertuan Agong, when acting while Parliament is not in session, to override all provisions of the Constitution, except those pertaining to any matter of Muslim law or the custom of the Malays, or any matter of native law or custom in a Borneo State, or to religion, citizenship, or language. It will be noted that of these truly inviolable rights, only those pertaining to religion affirmatively appear among the 'Fundamental Liberties'.

THE CASES—GENERAL

Judicial interpretation, particularly when acquiesced in by Parliament by refraining from amending a constitutional provision or enacting other 'clarifying' legislation, is the ultimate determinant of the meaning of constitutional language. Not all Fundamental Liberties' provisions have received judicial review. There are undoubtedly a number of reasons why this should be so. The Constitution is still a youthful document historically. Also, it is possible that some forbidden practices, such as slavery, may never occur. Other provisions may appear to potential litigants as so clear as not to warrant a judicial test. But judicial exegesis has occurred as to a number of provisions.

LIBERTY OF THE PERSON

Article 5(1). It is, of course, possible to be deprived of one's liberty by someone acting outside the law—even by a private individual. In *Munusamy* v. *Subramaniam & Ors.*,[23] the complaint was from a daughter who sought freedom to select a husband of her choice. In this case the High Court rejected an *ex parte* originating summons in chambers for application for a writ of *habeas corpus*. The complainant, having been mistaken in her procedure, received no determination on the substance of her petition. A more frequent loss of liberty can be expected to arise from governmental action, particularly in times of emergency. The meaning of the phrase, 'save in accordance with law', is relevant in issues of deprivation of life or liberty by governmental action. The same phrase appears in Article 13(1); and has there been interpreted by the Federal

Court. The case there involved an issue of taxation. But in addressing itself to the phrase, 'in accordance with law', the Court, through Gill C.J. (Malaya), in a unanimous decision, said, 'The result is that whenever a competent Legislature enacts a law in the exercise of any of its legislative powers, destroying or otherwise depriving a man of his property, the latter is precluded from questioning its reasonableness by invoking Article 13(1) of the Constitution, however arbitrary the law might palpably be.'[24] This is a holding which rejects the American concept of due process in favour of judicial deference to legislative intent. In *Comptroller-General of Inland Revenue* v. *N. P.*[25] the High Court specifically rejected any resort to natural justice in interpreting the phrase.

If, then, 'in accordance with law' has the same meaning in Article 5(1) as in Article 13(1), Article 5 litigation can be expected to be largely limited to the procedural questions of clauses (2), (3), and (4). Article 5(2) imposes on a High Court, or any judge thereof, the duty, on complaint made, to inquire into a charge of unlawful detention and to release the detainee if a determination is made that the detention is unlawful. The Article does not specify the procedure for making the complaint. As previously stated, in *Munusamy*[26] the High Court rejected the argument that a writ of *habeas corpus* could be proceeded with by way of *ex parte* originating summons under Article 5(2), and referred the complainant to Section 365 of the Criminal Procedure Code.

Article 5(3) extends two rights to the arrested person, that of being informed 'as soon as may be' of the grounds of his arrest and that of consulting and being defended by a legal practitioner of his choice. The phrase 'as soon as may be' is, of course, not precise. Its very expression makes it a source of litigation turning on the facts of each case in which it may be raised.[27] The right to consult and to be defended by a legal practitioner of one's choice seems not to be equivocal; but the exercise of the right is not without difficulty. Suffian L.P. has said for the Federal Court,

... the right of an arrested person to consult his lawyer begins from the moment of arrest, but I am of the opinion that the right cannot be exercised immediately after arrest. A balance has to be struck between the right of the arrested person to consult his lawyer on the one hand and on the other the duty of the police to protect the public from wrongdoers by apprehending them and collecting whatever evidence exists against them.[28]

In this case the accused was arrested on 26 December. His father instructed his solicitor on 30 December, who sought that day to interview the prisoner. The Lord President held that it was unreasonable for the solicitor 'to expect to be allowed to interview

Ooi on Monday, December 30'. On the contrary, his Lordship held that, 'it was quite reasonable of the police to give facilities to [the solicitor] to interview Ooi for the first time only on January 5, 1975'. The Court also rejected *habeas corpus* as an appropriate remedy for one denied access to his lawyer.

'Legal Practitioner' in Article 5(3) means one who has been admitted as an advocate and solicitor in the States of Malaysia.[29] If the legal practitioner is unwilling or unable to provide timely representation, the arrested person is obliged to seek other counsel.[30] It should be noted that clause (5) of Article 5 expressly states that clauses (3) and (4) do not apply to an enemy alien. Clause (4) provides that 'where a person is arrested and not released he shall without unreasonable delay, and in any case within twenty-four hours (excluding the time of any necessary journey) be produced before a magistrate and shall not be further detained in custody without the magistrate's authority'. The Constitution (Amendment) Act 1976 has extended the non-applicability of clause (4) to any person who is arrested or detained under the existing law relating to restricted residence. The amendment was given retrospective effect to Merdeka Day.

SLAVERY AND FORCED LABOUR

Article 6 is yet to be the subject of litigation.

RETROSPECTIVE CRIMINAL LAWS AND REPEATED TRIALS

Article 7(1) is substantive, not procedural, in character. Therefore, mere modification of procedure, such as a change from trial by jury to a trial by a judge alone, will not support a protest under this section.[31]

The following qualifications of the protection from repeated trials of Article 7(2) have received judicial recognition: The quashing of a conviction as a nullity has been held by the Federal Court to be no bar to a retrial.[32] Administrative detention is held not to be punishment for an offence and is, therefore, no bar to trial;[33] nor are trial and acquittal a bar to administrative detention.[34]

EQUALITY

Article 8(1) has two components, namely, equality before the law and equal protection of the law. It has been held that, before the bar of justice, princes of the royal houses are not to be treated differently from others. So in *Public Prosecutor* v. *Tengku Mahmood Iskander & Anor.*,[35] a High Court substituted a more severe sentence for a lesser one imposed by a lower court which had taken into account the exalted position of the accused. The Federal Court has held that it is not, however, a violation of equality before the law, nor of equal protection, for discretion to reside in a public prosecutor as whether to try an accused under ordinary criminal procedure or under Emergency Regulations in force, with their quite different procedure.[36]

No significant cases interpreting Article 8, clauses (2), (3), and (4) have been found.

Article 8(5)(a) excepts any provision of personal law from the general reach of the Article. The application of personal law may work to the disadvantage, rather than to the advantage, of the claimant. Thus when it was to the tax advantage of a Hindu not to be taxed under the Hindu Joint Families provision of the Income Tax Act 1967, he found himself bound by Hindu law, with the unfavourable consequences of the tax application.[37]

The power of legislation enacted under Emergency provisions to override Article 8 has been upheld by both the Federal Court[38] and the Privy Council.[39]

BANISHMENT AND FREEDOM OF MOVEMENT

Although the prohibition against the banishment of citizens appears absolute,[40] it must be read against the discretionary authority of the Government to deprive of their citizenship persons who are citizens by registration or by naturalization.[41] Such was the fate of one Chu Choon Yong, in a decision of the Federal Court.[42]

Since it is difficult to see how a law restricting freedom of movement would not relate to the security of the Federation, or some part thereof, or to public order, public health, or the punishment of offenders,[43] it is clear that limitations on this right are within the complete discretion of Parliament. This manifest fact is further underscored by Article 4(2)(a)[44] which relieves Parliament of any necessity of stating its reason for enacting a law restricting freedom of movement. The Federal Court has recognized this total power in Parliament.[45]

SPEECH, ASSEMBLY, AND ASSOCIATION

As with movement, speech, assembly, and association are only as free as Parliament chooses to have them be. These 'freedoms' are subject to the complete control of Parliament, being limited even by laws, such as the Sedition Act, 1948, enacted prior to the Constitution.[46] Moreover, prior restraint on freedom of speech may be exercised by an officer-in-charge of a Police District acting under the Police Act to regulate the conduct in public places of assembly and meeting, which officer may, in granting the licence to hold the meeting, proscribe subjects to be touched on in the speech.[47]

While the determination of what language is seditious is a mixed question of fact and law to be decided by the court, the cases do not suggest a liberal judicial reading of freedom of speech in favour of the political dissident opposed to the Government.[48]

RELIGION

Religious freedoms have not been a subject of meaningful litigation.

EDUCATION

Constitutional questions in respect to education have not arisen.

PROPERTY

As indicated above in the discussion of Article 5, the meaning of the important phrase 'in accordance with law' has been made clear in property cases. It contains no element of natural law or the American due process. In the words of Gill C.J., 'The result is that whenever a competent Legislature enacts a law in the exercise of any of its legislative powers, destroying or otherwise depriving a man of his property, the latter is precluded from questioning its reasonableness by invoking Article 13(1) of the Constitution, however arbitrary the law might palpably be.'[49]

However, Article 13(1) does prohibit illegal[50] and unreasonable[51] Executive Acts which have the effect of depriving one of his property.

In *Government of Malaysia & Anor.* v. *Selangor Pilot Association*,[52] the Privy Council drew a sharp distinction between 'deprivation' of property, which if by a legislature need not be compensated, and 'compulsory acquisition', which Article 13(2) contemplates occurring by 'law', and which requires adequate compensation. In the instant case, a law effectively terminated private pilotage business at Port Swettenham and placed all pilotage functions in a government agency. The private owners voluntarily sold certain physical assets to the Government Authority; but they sought additional compensation for 'goodwill'. While the Privy Council found that the restriction on the pilots' rights by a denial of licences did not amount to a deprivation of property, the majority went further to say that it also 'does not follow that such a provision which leads to deprivation, also leads to compulsory acquisition or use'. In this case it seems quite clear that 'goodwill', in its traditional meaning of the favour which management of a business wins from the public, was nothing the Government would have any interest in acquiring since the legislation gave the Government a pilotage monopoly. If the 'goodwill' in this instance was used in its traditional meaning by the complainants, it might have been something extinguished without being transferred.

One may venture that neither the precision of the holding in the *Selangor Pilot* case, nor the very broad dictum of Gill C.J. in *Arumugam Pillai* necessarily dispose of future cases which are conceivable, such as a confiscatory tax enactment.

SPECIAL POWERS AGAINST SUBVERSION AND EMERGENCY POWERS

Because of the overriding effect on the Fundamental Liberties provisions of these vast powers, no examination of Fundamental Liberties can be made without close consideration of them. As stated, *supra*, grant of these great powers appears in Articles 149 and 150; and the limitations on them in Article 151.

The powers to legislate against subversion in Article 149 and to legislate during a Proclamation of Emergency in Article 150 are similar in substance. The significant difference is procedural. Article 149 expands the power of Parliament, but not that of the Executive, whereas Article 150 invests the Yang di-Pertuan Agong with the authority to proclaim the Emergency and with the legislative power to act under the Proclamation unless and until Parliament is sitting.[53] He is charged with the duty of summoning Parliament 'as soon as may be practicable'; and Parliament may revoke the Proclamation of Emergency; but such revocation does not negate action taken by the Yang di-Pertuan Agong under ordinances which he may have promulgated pursuant to the Proclamation of Emergency.

The significant substantive difference between Articles 149 and 150 is that the latter specifically exempts from the reach of Emergency legislation matters of Muslim law or custom of the Malays, matters of native law or custom in a Borneo State, and matters relating to religion, citizenship, and language. Article 149 does not so limit legislation against subversion.

Since both Articles 149 and 150 can, when invoked, effectively suspend all Fundamental Liberties, with the exception of those noted in Article 150, it follows that the protections of Article 151, all of which are procedural, become of utmost importance to the citizen adversely affected by being caught within the sweep of one of those Articles.

The most cursory reading of Articles 149 and 150 reveals that the Constitution meant to invest Parliament with the broadest substantive powers to meet the threat of subversion and other emergencies; and the courts have interpreted those provisions favouring the power exercised. So in *Karam Singh* v. *Mentri Hal Ehwal Dalam Negeri, Malaysia*,[54] the Federal Court held, *inter alia*, that the question as to whether there was a reasonable cause for detention under Article 149 was a matter of opinion and policy, a decision entirely for the Executive. In *Eng Keock Cheng* v. *Public Prosecutor*,[55] Chief Justice Wylie, speaking for the Federal Court, said,

> The true effect of article 150 is that, subject to certain exceptions set out therein, Parliament has, during an Emergency, power to legislate on any subject and to any effect, even if inconsistencies with articles of the Constitution (including the provisions for Fundamental Liberties) are involved. This necessarily includes authority to delegate part of that power to legislate to some other authority, notwithstanding the existence of a written Constitution.[56]

Again the courts have held that detention made in the exercise of a valid legal power shifts the onus to the detainee to show that the power was exercised *mala fide* or improperly.[57] Moreover, the question as to whether there was reasonable cause for detention has been held to be a matter of opinion and policy, a decision entirely for the Executive.[58]

While the courts do liberally interpret the grant of substantive power to Parliament, they also recognize the importance for the protection of the individual of holding the Government to the procedural limitations of Article 151. Included in those protections is the requirement that a detainee be informed 'as soon as may be', of the grounds of his detention and the allegations of fact on which the order is based, although he is not entitled to facts which, in the opinion of any detaining authority, would be against the national interest. Furthermore, vagueness, insufficiency, or irrelevance of the allegations of fact supplied to the detainee will not render the detention unlawful but only permit the detainee to request particulars.[59] Withholding facts from the detainee may make difficult, in some instances, his ability to make the most effective representations against the order of detention. Undoubtedly the greatest procedural right of the detainee who is a citizen derives from the provision that he cannot be held for longer than three months unless an advisory board has considered his representations. In three companion cases the Federal Court ordered the release of citizens detained under the Emergency (Public Order and Prevention of Crime) Ordinance, 1969, when the evidence showed that an advisory board had not considered their representations within the constitutionally specified time.[60] As a result of the Constitution (Amendment) Act 1976, Article 151(1)(b) has been replaced by a new provision which states that 'no citizen shall continue to be detained ... unless an advisory board ... has considered any representations made by him ... and made recommendations thereon to the Yang di-Pertuan Agong within three months of receiving such representations, or within such longer period as the Yang di-Pertuan Agong may allow'. In future cases a detainee who is a citizen will find it extremely difficult to employ Article 151(1)(b) to challenge his detention successfully.

CONCLUSION

There is the familiar story of two persons examining the contents of the same vessel. The pessimist laments that it is half empty. The optimist rejoices that it is half full. Perhaps this story is not totally inapt as one contemplates Fundamental Liberties in the Constitution of Malaysia.

1. Harry E. Groves, 'Fundamental Liberties in the Constitution of the Federation of Malaya—A Comparative Study' (1959), 5 *Howard Law Journal* 190.

2. The Indian Constitution uses the term 'Fundamental Rights'. In the United States the related terms 'Civil Rights' and 'Civil Liberties' encompass much of the same subject matter.

3. Federal Constitution, Part II, Article 5.

4. Ibid., Article 6.

5. Ibid., Article 7.

6. Ibid., Article 8.

7. Ibid., Article 9.

8. Ibid., Article 10.

9. Ibid., Article 11.

10. Ibid., Article 12.

11. Ibid., Article 13.

12. Ibid., Article 6(1).

13. Ibid., Article 7.

14. Ibid., Article 9(1).

15. Ibid., Article 11.

16. Ibid., Article 12(3).

17. Ibid., Article 13(2).

18. Article 4(2)(a) is as follows:
    2. The validity of any law shall not be questioned on the ground that—
    (a) it imposes restrictions on the right mentioned in Article 9(2) but does not relate to the matters mentioned therein;

19. Article 4(2)(b) is as follows:
    2. The validity of any law shall not be questioned on the ground that—
    (b) it imposes such restrictions as are mentioned in Article 10(2) but those restrictions were not deemed necessary or expedient by Parliament for the purposes mentioned in that Article.

20. In the United States, this exception has been read into the Constitution by the United States Supreme Court. See, e.g., *Reynolds* v. *United States*, 98 U.S. 145, 25 L. Ed. 244 (1878).

21. Article 153 provides as follows:
    (1) It shall be the responsibility of the Yang di-Pertuan Agong to safeguard the

special position of the Malays and natives of any of the Borneo States and the legitimate interests of other communities in accordance with the provisions of this Article.

(2) Notwithstanding anything in this Constitution but subject to the provisions of Article 40 and of this Article, the Yang di-Pertuan Agong shall exercise his functions under this Constitution and federal law in such manner as may be necessary to safeguard the special position of the Malays and natives of any of the Borneo States and to ensure the reservation for Malays of such proportion as he may deem reasonable of positions in the public service (other than the public service of a State) and of scholarships, exhibitions and other similar educational or training privileges or special facilities given or accorded by the Federal Government and, when any permit or licence for the operation of any trade or business is required by federal law, then, subject to the provisions of that law and this Article, of such permits and licences.

(3) The Yang di-Pertuan Agong may, in order to ensure in accordance with Clause (2) the reservation to Malays and natives of any of the Borneo States of positions in the public service and of scholarships, exhibitions and other educational or training privileges or special facilities, give general directions as may be required for that purpose to any Commission to which Part X applies or to any authority charged with responsibility for the grant of such scholarships, exhibitions or other educational or training privileges or special facilities; and the Commission or authority shall duly comply with the directions.

(4) In exercising his functions under this Constitution and federal law in accordance with Clauses (1) to (3) the Yang di-Pertuan Agong shall not deprive any person of any public office held by him or of the continuance of any scholarship, exhibition or other educational or training privileges or special facilities enjoyed by him.

(5) This Article does not derogate from the provisions of Article 136.

(6) Where by existing federal law a permit or licence is required for the operation of any trade or business the Yang di-Pertuan Agong may exercise his functions under that law in such manner, or give such general directions to any authority charged under that law with the grant of such permits or licences, as may be required to ensure the reservation of such proportion of such permits or licences for Malays and natives of any of the Borneo States as the Yang di-Pertuan Agong may deem reasonable; and the authority shall duly comply with the directions.

(7) Nothing in this Article shall operate to deprive or authorise the deprivation of any person of any right, privilege, permit or licence accrued to or enjoyed or held by him or to authorise a refusal to renew to any person any such permit or licence or a refusal to grant to the heirs, successors or assigns of a person any permit or licence when the renewal or grant might reasonably be expected in the ordinary course of events.

(8) Notwithstanding anything in this Constitution, where by any federal law any permit or licence is required for the operation of any trade or business, that law may provide for the reservation of a proportion of such permits or licences for Malays and natives of any of the Borneo States; but no such law shall for the purpose of ensuring such a reservation—

(a) deprive or authorise the deprivation of any person of any right, privilege, permit or licence accrued to or enjoyed or held by him; or

(b) authorise a refusal to renew to any person any such permit or licence or a refusal to grant to the heirs, successors or assigns of any person any permit or licence when the renewal or grant might in accordance with the other provisions of the law reasonably be expected in the ordinary course of events, or prevent any person from transferring together with his business any transferable licence to operate that business; or

(c) where no permit or licence was previously required for the operation of the trade or business which immediately before the coming into force of the law he had been bona fide carrying on, or authorise a refusal subsequently to renew to any such person any permit or licence, or a refusal to grant to the heirs, successors or assigns of any such person any such permit or licence when the renewal or grant might in accordance with the other provisions of that law reasonably be expected in the ordinary course of events.

(8A) Notwithstanding anything in this Constitution, where in any University, College and other educational institution providing education after Malaysian Certificate of Education or its equivalent, the number of places offered by the authority responsible for the management of the University, College or such educational institution to candidates for any course of study is less than the number of candidates qualified for such places, it shall be lawful for the Yang di-Pertuan Agong by virtue of this Article to give such directions to the authority as may be required to ensure the reservation of such proportion of such places for Malays and natives of any of the Borneo States as the Yang di-Pertuan Agong may deem reasonable; and the authority shall duly comply with the directions.

(9) Nothing in this Article shall empower Parliament to restrict business or trade solely for the purpose of reservations for Malays and natives of any of the Borneo States.

(9A) In this Article the expression 'natives' in relation to a Borneo State shall have the meaning assigned to it in Article 161A.

(10) The Constitution of the State of any Ruler may make provision corresponding (with the necessary modifications) to the provisions of this Article.

22. Article 149 provides as follows:

(1) If an Act of Parliament recites that action has been taken or threatened by any substantial body of persons, whether inside or outside the Federation—

(a) to cause, or to cause a substantial number of citizens to fear, organised violence against persons or property; or

(b) to excite disaffection against the Yang di-Pertuan Agong or any Government in the Federation; or

(c) to promote feelings of ill-will and hostility between different races or other classes of the population likely to cause violence; or

(d) to procure the alteration, otherwise than by lawful means, of anything by law established; or

(e) which is prejudicial to the security of the Federation or any part thereof, any provision of that law designed to stop or prevent that action is valid notwithstanding that it is inconsistent with any of the provisions of Article 5, 9 or 10, or would apart from this Article be outside the legislative power of Parliament; and Article 79 shall not apply to a Bill for such an Act or any amendment to such a Bill.

(2) A law containing such a recital as is mentioned in Clause (1) shall, if not sooner repealed, cease to have effect if resolutions are passed by both Houses of Parliament annulling such law, but without prejudice to anything previously done by virtue thereof or to the power of Parliament to make a new law under this Article.

23. [1969] 2 M.L.J. 108.

24. *Arumugam Pillai* v. *Government of Malaysia* [1974] 2 M.L.J. 29.

25. [1973] 1 M.L.J. 165.

26. Op. cit. Note 23.

27. See, for example, *Aminah* v. *Superintendent of Prison, Pengkalan Chepa, Kelantan* [1968] 1 M.L.J. 92.

28. *Ooi Ah Phua* v. *Officer-in-Charge Criminal Investigations, Kedah/Perlis* [1975] 2 M.L.J. 198. See, also, *Hashim Bin Saud* v. *Yahaya Bin Hashim & Anor.* [1977] 2 M.L.J. 116.

29. *In Re G. G. Ponnambalam* [1969] 2 M.L.J. 263.

30. *Bakar Bin Ahmad* v. *Public Prosecutor* [1969] (Malacca Criminal Appeal No. 28 of 1968). Unreported. (See Jayakumar, *Constitutional Law Cases from Malaysia and Singapore*, 2nd ed., Malayan Law Journal Pte. Ltd, 1976 at p. 78.)

31. *Lim Sing Hiaw* v. *Public Prosecutor* [1965] 1 M.L.J. 85.

32. *Fan Yew Teng* v. *Public Prosecutor* [1975] 2 M.L.J. 235.

33. *Public Prosecutor* v. *Musa* [1970] 1 M.L.J. 101.

34. *Yeap Hock Seng @ Ah Seng* v. *Minister for Home Affairs, Malaysia & Ors.* [1975] 2 M.L.J. 279.

35. [1973] 1 M.L.J. 128.

36. *Mohamed Sidin* v. *Public Prosecutor* [1967] 1 M.L.J. 106.

37. *B.* v. *Comptroller of Inland Revenue* [1974] 2 M.L.J. 110.

38. *Eng Keock Cheng* v. *Public Prosecutor* [1966] 1 M.L.J. 18.

39. *Osman & Anor.* v. *Public Prosecutor* [1968] 2 M.L.J. 137.

40. *Kung Aik* v. *Public Prosecutor* [1970] 2 M.L.J. 174.

41. Federal Constitution, Article 25(1).

42. *Minister of Home Affairs* v. *Chu Choon Yong & Anor.* [1977] 2 M.L.J. 20.

43. Article 9(2) provides as follows:

9(2) Subject to Clause (3) and to any law relating to the security of the Federation or any part thereof, public order, public health, or the punishment of offenders, every citizen has the right to move freely throughout the Federation and to reside in any part thereof.

44. Note 18, *supra*.

45. *Assa Singh* v. *Mentri Besar, Johore* [1969] 2 M.L.J. 30.

46. *Public Prosecutor* v. *Ooi Kee Saik & Ors.* [1971] 2 M.L.J. 108.

47. *Madhavan Nair & Anor.* v. *Public Prosecutor* [1975] 2 M.L.J. 264.

48. Note 32, *supra*.

49. Note 24, *supra*.

50. *Philip Hoalim Jr. & Anor.* v. *State Commissioner, Penang* [1974] 2 M.L.J. 100; affd. [1976] 2 M.L.J. 231.

51. *Lai Tai* v. *The Collector of Land Revenue* [1960] M.L.J. 82.

52. [1977] 1 M.L.J. 133.

53. He may act both when a Parliament in being is not sitting or when Parliament has been dissolved and the general election to a new Parliament has not been completed. *Fan Yew Teng* v. *Public Prosecutor* [1975] 2 M.L.J. 235.

54. [1969] 2 M.L.J. 129.

55. [1966] 1 M.L.J. 18.

56. See, also, *Osman & Anor.* v. *Public Prosecutor* [1968] 2 M.L.J. 18.

57. *Karam Singh* v. *Mentri Hal Ehwal Dalam Negeri, Malaysia*, op. cit., note 54, *supra*.

58. Ibid.

59. Ibid.

60. *Re Tan Boon Liat @ Allen & Anor., et al.* v. *Mentri Hal Ehwal Dalam Negeri & Ors.* [1977] 2 M.L.J. 108.

✻ AHMAD IBRAHIM

3. The Position of Islam in the Constitution of Malaysia

IN the constitutional organization of the Muslim states that sprang up in South-East Asia can be seen the extension of established precedents concerning government and statecraft in the political history of Islam. The spread of Islam in Malaysia was accompanied by the rise of a series of autonomous sultanates which, possessing a known historical tradition, provided a basis for the constitution of Islamic political entities in the region.

The earliest written constitution in Malaysia is the Constitution of Johore promulgated in 1895.[1] This constitution was drafted by the legal advisers of Sultan Abubakar, a law firm in Singapore, but it did not attempt to set up a Western form of democratic government. Rather it set out in legal terms the political structure of Johore as it existed at that time with the addition of certain already defined checks on the Ruler and his prerogatives as 'sovereign Ruler and Possessor of the State of Johore and its dependencies'.

The preamble made it clear that it is the Sultan himself who is handing down the Constitution since it states that, 'We, in our name and for and on our own behalf and for and on behalf of our heirs and successors, the Sovereign Rulers and Possessors of this State, to wit the Sultans of Johore are pleased, willing and desirous' to make and grant the Constitution for the use of the Government, subjects and inhabitants of Johore. But in coming to the decision that such an act was proper, expedient and suitable at the time, the Sultan secured 'the advice, concurrence and assent of all the Members of our Council of State and other Chiefs and Elders of the country'.

Following the preamble the Constitution presents a list of definitions of the Malay terms used for the principal personages of the

State who have a voice in its affairs and participate in the election of the Ruler. The Ruler himself, it continues, 'shall be a person of the Malay race, of Royal blood, a descendant of the Johore sovereigns, a male and of the Muslim faith'. Normally the Sultan's heir is to be chosen from among his sons unless the Juma'ah Pangkuan Negeri (the supporters of the country or the Ahl-al-hall wa'l-'aqd, literally those with power to loosen and to bind) agree that all these are ineligible owing to their having some great and serious defect derogatory to the quality of a sovereign, that is to say, any infirmity such as insanity, blindness, dumbness or possessing some base qualities on account of which he would not be permitted by the Hukum Shara (Islamic Law) to become a sovereign. The various possibilities as to the succession are examined at length and the provisions for election vary to some extent in different cases, but the general power of election rests with the Juma'ah Pangkuan Negeri or Ahl-al-hall wa'l-'aqd. Provision is made for the appointment by the Juma'ah Majlis di-Raja (Council of the Royal Court) of a regent during the minority of a Sultan or his infirmity or illness or during his temporary absence from the country.

The Constitution originally contained a fundamental limitation on the power of the Sultan in that 'he may not in any manner surrender or make any agreement or plan to surrender the country or any part of the country to any European State or power or to any other State or nation' on the penalty of losing his throne and similar limitations are placed upon the Juma'ah Majlis di-Raja and the Juma'ah Pangkuan Negeri. It was also provided that the sovereign and the State of Johore shall always and permanently remain in a state and condition of amity and good understanding with other States (and especially and particularly with the British or English nation and government). A further limitation was that the Ruler may not appropriate for his own use a single duit more than the sum which shall be fixed from time to time by the Council of State (later the Legislative Assembly). Two councils were recognized by the Constitution as assisting the Ruler in the task of governing the country, the Council of Ministers and the Council of State. The members of the former were ex-officio members of the latter. The ministers individually and as members of the Council have the function of being assistants and coadjutors to the Sultan and it 'is expedient, necessary and advantageous to the Sultan to take the advice, opinion and counsel of that body in all affairs and cases concerning the interests of the country and the people'. The ministers must be Malays, subjects of the Sultan and professing the Muslim religion and are appointed by the Sultan. The Council of State contained in addition to the Ministers other members appointed by the Ruler with the advice or concurrence of the Council of Ministers and was the principal legislative body as well as an advisory council to the Sultan. Prior to 1914 its members were required to be Johore subjects although not necessarily Malays or Muslims, but after the Treaty with Britain the Council was opened to additional members who were not required to be Johore subjects nor to take the oath of allegiance to the Sultan. The Council of State later became the Legislative Assembly. In 1912 a third Council was added, the Executive Council, the members of which were appointed by the Sultan and sit at his pleasure. The Sultan could act in opposition to the advice of the Executive Council but must record in writing the grounds of his dissent.

The functions of the Executive Council were very broad, covering in general all routine matters of government, the initiation of legislation and 'other matters of general importance' in addition to its more specific duty of considering all applications for agricultural and mining lands and all contracts and tenders for public works.

Article VII of the Constitution provided that

... what is called the 'Religion of the State' for this territory and State of Johore is the Muslim Religion and such being the case, the Muslim Religion shall continuously and forever be, and be acknowledged and spoken of as the State religion; that is to say, on no account may any other religion be made or spoken of as the religion of the country, although all other religions are allowed and are always understood as proper to be allowed, to be practised in peace and harmony by the people professing them in all and every part of the Territory and Dependencies of the State of Johore.

Article LVIII provided that

All the laws and customs of the country shall be carried out and exercised with justice and fairness by all the Courts of Justice and by all Officers and Servants of the State between all the people of the country and the aliens who sojourn and reside under its protection, whether for a season or for a lengthened period, that is to say without their entertaining in the least degree more sympathy or regard or partiality towards those who profess the religion of the country, namely the Muslim religion or making any difference between those who are subjects of the State and those who are not.

In the case of *Wong Ah Fook* v. *State of Johore*[2] the plaintiff claimed a declaration that he had an absolute right to permit all persons to game at the gaming farm which he held under a concession from the Johore Government and that he was entitled to the return of all monies which he alleged he had paid under duress under agreements which he had been forced to sign. The main defence was that the State could not be liable for the acts of the Sultan as the supreme executive authority and the arguments put forward were that the State was governed by the Mohammedan law and under that law the sovereign's power is absolute; and secondly that by the Constitution of Johore no restriction was placed on the Sultan's authority. Whitley J. in his judgment referred to this argument and said:

... it is not true, as a general statement, that the State is governed by the Mohammedan law. It is governed by the laws of the country, and they in some respects are even antagonistic to the Mohammedan law.

The Constitution of 1895, ... enacts in Clause LVIII: 'All the laws and customs of the country shall be carried out and exercised with justice and fairness by all the Courts of Justice and by all officers and servants of the State'. There is no mention of the Mohammedan law here.

It was held that the defence plea failed and that the plaintiff was entitled to the declaration he asked for. The Sultan was not above the law and under the Constitution and by virtue of the declaration of 1908 (which amended the Constitution) and section 392 of the Civil Procedure Code the Courts of the State were competent to pronounce upon the legality of the Sultan's executive acts.

In the case of *Anchom binte Lampong* v. *Public Prosecutor*[3] it was argued, *inter alia*, that (a) Mohammedan law is one of the branches or ingredients of the law of the State of Johore and (b) that the Offences by Mohammedans Enactment was *ultra vires* the Constitution and was therefore void and of no effect. The Court of Appeal held that the Courts of the State have no jurisdiction to declare that an Enactment of the Legislature duly passed by the Council of State and assented to by the Ruler is *ultra vires* the Constitution. In doing so the Court relied mainly on Article LXIV of the Constitution, which has since been repealed. Poyser C.J. in the course of his judgment said:

It follows therefore that even if Enactment 47 of 1937 is contrary to the provisions of the Constitution, this Court cannot hold it to be so. I would only add that the Mohammedan law was never adopted in its entirety in the State of Johore. Mr. Braddell referred us to the early customary laws which establish this proposition. Such laws are set out in the Translation of the Malayan laws of the Principality of Johore, prepared by the late Thomas Braddell in 1855 and published in Volume IX of the Journal of the Indian Archipelago. The following is an example:- 'If a person who receives a blow on the face kill the assailant it shall be deemed no offence should he kill him within three days, but if after this period, the slayer shall be fined one catty, for by so doing he has conducted himself in an unmanly manner and this is the law of custom. But by the law of God the slayer in this case shall be put to death'. In recent years too, the majority of the Enactments probably contain provisions which are not in accordance with the Mohammedan law. Enactment No. 47 of 1937 is one of such enactments for under the

Mohammedan law the penalty for adultery is death but under the Johore law only imprisonment and fine.

Another example of a Malay State Constitution is the Constitution of Trengganu which was promulgated in 1911.[4] The preamble states that the Sultan 'the possessor and head of the Government of Trengganu in full sovereignty and with the consent of the members of the Cabinet of Ministers, the State Council, the chiefs and headmen of the State have considered after due debate and free discussion that it is fitting and incumbent ... to create and set up a law constituting the government of Trengganu'. The Constitution provides that the 'Raja who governs Trengganu must always be of Muslim religion and of the Malay race and of the lineage and descent of the Sultans of Trengganu'. Normally the Sultan's heir is to be chosen from the lineage of Sultan Zainal Abidin but if none survive or if those who survive are not eligible, another person may be elected by the State Council together with the Cabinet of Ministers and the Ahl-al-hall wa'l-'aqd (the Council of Regency, that is to say, the members of the two ranks of ministers and chiefs who are called *ahli alhilli wala'kod*, that is, men who have franchise in the setting up of the Raja and in matters of first importance). Where the Raja is a minor, a regent is chosen by the Ministers and when he is absent from the State, the State Council may appoint a Regent. Although all authority in the country and government is vested in the Raja yet it is stated, it is customary and obligatory on the Ruler to hold counsel with all his Ministers upon any question of government and of regulation of laws.

If the Raja considers that any act is for the public weal and betterment or any affair is likely to lead to trouble at a time when the members of the Council are not present he may straightaway act alone on his own responsibility but when the members of the Council are again present it is lawful for them to consider any regulations or laws which have been instituted by the Raja and if they are not agreed to by the Council they may be annulled.

Ministers are appointed

... to the chief offices in the Government with the express mandate of the Raja setting forth and explaining accordingly their correct titles and rank and various responsibilities and they may act as assistants and special advisers of the Raja in the several spheres of Government and when their departments have been established then all matters relevant to those departments are put in their personal charge.

The number of Ministers must not be less than eight or more than twelve and the head of the Ministers shall be the Chief Minister who is appointed leader of the State Council and further the Ministers appointed must be Muslims and subjects of Trengganu.

A State Council is constituted whose functions according to Chapter 37 are

... to assist the Raja and the Cabinet of Ministers in governing the country and its subjects in the way of making and adjusting and adding to the Laws and Regulations other than those concerning religion and Mohammedan law considering matters for the advancement of the country and its welfare putting up proposals for raising revenue, increasing trade, improving the condition of the peasants and rendering advice for maintaining the peace of the country and in the districts under it in the State of Trengganu and preserving good relations, friendship and concord with foreign governments.

It should be noted that religion and Muslim law are expressly excepted and cannot be 'adjusted or added to' by laws and regulations. Members of the State Council must be appointed from Trengganu subjects but it is not provided that they must all be of the Muslim religion and the Malay race.

Chapter 51 provides that

... whereas it has been asserted and laid down and established that for all time this Government of Trengganu is of the comity of Islam in Malaya that is it is called the State and official religion, no other religion whatever may be set up or referred to as the State religion, however many of other races or creeds are protected and allowed to shelter in the States and provinces of Trengganu.

Chapter 46 provides that

All laws and customs of the country must be forwarded and enforced justly and truly by all courts of the State and officers and administrative departments among the subjects of the country and foreigners who stop and take shelter in it whether temporarily or permanently.

The Constitution also provided in Chapter 53 that

The Raja is empowered by Order in Council to add to and extend this law from time to time provided that nothing is enacted contrary to its provisions or for the purpose of undermining the foundations and intention of this law and in like manner the Raja in Council or the State Council alone has the power and authority to interpret and confirm the provisions and appendages of all or any chapter or any word or any underlying intention included in this law and when this has been effected for the purpose of special clarity then all such clauses and commentaries which may be affirmed and decided shall become and be accepted as an integral portion of this law.

Chapter 14 provides that

... it is not right and not lawful in any way for the Raja to make a promise or proposal to release or surrender the country and its Government or any share of the authority of government or popular right to any other government whatever or into the power of any race, European or otherwise. If the Raja tries to evade this provision and limitation then he must be deemed to have broken the trust placed upon him and his action is unlawful. And thereupon it is not incumbent upon the government and all the subjects to remain loyal to him longer and he shall be dispossessed from his seat of government and a substitute set up in his place.

The Constitution of 1911 is now largely of historical interest as most of its provisions have been superseded by the Laws of the Constitution of Trengganu promulgated after the Federation was constituted in 1948. It may be noted that the Constitution of 1948 declares that the Religion of the State 'shall be the Muslim religion heretofore professed and practised in the State, provided that all other religions may be practised in peace and harmony by the persons professing them in any part of the State'.

Chapters 14, 37 and 53 of the Constitution of 1911 have also been superseded.

The early Malay State Constitutions—written or unwritten—show traces of the traditional Islamic polity. The Sultanate was the result of the assimilation of the spiritual and religious traditions originally associated with the institution of the Caliphate with the purely temporal authority that was the Sultan; the latter thus in addition to being a sovereign prince in the secular sense also came to maintain a close association with and responsibility for the Shariah. The Sultan was not entitled to any special exemption from the provisions of the Shariah law, being himself no more than a servant of the law. In theory neither the ruler nor any governmental organ has legislative powers in those matters that formed the exclusive substance of the Shariah law. The interpretation of the Shariah in relation to new situations was the prerogative of the learned *fuqaha* (jurists) including the mufti. The competence of the ruler was confined to the making of administrative regulations in those areas not the immediate concern of the substantive law of Islam, with the proviso that such regulations must not themselves lead to a breach of that law. This theory of non-interference in the Islamic law has been broken in practice by Muslim rulers in the past and in more modern times has been seriously affected by the legislative measures taken in the modern Muslim States. Notwithstanding the fact that the Ruler in each Malay State possesses discretionary powers, the Constitution provides for consultation with his ministers and advisers. The basis for this is the principle of *Shura* or consultation which was defended by the theorists of the classical sultanate on the ground that it would be advisable always to act on *nasihah* or advice for according to Ibn Tiqtaqa 'an error of judgment with consultation is better than a right decision made arbitrarily'.[5] Autocracy and despotism were denounced and consultation with the proper authorities—those distinguished for their knowledge, intelligence, and sound judgment—commended.

When the Reid Constitutional Commission was drafting the Constitution for the Federation of Malaya it considered the question whether there should be any statement in the Constitution to the effect that Islam should be the State religion. The Commission in its report[6] said:

There was universal agreement that if any such provision were inserted it must be made clear that it would not in any way affect the civil rights of the non-Muslims. In the memorandum submitted by the Alliance it was stated—'the religion of Malaysia shall be Islam. The observance of this principle shall not impose any disability on non-Muslim natives professing and practising their religions and shall not imply that the State is not a secular State'. There is nothing in the draft Constitution to affect the continuance of the present position in the States with regard to recognition of Islam or to prevent the recognition of Islam in the Federation by legislation or otherwise in any respect which does not prejudice the civil rights of individual non-Muslims. The majority of us think that it is best to leave the matter on this basis, looking to the fact that counsel for the Rulers said to us 'It is Their Highnesses' considered view that it would not be desirable to insert some declaration such as has been suggested that the Muslim faith or Islamic faith be the established religion in the Federation. Their Highnesses are not in favour of such a declaration being inserted and that is a matter of specific instruction in which I myself have played very little part'.

Mr. Justice Abdul Hamid, the Pakistani member of the Commission,[7] however felt that as the recommendation of the Alliance Party was unanimous, it should be accepted, and he suggested that a provision to the following effect should be inserted—'Islam shall be the religion of the State of Malaya, but nothing in this article shall prevent any citizen professing any religion other than Islam to profess and practise and propagate that religion, nor shall any citizen be under any disability by reason of his not being a Muslim'.

He said:

A provision like the one suggested above is innocuous. Not less than fifteen countries of the world have a provision of this type entrenched in their Constitutions. Among the Christian countries, which have such a provision in their Constitutions are Ireland (Article 6), Norway (Article 1), Denmark (Article 3), Spain (Article 6), Argentina (Article 2), Bolivia (Article 3), Panama (Article 36) and Paraguay (Article 3). Among the Muslim countries are Afghanistan (Article 1), Iran (Article 1), Iraq (Article 13), Jordan (Article 2), Saudi Arabia (Article

7) and Syria (Article 3). Thailand is an instance where Buddhism has been enjoined to be the religion of the King who is required by the Constitution to uphold that religion (Constitution of Thailand, Article 7). If in these countries a religion has been declared to be the religion of the State and that declaration has not been found to have caused hardships to anybody, no harm will ensue if such a declaration is included in the Constitution of Malaya. In fact in all the Constitutions of Malayan States a provision of this type already exists. All that is required is to transplant it from the State Constitutions and to embed it in the Federal.

The Rulers of the Malay States at first opposed the enactment of such a provision in the new Federal Constitution because they were told by their constitutional advisers that if the Federation had an official religion, the proposed Head of the Federation would logically become the Head of the official religion throughout the Federation and it was thought that this would be in conflict with the position of each of the Rulers as Head of the official religion in his own State. However it was explained by the Alliance Party that it was not intended to interfere with the position of the Rulers as Head of Islam in their own States and that the intention in making Islam the official religion of the Federation was primarily for ceremonial purposes, for instance to enable prayers to be offered in the Islamic way on official occasions such as the installation of the Yang di-Pertuan Agong, Merdeka Day, and similar occasions.[8] This explanation was accepted by the Rulers and accordingly Article 3 of the Federal Constitution enacts that Islam is the religion of the Federation. In conformity with previous practice the Article goes on to say that other religions may be practised in peace and harmony in any part of the Federation. In recognition of the representations made by the Rulers, Clause (2) of the Article states:

In every State other than States not having a Ruler the position of the Ruler as the Head of the Muslim religion in his State in the manner and to the extent acknowledged by the Constitution of that State and, subject to the Constitution, all rights, privileges, prerogatives and powers enjoyed by him as Head of that religion, are unaffected and unimpaired....

And in order to assure the non-Muslims that their civil rights are not affected Clause (4) provides that nothing in the Article (that is Article 3) derogates from any other provision of that Constitution.

Even before Merdeka it was found necessary in practice for the Malay States to act in concert in certain religious matters, for example in determining the first and last day of the fasting month. In 1949 the Conference of Rulers appointed a Standing Committee consisting of the Keeper of the Rulers' Seal as Chairman and two representatives from each Malay State to advise the Conference on religious matters with a view to achieving where possible uniformity throughout the Federation, and also to advise the Conference on matters specifically referred to it. In theory it was open for each Ruler to act separately in such religious matters but it was felt that there should be some uniformity and that the Yang di-Pertuan Agong should be given authority to represent each Ruler in certain acts, observances, and ceremonies. Accordingly it is provided in Clause (2) of Article 13 that 'in any acts, observances or ceremonies with respect to which the Conference of Rulers has agreed that they should extend to the Federation as a whole each of the other Rulers shall in his capacity of Head of the Muslim religion authorise the Yang di-Pertuan Agong to represent him'. The various State Constitutions have been correspondingly amended. This provision has been used for determining the commencement of fasting in Ramadan and the dates of the Hari Raya Puasa and the Hari Raya Haji. Another instance is the authority given by the Rulers to the Yang di-Pertuan Agong to issue *tauliahs* or letters of authority to religious teachers for the Armed Forces after the individual teachers have been duly chosen separately by the Rulers of the States.

Although Islam is the religion of the Federation, there is no Head of the Muslim religion for the whole of the Federation. The Yang di-Pertuan Agong continues to be the Head of the Muslim religion in his own State and it is provided that he shall be the Head of the Muslim religion in Malacca, Penang, in the Federal Territory, and in Sabah and Sarawak.[9] Each of the other States has its own Ruler as the Head of the Muslim religion in that State. The various State Constitutions moreover provide that the Ruler of the State may act in his discretion in the performance of any functions as Head of the Muslim religion, but it would appear that the Yang di-Pertuan Agong may only act on advice in performing his functions as Head of the Muslim religion in Malacca, Penang, the Federal Territory, Sabah, and Sarawak.

While the Constitutions of the Malay States provide that the religion of the State shall be Islam, this is not the case in Penang and Malacca. Neither the Federal Constitution nor the State Constitution provide that Islam is the State religion of either Malacca or Penang. In Sabah Islam has been formally declared as the religion of the State by a recent amendment to the State Constitution[10] but there is no similar provision in Sarawak. The position therefore is that Islam is the State religion in all the States of Malaysia except Malacca, Penang, and Sarawak. It may be noted that the former restriction that the function of the Conference of Rulers of agreeing or disagreeing to the extension of any religious acts, observances or ceremonies to the Federation as a whole shall not extend to Sabah or Sarawak has been removed.[11]

Article 8(2) of the Federal Constitution provides that:

Except as expressly authorised by this Constitution, there shall be no discrimination against citizens on the ground only of religion, race, descent or place of birth in any law or in the appointment to any office or employment under a public authority or in the administration of any law relating to the acquisition, holding or disposition of any property or the establishing or carrying on of any trade, business, profession, vocation or employment.

The Constitutions of the Malay States contained provisions that require that only a person of the Malay race who professes the religion of Islam can be appointed to be the Mentri Besar, but after Merdeka these provisions have been amended to enable a Ruler to appoint a non-Muslim as Mentri Besar provided that in the Ruler's judgment he is likely to command the confidence of the majority of the members of the State Legislative Assembly.[12] The Constitutions of the Malay States still provide that the State Secretary shall be of the Malay race and profess the Muslim religion.[13] These provisions which existed in the State Constitutions prior to Merdeka Day are saved by Article 8(5)(e) of the Federal Constitution.

The Rulers of the Malay States and therefore the Yang di-Pertuan Agong who is chosen by the Rulers among themselves must necessarily be Malays professing the religion of Islam, but there is nothing in the Federal Constitution which provides that the Prime Minister or any Minister or Federal high official must be a Muslim.

Article 11 of the Federal Constitution provides that every person has the right to profess and practise his religion and subject to Clause (4) to propagate it. Clause (4) provides that State law may control or restrict the propagation of any religious doctrine or belief among persons professing the Muslim religion. No person shall be compelled to pay any tax, the proceeds of which are specially allocated in whole or in part for the purposes of a religion other than his own. Every religious group has the right to manage its own affairs, to establish and maintain institutions for religious or charitable purposes and to acquire and own property and hold and administer it in accordance with law.

Provision has been made in the State laws in Malacca, Penang, Negri Sembilan, Perak, Kedah, Kelantan and Sabah[14] to restrict the propagation by any person of any religious doctrine or belief other than the religious doctrine and belief of the Muslim religion to any persons professing the Muslim religion and to make it an offence to do so. It may be noted the offences are cognizable by a civil court and not by the Shariah courts. State law also prohibits the teaching (except in one's own residence and in the presence only of members of one's own household) of any doctrine of the Muslim religion without written permission; and the teaching or expounding of any doctrine or the performance of a ceremony or act relating to the Muslim religion in any manner contrary to Muslim law.

Article 12 of the Federal Constitution provides that there shall be no discrimination against any citizen on the grounds only of religion, race, descent or place of birth (a) in the administration of any educational institution maintained by a public authority and in particular the admission of pupils or students or the payment of fees; or (b) in providing out of the funds of a public authority financial aid for the maintenance or education of pupils or students in any educational institution, whether or not maintained by a public authority and whether within or outside the Federation. Clause (2) of this Article formerly provided:

> Every religious group has the right to establish and maintain institutions for the education of children and provide therein instruction in its own religion and there shall be no discrimination on the ground only of religion in any law relating to such institutions or in the administration of any such law; but Federal or State law may provide for special financial aid for the establishment or maintenance of Muslim institutions or the instruction in the Muslim religion of persons professing that religion.

This has recently[15] been amended to read as follows:

> Every religious group has the right to establish and maintain institutions for the education of children in its own religion, and there shall be no discrimination on the ground only of religion in any law relating to such institutions or the administration of any such law; but it shall be lawful for the Federation or a State to establish or maintain or assist in establishing or maintaining Islamic institutions or provide or assist in providing instruction in the religion of Islam and incur such expenditure as may be necessary for the purpose.

It is not clear what changes are designed to be effected by the amendments except to make it unnecessary to have a Federal or State law to provide for financial aid for the maintenance and assistance of Islamic institutions and Islamic religious education. The amendment may however be interpreted to mean that religious groups cannot establish schools except for the education of children in their own religion, but then it is difficult to understand why there cannot be discrimination in such institutions on the ground only of religion. The words 'and provide therein instruction' have been omitted, but again it cannot be intended that no instruction in the religion can be given.

It may be noted that the powers under Clause (2) of Article 12 now extend to the whole of the Federation including Sabah and Sarawak.[16]

In the various States there is a Council of Muslim Religion known by various names whose principal function is to 'aid and advise the Ruler on all matters relating to the religion of the State and the Malay custom'. In such matters it is the chief authority in the State but is required to take notice of and to act in accordance with the Islamic law, Malay custom, and the written laws of the State. The power of the Council varies from State to State but generally it may issue *fatwas* on any matters referred to it, it has power to administer *wakafs*, it has power to act as the executor of the will or administrator of the estate of a deceased Muslim and it may hear appeals from Muslim courts.

There also exists in each State a Department of Religious Affairs responsible for the day-to-day administration of matters relating to the Muslim religion headed in each case by a lay administrator. Some of the members of the Department are also members of the Council and there is a close relationship between the two. There is legislation in each State for the administration of Muslim law and these provide for the setting up of Kathi's courts for the adjudication of disputes relating to Muslim family law and the trial of Muslim offences. They also provide for the registration of Muslim marriages, divorces, and revocations of divorce.

In most States apart from the lay head of the Religious Affairs Department the highest religious official is the Mufti whose principal function is to issue *fatwas* or to assist the Council of Religious Affairs to do so. In some States the prerogative of appointing the Mufti is exercised by the Ruler, although in other States he is appointed by the Ruler on the advice of the Ruler in Council or of the Council of Religion.

Although the Alliance Party had insisted that Islam should be declared in the Constitution as the official religion of the Federation, it did not ask that the Constitution should also declare, as did the Pakistan Constitution, that the State shall be an Islamic State. In the White Paper dealing with the Constitutional proposals (Legislative Council Paper No. 42 of 1957)[17] it is stated:

There has been included in the proposed Federal Constitution a declaration that Islam is the religion of the Federation. This will in no way affect the present position of the Federation as a secular state, and every person will have the right to profess and practise his own religion and the right to propagate his religion, although this last right is subject to any restrictions imposed by State law relating to the propagation of any religious doctrine or belief among persons professing the Muslim religion.

The position of each of their Highnesses as head of that religion in his State and the rights, privileges, prerogatives and powers enjoyed by him as head of that religion will be unaffected and unimpaired. Their Highnesses have agreed however to authorise the Yang di-Pertuan Agong to represent them in any acts, observances or ceremonies agreed to by the Conference of Rulers as extending to the Federation as a whole.

At present there is no head of the Muslim religion in either Malacca or Penang though in Penang the Government obtains advice in matters relating to the Muslim religion from a non-statutory Muslim Advisory Board. Since the Governors of the new States may not be persons professing the Muslim religion it is proposed that the Yang di-Pertuan Agong should be the head of religion in each of these states and that the Constitution of each should include provisions enabling the Legislature to regulate Muslim religious affairs and to constitute a Council to advise the Yang di-Pertuan Agong in such affairs. These Councils will be concerned solely with Muslim religious affairs and they will not be entitled to interfere in any way with the affairs of people of other religious groups; and the position of the Yang di-Pertuan Agong as head of the Muslim religion will not carry with it authority to intervene in any matters which are the concern of the State Governments or to require the State Governments to make financial provision exclusively for the benefit of the Muslim community.

If it is found necessary for purposes of co-ordination to establish a Muslim Department of Religious Affairs at federal level, the Yang di-Pertuan Agong will after consultation with the Conference of Rulers, cause such a Department to be set up as part of his establishment.

Early in 1958 a Muslim member introduced in the Federal Legislative Council the motion 'That this Council is of opinion that the serving of alcoholic drinks at all functions of the Federal Government ought to be prohibited'. In the event the following amended resolution was adopted 'That this Council is of opinion that the serving of alcoholic drinks to Muslims at all official functions of the Federal Government ought to be prohibited'. The Hon. Datuk Haji Yahya expressed the feeling of many Muslim leaders when he stated in his speech in favour of the original motion:

It would be sufficient if I remind our Islamic Government that it is pointless for the independent Federation Government to recognize itself as an Islamic Government if the teaching of Islam and the laws of Shara' are neglected and the honour of Islam sacrificed through actions forbidden by the Hukum Shara', one of which is to spend the revenue of the Islamic Government on things forbidden by the Almighty Allah, which could be avoided although the expenditure is meant for functions of non-Muslims. We have been officially recognized as an Islamic State. The State must therefore respect the rules of Islam and Islamic laws, as far as possible. I believe at any function given by an Islamic Government the function can go on smoothly without alcoholic drinks. An Islamic Government is a pure Government and if we challenge the sanctity of its laws, I am sure this is one way for our government to be condemned by the Almighty Allah who has the power to bring down tragedies to our country.

On the other hand the Prime Minister, Tunku Abdul Rahman, deplored the bringing in of religion and he went on to state, 'I would like to make it clear that this country is not an Islamic State as it is generally understood, we merely provide that Islam shall be the official religion of the State.'[18]

British influence in the Malay States came through the treaties that were made between the Malay Sultans and the British. The earliest of these was the Pangkor Engagement[19] made in 1874 between the Sultan and Malay Chiefs on the one hand and the British on the other under which it was agreed *inter alia* that 'the Sultan receive and provide residence for a British officer to be called the Resident, who shall be accredited to the Court and whose advice must be asked for and accepted upon all questions other than those touching Malay religion and custom'. In 1875 a British Resident was sent to Selangor. The Sultan had been advised or induced to ask for assistance and on 25 January 1875 the Governor issued a proclamation that the Sultan 'has asked for an English officer to assist him to open up and govern the country' and that the Governor had acceded to his request.[20] In Negri Sembilan a Resident had been requested by the Dato Klana of Sungei Ujong in 1874 and in 1889 when the Rulers of the respective States agreed to constitute their countries into a Confederation they expressed their desire 'that they may have the assistance of a British Resident in the administration of the government of the said Confederation'.[21] In Pahang in 1887 the Sultan was induced to accept a joint defence treaty and a British Agent having functions similar to those of a consular officer, but in 1888 the murder of a British subject provided the excuse for the appointment of a British Resident in order that 'he may assist us in matters relating to the Government of our country on a similar system to that existing in the Malay States under British protection'. The Sultan also stated

In asking this we trust that the British Government will assure to us and our successors all our proper privileges and powers according to our system of government and will undertake that they will not interfere with the old customs of our country which have good and proper reasons and also with all matters relating to our religion.[22]

Under the Treaty of Federation 1895[23] it was provided that the Rulers

... agree to accept a British officer to be styled the Resident-General as the agent and representative of the British Government under the Governor of the Straits Settlements. They undertake to provide him with suitable accommodation, with such salary as is determined by His Majesty's Government and to follow his advice in all matters of administration other than those touching the Muhammadan religion. The appointment of the Resident-General will not affect the obligations of the Malay Rulers towards the British Resident now existing or to be hereafter appointed to offices in the above Protected States.

Under the Agreement with the Government of Kelantan 1910,[24] it was agreed that

His Majesty the King of England reserves the right to appoint officers to be Adviser and Assistant Adviser to act as the representative (or agent) of His Majesty the King of England. The Raja of Kelantan engages to pay the Adviser and Assistant Adviser such salaries as His Majesty's Government shall determine and to provide them with suitable residences; and the Raja of Kelantan further undertakes to follow and give effect to the advice of the Adviser or, in his absence, of the Assistant Adviser in all matters of administration other than those touching the Mohammedan religion and Malay custom.

The agreement made in 1914[25] between the British Government and the State of Johore provided that

... the Sultan of the State and territory of Johore will receive and provide a suitable residence for a British officer to be called the General Adviser, who shall be accredited to his Court and live within the State and territory of Johore and whose advice must be asked and acted upon on all matters affecting the general administration of the country and on all questions other than those touching Malay religion and custom.

The Agreement between the British Government and the Government of Trengganu 1919[26] provided that

His Highness the Sultan of Trengganu will receive and provide a suitable residence for a British officer to be called the British Adviser, who shall live within the State of Trengganu and whose advice must be asked for and acted upon in all matters affecting the general administration of the country and all questions other than those touching the Muhammadan religion.

In the cases of Kedah and Perlis the respective agreements of 1923 and 1930[27] respectively provided that the Sultan (or the Rajah) will receive and provide a suitable residence for a British Adviser to advise on all matters connected with the government of the State other than those matters relating to Malay custom or Muhammedan religion and will accept such advice, provided that nothing in this clause shall in any way prejudice the right of the Sultan or his successors (or the Rajah or his successors) to address the High Commissioner of the Malay States or His Britannic Majesty if the Sultan (or the Rajah) so desires.

Despite the clauses excepting matters relating to the Mohammedan religion and Malay custom from the scope of the advice of the British Resident or British Adviser, we find that in all the Malay

States, the British did interfere in the administration of the Muslim law. The State Councils which were originally purely advisory became in time the legislative body for the States and although in theory the assent of the Ruler was necessary for the validity of the laws, in fact the State Councils were directed by the British Resident or the British Adviser. The British Advisers regarded the proper organization and supervision of the Kathis who administered the Muslim law of marriage and divorce and punished matrimonial offences and breaches of religious observances as matters which closely affected the peace and good order of the States. The appointments, salaries, suspensions, and dismissals of Kathis were decided by the State Council and as the Council minutes did not come into effect until approved by the Governor, we find that even the appointment of Kathis had to be approved by the Governor.[28]

Legislation was enacted in the Malay States for the registration of Muslim marriages and divorce, for the jurisdiction and supervision of the Kathis, and for the punishment to be imposed in cases of Muslim offences including adultery.

In every Malay State the independent jurisdiction of the Kathis was minimized, the more serious cases were transferred to the magistrates and the work of the Kathis was supervised in other ways. Thus in Perak the reports of cases and petitions for appeal were channelled through the European officers to the Chief Kathi and the Sultan. Thus even the administration of the Muslim law came under the control of the British Advisers.[29]

Moreover the scope for the application of the Muslim law and the jurisdiction of the Muslim law courts[30] was restricted by legislation. In 1937 the Civil Law Enactment[31] of the Federated Malay States provided that 'the common law of England and the rules of equity, as administered in England, at the commencement of this Enactment other than any modifications of such law or any such rules by statute shall be in force'. In fact the enactment merely gave statutory authority to what the courts, which had been set up and staffed on British advice, had been doing anyway. As Terrell Ag. C.J. said in the case of *Yong Joo Lin & Others* v. *Fung Poi Fong*[32]

Principles of English law have for many years been accepted in the Federated Malay States where no other provision has been made by statute ... section 2(1) of the Civil Law Enactment therefore merely gave statutory recognition to a practice which the courts had previously followed.

It might be noted that section 10 of the Enactment expressly provides that nothing in the Enactment affects the Muhammedan Law governing the relations of husband and wife.

Section 2 of the Civil Law Enactment, 1937, was extended to the Unfederated States of Johore, Kedah, Kelantan, Perlis, and Trengganu by the Civil Law (Extension) Ordinance, 1957.[33] The Civil Law Enactment, 1956[34] repealed the Civil Law Enactment, 1937 and section 3 thereof provided that

Save in so far as other provision has been or may hereafter be made by any written law in force in the Federation or any part thereof, the Court shall apply the common law of England and the rules of equity as administered in England at the date of the coming into force of this Ordinance. Provided always that the said common law and rules of equity shall be applied only in so far as the circumstances of the states and settlements comprised in the Federation and their respective inhabitants permit and subject to such qualifications as local circumstances render necessary.

Only Part VII of the Ordinance (which contains provisions relating to the disposal and devolution of property) is made inapplicable to Muslims. Nothing in that Part, it is provided, shall affect the disposal of any property according to Muslim law.[35] The saving in section 10 of the Enactment of 1937 in regard to the Mohammedan Law governing the relations of husband and wife was not however re-enacted.

The Federal Constitution sets out the subjects which are in the State list which includes:[36]

1. Except with respect to the Federal Territory, Muslim Law and personal and family law of persons professing the Muslim religion, including the Muslim Law relating to succession, testate and intestate, betrothal, marriage, divorce, dower, maintenance, adoption, legitimacy, guardianship, gifts, partitions, and non-charitable trusts; Muslim *wakafs* and the definition and regulation of charitable and religious trusts, the appointment of trustees and the incorporation of persons in respect of Muslim religious and charitable endowments, institutions, trusts, charities and charitable institutions operating wholly within the State; Malay customs; *Zakat Fitrah* and *Bait-ul-Mal* or similar Muslim revenue; mosques or any Muslim public place of worship; creation and punishment of offences by persons professing the Muslim religion against precepts of that religion, except in regard to matters included in the Federal List; the constitution, organization and procedure of Muslim courts, which shall have jurisdiction only over persons professing the Muslim religion and in respect only of any of the matters included in this paragraph, but shall not have jurisdiction in respect of offences except in so far as conferred by federal law; the control of propagation of doctrines and beliefs among persons professing the Muslim religion; the determination of matters of Muslim Law and doctrine and Malay custom.

It can be seen that the jurisdiction given to the State and to the Shariah courts is limited. Even in regard to the subjects included in the item in the State list, there are many federal laws which limit the scope and application of State laws. For example in the field of succession, testate and intestate, account has to be taken of the Probate and Administration Act[37] and the Small Estates (Distribution) Act,[38] with the result that the Kathis are only given the function of certifying the shares to be allotted to the beneficiaries under the Muslim law. In the field of the criminal law in particular the jurisdiction of the Shariah Courts is very limited. It has jurisdiction only over persons professing the Muslim religion and it has jurisdiction in respect of offences as is conferred by Federal law. The Muslim Courts (Criminal Jurisdiction) Act, 1965[39] provides that such jurisdiction shall not be exercised in respect of any offence punishable with imprisonment for a term exceeding six months or with any fine exceeding 1,000 dollars or with both. Thus for example the Shariah Courts are unable to exercise jurisdiction in respect of the *hadd* offence of *zinah*, where the punishment is fixed by the Holy Quran and the Sunnah.

Under the present constitutional structure the Sultan in theory may act in his discretion in the performance of his functions as Head of the Muslim religion[40] and the Sultan does have a great deal of influence on the appointment of the religious officials, especially the Mufti, and the direction of religious affairs in the State. The Sultans too are very jealous of their position as heads of the Muslim religion, so much so that we find that, through the influence of the respective Sultans, Kedah and Pahang have not participated in the National Council for Islamic affairs. *Fatwas* which are based on other than the orthodox doctrines of the Shafii school require the approval of the Sultan. Legislation however can only be exercised by a Bill passed by the Legislative Assembly and assented to by the Sultan[41] and to that extent the elected Ministers and members of the Legislative Assembly can influence the administration of Muslim law in the States. It might be noted that the Yang di-Pertuan Agong in the exercise of his functions as Head of the Muslim religion in Penang, Malacca, Sabah, and Sarawak has to act on advice[42] and here the influence of the Prime Minister and the Federal Ministers are more significant. The Sultan does continue to play an important part in the issue of *fatwas* or rulings on the Muslim religion and law. Under the various State enactments relating to the administration of Muslim law the power to issue *fatwas* is given to the Mufti, Fatwa Committee, or the Majlis Ugama Islam. In issuing such *fatwas* the person or body issuing the *fatwa* is required ordinarily to follow the orthodox tenets of the Shafii school, but where the public interest so requires the *fatwa* may be given according to the tenets of the other schools, but only with the special sanction of the Sultan.[43]

A further step to co-ordinate the administration of Islamic affairs was taken on 17 October 1968 by the establishment by the Conference of Rulers of the National Council for Islamic Affairs.[44] Its members are (a) a Chairman appointed by the Conference of Rulers (usually the Prime Minister is appointed); (b) a representative of each State in Peninsular Malaysia appointed by the Ruler concerned and in the case of Malacca and Penang by the Yang di-Pertuan Agong; and since July 1971 a representative also from Sabah and Sarawak, appointed by the Yang di-Pertuan Agong with the approval of the head of State in those States, after considering the advice of the Islamic Religious Council of the State concerned and (c) five persons appointed by the Yang di-Pertuan Agong with the consent of the Conference of Rulers. The functions of the National Council are (a) to advise and make recommendations on any matter referred to it by the Conference of Rulers, by any State Government or State Religious Council and (b) to advise the Conference of Rulers, State Governments, and State Religious Councils on matters concerning Islamic law or the administration of Islam and Islamic education with a view to imposing, standardizing, or encouraging uniformity in Islamic law and administration. It is expressly provided that the Council may not touch on the position, rights, privileges and sovereignty, and other powers of the Ruler as head of Islam in his State. Despite this safeguard, two States, that is Kedah and Pahang, have not agreed to appoint representatives to the Council.

The Council has a Committee of Muslim scholars known as the Fatwa Committee which considers matters pertaining to Islamic laws. The Committee comprises the Muftis of all the States which are members of the Council and five other Muslim scholars appointed by the Yang di-Pertuan Agong.

The Council has set up a number of Committees to co-ordinate and increase the efficiency of Islamic religious activities in all the States. They are:

(a) a task force to study the collection, administration and distribution of monies from *zakat*, *fitrah*, *Bait-ul-mal* and *wakaf*;

(b) a Committee to study the conditions of the Shariah courts and the position of Kathis;

(c) a Committee to study and streamline the laws pertaining to marriage and divorce; and

(d) a Committee to fix the First Day of Ramadan and the First Day of Shawal and to arrange Islamic Calendars.

The National Mosque is under the administration of the Council and so is the Islamic Research Centre. There is a separate organization dealing with Islamic missionary activities.

The Universiti Kebangsaan Malaysia was established in 1970 and it has a faculty of Islamic Studies. Steps have been taken to absorb the Nilam Puri Institute at Kota Bharu, Kelantan, into the University of Malaya to constitute faculties of Islamic Studies.

In the international sphere, Malaysia has been well-known for organizing the Quran Reading competitions and Malaysia has taken an active part in the Islamic Secretariat and its activities.

While Malaysia has undoubtedly achieved respect and honour in the world of Islam and the Government has done a great deal for Islamic education, culture, and propagation there are some who would wish the government to go further. One of the political parties in Malaysia is the Islamic Party or PAS, whose aims include the strengthening of Islam and Islamic law in Malaysia. Academics especially in the Faculty of Islam, Universiti Kebangsaan, have begun to query the Islamic content not only of the general laws followed in Malaysia but also of the Muslim law administered in the various States. In this respect the position of Islam and Islamic law in Malaysia is compared with that in other Muslim countries. In Egypt for example the Constitution provides that Islam is the State religion and that the principles of the Muslim Shariah shall be the basic source of jurisdiction.[45] In Syria it is similarly provided that Islamic jurisprudence shall be the main source of legislation.[46] In Saudi Arabia the King is declared to be bound by the statements of the Shariah and sentences may only be passed in accordance with the dictates of the Quran and the Sunnah of the Prophet.[47] In Pakistan the preamble to the Constitution begins in the name of Allah the Beneficient, the Merciful, and affirms the sovereignty of God. Sovereignty over the entire universe belongs to Allah Almighty alone and that the authority to be exercised by the people of Pakistan within the limits prescribed by Him is a sacred task.[48] The Constitution provides in effect that both the President and the Prime Minister must be Muslims.[49] It is also provided that all existing laws shall be brought into conformity with the injunctions of Islam as laid down in the Holy Quran and Sunnah and no law shall be enacted which is repugnant to the injunctions of Islam. It is however added that effect shall be given to those provisions only in the manner provided in the Constitution.[50] The steps to be taken by the State in respect of enforcing the Islamic way of life are set out in the chapter relating to principles of policy. These provisions are based on the principles of policy contained in the former Constitution of 1962 but in the existing Constitution they are not merely principles.[51] It is for example made obligatory for the President and the Governor of each province to cause to be prepared and laid before the National Assembly or the Provincial Assembly a report on the observance and implementation of the said principles of policy.[52] To give effect to the Islamic provisions it is provided that the Government shall set up a Council of Islamic Ideology whose task will be to make recommendations as to the measures for bringing existing laws into conformity with the injunctions of Islam.[53]

The functions of the Council shall be:

(a) to make recommendations to Parliament and the Provincial Assemblies as to the ways and means of enabling and encouraging the Muslims of Pakistan to order their lives individually and collectively in all respects in accordance with the principles and concepts of Islam as enunciated in the Holy Quran and Sunnah;

(b) to advise a House, a Provincial Assembly, the President or a Governor on any question referred to the Council as to whether a proposed law is or is not repugnant to the injunctions of Islam;

(c) to make recommendations as to the measures for bringing existing laws into conformity with the injunctions of Islam and the stages by which such measures should be brought into effect; and

(d) to compile in a suitable form, for the guidance of Parliament and the Provincial Assemblies, such injunctions of Islam as can be given legislative effect.[54]

The Constitution of Pakistan has itself been criticized in that it has not stated clearly that the Quran and the Sunnah shall be the chief sources of the law of the land. Moreover it is provided that the validity of an action or law shall not be called in question on the ground that it is not in accordance with the principles of policy and no action shall lie against the State, any organ or authority of the State or any person on such ground. The Islamic provisions, including the provision that no law shall be enacted which is repugnant to the injunctions of the Holy Quran and the Sunnah, can only be given effect to in the manner provided in the Constitution, which merely provides that the Council of Islamic Ideology can advise that the law is repugnant to the injunctions of Islam, whereupon the House, the Provincial Assembly, the President, or the Governor, shall reconsider the law so made.[55]

The supremacy of the Constitution was emphasized in the case of the *State* v. *Zia-ur-Rahman*[56] where Hamoodur Rahman C.J. said:

> The question was whether any document other than the Constitution itself can be given a similar or higher status or whether the judiciary can, in the exercise of its judicial power strike down any of the provisions of the Constitution itself either because it is in conflict with the law of God or of nature or of morality or some other solemn declaration which the people themselves may have adopted indicating the form of Government they wish to establish. Some of the provisions of the Constitution of Pakistan (1972) were challenged as being violative of the fundamental principles accepted

by the Objectives Resolution passed by the Constituent Assembly of Pakistan on 7 March 1949 and it was argued that the High Court was entitled to strike down such a provision. The contention was that the Objectives Resolution is a grund-norm for Pakistan; it was a supra-Constitutional document and stood above even the Constitution of Pakistan (1972) or any Constitution that may be formed in the future.

However, after a formal written Constitution has been lawfully adopted by a competent body and has been generally accepted by the people including the judiciary in the Constitution of the country, the judiciary cannot claim to declare any of its provisions *ultra vires* or void. This will be no part of its function of interpretation. Therefore however solemn or sacrosanct a document if it is not incorporated in the Constitution or does not form a part thereof it cannot control the Constitution. At any rate the Courts created under the Constitution will not have power to declare any provision of the Constitution itself as being in violation of such a document. If in fact that document contains the expression of the will of the vast majority of the people, then the need for correcting such a violation will lie with the people and not with the judiciary. It follows from this that under our system too the Objectives Resolution of 1949 even though it is a document which has been generally accepted and has never been repealed or removed will not have the same status or authority as the Constitution itself until it is incorporated within it or made part of it. If it appears only as a preamble to the Constitution then it will serve the same purpose as any other preamble serves, namely that in case of doubt as to the intent of the lawmaker it may be looked at to ascertain the true intent but it cannot control the substantive provisions thereof.

In *Asma Jilani* v. *Government of Punjab*[57] Hamoodur Rahman C.J. said:

In any event if a grund-norm is necessary for us I do not have to look to the western legal theorists to discover one. Our own grund-norm is enshrined in our doctrine that the legal sovereignty over the entire Universe belongs to Almighty Allah alone, and that the authority exercisable by the people within the limits prescribed by him is a sacred trust. This is an immutable and unalterable norm which was clearly accepted in the Objectives Resolution passed by the Constituent Assembly of Pakistan on 7 March 1949. This resolution has been described by Mr. Brohi as 'the cornerstone of Pakistan's legal edifice' and recognized even by the learned Attorney-General himself as the 'bond which binds the nation' and as a document from which the Constitution of Pakistan 'must draw its inspiration'. This has not been abrogated by anyone so far nor has this been departed or deviated from by any regime, military or civil. Indeed it cannot for it is one of the fundamental principles enshrined in the Holy Quran— 'Say O Allah Lord of Sovereignty. Thou givest sovereignty to whomsoever thou pleaseth; and thou taketh sovereignty from whomsoever thou pleaseth. Thou exaltest whomsoever thou pleaseth and thou abases whomsoever thou pleaseth'. (Al-Imran 3:27.)

Yaqub Ali J. in that case said:

Pakistan is an Islamic Republic. Its ideology is enshrined in the Objectives Resolution of 7 March 1949 which *inter alia* declares wherein the Muslims shall be enabled to order their lives in the individual and collective spheres in accordance with the teachings and requirements of Islam as set out in the Holy Quran and Sunnah.

Sajjad Ahmad J. said:

In Pakistan ... we do not have to depend on Kelsen or other jurists or legal philosophy for constitutional inspiration. Our grund-norms are derived from our Islamic faith, which is not merely a religion but is a way of life. These grund-norms are unchangeable and are inseparable from our polity. These are epitomised in the Objectives Resolution passed by the Constituent Assembly of Pakistan on 7-3-1949 and were incorporated in the First Constitution of the Islamic Republic of Pakistan of 1956 and repeated again in the Constitution of 1962. Its basic postulates are that Sovereignty belongs to Allah Almighty, which is delegated to the people of Pakistan who have to exercise the State powers and authority through their chosen representatives on the principles of democracy, freedom, equality, tolerance and social justice as enunciated by Islam, wherein the fundamental human rights are to be respected and the independence of the judiciary is to be fully secured. Can it be argued that any adventurer who may usurp control of the State power in Pakistan can violate all these norms and create a new norm of his own in derogation of the same? The State of Pakistan was created in perpetuity based on Islamic ideology and has to be run and governed on all the basic norms of that ideology, unless the body politic of Pakistan as a whole, God forbid, is reconstituted on an un-Islamic pattern which will of course mean total destruction of its original concept. The Objectives Resolution is not just a conventional preface. It embodies the spirit and the fundamental norms of the constitutional concept of Pakistan.

Salehuddin Ahmad J. said:

The corner-stone of the State of Pakistan is that the sovereignty rests with Allah and Pakistan is his delegatee in the matter of the governance of the State. It is natural therefore that the delegatee or for that matter any ruler, single or collective, in Pakistan can never have unlimited power.

In the latter case of *State* v. *Zia-ur-Rahman* (*supra*) Hamoodur Rahman C.J. referred to the case of *Asma Jilani* and said that it was contended that the Federal Court in that case had declared that the Objectives Resolution is the grund-norm of Pakistan and therefore impliedly it stands above even the Interim Constitution or any Constitution that may be found in future. 'I regret to have to point out that this is not correct', he said. Referring to the judgments delivered in *Asma Jilani's* case he said:

There is no mention in these observations ... of the Objectives Resolution being the grund-norm for Pakistan. The grund-norm referred to was something even above the Objectives Resolution which as Sajjad Ahmad J. puts it 'embodies the spirit and the fundamental norms of the constitutional concept of Pakistan'. It was expected by the Objectives Resolution itself to be translated into the Constitution. Even those who adopted the Objectives Resolution did not envisage that it would be a document above the Constitution. It is incorrect therefore to say that the Objectives Resolution of 7 March 1949 stands on a higher pedestal than the Constitution itself.

In Malaysia too it is the Constitution which is the Supreme law and it is significant that the definition of law which is contained in the Constitution does not mention Islamic law.[58] It is true that after Merdeka the Federal Parliament cannot make laws dealing with the law of Islam (except now for the Federal Territory) as Islamic law is a State responsibility but the State Legislatures can make laws and the laws cannot be held void because they contravene the Islamic law. The Civil Law Act, 1956, in effect makes the English common law and rules of equity the basic law to which recourse must be had if there is no written law in force in Malaysia. There are examples of laws made before Merdeka Day which contain provisions contrary to the Islamic law. In the case of *Ainan* v. *Syed Abubakar*[59] for example it was held that section 112 of the Evidence Ordinance (now the Evidence Act) applies to the exclusion of the Islamic law on the question of the legitimacy of a child. In *Tengku Mariam* v. *Commissioner for Religious Affairs, Trengganu*[60] the High Court held and the Federal Court was prepared to hold, that it was bound by the decisions of the Privy Council from India to hold that a *wakaf* for the benefit of the family of the deceased is bad, despite the validity of such a *wakaf* under the Islamic law. Post-Merdeka laws made by Parliament can only be made applicable to Muslims under the provisions of Article 76 of the Constitution, that is, they must be accepted by the States. The Guardianship of Infants Act, 1961, for example may apply to Muslims in a State if it is accepted by the State with the proviso that any provision in the Act which conflicts with the provisions of the Islamic law will not apply to Muslims. Despite this, in *Myriam* v. *Ariff*[61] it was held that the Guardianship of Infants Act, 1961, was applicable to enable the court to give the custody of a child to the mother even though the mother had married a stranger, if the court is satisfied that it is to the welfare of the child to grant such custody to the mother. The decision itself might perhaps be supported under the Islamic law but the learned Judge in his judgment said:[62]

In my endeavour to do justice, I propose to exercise my discretion and have regard primarily to the welfare of the children. In doing so it is not my intention to disregard the religion and custom of the parties concerned or the rules under the Muslim religion but that does not necessarily mean that the court must adhere strictly to rules laid down by the Muslim religion. The court has not I think, been deprived of its discretionary power.

In the case of *Anchom* v. *Public Prosecutor*[63] the Court of Appeal of Johore rejected an argument that the Offences by Mohammedans Enactment was void as it 'purports to revise, enlarge or amend the Mohammedan law' contrary to the Johore Constitution. As McElwaine C.J. said: 'The offence of which these persons were convicted would, had it been witnessed in its entirety by four witnesses, have been the crime of *zinah* punishable under Mohammedan law by sentencing to death'. The Offences against Mohammedans Enactment on the other hand provides that the offence of illegal sexual intercourse may be punished by fine or imprisonment. The Court of Appeal held that it had no power to construe the Constitution of Johore or to declare the law to be *ultra vires* the Constitution. Poyser C.J. in his judgment makes the significant remark:

I would add only that the Mohammedan law was never adopted in its entirety by the State of Johore ... in recent years too the majority of Enactments probably contain provisions which are not in accordance with the Mohammedan law. Enactment No. 47 of 1937 is one of such Enactments, for under Mohammedan law the penalty for adultery is death but under the Johore law only imprisonment and fine.

The same point has been forcefully made in criticisms of the various enactments for the administration of Muslim law in the States of Malaya—that is, that the *hadd* punishments provided under the Islamic law have been set aside and this therefore makes the laws not Islamic and makes it sinful for the Kathis to enforce the law. The point has been made that no human legislature or agency can tamper with the laws of God. But the dichotomy in the administration of the law in Malaysia continues.

1. Laws of the Constitution of Johore, *Malayan Constitutional Documents*, Vol. 2, Kuala Lumpur, 1962, p. 7ff; R. Braddell, *Legal Status of the Malay States*, Singapore, 1931, p. 23ff.

2. [1937] M.L.J. 128.

3. [1940] M.L.J. 22.

4. Laws of the Constitution of Trengganu, *Malayan Constitutional Documents*, Vol. 2, Kuala Lumpur, 1962, p. 383ff.

5. Ibn Tiqtaqa, *Al-Fakhri* (translated by C. E.J. Whiting), London, 1947, p. 21.

6. Report of the Federation of Malaya Constitutional Commission 1957, Kuala Lumpur, 1957, paragraph 169, p. 73.

7. Ibid., p. 100.

8. M. Suffian Hashim, 'The Relationship between Islam and the State in Malaya', *Intisari*, Vol. 1, No. 1, p. 8.

9. Federal Constitution, Article 3, as amended by Act A206 and Act A354.

10. Constitution of Sabah, Article 5A, added by the Constitution (Amendment) Act, 1973.

11. Constitution (Amendment) Act, 1976 (Act A354).

12. See for example Constitution of Selangor, 1959, Part II, Article LI and LIII.

13. See for example Constitution of Selangor, 1959, Part II, Article LII.

14. Malacca Administration of Muslim Law Enactment, 1959, s.159(2); Penang Administration of Muslim Law Enactment, 1959, s.157(2); Negeri Sembilan Administration of Muslim Law Enactment, 1960, s.159(2); Kedah Administration of Muslim Law Enactment, 1962, s.160(2); Kelantan Council of Religion and Malay Custom Enactment 1966, s.68(2); Sabah Administration of Muslim Law Enactment, 1977, s.93A.

15. Constitution (Amendment) Act, 1976 (Act A354).

16. Ibid.

17. Federation of Malaya Constitutional Proposals, 1957, Kuala Lumpur, 1957, pp. 18-19.

18. Official Report of Legislative Council Debates, 1 May 1958, Columns 4631 and 4671-2.

19. Maxwell and Gibson, *Treaties and Engagements affecting the Malay States and Borneo*, London, 1924, p. 28.

20. Ibid., p. 36.

21. Ibid., p. 64.

22. Ibid., pp. 66 and 69.

23. Ibid., p. 70.

24. Ibid., p. 109.

25. Ibid., p. 136.

26. Ibid., p. 113.

27. Ibid., p. 104.

28. See E. Sadka, *The Protected Malay States, 1874-1895*, Kuala Lumpur, 1968, p. 262ff.

29. Ibid.

30. i.e. the courts of the Chief Kathis and the Kathis.

31. F.M.S. No. 3 of 1937.

32. [1941] M.L.J. 63.

33. No. 49 of 1951.

34. No. 9 of 1956, Revised as the Civil Law Act, 1956 (Act 67).

35. Civil Law Act, 1956, s.25.

36. Federal Constitution, Ninth Schedule, List 2(1).

37. Act 97.

38. Act 98.

39. No. 23 of 1965.

40. See for example Constitution of the State of Johore, Second Part, Article VII(2).

41. See for example Constitution of the State of Johore, Second Part, Article XXXI.

42. Federal Constitution, Article 40.

43. See for example the Perak Administration of Muslim Law Enactment, 1965, s. 42.

44. See *Malaysia Year Book*, 1973 p. 57ff.

45. Constitution of the Arab Republic of Egypt, Article 2.·

46. Constitution of Syria, Article 3(2).

47. Constitution of Saudi Arabia.

48. Constitution of the Islamic Republic of Pakistan, Preamble.

49. Ibid., Articles 41 and 91.

50. Ibid., Article 227.

51. Ibid., Articles 29-40.

52. Ibid., Article 29.

53. Ibid., Article 228.

54. Ibid., Article 230.

55. Ibid., Articles 30 and 230(3).

56. P.L.D. 1973 S.C.49. See *Niaz Ahmad Khan* v. *Sind* P.L.J. 1977 Kar. 338.

57. P.L.D. 1972 S.C.139. See *Nusrat Bhutto* v. *Chief of Army Staff and Federation of Pakistan* P.L.J. 1978 S.C.47.

58. Federal Constitution, Article 160.

59. [1939] M.L.J. 209.

60. [1970] 1 M.L.J. 222.

61. [1971] 1 M.L.J. 265.

62. Ibid., at p. 269.

63. [1940] M.L.J. 22.

4. The Citizenship Laws of Malaysia

INTRODUCTION

THE concept of citizenship laws was introduced in several of the component states of the Federation of Malaysia long before the country achieved an independent and sovereign status. In view of the somewhat complex historical, social, and political structure of the various states, the development of the citizenship laws of Malaysia cannot be considered on an overall basis but rather it must be viewed separately in accordance with the political and constitutional nature of the different states at different times.

The Straits Settlements, consisting of Penang, Malacca, Labuan, and Singapore, was the first political entity to introduce naturalisation laws in this area. The Naturalisation Act of 1867[1] provided that, 'any person, whilst actually residing in the Colony, may present a memorial to the Governor in Council, praying that the privileges of naturalisation may be conferred upon him'.[2] It was also provided that 'such memorial shall state to the best of the knowledge and belief of the memorialist, his age, place of birth, place of residence, profession, trade or occupation, the length of time during which he has resided within the Colony, that he is permanently settled in the Colony, or is residing within the same, with intent to settle therein'.[3]

In 1904 the four States which made up the Federated Malay States, namely, Negri Sembilan, Pahang, Perak, and Selangor, introduced uniform naturalisation laws which were applicable to these States.[4] The Naturalisation Enactments provided that any person, not being a natural-born subject of the Ruler of any of the Federated Malay States who has resided in the Federated Malay States for a term of not less than five years and who intends when naturalised to reside permanently therein, may whilst actually residing in the State present to the Sultan a memorial 'praying that the privileges of naturalisation be conferred upon him'.[5] Section 8 of the Enactment then provided that such person if so granted a certificate of naturalisation 'shall be deemed a natural-born subject to his Highness the Sultan as if he had been born within the State, and shall be entitled within the State to all rights, privileges and capacities of a subject of the Sultan'.

However as far as the Unfederated Malay States, consisting of the independent States of Kedah, Perlis, Kelantan, Trengganu, and Johore, were concerned, no attempt was made to promulgate any similar legislation until the year 1948 when the Malayan Union was formed.

MALAYAN UNION

When the formation of the Malayan Union, comprising the nine Malay States and Penang and Malacca, was first proposed in 1946 the British Government attempted to introduce the concept of uniform local citizenship laws in Malaya. It was proposed that citizenship should be granted to all persons born in the Union and to all persons born in Singapore.[6] It was also suggested that citizenship ought to be granted to all persons who had been resident in the Malayan Union or Singapore for ten out of the fifteen years preceding 1942.[7]

The effect of these proposals would have been to accord political rights to practically the entire non-Malay population of the Union. The Malays completely rejected these proposals for fear of non-Malay domination in the political arena. Hence these proposals were not implemented.

FEDERATION OF MALAYA

The British Government then abandoned the proposals and initiated fresh talks with the Malay rulers with the view to the establishment of a new political unit—the Federation of Malaya. The Federation of Malaya was then set up pursuant to the Federation of Malaya Agreement 1948.[8]

It was felt that citizenship was an essential part of the policy for the establishment of the Federation of Malaya and as such it was proposed 'to create a common form of citizenship for all those who regard Malaya as their real home and as the object of their loyalty'.[9] The Committee set up to make proposals for the establishment of the Federation of Malaya when dealing with the question of citizenship found it the most 'difficult and delicate' issue. In an attempt to reach a compromise between 'the deep resentment felt by the Malay population throughout the Malay States' with the creation of the status of Malayan Union citizens and the policy of the British Government to grant citizenship to the non-Malays 'who regarded Malaya as their real home and as the object of their loyalty', the Committee recommended that Federal citizenship should be granted to 'any subject ... of His Highness the Ruler of any State'.[10] Basically, 'subject of His Highness the Ruler of any State'[11] was defined to mean any person who (*i*) belongs to an aboriginal tribe resident in that State, or (*ii*) is a Malay[12] born in that State or (*iii*) a Malay born outside the Malay State of a father who was a subject of the Ruler of that State or (*iv*) a person naturalised as a subject of that Ruler under any law. Besides the subjects of the Rulers, Federal citizenship was also conferred on (*i*) any British subject born in either of the Settlements and who is permanently resident[13] in the Federation;[14] (*ii*) any British subject born in the Federation and whose father was either born in the Federation or at the time of birth of such British subject a permanent resident;[15] (*iii*) any person born in the Federation who habitually speaks the Malay language and conforms to Malay customs;[16] (*iv*) any person born in the Federation, whose parents were also born in the Federation and who were permanent residents in the Federation[17] and (*v*) any person whose father is a Federal citizen.[18] Provision was also made for the acquisition of Federal citizenship by application: any person who was born in the Federation and had been resident there for ten out of the fifteen years preceding his application or any person who had resided in the Federation for fifteen out of twenty years preceding his application might apply for citizenship.[19] Minor children of such persons who are also residents in the Federation may also be granted such citizenship.[20]

The 1948 Agreement also provided for loss of Federal citizenship. 'Any person, except a subject of the Ruler of any State, who has been absent from the Federation for a continuous period of five years shall cease to be a Federal citizen.'[21] Furthermore, 'any Federal citizen by application who has done any voluntary act which is incompatible with his loyalty to the Federation may be declared to have ceased to be a Federal citizen'.[22]

It must be emphasized that Federal citizenship at this stage was 'not a nationality, neither could it develop into a nationality. It would not affect or impair, in any respect whatsoever, the status of British subjects in the settlements or the status of subjects of the Rulers in the Malay State. It is an addition to, and not a subtraction from nationality and could be a qualification for electoral rights, for membership of Councils and for employment in Government service ...'.[23] From an international law point of view, Federal citizens born in the Straits Settlements remained British subjects.

It must also be pointed out that the 1948 Agreement did not take into consideration the existing laws relating to State nationality. As mentioned earlier, as early as 1904 the four States of the Federated Malay States had introduced their own nationality laws. Even though none of the Malay States had any legislation defining the status of a subject of a Ruler, it was the practice to classify all non-Malays who were born and resident in a State as a subject of the Ruler by the principle of *jus soli*. This principle was also accepted by the Courts. In the case of *Chik Kwan* v. *The British Resident, Selangor*,[24] it was held that a Chinese born and resident in a Malay State became a subject of the Ruler of that State according to the general principle of international law. It was by virtue of this practice that the non-Malays, particularly the Chinese, were regarded as British-protected persons. Furthermore, the British Protectorate, Protected States and Protected Persons Order of 1949[25] provided that British-protected persons were those who were declared citizens or nationals of any State by any law of that State. In the absence of any such law, all persons born in the protected State would be treated as British-protected persons. Since the Federation by itself was not considered to be a separate legal entity and therefore not a protected State, Federal citizenship did not bestow the status of a 'British-protected person' on a Federal citizen. State nationality laws were still relevant in determining a British-protected person. Therefore, the Chinese who at this stage were subjects of the Rulers by the local laws and British-protected persons by international law were not subjects of the Rulers for the purpose of Federal citizenship.[26]

FEDERATION OF MALAYA AGREEMENT AS AMENDED

In 1952, the provisions dealing with Federal citizenship under the Federation of Malaya Agreement were amended. The two main reasons for this early revision were because of the change in the law of nationality of the United Kingdom and Colonies, which was brought about by the British Nationality Act 1948[27] and the emergence of Communist activity within the infant Federation.

The Federation of Malaya Agreement (Amendment) Ordinance 1952,[28] a Federal enactment, was introduced amending the law relating to Federal citizenship. Federal citizenship was abandoned and a new status of citizenship of the Federation of Malaya was introduced. At the same time, State Nationality Enactments were introduced in the nine Malay States.[29]

The new law, though largely based on the concept of State nationality, was more restrictive than its predecessor. Unlike the provisions relating to Federal citizenship under the unamended Federation of Malaya Agreement, the new provisions dealing with citizenship of the Federation of Malaya were not self-contained. There was a constant need for reference to other laws, particularly the State nationality laws, to determine whether a person was a citizen or not.

ACQUISITION

Citizenship under the Federal Enactment could be acquired by three means: (a) Operation of Law; (b) Registration and (c) Naturalisation. As these laws form the basis of citizenship under independent Malaya and subsequently Malaysia, it is proposed to deal with these provisions in detail.

(a) *Operation of Law*[30]

The Federal Enactment provided that the following persons shall be citizens of the Federation of Malaya by Operation of Law: (*i*) any subject of the Ruler of any State.[31] 'Subject of Ruler of any State' is defined to mean 'any person who under the written law in force in a State is a subject of His Highness the Ruler of that State'.[32] One then had to refer to the Nationality Enactment 1952 of the different States to determine who would qualify to be a 'subject of the Ruler of any State'. It must be pointed out that under the Uniform State Enactment, all the nine States of the Federation had a uniform law applicable to each of the States. By virtue of Section 4 of the State Enactment, it was provided that the following persons shall be subjects of the Ruler: any person belonging to an aboriginal tribe of Malaya; any Malay born in the State; any person born in the State, one of whose parents was also born in the Federation of Malaya; any person who was not a citizen of the United Kingdom and Colonies who was either born in the State and acquired Federal citizenship under the 1948 Agreement or even though not born in the State had acquired Federal citizenship by application under the 1948 Agreement. Furthermore, any person, wherever born, shall be a subject of the Ruler of the State if his father was also born in the State and at the time of the birth of such a person was or could have been a subject of the Ruler under the State Enactment, or if the father was a subject of the Ruler by Registration or by Naturalisation under the State Enactment.

Besides subjects of the Ruler of any State, any citizen of the United Kingdom and Colonies born in the Straits Settlements;[33] or born in the Federation of whom one of the parents was also born in the Federation;[34] or such citizen of the United Kingdom and Colonies wherever born but if born before February 1948 whose father was born in the Settlement and had at the time of such person's birth resided in the Federation for a continuous period of fifteen years;[35] or if born after February 1948, whose father was born in the Settlement and was at the time of such person's birth a Federal citizen under the Agreement before February 1948 or was a citizen of the Federation of Malaya,[36] then such person shall also be a citizen of the Federation of Malaya by Operation of Law. Furthermore, such citizen of the United Kingdom and Colonies whenever born could also acquire citizenship by Operation of Law if at the time of his birth, his father was a Federal citizen under the 1948 Agreement or a citizen of the Federation of Malaya by the grant of a Certificate of Citizenship or a Certificate of Naturalisation under the provisions of the Agreement or a citizen by Registration under the Agreement.[37]

Citizenship by Operation of Law was also granted to any other person who was a Federal citizen before February 1948[38] or any other person who has become a citizen of the United Kingdom and Colonies by Naturalisation under the British Nationality Act 1948 and who satisfied certain residential qualifications.[39]

(b) *Citizenship by Registration*

The Amended Federation of Malaya Agreement also provided for the acquisition of citizenship by Registration. Any person who is a citizen of the United Kingdom and Colonies and who has not been absent from the Federation for a continuous period of five years within the ten years immediately preceding his application shall be entitled to be registered as a citizen of the Federation of Malaya.[40] Provisions were also made for registration of women who were married to citizens of the Federation.[41] Such a woman had also to be a citizen of the United Kingdom and Colonies before she was entitled to be registered as a citizen.[42] A parent or guardian who is a citizen of the Federation of Malaya may also apply to register any minor child as a citizen of the Federation of Malaya.[43]

(c) *Naturalisation*

The High Commissioner was also given the power to grant a person a Certificate of Naturalisation if such person had resided in the Federation for ten out of the twelve years preceding his application and is of good character and is able to speak Malay or English with 'reasonable proficiency'.[44] Special provisions were also made for the granting of a Certificate of Naturalisation to persons who had served in the Forces.[45]

LOSS OF CITIZENSHIP

The Amended Act had detailed provisions for the loss of citizenship of the Federation of Malaya. A peculiar provision was Clause 132 which provided for loss of citizenship by Operation of Law. A person shall cease to be a citizen of the Federation of Malaya by Operation of Law if he ceases to be a subject of His Highness the Ruler of any State or a citizen of the United Kingdom and the Colonies. Absence from the Federation of Malaya for a period of five years without maintaining a 'substantial connection with the Federation' is another circumstance under which a person would lose his citizenship by Operation of Law. Likewise, a person would fall within the ambit of Clause 132 if he voluntarily acquires the nationality or citizenship of any other foreign country.[46]

Detailed provisions were also made for the deprivation of citizenship.[47] Anyone who had obtained citizenship by Registration or Naturalisation through false representation or concealment of any material facts may be deprived of his citizenship.[48] Furthermore, any person who has by act or speech been disloyal or disaffected towards the Federation, or during war had traded with an enemy or within five years of being a citizen been imprisoned for a period of more than twelve months may also be deprived of his citizenship.[49]

The overriding provision governing the loss of citizenship is that, if the effect of losing the citizenship of the Federation of Malaya would result in a person having no national status, then such person cannot lose the citizenship of the Federation of Malaya.[50]

CITIZENSHIP OF THE FEDERATION OF MALAYA UNDER THE 1957 CONSTITUTION

In 1957[51] when the Federation of Malaya achieved Independence, the citizenship laws were again changed. The new laws relating to citizenship were embodied in the Constitution and not as before in a Federal Ordinance which had to be read together with a number of State Enactments.[52]

ACQUISITION

To a very large extent the various categories of acquiring citizenship were retained: Operation of Law, Registration, and Naturalisation.[53]

(a) *Operation of Law*

All persons who were citizens of the Federation of Malaya before Merdeka Day became citizens of the independent Federation by Operation of Law.[54] Furthermore, every person born in the Federation on or after Merdeka Day also became a citizen by Operation of Law.[55] This unqualified principle of *jus soli* was applied in the Federation for the first time.[56] Any person born outside the Federation on or after Merdeka Day was also entitled to be a citizen of the Federation by Operation of Law if at the time of his birth his father was either (*i*) born in the Federation or (*ii*) the father was in service under the Federal or State Government.[57] If the father of such a child does not fulfil requirements (*i*) or (*ii*) above, such a child was still entitled to be a citizen by Operation of Law, if his father was a citizen of the Federation at the time of the birth and such birth had been registered at a Malayan Consulate within one year.[58]

In 1962, by a constitutional amendment,[59] the principle of *jus soli* as embodied in Article 14(1)(b) was amended. The new amendment provided that children whose parents were not citizens of the Federation or permanent residents would not become citizens by Operation of Law even if they were born within the Federation. This provision applied to all persons born within the Federation after September 1962.[60] However, if these qualifications cannot be fulfilled and as a consequence the child would be stateless, then such a child may become a citizen by Operation of Law.[61] As pointed out by the Solicitor General, 'this amendment curbed resort to the malpractice of a woman entering into the Federation merely to give birth to a child to have it acquire the status of Federal citizen'.[62]

(b) *Registration*

1. *Wives of citizens.* A woman who is married to a citizen is entitled to be registered as a citizen.[63] There were, however, certain qualifications to this rule. Firstly, the marriage must have been registered in accordance with any written law in force in the Federation.[64] Secondly, no person who had renounced or had been deprived of her citizenship under the Constitution or any earlier law, may qualify to become a citizen under this provision.[65] It was also provided that a woman who had acquired citizenship by Registration under this provision, may be deprived of such citizenship if her marriage to the citizen is terminated within two years of the marriage.[66]

It must also be mentioned that there is no similar provision for the granting of citizenship to husbands who were married to women who were citizens of the Federation.

This provision relating to the registration of wives was amended in 1962[67] so as to make the provision more stringent. Certain new qualifications were inserted by the amendment: (*i*) that she had resided continuously in the Federation for a period of not less than two years immediately preceding the date of the application; (*ii*) that she intends to reside permanently therein, and (*iii*) a qualification which was in force under the Federation of Malaya Agreement[68] and which was present in, other cases of registration:[69] that she must be of good character.[70] This new amendment was introduced largely to eliminate the possibility of acquisition of citizenship by a formal marriage of convenience entered into purely to enable acquisition of federal citizenship by a woman.

2. *Children.* Article 15 also provided that any parent or guardian may apply to register as a citizen any child whose father is a citizen of the Federation. Such a child is entitled to be registered as a citizen if the Government is satisfied that such child is ordinarily resident in the Federation and that he is of good character.[71]

Article 15 pertaining to the registration of children of citizens has also been subject to amendments. In 1962, Article 15(2) was substituted by a new provision which provided that subject to Article 18 the Federal Government may cause any person under the age of twenty-one years, being the child of *any citizen*, to be registered as a citizen upon application made to the Federal Government by his parent or guardian.[72] Furthermore, a new provision dealing with registration of children was also added. Article 15A provides that 'the Federal Government may, in such special circumstances as it thinks fit, cause any person under the age of twenty-one to be registered as a citizen'.

Two points are worth noting under these two new amendments: Article 15(2) is in more generous terms than its predecessor. Any child may be so registered under this provision so long as one of his parents is a citizen. The previous qualification that only children whose father was also a citizen could be registered is now removed.[73] Furthermore, the restrictions existing under the old law that the child must show that he is ordinarily resident in the Federation and that he is of good character is also removed. The other interesting point is that under the new Article 15A, the Federal Government may register any child under the age of twenty-one to be a citizen. There are no qualifications which such child should possess. However, it is not clear under what 'special circumstances'[74] the Government would invoke this provision to register any child. It may be that in the case where a child would be stateless, the Government may invoke this provision to register such a child as a citizen.

3. *Registration of persons born in the Federation before Merdeka Day.* Representations were made to the Reid Commission that the principle of *jus soli* as embodied in Article 14 should be given retrospective effect to all persons born in the Federation even before Merdeka Day. The Reid Commission was not satisfied that such an extension was desirable and therefore recommended that special provisions

should be made in the Constitution for the acquisition of citizenship by Registration.[75] Article 16 provided that any person above the age of eighteen who was born in the Federation is entitled upon application to be registered as a citizen if he had resided in the Federation during the seven years immediately preceding the application for a period of not less than five years[76] and that he intends to reside permanently in the Federation[77] and that he is of good character.[78] The Constitution drafters had also taken into consideration the recommendation of the Reid Commission 'that the language test should be waived in favour of all who make application within one year from Merdeka Day' but have provided that where an application is made within one year from Merdeka Day, the applicant must have an 'elementary knowledge of the Malay language'.[79]

4. *Registration of persons resident in the Federation on Merdeka Day.* The Reid Commission was sympathetic towards persons who were not born in the Federation, but who were resident in the Federation on Merdeka Day. They recommended that such persons should be entitled to citizenship as of right but on somewhat different terms from those who were born in the Federation.[80] The Commission pointed out

... that those to whom this recommendation applies are numerous, and in order that a sense of common nationality should develop, we think that it is important that those who have shown their loyalty to the Federation and have made it their permanent home, should participate in the rights and duties of citizenship. The only differences between the conditions which apply to applicants under this head and those which apply to applicants under the immediately preceding head, are that under this head: (*i*) the applicant must have resided in the Federation for eight out of the previous twelve years and (*ii*) that the language test should only be waived if the applicant is over forty-five years of age. It might be unreasonable in some cases to expect persons over forty-five years of age to learn Malay, and it might also be unreasonable in some cases to expect younger people to have an extensive knowledge of Malay. We therefore think that we are justified in recommending that the test should be waived entirely for those who apply promptly and are over forty-five, and that others should have to show only an elementary knowledge of the language.[81]

This recommendation was accepted by the drafters of the Constitution to a very large extent[82] except that they felt that such persons should not be entitled to citizenship as of right and that the Government should have discretion in so granting such citizenship.[83]

In early 1972, Article 17 was repealed.[84] It was pointed out by the Government that Article 17 was only intended as a transitional rule and having given ample opportunity to persons wishing to take advantage of the provision for four years, this special provision should be repealed.[85] The repeal, however, is without prejudice to any application for registration under the Article made before 1 July 1963.[86]

(c) *Naturalisation*

For all other persons who could not acquire citizenship of the Federation either by Operation of Law or by Registration, the only other means of obtaining citizenship was through Naturalisation.[87] The applicant has to comply with the following conditions: That he has attained the age of 21; that he is of good character;[88] that he has resided in the Federation for ten out of the preceding twelve years;[89] that he intends to reside there permanently;[90] that he has an adequate knowledge of the Malay language;[91] and that he should take an oath of allegiance.[92] The normal qualifications for Naturalisation are considerably modified in favour of members of Federation Forces who are at the time of application serving in prescribed Armed Forces of the Federation or who apply within five years, or within such longer period as may in any particular case be allowed, of their discharge from such Forces.[93] In such cases the applicant has merely to satisfy the Government: (*i*) that he has served satisfactorily in any such Forces for three years of full-time service or four years if part-time service[94] and (*ii*) that he intends to reside permanently in the Federation if the certificate be granted.[95] It is important to note that in such cases, the granting of a Certificate of Naturalisation is mandatory.[96]

The Constitution (Amendment) Act 1962,[97] again made some amendments to certain provisions dealing with Naturalisation. Article 19 was amended to add a further qualification to the application of a Certificate of Naturalisation. Besides the existing qualifications, any applicant for a Certificate of Naturalisation made after 1 October 1962[98] has also to show that he had resided continuously in the Federation for a period of not less than one year immediately preceding the date of application.[99]

As from 1 February 1963 by virtue of the same Act, Article 20 was repealed as it was felt that it was now obsolete.[100]

TERMINATION OF CITIZENSHIP

Provisions were also made under the Constitution for the termination of citizenship: Renunciation;[101] Deprivation of Citizenship on acquisition or exercise of foreign citizenship;[102] Special Grounds for deprivation of citizenship by registration and naturalisation[103] and the procedure to be complied with for deprivation.[104] As most of these provisions are similar to the provisions under the Malaysian

Constitution, these provisions will be dealt with in detail in the next part of this essay.[105]

CITIZENSHIP OF
THE FEDERATION OF MALAYSIA

Citizenship laws were again subjected to changes with the formation of Malaysia.[106] In September 1963 the Federation of Malaysia was formed, consisting of the original eleven States of the Federation of Malaya, together with Singapore and the Borneo States of Sabah and Sarawak. Citizenship laws were still contained under Part III of the Malaysian Constitution, though the provisions were amended to take into consideration the incorporation of the new States.[107] It is, however, interesting to note that the new law did not recast the law embodied under the 1957 Constitution. In fact, the provisions of the 1957 Constitution were re-enacted with the necessary amendments.[108] As such there was no provision for the conversion from the citizenship of the Federation of Malaya to citizenship of the Federation of Malaysia. Though these three new States became part of the Federation together with the other eleven States, these three States were not on equal footing with the other States. Special provisions were made in the Constitution which were applicable to these three States alone and not to the others. This was particularly so with regard to Singapore.[109] As a consequence, the concept of State citizenship as separate from Federal citizenship was to a certain extent re-introduced again, especially with regard to Singapore.[110] With the withdrawal of Singapore from the Federation in August 1965 the Constitution of Malaysia was again amended to repeal all provisions relating to Singapore.[111]

This essay will only deal with the citizenship laws as existing now and will not take into consideration the position before the repeal.

ACQUISITION

The three methods of acquiring citizenship are still retained under the Malaysian Constitution: Operation of Law, Registration, and Naturalisation.

(a) *Operation of Law*

Article 14 of the Malaysian Constitution provides that certain categories of persons born before Malaysia Day[112] and certain categories of persons born after Malaysia Day would be entitled to citizenship by Operation of Law. One then has to refer to the Second Schedule of the Constitution to determine who would qualify to be such citizens. The position becomes even more complex as one has to refer to the earlier Enactments relating to citizenship to determine whether a person is a citizen.[113]

1. *Persons born before Malaysia Day.* All persons who were citizens of the former Federation of Malaya before 31 August 1957, by virtue of the Federation of Malaya Agreement 1948 are entitled to be citizens of Malaysia by Operation of Law. For this purpose no distinction is drawn between those citizens of the former Federation of Malaya who acquired citizenship by Registration or Naturalisation and those who were citizens by Operation of Law.[114]

Persons born within the Federation of Malaya, acquire citizenship by Operation of Law by the principle, *jus soli*, only if they were born between 31 August 1957 and October 1962.[115] The *jus soli* principle as embodied in the 1957 Constitution is now confined to persons born after September 1962: such persons become citizens of the new Federation by Operation of Law only if one of their parents at the time of their birth is either a citizen or permanent resident of the Federation.[116] Furthermore, persons born after September 1962 would also become citizens by Operation of Law if they were not born citizens of any other country.[117] The latter provision and the one whereby citizenship is granted to any person born in the Federation even if neither of his parents is a citizen but only a permanent resident is a consequence of the amendment made to the *jus soli* principle as embodied in the 1957 Constitution.[118]

Similar provisions as embodied under the 1957 Constitution exist for persons born outside the Federation before Merdeka Day.[119] Such persons acquire citizenship if their father was a citizen of the Federation at the time of their birth and was either (*i*) born in the Federation or (*ii*) was in service under the Federation or State Government.[120] If the father of such person does not satisfy either requirement (*i*) or (*ii*) above, then such person can only become a citizen by Operation of Law if such birth had been registered at a Consulate within a year.[121]

It is difficult to appreciate the rationale underlying the restrictions imposed upon the qualifications of the father of a person born outside the Federation. In cases where such persons are born outside the Federation they can only acquire citizenship by Operation of Law if their father is a citizen of the Federation.[122] A distinction, however, is drawn between such fathers who were themselves born in the Federation and those who were not.[123] In the former case, children of such fathers acquired citizenship by Operation of Law even if such children were born outside the Federation. In the latter case, a further distinction is drawn between such fathers who were in the service of the Federal or State Government abroad and those who were not. If the father was in the service of the Federal or State

Government, then such children became citizens by Operation of Law automatically. If the father was not in the service of the Federal or State Government, his children only became citizens by Operation of Law if their birth was registered with a Consulate of the Federation. This latter requirement appears to be a departure from the usual case of citizenship by Operation of Law. The concept of citizenship by Operation of Law is that one acquires such citizenship without any act or procedure being complied with: in this respect the requirement that such birth be registered appears to vary from the usual understanding of the concept.[124]

Special provisions are also made for persons ordinarily resident in a Borneo State or Brunei to become citizens by Operation of Law if such persons were before Malaysia Day citizens of the United Kingdom and Colonies and were born either in the particular State concerned or became a citizen of such State by Registration or Naturalisation.[125]

2. *Persons born after Malaysia Day.* The provisions relating to persons born after Malaysia Day are similar to those relating to persons born after Merdeka Day.[126] All persons born after Malaysia Day can only acquire citizenship by Operation of Law depending on the status of their parents; if born within the Federation, one of the parents of such person must be a citizen or permanent resident[127] and if born outside the Federation, then the father of such a person must be a citizen and must satisfy one of the following three requirements: (*i*) born in the Federation; (*ii*) was in the service of the Federal or State Government;[128] or (*iii*) the birth was registered at a Consulate.[129] However, any person born within the Federation and not born a citizen of any country also becomes a citizen of the Federation by Operation of Law.[130]

Special provisions are made for persons born in Singapore: such persons become citizens by Operation of Law if one of their parents is a citizen of the Federation.[131]

(b) *Registration*

1. *Wives of citizens.*[132] Any married woman whose husband is a citizen is entitled to be registered as a citizen if the marriage was subsisting and the husband a citizen at the beginning of October 1962[133] or if she satisfies the Federal Government, that she has resided in the Federation throughout the two years preceding the date of the application and that she intends to do so permanently and that she is of good character.[134]

Again there are no similar provisions in favour of husbands who marry women who are citizens.[135]

2. *Children.*[136] To the already existing two provisions[137] dealing

with the registration of children, yet another provision was added in 1963, when Malaysia was formed.[138] Under this provision, any person under the age of twenty-one, who was born before the beginning of October 1962[139] and whose father is a citizen or was also a citizen at the beginning of October 1962, is entitled to be registered as a citizen. Such person must satisfy the Federal Government that he is ordinarily resident in the Federation and that he is of good character. The point to note under this provision is that, unlike the earlier two provisions, any such person who satisfies all the requirements is entitled to be registered as a citizen. But the qualification under the new provisions is more stringent and is restricted only to persons born before October 1962.[140]

3. *Persons born in the Federation before Merdeka Day.* This provision[141] is unamended except for certain minor modifications.[142] As such, persons born in the Federation are entitled to be registered as citizens if such persons have resided in the Federation for an aggregate of five years during the seven years immediately preceding the application;[143] intend to reside permanently in the Federation;[144] are of good character[145] and have an elementary knowledge of the Malay language.[146]

4. *Persons resident in Borneo States on Malaysia Day.* This is a new transitional provision[147] incorporated to take into consideration the joining of the Borneo States as part of Malaysia. Any person over the age of eighteen who on Malaysia Day was ordinarily resident in the Borneo States is entitled to be registered as a citizen if he applies to be so before September 1971. The usual qualifications are also imposed: must have resided in the Borneo States before Malaysia Day and after Malaysia Day in the Federation for a period of seven years;[148] and that he intends to reside permanently in the Federation[149] and is of good character.[150] Language requirements are also imposed.[151]

5. *Persons resident in the Federation on Merdeka Day.*[152] The provision dealing with the registration of persons resident in the Federation on Merdeka Day is now repealed,[153] but without prejudice to the operation of the provision with respect to any application for registration thereunder made before the coming into operation of the repeal.[154]

(c) *Naturalisation*[155]

The Federal Government may, upon application, grant a Certificate of Naturalisation to any person if satisfied that he has resided in the Federation for an aggregate of not less than ten years in the twelve years immediately preceding the date of the application for the certificate,[156] and which includes the twelve months immediately preceding that date[157] and intends to reside permanently in the Federation,[158] that he is of good character[159] and that he has an adequate knowledge of the Malay language.[160]

Clause (2) of Article 19 provides that 'The Federal Government may, in special circumstances as it thinks fit', grant a Certificate of Naturalisation to any person who applies and who satisfies all the conditions stipulated in Clause (1). The distinction between Clause (1) and (2) appears to be unclear. As originally enacted it may have been intended that Clause (1) should cover periods of residence in Singapore.[161] However, since the withdrawal of Singapore from the Federation, it is submitted that Clause (2) is now superfluous and of no effect and should be repealed.

The special provisions dealing with Naturalisation of members of the Forces have now been repealed, as the five-year period for which the provision was made has now expired.[162]

TERMINATION OF CITIZENSHIP

The Malaysian Constitution makes provision for the termination of citizenship under two different circumstances: Renunciation and Deprivation:

(a) *Renunciation*[163]

Any citizen above the age of twenty-one who is also or is about to become[164] a citizen of another country may renounce his citizenship of the Federation by making a declaration to that effect.[165] However, a declaration made during any war in which the Federation is engaged shall not be registered without the approval of the Federal Government.[166] Presumably, this was intended to prevent citizens from renouncing their citizenship so as to avoid national service.

(b) *Deprivation of Citizenship on Acquisition or Exercise of Foreign Citizenship*

Article 24 provides that if the Federal Government is satisfied that any citizen has acquired by Registration, Naturalisation or other voluntary and formal act, the citizenship of any other country, the Government may by order deprive such person of his citizenship.[167] Furthermore, if the Federal Government is satisfied that any citizen has voluntarily claimed and exercised in a foreign country[168] any rights available to him under the law of that country, such rights being accorded exclusively to citizens of that country, then an order may also be made to deprive such person of his citizenship.[169]

Since Commonwealth countries do not fall within the definition of 'foreign country' as defined by Article 160(2)[170] of the Constitution, it was found necessary to insert Clause (3) of Article 24. Where provision is in force under the law of any part of the Commonwealth for conferring on citizens of that part of the Commonwealth rights not available to other Commonwealth citizens, then an exercise of such rights by a Malaysian citizen in such part of the Commonwealth would be treated as though it was exercised in a foreign country. In such a case, such a citizen may be deprived of his citizenship. However, it would appear that if the right which was exercised by the Malaysian citizen in any part of the Commonwealth, was a right which was bestowed by that part of the Commonwealth to all other parts of the Commonwealth, then the exercise of such a right would not fall within the ambit of Article 24.[171] Therefore, to overcome this anomaly between Commonwealth and non-Commonwealth countries, Article 24 was amended in 1976. By virtue of the Constitution (Amendment) Act 1976,[172] Clause (3) of Article 24 was repealed, and the term 'a foreign country' in Clause (2) was amended to 'any country outside the Federation'. The effect of this amendment is to place Commonwealth countries and non-Commonwealth countries on the same footing for purposes of deprivation of citizenship.[173]

By virtue of Clause 3(A), it is provided that the exercise of a vote in any political election in a place outside the Federation shall be deemed to be a voluntary claim and exercise of a right available under the law of the place.[174] Furthermore, any citizen, who after 10 October 1963[175] applies for the issuance or renewal of a passport to the authorities of a country outside the Federation, or uses a passport issued by that country, may also be deprived of his citizenship under Article 24.[176]

If the Federal Government is satisfied that a woman who is a citizen by Registration under Article 15(1)[177] has acquired the citizenship of any country outside the Federation by virtue of her marriage to a person who is not a citizen, the Federal Government may by order deprive her of her citizenship.[178] It is also interesting to note that under Article 24 there is no requirement as it exists in the other provisions[179] dealing with deprivation that before an order of deprivation is made under Article 24 that the Federal Government has to be satisfied that it is not conducive to the public good that such a person should continue to be a citizen of the Federation.

(c) *Deprivation of Citizenship by Registration or Naturalisation*

Article 25 provides that the Federal Government may by order deprive of his citizenship any person who is a citizen by Registration under Article 16A[180] or 17[181] or a citizen by Naturalisation[182] if satisfied: (a) that such citizen has shown himself to be disloyal or disaffected towards the Federation;[183] (b) that he has, during any war in which the Federation is or was engaged, unlawfully traded or communicated with any enemy;[184] (c) that he has, within the period of five years beginning with the date of the registration or the grant of the certificate, been sentenced in any country to imprisonment for a term of more than twelve months or to a fine of more than $5,000;[185] (d) that he has, without the Federal Government's approval accepted, served in, or performed the duties of any office, post, or employment under the Government of any country outside the Federation[186] or any political sub-division thereof, or under any agency of such a Government, where an oath, affirmation or declaration of allegiance is required in respect of the office, post or employment;[187] (e) that any such citizen has been ordinarily resident in countries outside the Federation for a continuous period of five years and during that period has neither: been at any time in the service of the Federation or of an international organization of which the Federal Government was a member; nor registered annually at a consulate of the Federation his intention to retain his citizenship;[188] and (f) if any such citizen had obtained the registration or certificate of naturalisation by means of fraud, false representation or the concealment of any material fact, or was effected or granted by mistake.[189]

The Federal Government may also by order deprive of her citizenship any woman who is a citizen by Registration[190] under Clause (1) of Article 15 if satisfied that the marriage by virtue of which she was registered has been dissolved, otherwise than by death, within the period of two years beginning with the date of the marriage.[191]

No person shall be deprived of his citizenship under Articles 25, 26, or 26A unless the Federal Government is satisfied that it is not conducive to the public good that he should continue to be a citizen.[192] Neither can an order for deprivation be made on certain of the above grounds for deprivation if as a result of such deprivation such person would not be a citizen of any country.[193]

(d) *Deprivation of Citizenship of Child of Person losing Citizenship*

Where a person has renounced his citizenship[194] or been deprived of his citizenship under certain provisions relating to deprivation,[195] the Federal Government may by order deprive of his citizenship any child of that person under the age of twenty-one who has been registered as a citizen pursuant to this Constitution[196] and was so registered as being the child of that person or of that person's wife or husband.[197]

PROCEDURE FOR DEPRIVATION

Article 27 of the Constitution lays down the procedure for deprivation to be complied with by the Government: before making an order[198] the Federal Government shall give to the person against whom the order is proposed to be made notice in writing informing him of the ground on which the order is proposed to be made and of his right to have the case referred to a Committee of Inquiry.[199] If any person to whom such notice is given applies to have the case referred as aforesaid the Federal Government shall, and in any other case the Federal Government may, refer the case to the Committee of Inquiry consisting of a Chairman (being a person possessing judicial experience) and two other members appointed by the Government for that purpose.[200] In the case of any such reference, the Committee shall hold an inquiry in such manner as the Federal Government may direct, and submit its report to the Government; and the Federal Government shall have regard to the report in determining whether to make the order.[201]

The exact scope of Article 27 was interpreted by the Privy Council in the Malaysian case of *Lim Lian Geok* v. *Minister of Interior, Federation of Malaya*.[202]

A notice issued by the Registrar-General of Citizens under Article 27(1) of the Constitution informed the appellant, a Chinese-born school teacher and a citizen of the Federation by Registration of the then Federation of Malaya, that the Federal Government proposed to make an order under Article 25 of the Constitution depriving him of his citizenship on the ground, specified in Article 25(1)(a), that he had shown himself by act and speech to be disloyal and disaffected towards the Federation.

The notice proceeded to particularize the allegations against the appellant which included 'deliberate misrepresentation and inversion of Government education policy' and 'emotional appeals of an extreme communal nature calculated to provoke feelings of ill-will and hostility between different races in the Federation...'.[203]

The appellant was given one month during which he could have his case referred to a Committee of Inquiry under Article 27(2). The appellant, however, did not do so, but applied to the High Court for an order nisi prohibiting the respondent,[204] the Minister of Interior, from referring his case to a Committee of Inquiry. Among the several arguments put forward by the appellant, the one that is of interest to us is that which related to the form of the notice. He contended that the notice was defective as it was lacking in particulars:

> The main submissions which were presented to their Lordships related to the content and form of the notice. It was said that the notice was defective because it was lacking in particulars. It was said that before a person could or ought to be called upon to decide whether he would claim to have his case referred to a Committee of Inquiry he should be informed in the notice as to the details of what was alleged against him.[205]

The Privy Council, however, dismissed this argument by holding that:

... the word 'ground' in Article 27 refers to that part (or those parts) of Article 24 or 25 or 26 which is (or are) being involved. In the present case the appellant was informed by the notice that ... he had shown himself by act and speech to be disloyal and disaffected towards the Federation of Malaya. That was 'the ground'. What followed, under the headings (a) and (b), consisted of particulars of the 'ground' which had been previously stated.[206]

What then this amounts to is as follows: all that the Government has to do before depriving anyone of his citizenship is merely to state the provision of the Constitution which is being invoked by the Government to deprive such person of his citizenship. There is no constitutional requirement to give particulars of the said ground.

If this is the only requirement, then one wonders what purpose is really being served by such a safeguard. If the reference to the Committee of Inquiry is to be meaningful, then the said person should be given certain information so that he would be able to prepare his case. If only the 'ground' is given, then it would not be of much help. The Privy Council appreciated this need and pointed out that during certain stages the giving of particulars might be necessary. When the notice is first being given to the person, of the proposed action, there is no need for particulars to be given. Their Lordships, however, did not wish in any way to discourage the giving of any particulars in a notice wherever it was thought to be desirable to be given them. In such an instance, there was no need for full and elaborate particulars to be furnished. Their Lordships did not elaborate when it was 'desirable' to give any particulars at this stage. Probably, an instance where it would be desirable to give particulars at this stage would be in a case where the Government feels that the order might come as a surprise to the person against whom the order is proposed to be made, especially if the person has not been guilty of many acts which purported to constitute the 'ground' for such an order.

The Privy Council felt that once an inquiry is being held the person must be furnished with the particulars.

If there is an inquiry ... then the necessity of giving particulars might arise. Though there are no express provisions which require that any particulars that are reasonably desired should at that stage be given, their Lordships agreed ... that it is implicit in the procedure that this should be so. This (i.e. the holding of the inquiry) involves that the citizen concerned is to have every reasonable and proper opportunity to deal with the 'ground' (or grounds) on which a deprivation order is proposed. This in turn involves that he must have such reasonable information as he may seek to have in regard to the case against him so as to enable him to deal with it or to answer it or to make such representations in regard to it as he wished. There would not be a proper inquiry if the citizen concerned was denied such particulars as he might need to have or as he might reasonably request in order to be able to protect his own interest.[207]

The end result of this procedural safeguard is that at the first stage of giving notice the Government is not under an obligation to give particulars. If, however, an inquiry is being held, then sufficient particulars[208] must be given to the person. Otherwise, the inquiry would not be of much use since the person could not prepare his case fully.

The views of the Privy Council as to the furnishing of particulars now appears to be unclear in view of the recent decision of *Mak Sik Kwong* v. *Minister of Home Affairs*.[209] In this case, Abdoolcader J. in dealing with the procedure to be complied with by the Minister in making an order for deprivation held that 'for the purposes of the exercise of his powers in making an order of deprivation under Article 24(2) it was open to the respondent to take into consideration relevant confidential information such as intelligence reports and the like without disclosure to the citizen where such disclosure would be prejudicial to the public or national interests'.[210]

It would appear from this that there is no duty imposed on the Minister to disclose to the citizen 'particulars' upon which the order for deprivation is based. Even if the citizen were to apply for such 'particulars', then it will always be open to the Minister to seek refuge on the ground that such disclosure 'would be prejudicial to the public or national interests'.

It is rather unfortunate that the learned Judge did not consider in detail the views expressed by the Privy Council as to the granting of 'particulars' and information to the citizen when an inquiry under Article 27 has been set up. Though earlier in the judgment, the learned Judge had pointed out 'that the Constitution provided by Article 27 a scheme for the oblique application of the rules of natural justice and the concepts of fairness and impartiality by the intercalation at the instance of the citizen of (and, it is significant to note, at the discretion of the respondent in any other case where there is no such requisition by the citizen in which event the respondent is under no such obligation to refer to) a Committee of Inquiry to afford him the opportunity of making representations and being heard before the respondent arrives at his final satisfaction and makes an order of deprivation',[211] yet if the citizen is to be deprived of such particulars and information on the ground that such matters relate to the affairs of State, then one may have doubts as to the effect of such an inquiry. It is submitted that in cases where the Minister raises the defence of 'affairs of State' when a citizen applies for information, the Court should be slow in upholding such a defence. Otherwise, the procedure spelt out under Article 27 would provide no meaningful safeguard to a citizen.[212]

The case of *Mak Sik Kwong* also raises a number of other interesting issues relating to the procedure for the deprivation of citizenship under Article 27. Abdoolcader J. also spelt out in detail the procedure to be complied with by the Minister before he makes an order for deprivation under Article 24(2).

Under Article 24(2) the respondent (the Minister of Home Affairs) is required to satisfy himself that a citizen has voluntarily claimed and exercised in a foreign country any rights available to him under the law of that country, being rights accorded exclusively to its citizens, before making an order depriving that person of his citizenship. The process of satisfaction to this effect would appear to be that initially the respondent presumably receives reports and other information on the basis of which he comes to a provisional satisfaction. Thereupon Article 27 comes into operation and by virtue of its provisions a notice in writing will then have to be served on the citizen informing him of the ground on which the respondent proposes to deprive him of his citizenship and of his right to have his case referred to a Committee of Inquiry. In the course of such inquiry the citizen is given an opportunity to make representations and answer the case against him, and the Committee is obliged to submit its report to the respondent who then shall have regard to that report in finally determining whether to make an order of deprivation under Article 24(2).[213]

His Lordship then pointed out that 'there would appear to be two stages in the making of an order of deprivation of citizenship under Article 24(2), namely:
   (a) when the respondent satisfies himself of the matters required thereunder; and
   (b) when he makes the order of deprivation.
Even if the respondent is satisfied at the first stage, he is not bound or obliged to proceed to the second stage and make an order of deprivation, as the operative word in the second limb of Article 24(2) is 'may' and not 'shall' or 'must'.[214]

The question as to whether the order of the Minister is amenable to the writ of certiorari, in view of Clause 2 of Part II of the Second Schedule, was fully dealt with by the Court. This point will be discussed in the next part of this essay. The other point of interest relates to the proof of a law of a foreign country.

Article 24(2) provides that the Federal Government may deprive a citizen of his citizenship, if the Federal Government is satisfied that any citizen had voluntarily claimed and exercised in a foreign country any rights available to him under the law of that country being rights accorded exclusively to its citizens. Assuming then that an order for deprivation is made on the ground that a Federal citizen had voluntarily claimed and exercised a right in a foreign country, such right being accorded to citizens of that country alone, can a citizen challenge the order for deprivation on the ground that the Minister had erred in holding that the right which was exercised by the citizen was a right accorded exclusively to the citizens of that foreign country? In other words, can he challenge the order on the ground that the Minister had made a mistake as to the scope of the foreign law?

In the instant case, the citizen attempted to challenge the order of the Minister on the ground that the Minister acted on the mistaken belief that the citizen had exercised a right which was accorded exclusively to citizens of China. The Court in rejecting this argument held that an opinion upon a point of foreign law was a question of fact which was to be determined by the Minister and as such the Court would not interfere with the finding of the Minister on a question of fact:

> The matters to be considered by the respondent under Article 24(2) are pure questions of fact and asking me to entertain evidence in this connection is, in my view, tantamount to asking the Court to sit on appeal against the respondent's findings and re-try the matters entrusted to his discretion by the Constitution and his determination thereon. It is not the function or within the jurisdiction of the Court to do so. If the respondent erred at all in considering Chinese law for the purposes of his determination in this matter, he erred only on a question of evidence and fact resulting at the most only in an evidential error of law not going to jurisdiction, but there is no indication that he did indeed do so.[215]

The Court then held that 'the respondent had evidence of the applicant's residence and education in China without restriction and his final exit therefrom. Whether those facts were sufficient for the respondent to have arrived at his satisfaction for the purposes of Article 24(2) was a matter entirely for him to decide.'[216]

REVIEW

Section 2 of Part III of the Second Schedule of the Constitution provides that 'a decision of the Federal Government under Part III of this Constitution shall not be subject to appeal or review in any Court'. Does this therefore mean that the Courts have no jurisdiction whatsoever to determine the validity of any decision made by the Federal Government? Can a person challenge in Court a decision made by the Minister?

There are a number of Malaysian cases which have discussed the scope of this provision. In the case of *Soon Kok Leong* v. *Minister of Interior Malaysia*,[217] Ismail Khan J. in the High Court held that the provision did not exclude the application for an order of certiorari for excess of jurisdiction or for error of law on the face of the record. In a subsequent case, in *Re Soon Chi Hiang*,[218] Raja Azlan Shah J. held that 'it is true that the said order is not reviewable by the Court by virtue of paragraph 2 of Part III of the Second Schedule but that cannot take away by implication the judicial review by means of certiorari'.[219]

However, Ong Hock Sim J. in *Liew Shin Lai* v. *Minister of Home Affairs*[220] observed that an attempt to challenge the order of deprivation would be barred by virtue of Section 2. The Judge, in arriving at this view, made no reference to the earlier decisions nor did he consider the scope of Section 2 in detail. It is submitted that this view is wrong and decided *per incuriam*.

Abdoolcader J. in *Mak Sik Kwong* dealt with the scope of Section 2 in detail. After a full discussion of the cases dealing with such finality or privative clauses, he came to the view that 'the schedule provision does not preclude the Court from entertaining the application for an order of certiorari'.[221] In *Mak Sik Kwong (No. 2)*[222] the same Judge spelt out the circumstances under which the Court would interfere to review the decision of the Minister. He held that only if there was a 'jurisdictional defect' would the Court interfere.[223]

The conclusion one may draw from these cases is that the Malaysian Courts would not preclude themselves from reviewing an order of the Minister, even in the light of Section 2, if there has been some defect in the said order.

It should be noted in all the cases discussed above, the order in question related to the deprivation of citizenship. In these cases, it would appear to be clear that the Courts would interfere in certain cases when such an order is challenged. However, what is not clear is whether a Malaysian Court would also interfere with a decision of the Minister in the granting of a citizenship. As pointed out earlier, in certain cases of citizenship by Registration,[224] the Constitution provides that if the applicant satisfies all the requirements provided for by the Constitution, then such a person is to be registered as a citizen. Would the Courts on an application by such a person direct the Minister to register such a person as a citizen? Can the applicant apply for a writ of mandamus to compel the Minister to register such a person as a citizen?[225] There has been no Malaysian case on this point and the position appears to be unclear. It is the writer's view that even though some of these provisions bestow on the Government a certain amount of discretion by empowering it to make certain subjective conclusions like 'good character',[226] yet the Courts should not abdicate all their powers on the ground that such matters are best left to the executive alone to decide. The fact that the drafters of the Constitution provided that in these circumstances the applicant is *entitled* to be registered as a citizen whereas in certain other provisions express discretionary powers are granted to the Government whether to grant citizenship or not, appear to suggest that an applicant in the former case should be able to claim citizenship as of right—how else can such person claim such a right except through the assistance of the Courts?

CONCLUSION

Though the laws relating to citizenship have changed on a number of occasions through the various stages of the constitutional development of the country, it would seem that since 1957, when the citizenship laws of the country were first incorporated into the Constitution, there have only been four amendments to the provisions relating to citizenship: two of these amendments dealt with the formation of Malaysia and subsequently the separation of Singapore from the Federation. In effect, therefore, only the 1962 and the 1976 amendments altered the law to a significant extent. In fact, even the latter two amendments were made either to take into account changes in policy or to eradicate certain anomalies which were present. To this extent then there is much to be said for having the citizenship laws embodied in the Constitution. The intention of the drafters of the Constitution to embody these provisions in the Constitution so as 'to allay fears that they would be amended if they had been enacted as ordinary legislation' has to this extent been achieved. In fact, the provisions relating to citizenship are to a certain extent 'entrenched' under the Constitution. Article 150 (6A) provides that even if a Proclamation of Emergency is declared by the Yang di-Pertuan Agong under Article 150, no law shall be passed which is inconsistent with the provisions of the Constitution relating to citizenship. Furthermore, by virtue of the Sedition Act,[227] it is an offence under the Act to question the provisions of the Constitution relating to citizenship.

The importance of citizenship has been stressed by the Government over recent years by the introduction of various legislation providing for social benefits to citizens alone. The Employment (Restriction) Act[228] was introduced in 1968 to restrict the employment of non-citizens. Special employment permits are issued at the discretion of the Government for the employment of non-citizens. Employment in the Federal Civil Service is largely restricted to

Federal citizens. Priority is given to citizens for admission into local Universities. Tighter immigration laws have been introduced under the Immigration Act.[229] The consequence of all this legislation has been a large number of persons applying for citizenship. Unlike the Singapore Government,[230] the Federal Government has not spelt out any policies for the criteria to determine who would be granted citizenship by the Federal Government. It would be more desirable to spell out those policies rather than to leave the fate of the applicant at the complete discretion of the Government. As a result, the Government has been subjected to allegations that they have deliberately prolonged the consideration of these applications over an unduly long period and that this has caused a great deal of hardship to the applicants. During question time in Parliamentary sessions the Minister of Home Affairs is often queried on the delay in the processing of citizenship applications. Probably, a body in the nature of the Ombudsman should be set up by the Government to look into these complaints.[231]

1. Act VIII 1867, as amended by Ordinances 7 of 1870, 24 of 1919, 9 of 1928 and 21 of 1935, and consolidated as C. 86 of the Laws of Straits Settlements (1936).

2. Section 2.

3. Section 3.

4. Pahang Enactment No. 14 of 1904, Negri Sembilan Enactment No. 21 of 1904, Selangor Enactment No. 22, Perak Enactment No. 22 of 1904. See Laws of the Federated Malay States C.117 of 1935.

5. Section 2.

6. *Malayan Union and Singapore, Statement of Policy on Future Constitution*, January 1946, Cmd. 6724. HMSO (London) Paras. 2 and 10.

7. Ibid., Para. 10. See also *Malayan Union and Singapore, Summary of Proposed Constitutional Arrangements*, March 1949, Cmd. 6749, HMSO (London) Paras. 23-7.

8. G.N.6 of 1948. See Malayan Union and Federation of Malaya. Sub. Leg. 1948. Subsequently amended by L.N. 279/1949, O. 70/1949, O. 31/1950, L.N. 461/1951, O. 17/1951, L.N. 28/1952, G.N. 1814/1952, O. 23/1952, O. 1/1953, O. 27/1954, L.N. 509/1954, L.N. 767/1954, O. 39/1955, L.N. 419/1955, L.N. 463/1955. It was re-enacted in 1952 by Ordinance 23 of 1952.

9. See Preamble to the 1948 Agreement and also Para. 24 of *Federation of Malaya: Summary of Revised Constitutional Proposals*, July 1947, HMSO (London) Cmd. 7171.

10. Ibid., Para. 24(a). This recommendation was accepted by the drafters of the 1948 Agreement and was embodied in Clause 124(1)(a) of the Agreement.

11. Ibid., Para. 24. Embodied as Clause 124(3)(a) of the Agreement.

12. 'Malay' was defined in Clause 124(3)(b) as a person who (*i*) habitually speaks the Malay language; and (*ii*) professes the Muslim religion; and (*iii*) conforms to Malay custom.

13. 'Permanent resident' was defined in Clause 124(3)(c) as one 'who has completed a continuous period of fifteen years residence ...'.

14. Clause 124(1)(b).

15. Ibid., (c).

16. Ibid., (d).

17. Ibid., (e).

18. Ibid., (f).

19. Clause 125(1).

20. Ibid.

21. Clause 126(1).

22. Clause 126(a).

23. *Constitutional Proposals for Malaya, Report of the Working Committee*, Malayan Union Govt. Press, 1946.

24. (1931-2) F.M.S.L.R. 271; [1932] 1 M.L.J. 99.

25. S.I. No. 140. See also S.I. 1953, No. 1773.

26. The Indians and Ceylonese who were in the country were citizens of the United Kingdom and the Colonies.

27. 12 & 12 Geo.VI C. 56.

28. Federation of Malaya Agreement (Amendment) Ordinance 1952, Federal Ordinance No. 23 of 1952.

29. Johore No. 2 of 1952; Kedah No. 5 of 1952 (1371); Kelantan No. 2 of 1952; Negri Sembilan No. 2 of 1952; Pahang No. 2 of 1952; Perak No. 1 of 1952; Perlis No. 1 of 1952; Selangor No. 2 of 1952; Trengganu No. 3 of 1952. See Federal Ordinance and State and Settlement Enactment 1952.

30. Clause 125.

31. Clause 125(a).

32. Clause 124(f).

33. Clause 125(b).

34. Clause 125(c).

35. Clause 125(d)(*i*).

36. Clause 125(d)(*ii*).

37. Clause 125(e).

38. Clause 125(f).

39. Clause 125(g).

40. Clause 126. Clause 116 has to be read together with Clause 128 which imposes certain restrictions on the right to be registered as a citizen.

41. Clause 127 subject to Clause 128. See also the Proviso to the said Clause. There were, however, no residential requirements.

42. This provision was rather restrictive as it would not allow Chinese women who were not citizens of the United Kingdom and Colonies to be registered as citizens under this provision. See also comments by Clive Parry, *Nationality and Citizenship Laws of the Commonwealth and Ireland*, 1957, p. 393.

43. Clause 129.

44. Clause 131.

45. Clause 131(3).

46. Clause 132(6).

47. Clause 133.

48. Clause 133(2)(a).

49. Clause 133(2)(b), (c), (d) and (e).

50. Proviso (*i*) to Clause 133(2). However this restriction does not apply to any person who had been deprived of his citizenship under Clause 133(2)(a).

51. 31 August 1957. Commonly referred to as Merdeka Day.

52. Part III of the Constitution. For some of the effects of having it embodied in the Constitution, see Salleh Abbas, 'Amendment of the Malaysian Constitution', [1977] 2 M.L.J. (Supp.), ms. xxv, ms. xxvii.

53. See earlier part of this essay.

54. Article 14(1)(a).

55. Article 14(1)(b).

56. Except in cases of birth in the Straits Settlements as provided for under the earlier law.

57. Article 14(1)(c).

58. Article 14(1)(d).

59. Act 14 of 1962.

60. Date of coming into effect of the Amendment. L.N. 164/62.

61. Proviso (*ii*) to the amended Article 14(2).

62. See Note 52.

63. Article 15(1). See earlier position under old law on p. 74.

64. Article 15(3)—The laws providing for registration of marriages are the Registration of Marriages Ordinance No. 53 of 1952, Christian Marriage Ordinance No. 33 of 1956, Civil Marriage Ordinance No. 44 of 1952. Under the Law Reform (Marriage and Divorce) Act, No. 164 of 1976 (not in effect as yet), all this legislation would be repealed and henceforth all marriages have to be registered under the new Act S.25.

65. Article 18(2).

66. Article 26(2).

67. Act 14 of 1962. Amendment took effect from 10 September 1962, L.N. 164/62.

68. Clause 127, see p. 74.

69. Article 15(2); 16, 17.

70. Article 15(1)(c). There is no definition of 'good character' except that good character is presumed in the absence of criminal conviction. See Article 18(4).

71. Article 15(2).

72. Inserted by Section 3 of Act 14 of 1962. Emphasis added.

73. See the unamended Article 15.

74. There is no definition of what constitutes 'special circumstances'.

75. *Report of the Federation of Malaya Constitutional Commission* (1957), para. 38.

76. Article 16(a).

77. Article 16(b).

78. Article 16(c).

79. Article 16(d). See also para. 40 of Reid Commission Report.

80. Para. 41.

81. Para. 41.

82. Article 17.

83. See Para. 9. *Constitutional Proposals for the Federation of Malaya*, June 1957, Cmd. 210. Colonial Office, HMSO (London).

84. Act 14 of 1962.

85. *Parliamentary Debates (Dewan Ra'ayat)*, January 1962, Vol. III, 3rd Session. Col. 4169-70.

86. Section 5 of Act 14 of 1962.

87. Article 19.

88. Article 19(c).

89. Article 19(a).

90. Article 19(b).

91. Article 19(d).

92. Article 21.

93. Article 20.

94. Article 20(1)(a).

95. Article 20(1)(b).

96. Act 20(1) provides that the Federal Government *shall* grant a Certificate of Naturalisation.

97. Act 14 of 1962.

98. Date of coming into effect of the Amendment L.N. 164/62.

99. Article 19(e).

100. Section 7 of Act 14 of 1962.

101. Article 23.

102. Article 24.

103. Articles 25 to 26.

104. Article 27.

105. See p. 84.

106. Malaysia Act, No. 26 of 1963.

107. Malaysia Act, No. 26 of 1963.

108. The numbering of the Articles under the 1957 Constitution and the 1963 Constitution are identical.

109. See Article 14(3), Article 19(6), (7), (8) and Article 19A. All Articles have now been repealed. H. E. Groves, *The Constitution of Malaysia*, Malayan Publishing House, 1964, p. 171ff.

110. Article 14(2).

111. Constitution (Amendment) Act, 1966 (No. 59 of 1966).

112. 16 September 1963—L.N. 214/1963.

113. It is relevant to refer to the 1957 Constitution, the Federation of Malaya Agreement and to the State Nationality Acts. See earlier parts of this essay.

114. Article 14 together with Part I of the Second Schedule. Clause (1)(*i*). But for purposes of termination of citizenship they are treated differently. See Articles 28 and 28(4).

115. Part I, Second Schedule, Clause 1(1)(b).

116. Ibid., Clause 1(1)(c).

117. Ibid.

118. See p. 76.

119. See p. 76.

120. Part I, Second Schedule, Clause 1(1)(d).

121. Ibid., Clause 1(1)(e). The period for registration may be extended by the Federal Government.

122. Clauses 1(1)(d) and (e) of Part I of Second Schedule.

123. Ibid.

124. R. H. Hickling, *An Introduction to the Federal Constitution*, Fed. of Malaya Information Service, 1960, p. 24.

125. Second Schedule, Part I, Clause 2.

126. See above.

127. Second Schedule. Part II, Clause (a). The provision has to be read subject to Clause 2(1).

128. Ibid., Clause (b).

129. Ibid., Clause (c).

130. Ibid., Clause (e). Subject to Clauses 2(1), 2(2) and 2(3).

131. Ibid., Clause (d). Subject to Clause 2(1).

132. Article 15(1). See Citizenship Rules 1964, L.N. 82, for the different forms to be used for purposes of Registration and Naturalisation.

133. Date of coming into effect of the Amendment. See p. 76.

134. c.f. Situation under the 1957 Constitution. See pp. 76-7.

135. See the views of the Federation of Women Lawyers, Malaysia. 'Current Legislation in Peninsular Malaysia' [1975] 2 M.L.J. 1 xxv, para. 74.

136. Articles 15(2), (3) and 15A.

137. Articles 15(2) and 15A.

138. Article 15(3).

139. Date of coming into effect of the amendment.

140. This provision appears to have been a transitional provision, but to date it has not been repealed.

141. Article 16.

142. See Act 10 of 1960, 25 of 1963, 26 of 1963, and 59 of 1966.

143. Article 16(a).

144. Ibid., Clause (b).

145. Ibid., Clause (c).

146. Ibid., Clause (d). See Section 6 of Citizenship Rules 1964.

147. Article 16A. This provision has not been amended to date.

148. Article 16A(a).

149. Ibid., Clause (b).

150. Ibid., Clause (c).

151. Ibid., Clause (d). See Section 7 of Citizenship Rules 1964.

152. Article 17 (Now repealed). See p. 78.

153. Repealed by Act 14 of 1962.

154. Repealed in force from 1 July 1963. See Section 4 of Act 14 of 1962.

155. Article 19. Note also Clauses (5) and (9) of Article 19.

156. Article 19(3).

157. Ibid.

158. Article 19(1)(a)(i).

159. Ibid., (1)(b).

160. Ibid., (1)(c). See Section 8 of Citizenship Rules 1964.

161. Paragraph (a) (ii) before the repeal read as follows: '(ii) he has resided in Singapore for the required period and intends, if the certificate is granted, to do so permanently'.

162. Article 20. See p. 79. Repealed by Act 14 of 1962 in force from 1 February 1964.

163. Article 23. As to the form prescribed, see Section 36 of Citizenship Rules 1964.

164. See earlier position where one could only renounce Federal citizenship after becoming a citizen of another country. Present provision by Act 14 of 1962.

165. Article 23(1).

166. Ibid., Clause (2).

167. Article 24(1).

168. 'Foreign country' is defined under Article 160 of the Constitution not to include any part of the Commonwealth or the Republic of Ireland.

169. Article 24(2).

170. See Note 168.

171. For example, the right to vote in a political election as in the United Kingdom.

172. Act A354.

173. See view expressed by Salleh Abas, 'Amendment of The Malaysian Constitution' [1977] 2 M.L.J. (Supp). m.s. xxv, m.s. xxxix.

174. See view of Sheridan and Groves, '*The Constitution of Malaysia*', Oceana Publications, Inc., New York, 1967, pp. 58-60.

175. Date of coming into force of the amendment, Act 14 of 1962. L.N. 268 of 1963.

176. Article 24(3A). Added by Act 14 of 1962.

177. See p. 82.

178. Article 24(4).

179. See Article 26B(2).

180. Registration of persons resident in Borneo States on Malaysia Day. See also Article 28A.

181. Registration of persons resident in the Federation on Merdeka Day. Now repealed. See also Articles 28(1)(a) and 28A.

182. See p. 81. See Articles 28(1)(c) and 28A.

183. Article 25(1)(a).

184. Ibid., (b).

185. Ibid., (c).

186. 'Country Outside the Federation' was substituted for 'Foreign Country' by Act A354 in 1976.

187. Article 25(1A).

188. Article 25(2).

189. Article 26(1). Criminal proceedings may also be instituted in such cases: *P.P.* v. *Munusamy* [1967] M.L.J. 238; *P.P.* v. *Ramasami* [1970] 2 M.L.J. 71. See Section 16(1) of Part III of Second Schedule.

190. See Articles 28(1)(b) and 28A(3).

191. Article 26(2).

192. Article 26B(2).

193. Ibid.

194. Under Article 23.

195. Under Article 24(1) or 26(1)(a).

196. Under Article 15.

197. Article 26A.

198. This procedure is restricted to deprivation under Article 24, 25, or 26.

199. Article 27(1).

200. Ibid., Clause (2). See Section 38-40 of Citizenship Rules for Composition, Function and Powers of Committee of Inquiry.

201. Ibid., Clause (3).

202. [1964] 1 W.L.R. 554; [1964] 30 M.L.J. 158.

203. Ibid.

204. As to a discussion as to the propriety of the remedy sought—see S. Jayakumar, 'Deprivation of Citizenship', (1964) 6 Mal. L.R. 178.

205. [1964] 1 W.L.R. 554, 563.

206. Ibid., p. 565.

207. Ibid.

208. The Privy Council did not decide upon the issue whether a person can challenge the order on the ground that sufficient particulars were not furnished. It would seem that this would be a justiciable issue. See also Article mentioned in footnote 204.

209. [1975] 2 M.L.J. 168.

210. Ibid., p. 182.

211. Ibid., p. 181.

212. Maybe the general procedure for the disclosure of documents should be complied with.

213. *Supra*, p. 174.

214. *Supra*, p. 175.

215. *Supra*, p. 180.

216. Ibid.

217. [1968] M.L.J. 88.

218. [1969] 1 M.L.J. 218.

219. Ibid., p. 219.

220. [1970] 2 M.L.J. 7. See Notes by Jayakumar in [1970] 2 M.L.J. xviii. Vohrah [1970] 2 M.L.J. xxvi, and Jayakumar [1970] 2 M.L.J. lvii.

221. [1975] 2 M.L.J. 168, 172.

222. [1975] 2 M.L.J. 175.

223. As to the scope of 'Jurisdictional Defect', see p. 177. See also Jain, 'Development of Administrative Law in Malaysia Since Merdeka', [1977] 2 M.L.J. (Supp) m.s. ii.

224. See pp. 76-9.

225. See views of Suffian, *An Introduction to the Constitution of Malaysia*, 1976, 2nd ed., Government Printer, 1976, p. 259.

226. There is no definition of 'good character'. Article 18(4) was repealed by Act 25 of 1963.

227. Act 15. (Revised 1969).

228. No. 36 of 1968.

229. Immigration Ordinance No. 12 of 1959 and the Immigration Act No. 27 of 1963.

230. See Sinnadurai, 'Singapore Citizenship Laws' (1970), 12 Mal. L.R. 160.

231. Such a proposal for an ombudsman generally had earlier been rejected by the Government. Perhaps this should now be reconsidered.

* I am grateful to my student, Philip T. N. Koh, for his assistance in the preparation of this essay.

✻ F. A. TRINDADE

5. The Constitutional Position of the Yang di-Pertuan Agong[1]

THIRTEEN years ago, S. Jayakumar and I wrote an article entitled 'The Supreme Head of the Malaysian Federation'[2] in which we examined in some detail the provisions of the Malaysian Constitution which deal with the Yang di-Pertuan Agong. At that time the institution of the Yang di-Pertuan Agong was only in its seventh year—though the third holder was already in office, the first two holders having died after short terms in office—and there was a natural reluctance to assess that unique and new institution. We did however suggest that there was 'every indication that the creation of the office will, in time to come, be proved to be a wise one'.[3]

Now the institution has been in existence for twenty years and the sixth Yang di-Pertuan Agong is in office having been sworn in on 21 September 1975. Has the creation of the office proved to be a wise one? I think it is fair to say that the Yang di-Pertuan Agong has become 'a visible symbol of unity in a remarkably diverse nation'.[4] There is hardly any criticism of the institution that I have encountered and there has been no significant change to it during the last twenty years. The original institution created in 1957 continues to thrive in 1977 without any serious problems and though there have been some minor constitutional amendments and some discussion of the constitutional position of the Yang di-Pertuan Agong in a few decisions of the courts, they have been mainly elucidatory rather than innovative and much of what we wrote in 1964 about the office is still valid and relevant in 1977.[5]

THE OFFICE OF THE YANG DI-PERTUAN AGONG

This office was created by the Constitution of the Federation of Malaya on 31 August 1957. Article 32(1) stated: 'There shall be a Supreme Head of the Federation, to be called the Yang di-Pertuan Agong, who shall take precedence over all persons in the Federation ...'. During the course of the last twenty years this office has remained virtually untouched by the deluge of constitutional amendments. The Malaysia Act[6] increased some of the religious functions[7] of the Yang di-Pertuan Agong and this has been done again by the Constitution (Amendment) (No. 2) Act 1973[8] in relation to the Federal Territory and by the Constitution (Amendment) Act, 1976[9] in relation to Sabah and Sarawak. The 1976 Amendment Act has also effected a change in the disabilities of the Yang di-Pertuan Agong and the Raja Permaisuri Agong which will be dealt with later on in this essay.[10]

The office of the Yang di-Pertuan Agong is a unique and original institution. The Reid Commission[11] was directed by its terms of reference to include provision for 'a Constitutional Yang di-Pertuan Besar for the Federation to be chosen from among Their Highnesses the Rulers'. In recommending the creation of this office the Commission stated: 'He will be a symbol of the unity of the country'.[12] And this is an important facet of the Constitution, for by allowing each of the nine Rulers[13] the opportunity of assuming the office of the Supreme Head of the Federation, the Constitution tries to ensure that the people of the several States of the Federation identify themselves more closely with the Federation. The term of office is five years but due to the death of the first Yang di-Pertuan Agong on 1 April 1960 after less than three years in office, and the death of the second on 1 September 1960 after only a few months in office, the Rulers of six States, Negri Sembilan, Selangor, Perlis, Trengganu, Kedah and Kelantan, have already been elected during the first twenty years since the creation of the office.[14]

In order to be eligible for election to the office of the Yang di-Pertuan Agong a Ruler must be an adult, he must consent to be elected and he must be free from any physical or mental defect which might render him unsuitable for the office. He must also be first on the election list and receive the support of at least four other Rulers.[15] Since only the nine Rulers are qualified to be elected to the office of the Yang di-Pertuan Agong it follows that he must also be a male Malay and necessarily professing the Muslim religion.

Once he is elected the Yang di-Pertuan Agong must, before he exercises his functions, take and subscribe before the Conference of Rulers and in the presence of the Lord President of the Federal Court the oath of office[16] set out in Part I of the Fourth Schedule. The executive authority of the Federation is then vested in the Yang di-Pertuan Agong,[17] though it is exercisable not only by him but also *by the Cabinet or any Minister authorized by the Cabinet.*[18]

Although the term for which the Yang di-Pertuan Agong is elected is five years he may at any time resign his office. It is not necessary to obtain the approval of the Federal Parliament or even to inform them. All that is required is that the resignation must be in writing and that it must be addressed to the Conference of Rulers.[19]

By Article 35(1) Parliament is required to provide a Civil List[20] of the Yang di-Pertuan Agong. This Civil List is to be charged on the Consolidated Fund and it cannot be diminished during his continuance in office.

ELECTION TO THE OFFICE OF YANG DI-PERTUAN AGONG

The Constitution provides that the Yang di-Pertuan Agong shall be elected by the Conference of Rulers.[21] When the Conference of Rulers meets for this purpose it consists of the Yang di-Pertuan Besar of Negri Sembilan, the Raja of Perlis, and the seven Sultans of the other Malay States. When exercising its function of electing the Yang di-Pertuan Agong and the Timbalan Yang di-Pertuan Agong[22] the Conference of Rulers must act in accordance with the provisions of the Third Schedule. An important feature of this election is the election list. For the first election held in 1957 the list comprised the States of all the Rulers in the order in which Their Highnesses then recognized precedence among themselves. The order of precedence was based on the dates of accession to the thrones of the several States and the list in order of precedence was Johore, Pahang, Negri Sembilan, Selangor, Kedah, Perlis, Kelantan, Trengganu, and Perak. For subsequent elections the list has been varied so that the State whose Ruler was elected was omitted from the list and after each election any States preceding on the list the State whose Ruler was elected were transferred (in the order in which they were then on the list) to the end of the list. Whenever there is a change in the Ruler of a State on the list that State is transferred to the end of the list. When no State remains on the list because all the Rulers have been at some time the Yang di-Pertuan Agong or when no Ruler of a State then on the list is qualified for election or accepts office the list is to be reconstituted. The election list for the next Yang di-Pertuan Agong consists, in order of precedence, of Perak, Pahang, and Johore and unless the Rulers of these three States are not qualified for election or decline office, one of them will be the next Yang di-Pertuan Agong. The Table of the election lists for the Yang di-Pertuan Agong and the Table of States whose Rulers have already been elected which appears as an appendix to this essay will help the reader to understand better the process of electing the Yang di-Pertuan Agong.[23]

The purpose of the election list is to indicate to the Conference of Rulers who should be offered the office of the Yang di-Pertuan Agong and indeed section 2 of Part I of the Third Schedule states that

... the Conference of Rulers shall offer the office of Yang di-Pertuan Agong to the Ruler qualified for election whose State is first on the election list ... and if he does not accept the office, to the Ruler whose State is next on the list, and so on until a Ruler accepts the office.

A Ruler is not qualified to be elected if he is a minor or if he has notified the Keeper of the Rulers' Seal that he does not desire to be elected. This was probably done by the late Ruler of Johore in 1957 and the late Ruler of Pahang in 1970. If these two rulers did not voluntarily stand down then they must have been passed over, for the Conference of Rulers may by secret ballot resolve that any Ruler is not qualified to be elected because they believe that 'he is unsuitable by reason of infirmity of mind or body or *for any other cause* to exercise the functions of Yang di-Pertuan Agong'.[24] In our article in 1964 Jayakumar and I were critical of the unnecessarily wide discretion given to the Conference of Rulers to exclude any of their number from the office of Yang di-Pertuan Agong on any pretext whatever—particularly in view of the fact that there would be no redress for a Ruler who had been capriciously excluded, because the Constitution provides that 'the members of the Conference of Rulers may act in their discretion in any proceedings relating to ... the election or removal from office of the Yang di-Pertuan Agong or the election of the Timbalan Yang di-Pertuan Agong'.[25] However there has been no evidence during the last twenty years that that unnecessarily wide discretion has been abused, but even if it has we shall never know, as the proceedings of the Conference of Rulers in electing the Yang di-Pertuan Agong are kept secret and known only to the Rulers and the Keeper of the Rulers' Seal.

The election of the Timbalan Yang di-Pertuan Agong or Deputy Supreme Head of the Federation as he was formerly known is also conducted by the Conference of Rulers. The office of Timbalan Yang di-Pertuan Agong is usually offered to the Ruler who would be first entitled to be offered the office of Yang di-Pertuan Agong on the death of the Yang di-Pertuan Agong last elected. If he declines, the Ruler next on the list is offered the office until someone accepts the office. A Ruler who declines the office of Timbalan Yang di-Pertuan Agong does not lose his place on the election list for the office of Yang di-Pertuan Agong.

Once he is elected the Timbalan Yang di-Pertuan Agong exercises the functions and has the privileges of the Yang di-Pertuan Agong during any vacancy in that office and during any period during which the Yang di-Pertuan Agong is unable to exercise the functions of his office owing to illness, absence from the Federation, or for any other cause.[26] Until 1976 the Timbalan Yang di-Pertuan Agong could not exercise the functions of the Yang di-Pertuan Agong during his absence if it was expected to be less than fifteen days. However, by s. 10 of the Constitution (Amendment) Act 1976 the Timbalan Yang di-Pertuan Agong is given the power to exercise the functions of the Yang di-Pertuan Agong during any inability or absence of the Yang di-Pertuan Agong even if less than fifteen days if the Timbalan Yang di-Pertuan Agong 'is satisfied that it is necessary or expedient to exercise such functions'.

The Timbalan Yang di-Pertuan Agong is elected for a term of five years, if he is elected at the same time as the Yang di-Pertuan Agong. However, if he is elected during the term of a Yang di-Pertuan Agong, he can only be elected for the remainder of that term. If during the term of the Timbalan Yang di-Pertuan Agong a vacancy occurs in the office of the Yang di-Pertuan Agong, the term of the Timbalan expires as soon as a new Yang di-Pertuan Agong is elected.[27]

The Timbalan Yang di-Pertuan Agong is not automatically elected to the office of the Yang di-Pertuan Agong even when he is first on the election list for that office. This might seem anomalous, for the Conference of Rulers by electing him to be Timbalan Yang di-Pertuan Agong is tacitly acknowledging that he has all the necessary qualifications, because a Ruler is not qualified to be the Timbalan unless he is qualified to be elected Yang di-Pertuan Agong.[28] Nevertheless, the wide discretionary powers of the Conference of Rulers remain and a Timbalan who is at the top of the election list can it seems be passed over in the next election for the Yang di-Pertuan Agong.[29]

The Constitution provides that Parliament may entrust to a Ruler the exercise of the functions of the Yang di-Pertuan Agong either when there is no Timbalan Yang di-Pertuan Agong or when the Timbalan is ill, absent from the Federation, or cannot otherwise exercise the functions of the Yang di-Pertuan Agong.[30] By virtue of this provision Parliament enacted the Yang di-Pertuan Agong (Exercise of Functions) Ordinance, 1957.[31] Under this enactment the functions of the Yang di-Pertuan Agong are to be exercised by the Ruler who is first on the election list if he is able and willing to exercise such functions. If he is not able and willing then the functions are to be exercised by the Ruler next on the list and so on. The Conference of Rulers however can at the next meeting, by resolution, appoint any Ruler to exercise the functions of the Yang di-Pertuan Agong.

REMOVAL FROM OFFICE

Although the Yang di-Pertuan Agong is a Constitutional Monarch, 'bound by the Constitution to act at all times on the advice of the Cabinet',[32] he cannot be removed by the Cabinet or even by the Malaysian Parliament itself. In this respect, his position is stronger than that of the President of India who can be impeached[33] by both Houses of the Indian Parliament but not as strong as the English Monarch who cannot, it seems, be removed at all. For the Yang di-Pertuan Agong may be removed from office by the Conference of Rulers.[34] This may be effected at any time and for any reason and the decision cannot be questioned, because the Constitution provides that the members of the Conference of Rulers may act in their discretion in effecting the removal from office of the Yang di-Pertuan Agong.[35] All that is required is that a resolution of the Conference of Rulers to remove the Yang di-Pertuan Agong must have the support of at least five of the nine Rulers. In our 1964 article[36] Jayakumar and I thought that the removal of the Yang di-Pertuan Agong from so high an office should have been hedged with more safeguards than a simple majority of the nine Rulers. But Parliament has not seen fit, during the last twenty years, to impose any restrictions on the discretionary power of the Rulers to remove the Yang di-Pertuan Agong from office, provided at least five of them agree to do so. The Constitution also provides that the Yang di-Pertuan Agong must cease to hold office if he ceases to be a Ruler.[37]

Although the Timbalan Yang di-Pertuan Agong must cease to hold the office of Timbalan on ceasing to be a Ruler,[38] there is no provision in the Constitution for the removal of the Timbalan Yang di-Pertuan Agong from office. There seems to be no good reason why provision should not have been made in the Constitution for the removal of the Timbalan from office in the same way as the provisions which exist in the Constitution for the removal of the Yang di-Pertuan Agong from office. Jayakumar and I have suggested some good reasons why such provision should have been made and we have even suggested how this could be achieved with minor amendments to Article 33(2) and Article 38(6)(a). I do not wish to repeat those arguments now but merely draw attention to them.[39]

IMMUNITY OF THE YANG DI-PERTUAN AGONG

Article 32(1) of the Federal Constitution states that the Yang di-Pertuan Agong 'shall not be liable to any proceedings whatsoever in any court'. When the Timbalan Yang di-Pertuan Agong is exercising the functions of the Yang di-Pertuan Agong he is entitled to all the privileges of the Yang di-Pertuan Agong[40] and therefore entitled to this *complete immunity* from legal process during any period in which he assumes the office of the Yang di-Pertuan Agong. In our 1964 article[41] Jayakumar and I stated that no distinction has been made in the Malaysian Constitution between acts done in an official or personal capacity or between criminal and civil proceedings and we concluded that the wording of Article 32(1) suggests that the immunity from legal process of the Yang di-Pertuan Agong is complete and unqualified and applies to both civil and criminal proceedings and to acts done both in an official and in a personal capacity.

Since that time however we have had the decision of Pike C.J. (Borneo) in *Stephen Kalong Ningkan* v. *Tun Abang Haji Openg & Tawi Sli (No. 2)*[42] where the Proclamation of a State of Emergency made by the Yang di-Pertuan Agong on the advice of the Federal Cabinet on 14 September 1966 was challenged by the dismissed Chief Minister of Sarawak as being null, void, and of no effect by reason of the fact that it was not made *bona fide* but was made in *fraudem legis*. Counsel for the defendants had argued that since the power to proclaim a State of Emergency was vested in the Yang di-Pertuan Agong and since by Article 32(1) the Yang di-Pertuan Agong is not liable to any proceedings whatsoever in any court, the act of the Yang di-Pertuan Agong is not challengeable in any court. Pike C.J. rejected this argument of the defendants with the following words:

Article 32(1) only protects the Yang di-Pertuan Agong personally from proceedings in a court but cannot be construed to protect the Federal Government from action in the courts in respect of its acts committed in the name of the Yang di-Pertuan Agong, and when the Yang di-Pertuan Agong acts on the advice of the cabinet his act must be deemed to be the act of the Federal Government.[43]

Tun Suffian in his *Introduction to the Constitution of Malaysia*[44] appears to accept this statement of the position but one might well ask why it would have been necessary to say in Article 32(1) that the Yang di-Pertuan Agong 'shall not be liable to any proceedings whatsoever in any court' if it was merely intended to confer immunity from proceedings in a court only in his *personal* capacity. For, as every Yang di-Pertuan Agong must be a Ruler of a State, immunity from proceedings in a court in Malaysia in his *personal* capacity has already been conferred by Article 181(2) which states quite emphatically that 'no proceedings whatsoever shall be brought in any court against the Ruler of a State in his *personal* capacity'. It may therefore be possible that the immunity intended to be conferred by Article 32(1) of the Constitution is wider[44a] than that suggested by Pike C.J. in *Stephen Kalong Ningkan* v. *Tun Abang Haji Openg & Tawi Sli (No. 2)*.

There is one other matter which requires notice. In dealing with the legal immunity of the Yang di-Pertuan Agong, the following passage appears in Tun Suffian's book.[45]

It is significant that the Constitution merely says that the Yang di-Pertuan Agong shall not be liable to any proceedings in any court (that is to say, he cannot be sued): it does not say that His Majesty shall not be liable at all. It is therefore arguable that the law would still regard him as liable, especially in view of the fact that in his oath of office he has declared that he would carry out his duty in accordance with law and the constitution and that he would at all times uphold the rule of law and order in the country. This would become of practical importance should he voluntarily submit to the jurisdiction of the court (either by himself suing or by consenting to be sued) as undoubtedly he has the right to do, in which event the court may pass any lawful order binding on His Majesty.

Such a view of the legal immunity of the Yang di-Pertuan Agong is very restrictive indeed and in my view runs contrary to the very clear words of Article 32(1) which appear to confer on the Yang di-Pertuan Agong, a complete and unqualified immunity from the legal process.

DISABILITIES OF THE YANG DI-PERTUAN AGONG

The disabilities attached to this office are found in Article 34 of the Federal Constitution. During any period that a Ruler holds the office of the Yang di-Pertuan Agong he is not permitted to exercise his functions as Ruler of his State except those of Head of the Islamic religion.[46] He is allowed however to exercise as Ruler of his State any power vested in him to amend the Constitution of his State, and to appoint a Regent or a member of a Council of Regency in case the Regent or a member of the Council of Regency dies or becomes incapable of performing his duties.[47] The Yang di-Pertuan Agong cannot receive any emoluments of any kind from the State of which he is a Ruler,[48] but provision is made in pursuance of Article 35 of the Malaysian Constitution for the maintenance of the Yang di-Pertuan Agong out of public funds. The 1957 Civil List and the current Civil List are detailed earlier[49] in this essay.

Until 1976, Article 34(2) stated that 'the Yang di-Pertuan Agong shall not hold any office of profit'[50] but by section 12 of the Constitution (Amendment) Act 1976,[51] Article 34(2) has been amended to read 'the Yang di-Pertuan Agong shall not hold any appointment carrying any remuneration'. This, together with Article 34(3) which states that 'the Yang di-Pertuan Agong shall not actively engage in any commercial enterprise', would seem to preclude his participation in any business activity during his term of office. It was obviously felt desirable that the Yang di-Pertuan Agong should during his five-year term of office devote himself entirely to matters of that office. Finally, the Yang di-Pertuan Agong cannot be absent from the Federation without the consent of the Conference of Rulers for more than fifteen days, unless he is on a State visit to another country.[52]

If the Timbalan Yang di-Pertuan Agong or any other Ruler exercises the functions of the Yang di-Pertuan Agong for more than fifteen days, he is subject to all the disabilities to which the Yang di-Pertuan Agong is subject.[53]

Until 1976 the only disability to which the Raja Permaisuri Agong was subject was that she could not hold any office under the Federation. But by section 12 of the Constitution (Amendment) Act 1976,[54] Article 34(6) of the Constitution has been substituted with a new clause (6) which extends the application of Article 34(2) and (3) to the Raja Permaisuri Agong. The effect of this is that the Raja Permaisuri Agong cannot hold any appointment carrying any remuneration neither can she actively engage in any commercial enterprise. These disabilities of the Yang di-Pertuan Agong are now extended to his consort.

FUNCTIONS OF THE YANG DI-PERTUAN AGONG

WITH THE ADVICE OF THE CABINET

The Yang di-Pertuan Agong is a constitutional monarch and in exercising his functions under the Malaysian Constitution or federal law he must act with the advice of the Cabinet or of a Minister acting under the general authority of the Cabinet.[55] There are of course some functions which he exercises in his discretion and three of these are specifically mentioned in Article 40(2) of the Federal Constitution. We shall deal with those functions separately. There are other functions which he exercises after *consultation* with or on the *recommendation* of some person or body of persons other than the Cabinet,[56] but for the exercise of a vast majority of his functions the Yang di-Pertuan Agong must act as a constitutional monarch and seek the advice of his Cabinet. He appoints the Cabinet which will advise him in the exercise of his functions and he is entitled to receive any information concerning the government of the Federation which is available to the Cabinet.[57] When the Conference of Rulers deliberates on matters of national policy the Yang di-Pertuan Agong must be accompanied by the Prime Minister and the deliberations are among the functions exercised by the Yang di-Pertuan Agong in accordance with the advice of the Cabinet.[58]

IN HIS DISCRETION

One of the discretionary functions of the Yang di-Pertuan Agong is the appointment of a Prime Minister, but as Tun Suffian points out,[59] 'when appointing a Prime Minister, the Yang di-Pertuan Agong is not, however, completely free' as the Prime Minister must be a member of the House of Representatives and one who is 'likely to command the confidence of the majority of the members of that House'.[60] This discretion will, therefore, only be important when the majority party has no established leader but even then the prudent course would be to wait until the majority leader had been chosen in the party room.

The Yang di-Pertuan Agong may also act in his discretion in the withholding of consent to a request for the dissolution of Parliament. This may not seem an important function but if the Prime Minister ceases to command the confidence of the majority in the House of Representatives and the Yang di-Pertuan Agong refuses to accede to the request of the Prime Minister to dissolve Parliament to enable elections to be held to extricate him from his parliamentary difficulties, then the Prime Minister must tender the resignation of the Cabinet[61] and the Yang di-Pertuan Agong can appoint a new Prime Minister.

The Yang di-Pertuan Agong may also act in his discretion in determining when a meeting of the Conference of Rulers will be held. But this only applies to meetings concerned solely with the privileges, position, honours, and dignities of their Highnesses.[62] The Constitution ensures that Federal law will not usurp or qualify the discretionary functions of the Yang di-Pertuan Agong.[63]

The Yang di-Pertuan Agong in his discretion appoints members of the Public Services Commission[64] and the Railway Service Commission[65] in each case after *considering* the advice of the Prime Minister and after *consulting* the Conference of Rulers and he can in his discretion also appoint a member of the Commission constituted under Part X of the Constitution for a term shorter than the normal five-year term after *considering* the advice of the Prime Minister.[66]

ASSENT

For a Bill to become law it is necessary that it be passed by both Houses of Parliament[67] and be assented to by the Yang di-Pertuan

Agong.[68] The Yang di-Pertuan Agong signifies his assent to a Bill by causing the Public Seal to be affixed to the Bill. An air of unreality surrounds the assent of the Yang di-Pertuan Agong because the assent can never be withheld. This aspect of the Constitution was severely criticized by Mr. Justice Abdul Hamid in his note of dissent to the proposals of the Reid Commission where he said:

If this article is allowed to remain in the draft as it stands the Yang di-Pertuan (Besar) Agong will have no choice in the matter of assent. He shall be bound to assent to the Bill passed by the two Houses. In other words a Bill passed by the two Houses shall become law. If this is the intention, it is far better to approach this subject direct by saying ... that a Bill passed by the two Houses shall become law. No mention of assent is necessary at all. But if assent is to be mentioned the Constitution should give the power to the Yang di-Pertuan (Besar) Agong to accord assent or to withhold assent. In all constitutions the power to accord assent goes with the power to withhold assent.[69]

Nevertheless, it does not seem possible for the Yang di-Pertuan Agong to withhold assent to a Bill passed by both Houses of Parliament.

IN RELATION TO PARLIAMENT

Although the Yang di-Pertuan Agong is one of the constituent parts of Parliament,[70] there are certain functions which he exercises in relation to Parliament as a whole, and in relation to the Houses of Parliament separately. He can summon, prorogue, or dissolve Parliament.[71] And he may address either House of Parliament or both Houses jointly.[72] The Yang di-Pertuan Agong is also entrusted with the task of appointing thirty-two Senators.[73] Although the choice of Senators is not specifically left to the discretion of the Yang di-Pertuan Agong by the Constitution, it is arguable that this is what was intended because Article 45(2) of the Constitution indicates the Senators shall be persons who in the opinion of the Yang di-Pertuan Agong have rendered distinguished public service or have achieved distinction in the professions, commerce, industry, etc. The Yang di-Pertuan Agong can remove a disqualification for membership of either House of Parliament[74] which has been incurred because of an election offence[75] or because of a conviction for any other offence.[76] Finally, it is the Yang di-Pertuan Agong who appoints the Clerk to the Senate and the Clerk to the House of Representatives.[77] By an amendment to the Constitution in 1976 the Yang di-Pertuan Agong has been given power to make short-term appointments to the positions of Clerk to the Senate and Clerk to the House of Representatives from amongst the members of the public service. The appointment can be 'for such shorter period as he may deem fit'.[78]

IN RELATION TO THE PUBLIC SERVICES AND OTHER COMMISSIONS

Article 132 of the Federal Constitution states that for the purposes of the Constitution the public services are: (a) the armed forces; (b) the judicial and legal service; (c) the general public service of the Federation ; (d) the police force; (e) the railway service; (f) the joint public services mentioned in Article 133; (g) the public service of each State; and (h) the education service.[79]

The Yang di-Pertuan Agong exercises certain functions in relation to nearly all these services and, subject to the provisions of Federal law, he can regulate the qualifications for appointment and conditions of service of persons in the public services except of those persons in the public service of each State.[80]

In our 1964 article Jayakumar and I dealt with these functions in some detail and we also dealt with the functions which the Yang di-Pertuan Agong exercises in relation to the various public service Commissions and the Election Commission. The position has not changed sufficiently in this area to justify the treatment of those functions in the same detail again.[81]

IN RELATION TO THE JUDICIARY

The Lord President of the Federal Court, the Chief Justices of the High Courts, and the other judges of the Federal Court and of the High Courts are appointed by the Yang di-Pertuan Agong, acting on the advice of the Prime Minister, after consulting the Conference of Rulers.[82] Before tendering his advice on these appointments, apart from the appointment of the Lord President, the Prime Minister is required to consult the Lord President.[83] The Yang di-Pertuan Agong acting on the advice of the Lord President may also appoint for such purposes and for such period of time as he may specify any person who has held high judicial office in Malaysia to be an additional judge of the Federal Court. The normal retiring age of sixty-five years does not apply to these appointments.[84] By a recent amendment in 1976 for the dispatch of business of the High Court in Malaya, the Yang di-Pertuan Agong, acting on the advice of the Lord President, may by order appoint to be judicial commissioner for such period or such purposes as may be specified in the order any person qualified for appointment as a judge of a High Court. The person so appointed is given power to perform such functions of a judge of the High Court in Malaya as appear to him to require to be performed.[85]

When a judge of one High Court is being transferred to another High Court, the Yang di-Pertuan Agong can make the transfer on the recommendation of the Lord President, after consulting the

Chief Justices of the two High Courts. There is no need in such a case to seek the advice of the Prime Minister.[86]

The Yang di-Pertuan Agong can extend the tenure of office of a judge of the Federal Court beyond the age of sixty-five years but for not more than six months beyond that age.[87]

A judge of the Federal Court may resign his office by writing to the Yang di-Pertuan Agong,[88] but the Yang di-Pertuan Agong cannot remove a judge from office unless a tribunal appointed by him under Article 125(3) and (4) of the Federal Constitution recommends that he remove the judge from office. Pending the report of the tribunal, the Yang di-Pertuan Agong may on the recommendation of the Prime Minister and in the case of any other judge after consulting the Lord President, suspend a judge of the Federal Court from the exercise of his functions.[89] Before suspending a judge of a High Court other than the Chief Justice, the Yang di-Pertuan Agong is required to consult the Chief Justice of that court instead of the Lord President of the Federal Court.[90]

The Yang di-Pertuan Agong is entitled to refer to the Federal Court for its opinion any question as to the effect of any provision of the Constitution and the Federal Court must pronounce in open court its opinion on any question so referred to it.[91] The Yang di-Pertuan Agong is also responsible for making arrangements with the Queen of England for reference to the Judicial Committee of the Privy Council of appeals from the Federal Court.[92] These arrangements have been made and are set out in an Agreement between the Queen and the Yang di-Pertuan Agong, concluded on 4 March 1958, the text of which appears in the Federal *Government Gazette* of 10 April 1958 (Notification No. 1254).[93] However, as Tun Suffian points out in his article in this volume 'The Judiciary—During the First Twenty Years of Independence', an important development of the judiciary during the last twenty years is the curtailment[94] of appeals to the Privy Council with effect from 1 January 1978 and the consequent imposition of greater responsibility on the Federal Court. Only civil appeals that do not involve the Constitution may now be taken to the Privy Council.

Finally, the Yang di-Pertuan Agong is allowed to determine at what place in the Borneo States the High Court in Borneo will have its principal registry,[95] and he is given the authority to appoint a judicial commissioner for the dispatch of business of the High Court in Borneo in an area in which a judge of the Court is not for the time being available to attend to business of the Court.[96]

IN RELATION TO THE RELIGION OF ISLAM[97]

Islam is the religion of the Federation.[98] According to Ahmad Ibrahim

... the Rulers of the Malay States at first opposed the enactment of such a provision in the new Federal Constitution because they were told by their constitutional advisers that if the Federation had an official religion, the proposed Head of the Federation would logically become the Head of the official religion throughout the Federation and it was thought that this would be in conflict with the position of each of the Rulers as Head of the official religion in his own State.[99]

After satisfactory explanations[100] and a specific provision[101] preserving the position of each Ruler as Head of the Islamic religion in his own State, Article 3 of the Constitution, which makes Islam the religion of the Federation, was enacted. This explains why although Islam is the religion of the Federation, there is no Head of the Islamic religion for the whole of the Federation.

Although the Yang di-Pertuan Agong is precluded from exercising any functions in his own State while he is the Yang di-Pertuan Agong, an exception is made in the case of his functions in relation to the religion of Islam and he is allowed to remain the Head of the religion of Islam in his own State.[102] The Yang di-Pertuan Agong is also the Head of the religion of Islam in Malacca, Penang, in the Federal Territory and in Sabah and Sarawak.[103] Although each Ruler is Head of the Islamic religion in his own State, he can authorize the Yang di-Pertuan Agong to represent him in any acts, observances, or ceremonies with respect to which the Conference of Rulers has agreed that they should extend to the Federation as a whole.[104]

The Federal Constitution also provides in Article 42(10) that the power to grant pardons, reprieves, and respites in respect of, or to remit, suspend or commute sentences imposed by any Court established under any law regulating Islamic religious affairs in the States of Malacca, Penang, the Federal Territory, Sabah and Sarawak shall be exercisable by the Yang di-Pertuan Agong as Head of the religion of Islam in those States.

Ahmad Ibrahim states that while the

... various State Constitutions provide that the Ruler of the State may act in his discretion in the performance of any functions as Head of the Muslim religion, ... it would appear that the Yang di-Pertuan Agong may only act *on advice* in performing his functions as Head of the Muslim religion in Malacca, Penang, the Federal Territory, Sabah and Sarawak.[105]

This is undoubtedly true.

IN RELATION TO THE SPECIAL POSITION OF MALAYS

Article 153(1) of the Federal Constitution states that it is the responsibility of the Yang di-Pertuan Agong to safeguard the special position of the Malays and the legitimate interests of other communities in accordance with the provisions of that Article. The Yang di-Pertuan Agong is required to exercise his functions under the Constitution and federal law in such a way as to safeguard the special position of the Malays and is required to ensure that a reasonable proportion of positions in the public service and of scholarships and other educational privileges accorded by the Federal Government is reserved for Malays. He is also required to ensure that a reasonable proportion of any permits or licences which may be required by federal law for the operation of any trade or business is issued to Malays.[106] The Yang di-Pertuan Agong may give general directions to any authority or Commission to ensure that an adequate number of scholarships, exhibitions, etc., and positions in the public service is reserved for Malays when that authority or Commission is making its awards or appointments. And the Commission or authority must duly comply with the directions of the Yang di-Pertuan Agong.[107] An amendment of the Constitution in 1971[108] empowered the Yang di-Pertuan Agong

... to give directions to any university, college or other educational institution providing education at post secondary level where the number of places for any course of study is less than the number of candidates qualified for such places, to reserve for Malays (and natives of the Borneo States) such proportion of such places as the Yang di-Pertuan Agong deems reasonable. The intention of the amendments is to reserve places in those selected areas of study ... where the numbers of Malays and natives of the Borneo States are disproportionately small.[109]

IN AN EMERGENCY

The functions of the Yang di-Pertuan Agong in relation to a situation of emergency are found in Article 150 of the Federal Constitution. 'If the Yang di-Pertuan Agong is satisfied that a grave emergency exists whereby the security or economic life of the Federation or any part thereof is threatened, he may issue a Proclamation of Emergency' are the words used in Article 150(1) of the Constitution. But do the words 'if the Yang di-Pertuan Agong *is satisfied*' confer a *personal discretion* on the Yang di-Pertuan Agong to issue a Proclamation of Emergency?

Hickling in an article on 'The Prerogative in Malaysia' in 1975[110] argued that Article 150 did confer a personal discretion on the Yang di-Pertuan Agong. As he said:

...[T]he importation of a subjective state of mind in this context may well, given the unusual situation contemplated by the Article and the existence of a residue of prerogative powers, enable the Yang di-Pertuan Agong to legislate by Ordinance, at will: for the Article admits that such a method of legislation—which can overrule all provisions of the Constitution—can be adopted by the Yang di-Pertuan Agong, 'if [he is] satisfied that immediate action is required'. Here, then, is an unlimited power of legislation which could probably never be the subject of successful attack in any court. Such great powers have no doubt been entrusted to the Yang di-Pertuan Agong with the certain feeling that ... they will be reasonably exercised.[111]

And a few pages later:

Whether, therefore, the Yang di-Pertuan Agong must in exercising his powers under Article 150 act on the advice of the Cabinet or a Minister acting under Cabinet authority remains obscure: but the authoritative dicta cited strongly support a personal discretion remaining in him, in relation to the exercise of those constitutional powers requiring as a condition precedent to their exercise a subjective state of mind.[112]

Jayakumar in his essay on 'Emergency Powers in Malaysia' in this volume and elsewhere[113] does not accept this view, regarding it as an 'erroneous interpretation of the cases'. His view is that 'all the available judicial decisions as well as ordinary principles of interpretation, supported by the views of the Reid Constitutional Commission clearly establish that the Yang di-Pertuan Agong has to act on advice when issuing a Proclamation of Emergency'. As his essay appears in this volume I shall merely indicate that his views and arguments are found on pp. 335-6.

Part of the difficulty in this area is caused by the dicta of the several judges who heard the *Stephen Kalong Ningkan* cases[114] and appeal.[115] Hickling relies, for example, on the dictum of Barakbah L.P. in *Stephen Kalong Ningkan* v. *Government of Malaysia* in the Federal Court where he says 'in my opinion the Yang di-Pertuan Agong is the sole judge and once His Majesty is satisfied that a state of emergency exists it is not for the court to inquire as to whether or not he should have been satisfied'.[116] Whereas Jayakumar and Sinnadurai[117] both point out that while Barakbah L.P. did say that, he had earlier said that 'in an act of the nature of a Proclamation of Emergency, issued in accordance with the Constitution, in my opinion, it is incumbent on the court to assume that *the Government* is acting in the best interest of the State', etc.[118] And that it is only in the context of that statement that Barakbah L.P.'s statement about the '*sole judge*' should be read. And so the debate will go on.

If I might add a further observation, it is that the following portion of the Prime Minister of Malaysia's affidavit in *N. Madhavan Nair* v. *Government of Malaysia*[119] raises two questions:

9. I refer to paragraph 12 of the affidavit of K. Madhavan Nair and state that owing to the grave emergency threatening the security of the country during the 'May 13' incident, I personally presented the said Ordinance to

His Majesty the Yang Dipertuan Agung at Istana Negara for his consideration and approval. *Having considered the said Ordinance and after being satisfied* that immediate action was required for securing public safety, the defence of Malaysia, the maintenance of public order and of supplies and services essential to the life of the community, *His Majesty the Yang Dipertuan Agung approved the promulgation of the said Ordinance. His Majesty the Yang Dipertuan Agung signed the said Ordinance accordingly.* Immediate arrangement was then made to print and publish the said Ordinance in the Government Gazette.

Does the Government of Malaysia believe that the Yang di-Pertuan Agong must be *personally satisfied* that immediate action is required for securing public safety, etc. before he approves the promulgation and signs the Ordinance under Article 150(2) of the Federal Constitution? And if this is so, should the satisfaction of the Yang di-Pertuan Agong under Article 150(1) to issue a Proclamation of Emergency be treated any differently?

CONCLUSION

One commentator has described the office of the Yang di-Pertuan Agong as 'the essential one of the Malaysian constitution, without which all others become meaningless',[120] and another has said that in Malaysia, 'the position of the Yang di-Pertuan Agong has emerged as one of the strong cohesive forces in the federal structure'.[121] Yet, even though the Constitution has been amended twenty-three times in the course of the last twenty years,[122] very few of those amendments have concerned the office of the Yang di-Pertuan Agong. His functions in relation to the religion of Islam and the special position of the Malays have increased but only as a constitutional ruler acting on advice. There has been some consideration, in the courts and elsewhere, of the question whether the Yang di-Pertuan Agong has any personal discretion when he exercises the power to issue a Proclamation of Emergency. But the debate on that question has not been concluded. The amendments to Article 34 of the Constitution have attempted to ensure that the Yang di-Pertuan Agong and the Raja Permaisuri Agong do not hold any appointment carrying any remuneration and that they do not actively engage in any commercial enterprise. Other amendments have not been very significant and the enduring quality of the institution as originally created in 1957 is self evident.

APPENDIX

Table A. Election List for Yang Dipertuan Agung

Column 1	Column 2	Column 3	Column 4	Column 5	Column 6	Column 7	Column 8	Column 9	Column 10
Election list for election of first Yang Dipertuan Agung in 1957		Election list for election of second Yang Dipertuan Agung in 1960		Election list for election of third Yang Dipertuan Agung in 1960		Election list for election of fourth Yang Dipertuan Agung in 1965	Election list for election of fifth Yang Dipertuan Agung in 1970	Election list for sixth i.e. present Yang Dipertuan Agung in 1975	Election list for next Yang Dipertuan Agung
Johore	Selangor	Selangor	Perlis	Perlis	Trengganu	Trengganu	Pahang	Johore	Perak
Pahang	Kedah	Perlis	Kelantan	Trengganu	Perak	Pahang	Kedah	Kelantan	Pahang
N. Sembilan	Perlis	Kelantan	Trengganu	Perak	Pahang	Kedah	Johore	Perak	Johore
Selangor	Kelantan.	Trengganu	Perak	Pahang	Kedah	Johore	Kelantan	Pahang	
Kedah	Trengganu	Perak	Pahang	Kedah	Johore	Kelantan	Perak	(5.5.74)	
Perlis	Perak	Pahang	Kedah	Johore	Kelantan	Perak			
Kelantan	Johore	Kedah	Johore	Kelantan		(4.1.63)			
Trengganu	Pahang	(15 7.58)		(10.7.60)					
Perak		Johore							
		(8.5.59)							

Table B. States Whose Rulers Have Been Yang Dipertuan Agung

Column 1	Column 2	Column 3	Column 4	Column 5	Column 6
Negri Sembilan	Negri Sembilan	Negri Sembilan	Negri Sembilan	Negri Sembilan	Negri Sembilan
	Selangor	Selangor	Selangor	Selangor	Selangor
		Perlis	Perlis	Perlis	Perlis
			Trengganu	Trengganu	Trengganu
				Kedah	Kedah
					Kelantan

Note: Dates within brackets are dates of death of the different Rulers since Independence.

1. The words *Yang di-Pertuan Agong* literally 'one who is chief or head among the most prominent ones' will be used to denote the Supreme Head of the Malaysian Federation. Recently writers have begun to use *Yang Dipertuan Agung* but the words *Yang di-Pertuan Agong* used in the Malaysian Federal Constitution will be used in this essay.

2. (1966) 6 Mal. L.R. 280-302.

3. Ibid., at p. 302.

4. Groves, *The Constitution of Malaysia*, Malaysia Publications Ltd., Singapore, 1964.

5. Those familiar with the article mentioned in footnote 2 will know that I have drawn heavily on that article for some parts of this essay.

6. No. 26 of 1963, which amended the Constitution of the Federation of Malaya in order to provide for the admission of the former British colonies of North Borneo and Sarawak and the State of Singapore which subsequently seceded from the Malaysian Federation in 1965.

7. Malaysia Act, s.7.

8. Act A206, s.11.

9. Act A354, s.3.

10. Ibid., s.12.

11. The Federation of Malaya Constitutional Commission.

12. *The Report of the Federation of Malaya Constitutional Commission* (1957), p. 22.

13. The Governors of Penang, Malacca, Sabah, and Sarawak are not members of the Conference of Rulers when they meet to elect the Yang di-Pertuan Agong.

14. Details of the six elections are conveniently collected in Suffian, *An Introduction to the Constitution of Malaysia* (2nd ed.), 1976, pp. 28-32.

15. These provisions will be discussed more fully when the election of the Yang di-Pertuan Agong is considered.

16. The English translation of the oath of office is set out in Part III of the Fourth Schedule.

17. Federal Constitution, Article 39.

18. The words in italics were added by s.13 of the Constitution (Amendment) Act, 1962 (No. 14 of 1962), which was deemed to have come into force on Merdeka Day, i.e. 31 August 1957.

19. Federal Constitution, Article 32(3).

20. In Article 160(2) 'Civil List' is defined as the provision made for the maintenance of the Yang di-Pertuan Agong, his Consort, a Ruler, or Governor out of public funds. By the Civil Lists Ordinance, 1957, the following sums are payable, the current sums payable appear in brackets:

(a)	The Privy Purse	$180,000 per annum	($228,000 per annum)
(b)	Entertainment	$ 36,000 per annum	($ 87,600 per annum)
(c)	Salaries of the Household and Court	$177,000 per annum	($557,000 per annum)
(d)	Expenses of the Household and Court	$158,000 per annum	($400,000 per annum)
(e)	Royal Bounties, Alms and Special Services	$ 6,000 per annum	($ 20,000 per annum)
(f)	Cost of motor car	$ 52,000 (once during tenure of office)	

The Raja Permaisuri Agong receives an annual sum of $30,000 ($45,000).

The current sums appear in the Civil Lists (Amendment) Act, 1977.

21. Federal Constitution, Article 32(3).

22. The words 'Deputy Supreme Head' and 'Deputy Supreme Head of the Federation' are replaced by the words 'Timbalan Yang di-Pertuan Agong' wherever they appear in the Constitution by s.11 of the Constitution (Amendment) Act, 1976.

23. The tables are reproduced with the kind permission of Tun Mohamed Suffian, one of the co-editors of this volume.

24. Federal Constitution, Third Schedule, Part I, s.1(1)(c). Italics added.

25. Ibid., Article 38(6)(a).

26. Ibid., Article 33(1).

27. Ibid., Article 33(3).

28. Ibid., Third Schedule, Part II, s.5(a).

29. A more detailed treatment of this point appears on p. 285 of the article mentioned in footnote 2.

30. Federal Constitution, Article 33(5).

31. No. 72 of 1957:

32. *N. Madhavan Nair* v. *Government of Malaysia* [1975] 2 M.L.J. 286 per Chang Min Tat J.

33. Constitution of India, Article 61.

34. Federal Constitution, Article 32(3).

35. Ibid., Article 38(6)(a).

36. See footnote 2.

37. Federal Constitution, Article 32(3).

38. Ibid., Article 33(2).

39. See our article mentioned in footnote 2. See especially pp. 286-7 for our arguments and suggested amendments.

40. Federal Constitution, Article 33(1).

41. See footnote 2—the discussion on the Immunity of the Yang di-Pertuan Agong is at p. 288.

42. [1967] M.L.J. 46.

43. Ibid., at p. 47.

44. Op. cit., footnote 14, pp. 24-5.

44a. See Jayakumar's review of Suffian, *Introduction to the Constitution of Malaysia* (1976) 18 Mal. L.R. 365 at pp. 367-8.

45. Op. cit., footnote 14, pp. 25-6.

46. Federal Constitution, Article 34(1).

47. Ibid., Article 34(8)(a) and (b).

48. Ibid., Article 34(4).

49. See footnote 20.

50. Section 5 of the Malaysia Act 1963 redefined 'office of profit'. The new definition can be found in footnote 61 of our 1964 article.

51. Act A 354.

52. Federal Constitution, Article 34(5).

53. Ibid., Article 34(7).

54. Act A 354.

55. Federal Constitution, Article 40(1).

56. e.g. Ibid., Article 42(4)(a).

57. Ibid., Article 40(1).

58. Ibid., Article 38(3).
59. In *An Introduction to the Constitution of Malaysia*, p. 23.
60. Federal Constitution, Article 43(2)(a).
61. Ibid., Article 43(4).
62. Ibid., Article 40(2)(c).
63. Ibid., Article 40(3)(a).
64. Ibid., Article 139(4).
65. Ibid., Article 141(2).
66. Ibid., Article 143(1)(a).
67. Except in the case of Money Bills. See Article 68 of the Federal Constitution.
68. Federal Constitution, Article 66.
69. *Report of the Federation of Malaya Constitutional Commission* (1957), p. 102.
70. Federal Constitution, Article 44.
71. Ibid., Article 55(1), (2).
72. Ibid., Article 60.
73. Ibid., Article 45(1)(b).
74. Ibid., Article 48(3).
75. Ibid., Article 48(1)(d).
76. Ibid., Article 48(1)(e).
77. Ibid., Article 65(2).
78. Constitution (Amendment) Act 1976, Act A354, section 17.
79. Added by section 2 of the Constitution (Amendment) Act, 1973, Act A 193.
80. Federal Constitution, Article 132(2).
81. Op. cit., footnote 2, pp. 293-5.
82. Federal Constitution, Article 122B(1).
83. Ibid., Article 122B(2).
84. Ibid., Article 122(1A).
85. Section 27(b) of the Constitution (Amendment) Act 1976, Act A354.
86. Federal Constitution, Article 122C.
87. Ibid., Article 125(1).
88. Ibid., Article 125(2).
89. Ibid., Article 125(5).
90. Ibid., Article 125(9).
91. Ibid., Article 130.
92. Ibid., Article 131(1).

93. See also the Courts of Judicature Act, 1964 (No. 7 of 1964) and Agreement dated 10 December 1963 made between the Queen and the Yang di-Pertuan Agong (Malaysia L.N. 30 of 1964).

94. By an amendment to section 74 of the Courts of Judicature Act, 1964 (No. 7 of 1964) effected by section 13(3) of Act A 328/76. Tun Suffian deals with Privy Council appeals on pp. 246-7 of this volume.

95. Federal Constitution, Article 121(1)(b).

96. Ibid., Article 122A(3).

97. The expression 'religion of Islam' is substituted for 'Muslim religion'. See sections 44 and 45 of the Constitution (Amendment) Act 1976, Act A354.

98. Federal Constitution, Article 3(1).

99. 'The Position of Islam in the Constitution of Malaysia', pp. 49-50 of this volume of essays.

100. Ibid., p. 49.

101. Federal Constitution, Article 3(2).

102. Ibid., Article 34(1).

103. Ibid., Article 3, as amended by Act A 206 and Act A 354.

104. Ibid., Article 3(2).

105. Op. cit., p. 50 (emphasis added).

106. Federal Constitution, Article 153(2).

107. Ibid., Article 153(3).

108. Constitution (Amendment) Act, 1971 (Act No. A30).

109. Ahmad Ibrahim in the Introduction to the *Parliamentary Debates on the Constitution Amendment Bill 1971.*

110. 17 Mal. L.R. 207-32.

111. Ibid., pp. 220-1.

112. Ibid., p. 223.

113. S. Jayakumar, 'Emergency Powers in Malaysia: Can the Yang di-Pertuan Agong act in his personal discretion and capacity?' (1976) 18 Mal. L.R. 149.

114. *Stephen Kalong Ningkan* v. *Tun Abang Haji Openg and Tawi Sli* [1966] 2 M.L.J. 187; *Stephen Kalong Ningkan* v. *Tun Abang Haji Openg and Tawi Sli* (No. 2) [1967] 1 M.L.J. 46; and *Stephen Kalong Ningkan* v. *Government of Malaysia* [1968] 1 M.L.J. 119.

115. *Stephen Kalong Ningkan* v. *Government of Malaysia* [1968] 2 M.L.J. 238.

116. [1968] 1 M.L.J. 119 at 122.

117. (1968) 10 Mal. L.R. 130-3.

118. [1968] 1 M.L.J. 119 at 122.

119. [1975] 2 M.L.J. 286 at 288.

120. Hickling, op. cit., p. 219.

121. Groves, *The Constitution of Malaysia*, p. 42.

122. Salleh bin Abas, 'Amendment of the Malaysian Constitution' [1977] 2 M.L.J. xxxiv-xlix.

✻ M. PUTHUCHEARY

6. Ministerial Responsibility in Malaysia

MINISTERIAL responsibility to Parliament is an important convention of the parliamentary system of government. There are two separate but related parts to the convention: there is, first, the individual responsibility of each Minister to Parliament, and second, there is the collective responsibility of the Cabinet to Parliament. Individual responsibility requires that each Minister be accountable to Parliament for the conduct of his department. The act of every civil servant is regarded, by convention, as that of his Minister.[1] Consequently the Minister must be responsible to Parliament for every act or neglect of his department and cannot escape responsibility by blaming his civil servants. In cases where there appears to be gross negligence of duty or mismanagement of public funds, Parliament may censure the Minister and force him to resign from his post as Minister. Collective responsibility requires that all Ministers be jointly responsible as a team to Parliament. This means that individual ministers may not in public express views that contradict or criticize government policy nor may they vote against government policy. If a vote of no-confidence against the government is carried in Parliament, the whole Cabinet must resign *en bloc*.

This convention has been accepted at least in form as part of the parliamentary system of government which Malaysia adopted when it achieved its Independence. Under the Constitution, the Yang di-Pertuan Agong, on the advice of the Prime Minister, appoints Ministers from among the members of either House of Parliament, and the Cabinet of Ministers 'shall be collectively responsible to Parliament'.[2] Each member of Cabinet is responsible not only for decisions made in respect of his ministry but also is collectively responsible for decisions involving other ministries. If a minister disagrees with a Cabinet decision he is nevertheless obliged to defend it in public; if he feels unable to do so he should resign.[3] This pattern is repeated at the state level where the Mentri Besar or Chief Minister and the State Executive Council are responsible to the State Assembly.

The convention of ministerial responsibility underlies a very important aspect of parliamentary democracy: it means that ministers are answerable to Parliament for their actions or inactions in relation to their ministries. Ministers who act improperly or unsatisfactorily are liable to parliamentary censure. If they lose the confidence of the public and their parliamentary colleagues they must resign.

In order to play the role of watchdog of the public interest, Parliament has devised certain procedures to allow time for matters involving the work of ministers to be brought up for discussion. The most important procedure is the period allotted in each session to allow members of Parliament to put questions to Ministers about matters for which they are responsible to Parliament. It is during Question Time that information is obtained on the work of ministries and grievances ventilated about alleged mismanagement, unfair treatment or administrative bungling.

Ministers who do not answer questions satisfactorily face possible censure from Parliament and may even be forced to resign. In this way Parliament is able to 'hold' the Ministers responsible and accountable to Parliament. There is also time set aside when Parliament may discuss matters for which Ministers are responsible. Members of Parliament may put up a motion asking for an adjournment of the House for the purpose of discussing a definite matter of urgent public importance. Criticism can also be made against particular ministries during the Debate on the Budget when a member of Parliament may propose a reduction in the Minister's salary to indicate disapproval. During meetings of the Public Accounts Committee of Parliament, members of the Committee are given opportunities to ascertain 'whether any department has spent more money than Parliament has granted or has spent money on objects other than those for which Parliament granted it'.[4]

But in practice it is extremely difficult for Parliament to enforce ministerial responsibility. The main reason for this is the emphasis that has been given to party solidarity and party discipline so that members of Parliament are obliged to follow the wishes of the party rather than to vote according to their own conscience. Thus, as pointed out by Birch, the convention of ministerial responsibility ... does not occupy the place in the present political system that is commonly claimed for it. It purports to provide an effective sanction for government blunders, but it does not normally do so.... A crisis that would have brought down a government a hundred years ago now acts as an opportunity for its Parliamentary supporters to give an impressive display of party loyalty, and stimulates its leaders to hold on to the reins of power until public attention is diverted to a sphere of policy which puts the government in a more favourable light.[5]

Finer went even further to disclaim the convention as little more than a myth.[6] When the ruling party is strong in Parliament, most charges of improper or inefficient conduct in ministries are 'stifled under the blanket of party solidarity'. Only when there is a minority Government or where the Minister seriously alienates his own back-benchers does the issue of individual culpability of the Minister even arise. And even in such cases there is no guarantee that the Minister will be forced to resign. Finer indicated that there were in fact more Ministers that 'got away' than Ministers who did not, in the last century in Britain. He counted twenty resignations of Ministers due to parliamentary censure—'a tiny number compared with the known cases of mismanagement and blunderings'.

But even though there may be difficulties in enforcing ministerial responsibility in Britain there is a general consensus in society that ministers are liable to lose their office should they be guilty of mismanagement or administrative blunderings. The press and other mass media make it their business to inform the public about specific cases of mismanagement or improper use of public funds and there is an openness and frankness in public discussions on matters of public interest. In such an atmosphere it is very dangerous for a minister deliberately to withhold information or to disregard questions put to him concerning the work of his ministry. He must not appear to be arrogant or highhanded in his replies to questions put to him in Parliament lest he offends not only the opposition members but also his own party backbenchers.[7] Most of all he must be 'sensitive to what the public will or won't stand'.[8] As pointed out by Lord Morrison,

> The House of Commons is generous to a Minister who has told the truth, admitted a mistake, and apologized: but it will come down hard on a Minister who takes the line that he will defend himself and his Department whether they are right or wrong or who shuffles about evasively rather than admit that a blunder or an innocent mistake has been made.[9]

In particular the role of the opposition in bringing up matters concerning maladministration in government departments is well recognized in Britain and the opposition is therefore given adequate opportunities in Parliament to make criticisms and ventilate griev-ances. As Jennings pointed out:

Attacks upon the Government and upon individual ministers are the function of the opposition. The duty of the opposition is to oppose.... It is the public duty of the opposition to raise such questions. It is a duty hardly less important than that of the government. 'Her Majesty's Opposition' is second in importance to 'Her Majesty's Government'. The apparent absurdity that the opposition asks for parliamentary time to be set aside by the government in order that the opposition may censure the government or that the government is asked to move a vote of supplies for the Ministry of Labour in order that the opposition may attack the Minister of Labour, is not an absurdity at all. It is the recognition by both sides of the House that the government governs openly and honestly and that it is prepared to meet criticism not by secret police and concentration camps but by rational argument.[10]

When Malaysia (then called Malaya) achieved its Independence in 1957 it adopted a parliamentary form of government. The Cabinet is appointed from among the members of either House of Parliament and, as expressly provided by Article 43(3) of the Federal Constitution, is collectively responsible to Parliament. Thus, formally at least, the convention of ministerial responsibility is applicable in the Malaysian situation.

But political realities in Malaysia dictate a kind of democracy and a style of politics that is very different from the British experience. Although the democratic process has been accepted it has been accepted only with some modifications. In fact it is generally believed that the concepts and precepts of a Westminster-type democracy are irrelevant to Malaysia's needs and thus to 'mimic the democracy of Westminster in 1957 without the comparative economic and social foundation is to court self-destruction'.[11]

In particular there appears to be a consensus in the community for a strong government to maintain political stability and to bring about national unity through correcting the economic imbalance among the various races in the country. This point was emphasized by the former Prime Minister, the late Tun Abdul Razak, just before Parliamentary democracy was reintroduced after the 1969 riots. He said:

Ours is a young nation and the democratic system is still new to our country. We cannot practise the democratic process as it is practised in such developed nations as Britain, Sweden or the U.S. We must understand the background of the democratic evolution of those countries.... National unity cannot be achieved in Malaysia unless the economic imbalance existing among the communities is rectified and unless the nation's prosperity is enjoyed much more equitably among the people.[12]

Thus democratic values appear to be less important than other values such as political stability and socio-economic development.

James Scott in his book *Political Ideology in Malaysia* concluded that Malaysia's commitment to democratic values is 'more formalistic in the sense that it tends to weaken quickly when it threatens other values like security, stability and so forth'.[13]

It is in this context that one can understand the application of ministerial responsibility in Malaysia. Generally the opposition is regarded at best as unnecessary and at worst as evil. Thus the time given to the opposition in Parliament is considerably reduced. The number of oral questions that a member of Parliament may ask in Parliament is limited to twenty questions per meeting.[14] Furthermore as the time allotted for asking questions is limited to half an hour at each sitting of Parliament the order in which the questions are listed is important. In this matter the opposition feels that their questions are listed towards the end, thus reducing the number of questions answered orally.[15] And even when questions are answered orally they are seldom answered adequately and to the satisfaction of the questioner.[16]

There are of course other times when members of Parliament may bring up matters concerning the workings of particular ministers. A member may move an adjournment of the House for the purpose of discussing a definite matter of public importance. But for a motion of this nature to be accepted, three conditions must be satisfied—the matter must be urgent, it must be of a specific nature, and it must be of public importance. And as it is the Speaker, and not the House, who decides whether or not to allow the adjournment it is to be expected that there have been very few occasions when a motion of this nature is accepted.[17]

Other times when members of Parliament may bring up matters concerning the administration of ministries is during the debates on the Royal Address, on the budget, and on the report of the Public Accounts Committee. And during the Adjournment Speech at the end of the day's sitting any member may address the House on 'any matter of administration for which the Government may reply; but no such address may be made during the first meeting of the session or during the meeting at which the supply bill is considered'.[18] But these occasions are not as important as Question Time as the Minister may choose not to refer to the specific points made by the opposition member, when giving his reply to the member's question during the debate. Furthermore the lateness of hour and the lack of a quorum reduces the effectiveness of the half-hour adjournment debate at the end of each day's business as an occasion for ventilating grievances.

The Public Accounts Committee which is required to look into the accounts of the federal ministries and departments also does not appear to be an effective tool for checking wasteful expenditure. First, the Public Accounts Committee does not examine the accounts in time to be of much use. For example the accounts of 1973 were only just being examined by the Public Accounts Committee in 1977! Secondly, the usual practice in Britain of appointing the Chairman of the Public Accounts Committee from the opposition members is not followed in Malaysia despite several appeals from the opposition for this to be done on the grounds that the Government cannot be both a defendant and a judge.[19]

These procedures together with the strength of the ruling party in Parliament have resulted in the weakening of the Malaysian Parliament as a forum for public debate. There is no doubt that ministerial responsibility is more real in Britain than it is in Malaysia.

In Britain, despite the difficulties mentioned by Finer in forcing ministers to resign from their office there is still a general consensus in the society that ministers are responsible to Parliament and the public has a right to know what is going on and to publicly censure the minister by forcing him to resign. The opposition parties and the mass media have an important role in holding ministers responsible to Parliament and to the public. In Malaysia the political situation is very different. There is no consensus in society that ministers who act improperly in relation to their ministries and departments must resign. Instead there is a general feeling that the government which is in power has every right to decide who shall be ministers and to do whatever it considers best in order to strengthen its position and stay in power. Charges of mismanagement and corruption therefore do not appear to have the same degree of public disapproval that they have in Western democratic countries. In addition there is a veil of secrecy that hides most government activities from the public so that even if the public wants to know what is going on it is extremely difficult for it to find out. The press and other mass media do not play the role of providing a forum for public discussion on matters of public interest either because of Government's objections to any criticism or because of their own self-censorship.

There appears to be a general unwillingness to debate matters of public interest in an open and frank manner. This unwillingness is seen in the way charges that are brought up in Parliament are dealt with. Ministers usually answer questions in a perfunctory manner revealing as little information as possible. Even in cases of alleged maladministration involving loss of lives or alleged corruption involving millions of dollars the Government prefers not to divulge the full details but to appoint internal committees to investigate and report directly to the Minister concerned. Action is then taken to deal with the matter without 'washing the dirty linen in public'. An example of the way charges against Government departments are dealt with is seen in the recent charges of maladministration in the Malacca hospital resulting in several deaths in July and August 1973.[20] When this matter was brought to the attention of the public by the leader of the opposition the Minister of Health responded by 'ordering a full investigation into the deaths'.[21] But the committee which was appointed to investigate the matter was composed of professional men and civil servants appointed by the Minister and its proceedings and deliberations were not made public. Furthermore the public was not informed of the findings of the committee or of any action taken by the Ministry of Health to prevent a recurrence of the tragedy. The opposition leader attempted to bring the matter up in Parliament by proposing a cut in the Minister's salary during the debate on the budget for the Ministry of Health but the motion was defeated because the Government backbenchers voted solidly against it. Thus the public was not given any opportunity to learn more fully about the matter. What is perhaps even more surprising was the lack of reporting of the matter in the press. The speech made by the opposition member was not even reported in the English language press.[22] And little public interest appears to have been aroused concerning the whole episode. The call by the opposition for the Minister concerned either to publicly discipline and dismiss the hospital officers responsible for the deaths and pay compensation to the bereaved families or resign from his post as Minister of Health appears to have been ignored by the Government and general public as the ravings of a frustrated and desperate opposition, wanting to use every opportunity to attack the Government and gain some political advantage for itself. Two years after this episode, the Malacca hospital again came into the limelight when another charge of maladministration of the hospital was made, this time resulting in an abnormally high rate of infant deaths at the hospital. The Minister responded by ordering a public inquiry into the deaths but so far, about two years after the alleged incident, the findings and report of the inquiry have not been made known to the public.

Two important lessons on Ministerial responsibility can be learned from this case study. Firstly, the erring Minister did not stand alone but was supported by his colleagues in the Cabinet and by his own backbenchers. The convention of collective responsibility thus becomes important in achieving party solidarity but it tends to prevent the full operation of the convention of individual responsibility. Backbenchers who may agree with the opposition that a particular minister should resign are dissuaded from supporting the opposition by the party whip and the fear that any dissent within the ruling party endangers the whole Government. Thus the need to support one's own leaders especially in times of crisis reduces the opportunities given to backbenchers to vote according to their own consciences and not according to the wishes of the party. In this particular case, the motion to cut the Minister's salary was defeated because Government backbenchers voted solidly against the motion. Only one Government backbencher abstained.[23]

Secondly, the case study on the Malacca hospital deaths revealed another reality of Malaysian politics. The attitude of the public has remained apathetic and indifferent. A matter which would have raised a hue and cry in almost any country purporting to be democratic has hardly touched the majority of the people and was not even considered worthy of some comment in the local newspapers. It is four years since the matter was first brought to public attention but so far there has been no official disclosure on the findings of the investigating committee or the action taken by the Government. All that the Minister has said so far is that the matter has been investigated and action has been taken to prevent a similar occurrence. The secrecy that surrounds all Government activities, the inability of the press and other mass media to sharpen public interest in the matter and the inarticulate and apathetic public have allowed the Minister to evade his responsibility to Parliament and to the public.

It is therefore not surprising that there have been only two cases in the history of Parliamentary democracy in Malaysia when Ministers were forced to resign from the Cabinet.[24] But even in these two cases they were not the result of Parliamentary censure over maladministration or misconduct in connexion with their ministerial duties. As such they cannot be regarded strictly as the result of the proper enforcement of the convention of ministerial responsibility. In the first case, the Minister of Agriculture was forced to resign because of disagreements with other members of the Cabinet and not because he had publicly expressed criticisms against government policies. The ability to work together is especially important in maintaining Cabinet solidarity when the government consists of several political parties with different and sometimes conflicting interests. The Prime Minister, in forcing the Minister to resign emphasized the need for the responsibility of every Minister to work together as a united body of men. He complained to the Minister that:

Throughout your term of office as Minister of Agriculture you have done many things without consulting your colleagues, most of whom, including myself, are in the dark as to what goes on in your Ministry.... If you feel you cannot work with the members of the Cabinet and cannot give your loyalty to me, then I say there is no point in your being there.[25]

In the second case the Minister of Education was forced to resign because he had lost a court case in which he had sued a member of the opposition for libel and slander in connexion with statements made by the opposition member charging the Minister with corruption and misuse of public office for personal gain. When the court decision was known there was pressure both from the opposition and from within the Government for him to resign.[26]

These two cases highlight some important political realities in Malaysia. In the case of Aziz Ishak, the Minister of Agriculture, the Prime Minister was at first reluctant to sack him. An open confrontation such as a dismissal would only generate resentment, and in Malay social tradition this should be avoided as far as possible. Thus in cases of disagreements attempts are made to solve the problems amicably without 'loss of face'. Ministers that are found to be lacking in ability to discharge their functions as ministers or to be corrupt are therefore removed quietly without the public getting to know the real reason for their removal. They are either transferred to another (and less important) ministry in a Cabinet reshuffle or they are given a non-ministerial post either within the Government or in a statutory authority. Some are offered a diplomatic post overseas. Thus when Aziz Ishak came into conflict with his colleagues over matters in the Ministry of Agriculture, the Prime Minister reshuffled the Cabinet and transferred him out of Agriculture and into Health. But Aziz Ishak refused the appointment and resigned. If however he had remained a loyal backbencher in Parliament he might have been able to gain sufficient sympathy to return to the Cabinet. But instead Aziz Ishak became a bitter opponent of the Government while remaining in the party. He attacked his former Cabinet colleagues openly, both in and out of Parliament. This was in direct contradiction to Malay traditions of behaviour and could not be tolerated. He was therefore expelled not only from the leadership but from the party.

The importance of loyalty in Malaysian politics is demonstrated in the second case. Rahman Talib, the Minister of Education, was a close friend of the Prime Minister and his loyal supporter. It is certain that had he not lost the libel case he would have remained in the Cabinet as long as he retained his seat in Parliament. But his resignation from the Cabinet after the court decision was known was immediately followed by an offer of an ambassadorial position overseas, thus negating any public disapproval that might have been registered by the resignation. In fact, the Prime Minister and other Cabinet colleagues went out of their way to praise him for his past services. The Prime Minister declared in a letter to him that 'your colleagues and I are convinced of your innocence'.[27] Furthermore when it was discovered that his costs of litigation had been paid by the government through some disguised item in the budget, the government justified it on the grounds that he was a public officer.[28] What is more revealing is that the party whip was again used to secure voting along party lines.

The Cabinet support for Rahman Talib illustrates three important aspects of Malaysian politics. First, it shows that loyalty is valued much more highly than many other virtues, even personal integrity. There appears to be a difference in attitude towards corruption in Western and non-Western political cultures. In the West political leaders who have been convicted of corruption would be discredited in the eyes of the public and therefore no political party would run the risk of putting up such people as candidates lest the whole party is discredited. But in Malaysia, as perhaps in other Asian countries, charges of corruption do not necessarily discredit such leaders. As one writer put it:

... as long as their capacity for mass mobilization rested heavily on ascriptive and ideological criteria, charges of corruption would not discredit such leaders in their communal constituencies; rather their dismissal would generate local resentment and an invitation to apply their capacities against the government. Fairness aside, political realism argued for a broad-minded attitude toward their lapses in the face of materialistic temptations provided always that they remained loyal to the political system and, of course, to him [the Prime Minister] personally.[29]

Second, the party leaders appear to have complete control over their own rank and file. This is because party members are aware that the plums of office go to those who acquiesce with the decisions of their leaders and who are not 'troublemakers'. In Malaysia the ruling party has always enjoyed a position of strength in Parliament and therefore has had little difficulty in getting the necessary votes to support their proposals. Even for the decision to pay Rahman Talib's legal costs from Government funds, a matter which by any standards of Government accounting practice must be considered irregular, there was no difficulty in getting the necessary party support to ensure parliamentary approval for the action.

Third, the Rahman Talib case showed that the party's position was not adversely affected by the incident and that, despite the fact that the Prime Minister and his colleagues rallied to the support of the erring Minister, there was little danger of a vote of no confidence being passed on the government as a whole. This reflects not only the strength of the ruling party in Parliament but also the different value orientations between Western and non-Western cultural patterns. Although the party did suffer a temporary setback in its popularity as a result of the incident, it was able to regain its position of power without much difficulty.

Thus the political environment of Malaysia does not appear to have the characteristics that allow the convention of ministerial responsibility to operate fully and effectively. This does not mean to say, of course, that because of this there is no ministerial responsibility or that ministerial irresponsibility is the result. All it means is that the government prefers to deal with problems of maladministration or mismanagement of government funds through more internal methods rather than to discuss these matters in open debate in Parliament. Within the executive branch of Government there are several agencies especially created to look into matters involving maladministration and corruption.[30]

But, however effective these internal checks may be in achieving some degree of control over the workings of ministers and civil servants, there is no doubt that it cannot take the place of parliamentary controls that are made effective through the enforcement of the convention of ministerial responsibility. The socio-political environment and the style of politics that has evolved in Malaysia since Independence, however, are inimical to the development of a system in which the convention of ministerial responsibility can operate fully. Thus, for the time being at least, the convention can be said to operate in Malaysia more in form than in reality.

1. Sir Ivor Jennings, *The Law and the Constitution*, University of London Press, London, 4th ed., 1952, pp. 189-90, and E. C. S. Wade and G. G. Phillips, *Constitutional Law*, Longmans, London, 4th ed., 1950, pp. 63-5.

2. The Federal Constitution, Article 43.

3. M. Suffian, *An Introduction to the Constitution of Malaysia*, Government Printer, 1976, p. 53.

4. L. A. Abraham and S. C. Hawtrey, *A Parliamentary Dictionary*, London, Butterworths, 1964, pp. 160-1.

5. F. A. H. Birch, *Representative and Responsible Government*, George Allen and Unwin, London, 1964, pp. 137-8.

6. S. E. Finer, 'The Individual Responsibility of Ministers', *Public Administration*, Vol. XXXIV, Winter 1956.

7. 'The Minister's primary task is to say neither too little, so as to suggest that he is hiding something, nor too much. Smart repartee challenges a reply and nasty language is apt to annoy. The most successful minister in this ordeal is often he who says very little at great length and in a bland and confidential manner.' Sir Ivor Jennings, *Parliament*, Cambridge University Press, 1957, p. 107.

8. D. N. Chester, 'The Crichel Down Case', *Public Administration*, Vol. XXXII, Winter 1954, pp. 393-4.

9. Rt. Hon. Lord Morrison, *Government and Parliament*, Oxford University Press, London, 3rd ed., 1964, pp. 332-3.

10. Sir Ivor Jennings, *Cabinet Government*, Cambridge University Press, 3rd ed., 1959, p. 499.

11. Tan Sri Ghazalie Shafie's speech in the Senate on the Constitutional Amendments. Quoted in the *Straits Times*, 7 March 1971. See also Tun Razak's

address to the 17th Commonwealth Parliamentary Association conference in Kuala Lumpur on 13 September 1971 and quoted in the *Straits Times*, 14 September 1971.

12. Speech to Alliance members of Parliament and Assemblymen on the eve of the opening in Parliament after the emergency. Quoted in the *Straits Times*, 18 February 1971.

13. James C. Scott, *Political Ideology in Malaysia,* Yale University Press, 1968, p. 177.

14 *Standing Orders of the Dewan Ra'ayat of Malaysia,* paragraphs 21-24. There are usually four to six meetings in a year, each meeting lasting between two weeks and about two months.

15. Interview with Lim Kit Siang, the leader of the Opposition, July 1977. The advantage of the oral question is that it can be followed by a supplementary question which the Minister must answer immediately. As notice of oral questions must be given at least fourteen working days before the commencement of the meeting the tendency is for the opposition to ask the more innocuous question first, saving the crucial one for the supplementary question which does not require notice and which must be answered by the Minister then and there without referring to his civil servants or political advisers.

16. When a member of Parliament complained that the answer given by the Minister was not adequate or satisfactory, the Speaker pointed out that 'the Minister is not obliged to answer the question until you are satisfied!' *Official Reports of the Dewan Ra'ayat* (House of Representatives), 7 May 1973.

17. *Standing Orders of the Dewan Ra'ayat of Malaysia*, para. 18. There has not been a single motion passed to debate a matter of grave public importance in the last five years. Interview with Datuk Azizul Rahman, Clerk to the Dewan Ra'ayat, Parliament, 18 August 1977.

18. *Standing Orders of the Dewan Ra'ayat of Malaysia*, para. 18.

19. When the Auditor-General's Report on the accounts of 1958 indicated certain irregularities in the disbursements of government funds, the government issued a Command Paper No. 14 of 1960 in which these irregularities were justified on the grounds that conditions had changed and that 'those changed conditions must be taken into consideration before any judgement is passed for or against those responsible for the disbursement of government funds'. One of the charges made was that in the 'desire to achieve quick results, government had overlooked certain procedures, accounting and financial'. See *Official Report of the Dewan Ra'ayat*, 28 April 1960, Col. 878.

20. According to the Minister of Health 12 deaths were involved while the opposition claimed that 107 deaths were involved.

21. *Straits Times*, 25 August 1973.

22. The opposition party then published the speech of its leader with the caption 'The Malacca Hospital Mass Deaths—the speech the Straits Times Blacked Out', DAP publication, Kuala Lumpur.

23. Ibid.

24. The case of Aziz Ishak who resigned as Minister of Agriculture in September 1962, and the case of Rahman Talib who resigned as Minister of Education in December 1964.

25. Letter from Tunku Abdul Rahman to Abdul Aziz bin Ishak, 24 July 1962, quoted in Karl von Vorys, *Democracy without Consensus,* Oxford University Press, Singapore, 1976, pp. 179-80.

26. Rahman Talib, the Minister of Education, sued an opposition member of Parliament, D. R. Seenivasagam, for libel and slander when the latter repeated his allegations of corruption outside Parliament. The Court acquitted the member of Parliament on grounds of justification. See *Abdul Rahman Talib* v. *Seenivasagam & Anor.* [1965] 31 M.L.J. 142 (H.C.) and [1966] 2 M.L.J. 66 (F.C.).

27. *Straits Times*, 8 December 1964.

28. When it was pointed out in Parliament that the charges of corruption were not connected with his ministerial duties and therefore should not be paid from government funds, the Prime Minister insisted that the charges were made against a Minister who was a public officer and who was therefore eligible for this privilege provided he obtained prior approval from the Cabinet. *Parliamentary Debates* (Dewan Ra'ayat), 18 November 1965, Col. 2976.

29. Karl von Vorys, op. cit., p. 192.

30. Apart from internal departmental committees appointed on an *ad hoc* basis to look into specific matters, there are government agencies such as the National Bureau of Investigation and the National Complaints Bureau to investigate matters involving alleged corruption and maladministration.

7. The Malaysian Parliament

INTRODUCTION

HISTORY, politics, and the legal system then existing in a country play a major role in the shaping of a legislative body. Its composition, powers, duties, privileges, and prerogatives are all determined by the political parties then in power. Although the powers and functions of the legislatures all the world over are basically the same—to legislate—the mode of election to the legislature, its composition, its tiers, rights and privileges, and a host of other things are different from country to country.

Some legislatures are unicameral, while others are bicameral. Like those of Australia, India, or the United States, the Malaysian Parliament is bicameral. Unlike them, it is bicameral at the federal level and unicameral at the State level. The Upper House is designated as the Senate or Dewan Negara, and the Lower House as the House of Representatives or Dewan Ra'ayat. The two Houses together with the Yang di-Pertuan Agong constitute Parliament.

SOME HISTORICAL PERSPECTIVES

In 1956, the framers of the Malayan Constitution were given the task of proposing a workable Constitution for the new Federation of Malaya yet to be born. After looking at the Federation of Malaya Agreement, 1948 and model constitutions from India, the United States, and elsewhere, they decided to divide the power into three branches of government—legislative, executive, and judiciary, but they looked on the legislative branch as the source of governmental energy and the seat of national power. They looked upon Parliament as the main channel of democratic impulses. In so doing, they had to face a perplexing and controversial question involving the nature of the legislative branch of the government. To continue with the precedent, that is to have a unicameral legislature, would be unfair to the smaller States such as Perlis which has only two seats in the Parliament. To have a bicameral legislature would be to depart from the normal convention, because the then Federal Legislative Council was a unicameral legislature. Finally, after looking at the Western experiences, especially the United States and the British models, the framers came to a compromise—a bicameral legislature; but the Upper House should be different from that of the United Kingdom and the United States—again another compromise.[1] The justification for having a bicameral legislature was that the then Federation of Malaya was a federation like that of India or Australia and being a federation, the interests of the component States as opposed to the interest of the populace must be given higher priority. The Upper House was to represent areas rather than numbers. Moreover, by having a bicameral legislature, it would, as it was hoped, provide a check against hasty legislation. In other words, the role of the Upper House was to be a revising chamber.

Initially, the Upper House was to be modelled after the House of Lords in the United Kingdom, where the members were to be appointed. Gradually, the United States model where all members were elected was to be adopted. Hence a provision for this arrangement was made in Article 45(4) of the Malaysian Constitution, although at present it is still in 'cold storage'.

THE CONSTITUTION OF PARLIAMENT

Parliament consists of the Yang di-Pertuan Agong, the Dewan Negara, and the Dewan Ra'ayat.[2] The three institutions acting together enact laws. Although a constituent part of Parliament the Yang di-Pertuan Agong does not sit in Parliament, nor does he have the final say as to which laws should or should not be enacted, because in legislative matters he acts on the advice of the Cabinet.[3] The Yang di-Pertuan Agong may address either House of Parliament or both Houses jointly,[4] but in practice he addresses both Houses jointly at the opening of each session of Parliament.

The Yang di-Pertuan Agong summons Parliament from time to time, but he cannot, except during an emergency,[5] allow six months to elapse between the last sitting in one session and the date appointed for its first meeting in the next session.[6] He may prorogue or dissolve Parliament.[7] Unless sooner dissolved, Parliament continues for five years from the date of its first meeting, and at the end of the five-year period it is automatically dissolved. Whenever Parliament is dissolved, a general election has to be held within 60 days in the States of Malaya and 90 days in Sabah and Sarawak from the date of the dissolution and the new Parliament shall be summoned to meet again on a date not later than 120 days from the date of the dissolution.[8] This 60 and 90 day distinction between the States of Malaya on the one hand and Sabah and Sarawak on the other should be abolished. It creates difficulties for the students, administrative difficulties for the civil servants, and confusion even to the politicians. More important, it creates disunity between the two component regions. If communications in the Borneo States was the reason for the longer 90 day period, it should no longer be a problem after three Malaysia Plans. It is submitted that a uniform period should be substituted, either 60 or 90 days for both territories.

In the exercise of summoning Parliament, reading the speech from the throne and a host of other Parliamentary business, the Yang di-Pertuan Agong must act on the advice of the Cabinet,[9] but in withholding consent to a request for the dissolution of Parliament he acts in his own discretion.[10]

THE DEWAN NEGARA

The upper chambers of national legislative bodies are frequently identified more with honour than with authority. The House of Lords in England, for example, is made up of nobles both temporal and spiritual, many of whom represent the most aristocratic ancestral lines; but, although its prestige is enormous in certain circles, it long ago yielded final power in controversial matters to the House of Commons.[11]

This statement is true in Malaysia, for the Senate is less powerful and less influential than the Dewan Ra'ayat in terms of its membership, the power in relation to money Bills, in terms of remuneration of its members, the qualification of members to the prime ministership, and a host of other things.

In a few socialist countries, the Upper House was abolished,[12] and in others they were not created,[13] for reasons better known to themselves. In India, the *Rajya Sabha* or the Upper House, was described as a 'Rolls Royce institution in a bullock-cart country'.[14] In England, the House of Lords was described as 'a yawning and sleeping chamber for the aristocrats, the public service pensioners and retired ambassadors'.[15]

The Dewan Negara is designed to fulfil a number of purposes. First, it has been envisaged as a forum to which seasoned and experienced politicians and public men might get an easy access without undergoing the din and bustle of a general election which is inevitable for finding a seat in the Dewan Ra'ayat. In this way, experience and talent are not lost to the country and the senior public men are enabled to apply their mature judgment and wisdom to solving questions of public importance facing the country. The value of the Upper House, therefore, lies in the talent, experience and knowledge which it can harness to the service of the country which might not be available otherwise. Secondly, the Dewan Negara serves as a debating chamber to hold dignified debates and it acts as a revising chamber over the Dewan Ra'ayat which, being a popular chamber, may at times be swayed to act hastily under pressure of public opinion or in the heat of passion of the moment. The existence of two debating chambers means that all proposals and programmes of the government are discussed twice and that these will be adopted after mature and calm consideration, and thus precipitous action may be prevented. Usually, discussions in the Dewan Negara are somewhat on a less politically partisan basis. As a revising chamber, the Dewan Negara may also help in improving Bills passed by the Dewan Ra'ayat. Lastly, the Dewan Negara is designed to serve as a chamber where the States of the Federation are, to some extent, represented as States in keeping with the federal principle and, therefore, the House has been given some federal functions to discharge on the theory, and in its character, of a House representing the States rather than the people.[16] In practice, however, the Dewan Negara does not act as a champion of local interests, or as a battleground between the Centre and the States. Even though the twenty-six members are elected by the State Legislatures, the members of the Dewan Negara vote, not at the dictate of the State concerned, but according to their own views and party affiliation. There is no provision in the Constitution requiring the members of this House to vote as the instructed delegates of the State Government or the Legislature concerned. They are not subject to any direct control of the State they seek to represent. The Dewan Negara has thus emerged as a forum where problems are discussed and considered from a national rather than a local plane.[17]

COMPOSITION OF DEWAN NEGARA

In comparison with the Dewan Ra'ayat, the Dewan Negara is a reasonably small body consisting of 58 members, 26 of whom are chosen by indirect election from the States, and the other 32 are appointed by the Yang di-Pertuan Agong.[18] The two elected members from each State, irrespective of size and population, provide equal representation to State interests in Parliament.[19] The remaining thirty-two members are appointed by the Yang di-Pertuan Agong, on the advice of the Cabinet.[20] The Constitution directs that the appointed members should be persons who have rendered distinguished public service or have achieved distinction in the professions, commerce, industry, agriculture, cultural activities, or social service, or are representative of racial minorities or are capable of representing the interests of the *orang asli*.[21] Whether the future will see an enlargement depends entirely upon the will of Parliament itself to invoke Article 45(4) of the Constitution which empowers it to increase the number, and to change its composition and structure.

It is of interest to note at this point that unlike the States, the Federal Capital Territory is not represented in the Senate. This is because the Federal Capital Territory does not have a legislature of its own. What it has is a City Council whose members are appointed by the Government. Secondly, the Federal Capital Territory is the direct responsibility of the Federal Government and not of the States. Therefore, there is no necessity to have two representatives in the Senate from the Federal Capital Territory. Furthermore, the Yang di-Pertuan Agong, in exercising his power of appointment of the thirty-two Senators under Article 45(2), may look for someone who habitually resides in Kuala Lumpur. It is submitted that this should be so, for someone must champion the interests of the City.

By not having direct elections to the Senate, and by keeping the power of appointment in the hands of the Cabinet (in that the Cabinet will advise the Yang di-Pertuan Agong to make the appointment of the thirty-two members) the party in power by appointing only supporters of the Government can ensure that Bills introduced by the Government will have a smooth passage in the Senate.[22] It is some sort of patronage system.[23] In the early days of independence, some Senators were appointed from among those who lost in the general elections to the House of Representatives. This was true in the 1959, 1964 and the 1969 General Elections, when no less than forty Senators were appointed from among the losers. Fortunately however, the present trend is to appoint persons of political maturity and seniority to the Senate so that they do not have to concern themselves with the rigours of electioneering.

If we were to have a referendum today on the question of whether Senators should be elected or appointed, 99.9 per cent of the electorate would vote for an election, because they want to see democracy at work. But since politicians decide for the masses on many important political issues, the masses virtually have no say at all. They have to follow what the politicians have said and what they have to say.

THE HOUSE OF REPRESENTATIVES

The Dewan Ra'ayat is a democratic chamber popularly elected directly by the people on the basis of adult suffrage. It is designed to reflect the popular will and in this lies its source of strength. The Constitution specifies that the Prime Minister must be a member of the House of Representatives,[24] and the House of Representatives has the final say in money Bills such as taxation and expenditure of public money.[25]

Ordinarily, the life of Parliament[26] is five years, whereupon it stands dissolved. It may be dissolved at any time during the period of its normal life by the Yang di-Pertuan Agong, acting within his discretion[27] upon the request of the Prime Minister.[28] The last three Parliaments were dissolved at five-year intervals, namely in 1964, 1969, and 1974.[29]

The word 'Parliament' in the Constitution is very ambiguous, for it means many things. Article 44 spells out the institution of Parliament as consisting of the Yang di-Pertuan Agong, the Dewan Negara, and the Dewan Ra'ayat. However, Article 55 goes on to say that the Yang di-Pertuan Agong may dissolve Parliament. This does not mean that the Yang di-Pertuan Agong may dissolve all the three institutions, because by virtue of Article 45(3) the term of office of a member of the Senate is six years and shall *not be affected by a dissolution of Parliament*. What was envisaged was that the phrase 'dissolution of Parliament' in Articles 40, 43, and 55 was meant to be the House of Representatives and not the entire Parliament.

Unless such an interpretation is given to Article 55, the whole concept of 'dissolution of Parliament' is lost. It is submitted that in order to avoid confusion and to give clarity to the words and phrases used in the Constitution, Article 55(5) should be added to read as follows:

55(5). For purposes of this Article, Clause (2) of Article 40, Clause (2) of Article 43 and Clause (3) of Article 45, 'Parliament' means the House of Representatives.

This is what is clearly intended by the framers of the Constitution.

MEMBERSHIP OF THE HOUSE

The size of the House of Representatives is based on population. With a population of 6,661,000 in 1959, the First Parliament of 1959 had 104 members. This works out to one member of Parliament to 64,000 people. In the Second Parliament of 1964, the number of members was enlarged to 159, as a result of the formation of Malaysia, whereby Sabah, Sarawak, and Singapore were represented for the first time in the Malaysian Parliament. In the 1969 Election, the number was reduced to 144 after the separation of Singapore from Malaysia. It was again increased to 154 in the Fourth Parliament following the 1974 general election. Table I gives a general view, on a pro-rata basis of the First to the Fourth Parliaments.

TABLE I
Number of Parliamentary Seats and Population
First to Fourth Parliament, 1959-1974

Parliament	Year of Election	Number of Seats	Number of Population	Ratio of M.P.s to Population
First	1959	104[a]	6,661,000[a]	1 : 64,048
Second	1964	159	11,065,491[b]	1 : 69,591
Third	1969	144	10,452,309[c]	1 : 72,583
Fourth	1974	154	11,759,949[d]	1 : 76,357

[a]Figures represent seats and population for Federation of Malaya only.
[b]The total is obtained by combining the population for Peninsular Malaysia, Sabah, Sarawak, and Singapore. Malaysia, Official Yearbook, 1965, and Singapore Yearbook, 1965.
[c]1970 Population Census, Malaysia, Official Yearbook, 1972 at p. 23.
[d]Malaysia, Official Yearbook, 1975, at p. 3.

'Family Planning' is unknown to the House of Representatives. Some constituencies have as few as 13,345 voters,[30] while others have as many as 58,261 voters.[31] Originally, it was intended that there should be a rural bias in the proportion of 1 : 2 in favour of rural constituencies.[32] However, for political and other reasons known to Parliament itself, Parliament in 1974 thought fit to adopt a new scheme whereby the constituencies were to be finally determined by the House itself on the recommendation of the Election Commission. As a result, some States have fewer seats and some have more when compared with the previous Parliament. Kelantan and Pahang gained two seats each, while Kedah, Penang, Perak, and Trengganu gained one seat each, but Selangor lost three seats as a result of the creation of the Federal Capital Territory. The other six States remained the same.

However, in spite of the redistribution of seats in the 1974 elections, the number of seats are not proportionate to the relative populations of the country, 'but resulted from hard political bargaining preceding the formation of the Federation and taking into account, *inter alia*, the large land area of the Borneo States'.[33] Further, the population of a State is not the sole factor in determining the number of seats for each State, for other factors must be taken into account, such as the number of voters on the electoral roll, the age distribution of the population,[34] citizenship factors,[35] communication problems in rural constituencies, the rate of development in the State, mobility of the rural population to urban areas, the freedom to stand in any constituency without any residential qualifications (except for Sabah and Sarawak), and a host of other factors which are thought reasonable by Parliament.

WOMEN IN THE MALE-DOMINATED HOUSE

Running Parliamentary business would appear to be still dominated by the male sex. Running the government business is still an all-but-one male affair. This trend will remain so for the next century or so.

The Dewan Ra'ayat has 6 female members against 148 male members. This works out at 3.9 per cent of the females in the male-dominated House. The Dewan Negara has 7 female members against 51 male members, namely 12 per cent—a fairer representation. Population-wise, the number of males to females is about even, 51 males to 49 females.[36] The women libbers and equal rights fighters, especially the *Wanita* UMNO, have been campaigning for an increased representation for females. Although the number will be increased from time to time, a substantial increase is not likely to occur.

QUALIFICATIONS AND DISQUALIFICATIONS

Much has been said elsewhere about the qualifications and disqualifications of a member of Parliament.[37] Suffice it to mention here that they are not onerous. The Constitution provides a minimum age of 30 years for membership of the Dewan Negara and 21 years for membership of the Dewan Ra'ayat. Other qualifications are the same for both Houses, namely citizenship of the Federation, residence in Malaysia and absence of any disqualification.[38]

Disqualifications are the same for membership in both Houses. They are laid down in Article 48 of the Constitution.

A person is disqualified for being a member of either House of Parliament if:

(a) he is and has been found or declared to be of unsound mind; or

(b) he is an undischarged bankrupt;[39] or

(c) he holds an office of profit; or

(d) having been nominated for election to either House of Parliament or to the Legislative Assembly of a State, or having acted as election agent to a person so nominated, he has failed to lodge any return of election expenses required by law within the time and in the manner so required; or

(e) he has been convicted of an offence by a court of law in the Federation (or, before Malaysia Day, in the territories comprised in a Borneo State or in Singapore) and sentenced to imprisonment for a term of not less than one year or to a fine of not less than two thousand dollars and has not received a free pardon;[40] or

(f) he has voluntarily acquired citizenship of, or exercised rights of citizenship in, a foreign country or has made a declaration of allegiance to a foreign country.

The provisions of our Constitution are vague in many areas which lead to various interpretations. For example, who decides that a member of Parliament is of unsound mind? In India, Article 102 of the Indian Constitution provides that 'a member is disqualified if a competent court has declared him to be of unsound mind'. In Malaysia, since the Constitution is silent on the declaring authority, the Mental Disorders Ordinance, 1952[41] has to be invoked, i.e. two qualified medical practitioners must pronounce that a member of Parliament is of unsound mind.

The phrase 'holding an office of profit' generally refers to any full-time employment in any of the public services. The rationale for disqualifying the holder of an office of profit from being a member of Parliament is aptly described by Jain, as follows:

Dependence of a large number of members of Parliament on government favours and patronage would weaken the position of Parliament *vis-à-vis* the executive; for, such members may be tempted to support the government without considering any problem with an open mind. This is the rationale behind the constitutional provision debarring a holder of an office of profit under the government from being elected to a House of Parliament.

It is thus designed to protect the democratic fabric of the country from being corrupted and polluted by executive patronage. It ensures that Parliament does not contain persons who may be obligated to the government, and thus be amenable to its influence, because they are receiving favours and benefits from it. The provision secures independence of members of Parliament from the influence of the government and thus seeks to reduce the risk of conflict between duty and self-interest in them so that they may discharge their functions and criticize the government, if necessary, without fear or favour.[42]

In the light of recent developments in the 'public service', as envisaged by the Cabinet Committee on Salary, the phrase 'public service' becomes ambiguous. Formerly, members of statutory bodies, universities, and employees of local authorities were allowed to seek election,[43] or to accept appointment to the Senate.[44]

However, in view of the Cabinet Committee Salary Report replacing the earlier Salary Reports, a doubt has arisen as to whether a member of a statutory body or of a local authority is or is not holding an office of profit. Attempts have now been made by the various authorities through subordinate legislation to bar their members from active politics. Parliament is free to declare any office one of profit,[45] but as each House is empowered to decide the question of disqualification, and such decision is final,[46] it is a matter of some embarrassment for the elected members of each House. To avoid unnecessary litigation, great risk on the part of potential candidates, and a great sum of money involved in an election, specific laws are needed to redefine the phrase 'office of profit' in addition to that given in the Constitution. Alternatively an amendment to the Constitution to clarify the position should be made.

Clause (1)(e) of Article 48 raises a point of some academic interest. What was the intention of the framers of the Constitution in providing for such phrases as 'convicted in the Federation of an offence', 'and having been sentenced to an imprisonment of not less than one year or to a fine of not less than two thousand dollars'? Suppose a member was sentenced to four years imprisonment in a neighbouring country immediately after he was elected[47] or he was convicted of a serious criminal offence under the Penal Code in a court in the Federation but was sentenced only to nine months imprisonment, or he was convicted of an offence under the Road Traffic Ordinance but was sentenced to six months imprisonment AND a fine of $1,000, would he still be a member and retain his seat? The answer is in the positive. Going back to the spirit of the Constitution, it is submitted that in order to have a House of members free from crime and corruption, and in order to provide a model Parliament, such provisions as corrupt practices at an election, conviction for an offence resulting in imprisonment for two or more years, or for an offence under the Penal Code, or Prevention of Corruption Act, or Dangerous Drugs Act, or having an interest or share in a contract for supply of goods and services to the Government, or being an employee of a wholly or partly owned Government corporation such as Petronas,[48] MAS, MISC, or SEDCs, or dismissal from government service, should be included as a disqualification for being a member of Parliament.[49]

The Yang di-Pertuan Agong is empowered to remove any disqualifications under paragraphs (d) and (e) of clause (1), namely the offence of failure to lodge a return of election expenses,[50] and conviction and sentence for a criminal offence. Both disqualifications, if not removed, cease to be applicable after five years.[51]

DUAL MEMBERSHIP

Dual membership in both Houses of Parliament simultaneously is prohibited, nor can one represent more than one constituency, or be elected to the Senate for more than one State, nor be both an elected and an appointed member of the Senate.[52] However, in the absence of residential qualification either in the Constitutions or in the Election Rules, concurrent membership in either House of Parliament and a State Legislative Assembly is not forbidden and is, in fact, common. At present, the Chief Ministers of the three States of Penang, Sabah, and Sarawak who are members of their own respective State Legislative Assemblies are concurrently members of the national Parliament. In addition, a great majority of the members of the opposition are holding concurrent membership. To make matters worse, at one time between 1959 and 1974, three members of the People's Progressive Party were holding triple membership in the three tiers of government, namely the elected membership of the Ipoh Municipality, the State Legislative Assembly of Perak, and the Federal Parliament at one and the same time.

Although residential qualification in the constituency is not governed by the Constitution, custom and usage play a great part in the election. With the exception of the 1959 and 1964 general elections, the 1969 and 1974 general elections saw a dividing line between 'locals' and 'outsiders'. In the 1959 general election, for example, eight PAS members were 'outsiders'—in that they were not natives of Kelantan or Trengganu. Dato' Onn bin Jaafar of the Party Negara who was from Johore won a seat in Trengganu. The two later elections rejected 'outsiders' in preference to the locals or natives of that State.

The concept of 'representation' would be meaningless if the Constitution were to allow a 'foreign member' to reside 400 miles away from his constituency, unless he is appointed a member of the administration. It is submitted that a provision should be included in the Election Rules to the effect that a candidate must 'ordinarily be a resident' in a particular constituency for a minimum period of five years, unless prior to the candidature, he has served the Government in some capacity.

Twenty years experience is enough for us to judge the merits and demerits of dual membership; the demerits far outweigh its merits. The effectiveness of being a representative of the people in two constituencies, hundreds of miles apart, is lost. Unless a member can mobilize all the machinery, money, time and energy, and other things necessary to help him in the conduct of his parliamentary and State Legislative Assembly business simultaneously, effective representation is not possible. The running of parliamentary business effectively is time-consuming, energy-wasting, and requires great effort. Secondly, the sessions of the Federal Parliament and of the State Legislative Assemblies, especially the budget session, are held almost simultaneously, and the House of Representatives normally runs a marathon session of some forty days towards the end of the year. As a result of dual membership, absenteeism in one legislature or another is unavoidable. Thirdly, monopoly of seats is bad and should be avoided at all costs. Fourthly, in a country where democracy is at work, membership of the State Legislative Assemblies should be spread over as many aspiring members of a political party as possible. To say that only a few party leaders are capable of representing the people at both the Federal and State levels would be tantamount to denying the right of others to participate in a democracy.

It has been the policy of the Alliance Party, though not of the Barisan Nasional, to avoid duplication or triplication of membership. The Alliance Party did not subscribe to the monopolistic thinking of other parties. It subscribed, however, to the spreading of membership of the legislatures to as many people down the line of the party hierarchy so as to reach the maximum number of party affiliates. It provides a training ground for young and dedicated politicians who aspire to move up the hierarchy. Moreover, the Alliance Party, especially UMNO, has the greatest number of members reaching the grass-root level. Therefore it can afford to 'spare' candidates at any level. This policy as adopted by the Alliance Party is in line with the Indian practice. In India, no person can be a member of Parliament and a State Legislature simultaneously.[53] It is submitted that the Indian provision on the prohibition and the practice adhered to by the Alliance Party should be carefully considered by Parliament, for the demerits, if any, of dual or triple membership far outweigh its merits. It is not too far-fetched to suggest that Parliamentary reform is necessary to abolish dual membership.

TERMINATION OF MEMBERSHIP

A member of any House may resign his seat. In practice, however, none have resigned from the House of Representatives,[54] although many have resigned from the Senate in order to contest the various general elections. Some of the members of the Cabinet today have at one time or another been in the Senate,[55] and there is also a transfer of membership from the Lower House to the Upper House after a general election on the occasion of 'retirement' from the Lower House and from the active politics of representing a constituency.

The Constitution also provides that if a member of either House is absent without leave of the House from every sitting of that House for a period of six months, the House may declare his seat vacant.[56]

The House is quite generous in granting leave of absence.[57]

Article 53 provides that questions concerning the disqualification of members are decided by the House concerned, the decisions of which are final. A disqualification may either exist when a person seeks to become a member and if he is already disqualified he is not entitled to be chosen as a member, or may arise after he has become a member and in such a case he will cease to be a member. The election or appointment of a disqualified person is void; and if disqualification arises subsequent to a member taking a seat, his seat becomes vacant. However, by virtue of Article 62(2), the presence or participation of persons so disqualified will not invalidate any legislative proceedings.

THE OFFICERS OF PARLIAMENT

THE SPEAKER OF THE DEWAN RA'AYAT

The Speaker is the chief officer of the Dewan Ra'ayat. He presides at its meetings.[58] The Dewan Ra'ayat elects a Speaker and a Deputy Speaker at the first sitting following a general election,[59] or following the death of the Speaker.[60] Originally, the Speaker must be elected from among its own members. However, for various reasons, Article 57 of the Constitution was amended in 1964[61] by providing that:

(1) The House of Representatives shall from time to time elect:
    (a) as Yang di-Pertua Dewan Ra'ayat (Speaker) a person who either is a member of the House or is qualified for election as such a member, and
    (b) as Deputy Speaker, a person who is a member of the House.

The two former Speakers were not members of the House, but the present one is. Once a non-member is elected as Speaker, he automatically becomes a member of the House by virtue of holding his office, additional to the members elected by popular votes in the general election.[62]

The Deputy Speaker is also elected by the House itself from amongst its members. He performs the duties of the Speaker in the latter's absence. If both the Speaker and his Deputy are absent, then any member, upon the motion of a Minister, may be called upon to preside.[63]

The office of the Speaker enjoys great honour, dignity, prestige, position, and authority not only within the four walls of the House, but also outside. Protocol-wise, he is number one man inside, and number four man outside, for he takes precedence next after the Yang di-Pertuan Agong, the Raja Permaisuri Agong, and the President of the Senate. He even takes precedence over the Prime Minister.

Authority-wise, he has extensive powers to regulate the proceedings of the House. He interprets and declares the rules, procedures, and customs of the House. 'He is the spokesman of the House in its collective capacity.'[64] In many instances, he has discretionary powers to allow or not to allow questions to be asked,[65] or to determine whether a Minister can refuse to answer a question[66] or supplementary questions,[67] or questions asked without notice[68] or to order the discontinuance of repetitious speech-making[69] or to order the withdrawal of a member[70] or to adjourn or suspend a sitting,[71] and a host of other powers befitting the chair of an omnipotent House. In simple layman's language the Speaker has all the necessary powers to ensure order, respect, decorum, and the smooth running of the debate of parliamentarians in the House.[72]

In order to ensure the independence and impartiality of the Speaker and the Deputy Speaker, the Constitution also formally makes certain significant provisions[73] in addition to that of the Standing Order. Their salaries and allowances are to be fixed by a law made by Parliament and are not subject to the annual vote of Parliament and are charged to the Consolidated Fund.[74] 'There is thus no special opportunity to criticize their work and conduct in Parliament.'[75] Further, none of them can be removed from office except by a resolution passed by a special majority of the House itself.

THE PRESIDENT OF THE DEWAN NEGARA

Generally speaking, what has been said about the Speaker of the Dewan Ra'ayat is applicable *mutatis mutandis* to the President of the Dewan Negara and about the Deputy Speaker of the Dewan Ra'ayat to the Deputy President, except that the Dewan Negara elects a President and a Deputy President from amongst its own members. They vacate their offices as soon as they cease to be members of the Senate.

Because the life of the Senate is continuous and thereby is not affected by the dissolution of Parliament, the term of office of the President is not prescribed by law. Two factors however are significant, that an election is required upon a vacancy in the office of the President and that his term as a member is not expected to expire in a short period of time. Thus if he is elected President on the eve of expiry of his term, some announcement has to be made for the renewal of the term. Otherwise it is meaningless or even futile to elect a President for only one or two sittings. The same is true with regard to the Deputy President.

FUNCTIONS OF PARLIAMENT

Parliament is not only a legislative body, but also a deliberative institution. Broadly, we may divide its powers into seven broad areas, namely: legislation; finance; deliberation and discussion; control over the executive; amendatory powers; housekeeping; and disciplinary.

1. THE LEGISLATIVE AUTHORITY OF PARLIAMENT

The primary role of Parliament is to legislate. Article 44 provides that the legislative authority of the Federation shall be vested in a Parliament. Article 66 again spells out the law-making procedure, through Bills passed by both Houses and assented to by the Yang di-Pertuan Agong. Article 159 gives the power to Parliament to amend the Constitution if it so wishes, mostly by a two-thirds majority. With the exception of Articles 2, 38, 70, 71, 153, and 181, Parliament, and Parliament alone, has sovereign and paramount power to legislate. But to what extent can Parliament legislate? Within the limits of its own spheres, namely the Federal and Concurrent List,[76] and in some cases even in the State List,[77] the authority of Parliament to legislate is almost absolute and the properly enacted laws of a sovereign Parliament are unchallengeable. Article 44 provides:

> The legislative authority of the Federation shall be vested in a Parliament, which, shall consist of the Yang di-Pertuan Agong and two Majlis (Houses of Parliament) to be known as the Dewan Negara (Senate) and the Dewan Ra'ayat (House of Representatives).

Nowhere in the Constitution is it stated that Parliament can delegate its legislative powers to another body. However, Parliament in exercising its legislative authority often delegates its legislative powers to another body. The practice is based on the assumption that if the British Parliament is empowered to delegate, other Parliaments also have power to delegate. It is submitted that we have been too much swayed by the British practices, without realizing that our Constitution is a *written one*—and the British is largely unwritten. 'The question whether legislative power can be delegated cannot arise in England since Parliament is supreme and there are no legal limitations on its powers. But the question has arisen with reference to the Constitution established by the British Parliament.'[78]

We are not in England. We are in Malaysia. Our Parliament is not supreme. Our Constitution is. It is submitted that we, knowingly or unknowingly, consciously or unconsciously, have been following the concept of 'delegated legislation' as it existed in England. There must be a source of power in the Constitution before our Parliament can delegate its legislative power to some other subordinate authorities. In the past, Parliament has given to itself the power to delegate without knowing that it has no such power because the Constitution confers upon Parliament, and no one else, the power to legislate.

Again, we cannot be swayed with the decision of the Privy Council on the doctrine of *delegatus non potest delegare*. The Privy Council rejected the doctrine as founded on a mistaken view of the powers of legislatures established by the British Parliament, like the Australian or Canadian Legislatures, and indeed of the nature and principles of legislation, and affirmed the position that the legislatures acting within their powers had, and were intended to have, plenary powers of legislation as large, and of the same nature, as those of the British Parliament itself. Thus, by 1885 the theory that the colonial legislatures established by the British Parliament were its delegates was decisively rejected and the doctrine of supremacy within limits was finally affirmed.[79]

Again, it is submitted that Section 3 of the Civil Law Act, 1956 (which deals with the application of U.K. common law, rules of equity, and certain statutes), does not apply in this case because the Act is subordinate to the Constitution. It does not apply to the constitutional principles.

It is interesting to compare the legislative power in Article 44 with Article 150 in which the Yang di-Pertuan Agong is empowered by the Constitution, during an emergency, to promulgate ordinances having the force of law. In *Eng Keock Cheng* v. *Public Prosecutor*[80] the question of delegation was raised. Wylie C.J. (Borneo) said:

The true effect of article 150 is that, subject to certain exceptions set out therein, Parliament has, during an emergency, power to legislate on any subject to any effect, even if inconsistencies with articles of the Constitution (including the provisions for fundamental liberties) are involved. This necessarily includes authority to delegate part of that power to legislate to some other authority, notwithstanding the existence of a written Constitution.... The Emergency (Criminal Trials) Regulations, 1964, have been made under section 2 of the Act. Their subject-matter is clearly within the language already quoted, as they provide for special provisions in respect of procedure in criminal cases. On this subject, His Majesty has been given power to make such regulations as he deems necessary or expedient for the purposes set out in section 2, as has earlier been concluded, the effect of subsection (4) is that this power cannot be limited by reference to the provisions of the Constitution. Parliament has expressly enacted that the regulations are to be valid notwithstanding any inconsistency with the provisions of the Constitution, an enactment which it was not beyond the power of Parliament to make.

It is therefore unnecessary to express any opinion as to whether the regulations are inconsistent with article 8 or any other provision in the Constitution....

In *Osman & Ors.* v. *Public Prosecutor*,[81] the Privy Council held that essential regulations made by the Yang di-Pertuan Agong under section 2 of the Emergency (Essential Powers) Act, No. 30 of 1964, an Act enacted by Parliament during an emergency by virtue of Article 150, are valid even if they are inconsistent with the Constitution.

Again in 1976, the same question was put to the test in the Federal Court in *Public Prosecutor* v. *Khong Teng Khen & Anor.*[82] It was held that it was lawful for the Yang di-Pertuan Agong to delegate under section 2 of the Emergency (Essential Powers) Ordinance, 1969 power to himself to make regulations inconsistent with the Constitution.

These three cases are emergency cases, in which not only Parliament but also the Yang di-Pertuan Agong are given wide powers to legislate notwithstanding that they are inconsistent with the provisions of the Constitution. Article 150 is specific, that is a provision dealing with emergency; therefore wide powers are necessary. But Article 44 speaks about normal times, and there is no specific provision with regard to delegation.

Therefore, it is submitted that the silence on delegation in Article 44 cannot be taken as implied consent to delegate the legislative power of Parliament to any other authority, for the power to delegate must be specified in the Constitution itself.

Before someone takes the matter before the Court to have the whole subordinate legislation declared unconstitutional for violating Article 44, it is submitted that Article 44 should be amended to include the following clauses:

44(2). In exercising its legislative authority, Parliament may by law delegate its legislative power to other bodies prescribed in the Act of Parliament.

44(3). Clause (2) of Article 44 shall be deemed to have effect from Merdeka Day.

2. FINANCE

For purposes of this essay, suffice it to mention that Parliament, and only Parliament, has power to levy any taxes or rates. The Executive has no power to impose any taxes. Article 96 provides that no tax or rate shall be levied by or for the purposes of the

Federation except by or under the authority of Federal law. The principle on which parliamentary control of finance is based is the doctrine that Parliament is the custodian of the public purse. This function is very important as it enables Parliament to exercise some form of control over the Executive, through discussions during the Budget debate. It is to be noted that by virtue of Article 68, financial powers have been concentrated in the Dewan Ra'ayat, and the Dewan Negara has no choice except to agree. Therefore in financial matters, the Dewan Negara plays only a subsidiary role. Again, Parliament cannot act on its own motion, for it has to act in response to a request made by the Executive.

The power of Parliament includes granting of money for expenses on public services, imposition of taxes, and authorization of loans. During the Budget debate, the members take the opportunity to discuss not only the dollars and cents, but also the Government's policies and its administrative machinery. The Budget debate has always been lively, for members take the opportunity to air their grievances, and ministers defend the Government's policies.

3. DELIBERATION AND DISCUSSION

Parliament is constantly engaged in deliberation and discussion of important public issues and airing public grievances. This is constantly done through legislation, control of public finance, debate on the Royal address, and through question time. Parliamentary questions provide an effective check on the day-to-day administration and an opportunity for concentrating public attention on topics of current concern. They are of value in securing redress of individual grievances,[83] for 'civil servants are aware that departmental action for which they are responsible to their Minister may result in a parliamentary question which may embarrass him in the House'.[84] Stressing the importance of this procedure, Ilbert observes,

There is no more valuable safeguard against maladministration, no more effective method of bringing the searchlight of criticism to bear on the action or inaction of responsible Ministers and their subordinates. A Minister has to be constantly asking himself not merely whether his proceedings and the proceedings of those for whom he is responsible are legally or technically defensible, but what kind of answer he can give if questioned about them in the House and how that answer will be received.[85]

4. CONTROL OVER THE EXECUTIVE

In any parliamentary form of government, the Executive is made subordinate to the legislature and responsible to it. Article 43(3)

provides that the Cabinet shall be collectively responsible to Parliament and by Article 43(4), if the Prime Minister ceases to command the confidence of the majority of the members of the House of Representatives, then unless at his request the Yang di-Pertuan Agong dissolves Parliament, the Prime Minister shall tender the resignation of the Cabinet. An important function of Parliament, therefore, is to control the Executive, criticize and supervise the administration and influence the policies of the government.[86]

5. AMENDATORY POWERS

The Executive proposes amendments to the Constitution and Parliament accepts or rejects them. In practice, however, Parliament accepts the proposal almost *in toto*. Article 159 empowers Parliament to amend the Constitution from time to time. However, there are certain limitations to the amendment of Articles 10(4), 14-31, 38, 63(4), 70, 71(1), 72(4), 152, 153 and 159(5) in that these Articles cannot be amended without the consent of the Conference of Rulers.

During the past twenty years, Parliament has amended the Constitution no less than twenty times,[87] involving fourteen Articles relating to Parliament, namely 45, 46, 48, 50, 53, 54, 55, 56, 57, 61, 62, 63, 65 and 67.

6. HOUSEKEEPING POWERS

The Constitution authorizes Parliament to enact the necessary laws to provide for its own maintenance and to give such House the power to make its own procedures. Article 58 provides that Parliament shall by law provide for the remuneration of the President and Deputy President of the Senate and the Speaker and Deputy Speaker of the House of Representatives, and the remuneration so provided for the President of the Senate and the Speaker of the House of Representatives shall be charged to the Consolidated Fund. Article 64 further provides that Parliament shall by law provide for the remuneration of members of each House. It is interesting to note that remuneration of the two principal officers of Parliament only, namely the President and the Speaker, are to be charged to the Consolidated Fund. The two Deputies as well as the members themselves are not covered. Therefore, the remuneration of the Deputy Speaker or the Deputy President is subject to debate in Parliament.

In exercise of these housekeeping powers, Parliament has passed several Acts of Parliament, namely President of the Senate (Remuneration) Act, 1960,[88] Speaker (Remuneration) Act, 1960,[89] Parliament (Members Remuneration) Act, 1960,[90] Members of the

Administration and Members of Parliament (Pensions and Gratuities) Act, 1971,[91] Parliamentary Services Act, 1963,[92] and Houses of Parliament (Privileges and Powers) Ordinance, 1952.[93] In addition, Parliament has, in exercise of the powers conferred by Article 62, adopted Standing Orders of its own; the Senate, the Standing Orders of the Dewan Negara, and the House of Representatives, the Standing Orders of the Dewan Ra'ayat.

7. POWER TO PUNISH FOR ITS CONTEMPT

This heading is discussed under the Powers and Privileges of Parliament.

A COMPARISON OF THE TWO HOUSES

It is interesting to make a comparison of the two Houses of Parliament with regard to their composition, powers, qualifications, and remuneration. (See Table II.)

COMPOSITION

The Senate has 58 members and the House of Representatives 154. Proportionately it is 1 : 3. Some countries have a proportion of 1 : 2, some others 1 : 4. Australia has 1 : 2 (64 against 125); and India has 1 : 2 (250 against 525). In the United Kingdom the position is reversed, whereby the membership of the House of Lords exceeds that of the House of Commons, 850 against 635. In the final analysis, the pattern seems to range from 1 : 2 to 1 : 4.

POWERS

The Malaysian Senate is less powerful than the House of Representatives. Although the Upper House has power to originate any Bill, money Bills must originate in the House of Representatives. Although it has a delaying power, the period is limited to one month for money Bills and one year for other Bills.

AGE

The minimum age for the Dewan Negara is 30 years while the minimum age for the Dewan Ra'ayat is 21 years. It is difficult to understand the logic of the distinction. If the Dewan Negara is supposed to be filled by mature experienced adults to revise the hasty bills passed by the Dewan Ra'ayat, then it is submitted it does not serve the purpose, for, to put it extremely, a person is mature enough to be a Prime Minister at the age of 21, yet he is too immature to be a Senator, because the Constitution specifies that the Prime Minister must be a member of the Dewan Ra'ayat. Unless the minimum age of a Prime Minister is specified at 30, the distinction would be superfluous.

REMUNERATION

Not only the composition and powers differ between the two Houses, remuneration also differs. Though both are members of Parliament, each member from the Dewan Ra'ayat gets an allowance of $1,500 per month and each member of the Dewan Negara receives a reduced sum of $1,000 per month, though other benefits are the same. Presumably, the members from the Dewan Ra'ayat are obliged to meet the voters in their respective constituencies, but not the Senators, and therefore they have to incur additional financial burdens.

TABLE II

A Comparison between the Two Houses of Parliament

| The Differences | The Houses | |
	Dewan Negara	Dewan Ra'ayat
Number in the Chamber	58	154
Qualification—minimum age	30	21
Remuneration	$1,000 per month	$1,500 per month
Term of Appointment/Election	6 years	5 years or sooner
Mode of Appointment	Indirectly elected/ appointed	Elected
Office of Prime Minister	Disqualified	Qualified
Powers of the House	No power in Money Bills	Have power in Money Bills
Dissolution of Parliament	Not Affected	Affected

CONCLUSION

DO WE NEED PARLIAMENTARY REFORM?

As we grow up from infancy through adolescence to adulthood, we need to look back and assess our past performance in preparation for the future. As we gain maturity with the coming of age and with breadth of twenty years' experience behind us, we need to ask ourselves these questions: 'Are we happy and contented with the present Constitution?' 'Does it reflect the true aspiration of our peoples, in particular, do we need parliamentary reform?'

At present, the principles of true democracy have not been followed in the general elections. The Westminster Model of democracy has been used as a guiding principle. It is based on a simple majority—the winner is elected. A candidate who obtains 5,500 votes in a four-cornered fight out of a total of 20,000 votes cast is declared the winner, while the other three candidates having a combined total of 14,500 votes are declared losers. In countries which adhere to true democratic principles, such as Australia, a candidate must secure an absolute majority of votes before he can be declared a winner. This principle of absolute majority is followed in Malaysia in the election of the Speaker of the Dewan Ra'ayat and the President of the Senate. Going through the election records, from 1959 to 1974, one will find that forty-eight seats have been won on the basis of 'he who gets the biggest vote wins'. Some winners have had as low as 20 per cent of the votes cast, and the biggest was 42 per cent.[94]

It is submitted that the working of parliamentary democracy as operating in Malaysia at present should be reformed. The present system is to the advantage of the party in power, because the votes cast for the third and fourth candidates in a four-cornered fight are really votes cast against the first two candidates. If there is no choice, most of the voters will vote for the party in power. In this way, it will help to provide a way for a two-party system of government. The Australian model needs to be carefully studied, for the merits of absolute majority outweigh its demerits.

Secondly, a reform of the Senate as an Upper House and a revising chamber is necessary. The present set-up does not reflect the value of the democratic system of government, because the majority of the members, 32 in number, are appointed as against 26 indirectly elected. No popular element is involved for they are not elected by the people, they do not enjoy equal status with the Lower House in terms of powers, members' remuneration and responsibilities, although they enjoy the same privileges and immunities.

Alternatively, a new arrangement may be made for the composition of the Upper House. It is recommended that in order to reflect a true Malaysian democracy that we cherish, a partly elected and partly appointed chamber is envisaged. Let us say we retain the magic figure of 58. We also retain the 2 senators elected by the State Legislative Assemblies, but we redistribute the 32 members appointed by the Yang di-Pertuan Agong. The Yang di-Pertuan Agong shall have power to appoint, let us say, 12 members to represent vested interests as envisaged by Article 45(2), and the balance of 20 are to be equitably distributed, according to some principle, among the votes cast for the various parties in the general election. The best arrangement is on the basis of percentage of votes cast for that party.

Let us say six parties have contested the general election, and the following are the votes cast for the various parties:

Party Contested	Votes Cast	Percentage	Seats in the Senate
Party A	3,000,000	60	12
Party B	1,000,000	20	4
Party C	500,000	10	2
Party D	250,000	5	1
Party E	200,000	4	1
Party F	50,000	1	No Seat
Total	5,000,000	100	20 seats

The chairman of the Election Commission will then notify the Clerk of the Senate of the votes cast, the percentage obtained and the number of seats to be allocated to that party. Party A will then nominate the twelve members to the Senate, followed by Parties B, C, D and E.

Thirdly, at present, the voices of the minority parties who have lost in the election are not heard in Parliament, and everybody turns a deaf ear to their grievances. By having this unique arrangement (for Malaysia is fond of creating unique institutions like the election of the Yang di-Pertuan Agong), a true principle of democracy will be at work. The voices of thousands of voters who voted for minority parties but whose representatives have lost by a slim majority can now be heard if that party can command a significant percentage sufficient to be accorded some recognition. After all, we believe in democracy. We adhere to democratic principles, and therefore we must see that democracy is at work. We need dissenting opinions, we need constructive criticism, we need to hear what the small men in the small parties have to say, for they are also citizens of the country.[95]

It is submitted that the time has come for Parliament seriously to consider invoking the already entrenched Article 45(4) of the Constitution. By having a fully elected Senate like that of the United States, more powers may be vested in it, especially the power of checking the work of the Executive.

Fourthly, States are allocated a number of parliamentary seats ranging from two in Perlis to twenty-four in Sarawak. States are again divided into electoral constituencies. By and large, they are political in nature and, of course, partisan in character. As such, some constituencies have been deliberately 'gerrymandered'. The purpose is not only to secure for the party in power the majority of the seats in the Parliament and also in the State Legislative Assemblies, but to get a lion's share of the seats, though not of the votes. Therefore it is not strange to find a constituency in the shape of two American Continents joined together to form a parliamentary constituency.[96] Whether such an arrangement will work to the advantage of the party in power is not quite certain.[97] But one thing is sure, gerrymandering of rural-urban constituencies will create many administrative problems not only for the Election Commission, but also for the voters, the constituents, and the general public. It confuses not only the voters but the party workers of the ruling party. Therefore, reform on the demarcation of boundaries of the constituencies is necessary. Gerrymandering should be reduced to a minimum. Some principles or guidelines need to be determined so as to avoid unnecessary confusion and administrative inconvenience.

Fifthly, Members of Parliament are representatives of the people in Parliament. Their roles are varied, ranging from full-time representatives in the case of some members, to part-time representatives in the case of others. The former are composed of full-time politicians who have retired from active professions, business, trade, or industry. The latter are composed of politicians who are actively engaged in their own profession, trade, business, or industry. To some, the allowance of $1,500 per month (in the case of members of the Dewan Ra'ayat) or $1,000 per month (in the case of members of the Dewan Negara) is a meagre sum. To others, such sums are inadequate to make ends meet. The object of paying such a remuneration is to compensate for the time lost and energy consumed while attending to parliamentary business. Therefore, their remuneration should be increased to a level which will enable them to devote their full attention to parliamentary business.

1. See *Report of the Constitutional Commission*, Kuala Lumpur, Government Printer, 1957.

2. Malaysia, Federal Constitution, Article 44.

3. Article 40.

4. Article 60.

5. During the 1969 Emergency, Parliament was not summoned for a period of

almost two years. The Second Parliament was dissolved in March 1969, and the Third Parliament was summoned only in February 1971.

6. Article 55(1).

7. Article 55(2).

8. Article 55(4).

9. Article 40(1).

10. Article 40(2).

11. Harold Zink, *Government and Politics in the United States*, New York, MacMillan, 1942, p. 367.

12. Sri Lanka abolished the Upper House in 1971.

13. Singapore did not establish one when it became independent in 1965.

14. N. N. Agarwal, V. Bhusham and V. Bhaguran, *Principles of Political Science,* Delhi, Ram Chand, 1969, p. 374.

15. H. Laski, *Parliamentary Government in England*, London, 1959, p. 112.

16. See Morris-Jones, *Parliament in India*, p. 256.

17. Because of the similarities of the Dewan Negara in Malaysia with that of *Rajya Sabha* of the Indian Parliament, this paragraph is quoted *mutatis mutandis* from M. P. Jain, *Indian Constitutional Law*, Bombay, Tripathi, 1970, p. 15.

18. Article 45(1) and (2).

19. See Tun Mohamed Suffian, *An Introduction to the Malaysian Constitution*, 2nd ed., Kuala Lumpur, Government Printer, 1977, p. 60.

20. See Article 40(1).

21. Article 45(2).

22. Harry E. Groves, *The Constitution of Malaysia*, Malaysia Publications Ltd., Singapore, 1964.

23. Ibid.

24. Article 43(1).

25. Article 68.

26. The word 'Parliament' is used in the Constitution. See Article 55.

27. Article 40(2).

28. So far, no request has been turned down, although at the State level the request for the dissolution of the Legislative Assembly of Trengganu was turned down by the Ruler in 1961, and that of the Kelantan Legislative Assembly by the Regent of Kelantan in 1977.

29. There are strong rumours that the Fourth Parliament will be dissolved in 1978, giving it a life-span of four years.

30. The Constituency of Sepang in Selangor in the 1959 Election.

31. The Constituency of Bangsar in Selangor in the 1964 Election.

32. See the Thirteenth Schedule to the 1957 Constitution.

33. Groves, op. cit., p. 66.

34. Some States have more children below 21 years than others. See the 1970 Population Census.

35. Some States have more non-citizens than others. Nearly half a million of the population are non-citizens.

36. 1970 Population Census.

37. See Harry E. Groves, *The Constitution of Malaysia*, Malaysia Publications, Singapore, 1964, Chap. V; Tun Mohd. Suffian, *An Introduction to the Constitution of Malaysia*, Kuala Lumpur, Government Printer, 1977; L. A. Sheridan & H. E. Groves, *The Constitution of Malaysia*, Oceana Publications, New York, 1967; L. A. Sheridan, *Malaya, Singapore, and the Borneo States: The Development of its Laws and*

Constitutions, London, Stevens, 1960.

38. Article 47.

39. A person is qualified after he has been discharged.

40. Dr. Burhanuddin Al-Hilmy did not contest the 1964 General Election after having been fined a sum in excess of $2,000 for an offence under the Companies Act.

41. No. 31 of 1952.

42. Jain, op. cit., pp. 22-3.

43. Dr. Neo Yee Pan and Dr. Goh Cheng Teik of the University of Malaya were elected to the House of Representatives in the 1974 Election, but resigned from the University after they were appointed Parliamentary Secretaries.

44. Senator Rafidah Aziz was appointed to the Senate when she was a full-time academician at the University of Malaya.

45. Article 160.

46. Article 53.

47. There are instances where government officers have been sentenced to imprisonment outside Malaysia. See *Augustine* v. *Commissioner of Police* [1964] 30 M.L.J. 438.

48. Datuk Mohd. Najib was elected to the Pekan Constituency in Pahang in the 1976 by-election when he was still an employee of PETRONAS, a wholly-owned government corporation.

49. Some of these provisions are made in the Representation of the People Act, 1951 of India.

50. Mr. Lim Kit Siang obtained a free pardon in 1975 for an offence of failure to lodge a return of election expenses.

51. Article 48(5).

52. Article 49.

53. Article 101(2) of the Indian Constitution.

54. A DAP opposition member Mr. Fan Yew Teng who was convicted and fined $2,000 for an offence under the Sedition Act, 1948 has indicated that he is not going to attend the rest of the 1977 Session of Parliament.

55. For example, Datuk Seri Dr. Mahathir Mohamad, Tan Sri Abdul Kadir Yusoff, Datin Paduka Hajjah Aishah Ghani, Tan Sri Mohamed Ghazali Shafie.

56. Article 52.

57. Tun Datuk Mustapha bin Datuk Harun and Mr. Lim Kit Siang were given such leave of absence. But no leave was granted to Mr. Fan Yew Teng after his conviction.

58. Dewan Ra'ayat, Standing Order, 7.

59. Ibid., S.O. 1-4.

60. Ibid., S.O. 2. The former Speaker, Tan Sri Datuk Nik Ahmed Kamil, died in office in December 1977.

61. The Constitution (Amendment) Act, No. 19/1964, in force from 30 July 1964.

62. Article 57(1A).

63. S.O. 7(1).

64. Ilbert, *Parliament*, 1973, p. 125.

65. S.O. 23.

66. Ibid.

67. S.O. 44.

68. S.O. 22.

69. S.O. 44.

70. Ibid.

71. S.O. 44.

72. Jain, op. cit., p. 38.

73. Article 58.

74. President of the Senate (Remuneration) Act, No. 2 of 1960 and Speaker (Remuneration) Act, No. 7 of 1960.

75. Jain, op. cit., p. 32.

76. Article 74 and Ninth Schedule.

77. Article 76.

78. H. M. Seervai, *Constitutional Law of India*, Bombay, Tripathi, 1976, Vol. 2, p. 1185.

79. *R.* v. *Burah* (1883) 9 A.C. 117; *Powell* v. *Apollo Candle Co.* (1885) 10 A.C. 282, putting an end to the doctrine that colonial legislatures were delegates of the British Parliament.

80. [1966] 1 M.L.J. 18.

81. [1968] 2 M.L.J. 137.

82. [1976] 2 M.L.J. 166.

83. Jain, op. cit., p. 59.

84. Wade and Bradley, *Constitutional Law*, Longmans, London, 7th ed., 1965, p. 125.

85. Ilbert, op. cit., p. 98.

86. Jain, op. cit., p. 38.

87. For a full list of amendments, see [1977] 2 M.L.J. cxv.

88. No. 2 of 1960.

89. No. 7 of 1960.

90. No. 4 of 1960.

91. Act No. 23.

92. No. 12 of 1963.

93. No. 15 of 1952.

94. The following constituencies were won on a basis of simple majority in the 1959 Election: Seremban Barat, Seremban Timor, Bruas, Sitiawan, Kuala Kangsar, Kampar, Bagan, Seberang Tengah, Seberang Selatan, Penang Selatan, Bangsar, Bukit Bintang, Setapak, Kuala Selangor, Sepang and Kapar. 1964 Election: Tanjong, Dato Keramat, Penang Selatan, Larut Selatan, Ulu Kinta, Kampar, Batu, Bangsar, Bukit Bintang, Damansara, Port Dickson, Seremban Timor, and Bandar Melaka. 1969 Election: Perlis Utara, Alor Setar, Sungei Petani, Lumut Selatan, Bruas, Tanjong Malim, Kuantan and Kapar. 1974 Election: Tanjong, Jelutong, Sungei Siput, Kinta, Bruas, Batu Gajah, Lumut, Petaling, Kepong, Serian, Ulu Rejang.

95. Following this arrangement, DAP will have 3 seats in the Senate, Pekemas 2 seats, Parti Ra'ayat Socialist Malaysia, 1 seat.

96. The constituency of Mantin in Negri Sembilan in the 1974 Election is an example.

97. The three constituencies in Negri Sembilan (Mantin, Seremban Timor, and Seremban Barat) have always been held by the DAP, the opposition party.

⁂ TAN SRI DATUK
MOHD. SALLEH BIN ABAS

8. Federalism in Malaysia—
Changes in the First Twenty Years

INTRODUCTION: THE CONCEPT OF FEDERALISM

IN order to find a definition in which I can give a historical interpretation of the changes in the Constitution of this country, it is necessary to elucidate the federal idea as an evolutionary process. The
choice of a definition must go beyond an identification function
'because no federal state in the world, which possessed real political
life, was conceivable without a continuous conflict between unitary
and federal efforts'.[1]

For this reason it has been argued that the identification definition
is not inconsistent with the evolutionary concept. The two ap-
proaches may be fused together as

... an institutional arrangement reflecting a particular social pattern present in a society or group of societies, initially formulated in a bargaining
process involving two different levels of governments seeking agreement on
common aims and interests, and constantly being reformulated in practice
in response to changes in the social pattern ... and in response to shifts in
loyalties from one level of government to another.[2]

The identification process has brought about various results. To
Riker, the following characteristics must emerge, *viz.* (i) two levels of
government rule the same land and people, (ii) each level has at least
one area of action in which it is autonomous and (iii) there is some
guarantee of autonomy of each government in its own sphere.[3]

Wheare insists on the existence of co-ordinate independent governments at Federal and State levels and sees it as a 'method of

dividing powers so that the general and regional governments are each within a sphere, co-ordinate and independent'.[4] This is Wheare's 'federal principle'.

With the foregoing before us, changes in a federal system are acceptable, indeed, imperative. Their significance must be seen in the objectives and compromises of the bargaining process and from this may be drawn the factors for the successful maintenance of a particular federation.

HISTORICAL BACKGROUND: 1895-1957[5]

The relative emphasis assigned to the historical milieu of the federal idea in the Federation of Malaya covering a period transcending six decades before 1957 needs some justification. The subject requires an understanding of the reasons and motivations of this system of constitution and government. And those ideas must be traced to their origin; hence to a point when the system was initially introduced and the reasons therefor. For Malaya this date is 1895 when the Federated Malay States comprising Perak, Selangor, Negri Sembilan, and Pahang were 'federated' under the authority of a British Resident-general.

Federalism in Malaya is to a certain extent a tried system. First introduced in 1895, it was succeeded by varying governmental exercises running through centralized and decentralized forms followed by an abortive attempt at unitary government.[6] Finally there was a swing-back to the federal system in 1957, which system is the pattern for the Malaysian Federation after suitable amendments.

THE FEDERATED MALAY STATES (1895)

Malaya in the 1800s was politically divided. The nine Malay States of Perak, Selangor, Negri Sembilan, Pahang, Johore, Kelantan, Trengganu, Kedah, and Perlis were under varying degrees of British influence. By 1895, just before the Federation, Perak, Selangor, Negri Sembilan and Pahang had accepted British Advisers who were in fact the effective rulers while the Malay Sultans had lost a substantial part of their powers. The reasons put forward have been numerous. The Settlements of Penang and Singapore had expressed demands that the hinterland which was rich in resources be brought under British control for their welfare and prosperity as trading places. 1873 marked the turning point in the British colonial attitude in respect of the Malay States. Britain found it 'incumbent to employ such influence as they possessed with the native princes, to rescue if possible, these fertile and productive countries from the ruin which must befall them if the present disorders continue unchecked'.[7] These disorders were allegedly occasioned by piracy and various rival claimants to the Sultanates. The only observation I would want to make on this point has been very succinctly put by Alfred P. Rubin. He says:

[T]he Malay Rulers' lack of foresight and lack of flexibility are more than matched by the European penchant for using the theories and concepts of international law to justify in a multitude of legalistic generalities acts that could not be reconciled with the rules of international law that were held to apply in Europe.[8]

By accepting a British Resident, the States concerned agreed to the appointment of a British officer whose advice must be followed in all matters except Malay religion and custom. The States undertook that they would have no dealings with other foreign powers except through Britain. In return, Britain promised protection against external threats.

Under the rule of the separate Residents, each State developed at its own pace and emphasis. There was no co-ordination amongst them. Each constituent State still continued to be administered by the Resident who was ultimately responsible to the Resident-general. In theory the latter worked under the direction and control of the colonial governor. Each government department was responsible to the relevant Resident. But more important departments were headed by two officers, one State and the other Federal.

It was a centralized form of government. Although the State Councils retained their legislative powers, it was the Adviser (a Federal officer) who drafted the laws. The State Councils merely ratified laws made by the Federal Government. To the extent that there was some independence and sovereignty of the States and Malay Rulers, it was merely a fiction. They were under an obligation to adhere to the advice of the Residents in all matters except Malay religion and culture. The Conference of Malay Rulers as established was some measure of recognition of some participation by the Malay Rulers in government.

The tendency for a central bias was evident in the growing powers of the central government *vis-à-vis* the status of the constituent states. By 1909 state powers (including that of the Malay Rulers) were reduced to matters of local importance and the execution of the directions of the Federal Government. State dissatisfaction was apparent: as a result the powers of the Resident-general were reduced to accommodate these demands. But the tussle between centralization and decentralization continued until the outbreak of the First World War.

THE UNFEDERATED MALAY STATES

Meanwhile, the unfederated States of Kelantan, Trengganu, Kedah, and Perlis were anxious not to fall under direct control of the British. The example of the Federated Malay States, whose Malay Rulers were robbed of their sovereignty, heightened their anxiety to maintain independence. But they were also helpless in their quest to shed Siamese suzerainty, which was often reasserted by war threats. For this reason, Britain managed to conclude various arrangements with these States, whereby the latter were promised protection in return for control of their foreign affairs and considerable influence in their governments. Thus Britain consolidated her powers in the Malay States of Kelantan, Trengganu, Kedah, and Perlis.

The Settlements of Penang and Malacca were by 1895 colonies, transfer having been effected from the East India Company.

THE MALAYAN UNION (1946)

The foregoing state of affairs continued substantially until 1946. As a result of the Second World War and the need to constitute a politically viable state of Malaya the British government mooted the idea of the Malayan Union, comprising the Malay States and the Settlements of Penang and Malacca as a unitary state. It was not really the first movement, the British having attempted in the mid-1930s to implement this system. It was considered that the post-war period provided the opportune moment for revolutionary reform.

In the British scheme, it was hoped that Malaya would be granted independence in the future. When the eventuality arose this political unit would be able to stand on its feet both economically and politically. The Malayan Union of 1946 proved abortive. The Malays opposed the union; its basis rejected their special position as sons of the soil. The liberal franchise laws would disturb the Malay-Chinese balance. They did not wish to be overwhelmed by a race which had little, if any, real loyalty and commitment to the country.[9] Centralization would also deprive the Malay Rulers of their power.

On the other hand, the two Straits Settlements of Penang and Malacca were not totally encouraged to join such a unitary state where the identity of each constituent state would eventually be eradicated. Indeed, the Straits Settlements Chinese were reluctant to give up their status as British subjects. The British attempt to draw up a system which was supposed to have taken account of the interests of the Malay Rulers and the population was not totally beyond reproach. All these factors put together could not have supported even the initial years of the union; it was doomed from the start.

Be that as it may, the Malayan Union is a landmark in the history of Malay politics in that 1946 saw the birth of concerted Malay nationalism in the founding of the United Malay National Organisation (UMNO).[10] But another consequence of this resistance was the intensification of the latent animosity between the two dominant races, the Malays and the Chinese.

After this failure, the British had to find a more acceptable political arrangement. By then the British attitude had changed considerably; the Malay rejection of the Malayan Union served as a caution that this hostility and lack of co-operation could degenerate into a completely anti-British attitude. The alternative chosen was the Federal system embracing the Malay States and the Settlements of Penang and Malacca. This proposed dual governmental set-up would secure the twin objectives, *viz*., a sufficiently big state and the integrity of the individual states and their Rulers. It was conceived as a pro-centre arrangement; the Federal Government would have a preponderance of power.

OPPOSITION TO AND THE SUCCESSFUL MAINTENANCE OF THE FEDERATION

Although this Federation was to survive until 1963, and as an independent nation after 1957, it was not free from internal opposition. Four attempts at secession threatened the Federation; by Penang between 1948 and 1949 and again between 1953 and 1957, by Johore and Kelantan separately between 1955 and 1956.

Penang was disenchanted by the dismantling of the Straits Settlements which had also comprised Singapore. Where previously the Chinese population was the dominant majority, the influence and status this gave would be lost when united with the Malay States. Further, the Penang Chinese had identified themselves as British subjects with loyalties to Britain. The loss by Penang of its free port status was an additional grievance to a population which was largely composed of traders. This placed them at a certain disadvantage when compared to the position of Singapore traders. Not only were they economically 'deprived' but the Straits-born Chinese did not see much opportunity for political equality with the Malays and would therefore lose out in comparison with the Singapore Chinese who were advancing in political participation and maturity. But this resistance to federate had to contend with Malay and British opposition. Although this opposition was differently motivated, it was apparent that the British were not prepared to go against Malay opinion. Thus this attempt at secession was not able to marshal concerted movement and soon died. The Federal Government too agreed to eliminate the problem of the Penang traders by passing the Customs Duties (Penang) Bill 1949 and the Rubber Excise (Penang) Bill 1949[11] which removed the difficulty occasioned by the loss of free port status.

Again between 1953 and 1957 Penang tried to secede, but like the earlier attempt it was disorganized and short-lived. It was directed against Malay domination in the Federal Government and motivated by Chinese fear of lack of political eminence and power in the new set-up. Set against this UMNO was faced with the dual task of moderating extremist Malay demands and meeting the Chinese grievances at some meaningful level. UMNO agreed that the franchise policy regarding the Straits-born Chinese be relaxed and *jus soli* was accorded. At the same time these citizens were allowed to retain their status as British subjects.

Johore too did not view the federal idea with much favour. The fact that federation would bring about the abolition of British Advisers did not endear the idea to the Johore Ruler who regarded the Adviser as an essential officer for the smooth running of the state. Speculation that the Ruler might also have been anxious to retain his personal power and social standing has been made. However, as circumstances then indicated it was apparent that if Johore was adamant in its opposition, it had also to reconcile itself to the idea of being the lone objector among the Malay States. It finally succumbed to Kuala Lumpur's persuasion and signed the 1957 Federation of Malaya Agreement.

Initially Kelantan also resisted the Federation. Kelantan saw the Federation as a likely loss of Malay rights to the Chinese. The objective of the Kelantan Malay United Front which championed this cause was amongst others the restoration of the supremacy of the Islamic religion, the Malay language, and Malay customs. The movement however obtained only minimal support. Its poor financial condition did not make the idea of secession attractive or even possible. This was the last resistance to the 1957 Federation.

The foregoing demonstrates that the most important single factor for the maintenance of the Federation is the will of the populace. The 'separatists' patent helplessness'[12] is nothing more than insufficient support for a concerted will. That will should be considered in any federal-state manoeuvres to ensure the continued well-being of the Federation.

THE 1957 CONSTITUTION AS A FEDERAL CONSTITUTION

The choice of a system of government is influenced by circumstances both of the nation and its people. Whatever the basis, the relationship between the government and its citizens may be likened to that of trustee and beneficiary. A federal government does not detract from it simply because it is a second level of government in the dual set-up. When the federal State unites the individual States, the citizens of such individual States become at the same time also citizens of the federal State. These citizens through their States have given life to the Federal Government whose basis coincides with that of the State governments, *viz*., the will of the citizens. As a trustee the Federal Government owes it to the citizens to ensure that the Constitution, which regulates the basic framework of its relationship with States and the citizens, be honoured both in the letter and in spirit.

THE FEDERAL-STATE RELATIONSHIP

The federal-state relationship and allocation of powers reveal a federal constitution with a central bias.[13] This was the express intention of the Reid Commission[14] and was one of the terms of reference of the Working Committee for the drafting of the Constitution, the others being:

(a) that the identity of each of the Malay States and Settlements of Penang and Malacca be preserved,

(b) that it should provide a suitable constitutional framework for the then pending independence and should provide a suitable franchise policy, according political rights to those who are loyal to the country while taking into consideration the position of the Malay population because they do not have an alternative homeland or allegiance.[15]

A FEDERAL BIAS AND THE CONSTITUTIONAL GUARANTEES OF STATE CONSTITUTIONS

As considerable difficulty had to be overcome because of the anxiety of the Rulers of the Malay States that they should maintain their status as Heads of States, the care taken to ensure the continuance of State governments with meaningful attributes of such governments is reflected in the relative independence of the States. Each State government is, within defined legislative and executive powers, independent. The legislative powers are divided into the Federal, State and Concurrent Lists; residuary powers remain with the States. The nature and extent of such Federal powers clearly reveal a Federal preponderance. Matters of local importance remain with the States but it is evident that matters of the first level of governmental importance like external affairs, defence, internal security, finance, civil law and procedure, and the administration of justice, citizenship, trade, commerce and industry, are within Federal competence.[16] Where any State law is inconsistent with Federal law, the latter prevails and to the extent of the inconsistency the State law is void.[17]

Division of executive authority similarly is in favour of the Federal Government, the extent of Federal and State powers being co-extensive with their respective legislative powers. In respect of matters under the Concurrent List, the Federal executive authority is determined by the particular legislation. In matters exclusively in the State List, Federal executive authority may be exercised for the limited purposes, *inter alia*, of inquiries, surveys, and statistics; research, the provision and maintenance of experimental stations, advice and technical assistance to States. The Federal Government may also inspect State activities where the department and work are in respect of matters not exclusively within State legislative competence. Further, a State shall so exercise its executive authority as to ensure compliance with any Federal law applying to that State, and as not to impede the exercise of the executive authority of the Federation.[18]

The financial provisions in Part VII of the Constitution allocate the important sources of revenue to the Federal Government. Except for revenue from lands and forests, there are no significant sources for the States. The Federal Government is also the main taxing authority[19] and controls the borrowing powers[20] of the States. Where a deficit occurs, the Federal Government supplements by way of allocations and grants.[21]

The Reid Commission sought to guarantee State independence by defining in a more specific form the revenue that is to accrue to State governments. It provides for a formula based on the population[22] and the mileage of roads[23] in the State and a certain percentage of certain taxes collected. But the idea remains that the State would chiefly remain financially dependent on the Federal Government.

In addition to the above, the Federal Government is also empowered to assume powers of a unitary state under circumstances of emergency. Article 150 enables the Federal authority in an emergency to legislate in respect of matters exclusively within States' jurisdiction. Outside an emergency, it may legislate on State subjects only for the limited purposes outlined below:

(a) for the purpose of implementing any treaty, agreement or convention between the Federation and any other country, or any decision of an international organization of which the Federation is a member; or

(b) for the purpose of promoting uniformity of the laws of two or more States; or

(c) if so requested by the Legislative Assembly of any State.[24]

Side by side with this bias for the centre, there are however certain constitutional guarantees[25] for State constitutions. But whatever guarantees there are, perhaps the most important is the process of amendment of the Constitution. Described as the cornerstone of a constitution, the process determines the efficacy of the constitution. This Constitution provides three methods of amendment[26] and these are:

(a) by an Act requiring a simple majority;
(b) by an Act requiring a two-thirds majority in both Houses of Parliament at the second and third readings; and
(c) by an Act which having satisfied the conditions in (b), further obtains the consent of the Conference of Rulers.

The second method provides the general method to be employed with respect to the majority of the constitutional provisions; the third method directs itself to matters relating to the Conference of Rulers, the precedence of Rulers, the Federal guarantee of Rulers, and the special position and privileges of the Malays. As more detailed observations will be made on the amendment process in a later part of this essay, it may be sufficient here merely to note the case of *The Government of the State of Kelantan* v. *The Government of the Federation of Malaya and Tunku Abdul Rahman Putra Al-Haj*[27] as an interpretation of the amendment process.

In this case, the State of Kelantan asked for a declaration that the Malaysia Agreement, signed by the Federation of Malaya, the United Kingdom, Sabah, Sarawak, and Singapore on 9 July 1963 and the subsequent Malaysia Act, 1963 were null and void or alternatively not binding on the State of Kelantan. The State's arguments were, *inter alia*, that as Malaysia involved the consent of all the constituent States of the existing Federation of Malaya, the acts of the Federal Government were null and void as Kelantan had given no consent. In rejecting these arguments, Thomson C.J. reasoned that the formation of Malaysia by merger with Singapore, Sabah, and Sarawak was not something so 'fundamentally revolutionary' as to require the consent of the States. This has been criticized partly because the test is 'too vague and lacks definite criterion for its determination'.[28] But, it is submitted that some limit for this concept may be found in the following passage of the judgment:

It is true in a sense that the new Federation is something different from the old one. It will contain more States. It will have a different name. But if that state of affairs be brought about by means contained in the Constitution itself and which were contained in it at the time of the 1957 Agreement, of which it is an integral part, I cannot see how it can possibly be made out that there has been any breach of any foundation pact among the original parties. In bringing about these changes Parliament has done no more than exercise the powers which were given to it in 1957 by the constituent States including the State of Kelantan.[29]

This is consistent with the concept of Parliamentary supremacy which is fundamental to a Westminster type of democracy of which the Federation claims to be an example.

The Reid Commission had attempted to provide a further guarantee of State Constitutions in the structure and powers of the Upper House, the Senate.[30] The Senate was originally composed of 22 Senators appointed by States and 16 appointed by the Yang di-Pertuan Agong. This proportion in favour of State Senators was designed to constitute a restraining safeguard against constitutional amendments requiring a two-thirds majority in both Houses. This function of the Senate could only be realized if those State Senators continued to identify themselves as guardians of State interests but it is a trite observation that these Senators, paid by and associated with the Federal Government, soon forget this aspect of their role and link *vis-à-vis* the States.

From the foregoing it may be fair to say that States do not have much real power to guarantee their independence. Further if it is remembered that the preponderance of financial powers is with the Federal Government, such power is further diminished. The Federal Government's financial power can be used as a lever to require States to fall in line with Federal policies; the possibility of the abuse of this power should not be totally discounted.

The financial dependence of States as earlier alluded to must have proved difficult for a State whose government is controlled by a party different from the party that rules at Federal level. If starved of finance a politically 'wayward' state may be forced to seek some other means of finance. Kelantan in the 1960s is a good example.

Kelantan had been a strong Pan-Malayan Islamic Party (an opposition party) stronghold. The 1959 general elections campaign by the Alliance (the party in government) in Kelantan was highly intense. And as not unusual in politics, a significant inducement was proferred, this time in a promise to build a bridge over the Kelantan River—the Sultan Putera Yahya Bridge. Road signs indicating the proposed constructions were testimony of that promise. However, the Pan-Malayan Islamic Party was returned to power and with that Kelantan was also forced to finance the proposed bridge. It may have been for reasons of necessity or the impelling political need to 'deliver the goods' that Kelantan undertook to build the bridge. This was not without heavy cost. Kelantan gave a timber concession to a private company getting in return 'prepayment of royalties' amounting to M$2.5 million. It was in effect a borrowing arrangement for which large tracts of timber land were pledged as security. Subsequent years reveal the folly of the venture because it was realized that land of that extent and importance is not an appropriate matter for the granting of this concession.

Whatever the political realities may be, the ultimate burden is with the *ra'ayat*—the people. It is therefore with considerable relief that we see a changed attitude of the Federal Government as regards the allocation of funds. Allocations to the States under the Third Malaysia Plan (1976-1980) show a commendable rationale, in that

... the distribution of development expenditure by States has been based on the need ... to redirect development expenditure to the poorer States as well as the depressed areas in the other States. The priority States are Kedah, Perlis, Kelantan, Trengganu, and Malacca, as they are the lowest income States in the country with income levels well below those of other States.[31]

But of even greater significance is the Federal Government's attitude in the settlement of the petroleum matter with the States. When the Petroleum Development Act 1974 was to be enacted the property and control over petroleum within the three-mile limit had to be transferred completely from the States to the Federal Government. In regard to petroleum lying outside this limit it was the view of the Federal Government that it did not belong to the States. Nevertheless as a gesture of goodwill and to maintain harmony within the Federation, the Federal Government was prepared to make some kind of payment to the relevant States. The moral responsibility reflected in this arrangement shows a more enlightened attitude of the Federal Government towards its role and responsibility to the States and the *ra'ayat*.

CONSTITUTIONAL AMENDMENTS, 1957-1962

Briefly, these amendments show a bias for the Federal Government. In 1960, for the sake of co-ordination, the National Council for Local Government (NCLG)[32] was constituted, consisting of one representative from each State and ten representatives of the Federal Government. Here, through the organization, the Federal power to co-ordinate is effected through a national body: it is a further inroad into State matters.

The example of the NCLG as a national body to formulate policies and advise on matters within State jurisdiction has other equivalents, in the National Land Council[33] for example.

Article 34 was also amended[34] to enable the Yang di-Pertuan Agong to amend the Constitution of a State of which he is the Ruler for the purpose of bringing that State Constitution into accord with the Federation. This goes beyond the amendments relating to the essential provisions contemplated under Article 71.

Article 159 was amended[35] excepting amendments 'made for or in connexion with the admission of any State to the Federation or its association with the States thereof, or any modification made as to the application of this Constitution to a State previously so admitted or constituted'. Hence, a simple majority is sufficient to 'modify' the application of the Federal Constitution to a State. The scope of 'modification' is not clear. In conjunction with this, it has been noted that Article 63 protects the propriety of acts of the Legislature as privileged;[36] hence may be seen the full implication of this amendment.

Up to 1962, the power of Parliament to legislate for States for the purpose of ensuring uniformity of law excluded the subject of 'mining leases'. Amendments in 1962 removed this disability and as a *quid pro quo* Article 110[37] was also amended. The Federal Government is enabled to assign a proportion of the export duty on minerals other than tin to the States and in consequence empowers the Federal Government to control the royalties charged under the mining leases. This was prompted by agitation by the mining industry which previously had to pay fees to the States in respect of the mining leases, besides other forms of taxes and charges in relation to these industries. The consequential enactments[38] relieve miners of further payments of fees or similar charges for mining leases.

That was the Constitution as at 1962; it was pro-centre. Fortunately the exercise of the Federal powers up to then demonstrated a reasonable observance of the spirit of the Constitution.

THE FORMATION OF MALAYSIA

The various inhibiting factors[39] to the formation of Malaysia in 1963 are shown in the final arrangements. The Government of Malaya found the idea attractive for two main reasons. Firstly, the communist expansion in Singapore had to be contained; it was too close a neighbour for the security of the two countries to be considered as independent of the other. Paradoxically, the Federal Government attempted to contain this expansion and ward off the communist threat by including Singapore within its territorial jurisdiction. Secondly, the States of Sabah and Sarawak with a predominantly non-Chinese population would help to balance a federation which would otherwise be overwhelmingly Chinese with a Malaya-Singapore merger.

For Sabah and Sarawak the choice had really been independence within Malaysia or continuation as British colonies. They were not as yet able to be independent on their own; British withdrawal was imminent, targeted to be by 1972, and the defence problem was one of their major preoccupations. Also, merger with Singapore would bring certain economic advantages.

Singapore was at that point still a British colony although independent in all internal affairs. For almost similar reasons, it was only through merger with Malaysia that Singapore could hope for early independence.

R. S. Milne and K. J. Ratnam describe the Malaysian bargaining process thus: 'There is ... an investment of utilitarian assets by the élite units in exchange for some symbolic (identitive) gratification, such as that gained from the status of leadership.'[40]

With the admission of the new States by virtue of the Malaysia Act[41] several changes were made to the Federal Constitution to reflect the terms of the Agreement[42] between the Federation Government, the British Government, and each of the three new constituent States. The arrangements for the new Federation were further clarified and amplified in the Inter-Governmental Committee Report 1962.[43]

The relationships between the Federal Government and each of these new States are not similar because of the differences of the bargaining processes. It has been said that paradoxically the weakness of Sabah and Sarawak gave them a better edge in the bargain. Substantially the form and substance of the Federation of Malaya Constitution remained and there was no change effected in respect of the original States. But the division of powers between the Federal Government on the one hand and each of the State Governments of Singapore, Sabah, and Sarawak on the other is considerably different.[44] The State List (for Sabah and Sarawak) is more extensive; for Singapore it was even more so. It must be remembered that when Singapore joined the Federation she was an independent government except for defence and external affairs. Similarly, the supplementary Concurrent List for Sabah and Sarawak is more extensive.

Special arrangements regarding religion, the national language, the position of the natives in Sabah and Sarawak, and immigration are made in the Constitution and the Inter-Governmental Committee Report.[45] To implement these special arrangements on immigration, the Federation passed the Immigration Act, 1959/1963 by which Sabah and Sarawak retain the powers of control and entry into and residence in these States. They are also empowered to treat Federal citizens as non-citizens for these purposes.[46]

The functions and powers of the various consultative bodies mentioned earlier are not the same in respect of Sabah and Sarawak;[47] indeed this facility of control is absent in respect of these States.

The constitutional guarantees of State Constitutions are more definite in respect of Sabah and Sarawak. However before this is elaborated upon, it must be noted that Article 150 (emergency powers) remains unchanged even in respect of these States. Articles 71, 159 and 161E guarantee the constitutions of these two States. Article 71, dealing with the essential provisions which a State Constitution has to incorporate, applies to Sabah and Sarawak with modifications. Effectively, up to 1975, their constitutions as on Malaysia Day may continue.[48]

The amendment process as contained in Article 159 has been referred to earlier. With the incorporation of Sabah and Sarawak a fourth method of amendment was introduced.[49] This requires a two-thirds majority in both Houses at the second and third readings, and further, the consent of the governor of the State (Sabah or Sarawak) concerned. The subject matters which call for this process are provided for in Article 161E and relate to citizenship, immigration, the constitution and jurisdiction of the High Court in Borneo, appointment, removal and suspension of judges of that Court, the State Legislative List, the Federal-State financial arrangements, religion, official language, special treatment of natives, and the allocation to the State of representatives in the House of Representatives before the end of August 1970. Even as regards the amendment process, the States of Sabah and Sarawak have a different relationship with the Federation, one which definitely secures greater independence.

In relation to the Senate as a constitutional safeguard, the arrangement under Malaysia originally left the proportion of State Senators to federally appointed Senators at 28 to 22. But soon in 1964, the appointed Senators outnumbered the State Senators by 32 to 28;[50] the separation of Singapore reduced the latter group further to 26. Whatever potential the Senate had originally under the 1957 Constitution and later under the Malaysian modification was lost by this modification.

The Malaysian arrangement therefore prescribes a different Federal-State relationship for Sabah and Sarawak as compared with that of the original eleven States. Additional sources of revenue are available to Sabah and Sarawak. For example, both States may make laws imposing sales tax,[51] are assigned import and excise duties on petroleum goods, export duty on timber and other forest products, revenues from ports and harbours (excepting federal ports and harbours).[52] Both States also receive additional grants from the Federal Government.[53]

CHANGES IN THE CONSTITUTION, 1963-1977

In 1965, the Constitution had to be amended again to effect the secession of Singapore from the Federation. The Constitution and Malaysia (Singapore Amendment) Act, 1965 was preceded by the Separation of Singapore Agreement, 1965. Consequential amendments were effected through further amendments in 1966.[54]

It is worth noting that the Constitution does not provide for secession. Is such a provision necessary? India, Australia, and the U.S.A. similarly do not have such a provision. It has sometimes been advanced that one of the main reasons for the disintegration of the short-lived West Indian Federation was the lack of such a provision;[55] the Federation being a package deal, the withdrawal of any one constituent State meant a complete disintegration. Some literature on the U.S. Constitution suggests that the decision to federate is irrevocable; others feel that the subject falls under treaty law. The example of Singapore in 1965 suggests that it must be effected through agreement and no unilateral action is enough to support a secession.

The same inquiry may be directed to the subject of expulsion. If expulsion through a two-thirds majority is possible, the implication of the present allocation of seats in Parliament—104 (Malaya), 16 (Sabah) and 24 (Sarawak)—is worth some consideration.

The resolution of the foregoing lies in an understanding of the full import of Article 159 which prescribes the methods of amendment to the Constitution. The matters within the purview of this Article include 'addition and repeal' in respect of the Constitution. The observation[56] made in the earlier part of this essay referring to the scope of matters which may be amended is pertinent in this regard. Also, the secession of Singapore was a pragmatic solution. The Federal power could have been exercised to prevent Singapore from seceding but such decision must also be accompanied by the will and capacity to force an unwilling State to remain a member at whatever cost.

After 1966 no further important amendments bearing on the federal aspects of the Constitution were made until 1971. Article 153 was amended by the Constitution (Amendment) Act, 1971[57] to 'provide for parity of natives of any of the Borneo States with Malays in West Malaysia'. Two objectives are served. Firstly, while prior to this amendment, the natives were entitled to reservations in the public service, there was no such reservation of scholarships, and training and education facilities; this amendment secures this objective. Secondly, priority is secured for places in institutions of higher education where the places of study offered is less than the number of qualified persons.

This Act also increased the relevance of the consent of the Conference of Rulers for amendments of the Constitution. Article 159(5) entrenched those provisions relating to matters regarded as 'sensitive' by requiring the consent of the Conference and this procedure for amendment also applies as regards the amendment itself.

In 1973, in contemplation of the establishment of the Federal Territory out of part of the territory of the State of Selangor, the Constitution was amended to provide that the definition of territory of a State be amended by a simple majority if the amendment is consequential upon consent given by the Legislative Assembly of the State and the Conference of Rulers.[58] By a further amendment Act in 1973,[59] the Federal Territory was established after passage in the Legislative Assembly of Selangor of an Enactment to that effect. The Conference of Rulers had also given their consent. The jurisdiction and sovereignty over the Federal Territory now vest in the Federal Government. Transitional provisions in respect of State laws were made; otherwise all executive and legislative powers vest in the Federation. Consequential upon this, the membership of the House of Representatives was reconstituted and two seats are allocated to the Federal Territory.[60]

Up to 1976,[61] the Constitution seemed to indicate a federation of the Federation of Malaya with the States of Sabah and Sarawak, the original States of the earlier Federation being described together under the style of 'the States of Malaya, namely, Johore, Kedah, Kelantan, etc.'. To correct this awkwardness, the Malayan States are subsequently enumerated with all the other constituent States in alphabetical order.

This Act also effected a new relationship between the Yang di-Pertuan Agong and the States of Sabah and Sarawak. Initially, as part of the special arrangements on religion the Yang di-Pertuan Agong was not accorded the status of Head of the Muslim religion in these States, unlike the situation in the former colonies of Malacca and Penang. This difference was finally abolished in 1976,[62] so that the Yang di-Pertuan Agong is now Head of Islam in Sabah, Sarawak, Penang, and Malacca.

Along with the foregoing, the same Act also increased the Federal List, taking away prevention and extinguishment of fire from the Concurrent List in respect of all Malay States, Penang, and Malacca.[63] Finally in 1977, further amendments were required; the objective was to increase the capitation grants to the poorer States.[64]

It has been remarked that the frequent need to amend the Constitution is in stark contrast to the American Constitution which in its span of 182 years, has been amended only twenty-six times.[65] If we refer again to J. Rudolph Jr.'s idea[66] of the constitution as a revolutionary process and that changes are imperative, especially in the earlier years to find a balance, the comparison should not unduly worry the observer.

CITIZENSHIP AND NATION BUILDING

This subject has been taken up separately because of its importance as far back as 1946. The importance of providing a reasonable franchise policy has been a dominant factor; by 'reasonable' is meant that it should serve two purposes. The policy must be broad enough to enable those who have attachments of birth and/or a suitable residence period to become citizens. On the other hand this basis should be limited in order that the interests of the Malays (and the natives of Sabah and Sarawak) be protected as persons who have no alternative home and allegiance. Failure to find this balance was responsible for the failure of the 1946 Malayan Union.

The 1948 formulation of the citizenship policy preserved the status of the Malays. Citizenship status was conferred upon them automatically. It reflects an assimilationist policy giving the definition of 'Malay' a cultural meaning.[67] Generally this was a swing-back to the pre-Malayan Union days of recognizing Malaya as mainly a Malay country and if others were to be accorded the status of citizens, they must demonstrate a suitable degree of assimilation of the Malay culture.

The preparation of the 1957 Constitution further increased the significance of the citizenship laws with independence round the corner. It witnessed a broadening of the base for citizenship. The principle of *jus soli* for births after Merdeka Day (Independence Day) was accepted without qualification.[68] However, citizenship on the basis of United Kingdom citizenship though permissible was limited to a stipulated period by Article 170; it had the effect of making Federal citizenship more distinct in that non-local qualifications would not be a permanent basis.

In 1962, the citizenship laws were tightened up by further localizing the requirements; *jus soli* was qualified.[69] In cases where qualified persons were previously 'entitled' to citizenship, these amendments made this a 'discretion' of the authority.[70]

In addition to the considerations alluded to in the foregoing, the 1963 modifications of the citizenship laws had also to take into account the following:

(a) the recognition of the natives of Sabah and Sarawak and their special interests; and

(b) the special position of Singapore; the bargain with Singapore for its greater autonomy is reflected in these provisions.[71]

Generally speaking, birth and residence in the States admit of qualification for citizenship of the Federation. Such residence and birth in Singapore however were not recognized for the purpose of citizenship in the Federation. It was also possible to retain the status of a Federal citizen if the subject had had his Singapore citizenship withdrawn. This would be so where citizenship in the Federation was granted on qualification such as would apply to a foreigner.[72] The effects of such citizenship were however limited and the citizen concerned could not exercise the normal political rights in Singapore.

At least until 1957 citizenship in the Federation did not confer the status of nationality as understood in international law. This was not possible because the Federation was not a nation but a multiple dependency under the colonial rule of the British Government. In fact the 1957 Constitution too has often been criticized for this. Prior to 1976, it was legally permissible for a Malayan (Malaysian, after 1963) citizen to retain his Commonwealth citizenship and exercise rights, the nature of which is generally those accorded to citizens only. This observation refers to British subjects under the British Nationality Act, 1948. This capacity was restricted from October 1963 whereby the use of a passport issued by a foreign authority as a travel document is deemed to be the voluntary claim and exercise of a right exclusive to its citizens only. This use constitutes a ground for deprivation of citizenship by the Federation.

STATE PAROCHIALISM AND NATION BUILDING

It may be reiterated here that the 1957 Constitution was conceived as a Federation with a strong bias for the centre. Up to 1963 and even to date, this relationship between the Federal Government and each of the original eleven States, has existed *de jure* and *de facto*. The 1963 merger with Sabah and Sarawak is not to be regarded as a substantial shift in that policy; the constitutional arrangements and the Inter-Governmental Committee Report which gave far greater autonomy to Sabah and Sarawak in matters which are Federal in relation to the original States were meant to provide an interim measure before a suitable degree of assimilation is achieved.[73] It is unlikely that Malaysia could ever be a true nation if factors inhibitive to nation building are to be maintained permanently. Initially contemplated to extend only for the first five-year period, these factors have persisted well beyond 1968. Some of these differences are noted in a later part of this essay.[74]

Malaysia cannot afford economic parochialism in the States. The reasons for the 1895 Federation highlighted the need for economic co-ordination in the development of the rubber and tin industries. In fact any national economy requires co-ordination. 'A prime necessity in any federal government which is to survive is some flexible means of prohibiting the tendency of member States to go their own economic ways, to the community detriment.'[75] Of the significance of this power in the U.S.A. federal system, Justice Holmes said,

> I do not think the U.S. would come to an end if we lost our power to declare an act of Congress void. I do not think the Union would be imperilled if we did not make that declaration as to the laws of the several States. For one in my place sees how often a local policy prevails with those who are not trained to national views and how often action is taken that embodies what the common clause is meant to end.[76]

For reasons of history and national aspirations, a typically local matter may assume national importance. It is with this observation that the following selected areas are discussed and justified for federal 'interference'.

Firstly, industrialization: it is a federal function. The powers to incorporate for the main purpose of trade, commerce, and industry is also a Federal function. By the Incorporation (State Legislatures Competency) Act, 1962, State Governments are empowered to make laws with respect to the incorporation of certain persons and bodies within a State in relation to, *inter alia*, the development of urban and rural areas. On this legal basis, the State Economic Development Corporations were established and they in turn fanned out into various subsidiaries and sub-subsidiaries, and by the end of 1976 this number totalled 436. There was until 1976 no facility for the Federal Government to monitor their progress. The Federal Industrial Development Authority through its advisory capacity in matters of industrialization assists in providing some form of co-ordination in instances where such bodies approach the Authority for advice. Otherwise, there is every possibility of competition and duplication between State and Federal governments. This inevitably results in waste. The financial burden of State projects, however, is not always independent of Federal resources. The Federal Government provides loans to States (sometimes after borrowing the necessary money from other institutions, e.g. the World Bank and Asian Development Bank) or guarantees State borrowings. The amounts involved are substantial.[77]

There has been considerable concern by the Federal Government regarding the viability of these State projects and in 1976 the Incorporation (State Legislatures Competency) Act, 1962 was amended[78] to provide for some control and supervision by the Federal Government.

The justification for Federal interference or need for recommending that government assume a firm posture in its business dealings is apparent in the numerous failures or near failures of government projects. Over-anxiety of State governments to launch projects has sometimes made them neglect the need for feasibility studies. In one project it was found that of the 27,000 acres assigned for the planting of the crop, the larger part of 20,000 acres was not suited for such cultivation. This was never foreseen because no feasibility study had been undertaken.

In a few cases the government party has to make payment for which there is no real reason. Such payments are sometimes prompted by a compelling need to negotiate for a variation or termination of an agreement which the government finds is not profitable for its purpose. Such discovery made at a subsequent date in some cases is also accompanied by the further difficulty of terminating the agreement. Often a hasty negotiation has landed the government party with an agreement which is one-sided in favour of the other party. For example, in 1968, the State of Malacca contracted with a private developer company for the construction of a satellite town and housing estate in Ayer Keroh. The consideration included, *inter alia*, payment of an administrative fee for the supervision and management of the whole of the development area at a fixed rate of seven per centum of all costs of the plan, fees, and other charges. The company claims that the seven per centum refers to all works carried out in the development area whether by the company or other persons. The contract, being loosely worded, leaves room for various interpretations.

Apart from lack of care in the negotiation of agreements, the insufficiency of feasibility studies and the anxiety of State governments to launch projects, it is a common allegation of the Malaysian people that these government projects are further disadvantaged by lack of managerial and technical skills on the part of the staff employed. Mismanagement of funds is a common problem. To a very large extent the recruitment of personnel for government corporations is left to the individual corporation concerned. The independence enjoyed in this area was meant to be an additional facility for the corporation to attract the right kind of expertise. With this same independence, however, there is every possibility of abuse of discretion. It is questionable whether this freedom to hire and fire is correctly exercised.

Secondly, housing: this is a State function. But although this may be regarded as a local matter '... there are countries, like Malaysia, which regard the provision of housing not merely as a basic need of the individual and their commitment within the context of pleasant environment but also have to regard housing as an instrument for the attainment of national goals beyond social objectives'.[79] In Malaysia, among other things, housing is employed to restructure society and to break down the barriers among the social groups. Certain other aspects related to housing, namely, land utilization control, building control and the squatter problem are important to all States and a national problem. Further, for a large part of the financial commitments of the housing project and the professional and technical expertise required by States in public housing, the source is still the Federal Government. Therefore it can be expected that a certain degree of control would shift from the State to the Federal sphere. This accountability factor is the primary cause for State reluctance to borrow from the Federal Government. It is, however, a reluctance which they can ill afford, looking at their capacity to meet the public demand. Only three States, Selangor, Pahang, and Johore have shown sufficient capacity under the Second Malaysia Plan period.[80]

It is the view of the Ministry of Housing and New Villages that because of various constraints, it may be necessary to regrade housing standards. While this may be an economic answer to these constraints, it is unlikely that any proposed development under State control will willingly conform to such regrading of standards, for fear of criticism.

From the above it may be seen that at least two factors make it desirable that some Federal control be given a legal basis. These factors are

(*i*) the inevitable Federal financial and other involvement in State projects necessitated by lack of State capacity, and

(*ii*) the difficulty of streamlining development to cope with national objectives.

Thirdly, local government: this is an area under the State List where the Federal Government has through a national body, the National Council for Local Government (NCLG), the power to co-ordinate the development of local governments. Although the advice and policies drawn up by the NCLG are binding on the States, past experience has indicated little compliance with this. For the sake of good relations between these two levels of government, the Federal Government has been reluctant to insist on its authority.

The Inter-Governmental Committee Report, 1962 provides for considerable State autonomy for Sabah and Sarawak in matters of education, leaving the policy and system of education to the State governments. Because of the National Language issue, the alignment of Federal and State policy becomes more difficult. Only recently has it become possible to have a comprehensive national policy.

This leaves the National Language issue still outstanding. National aspiration to make Malay, already the National Language, the sole official language is not unmindful of the practical difficulties involved. It provides bridging relief in that English is to continue as a joint official language. The Malaysian Report of the Inter-Governmental Committee Report, 1962 provides that English is to continue for limited official use in Sabah and Sarawak for a period up to ten years and 'thereafter until the State Legislature otherwise provides ...'.[81] This takes into consideration the additional difficulty of these States in that there are other native languages which have sometimes been advanced as arguments against accepting Malay as the sole official language.

The civil services in Sarawak and Sabah on Malaysia Day were split into Federal and State services, the former comprising those which dealt with matters now allocated as Federal matters. But they are not in fact integrated with the Federal service in Peninsular Malaysia. Malayan officials appointed to the Federal service in these States evoked resentment. Legally there is no prohibition against such appointments although Borneonization is of course to be given priority.

The Judiciary is still divided into two separate High Courts, the High Court in the States of Malaya and the High Court in Borneo, with separate registries. The legal profession is likewise still divided although the Legal Profession Act, 1976, has been brought into force. The object of this Act is to consolidate the law relating to the profession in respect of Malaysia; it has not however been applied to Sabah and Sarawak.

Where both Federal and State laws cover the same subject matter, the choice may well be influenced by a sense of competition. It is not unlikely that the Federal or State Authority may disregard less obvious difficulties in its anxiety to act. The case of the arrest and detention of Datuk James Wong in Sarawak in 1975[82] under the Public Security Ordinance, Sarawak, 1962 was not without difficulty. The Ordinance has effect only in regard to Sarawak so that detention outside Sarawak is beyond the scope of the Ordinance. The Internal Security Act, 1960,[83] applies to Sarawak as from Malaysia Day, 16 September 1963. If recourse had been made to this Act, instead of the Ordinance, the Datuk's detention, being within Malaysia (though outside Sarawak), would have been lawful.

If differences in federal-state relationships are sympathetically viewed because of the peculiar difficulties of certain States and the need for an interim period, the Federal Government may also consider that these differences may be looked upon as some form of discrimination. As much as the other States may want to observe the spirit of federalism, they cannot be unaware of this 'discrimination' which, albeit accepted during the initial years, becomes mere parochialism after that. The comments[84] on the method of government will have reference here.

THE JUDICIAL SYSTEM AND METHOD OF GOVERNMENT

However precise and efficacious the Constitution may be to define the system of federalism, the judicial system and the method of government are of equal importance.

THE JUDICIAL SYSTEM

The judiciary which must be the final arbiter of any conflict between State and Federal interests must demonstrate impartiality. The judicial powers in the Federation are vested in the Federal Court and the High Courts of the States of Malaya and Borneo and such courts as may be provided by federal law.[85] The most important power of the Federal Court of relevance to this essay is its original jurisdiction to determine:

(a) any question whether a law made by Parliament or by the Legislature of a State is invalid on the ground that it makes provision with respect to a matter with respect to which Parliament or, as the case may be, the Legislature of the State has no power to make laws; and

(b) disputes on any other question between States or between the Federation and any State.[86]

From the Federal Court there was an appeal to the Yang di-Pertuan Agong who referred the matter to the Judicial Committee of the Privy Council,[87] but this appeal has been abolished from 1 January 1978. The impartiality of the judges is secured by a constitutional guarantee of their tenure and remuneration.[88] Their judicial conduct is also privileged from parliamentary discussion.[89] Removal of judges is excluded from the powers of the Executive and the Legislature; this function is assigned to a tribunal of judges and ex-judges.[90]

METHOD OF GOVERNMENT

With a Constitution as lengthy as the Federal Constitution where nearly every aspect of government is covered one is tempted to suspect that any shortcoming in the government must lie in the method of government and a lack of goodwill of responsible bodies.

The last twenty years have seen a mushroom growth of various public corporations whether established by statute or under the Companies Act, 1965—to say nothing of the various degrees of government investment participation as equity holders or in joint-ventures. These corporations have a purpose to serve. Not being Government departments, they are not bound by the red tape of bureaucracy by being part of a vast Government hierarchy. Also, these corporations enable Government to serve various objectives, not merely economic in the financial sense but more importantly the socio-economic objectives of the country.

But the establishment of these corporations in Malaya (Malaysia after 1963) has far outstripped the government capacity to exercise control over them. With respect to Federal corporations, where the conduct of such corporations is accountable to the Ministers concerned or where government representatives sit on the Board of Directors, the control may be reasonably effective. But even this is doubtful. For reasons ranging from personalities of the government watchdogs and the supervisory bodies' lack of capacity for effective control, it has been intimated to me that this control in fact is illusory. State corporations pose a further problem. They have sometimes been used to circumvent the limitations imposed by the Constitution on the borrowing powers of States: the effect of Article 112 carried to its logical end must necessarily preclude borrowing by State corporations because although such corporations are separate legal entities, the financial implications on State governments are obvious. This prohibition in practice has not inhibited such borrowing. Finally in 1961, the Public Authorities (Control of Borrowing) Act, 1961, was passed to correct this anomaly. But whatever the intention of the Legislature was, its implementation has not been extended to deal with the problem as it relates to State development corporations.

To date, the relevant Ministry has attempted to make periodic progress evaluation of performance by corporations under its purview. It would seem that the returns to be filled by these corporations merely reflect on the financial aspects of the corporations; the socio-economic aspects must surely be considered. In the event that a corporation is regarded as not fulfilling the purpose, the Ministry would recommend further study—and for this it feels that outside consultants have to be employed.

Lack of skill and proper training of personnel seem to be a common malaise in the various government departments. And when a federal authority has to formulate national policies and advise on a specific field, it can be further frustrated by a similar lack of capacity by State governments. The Land Department is especially beset by this. But lack of capacity of States often means a loss of finance not only to the States but to the Federal Government as well. The Treasury feels that some States do not have the capacity to carry out development projects effectively. A project demands not only direct government involvement in terms of finance by way of grants or loans but the laying of infrastructure by the Federal Government.

Of State financial capacity, it must be remembered that some States are too poor even to support the necessary apparatus of a State government or if they are well endowed their resources are not properly exploited. Hence, the Federal Government is often burdened with bad debts.

Added to this, the Federal Government now is supporting a growing Cabinet and its attendant staff. The justification for the recent tendency for an increased number of Deputy Ministers may lie in politics but the financial burden is substantial and this burden is borne by the public. The appointment of a Deputy Minister carries with it the appointment of a complement of staff. The office of a Deputy and a Parliamentary Secretary could be made in the alternative to 'stand in' for the Minister. But two or three 'stand ins' may be a luxury the country could ill afford.

Lastly, goodwill: it cannot be over-emphasized that without it, the continued well-being of the Federation is at stake. Even though the constitutional provisions tend towards a bias for the Federal Government, in fact the Federal Government has shown itself hesitant in insisting on its rights for the sake of good relations. The NCLG for example has every authority to require States to comply with its decisions but so far it has preferred to use persuasion. The Federal Government also paid as a reimbursement a handsome sum for Sabah's Television Project which it originally did not undertake for reasons of priority. Sabah, however, insisted on the project, paid the costs and duly asked the Federal Government for reimbursement.

CONCLUSION

The evolution of our Constitution has been geared to accommodate our peculiar problems. For this reason, this evolution should not be appraised in the light of other constitutions. In the words of Thomson C.J. '... the Constitution is primarily to be interpreted within its own four walls and not in the light of analogies drawn from other countries such as Great Britain, the United States of America, or Australia'.[91]

This evolution has not, however, departed from its original expressed principle; the Federation is to have a strong central government. As such, State parochialism is not within its contemplation; State parochialism is insistence of a State to be differently treated *vis-à-vis* other States within the Federation beyond the degree necessitated by relevant peculiar characteristics in the initial years. Nation building demands an assimilation of all into the one national identity.

In as much as this requires observance of the idea of federalism not only in letter but in spirit by States, the Federal Government has definite responsibilities to the States and the *ra'ayat*. Such responsibilities should be borne with goodwill and a sense of fairness to all. Likewise, the States should not impose on the Federal Government and take undue advantage of its goodwill.[92]

The Federation is still in its early years, and therefore the frequency of constitutional amendments is nothing more than the accommodation of necessary adjustments. But improvements in the letter of the Constitution alone cannot make up for any deficiency in good administration and continued goodwill. The Constitution must not only be seen as a document but also as law-in-action.[93]

1. See Sobei Mogi, *The Problem of Federalism*, Vol. II, George Allen and Unwin Ltd., London, 1931, p. 796 where he quotes Triepel.

2. R. Rudolph Jr., *Federalism and Nation Building: India, Pakistan, Malaysia and Nigeria*, University Microfilms Ltd., High Wycombe, England, 1971, p. 11.

3. William H. Riker, *Federalism: Origin, Operation, Significance*, Little, Brown and Company, Boston, 1964, p. 11.

4. K. C. Wheare, *Federal Government*, Oxford University Press, London, 1963, p. 10. Wheare explains at p. 15 that it would not be sensible to apply the 'federal principle' completely and without exception to all constitutions.

Ahmad Ibrahim, 'Malaysia as a Federation', (1974) 1 *Journal of Malaysian and Comparative Law*, 27, limits the application of Wheare's 'federal principle' because it was based on the earlier federations such as the U.S.A. and Australia.

5. This historical background was largely drawn from (*i*) Alfred P. Rubin, *International Personality of the Malay Peninsula*, Penerbit Universiti Malaya, Kuala Lumpur, 1974, (*ii*) Ginsburg and Roberts, *Malaya*, University of Washington Press, Seattle, 1958.

6. The Malayan Union of 1946.

7. Ginsburg and Roberts, op. cit., p. 42.

8. Rubin, op. cit., p. 280.

9. For a brief account of the communal problem in early Malayan history, see K. J. Ratnam, *The Problem of National Unity*, University of Malaya Press, Kuala Lumpur, 1965.

10. The Malayan Union proposal sought to withdraw Malay rights; initially Malay nationalism was largely influenced by the Muslim reformist movement in Arabia, Indonesian nationalism, and Japanese expansion.

11. Subsequently published as Ordinances 11 and 12 of 1949 respectively.

12. Mohamed Nordin Sopiee, *From Malayan Union to Singapore Separation*, Penerbit Universiti Malaya, Kuala Lumpur, 1974, p. 88. He attributes the successful maintenance of the Federation to

(a) the monopoly of 'system-transformation' authority by the Central Government,

(b) the separatists' patent helplessness due to deficiencies in resources and the difficult task of getting support of the Central Government, and

(c) the strong commitment of the Central Government and UMNO, the dominant Malay political party.

13. In assessing whether a State has a central bias or not, we must examine the nature of those areas where the respective governments are 'independent and co-ordinate'. This observation was made in criticism of Wheare's 'federal principle' in Mackenzie and Chapman, 'Federalism and Regionalism', (1951) 14 *Modern Law Review*, at p. 187.

14. *Report of the Federation of Malaya Constitutional Commission, 1957*, Government Press, 1957.

15. Ibid., p. 2.

16. Ninth Schedule.

17. Article 75.

18. Articles 80-81, 93-95.

19. Article 96.

20. Article 111.

21. Payments are authorized under Article 109(3), (5) and (6).

22. Tenth Schedule, Part I.

23. Tenth Schedule, Part II.

24. Article 76.

25. Article 71, the Conference of Rulers (Article 38) and its relevance to constitutional amendments.

26. Article 159.

27. [1963] M.L.J. 355.

28. H. P. Lee, 'The Amendment Process', (1974) 1 *Journal of Malaysian and Comparative Law*, 192.

29. [1963] M.L.J. 355 at p. 359 (per Thomson C.J.).

30. *Report of the Federation of Malaya Constitutional Commission, 1957*, op. cit., at paras. 61-3.

31. *Third Malaysia Plan, 1976-1980*, Government Press, 1976, p. 234.

32. Constitution (Amendment) Act, 1960, section 12.

33. Article 91.

34. Constitution (Amendment) Act, 1960, section 3.

35. Emergency (Federal Constitution and Constitution of Sarawak) Act, 1966, section 3(1)(a).

36. R. H. Hickling, 'The First Five Years of the Federation of Malaya Constitution', (1962) 4 Mal. L.R. 183.

37. Constitution (Amendment) Act, 1962, sections 17 and 19 respectively.

38. (*i*) Assignment of Revenue (Export Duty on Iron Ore) Act, 1962.
(*ii*) Assignment of Export Duty (Mineral Ores) Act, 1964.

39. For some critical analysis of the merger, see
(*i*) Means, *Malaysian Politics*, University of London Press, London, 1970;
(*ii*) R. S. Milne and K. J. Ratnam, *Malaysia—New States in a New Nation*, Frank Cass, London, 1974.

40. Milne and Ratnam, op. cit., p. 20.

41. Act No. 26/1963.

42. Malaysia Agreement.

43. *Malaysia, Report of the Inter-Governmental Committee 1962*, Government Press, Kuala Lumpur, 1963. (Hereinafter referred to as IGC in the footnotes.)

44. Ninth Schedule.

45. At paras. 16, 28, and 29.

46. Immigration Act 1959/1963, proviso to section 66(3).

47. *IGC Report*, op. cit., at para. 23 (NCLG) and para. 22(4) (National Land Council).

48. Clause 4 read with clause 7 of Article 71.

49. Article 159 read with Article 161E(2).

50. Constitution (Amendment) Act, 1964, section 6.

51. *IGC Report*, para. 24.

52. Tenth Schedule, Part V.

53. Tenth Schedule, Part IV, para. 2 (for Sabah) and para. 1 (for Sarawak).

54. Constitution (Amendment) Act, 1966.

55. J. H. Proctor Jr., 'Constitutional Defects and the Collapse of the West Indian Federation', (1964) *Public Law*, 125.

56. *Infra*, pp. 171-2.

57. Act A30 of 1971, section 6.

58. Constitution (Amendment) Act, 1973.

59. Constitution (Amendment) (No. 2) Act, 1973.

60. Section 12.

61. Article 1(2) as amended by the Constitution (Amendment) Act, 1976.

62. Constitution (Amendment) Act, 1976, section 3.

63. Section 48.

64. Capitation Grant Act, 1977.

65. H. P. Lee, op. cit., p. 186. In comparison the Federal Constitution has, up to date, been amended twenty-three times.

66. *Infra*, pp. 163-4.

67. State Nationality Enactments—
    (*i*) Johore 2/1952.
    (*ii*) Kedah 5/1371 (1952).
    (*iii*) Kelantan 2/1952.
    (*iv*) Negri Sembilan 2/1952.
    (*v*) Pahang 2/1952.
    (*vi*) Perak 1/1952.
    (*vii*) Perlis 1/1952.
    (*viii*) Selangor 2/1952.
    (*ix*) Trengganu 3/1952, define 'Malay' as a person who (a) habitually speaks the Malay language; and (b) professes the Muslim religion; and (c) conforms to Malay custom.
    The reference to 'subject of His Highness the Ruler of any State' refers to the State Nationality Enactments.

68. *Report of the Federation of Malaya Constitutional Commission 1957*, op. cit., p. 14.

69. Constitution (Amendment) Act, 1962, section 2(4) restricts further its application where 'neither of his parents was a citizen of the Federation and neither of them was a permanent resident ...'.

70. Constitution (Amendment) Act, 1962, section 3(1); in respect of registration of wives a two-year residence period is required.

71. Malaysia Bill—Explanatory Note at para. 4.

72. Malaysia Act, Act 26/1963, section 28.

73. *IGC Report* Annex A deals with the Legislative Lists, Administrative Arrangements and Assurances. In relation to the Public Service (Annex B) it is noted '...[I]f the safeguards provided for Borneonisation were used for the permanent exclusion of Malayan officers from Federal posts in the Borneo States, Federal policies could not take full account of the views of the Borneo States'.

74. *Supra* at pp. 183-4.

75. Robert R. Bowie, and Carl J. Friedrich, *Studies in Federation*, Little, Brown and Company, Boston, 1954, p. 313.

76. Ibid, p. 313.

77. For example Federal loans to States and State Economic Development Corporations for 1975 and 1976 are as follows:

	States (Million Ringgit)	SEDCs (Million Ringgit)
1975	47.452	63.8
1976	53.93	53.93

78. Incorporation (State Legislative Competency) (Amendment) Act, 1976.

79. Ahmad b. Ahmad Rahim, Secretary-General, Ministry of Housing and New Villages.

80. Mainly drawn from my interview with Ahmad b. Ahmad Rahim.

81. At para. 28; Article 161.

82. *Datuk James Wong Kim Min* v. *Minister of Home Affairs, Malaysia & Ors.* [1976] 2 M.L.J. 245.

83. Extended to Sabah and Sarawak by the Modification of Laws (Internal Security and Public Order) (Borneo States) Order, 1963.

84. *Supra* at pp. 185-7.

85. Article 121.

86. Article 128.

87. Article 131.

88. Article 125.

89. Article 127.

90. Article 125(4).

91. Thomson C.J. in *Government of the State of Kelantan* v. *Government of the Federation of Malaysia and Tunku Abdul Rahman Putra Al-haj* [1963] M.L.J. 355.

92. Sabah under Tun Mustapha's régime had even gone to the extent of establishing its own Sabah Airlines. Shortly before the late Tun Fuad was sworn in as the new Chief Minister in April 1976, he said, 'We do not want the State airline when we already have the national airline.... They are [sic] completely unnecessary'. *The Straits Times*, 16 April 1976, p. 1.

93. '... [f]ederal constitutions do not alone make for federal governments and political practice frequently vitiates legal forms.' Rudolph Jr., op. cit., p. 16.

※ TAN SRI D. B. W. GOOD

9. Problems of Harmonizing the Laws in the Malaysian Federation

THIS is not a legal treatise, learned or otherwise, but a stark recital of facts which are on historical record.

The expression 'harmonization' was adopted, at the inter-Governmental talks in 1962 which led to the establishment of Malaysia in 1963, as an alternative to 'consolidation', which is not quite the same thing. Consolidation is designed to achieve harmonization, but harmonization can be achieved, in a federation of states having a different historical, social, and cultural background, by means other than full consolidation, e.g. by the modification of the existing laws of one or more states of the federation to bring them into conformity with the Constitution by which new states were added to the original federation and to avoid conflict with the laws of other states having parallel and contemporaneous effect on similar subject-matter, or by the extension of the laws of a part of the federation to the remainder, with appropriate modifications where necessary. This is how the process of harmonization began in 1963. It is still going on.

Because harmonization is inextricably bound up with law revision, this essay will inevitably be largely about law revision although the expression does not occur in the heading. To avoid cluttering up parliamentary business with a vast work-load of statute law revision bills, a short-cut method of law revision without resorting to legislation by Parliament was devised as the tool with which to fashion harmonization. This will be explained in detail later.

Let us begin by taking a look at the state of the law in Malaya from the end of the war in the Far East in 1945 until the Federation of Malaya with the addition of Sabah, Sarawak, and Singapore became the Malaysian Federation (or, more strictly, the Federation known as Malaysia)[1] on 16 September 1973.

When Oliver Cromwell described the English law of real property as 'a tortuous and ungodly jumble'[2] he might have been speaking prophetically of the laws of Malaya almost three centuries after the words were spoken. And, by a sequence of events which will be described later, the confusion existing in 1945 had become even more confused by 1963.

The late Dr. W. Blake Odgers described the relationship between the State, the law and the community in the following words:

A State may be roughly defined as a political community which governs itself. It governs itself by means of laws. It is essential to the welfare of the community that in every State there should exist an authoritative body of law, readily accessible, easily intelligible, and strictly and impartially enforced.[3]

The requirement of accessibility is, unfortunately, not always present in Malaysia. Until the 1965 reprint of federal laws of Sabah and Sarawak[4] there were not more than two or three copies of these laws available in the federal capital, and instances occurred of Ministries responsible for their enforcement being unable to comment on proposed amendments because they did not have copies of the law which it was proposed to amend. Only one master copy, in the library of the Attorney-General's Chambers in Kuala Lumpur, could be guaranteed to contain all the amendments up to date. This was a premium that had to be paid for the urgency of constitutional change. Politics dictate the speed of change; the legislative processes necessary for giving effect to the political decisions have to follow at the best speed that the available draftsmen, always too few, and the Government Printer, always over-pressed, can contrive to make. The revision of the laws becomes a continuous battle with backlog.

The availability of the older laws, the pre-war laws of the States of Malaya, was found to be in an even sorrier state. The Commissioner for Law Revision and his one and only professional assistant had to pay two visits to each of the twelve State capitals outside Kuala Lumpur, a total of over 7,000 miles, in order to make absolutely certain what laws were still in force, and to discuss with the State Legal Advisers which of them could safely be repealed as spent, obsolete, or redundant, and which required replacement by federal legislation. We found in some places that the only complete but not always reliable copy of the State laws reposed, as precious as the Crown Jewels, in the safe of the State Secretariat, and that in some cases all that had survived was a typed copy, made by some industrious typist half a century previously, stained, before the days of air-conditioning, by the all-permeating humidity of the local climate, nibbled by 'silver-fish' and chewed by cockroaches. In a few cases the texts of enactments which we knew existed and had not been repealed, were not available at all. We had to assume that they were obsolete.

These practical difficulties, which beset the path of law revision, particularly in Peninsular Malaya (as distinct from Malaysia), are the result of a series of historical accidents such as probably no other country has had to endure in so comparatively short a space of time. In colonial territories, and territories which formerly followed the colonial pattern, the practice had been to produce, at intervals of about fifteen years, bound revised editions of the statutes arranged, not chronologically, but either alphabetically (as in the Sabah edition of 1953), or by grouped subject-matters (as in the Sarawak edition of 1958). This became the conventional form of revised editions for all the former colonial territories. No such revision had taken place in Malaya since before the war. The laws of the Federated Malay States (Negri Sembilan, Pahang, Perak, and Selangor) and of Kedah were revised in 1934, those of Johore in 1935, and those of Malacca and Penang in 1936, when these two States were still part of the Straits Settlements. A revised edition of the laws of Trengganu up to 20 February 1939 (the first day of the Muslim year 1358) was printed in 1941 but it was never brought into force because the Japanese invaded Malaya in that year. Nearly four years of enemy occupation, followed after an interval of less than three years of peaceful conditions by the Emergency of 1948 to 1960, followed by the emergency known as 'Confrontation' from 1963 to 1966, together with four major constitutional changes (the Malayan Union in 1946, the first Federation of Malaya in 1948, the independent Federation of Malaya in 1957, and Malaysia in 1963), combined to make the task of law revision virtually impracticable from the beginning of the second world war. A start was made in 1959 by Mr. R. H. Hickling on a revised edition of the laws of the Federation of Malaya, after the modifications consequent upon Merdeka had been made by a series of orders made in 1957, 1958, and 1959. The first volume was in proof towards the end of 1962, by which time the preliminary talks leading to the establishment of Malaysia were taking place and the project was shelved, as it was realized that what would be required was a revision of the laws, not of Malaya but of Malaysia. This was the point at which the writer took over from Mr. Hickling. The task of modifying the laws in consequence of the passing of the Malaysia Act was begun in 1963 and is still proceeding under a new Commissioner, Mr. Shiv Charan Singh. Even in this apparently straightforward exercise unforeseen delay was caused by the separation of Singapore from Malaysia in August 1965, resulting in the consequential operation of unscrambling the incompatible ingredients in the Malaysian omelette.

It became obvious at a very early stage of the task of law revision that a conventional revised edition would be out of the question, at any rate for some years—possibly many years—to come. This will be dealt with in detail later. The laws are in a phase of constant change and a revised edition would be out of date by the time it was printed. 'Malaysia' modifications (i.e. consequent upon the passing of the Malaysia Act), and modifications consequent upon the separation of Singapore, if any still remain to be made, will continue to be made until Parliament decides that they are to stop. In this respect the Malaysia Act differs from the 1957 'Merdeka' Constitution which required all modifications to existing laws to be made within two years, which resulted in an awesome proliferation of modification orders in the years 1957, 1958 and 1959. The repeal and replacement of obsolete federal laws, or of laws on federal subjects which are still to be found in the statute books of the States, is a task which could still take years to complete. The work of consolidating the laws on federal subjects, which took place from 1948 to 1957, was never completed. The list of federal subjects itself has undergone two overhauls, one in 1957 and another in 1963, since it was first promulgated as a Schedule to the Federation of Malaya Agreement in 1948. There are still a number of important federal subjects which rely on legislation having effect in the States of Malaya, in the individual component States or in pairs or groups of States. In alphabetical order, Appraisers, Auctions, Gold Buyers, Mineral Ores, Mining, Petition Writers, Quarantine and Prevention of Disease, Rubber Dealers, Rubber Regulation, Rubber Supervision, Theatres and Places of Public Amusement, Water Supply, Weights and Measures, and Women and Girls Protection are the subject of multiple legislation extending, in many cases, to seven separate enactments. In a few cases, e.g. Weights and Measures, pan-Malaysian legislation has been drafted but not yet been brought into force. These are all federal matters which could, should, and eventually will be governed by a single Act of Parliament on each subject.

This multiplicity of legislation is further multiplied if one includes Sabah and Sarawak, for while a vast amount of consolidation of the Malayan laws was carried out in the years 1948 to 1959, not enough headway has been made since Malaysia Day in producing legislation on a pan-Malaysian scale extending to the new States of Sabah and Sarawak. Thus each of the following diverse subjects, taken at random—Advocates; Designs; Patents and Trade Marks;

Excise; Moneylenders; Poisons and Dangerous Drugs; Post Office; Prisons; and Registration of Dentists is the subject of one law in the States of Malaya, another in Sabah, and another in Sarawak. There are no great differences between them—they are for the most part based on common models—and in the majority of cases the differences can readily be reconciled and the laws consolidated. But in certain cases political obstacles, or differences in local conditions, make complete and immediate reconciliation impossible. An example of this is to be found in the consolidation of the Criminal Procedure Codes, of which there were four in force in Malaysia until 10 January 1976: one in the former Malay States, one in the former Settlements of Penang and Malacca, one each in Sabah and Sarawak. Penang and Malacca pressed for the retention of trial by jury in all criminal trials in the High Court; in the other nine States of Malaya trial by jury is restricted to capital cases other than emergency procedure cases (trial with the aid of assessors was abandoned in 1957) while in Sabah and Sarawak there is no trial by jury but capital cases are tried with assessors. None of the components of Malaysia desired any change in the existing arrangements, and although this is a matter about which Parliament is empowered by the Constitution to make laws, consideration had, for political reasons, to be given to strong local feeling. In the event, Penang and Malacca lost their juries except in capital cases, while provision was made for trial by jury in Sabah and Sarawak with a stay of execution on its implementation. This is one of a number of examples which could be quoted to demonstrate that the reconciliation of differences in the laws in force in different parts of Malaysia is not always a matter of mere drafting.

Examples of the problems of harmonization which beset the draftsman in dealing with laws which could not be fully integrated owing to the need to perpetuate differences enforced by local circumstances, and also by compromises agreed to in the pre-Malaysia Constitutional talks, could be multiplied beyond the point of tedium. A few will be enough to illustrate the point.

One of the commonest problems of harmonization concerns the transfer of statutory powers and functions, exercised by federal authorities in Peninsular Malaysia, to appropriate authorities in East Malaysia. This involved problems of communication and accessibility. The statutory pattern is that the powers and functions necessary to give effect to a law are vested in the Minister, who is empowered to make rules and orders by public notification in the Gazette, and to give administrative directions for specified purposes. Now, it is all very well saying that the Minister may do this or that, but he cannot exercise his discretion unless he is briefed, and the persons whose duty it is to brief him are the civil servants in his Ministry. But they live in Kuala Lumpur, and decisions have to be taken which will have effect in Sabah and Sarawak many hundreds of miles away across the sea; so that if there is to be consultation with the people on the ground who have to implement or operate the decisions of Kuala Lumpur in East Malaysia, officials in Kuching or Kota Kinabalu have to fly to Kuala Lumpur or Ministry officials have to fly to East Malaysia. This is a very expensive way of briefing the Minister. It also causes delay, and decisions have often to be taken urgently. To overcome this difficulty, the drafting team invented a functionary whom we called the Local Federal Authority. This could be any person appointed by the Minister to exercise his statutory functions under federal laws in Sabah and Sarawak, either generally or *ad hoc*. In practice however, ministerial authority was delegated to the Federal Secretary in Kuching and the Deputy Federal Secretary in Kota Kinabalu, who were senior civil servants posted from Kuala Lumpur to represent the Federal Government in Sarawak and Sabah respectively. In some cases, however, the Governments of Sabah and Sarawak requested either a direct authorization or delegated authority to a State Minister or official, and this has been granted in a few cases as a matter of general convenience. But it must be remembered that we are speaking of federal powers under federal laws, and that the ultimate control of their exercise remains always with the Minister.

In 1963 an Immigration Act was passed by Parliament which extended the Immigration Ordinance of 1959 to Sabah and Sarawak as a general law for the Federation as a whole, but also, subject to and in accordance with the provisions of Part II of the Act, as a special law for each of the Borneo States. Part II of the 1963 Act is now Part VII of the revised Immigration Act, Laws of Malaysia Act 155. This had to be done in this way because although immigration is a federal subject and the federal law was extended to East Malaysia in 1963 certain exceptions to federal control over immigration had been agreed to at the constitutional talks in 1962-3 and effect had to be given to the agreement. In the result, the State Authority in Sabah and Sarawak was given a measure of control over immigration into those States and in consequence of this the immigration law could not be fully harmonized.

One very difficult exercise was the attempt to harmonize the education laws. Education is a federal subject but the Report of the Inter-Governmental Committee, 1962, which was adopted by the contracting parties in the London Agreement of 1963, put a stay of execution on any changes in the educational systems operating in Sabah and Sarawak under their own State laws until those States otherwise agreed. After prolonged consultation between the Federal Government and the Governments of Sabah and Sarawak, the Education Act, 1961, of the former Federation of Malaya was extended to Sarawak in 1975 and to Sabah in 1976 with substantial modifications designed to preserve parts of the systems of education followed in those States under their own laws; so that when those laws were repealed by the extension order some of their provisions were written into the extended Act to meet local conditions.

The judicial system was harmonized, so far as the superior Courts, i.e. the Federal Court and the High Court, are concerned, by the Courts of Judicature Act, 1964 (now revised as Act 91). The Subordinate Courts Act (Act 92) is ready for extension to East Malaysia but has not yet been extended and the organization and jurisdiction of the subordinate Courts in Peninsular Malaysia and East Malaysia differ in a number of respects. The Legal Profession Act (Act 166) does not apply in East Malaysia, and Sabah and Sarawak have retained their respective Advocates Ordinances. The Medical Act, 1971 (Act 50) applies throughout Malaysia, but the Dental Act, 1971, designed as a pan-Malaysian law, has not yet been brought into force.

The inclusion of Sabah and Sarawak in the federal legislative framework is further complicated by substantial differences in the legislative lists, as between the Federation and the States of Malaya on the one hand and the Federation and the Borneo States on the other. The report of the Inter-Governmental Committee, 1962, made a number of important recommendations, adopted by the contracting Governments in Article VIII of the London Agreement, which place the Borneo States in a special position *vis-à-vis* the Federal Parliament, and in general confer upon them legislative powers greater than those enjoyed by the States of Malaya, as a glance at the supplementary legislative lists (IIA and IIIA, in the Ninth Schedule to the Constitution) will show. A draftsman setting out to extend existing federal laws of the States of Malaya to the Borneo States, or to draft consolidated pan-Malaysian laws, must keep open before him the Ninth Schedule to the Constitution and Annex A to the Inter-Governmental Committee's Report; otherwise he will find himself bombarded with protests and cries of *ultra vires* by those guardians of the constitutional rights of the Borneo States, the State Attorneys-General of Sabah and Sarawak: and rightly so. The simple answer is, of course, collaboration. The legal officers of the Federation and of the States are colleagues working towards a common goal.

There are in force in Malaysia today laws belonging to, or a legacy

from, forty-three systems which have existed from time to time. They
are:

The pre-war laws of the former Straits Settlements, some of which
still apply in Penang and Malacca.

The pre-war laws of the former Federated Malay States, many of
which still apply in the States of Negri Sembilan, Pahang,
Perak, and Selangor.

The pre-war individual State enactments passed by the legislatures of each of the four former Federated Malay States, which
apply in one State only, and not in all four.

The pre-war laws of each of the five former unfederated States.

A sole survivor of the British Military Administration Proclamations, 1945 (many of which had survived in the statute book
until they were repealed in 1965).

Ordinances of the Malayan Union, 1946-8.

Ordinances of the first Federation of Malaya, 1948-57.

Enactments passed by the Councils of State of the eleven States of
the Federation of Malaya, 1948-57.

Ordinances of the Legislative Council of the independent Federation of Malaya, 1957-9.[5]

Acts of Parliament, 1959 to date.

State Enactments passed by eleven State Legislative Assemblies
since Merdeka Day, 1957.

Laws of the former Colony of North Borneo.

Laws of the former State of Sarawak under the Rajahs, kept in
force by the Omission Schedule to the Revised Edition of the
Laws Ordinance, 1956 Sarawak No. 4/56.

Laws of the Colony of Sarawak, 1946-63.

Laws passed by the Legislative Assemblies of Sabah and Sarawak
since Malaysia Day.

A layman might be forgiven for supposing that among the more
unhappy legacies of British administration has been a mass of statute law of such confusion, complexity and difficulty of access as to
merit the comment of Buckle that 'the more a man knows of the
history of legislation, the more he will wonder that nations should
have been able to advance in the face of the formidable impediments
which the legislators have thrown in their way'.[6] It is, one hopes, not
unreasonable to suppose that the present confusion of our laws could
not have been brought about by design but is the melancholy consequence of historical events.

The end-result of all these extraordinary complexities has been a
break-away from the conventional form of law revision. It was
decided, firstly, that the exercise was on too large a scale for a
conventional revised edition consisting of a set of volumes of laws all

coming into force together on an appointed date. So great is the demand for copies of the laws that it would be impracticable and unreasonable to wait for the completion of the exercise before making available those most urgently needed. It was therefore decided to proceed on the loose-leaf system, so that individual laws could be published as soon as they were ready, and so that they could be assigned priority according to the importance of their subject-matter and the urgency of the demand for them. This method, too, has the advantageous side-effect that, with the loose-leaf binders available from the Government Printer, users of the laws can arrange them in the order most convenient to them; and a person who needs for his profession or business the texts of only a few laws does not have to buy a whole expensive set.

It was decided, secondly, that because the circumstances peculiar to Malaysia involve the taking of decisions outside the scope of a Commissioner preparing a conventional revised edition (whose functions are largely mechanical), unusually wide powers should be given to the Commissioner but that a safeguard should be introduced to ensure that he does not overstep them.

With this in view the Revision of Laws Act, 1968, which came into force on 1 January 1969, established a Law Revision Committee of from five to seven members, to be appointed by the Lord President of the Federal Court. Its function is to 'vet' the amendments to laws made by the Commissioner in the course of revision, and to certify that they are *intra vires* the powers conferred upon him by the Revision of Laws Act. Accompanying each revised law the Commissioner sends to the Committee are:

(*i*) a list of the amendments which have been made from time to time by law, with references to the amending laws and to the dates on which they came into force; and

(*ii*) a list of the amendments made by himself under the Revision of Laws Act, quoting his authority for making each amendment.

It was decided, thirdly, to establish law revision in Malaysia as a continuing process. A conventional revised edition is prepared as a single, distinct operation: when it has been published the Commissioner is *functus officio*, and a fresh enabling law is required for every subsequent revised edition. The Revision of Laws Act is, on the contrary, designed to enable any federal law in force in Malaysia to be revised at any time. Even before all the laws have been revised it is expected that some of them will have to be revised: such is the tempo of legislative change in a fast-developing country. And furthermore, what we have been considering so far is 'superior' legislation, i.e. an accumulation of laws passed by the various legislatures which from time to time have made laws for the component parts of Malaysia. Mention must also be made of the no less voluminous collection of subsidiary legislation, statutory regulations, rules, orders, and by-laws which have been made by different authorities under the parent legislation. Ideally, when a law is revised, all the subsidiary legislation made under it should be revised also. In practice, this will rarely occur, and the revision of subsidiary legislation will have to await its turn, or it will have to be replaced by new subsidiary legislation made under the revised laws. The latter would be the more expeditious course, because any necessary rules, orders, etc. would then be made as current rather than revised subsidiary legislation as and when required. The former subsidiary legislation would be saved until replaced.

Unhappily, the programme was soon to suffer a serious set-back. The first law to be revised was the Election Offences Ordinance, which was urgently required for the General Election on 9 May 1969. It was published on 10 April. Other revised laws in course of preparation were almost ready to go to the Law Revision Committee when the events of 13 May occurred and a state of emergency was proclaimed. Thereafter, and for the rest of 1969, the Commissioner and his staff had to be diverted to emergency drafting, and law revision, being a matter of less demanding urgency, was temporarily relegated to a subordinate position in the priority list. The redeployment of staff for unforeseen commitments arising from the emergency delayed the overall programme of law revision for over a year.

In order to determine where the legislative functions of Parliament cease and those of the State legislatures begin, and where they overlap, it was necessary to sort the present laws into four categories (1) Federal; (2) State; (3) Concurrent; and (4) Hybrid (that is, containing the ingredients of two or more of the other categories). Parliament can pass laws about (1), (3), and parts of (4); State Legislatures can pass laws about (2), (3), and the remainder of (4). It was necessary to study all the laws of the States of Malaya, Sabah, Sarawak and, of course, (at that stage) Singapore (in all about 50,000 pages), in order to place every law in its proper category. In the course of this survey many instances were found of laws that were obsolete or spent. A series of Statute Law Revision Acts was passed by Parliament in August 1965 repealing about 350 of them. Another 700 out-of-date laws on State subjects were also discovered, which were left for repeal by the State Legislatures.

A further exercise resulting from the overall survey of existing laws is the process of 'dehybridisation' of hybrid laws, a task which may be tackled in either of two ways:

   (a) an enactment may be dissected and re-enacted as to its federal parts by Parliament and as to its State parts by the State Legislature or Legislatures concerned; or

   (b) with the concurrence of the Federal and State Governments an enactment which is for the most part federal but in some parts State may be dealt with as a federal law and re-enacted *in toto* by Parliament, while one which is mainly State but partly federal may be treated as State law and re-enacted by the State Legislature.

To clear the decks, declaratory orders under section 74(2) of the Malaysia Act were made in May 1965, with the concurrence of the Heads of the two States concerned, declaring 120 Sabah Ordinances and 108 Sarawak Ordinances to be federal laws. This leaves Parliament, or the Federal Government, as the case may be, free without further concurrence (or even consultation, except as a matter of prudence) to repeal and replace, or to modify, any of the laws enumerated in these Orders.

The Malaysia Act provided for the extension to the Borneo States of laws of the former Federation of Malaya, now known as the States of Malaya, West Malaysia or Peninsular Malaysia. This has proved in practice to be a useful and expeditious method of providing, without having to take up the time of Parliament, a single pan-Malaysian law on any given subject. But it was found to be too restrictive. Because the laws of the Borneo States were revised so much more recently than those of the States of Malaya, many Ordinances, particularly those of Sarawak which were revised at the end of 1958, were thought to be more suitable for extension than Malayan laws of more ancient vintage. Section 74 of the Malaysia Act was therefore amended by Act No. 31 of 1965 to enable any federal law in force in any part of Malaysia to be extended throughout Malaysia or to any State or States thereof. The power has not yet been much used for the purpose of 'reverse extensions', but it is convenient for the draftsman to have it in his armoury so that he can select the best available model as the basis of a consolidated Malaysian law.

The commonest reaction of human beings, even the more enlightened ones, to proposals for change is 'leave well alone'—the *laissez faire* attitude which has been a feature of many administrations in the history of government. Except in the socio-economic field where dedicated reformers want to change everything because everything that exists in their special field is *ipso facto* wrong, most people, if things have been going well for some time, have a built-in resistance to change. This does not apply to material things, to which the principle of 'keeping up with the Jones's' applies. A man will buy a new car although he already has a perfectly good one, because he does not want to lag behind in the rat-race for social prestige. But in matters of law and administration he tends to be ultra-conservative unless he is activated by political propaganda. In the kind of law revision of which we are speaking, which is purely for the sake of harmonization, there is no element of politics or of economic or social reform.

Proposals to extend federal laws to replace the corresponding laws of East Malaysia sometimes turned out to be a hard sell: not because the Governments of Sabah and Sarawak have been unco-operative—far from it. In many cases, probably the majority, the green light for the 'all clear' was given without question. But sometimes a red warning light appeared, usually because tradition was preferred to novelty, and East Malaysia could see no need to change things to which they had grown accustomed. For the sake of harmonization, and for no other reason, this natural initial resistance had to be overcome by consultation and sometimes persuasion, and the light remained at amber for a long time before the green light appeared. And it must be emphasized that these were federal laws which by prior agreement between the contracting parties, the Federal Government was fully entitled, subject to stays of execution or other qualifications expressed in the Report of the Inter-Governmental Committee, 1962, to impose without the concurrence of the State Governments and without any consultation. But the Federal Government never used the steam-roller, except in matters affecting national security or other emergency situations.

In the writer's experience as Commissioner of Law Revision, a proposal to harmonize, for example, the laws relating to criminal procedure, evidence or interpretation by the Malaysianization of the laws of the former Federation of Malaya on these subjects produces a reaction such as 'We have had ours for x years, they have worked well and everyone here has grown used to them. Why change them?'—to which, of course, the only valid answer is 'Why not?' The issue then becomes one of convincing the intended recipients that this is not a case of change for the sake of change but change in the interests of harmonization, and that harmonization, though perhaps not necessary, is desirable.

Harmonization may be desirable for strictly practical reasons. The Federal Court, which is the highest court of appeal in Malaysia (and has, on 1 January 1978 become the ultimate court of appeal in constitutional and criminal appeals when the Judicial Committee of the Privy Council ceased to advise the Yang di-Pertuan Agong in appeals from the Federal Court) is a peripatetic Court. When it sat in Sabah or Sarawak it had to apply different rules of criminal procedure from those which applied in Peninsular Malaysia until the Criminal Procedure Code was Malaysianized on 10 January 1976, and it had to apply the Criminal Procedure Code of the former Straits Settlements when it sat in Penang. The Evidence Act (Act 56) did not become pan-Malaysian until 1 November 1971. The laws about interpretation of statutes have not yet been harmonized. There are two in force in Peninsular Malaysia, one applicable to laws passed before 18 May 1967, and the other to laws passed on or after that date, one in Sarawak and two in Sabah, one applicable to laws of the former colony of North Borneo which became federal laws on Malaysia Day and the other to Sabah State laws including those inherited from North Borneo.

It does not require much imagination to sympathize with the Judges of the Federal Court who have to address their minds to selecting the relevant law out of this *mélange*, which must tend to make proceedings longer and their Lordships' patience shorter. Similar difficulties are experienced by the heads, officers, and staff of federal departments serving in Sabah or Sarawak. Some are fortunate in that the laws under which the department operates and which it is their duty to enforce have been imported from Peninsular Malaysia. Others (e.g. the Prisons Department) have had to learn unfamiliar new laws.

When harmonization by way of the extension to East Malaysia of an existing law of Peninsular Malaysia has been agreed with the State Governments, that is not the end of the problem. Consideration has then to be given to necessary modifications to fit that law to special local conditions. Specific reference has been made in this paper to a special exception in the Criminal Procedure Code postponing indefinitely (i.e. until a date to be determined by the appropriate Minister who will undoubtedly consider the wishes of the Sabah and Sarawak Governments) the introduction of trial by jury in East Malaysia. There are many other considerations which vary or limit the practical application of particular provisions of extended laws: different customs, e.g. about marriage, land tenure, native courts; shortage of qualified personnel in outlying areas; and, in Sarawak, sheer size, lack of rail communication and paucity of roads, making it difficult for the people to comply with requirements such as attendance in person at registries or offices which are situated in the principal towns. The solution of these difficulties is administrative, technical, and financial and depends on the speed of development. But so far as the laws are concerned special exceptions have to be made to suit local circumstances, and this calls for detailed consultations at civil service level even after the decision has been taken in principle to extend a federal law.

A further circumstance which has occasionally hampered the speedy progress of the process of harmonization is political change. In 1966 in Sarawak and in 1976 in Sabah there were changes of government; and although changes of government do not necessarily result in major changes of policy, particularly in matters which are mainly non-contentious, policy decisions still have to be negotiated and it is more difficult to get a quick response from a new government than from one which has held office for a long time and has grown accustomed to the problems involved.

The course of law revision in Malaysia may be described as a series of overlapping phases:

Phase I may be called the phase of modification and extension. Two hundred and ten orders either extending federal laws with modifications or modifying pre-Malaysia laws of the Borneo States (in some cases several laws in one Order), to bring them into line with the Federal Constitution, have been made. This is a holding device, to keep the machinery of Government turning over until time can be found for repeal and replacement by new legislation.

Phase II is the reprinting of existing laws as modified, including the consolidation of all amending statutes in the principal statute. This comes close to the conventional practice of law revision, except as to the format in which the reprints come off the press. A reprint does not revise, it merely consolidates in one text the original law with all subsequent amendments to it. It is standard practice, save in most exceptional cases of urgency or because it is of little public interest, that when a law is extended, the extension order is not published until sufficient copies of a consolidated reprint are available for Bench and Bar, Ministries and Government Departments, commercial houses, and the general public, in the territory to which the law is extended. These reprints, which form the nucleus of the revised edition in the shape that it will take for some years to come, are being produced all the time concurrently with the winding-up of Phase I.

Phase III is the phase of consolidation by way of repeal and replacement. Many consolidating Acts for Malaysia have been passed by Parliament since Malaysia Day. Many more remain to be done, and a fair number have been passed by Parliament but not yet brought into force, mainly because of administrative problems. The recipients are not ready to accept the federal bounty, or the Federal Government is not ready to set up the necessary machinery.

It may be mentioned purely as a matter of general interest that the English technique of amending statutes by separate Acts to be read with, but not verbally incorporated in, the principal Act, was introduced into Malaysia in 1961 by an English draftsman on loan to the Malayan Government, but was abandoned in 1963 as being too complicated for our straightforward approach to the drafting and at a later stage to the construction of statutes. Malaysia favours the 'for A substitute B' formula. To overcome the difficulty experienced by the draftsman when preparing a consolidated reprint of a law which has been amended in the English fashion, the Reprint of Federal Laws Act, 1965 has been amended by the inclusion of the definition—' "amendment" includes, for the purposes of section 4, any variation or extension of any law, whether such variation or extension is made by substitution, construction, variation or otherwise, so long as, in effect, the provision concerned alters the original law'. This amendment enables the Commissioner, in preparing a reprint, to write into it the substance of any provisions, however expressed, varying the effect or changing the construction of the original law. It is a useful power, but one that has to be exercised sparingly and with caution.

The task of harmonizing the laws by way of law revision inevitably includes an element of law reform. The Commissioner of Law Revision studying a law with a view to harmonizing its provisions with those of other laws (whether by consolidation or not) is in a position to detect anomalies and anachronisms. He is also the recipient of suggestions from Ministries, Judges, Law Officers, and members of the Bar for substantive improvements in the law that he is revising. If the proposals would be *ultra vires* his authority under the Revision of Laws Act, 1969 because they involve policy decisions or material changes in the content of the law, he must take instructions from the appropriate Ministry or Ministries. If the proposed amendment could affect the position in a State, he will, if he is prudent, consult the Legal Adviser of the State, even if the law is purely federal in content, in order to avoid any unforeseen consequences due to inadequate knowledge on his part of the laws and local conditions of the State or States concerned. And if there are likely to be differences of opinion about the need for, or desirability of, a proposed reforming amendment, or about the way in which the reform should be implemented, it is wise, and generally recognized to be wise, to have full consultation between the Federal Government and the Governments of all the States which will be affected by any proposed change in the law. A federation being what it is, bulldozing is to be avoided even though the subject-matter of the projected measure is expressed by the Constitution to be federal. It is better to postpone the decision until agreement has been reached than to reach disagreement by over-hasty action. It may be frustrating for the draftsman who could complete the job in a fraction of the time taken up by consultation, but that is how federalism works.

1. Article 1(1) of the Constitution of Malaysia.

2. I am indebted to my friend Mr. R. H. Hickling for this quotation. Mr. Hickling was my predecessor as Commissioner of Law Revision and is a co-contributor to this book.

3. I am also indebted to Mr. R. H. Hickling for this quotation.

4. This expression may appear to be a contradiction in terms. In the context of a law having effect in a State and not throughout the Federation, it means an existing law of that State which on Malaysia Day became a federal law by virtue of Article 74 of the Constitution and of the Ninth Schedule thereto.

5. Provision was made in the 1957 Constitution for a fully elected Parliament to replace the former Legislative Council, which was originally nominated by the High Commissioner (or Governor during the Malayan Union, 1946-8) and became a partly elected, partly *ex officio* body in 1955. Parliament did not sit until 1959 as the work of delineating and declaring constituencies, preparing electoral lists and preparing for and holding elections took two years. Transitional provisions in the Constitution enabled the Legislative Council to continue until Parliament was established.

6. I am again indebted to Mr. R. H. Hickling for the quotation.

10. Developments in the Law concerning Elections in Malaysia

ELECTIONS are a means of making political choices by voting. They are used in the selection of leaders and in the determination of issues. This concept of elections implies that the voters are presented with alternatives, that they can choose among a number of proposals designed to settle an issue of public concern. The presence of alternatives is a necessary condition, for although electoral forms may be employed to demonstrate popular support for incumbent leaders and their policies, the absence of alternatives disqualifies such devices as genuine elections.

The principal laws relating to elections in Malaysia are embodied in Part VIII (consisting of Articles 113-120, together with the Thirteenth Schedule) of the Federal Constitution. An Election Commission is constituted by Articles 113 and 114 for the purposes of conducting elections, keeping electoral rolls and reviewing the division of the country into constituencies. Service with and assistance to the Election Commission are governed by Article 115. Article 116 and the Thirteenth Schedule provide for the federal constituencies, while Article 117 relates to constituencies for State elections. Other provisions in this Part deal with challenges to elections by election petition (Articles 118 and 118A), qualification to vote (Article 119), and the machinery for direct election of senators should this be introduced (Article 120).[1]

Parliament and a State Legislative Assembly each have a life of five years and so, unless either is sooner dissolved, there is a general election every five years, held within 60 days in Peninsular Malaysia and 90 days in Sabah and Sarawak from the date of the dissolution. Federal and State general elections for Peninsular

Malaysia in 1964, 1969 and 1974 were held simultaneously to save time and money.[2] According to Article 119 of the Federal Constitution, every citizen who on the qualifying date

(a) has attained the age of 21 years; and

(b) is resident in a constituency or, if not so resident, is an absent voter,

is entitled to vote in that constituency in any election to the House of Representatives or the Legislative Assembly, unless he is disqualified under clause (3) of Article 119 or under any law relating to offences committed in connexion with elections. No person may in the same election vote in more than one constituency. If a person is in a constituency by reason only of being a patient in a place for the reception or treatment of persons suffering from mental illness or mental defectiveness or if he is being detained in custody, he cannot vote in that constituency. A person is (according to clause (3) of Article 119) disqualified from being an elector in any election to the House of Representatives or the Legislative Assembly if

(a) on the qualifying date he is detained as a person of unsound mind or is serving a sentence of imprisonment; or

(b) having before the qualifying date been convicted in any part of the Commonwealth of an offence and sentenced to death or imprisonment for a term exceeding twelve months, he remains liable on the qualifying date to suffer any punishment for that offence.

'Qualifying date' means the date by reference to which the electoral rolls are prepared or revised.[3]

Besides the Federal Constitution, the legislative framework for the holding of elections in Malaysia consists of the following:

1. Federation of Malaya Agreement, 1948
2. Sedition Act, 1948
3. Registration of Electors Ordinance, 1954
4. Election Offences Ordinance, 1954
5. Registration of Electors Regulations, 1955
6. Election Offences (Amendment) Ordinance, 1955
7. Election Commission Ordinance, 1957
8. Elections Ordinance, 1958
9. Elections (Conduct of Elections) Regulations, 1959
10. Elections (Control of Motor Vehicles and Vessels) Regulations, 1959
11. Elections (Postal Voting) Regulations, 1959
12. Local Government Elections Act, 1960
13. Election Offences (Amendment) Act, 1961
14. Election Act, 1963
15. Malaysia Act, 1963

16. Election Offences (Amendment) Act, 1964
17. Elections (Amendment) Act, 1965
18. Elections (Registration of Electors) Regulations, 1971

THE GENERAL ELECTION OF 1955

Polling for the first elections to the Legislative Council of the Federation of Malaya took place on 27 July 1955, eighteen months after the publication of the Report of the Committee appointed to examine the question of Elections to the Federal Legislative Council thirteen months after the submission of the Report of the Constituency Delineation Commission recommending boundaries for the Federation's fifty-two constituencies, and just over nine months after the beginning of the period of the registration of electors. Before 27 July 1955, only some twenty-five per cent of the registered electorate had had the opportunity to vote at any previous election. Whilst Johore, Trengganu, and Penang had held their respective State and Settlement elections, and there had been numerous Municipal, Town Council, and Local Council elections in different parts of the Federation, the mass of the electorate living in rural areas voted for the first time at the Federal Elections.

The registration of electors for the General Election was conducted in accordance with the provisions of the Registration of Electors Ordinance, 1954, and the Registration of Electors Regulations, 1955. The Ordinance was passed by the Legislative Council on 18 August 1954 and received the assent of the High Commissioner and Their Highnesses the Rulers in September 1954. The Registration of Electors Ordinance provided for the voluntary registration of Federal electors in all States and Settlements and of State and Settlement electors in respect of those States and Settlements whose Councils had passed a resolution bringing the provisions of the Ordinance into force in relation to the registration of State and Settlement electors. Every Federal constituency constituted a separate registration area for registration purposes and each polling district constituted a separate registration unit.

Special measures were taken to facilitate registration of potential electors in the Armed Forces and in the Police with a view to making arrangements for postal voting somewhat similar to the system in force in the United Kingdom. Central arrangements were made for the distribution of application forms for registration to the various units in the Armed Forces and each unit arranged to make application forms available both to serving personnel with the necessary qualifications and also to wives of serving personnel wherever such wives had the correct qualifications and were living in accommodation provided by the Armed Forces. Each completed registration form was despatched by the applicant's military unit direct to the Elections Officer in the State or Settlement containing the town or *kampung* which the applicant regarded as his home; and he was then registered in the appropriate registration area.

The 52 seats were contested by 129 candidates of whom 18 were Independents and the remainder distributed among the following political parties:

1. Alliance	52
2. Party Negara	30
3. Pan-Malayan Islamic Party	11
4. National Association of Perak	9
5. Labour Party	4
6. Perak Malay League	3
7. Perak Progressive Party	2

The Alliance won 51 of the 52 seats, securing 81.7 per cent of the electoral votes. The only seat lost by the Alliance was the Krian constituency of Perak which was won by the Pan-Malayan Islamic Party.[4]

THE GENERAL ELECTION OF 1959

The Parliamentary and State elections held in 1959 were significant in Malaysian history as being the first elections held after the achievement of Independence and the first elections to result in the creation of entirely elected legislatures both at Federal and State levels. They were also the first elections to be held under the supervision of the independent Election Commission established under Articles 113-120 of the Constitution of the Federation of Malaya. The essential preliminaries to the holding of elections—the delimitation of the constituencies and a major revision of the electoral rolls, were carried out by the Election Commission in 1958. Thereafter, in 1959, after the dissolution of the State Councils and the Federal Legislative Council, writs for elections to the State Legislative Assemblies were issued on various dates during the month of April, and for the general elections to the Dewan Ra'ayat on 1 July. Where constituencies were contested, the polling days for elections to State Legislative Assemblies occurred during the months of May and June, and for the elections to the Dewan Ra'ayat on 19 August 1959.

Article 113 of the Constitution (as it then stood) indicated that the Election Commission should conduct elections to the House of Representatives and to the Legislative Assemblies of the States and also that it should delimit the constituencies and prepare and revise the electoral rolls for such elections. The Commission was established shortly after the attainment of Merdeka in 1957 and in accordance with the provisions of the Constitution at once proceeded to plan for the holding of the first elections to the State and Federal Legislatures. Although under Article 116 of the Constitution provision was made for the allocation among the various States of 100 Federal constituencies the boundaries of which should be delimited by the Commission in accordance with certain clearly defined principles, Article 171 of the Constitution indicated that for the purpose of the first elections to be held after Independence, Article 116 should not apply but that on the occasion of those elections, the Federation should be divided into constituencies by dividing into two, each of the constituencies delimited for the purpose of elections to the Legislative Council under the Federation of Malaya Agreement, 1948. Accordingly in 1958 the Commission proceeded to divide the 52 existing constituencies into 104 new constituencies endeavouring when doing so to provide as far as possible for an approximate equality of population in the constituencies created. The then Article 171 of the Constitution also provided for the number of constituencies for the purpose of the first elections to be held to the Legislative Assemblies of the several States. The number of constituencies in each State is a multiple of the number of Parliamentary constituencies, and therefore at the time of delineating the boundaries of the Parliamentary constituencies in 1958 the Commission proceeded to subdivide each of the Parliamentary constituencies into a number of State constituencies to provide for the election of the appropriate number of representatives determined by law to each Legislative Assembly.

The registered electorate in 1959 was approximately double that of 1955, partly due to the large number of persons who had qualified for citizenship in the intervening years. On 18 August 1959, 2,110,495 voters cast their votes—over twice as many votes as had been cast at the first Federal elections. Again the Alliance emerged the victor, but with greatly diminished percentages compared to those of 1955. It controlled 74 seats, while the opposition parties won 30 seats. The election returns gave evidence of continued popular support for the Alliance, but its overall majority dropped from 81.7 per cent in 1955 to 51.5 per cent in 1959.[5]

THE GENERAL ELECTION OF 1964

The Alliance Government's term of office did not expire until August 1964. Even so, the Federal Government decided to hold State and Federal elections on 25 April. Several motives have been suggested for the earlier date. The Alliance had won several decisive by-election victories during the previous year, demonstrating that it continued to command overwhelming support at the polls. Malaya, with the inclusion of Sabah, Sarawak, and Singapore had, to the displeasure of neighbouring Indonesia, just become Malaysia. Indonesia's propaganda against Malaysia played on the theme that Malaysia was established without popular support. It was felt that a decisive Alliance victory would provide irrefutable evidence that Malaysia was endorsed by the public and was not a 'neo-colonial plot' as charged by Indonesia. The election would also force the anti-Malaysia opposition parties to choose between supporting Malaysia as a *fait accompli* or give the appearance of rendering aid and comfort to Malaysia's foreign attackers. It is uncertain whether the Alliance expected elections during that period of foreign crisis would make the opposition more moderate, or more radical and tend to force them into league with Malaysia's attackers abroad. In any event, the opposition parties were vulnerable. As soon as the elections were announced, the opposition parties began negotiations to pool their strength. However, the construction of a united front of opposition parties was even more difficult than in previous elections because of sharp communal differences and because of their conflicting reasons for opposing Malaysia.[6]

Prior to the polling date Indonesian agents engineered a number of incidents designed to influence the outcome of the elections in favour of the anti-Malaysia parties. It would appear, however, that terrorism produced the opposite effect, for, after the votes were counted, the Alliance had once again gained a decisive victory, improving on its 1959 record. They won 123 out of the 159 Parliamentary seats and 240 out of the 282 State seats. The electoral votes in favour of the Alliance improved from 51.8 per cent in 1959 to 58.3 per cent.[7]

THE GENERAL ELECTION OF 1969

The election of 1969 will go down as one of the most explosive and tragic events in Malaysian history. The intricacies and problems created by this election have been discussed at great length by various legal, social, and economic analysts and it is not the aim here to elaborate on what has already been aptly analysed elsewhere.[8]

Suffice it to note that a sort of premonition of impending disaster was felt, months before the election, by the government, for steps were in fact taken to prevent the occurrence of what eventually took place: for the first time in election history an Electoral Behaviour Code along the following lines was adopted:

1. Exemplary behaviour should be shown by political leaders, candidates, their election and other agents, supporters, helpers, and workers.

2. Personal criticisms levelled against any individual should be confined only to his political activities and views.

3. Political speakers should reply to their opponents from their own platforms.

4. The wearing of distinctive headgear and uniform clothing by persons collectively should be avoided.

5. The race or religion of any individual should not be mentioned with the intention of ridiculing, insulting, or bringing him into contempt.

6. The carrying of weapons by candidates, their election and other agents, supporters, helpers and workers should be considered wholly undesirable.

7. Political leaders, candidates, their election and other agents, supporters, helpers, and workers should refrain from tearing down or defacing election posters and/or banners of rival parties or candidates.

8. Political leaders and candidates should ensure that all posters and/or banners put up on their behalf are removed immediately after the election.

9. Political leaders and candidates should avoid using or employing members of Secret Societies and other undesirable elements at assemblies/meetings or in house-to-house canvassing.

10. In a candidate's booth, only sufficient food and refreshments required for consumption by persons manning the booth should be stored.

11. Political leaders, candidates, their election and other agents, supporters, helpers and workers should not take part in propagating their party platform at any function organized by Government officers.

Towards the end of 1968 it was reported that a political party had instructed all its members in the House of Representatives and in the various State Legislative Assemblies to resign their seats on staggered dates. As the law stood at the time, it was necessary to fill any vacant seat within sixty days from the date on which a vacancy was established. The Government decided that the holding of by-elections would cause considerable inconvenience to the electorate as Parliament and State Assemblies would in any case be dissolved by 18 May 1969 and a general election held thereafter. To meet this unusual situation Article 54(2) of the Constitution was amended whereby casual vacancies occurring within six months of the date on which Parliament would stand dissolved, need not be filled. This amendment was made to apply to State Assemblies as well. As a result of this, although a number of vacancies occurred in the House of Representatives and State Assemblies, no by-elections were held. In addition, the following amendments were made:

(a) The Election Offences Act, 1954

Amendments were made to this Act in 1969, the effect of which were as follows:

(*i*) the limit of expenses that may be incurred by a candidate or his election agent was increased from $10,000 to $20,000 in the case of an election to the House of Representatives, and from $7,500 to $15,000 in the case of an election to a State Legislative Assembly;

(*ii*) the penalty for the offence of treating, undue influence, and bribery was increased from six months' imprisonment and a fine of $500 to twelve months' imprisonment and a fine of not less than $250 and not more than $1,000;

(*iii*) the provisions relating to personal expenses of candidates were dispensed with.

(b) Elections (Conduct of Elections) Regulations, 1959

The Elections (Conduct of Elections) (Amendment) Regulations, 1968, made by the Election Commission, were approved by the Yang di-Pertuan Agong on 20 December 1968. The amendments were made for the purpose of uniformity and bringing into line similar regulations which were applicable to the Borneo States.

Two notable amendments were:

(*i*) In relation to election deposits by intending candidates, it was provided that candidates who pay their election deposits to a Government Department authorized by the Returning Officer should produce the deposit receipt to the Returning Officer within the hours of 10 o'clock in the forenoon and 12 o'clock on nomination day. Failure to do so would render the nomination of such candidate invalid; and

(*ii*) The insertion into the Regulations of a new provision making it obligatory for a Returning Officer to order a recount of votes upon the application of any candidate or his election agent if the number of votes for all the candidates together with the rejected votes varies from the number of ballot papers found in the ballot boxes by one per centum or more, or if the difference between the number of votes cast for the leading candidate and the number of votes cast for the next leading candidate was two per centum or less of the total number of votes cast.

(c) Elections (Postal Voting) Regulations, 1959

The Elections (Postal Voting) (Amendment) Regulations, 1968 were approved at the same time. With this amendment, a new procedure was introduced enabling certain categories of voters to apply for postal votes if they wished to vote by post.

Although the Alliance won 66 out of the 113 Parliamentary seats it gained only 48.4 per cent of the total electoral votes and for the first time in Malaysian history, the Alliance failed to secure its ⅔ Parliamentary majority. In State elections the Alliance lost control of Penang, Perak, and Kelantan, while in Selangor it gained half the seats in the State Assembly, creating a potential deadlock with the combined opposition.[9] What happened next has now become common knowledge in this country—the riots of 13 May, the suspension of Parliament, and the assumption of virtually dictatorial powers by the then Deputy Prime Minister.

THE GENERAL ELECTION OF 1974

General elections to the House of Representatives and the State Legislative Assemblies, except the State Legislative Assembly of Sabah, were held on 24 August 1974 to elect members to the 154 seats of the House of Representatives and 360 seats of the various State Legislative Assemblies. These were the fourth Parliamentary and State general elections held in the States of Malaya since Independence and the third since the formation of Malaysia. In the case of Sabah and Sarawak, these were the second direct elections to the House of Representatives and likewise to the State Legislative Assembly of Sarawak. Both the general elections to the House of Representatives and State Legislative Assemblies, except the State Legislative Assembly of Sabah, were held simultaneously on 24 August 1974. Even though polling was completed within one day in the States of Malaya, owing to difficulties in communication and transportation in Sabah and Sarawak polling had to be staggered and it took two to three weeks to complete.

According to Article 46 of the Federal Constitution, the House of Representatives shall consist of 154 elected members, 114 of whom shall be from the States of Malaya, 16 from Sabah, and 24 from Sarawak. The number of elected members in the States of Malaya was increased from 104 to 114 and the number allocated to each State is laid down in Article 46 of the Constitution which was amended *vide* Constitution (Amendment) (No. 2) Act, 1973 (A206). Section 4 of Schedule Eight Part I of the Federal Constitution stipulates that each State Legislative Assembly shall consist of such number of elected members as its Legislature may by law provide, and the number shall be the same as or a multiple of the number of Federal constituencies of each State. The number of members of the House of Representatives and the State Legisla-

tive Assemblies according to each State fixed by the Federal and
State Constitutions were as follows:

	House of Representatives	State Legislative Assemblies
Johore	16	32(x2)
Kedah	13	26(x2)
Kelantan	12	36(x3)
Malacca	4	20(x5)
Negri Sembilan	6	24(x4)
Pahang	8	32(x4)
Perak	21	42(x2)
Perlis	2	12(x6)
Penang	9	27(x3)
Sabah	16	48(x3)
Sarawak	24	48(x2)
Selangor	11	33(x3)
Trengganu	7	28(x4)
Federal Territory	5	—
Total	154	408

With the change in the number of members of the House of Representatives and the various State Legislative Assemblies, it was
the responsibility of the Election Commission to delimit the
number of Federal and State constituencies according to the
number of members fixed for each State by the Constitution. All
114 Federal constituencies and 312 State constituencies of the
States of Malaya and 16 Federal constituencies and 48 State constituencies of the State of Sabah were delimited in accordance
with the principles laid down in the Thirteenth Schedule of the
Federal Constitution in 1973/74 and the new boundaries of the
said constituencies were passed by the House of Representatives
on 24 July 1974.

Prior to the General Election, the Elections (Conduct of Elections) Regulations, 1959 were amended as follows:

(a) Regulation 3 was amended by adding a new sub-paragraph
5 which provides that in the event polling cannot be held or after
being held cannot be completed, the Election Commission can
suspend such polling and fix new dates for polling or complete
such polling as it deems fit.

(b) Regulation 4(4) was amended to allow Returning Officers
to give free copies of nomination papers and statutory declarations

from the date the election writ was issued to 11.00 o'clock and not 12.30 in the afternoon on nomination day. This amendment was in line with the amendment to Regulation 6(2) which requires nomination papers to be handed in between 9.00 o'clock to 11.00 o'clock in the forenoon on nomination day.

(c) Regulation 5 was amended by increasing the election deposits for the State and Parliamentary elections from $250 to $500 and from $500 to $1,000 respectively. The amendment was intended to take into account the value of the currency at that time and also to ensure that only genuine candidates contested the elections. The Government however had initially agreed to increase the deposit even higher from $500 to $750 and from $1,000 to $1,500 for the State and Parliamentary elections respectively but later decided to rescind its decision made on 9 July 1974 as it conflicted with the Elections Act, 1958. The Government then agreed to the original suggestion of the Election Commission since it was more consistent with the provision of the Elections Act.

(d) Regulation 5(1) was amended to allow candidates to pay their election deposits not later than 11.00 o'clock in the forenoon on nomination day and submit the deposit receipt to the Returning Officer between 9.00 o'clock and 11.00 o'clock in the forenoon on nomination day since the period fixed for the receiving of nomination papers was between 9.00 o'clock and 11.00 o'clock in the forenoon.

(e) Regulations 6 and 7 were amended so that nomination period was fixed between 9.00 o'clock in the forenoon and 12.30 in the afternoon; receiving of nomination between 9.00 o'clock and 11.00 o'clock in the forenoon and objection period between 11.00 o'clock in the forenoon and 12.30 in the afternoon, thus bringing these various periods within office hours.

(f) Regulation 9(1) was amended to allow a candidate to withdraw at or before 11.00 o'clock in the forenoon on nomination day to coincide with the period allowed for the handing in of nomination papers to Returning Officers.

(g) Regulation 11(2)(b) was amended to allow the Returning Officer to give the sole independent candidate in any contested election an election symbol of his choice without having to draw lots.

(h) Regulation 17(3) was amended so that the serial numbers of the ballot paper could be printed on the front and not on the back of the ballot paper as this would reduce the printing time to half.

(i) Regulation 19(2) was amended to enable the Presiding

Officer to initial or to put his official mark on the front and not on the back of the ballot paper.

(j) Regulation 19(7) required that the notice to voters at polling stations be in the National Language and in English and any other language or languages directed by the Election Commission. The Election Commission was of the opinion that the use of the English language in such a notice need not be made compulsory. However the Election Commission should be able to direct the use of the English language if and when necessary. This regulation was therefore amended accordingly.

(k) Regulation 30 was amended to enable a candidate to inform the Presiding Officer which of his names other than his surname or his personal name in the nomination paper he desired to be specified in initials before 12.30 and not 1.30 in the afternoon.

(l) The Election Notice was amended as a result of the above amendments.

(m) Action was also taken to simplify the filling in of Nomination Papers. In addition the statutory declaration was exempted from stamp duty further to guarantee the secrecy of the nomination.

The Federal and the various State Constitutions provide that unless earlier dissolved the House of Representatives and State Legislative Assemblies respectively will stand dissolved five years from the date of their first meeting after a general election.[10] In the case of the former the first meeting was held on 20 February 1971 while the latter held their first meetings on different dates much later. This means that unless earlier dissolved the House of Representatives stands dissolved on 19 February 1976. The House of Representatives and all State Legislative Assemblies except the State Legislative Assembly of Sabah were dissolved on 31 July 1974 and they were thus dissolved much earlier than the permitted five-year term and this was the first time they were so dissolved. The snap dissolution of the House of Representatives, just a week after it passed the delimitation of new Parliamentary and State constituencies including those in the Federal Territory which was created on 1 February 1974, did not give sufficient time to the Election Commission to prepare a more satisfactory electoral roll, or the electors to acquaint themselves with the new constituencies. The Election Commission was therefore unable to conduct a special registration exercise for electors as it normally did before a general election and as such the Election Commission had no choice but to rearrange the existing rolls according to the new constituencies.

In order to ensure that the elections would be carried out orderly and peacefully, the Election Commission invited all political parties to a meeting to formulate an electoral code of conduct. However only the National Front, the Democratic Action Party, and PEKEMAS attended the meeting. The Police were also present at the meeting and the codes of conduct that were agreed upon were similar to those adopted before the 1969 General Election. Candidates began campaigning as soon as they were allowed by the authorities concerned after nomination day. Campaigns were much more orderly and peaceful than those in 1969. With the amendments to the Sedition Act, 1948 which among other things made it an offence for anyone to question any matter relating to the rights, status, privilege and sovereignty or prerogative established or protected by provisions of Part III of the Federal Constitution or Articles 152, 153 or 181 a much more peaceful atmosphere was maintained. Nevertheless one political party put up their posters written in Mandarin which touched upon the question of language but the Police were quick to pull them down.

Polling for the States of Malaya was held on 24 August 1974. In the case of Sabah polling was held for two weeks from 24 August 1974 to 7 September 1974 while in the case of Sarawak polling was extended to three weeks from 24 August to 14 September 1974. Candidates from eight political parties contested the 154 Parliamentary seats and 360 State Legislative Assemblies seats except Sabah, but candidates from only four political parties achieved some form of success while the others failed even to secure a seat. The National Front (an enlarged Alliance Party) won 135 of the 154 Parliamentary seats and also secured control of all the State Legislative Assemblies. Sixty point seven per cent of the electorate voted for the Front.[11]

THE CONCEPT OF FREE ELECTIONS

In the name of 'democracy', the phrase 'free elections' has become a parrot cry of nationalist politicians, particularly in dependent territories during the colonial era. Their use of the phrase has often implied that free elections are an end in themselves, instead of being a means to an end, namely, good government, responsive to the popular will.

If democracy is the desired end, it can be achieved by other means than by free elections. For example, in the ancient Greek city-state of Athens, in the fifth century B.C., some of the highest offices in the state were filled simply by drawing lots. The Athenians regarded this as being the most perfect of all democratic devices, since every citizen had an equal chance to occupy the highest offices of state. It would be a bold Malaysian politician in modern times who would advocate this system of selection in the name of democracy.

Free elections, then, are not an end in themselves, but they have three features which are extremely useful in the establishment and maintenance of a satisfactory system of representative government:

(*i*) They create a sentiment of popular consent and participation in public affairs. The people feel that they have been consulted, and have indicated their wishes, in the broad field of national policy, and are therefore willing to accept the legitimacy of the power exercised by those put into positions of authority by the electoral system.

(*ii*) Free elections make it possible for one government to succeed another in an orderly manner, without violence or bloodshed.

(*iii*) Free elections emphasize the responsibility of the government to the people. Politicians dare not become too out of touch with public opinion, since they know that this will adversely affect their political interest at the next election.

There are, according to Mackenzie,[12] four prerequisites for elections which can be claimed to be free:

(*i*) The country must have an independent judiciary, free from political influence or control, which can interpret the electoral laws fairly and impartially.

(*ii*) There must be an honest, competent, non-partisan administration to run the elections.

(*iii*) There must be a developed system of political parties, since, if this is not so, the voter may not be clear what policies the candidate stands for, or which potential government he would support if elected.

(*iv*) There must be general acceptance, both by the politicians and by the general public, of what might vaguely be described as the 'rules of the game'. Candidates must play fair; they must not try to evade legal restrictions upon their electoral activities, such as bribery or misrepresentation, either in the letter or in the spirit of the law, nor must they refuse to admit defeat if the verdict of the ballot boxes goes against them. Equally, the voters who supported defeated candidates must accept the decision of the majority.

In further tracing the developments in the law concerning elections in Malaysia, the extent to which the above four prerequisites is followed in Malaysia is next discussed.

THE INDEPENDENCE OF THE JUDICIARY

The Judiciary in Malaysia performs a relatively effective task of checking any abuses of legislative or executive powers. This is made possible by the relative independence which it enjoys *vis-à-vis* the legislative and executive branches of government. Judicial independence in relation to tenure and remuneration is secured by constitutional provisions. Judges are paid fixed salaries charged to the Consolidated Funds and they hold office till sixty-five and this may be extended for another six months with the approval of the Yang di-Pertuan Agong. Their conduct may not be the subject of discussion in the State Assembly and although it may be discussed in Parliament, there is a requirement that it may be done only on a substantive motion of which notice has been given by not less than one-quarter of the total number of members of that House.

Judges do not hold office at the pleasure of the Yang di-Pertuan Agong and they can be removed from office for only two reasons: misbehaviour or inability properly to discharge the functions of their office. Any action for removal from office for the above reasons is subject to a rigorous procedure. A necessary ingredient of judicial independence in this country is its power to declare invalid any law or executive act repugnant to the Constitution.[13]

It is possible to bring an action against the Government in this country and the number of instances in which the Government has been found by the court to be in the wrong speaks well for the Judiciary's independence. Thus in the celebrated case of *Stephen Kalong Ningkan* v. *Tun Abang Haji Openg and Tawi Sli*[14] the court held that the purported dismissal by the Governor of Sarawak of Dato Ningkan from his post of Chief Minister, Sarawak, was *ultra vires* the Constitution and therefore null and void. In *Koh Yin Chye* v. *Leong Kee Nyean*[15] the court declared the election of a member of the ruling Alliance party void when it found the candidate guilty of a corrupt election practice. In *Fan Yew Teng* v. *Setia Usaha, Dewan Ra'ayat & Ors.*[16] an attempt was made by the Government to unseat the plaintiff from his position as a member of Parliament by virtue of his conviction and fine of $2,000 in default six months' imprisonment for sedition. The plaintiff had appealed against his sentence but while his appeal was pending in the Federal Court, he was informed by letter dated 4 February 1975, by the Setia Usaha Dewan Ra'ayat (Secretary, House of Representatives) that because of the conviction and sentence he had been disqualified by Article 48(1)(e) and that by virtue of Article 50(1) his seat had become vacant. By writ of election dated 17 February 1975, the Secretary to the Election Commission directed the

Returning Officer for Menglembu, the plaintiff's constituency, to hold a by-election and a notice of by-election was published on 20 February. The plaintiff argued that his conviction and sentence did not make him lose his seat automatically and that he was entitled to show cause against any move to unseat him under Article 53. The defendants argued that Article 53 applied only where there was any doubt about disqualification but not here because there was no doubt. Mohamed Azmi J. held that the conviction and sentence did not automatically render the plaintiff's seat vacant and declared that the by-election could not therefore be held. The learned judge drew a distinction between on the one hand Article 48(1) which he said dealt with both pre-election and post-election disqualification, and on the other Articles 50(1) and 53 which dealt only with post-election disqualification.

In 1965 an attempt by an unsuccessful Alliance candidate to challenge the election of an opposition candidate failed even though the court found that there was a transgression of the law. In that case, *Ishak Hamid* v. *Mustapha*,[17] the applicant had contended that the statutory declaration submitted by the respondent with his nomination papers was invalid as the stamp on it had not been cancelled in the prescribed manner and therefore the returning officer was wrong in accepting the nomination papers of the respondent. The court agreed that as the stamp on the statutory declaration had not been cancelled in the prescribed manner the statutory declaration must be deemed to be unstamped and therefore inadmissible in evidence and could not be acted on for any purpose; and as there was no valid statutory declaration, the returning officer should have rejected the respondent's nomination papers and as this was not done in this case there was a non-compliance with the provisions of the regulations relating to elections. However, the court held that despite the transgression of the law by the returning officer the election in this case had substantially been conducted in accordance with the principles of the law and therefore as the non-compliance of the law by the returning officer had not affected the result of the election, the respondent must be held to have been duly elected.

The Executive has however from time to time modified or negatived decisions of the Court not in its favour by taking advantage of its majority in Parliament to introduce frequently laws for the purpose of 'remedying' those judgments. Two recent cases, namely, *Government of Malaysia* v. *Zainal bin Hashim*[18] and *Loh Kooi Choon* v. *Government of Malaysia*,[19] illustrate the extent to which the Executive will utilize its powers to, in effect, 'wrong a right'. Although such steps in no way affect the independence of the

Judiciary (in the *Zainal bin Hashim* case, for example, Suffian L. P., in fact condemned the Government's action by compelling them to pay costs to the plaintiff who lost the case),[20] they do, however, incur the suspicion of the lay public that the Judiciary is simply another organ of the Executive and has invariably to toe the Government's line.

THE ELECTION COMMISSION

The requirement that an Election Commission should be honest, competent and non-partisan was incorporated by the framers of the Federal Constitution in 1957. The Constitution establishes an Election Commission which is independent of the Government. The members are appointed by the Yang di-Pertuan Agong after consultation with the Conference of Rulers. The Commission consists of a chairman and three other members. In appointing them the Yang di-Pertuan Agong is constitutionally required to have regard to the importance of securing a Commission which enjoys public confidence. To ensure that the Commission cannot be interfered with by the Government, the Constitution provides that a member may not be removed from office except on the same grounds and in the same manner as a judge. Notwithstanding this, he automatically ceases to hold office on reaching the age of sixty-five years and, further, the Yang di-Pertuan Agong may remove him from office if he

(a) is an undischarged bankrupt; or

(b) engages in any public office or employment outside the duties of his office; or

(c) is a member of either House of Parliament or of the Legislative Assembly of a State.

The remuneration of election commissioners is charged on the Consolidated Fund and is thus removed from annual debate and approval by Parliament. The remuneration may not be altered to their disadvantage after their appointment.[21]

As is the case with the Judiciary, the independence of the Elections Commission is similarly qualified by the powers available to the Executive. By Act 14 of 1962, for example, the power to delimit Parliamentary constituencies was transferred from the Elections Commission to Parliament and the formula for the delimitation of constituencies under a 'quota' system which was written into the original Constitution was abolished. Certain new principles were introduced in Part I of a new Thirteenth Schedule to the Constitution. Of these principles the most important one is that permitting a weightage of up to 2 : 1 in favour of rural constituencies: a provision presumably designed (since no explanation is afforded by the Explanatory Memorandum to the Bill) to ensure that the interests of the rural areas are adequately represented. As Hickling, a noted authority on the Malaysian Constitution puts it, it is possible that the majority of workers in rural areas are Malays. Certainly the argument was advanced in a criticism of the proposal. Yet in view of the apparent drift of the rural population to the towns, it is suggested that any such criticism may be invalid. However, the abolition of the powers of an independent Commission, Hickling adds, smacks a little of expediency: and expediency can be a dangerous policy. Indeed, these particular amendments, coupled with those affecting the Service Commissions, suggest that the Federation is intent upon destroying the relics of a paternal policy, embedded in the original Constitution, under which a number of independent bodies (in addition to the Supreme Court) shared, with the legislature, the authority of the Federation. The present policy is, no doubt, in line with orthodox constitutional doctrine in the United Kingdom: but there Parliament has lost much of its authority and most of its magic and it seems an unfortunate example to follow. Power is properly assumed by politicians, but the increasing complexity of life compels them to rely heavily on the civil service and, of this benighted body of men, those fare best who think least: for who would move one step, if by doing so he put a foot wrong? The original architects of the Constitution may have been wiser than we know, in creating a complex division of powers designed to frustrate the politician and alarm the law student. To transfer all powers to the myth of a legislature and the reality of an executive is to make the way straight for authoritarian rule. This may not be a fear for today, but what of tomorrow, when these powers may be in other hands?[22]

The 1962 amendments have also incurred the wrath of Professor H. E. Groves, who in no uncertain terms made known his observations:

It is apparent that the [1962] amendments as to elections have converted a formerly independent Elections Commission, whose decisions became law and whose members enjoyed permanent tenure, into an advisory body of men of no certain tenure whose terms of office, except for remuneration, are subject to the whims of Parliament. The vital power of determining the size of constituencies as well as their boundaries is now taken from a Commission, which the Constitution-makers had apparently wished, by tenure and status, to make independent and disinterested, and has been made completely political by giving this power to a transient majority of Parliament, whose temptation to gerrymander districts and manipulate the varying numerical possibilities between 'rural' and 'urban' constituencies for political advantage is manifest. It is, perhaps, not unworthy of comment that the Constitution does not offer any criteria for the determination of what is 'rural' and what 'urban'.[23]

POLITICAL PARTIES

As with most constitutions, that of Malaysia is silent on the subject of political parties. Yet democratic government here, as elsewhere, could scarcely function except upon a structure of party politics.[24]

There are approximately twenty-seven political parties in Malaysia.[25] The formation of a political party is subject to the rules as laid down under the Societies Act 1966 as amended. Section 7(1) of the Act however empowers the Registrar of Societies to refuse registration of a political party:

(a) which in the opinion of the minister is likely to affect the interest of the security of the Federation or any part thereof, public order or morality; or

(b) which is an organization or group of a political nature established or having affiliation or connexion outside the Federation; or

(c) which is an organization or group established or having affiliation or connexion outside the Federation.

The Malaysian Communist Party, banned since colonial days, has never applied for registration under the Act. However, even if it did, registration would have been refused under the above provisions. The People's Action Party which had representatives in the Malaysian Parliament before the secession of Singapore in 1965, was not allowed to function in this country upon similar grounds.

Almost all the major parties are formed along racial lines. Temporary mergers of political parties for the purpose of overcoming racial barriers during a General Election are common occurrences. The existence of numerous political parties in the country augurs well for democracy but it is doubtful whether the tragic events which occurred during the aftermath of the May 1969 General Election could not recur unless political parties based upon racial groups are abolished altogether.

RULES OF THE GAME

That Malaysian politicians and the general public on the whole have to a certain extent adhered to the 'rules of the game' of elections is not in dispute. There have been no dirty tricks[26] of the kind that have been used in elections in the United States in recent years. Nevertheless there *were* incursions against the 'rules'. Many were minor but some others, though few in number, had appalling consequences.[27] The 13 May riots of 1969 resulted, in a way, from the reluctance of voters of defeated candidates to accept the adverse verdict of the election against them. The impression is given that the recent imposition of Federal rule in Kelantan is said to have been the result of the reluctance of the ruling national coalition party to accept the fact that it cannot hope to wrest power from the Party Islam through a fair and clean general election.

Granted the prerequisites outlined above, there are many different electoral systems which can be used in free elections. The one adopted in Malaysia is the 'first past the post' system which was established during the colonial period. The technical term for this system is the 'simple plurality system', because the candidate who secures the greatest number of votes, even though he may not have secured a majority of all the votes cast, is declared elected. Despite its simplicity, this system has one serious disadvantage from the point of view of the purists, namely, that it is liable to produce an overall result which does not accurately reflect the voting strength of the various parties contesting the election. In the 1969 General Election, for example, the Federal Government was elected on the votes of a minority of the total electorate. This system does however have one major advantage from the practical point of view, namely that it usually produces a government with an adequate working majority in Parliament.

Finally, the existing system of representation in both the Malaysian Parliament and State Assemblies is a local or territorial one, the members being elected for constituencies determined on geographical lines. They thus represent the inhabitants of a certain area, and have, broadly speaking, nothing in common except residence in that area. It has often been suggested that this system should be replaced by vocational or functional representation. This means that vocations or 'interests' would be the basis of representation instead of a geographical area—the soviet system. It is argued that the increasing complexity of legislation and especially its growing concern with industrial and commercial matters, makes it advisable for interests rather than localities to be represented. It is true that this principle is to some extent adopted in practice, though not in theory, for trade union leaders, for instance, are regarded as representing their unions rather than their nominal constituencies, and the connexion between a prominent cabinet minister and his constituency is often a slight one. It is also true that many localities are so closely identified with certain localized industries that their representatives may almost be said to represent the industry itself. A complete system of vocational representation, therefore, would be to a large extent simply an extension and formal recognition of a system which is already partially in operation. Whether such a system would be an improvement on the existing one is a very controversial question. It may be argued on the one hand that legislation is becoming increasingly concerned with sectional interests and economic matters, affecting particular industries or groups of people rather than the entire population, and that therefore representation should be based on these sectional interests. There is obviously something to be said for this. Already it is customary for vocational associations to be consulted by the Government when legislation affecting them is being drafted, so that their views are taken into account. But there is also much to be said on the other side. It may be argued that these sectional interests are already quite sufficiently separated from each other—perhaps too much so, in some cases— and that the general basis of a common citizenship is more in need of emphasis. After all, a man is a citizen first and a worker second. Only part of his time and part of his mind are devoted to his daily vocation, and the tendency is for less and less of his time to be taken up with work, and for more and more attention to be given to providing for the non-working hours. Again, about half the electors are now women, and of these a very large number are housewives only, and would not fall into any vocational group except that of housewives, which is not a satisfactory kind of group. That, indeed, is one of the very serious practical difficulties which would have to be faced in formulating a scheme of functional representation. To classify some five million electors on a vocational basis, and then assign to them their representatives so as to give general satisfaction and provide a workable legislative assembly, would be a well-nigh impossible task. Apart from the innumerable subdivisions of modern industry there is all the overlapping between trades and professions, as well as the problem of the non-working elector. On practical grounds, there-fore, the system appears to be as impracticable as it is undesirable in principle.

In any democratic society, the conduct of elections of the people's representatives has to be properly regulated. The various amend-ments to the election laws in this country made since 1957 have been made consequent upon the country's experience during that period. By and large the laws as they now stand satisfactorily regulate the conduct and are acceptable to all political parties.

1. L. A. Sheridan and H. E. Groves, *The Constitution of Malaysia*, Oceana Publications, New York, 1967, p. 159.

2. Tun Mohamed Suffian, *An Introduction to the Constitution of Malaysia*, Government Printer, Kuala Lumpur, 2nd ed., 1976, p. 93.

3. Ibid., pp. 90-1.

4. See *Report on the First Election of Members to the Legislative Council of the Federation of Malaya (1955)*, Government Printer, Kuala Lumpur, 1955.

5. See *Report on the Parliamentary and State Elections (1959)*, Government Printer, Kuala Lumpur, 1960.

6. G. Means, *Malaysian Politics*, Hodder & Stoughton, London, 1976, pp. 335-6.

7. See *Report on the Parliamentary and State Elections (1964)*, Government Printer, Kuala Lumpur, 1964.

8. See, e.g., Tunku Abdul Rahman, *May 13: Before and After*, Utusan Melayu Press, Kuala Lumpur, 1969; Gagliano, *Communal Violence in Malaysia (1969): The Political Aftermath*, Ohio University, Center for International Studies, Athens, 1970; Goh Cheng Teik, *The May Thirteenth Incident and Democracy in Malaysia*, Oxford University Press, Kuala Lumpur, 1971; Mahathir bin Mohamad, *The Malay Dilemma*, The Asia Pacific Press, Singapore, 1970; Means, op. cit.; Slimming, *Malaysia: Death of Democracy*, John Murray, London, 1969; K. Von Vorys, *Democracy without Consensus*, Princeton University Press, New Jersey, 1975; *Report on the May 13 Tragedy (1969)*, the National Operations Council, Kuala Lumpur, 1969.

9. See *Report on the Parliamentary and State Legislative Assembly General Elections (1969)*, Government Printer, Kuala Lumpur, 1972.

10. See also pp. 209-10 above.

11. See *Report on the Parliamentary and State Legislative Assembly General Elections (1974)*, Government Printer, Kuala Lumpur, 1975.

12. W. J. M. Mackenzie, *Free Elections*, Allen and Unwin, 1958.

13. Wu Min Aun, *An Introduction to the Malaysian Legal System*, Heinemann, Kuala Lumpur, 1975, p. 64.

14. [1966] 2 M.L.J. 187.

15. [1961] 2 M.L.J. 67

16. [1975] 2 M.L.J. 41.

17. [1965] 2 M.L.J. 18.

18. [1977] 2 M.L.J. 254.

19. [1977] 2 M.L.J. 187.

20. 'The Government have used their power to deprive the plaintiff of a right that was vested in him under the judgement appealed from and as they are the most powerful body in the country we do not think it unfair that they should also pay the plaintiff costs of this appeal also,' per Suffian L.P.

21. Suffian, op. cit. at p. 85.

22. R. H. Hickling, 'The First Five Years of the Federation of Malaya Constitution' (1962) 4 Mal. L.R. 183 at pp. 191-2.

23. H. E. Groves, 'Constitution (Amendment) Act 1962' (1962) 4 Mal. L. R. 329.

24. H. E. Groves, *The Constitution of Malaysia*, Malaysia Publications Ltd., Singapore, 1964, p. 80.

25. See *Information Malaysia 1976/77*, Berita Publishing Sdn. Bhd., Kuala Lumpur, 1977.

26. One of the dirty tricks in fact played by supporters of the Democratic Party during the 1972 U.S. Presidential Elections campaign involved pickets of pregnant mothers carrying banners with the words 'Nixon did this to me'. For more insight of 'dirty tricks' practised at U.S. elections, see Jaworski, *The Right and the Power*, Reader's Digest Press, New York, 1976, pp. 18, 39-40, 41, 76, 289.

27. As Von Vorys, op. cit. at pp. 285-6 observed '... the (Election) campaign had broken the bounds of constitutional restraint.... And two events which must have had a profound effect on the campaign were yet to come. First, came the release of some pictures by the PMIP. One showed Khir Johari and his wife dressed in mandarin clothes. It had been used as a greeting card from Chinese New Year and may have seemed clever or cute to the Minister of Education. Two days before Elections the PMIP flooded the *kampongs* with reproductions, distributing some 50,000 in Kedah alone. The other circulated more surreptitiously depicted the Prime Minister eating with chopsticks with a roast suckling pig in the middle of the table. It was, to be sure, a composite, but few knew that....'

11. The Judiciary—During the First Twenty Years of Independence

THE Malaysian Constitution, which as the Malayan Constitution came into force twenty years ago, has proved to be a strong foundation on which to base a system of government capable of securing an efficient executive sensitive to the need for political stability without which there can be no economic stability and no prosperity for the newly independent nation.

There is no doubt that since 31 August 1957 the country has gone from strength to strength, as can be seen from the increase in the number of companies, firms, and factories all over the country, in the increase of employment, the increase in the number of home-owning citizens, in the number of motor vehicles on the road, in the number of schools and universities that provide more opportunities for more citizens, and generally in the growing number of the middle class that hardly existed before the last war. The most dramatic evidence of the advance achieved by the country is the value of the Malaysian dollar, which is today worth in terms of sterling double what it was at Independence.

Many factors have been responsible for the steady progress made by the country in so many areas. Not least is the contribution made by the judiciary that has quietly maintained the supremacy of the Constitution and the rule of law, and determined the matters that come up before it fairly and impartially, without fear or favour. The reputation that it enjoys of being able to decide without interference from the executive or the legislature, or indeed from anybody, contributes to confidence on the part of the members of the public generally that should they get involved in any dispute with the executive or with each other they can be sure of a fair and patient hearing and that their disputes will be determined impartially and honestly in accordance with law and justice. It is therefore appropriate that I should be invited to review the developments that have taken place in regard to the judiciary during the first twenty years of Independence.

Apart from transitional provisions the present Constitution contains sixteen Articles dealing with the judiciary. Originally it contained only twelve Articles, but Act 26/1963 which brought into being Malaysia added Articles 122A, 122B, and 122C with effect from Malaysia Day, 16 September 1963, and in 1976 Act A354 added Article 125A. This is in contrast to the Federation of Malaya Agreement, 1948, the Constitution in force immediately before Independence, which, apart from transitional provisions, had only seven clauses dealing with the judiciary.

INDEPENDENCE OF THE JUDICIARY

The first important development in regard to the judiciary in the first twenty years of Merdeka is the formal securing of the independence of the judiciary by the Merdeka Constitution. Before Independence, Malayan judges held office at the pleasure of the Crown, as can be seen from *Terrell* v. *Secretary of State*,[1] so that at least in theory they could be dismissed for any or no reason, but after Independence they no longer hold office at the pleasure of the Crown. The Merdeka Constitution contains express provisions to secure the independence of the judiciary from control or interference by the executive and the legislature.

As regards judges of superior courts, they may be removed from office by His Majesty only on the ground of misbehaviour or of inability from infirmity of body or mind or any other cause, properly to discharge the functions of their office—and then only on the recommendation of a tribunal consisting of five judges. They cannot be removed from office in any other way. Secondly, a judge's remuneration and other terms of office (including pension rights) may not be altered to his disadvantage after his appointment. Thirdly, his remuneration is charged on the Consolidated Fund, and must be incorporated in an Act of Parliament, which means that it is thereafter payable every year without the necessity for annual parliamentary approval, unlike the salary of members of the public service. Fourthly, the conduct of a judge may not be discussed in either House of Parliament except on a substantive motion of which notice has been given by at least a quarter of the number of members of that House, and may not be discussed in a State Assembly at all. Fifthly, since 1963 a judge is entitled to his pension, unlike civil servants who are only eligible for theirs.

It is worth repeating that judges should be independent, not to bolster their ego but in order to serve members of the public whose disputes with each other or with the Government should be determined impartially by persons who are free to decide simply in accordance with law and their conscience.

A Malaysian judge does not, however, hold office for life, for under the Constitution he has to retire at the age of sixty-five. Thereafter he may remain in office only for a further period of six months, if His Majesty so approves. Since the addition[2] of clause (1A) to Article 122, he may however be appointed an additional Federal Judge, as happened to the late Tan Sri MacIntyre on his retiring from the High Court, Malaya, at the age of sixty-five.

In the case of subordinate judges such as presidents of sessions courts and magistrates, they still hold office at the pleasure of His Majesty, but their appointments, promotions, transfers, and discipline are outside the control of the Government—these matters are decided by an independent Judicial and Legal Service Commission.

In the case of members of the general public service who sometimes do duty on the subordinate bench, they may not be disciplined in regard to their judicial duties except with the consent of the Judicial and Legal Service Commission.[3]

TEMPORARY JUDGES

Since before Independence judges served at the pleasure of the Crown, it was possible to appoint acting judges. Though under the present Constitution a judge does not hold office at the pleasure of the Crown, yet it allows the appointment of temporary judges in one of four ways:

(a) As an additional Federal judge appointed under clause (1A) of Article 122 by the Yang di-Pertuan Agong on the advice of the Lord President. The Conference of Rulers need not be consulted. He may be appointed even if over the age of sixty-five, but he must have held high judicial office in the Federation.

(b) If he is 'designated' to sit as a judge of a High Court either in Malaya or in Borneo under clause (2) of Article 122A.[4] He must be qualified for appointment as a judge and designated by the Yang di-Pertuan Agong acting on the advice of the Prime Minister after consulting the Conference of Rulers, and the Chief Justice of the High Court concerned. So far nobody has ever been designated to sit as a judge.

(c) As a judicial commissioner under clauses (3) and (4) of Article 122A,[5] 'for the despatch of business of the High Court in Borneo in an area in which a judge of the court is not for the time being available'. The appointee need not be a person qualified for appointment as a judge; he need only be an advocate or a person professionally qualified to be admitted an advocate of the court. The appointment is made by the Yang di-Pertuan Agong acting on the advice of the Lord President, or for an area in either State by the Governor of the State acting on the advice of the Chief Justice, Borneo, and the appointment will be for such period or for such purposes as may be specified in the order of appointment. The judicial commissioner's power is, however, rather limited, because the order appointing him may impose limitations and conditions, and he has power, first, only in the area for which he is appointed, and, secondly, only to perform such functions of a judge of the High Court, Borneo, as appear to him to require to be performed without delay.

Provisions similar to clauses (3) and (4) existed in Borneo even before Malaysia Day and were resorted to when a judge was sick or absent on short leave. Since Malaysia Day, most senior stipendiary magistrates in Borneo have at one time or another been appointed by the Governor as judicial commissioners for very short periods when judges were away. Because clause (4) says that the power of a judicial commissioner is limited to such functions as appear to him to require to be performed without delay, these stipendiary magistrates continued with their ordinary court work but held themselves ready to deal with any urgent business, such as *habeas corpus*, injunctions, stay of execution, and so on. Only Mr. John Williams and Tan Sri Datuk Lee Hun Hoe, the present Chief Justice, Borneo, were appointed for more than six months. They were both later appointed judges.

(d) In 1976, Parliament by Act A354/76, section 27(b), allowed the appointment of temporary judges by a fourth way. A new clause (5)[6] to Article 122A provides that for the despatch of business of the High Court in Malaya His Majesty, acting on the advice of the Lord President, may appoint to be judicial commissioner any person qualified for appointment as a judge of the High Court. So far nobody has yet been appointed judicial commissioner under this new provision.

The intention is to make these appointments from among senior members of the Bar and senior officers of the service as and when required, particularly to help out when a regular judge is sick or on leave, or is away chairing a Royal Commission, and also in areas where there is no resident judge and it is desired to clear mounting backlog. These judicial commissioners will do the same kind of work as Recorders in England.

It will be noted that appointments under the new clause (5) can be made by His Majesty simply on the advice of the Lord President—without reference to the Conference of Rulers. Though the new clause (5) omits mention of the Prime Minister, he will of course be consulted since the Lord President communicates with the Palace through the Prime Minister's Department.

THE MINISTER OF JUSTICE

The second development as regards the judiciary is the abolition of the Minister of Justice in 1970.

The first Minister of Justice[7] (appointed in September 1957) was Datuk Suleiman bin Datuk A. Rahman who was also Minister of the Interior. He was followed (in September 1959) by the late Tun Leong Yew Koh who subsequently became Governor of Malacca. He was responsible only for the courts, meaning their administrative requirements and problems; he had no say in decisions of judges or magistrates, nor in their appointments, promotions, transfers, or disciplining. He had no responsibility for other departments. His court responsibility meant that he had to see that the judiciary had enough judges, magistrates, and support staff, enough courthouses, books, typewriters, stationery, and so on—so that it may provide an efficient public service, for the judiciary does provide an essential public service, in the same way as do the Water Department, the Telecommunications Department, the Post Office, the National Electricity Board, and so on. He and his staff went round the country looking at courthouses, talking to staff on the ground, and finding out what facilities were lacking. Then they did battle on behalf of the judiciary with the Treasury and the Establishment Office for the necessary money and staff, with the Ministry of Works for priority to be given to court buildings, and with State Governments for necessary land. This spared the head of the judiciary from administrative headaches and freed him to concentrate on hearing cases and writing judgments. In Cabinet the Minister of Justice was always available to defend proposals to improve the machinery of justice, in the same way as the Minister of Law was—and is—available in Cabinet and Parliament to press proposals to strengthen the Attorney-General's Department. Thus the case for the judiciary could not be lost by default.

Some of Tun Leong Yew Koh's successors were only part-time Ministers of Justice responsible for other departments also. Only two of them were full-time Ministers of Justice: Encik Bahaman bin Shamsuddin, and Datuk Haji Ghani Gilong, the last Minister of Justice.

In 1970 the separate Ministry of Justice was abolished on the ground that its existence was inconsistent with the independence of the judiciary. Responsibility in Cabinet and Parliament for the machinery of justice was transferred to the Prime Minister and most of the staff of the defunct ministry transferred to the courts. There are two schools of thought about this.

One school holds the view that the executive should have no say in the running of courts and their staff which should be the sole responsibility of the head of the judiciary. This view has prevailed in the Philippines since the 1973 Constitution. But for this view to mean anything, the relation between the head of the executive and the head of the judiciary must be very good, for the judiciary requires funds for staff and equipment, and these funds are controlled by the executive. So the head of the judiciary should be a good administrator and a good diplomat. He has to give thought to administrative and financial matters, which, though not always difficult, are usually very time-consuming, and he must be skilled in persuading the executive to give him the necessary funds to implement his plans.

The other school of thought holds the view that the head of the judiciary and his fellow judges should be free to concentrate solely on judicial work, and not be troubled by matters that are best handled by experts trained and skilled in administration. Examples of such matters are the right number of judges and magistrates and their support staff, their salaries and conditions of service, extensions to court buildings and the construction of new ones, money for equipment such as books, telephones, typewriters, stationery, and so on. It is very time-consuming and often exasperating for the head of the judiciary or his officials to have to argue over these matters with the Treasury and other ministries, who have to meet the competing claims of other and vote-winning projects.

Today, in the absence of a Minister of Justice, the Lord President and the two Chief Justices, in addition to sitting in court and writing judgments and worrying about the Federal and High Courts, have to worry about subordinate courts and their staff and administrative needs. In England and in New Zealand the Chief Justices are not troubled by problems of subordinate courts. In England the Lord Chancellor attends to them, and in New Zealand the Minister of Justice.

Probably the time will return when in Malaysia too the Lord President should be freed to look only after the affairs of the Federal Court, and each of the two Chief Justices only after the affairs of their respective High Courts, with a Minister of Justice looking after the multifarious problems relating to the administrative needs of all courts, especially the multifarious needs of subordinate courts, where the bulk of judicial work is done. The present arrangement whereby the Prime Minister is responsible in Cabinet and Parliament for the machinery of justice, while splendid in concept, does not work well in practice. He and his staff have a thousand and one problems, political and otherwise, all urgent, and while they have the power to implement suggestions emanating from the judiciary they do not have the time to give much thought to them.

While on the subject of the Minister of Justice, it is well worth remarking that in Malaysia there seems to be some confusion regarding the functions and responsibilities of the Attorney-General who is also the Minister of Law. Not only the public, whose ignorance may be excused, even some State Governments and some senior civil servants are under the impression that the Minister of Law is responsible for judges and the smooth running of the courts. A senior official of the Kelantan Government who was engaged in devising a programme for the official opening of a new courthouse was surprised to be told that the Lord President was head of a separate and distinct branch of government and had no minister, and that the Minister of Law was only the Government's legal adviser, representing Government in court and having no say in the running of the judiciary. In one year the Public Services Department lumped the staff of the judicial and legal departments in one list. This confusion has been caused in part by the practice—in my view undesirable—of the Minister of Law being sometimes assigned by the Government to answer parliamentary questions on courts.

POWER TO INTERPRET THE CONSTITUTION

The third important development in regard to the judiciary is that today, unlike before Independence, judges have power (and indeed the duty) to interpret the Constitution (in cases and controversies actually before them). This is implicit from the Constitution which does not have a provision corresponding to clause 153 of the Federation of Malaya Agreement, 1948, which expressly reserved the power to interpret that agreement to an Interpretation Tribunal.[8]

Courts have power to interpret written law; by virtue of section 2 of the Federal Constitution Ordinance, 1957, the Constitution has the force of law; as it is written it is therefore written law; and it follows that courts have power to interpret the Constitution. *All* courts have this power, not only the Federal Court.

Doubt that courts other than the Federal Court have this power is caused by misunderstanding of the effect of clause (2) of Article 128. The effect of that clause is not to prevent any court other than the Federal Court from interpreting the Constitution. Its effect is merely this, that where in any proceeding before any other court a question arises as to the effect of any provision of the Constitution, if rules of court so provide, that question must be referred to the Federal Court, whereupon the Federal Court must determine the question and remit the case to the other court for disposal in accordance with the determination. In practice constitutional questions often arise in the High Court but never in subordinate courts.

POWER TO DECLARE LAWS INVALID

The fourth important development is that unlike before Independence,[9] now, courts have power to declare law enacted by the legislature void:

(a) in the case of both federal and state written law, because it is inconsistent with the Constitution;[10]

(b) in the case of federal written law, because it is outside the power of Parliament to enact, and in the case of state written law, because it is outside the power of the state legislature to enact;[11]

(c) in the case of state written law, because it is inconsistent with federal law.[12]

The power to declare invalid any law on grounds (a) and (c) is not subject to any restrictions, and may be exercised by the courts in the ordinary way, so that the question may be determined by any court in the land.

The power to declare any law invalid on ground (b) is however subject to three restrictions prescribed by the Constitution.

First, clause (3) of Article 4 provides that the validity of any law made by Parliament or by a state legislature may not be questioned on the ground that it makes provisions with respect to any matter with respect to which Parliament or, as the case may be, the legislature of a State has no power to make laws, except in three types of proceedings:

(i) in proceedings for a declaration that the law is invalid on that ground; or

(ii) if the law was made by Parliament, in proceedings between the Federation and one or more States; or

(iii) if the law was made by a state legislature, in proceedings between the Federation and that State.

It will be noted that proceedings of types (ii) and (iii) are brought by the Government. Proceedings of type (i) may be brought by any person, but he must specifically ask for a declaration[13] that the law impugned is invalid on the ground that it is outside the competence of the relevant legislature.

Secondly, clause (4) of Article 4 provides that proceedings of type (*i*) may not be commenced by an individual without the leave of a judge of the Federal Court, and the Federation is entitled to be a party to such proceedings and so is any State that would or might be a party to proceedings brought for the same purpose under (*ii*) or (*iii*) above.

Thirdly, clause (1) of Article 128 provides that only the Federal Court has jurisdiction to determine any question whether a law made by Parliament or by a state legislature is invalid on the ground that it makes provision with respect to a matter with respect to which Parliament or, as the case may be, the state legislature has no power to make laws.[14] No other court has this jurisdiction.

LOCALIZATION OF THE JUDICIARY

The fifth important development of the judiciary is its complete localization which occurred in 1969 when the last expatriate judge (Mr. Justice W. J. Silke, Kuching) left on retirement.

Before the last war, only one local man (the late Raja Musa) had been appointed High Court judge; after the war, first Datuk A. Hamid bin Mustapha was appointed (1952) and then Syed Sheh Barakbah (1956). In the year of Independence (1957) out of fourteen judges listed, only two were local. In the same year Datuk A. Hamid retired. Then in 1958 the late H. T. Ong (later Tan Sri) and Ismail Khan (later Tan Sri) were appointed, followed in 1959 by Azmi bin Mohamed (later Tun) and Mahmud M. Hashim, bringing the number of local judges that year to five. This number remained unchanged until 1961 when I was appointed. The last expatriate in Malaya, Tun Sir James Thomson, retired in 1966 and in Borneo (Silke) in 1969. Today[15] all twenty-eight judges are Malaysian.

Expatriate judges had a high reputation for being impartial and fair and fearless, and appearing in court before any of them one sometimes wondered whether after they had all gone the judiciary would enjoy the same high reputation. Experience since has shown that one need not have wondered.

, Subordinate courts had for many years before Independence been manned by a fairly large number of local lawyers, and their localization presented fewer problems and was achieved in a much shorter time.

The credit for successful localization should be given to the late Sir Charles Mathew, then Chief Justice, Malaya, and to his successor, Tun Sir James Thomson (subsequently Lord President). They watched over their young magistrates sympathetically and carefully and had promising ones sent to London on government scholarship to qualify as barristers and return to the junior bench or to serve in the Attorney-General's Chambers. This took some doing because in the early years of Independence top priority was given to the training of administrators to take over from expatriates in the civil service who were to remain for five years after Independence—unlike expatriate officers in the judicial and legal service who undertook to remain two years longer. So in the 1950s many able young men sent to U.K. to get a university law degree were expressly forbidden to read for the bar, in case later they should get snapped up by the judicial and legal service or, worse, leave for private practice a few years after their return. (Many of these men are now very senior officers in various important ministries.)

DIRECT APPOINTMENTS FROM THE BAR

The sixth important development in the judiciary during the last twenty years was the increase in the number of direct appointments from practising members of the local Bar.

Between the end of the Second World War and Independence a few direct appointments were made, but all of expatriates, namely Mr. Hastings, Mr. Bostock-Hill, and Mr. F. A. Briggs.

The first local man to be appointed direct from the Bar was the late Tan Sri H. T. Ong, followed a month later by Tan Sri Ismail Khan. Both retired as Chief Justice, the first of the High Court, Malaya, and the other as Chief Justice, High Court, Borneo.

Since then eight practising members of the Bar have been appointed, namely: Tan Sri MacIntyre (1964—he came through the diplomatic service); Tan Sri S. M. Yong (1965); Datuk Chang Min Tat (1966); the late Narain Sharma (1969); in Borneo, George Seah (1969); Fred Arulanandom (1974); Datuk Eusoffe Abdoolcader (1974); and Datuk Mohamed Zahir (1975).

Three of these—S. M. Yong, George Seah, and Zahir—had been very active in politics before their appointments, but nobody can say that in their work they ever allowed their decisions to be influenced by political considerations. Out of twenty-eight judges today,[16] five are direct appointees from the Bar.

Finding a private practitioner who is willing to be elevated is not easy. Those who are suitable are not always willing because they have been used to heavy expenses to support their children in school or university—or even racehorses—and cannot afford to maintain their family or interests on a judge's salary, or simply because they prefer the freedom of private practice which allows them to dabble in business or politics or both, and know that the constraints of a judge's life, not only on the bench but also off it, will irk them. Also they know that after retirement they are not expected to return to practice of the law however much they may need to financially, as the Bar frowns on retired judges re-entering practice. Those who are willing may not be suitable, and the few (their number is tiny) who lobby for elevation have to be courteously fobbed off.

The presence of direct appointees from the Bar has no doubt strengthened the judiciary, as usually they have expertise in special branches of the civil law and are familiar with what goes on during the sparring stage leading to actual trial, and fill in the gaps in the experience and knowledge of those appointed from the service. Direct appointees too benefit from working side by side with service appointees, for the latter have special knowledge of police and government procedures and are used to listening quietly and court-eously before making up their minds. There are about 500,000 government servants, and a good one has learned to be a team worker, to get on with his superiors, equals and subordinates. This is good discipline for him—it makes him tolerant and understanding of others' points of view, a quality helpful to a judge.

JUDICIARY STILL UNPOLITICIZED

The sixth feature of the judiciary since Independence is that, unlike the civil service, it has remained completely unpoliticized. Before Independence there were no politicians in power, and the civil service, especially the Malayan Civil Service and its equivalents in Sabah and Sarawak, *was* the Government. After Independence power was transferred to local politicians, as is natural in a par-liamentary democracy, and it is they who decide policy and see that it is implemented. As a result, the role of the civil service has changed. Now, they gather and analyse the evidence and marshal the facts on a particular problem; they advise their political masters on the various options open, taking care to point out the repercus-sions that are likely to arise from each option; and once a decision has been taken the civil servants implement it. Thus it is inevitable that the public service should have become politicized. The judiciary, on the other hand, in determining the disputes that come up before them is under a duty to do so impartially without fear or favour and the Constitution forbids the executive and the legislature from telling them how a case should be decided. In fairness to the executive and the legislature, it must be said that they have never at any time tried to influence the judiciary.

PROFESSIONALISM IN SUBORDINATE COURTS

The seventh important development of the judiciary during the last twenty years is the increasing professionalism of subordinate courts. Before the war, administrative officers such as D.O.s and A.D.O.s did part-time duty sitting as magistrates. The pace of life was slower and they had time to do it. Though not qualified as lawyers, all of them had been given some training in law, especially criminal law, the law of criminal procedure, and the law of evidence, and they did well sitting as magistrates. Also, the experience of actually trying cases gave them a good insight into the impact of the law on the citizen and instilled into them the conviction that the law was not something abstract to be read in the quiet of the study. Also, it instilled into them a sense of fair play (the desirability of considering the evidence before making up their minds), a very important quality in an administrator. Finally, when eventually they rose to high positions in the Treasury and the Establishment Office, unlike their modern counterparts, they were familiar with administrative problems affecting the courts and their staff and listened with understanding and sympathy to proposals to improve the machinery of justice.

In the days immediately after the Japanese surrender administrative officers had to give top priority to rehabilitating the country from the ravages of war. When the emergency broke out (1948) security became the top priority. D.O.s and A.D.O.s then found sitting on the bench very inconvenient. Also, the number of lawyers had increased gradually, and trying a case became more time-consuming. Government then decided that the judicial work of D.O.s should be taken over by qualified lawyers appointed magistrates full-time, travelling on circuit to various districts. I was the first full-time circuit magistrate appointed, in Malacca in 1948.

As salaries in Government were not attractive, few lawyers were willing to serve in the public service, and consequently the implementation of this policy took some time. (A number of expatriate lawyers arrived with the reoccupation forces and served with the British Military Administration and subsequently with the Malayan Union, but thereafter most of them left to go into private practice.) Even today, while it is true that D.O.s and A.D.O.s do very little work on the bench, certainly in Peninsular Malaysia, we have not succeeded in employing only qualified lawyers as magistrates. Fortunately we are able to persuade some retired civil servants with judicial experience to return to serve as magistrates, but these officers will gradually be replaced as more lawyers become available.

In Sabah and Sarawak, however, the population is comparatively sparse and scattered, and it is uneconomic to employ magistrates in every division. Consequently they are concentrated in the major centres, and because of distance they are unable to cover every area where their service is required and as a result it is still necessary for administrative officers to sit on the bench in many places. The State Governments have asked for this work to be taken over wholly by the judiciary and the intention is to do so. But there is an acute shortage of lawyers in Borneo and the few that there are find private practice, or business or politics or a bit of each more attractive, so the implementation of this intention will take much longer than in Peninsular Malaysia.

INCREASED JURISDICTION OF SUBORDINATE COURTS

In view of the increased professionalism of subordinate courts, the legislature has continued its pre-Independence policy of gradually increasing the jurisdiction of presidents of sessions courts and of magistrates.

As regards criminal matters, immediately before Independence a sessions court had jurisdiction under section 63(1) of the Courts Ordinance No. 43 of 1948, to try all offences for which the imprisonment provided by law did not exceed 7 years or which were punishable with fine only and certain specified grave offences under the Penal Code, but under section 64(1) it could pass only a sentence not exceeding

(a) 3 years' imprisonment;
(b) a fine of $4,000;
(c) whipping up to 12 strokes; or
(d) any combination of the above sentences.

Notwithstanding section 63(1), a sessions court could try any offences not punishable with death or imprisonment for life if both the Public Prosecutor and the accused consented.

Notwithstanding section 64(1), a sessions court could impose the maximum sentence prescribed by law if it considered it just to do so by reason of the previous conviction or of the antecedents of the accused, in which case it should record its reason for so doing.

In 1969 this jurisdiction was increased by the Emergency (Essential Powers) Ordinance No. 14, 1969,[17] which was subsequently made permanent by the Courts (Amendment) Act A33 of 1971.

Now a sessions court has jurisdiction to try all offences for which the maximum imprisonment provided by law does not exceed 10 years. Also the Yang di-Pertuan Agong may, on the advice of the Chief Justice, confer on any president of the sessions court special jurisdiction to try offences for which the term of imprisonment provided by law does not exceed 14 years.

As regards sentences, a sessions court may now pass any sentence not exceeding

    (a) 5 years' imprisonment or, in the case of a president conferred with special jurisdiction, 7 years' imprisonment;

    (b) a fine of $10,000, or, in the case of a president with special jurisdiction, a fine of $20,000;

    (c) whipping up to 12 strokes; or

    (d) any sentence combining any of the above.

Act A33 also empowers a president with special jurisdiction to try offences under sections 326, 329, 376, and 377 of the Penal Code and section 30 of the Arms Act, 1960, all punishable with more than 7 years' imprisonment.

In addition he may also try the following offences punishable with life, namely under section 39B of the Dangerous Drugs Ordinance, 1952, and sections 4 and 5 of the Firearms (Increased Penalty) Act, 1971, and may impose the full punishment.

As regards civil matters, immediately before Independence a sessions court had jurisdiction to try all civil suits where the value of the subject matter did not exceed $2,000, section 65(1). The same Emergency Regulation subsequently confirmed by Act A33 has increased this upper limit to $5,000. Act A33 also provides that a president with special jurisdiction may try suits of a value not exceeding $10,000.

As regards magistrates, immediately before Independence a first-class magistrate had jurisdiction to try all offences for which the maximum imprisonment provided by law did not exceed 3 years or which were punishable with fine only and certain specified grave offences under the Penal Code, section 85 of the Courts Ordinance No. 43 of 1948. The Emergency (Essential Powers) Ordinance No. 14, 1969, increased this upper limit to 5 years, which increase has been made permanent by Act A33.

Immediately before Independence a first-class magistrate had power to pass any sentence allowed by law not exceeding

    (a) 12 months' imprisonment;

    (b) a fine of $2,000;

    (c) whipping up to 6 strokes; or

    (d) any sentence combining any of the sentences above.

In exceptional cases he could impose the full punishment, in which case he had to record his reason for doing so, section 87(1) of the Courts Ordinance No. 43 of 1948. The Emergency (Essential Powers) Ordinance No. 14, 1969, since made permanent by Act A33, empowers a first-class magistrate to impose a maximum sentence of 2 years' imprisonment and a fine of $5,000.

In civil matters, immediately before Independence a first-class magistrate had jurisdiction to try all civil suits of a value not exceeding $1,000, section 90 of the Courts Ordinance No. 43 of 1948. This upper limit was increased to $2,000 by the Emergency (Essential Powers) Ordinance No. 14 of 1969, which increase was made permanent by Act A33.

INCREASED RESPONSIBILITY OF THE HEAD OF THE JUDICIARY

The eighth important development in the judiciary during the last twenty years is the increase in the responsibility of its head arising out of Sabah and Sarawak joining Malaya (1963) to form Malaysia. Sabah and Sarawak are served by a separate High Court (that of Borneo). It is true that local problems affecting the courts in Borneo are looked into and may be solved by the Chief Justice in Kuching, but some problems require solution at a higher level, and the Lord President has then to be brought into the picture. Also he has periodically to visit the courts there, especially in outlying areas, to familiarize himself with living and working conditions on the ground, so that he is aware of the difficulties of judges and magistrates and their staff there. Everything may look rosy from Kuala Lumpur, but things look different in Sabah and Sarawak. All this work requires careful planning and occupies much time. On top of this, the Federal Court sits in East Malaysia twice a year, spending a week at each sitting, and the Lord President is expected to preside at those sittings. All this has resulted in adding an extra burden on his shoulders.

THE INCREASE IN WORKLOAD

The ninth notable feature of the judiciary during the first twenty years of independence is the increase in the workload of all courts at every level throughout the country. Increased prosperity should in theory bring down the crime rate, but in fact it has had the opposite effect. The sight of prosperous neighbours fills many with envy and a desire for instant wealth, which can be achieved by cheating, thieving, burglary, and robbery. The increases in population, in the standard of education, and in the number of lawyers have also had the effect of bringing more civil business to the courts. An educated citizenry is more aware of its rights and the existence of a fairly competitive bar makes it possible for more Malaysians to resort to court to assert their rights.

Running-down actions threaten to swamp the High Court in Peninsular Malaysia which spends about 60 per cent of its time determining which motorists are responsible for persons killed or maimed on the roads. The move by the Government to follow the

New Zealand no-fault insurance scheme will be welcomed not only by victims of traffic accidents (who will not mind receiving less compensation, knowing that they will in any event get it, and get it quickly and without losing a good part of it to legal fees), but also by judges who can then devote more time to other—more interesting—work.

THE PRIVY COUNCIL

The tenth important development of the judiciary during the last twenty years is the curtailment[18] of appeals to the Privy Council with effect from 1 January 1978, and the consequent imposition of greater responsibility on the Federal Court.

Before Independence, the Rulers by clause 83 of the Federation of Malaya Agreement, 1948, severally requested the British sovereign to receive appeals to the Privy Council from the Malayan Supreme Court and in respect of each of their states severally conferred upon the British sovereign power and jurisdiction so to do, which power and jurisdiction the British sovereign accepted. By subclause (5) of clause 77 of the Constitution, the powers and procedure of the Supreme Court and provisions relating to appeals therefrom to the Privy Council were to be prescribed by federal Ordinance.

On Independence, appeals to the Privy Council were retained. The inconsistency of such appeals from an independent country with its own head of state to another country with a separate head of state was overcome neatly by providing that in law such appeals are addressed not direct to the Privy Council but to the Yang di-Pertuan Agong who refers them for advice to the Privy Council who advises thereon not the British sovereign but the Yang di-Pertuan Agong. It is implicit that the Malaysian Parliament may at any time curtail or even abolish altogether such appeals.

Article 131 of the Merdeka Constitution provides that the Yang di-Pertuan Agong may make arrangements with the British sovereign for the reference to the Privy Council of appeals from the Federal Court, and such arrangements were made in an Agreement concluded between the British sovereign and the Yang di-Pertuan Agong on 4 March 1958, and published in the Federal Government Gazette of 10 April 1958.[19]

Clause (4) of Article 131 further provides that on receiving from the British Government in the United Kingdom the report or recommendation of the Judicial Committee of the Privy Council in respect of an appeal under this Article, the Yang di-Pertuan Agong shall make such order as may be necessary to give effect thereto.

Clause (1) of Article 131 also provides that, subject to the provisions of that Article, an appeal shall lie from the Federal Court to the Yang di-Pertuan Agong in any case where such appeal is allowed by federal law, and in respect of which provision for reference to the said Committee is made by or under the enactments regulating the proceedings of the said Committee.

The British sovereign appoints to the Judicial Committee judges from countries from which appeals lie to that Committee—but only on the recommendation of the government of those countries, e.g. the late Sir Hugh Wooding, Chief Justice of the West Indies. Current appointees are the Chief Justices of Australia and New Zealand. No such appointments have however been recommended from Malaysia.

From 4 October 1975, decisions of the Federal Court in criminal cases tried under the Essential (Security Cases) Regulations, 1975,[20] may not be appealed to the Privy Council.

The decision to curtail appeals to the Privy Council in criminal and constitutional matters was given effect to by amendments to section 74 of the Courts of Judicature Act 7 of 1964.[21] As regards constitutional matters, the amended subsection (3) of section 74 of the Courts of Judicature Act 7 of 1964 provides:

'(3)... no appeal shall lie from the Federal Court to the [Privy Council]—
   (a) from any decision as to the effect of any provision of the Constitution including the validity of any written law relating to such provision; and
   (b) from any opinion pronounced on a reference under Article 130 of the Constitution.'

(A new subsection (4) of section 74 provides that a certificate by the Federal Court that a decision falls within subsection (3) is final and shall not be subject to appeal to [the Privy Council].)

Thus today only civil appeals that do not involve the Constitution may be taken to the Privy Council.

The Federal Court has always been careful to make the right decisions, but now it has to be extra careful in making the right decisions in criminal and constitutional matters, because their mistakes are final. It may well be that criminal and constitutional appeals that come up before it should always be heard by a minimum of five judges.[22]

DISAPPEARANCE OF THE SUPREME COURT

The eleventh important development is the disappearance from the scene of the Supreme Court, consisting of the Court of Appeal and the High Court of Malaya, and its replacement by the Federal

Court and two High Courts of co-ordinate jurisdiction, namely that of Malaya and that of Borneo.

Before Independence, the Federation of Malaya Agreement, 1948, by clause 77 established a Supreme Court, a 'court of un-limited civil and criminal jurisdiction' which was but a continua-tion of the pre-1948 Supreme Court. The 1957 Constitution uses for the first time the expression 'judicial power', which, according to Article 121, 'shall be vested in a Supreme Court and such inferior courts as may be provided by federal law'.

In 1957 too the Supreme Court was but a continuation of the pre-Independence Supreme Court.

In 1963 with the formation of Malaysia, the Supreme Court disappeared from the scene when Article 121 was amended[23] to provide that the judicial power of the Federation shall be vested in three High Courts of co-ordinate jurisdiction and status and in such inferior courts as may be provided by federal law—the three High Courts being those of Malaya, Singapore, and Borneo. Since the departure of Singapore in 1965, there are now two, each headed by its own Chief Justice.

THE FEDERAL COURT

From Malaysia Day, 16 September 1963, with the abolition of the Supreme Court, the Court of Appeal was abolished and replaced by the Federal Court. In effect this was only a renaming exercise.

The Federal Court consists of the Lord President, the two Chief Justices, and four Federal Judges. Usually it sits in a panel of three and occasionally in a panel of five. A High Court judge nominated by the Lord President may also sit on it. It is presided over by the Lord President or by the most senior judge. It travels on circuit to the major state capitals.

The Federal Court is different from the old Court of Appeal as follows. Apart from hearing appeals from the two High Courts, which forms the bulk of its work, it has three other kinds of jurisdic-tion:

1. exclusive original jurisdiction under Article 128(1)—
   (a) to determine whether a law made by Parliament or by the legislature of a state is invalid on the ground that it makes provision with respect to a matter with respect to which the particular legislature has no power to make laws; and
   (b) disputes or any other question between states or between the Federation and any state;
2. referral jurisdiction under clause (2) of Article 128. Under this where in any proceeding before another court a question arises as to

the effect of any provision of the Constitution, the Federal Court has jurisdiction to determine the question and remit the case to the other court to be disposed of in accordance with the determination; and

3. advisory jurisdiction under Article 130 which gives power to His Majesty the Yang di-Pertuan Agong to refer to the Federal Court for its opinion any question as to the effect of any provision of the Constitution which has arisen or appears to him likely to arise.

The Federal Court has never had occasion to exercise jurisdiction (1) above; it has had occasion to do so several times in the case of jurisdiction (2)—see for example *Assa Singh* v. *Mentri Besar, Johore*[24]—and it had occasion to exercise jurisdiction (3) once, in *Government of Malaysia* v. *The Government of the State of Kelantan*.[25]

Considering the country's size, there should be no need for two separate High Courts, but when Singapore and Borneo joined Malaya to form Malaysia in 1963, it would not have been politically acceptable to merge the then already existing Supreme Court of Singapore and that of Borneo into the then High Court of Malaya, and abolish the office of the two Chief Justices of Singapore and Borneo and put the two of them under the Chief Justice of the new Malaysia. So the decision was taken to retain the two Supreme Courts as the High Court of Singapore and that of Borneo, each headed by its respective incumbent Chief Justice; to retain the High Court, Malaya, also headed by a newly created Chief Justice; and to create a new office of Chief Justice, Malaysia, above the three offices. This last was named Lord President, following the example of Scotland, the native land of Tun Sir James Thomson, the then Chief Justice, Malaya, and Lord President designate.

THE JUDICIARY MORE FEDERAL

The twelfth important development in regard to the judiciary is that today it is more federal and less state.

Before Independence, the machinery of justice was hybrid, i.e. partly federal and partly state, for the Federation of Malaya Agreement, 1948, provided that the establishment, jurisdiction, and powers of all courts (except Muslim religious courts) were matters with respect to which the federal legislature had power to make laws, but any federal law made must confer executive authority on states and settlements (except so far as matters of policy common to two or more states and settlements were involved) over—

1. the appointment of presidents of sessions courts to be by the High Commissioner on the recommendation of the Chief Justice;

2. the appointment of first-class magistrates (other than *ex officio* first-class magistrates) to be in a Settlement by the High Commis-

sioner, and in a Malay State by the Ruler, in each case on the recommendation of the Chief Justice;

3. the appointment of magistrates, other than first-class magistrates, to be, in a Settlement by the High Commissioner, and in a Malay State by the Ruler.

Thus it will be seen that in the case of the appointment of subordinate judges, legislative authority was with the Federal Government but executive authority was shared in the case of first-class magistrates between the Federal and State Governments.

In the case of superior judges too authority was shared, for the Agreement provided that the Chief Justice and judges of the Supreme Court were to be appointed by the High Commissioner for and on behalf of the British sovereign and of the Rulers.

Under the present Constitution, the administration of justice including the Constitution and organization of all courts other than Muslim courts and the jurisdiction and powers of all such courts, is a wholly federal subject, except as regards the appointment of superior judges—so that constitutionally Parliament may legislate to provide that appointments of all magistrates be made solely by a federal authority, contrary to the current law set out in the Subordinate Courts Act.[26] But Parliament may not do so regarding superior judges, for Article 122B expressly provides that the Conference of Rulers must be consulted regarding the appointments of the Lord President, every Chief Justice, every Federal and High Court judge. In the case of the appointment of the Chief Justice of Borneo, the Prime Minister is required to consult the Chief Ministers of Sabah and Sarawak and, as has been seen, the Governor of each of these States has the right under Article 122A(3) to appoint on the advice of the Chief Justice, Borneo, a judicial commissioner for an area in the State.

Also, under the present Constitution the posting of superior judges to a State constitutionally may be done by the head of the judiciary without the concurrence of any federal authority or prior consultation with the State. Such concurrence and prior consultation were necessary prior to Independence, because the Federation of Malaya Agreement provided that arrangements for the duties and places of residence of judges made by the Chief Justice required the concurrence of the High Commissioner and that no judge could be appointed to reside in a Malay State unless the Ruler had been consulted first. There is no similar provision in the present Constitution.

However, the practice in Peninsular Malaysia is to consult the Ruler or Governor before a judge is posted to his State, and other arrangements are made if there is objection or even if the Ruler or

Governor expresses unhappiness. In Sabah and Sarawak the pre-Independence practice is followed whereby the Governor and State Government are only informed of the posting of a judge to their State.

In principle this practice should also be followed in Peninsular Malaysia; if the independence of the judiciary is to mean anything, no State's objection should prevail over the decision of the head of the judiciary to post a judge to that State.

The Federal Government has no say in the posting of judges, and there is no good reason why State Governments should have a say.

JUDICIAL AND LEGAL SERVICE COMMISSION

The thirteenth important development as regards the judiciary within the first twenty years of Merdeka is the establishment in 1957 of an independent service commission, the Judicial and Legal Service Commission, to appoint, confirm, promote, transfer, and discipline officers of the Judicial and Legal Service; its abolition in 1960; and then its revival on Malaysia Day in 1963.

Before Independence the Secretary of State in London dealt with these matters. After Independence they were dealt with by the Judicial and Legal Service Commission established by Article 138.

The Commission consisted of the Chief Justice as Chairman; the Attorney-General; the senior puisne judge; the Deputy Chairman of the Public Services Commission; and one or more other members appointed by the Yang di-Pertuan Agong, after consultation with the Chief Justice, from among judges or former judges. The Commission had no jurisdiction over the Chief Justice and other judges and the Attorney-General. Its function was to promote, confirm, emplace on the permanent or pensionable establishment, transfer (if a change of rank was involved), and exercise disciplinary control over members of the Judicial and Legal Service.

In addition, it must be consulted by the Yang di-Pertuan Agong before appointing an Attorney-General; it recommended the appointment of members of the Tribunal appointed by the Yang di-Pertuan Agong under Article 125 to enquire into the conduct of a judge; it recommended to the Yang di-Pertuan Agong that a judge be suspended pending reference to and report by the Tribunal.

It would appear that these recommendations were not binding.

The Commission also made recommendations on appointments of judges other than the Chief Justice, but these recommendations must be acted on by the Yang di-Pertuan Agong, after consulting the Conference of Rulers, Article 122(3). Before acting on such a recommendation the Yang di-Pertuan Agong could once refer it back to the Commission for reconsideration, Article 122(4).

In 1960, however, the Judicial and Legal Service Commission was abolished[27] and its functions in regard to members of the Judicial and Legal Service other than the Chief Justice and other judges were transferred to the independent Public Services Commission established on Independence by Article 139.

But thereafter the Attorney-General could be appointed by His Majesty simply on the advice of the Prime Minister without reference to any other authority, and a Tribunal appointed to enquire into the conduct of a judge could be appointed by His Majesty without reference to any authority except the Prime Minister.

As regards appointments of judges other than the Chief Justice, thereafter His Majesty could simply make them on the advice of the Prime Minister after consulting the Conference of Rulers and considering the advice of the Chief Justice.

In 1963, however, the Commission was revived with effect from 16 September 1963.[28] At the same time a branch of the Commission was established in the Borneo States with jurisdiction over members of the service employed in Borneo, Article 146A.

The main branch consisted of the Chairman of the Public Services Commission, as Chairman; the Attorney-General, or (since Act A354/76, section 31(b)), if the Attorney-General is a member of Parliament or is appointed otherwise than from among members of the Judicial and Legal Service, the Solicitor-General; and one or more other members appointed by the Yang di-Pertuan Agong after consultation with the Lord President, from among persons who are or have been, or (since Act A354/76, section 30(c)) are qualified to be judges or who were before Malaysia Day judges of the Supreme Court.

The Commission appoints, confirms, emplaces on the permanent or pensionable establishment, promotes, transfers (if a change of rank is involved), and exercises disciplinary control over members of the Judicial and Legal Service. It does not, however, have anything to do with the appointment of the Attorney-General, judges, or the Tribunal to enquire into the conduct of judges.

The Borneo branch of the Commission consisted of the Chief Justice of the High Court in Borneo (Chairman); the State Legal Adviser of each of the Borneo States; the Chairman of the State Public Service Commission in each of the Borneo States; and two persons designated by the Federal Government from among the members of the main body of the Judicial and Legal Service Commission or the Public Services Commission. The jurisdiction of this branch also extended to members of the public service of a Borneo State seconded to the Judicial and Legal Service.

Clause (6) of Article 146A provided that that Article was to have effect until the end of August 1968, and thereafter until the Federal Government determined to the contrary.

The Federal Government has decided to abolish the branch and that decision was given effect to by Act A354/76, section 35, effective from 26 August 1976.

Thus members of the Judicial and Legal Service employed in the Borneo States are now within the jurisdiction of the Commission based in Kuala Lumpur.

His Majesty has on the recommendation of the Lord President appointed to the Commission as members from Borneo the Chief Justice, High Court, Borneo; Mr. Justice B. T. H. Lee; and the State Attorney-General of Sarawak.[29]

Officers of the State Attorney-General's Chambers in Sarawak (other than the State Attorney-General) are members of the Federal Judicial and Legal Service, while those in the State Attorney-General's Chambers of Sabah are not; they are members of the State Service of Sabah. That is why the State Attorney-General of Sabah has not been appointed a member of the Commission.

It was thought that the Judicial and Legal Service Commission was abolished in 1960 on the recommendation of the then Federal Attorney-General, who considered that the judges who were in the majority were not sufficiently understanding of the need of the Attorney-General's Department for high quality staff.

Officers of the Judicial and Legal Service man not only the Judicial department but also the various departments under the Attorney-General's jurisdiction, and they are interchangeable between the various departments. An unsympathetic Chief Justice may starve the Attorney-General's Department of experienced staff and vice versa, and accordingly understanding of each other's needs is essential. To have a separate subordinate judicial service, as in India, is impractical; it will be a small service and promotion prospects within it will be limited, and consequently the service will have difficulty recruiting and retaining good officers.

OTHER DEVELOPMENTS

Other judicial developments may now be noticed.

POWER OF FEDERAL JUDGE

When a High Court judge was appointed Federal Judge, did he cease to have the power of a High Court judge? I do not think so, because his appointment was not revoked when he became a Federal judge; but in 1966 a new clause (10) was added[30] to Article 125 providing that a High Court judge appointed a Federal judge shall with effect from 19 September 1966, cease to be a judge of the High Court, except only for the purpose of giving judgment in a case tried by him prior to his appointment as a Federal judge. This amendment was made to stop Federal judges from interfering with decisions of magistrates and presidents of sessions courts. It is clear that after that a High Court judge on promotion to the Federal Court ceased to have the power of a High Court judge except for the limited purpose stated.

Then in 1971 this new clause was deleted by Act A31 effective from *19 September 1966*; as if Parliament intended that the new clause (10) had never existed. What was the position then? In my view it is clear that a High Court judge appointed to the Federal Court before or after that date continues to have the power of a High Court judge, but there was doubt in some minds as regards the true position. Many cases have been tried and decided by Federal judges sitting alone in the High Court, to help clear backlog especially in outlying places like Muar, Raub, and even in Kuala Lumpur. In particular, an ex-Mentri Besar of Selangor was tried and convicted by a Federal judge sitting alone in the High Court, *P.P.* v. *Datuk Harun bin Haji Idris*,[31] and one of his grounds of appeal was that he should have been tried in the High Court by a High Court judge and that his trial before and conviction by a Federal judge were a nullity. This ground was abandoned, because before the appeal came up for hearing the Constitution was amended[32] by Act A354 and the opportunity was taken to add a new Article 125A declaring that with effect from Merdeka Day a Federal judge may exercise the power of a High Court judge. The opportunity was also taken to declare that the Lord President may also do so, and that a judge of one High Court may exercise the power of a judge of another. No mention is made of the Chief Justice, since he is necessarily a judge of the High Court of which he is Chief.

It is convenient to allow a Federal judge to exercise the power of a High Court judge, so that if, for instance, a High Court judge suddenly falls ill or goes on leave his list may be taken care of by a Federal judge who happens to be free, rather than have all the cases taken off the list causing inconvenience to parties, counsel, and witnesses.

TRANSFER OF JUDGES FROM ONE HIGH COURT TO ANOTHER

A judge may be transferred from one High Court to another simply by the Yang di-Pertuan Agong on the recommendation of the Lord President after consulting the two Chief Justices, Article 122C. In practice no such transfers have been made. Before 1 January 1970, such transfers were difficult to make because the basic salaries of judges in Borneo were lower than those of judges in Peninsular Malaysia. Even now they are still difficult to make, because of the difficulty of finding replacements for the judges transferred.

NUMBER OF JUDGES

The number of judges, apart from the Lord President and the two Chief Justices, was fixed by the Constitution at four in the case of Federal judges—apart from additional Federal judges appointed under clause (1A) of Article 122—and at between four and twelve in the case of the High Court, Malaya, and at between four and eight in the case of the High Court, Borneo. But Parliament was expressly given power to change this number, and in 1969 it increased the number of judges of the High Court, Malaya, to fifteen.[33] Act A354/76 has transferred this power to change the number to the Yang di-Pertuan Agong, and His Majesty has increased the number of judges of the High Court, Malaya, to sixteen with effect from 1 January 1978.[34]

At present, apart from the two Chief Justices, there are sixteen High Court judges in Peninsular Malaysia and five in Sabah and Sarawak.[35]

UNIFORMITY OF LAWS

Laws should be certain and easily accessible. In a new federation like Malaysia, there are still many statutes on the same subject, applying in different parts of the country, and the work of harmonizing the written law, which is the avowed policy of the government, continues apace, albeit slowly. Fortunately, the superior courts are governed by one statute, the Courts of Judicature Act, 1964, and their procedure by the Rules of the old Supreme Court enacted in 1957 which have been applied throughout the country; the Evidence Ordinances of the different territories have been replaced by one that applies throughout Malaysia, the Evidence Act 56, and likewise the Criminal Procedure Code. A policy decision has been taken to apply the Malayan Subordinate Courts Act 92 to Sabah and Sarawak.

Having two or three statutes governing the same subject is confusing not only to lawyers with clients in several states, but also to the Federal Court which is expected to be au fait with all statutes in force.

It is the hope that the work of harmonizing the law will continue apace.

GOVERNMENT, THE ATTORNEY-GENERAL, THE BAR, AND LEGAL EDUCATION

No account of the judiciary is complete without mention of the Government, the Attorney-General, the Bar, and Legal Education.

During the last twenty years the Government, while slow to respond to proposals to improve the machinery of justice, continues to give it support by respecting its decisions and giving effect to them, and generally by upholding the independence of the judiciary.

With the Attorney-General too, as the foremost officer of the court, the judiciary enjoys cordial relations, despite the fact that the Government does not always win its cases.

The Bar is still fragmented into three, the Bar of Malaya, that of Sabah, and that of Sarawak, but the intention is to replace all three by the Malaysian Bar under the new Legal Profession Act, 1976, Act 166. Most of the existing members of the Bar are products of the English Inns of Court and in Sabah and Sarawak many of them qualify by virtue of being members of the Bar in Australia or New Zealand. Since 1957 however it has become possible for Malayans (now Malaysians) to become lawyers by entering the Law Faculty of the University of Singapore and the more recently opened (1972) Law Faculty at the University of Malaya in Kuala Lumpur. However, the student intake at Kuala Lumpur was and is small (about fifty per year), but there are plans afoot to increase it. As more and more senior lawyers retire, the majority at the Bar will consist of locally produced lawyers, and judging by some of them who appear in court before us there need be no fear about a drop in quality. Local law graduates have the advantage of being taught local law and therefore of being of almost immediate use as magistrates or in law firms, but London-trained barristers have more self-assurance and social poise and an easier command of English, which will continue to be of value to lawyers in Malaysia for a long time to come, if they wish to be competitive—in the same way as knowledge of Arabic will long remain important to those specializing in Muslim Law.

THE NATIONAL LANGUAGE

There has been increasing use of the national language, especially in subordinate courts.

In a court of justice parties and witnesses should be entitled to use any language they like. In Kedah and Perlis, even some Malays after giving evidence briefly in Malay would stop and ask permission to continue in Thai, and in a court of justice they should be and are given permission to do so. Nobody should be compelled to use a language in which he is not at home, and the Judicial Department employs skilled interpreters to help. In the business of arriving at the truth and doing justice, judges, presidents, and magistrates do everything to make it possible for parties and witnesses to be heard and understood by the court, and vice versa.

The use of the national language varies from place to place. In Alor Star over ten years ago when I was judge there, even in the High Court quite a number of cases were conducted almost entirely in the national language when there was no risk of injustice, because everybody present including counsel knew the language well.

I am of the view that the use of the national language cannot be rushed in a court of law without risk of doing injustice. Courts are not a political forum.

CONCLUSION

During the first twenty years of Independence the courts continue to enjoy public acceptance and confidence—due to the way they do their work (they sit in public in the presence of the press and of whoever wishes to come and attend), and to the reputation for fairness and impartiality they inherited from before Independence and which they have since enhanced.

The courts protect the citizen from bullying, victimization, and tyranny. By stoutly upholding the Constitution and enforcing the rule of law, they inspire in the bully, the wicked, and the rich and powerful with a salutary fear of retribution for any unlawful act or omission.

If the courts maintain their present standards in the future they will no doubt continue to enjoy public acceptance and confidence.

Appendix

This appendix on the Judiciary in Sabah and Sarawak has been prepared by Tan Sri Datuk Lee Hun Hoe, Chief Justice, High Court, Borneo.

SUPERIOR COURTS

Long before the formation of Malaysia, there was in Borneo what was popularly known as the Combined Judiciary with jurisdiction over Sarawak, North Borneo (now Sabah), and Brunei. The Sarawak, North Borneo and Brunei (Courts) Order in Council, 1951, established one superior court of record styled as the Supreme Court of Sarawak, North Borneo and Brunei consisting of the High Court of Sarawak, North Borneo and Brunei and the Court of Appeal of Sarawak, North Borneo and Brunei. This superior court came into existence on 1 December 1951, and represented one of the earliest steps taken to bring about unification of the three Borneo States in which it had jurisdiction. Progress in this direction eventually led to the formation of Malaysia in 1963.

After Malaysia Day, the superior court ceased to exercise jurisdiction over Brunei which did not join the Federation. The Combined Judiciary disappeared. The jurisdiction of the High Court of Sarawak, North Borneo and Brunei was assumed in Malaysia by the High Court in Borneo with jurisdiction in Sarawak and Sabah. In the same way the appellate jurisdiction of the Court of Appeal of Sarawak, North Borneo and Brunei was assumed by the Federal Court. Subsections (3) and (4) of section 88 of the Malaysia Act No. 26 of 1963 explain the position very clearly and read as follows:

(3) Anything done before Malaysia Day in or in connection with or with a view to any proceedings in the Court of Appeal of the Federation [of Malaya] or of Sarawak, North Borneo and Brunei, ... shall on and after that day be of the like effect as if that court were one and the same court with the Federal Court.

(4) Anything done before Malaysia Day in or in connection with or with a view to any proceedings in the High Court of the Federation, or of Sarawak, North Borneo and Brunei, ... shall on and after that day be of the like effect as if those High Courts were respectively one and the same court with the High Court in Malaya, the High Court in Borneo....

Although the Court of Appeal of Sarawak, North Borneo and Brunei ceased to exist, its ghost still haunts the courts. In 1970, a few years after Singapore had left Malaysia, the High Court of Singapore consisting of three judges held in *Mah Kah Yew* v. *Public Prosecutor*[36] that it was bound by a 1955 decision of the Court of Appeal of Sarawak, North Borneo and Brunei in the case of *Public Prosecutor* v. *Mills*[37] as under subsection (3) of section 88 of the Malaysia Act such decision had 'the like effect as if that court were one and the same court with the Federal Court'. See also *Public Prosecutor* v. *Adnan bin Khamis*[38] and *Public Prosecutor* v. *Joseph Chin Saiko*.[39]

As in Peninsular Malaysia, the superior court judges in the two States were also expatriates and the first local man (Tan Sri Datuk Lee Hun Hoe) was only appointed a High Court judge in 1965. The process of complete Malaysianization of the superior court in Sabah and Sarawak only became a reality in 1969 with the departure of the last expatriate judge (Mr. Justice W. J. Silke) on the expiry of his contract.

The High Court in Malaya and the High Court in Borneo have equal and co-ordinate jurisdiction. The judges take precedence among themselves according to the dates of their appointments. The judges receive the same basic salary and enjoy similar privileges.

SUBORDINATE COURTS

The Inferior or Subordinate Courts in Sabah and Sarawak are governed by their respective Subordinate Courts Ordinance which make provisions for three main classes of Magistrates, namely, First Class Magistrates, Second Class Magistrates, and Third Class Magistrates. First Class Magistrates are all legally qualified persons. Professionalism of the Subordinate Courts in the two States only began in the early 1950s. Where the Governor, by a warrant, declares a First Class Magistrate in his State to be a Stipendiary Magistrate, then he may pass sentence of imprisonment for a term not exceeding three years and impose a fine not exceeding $5,000/-. He may also be empowered to try certain offences normally dealt with by the High Court if the Governor includes those offences in the warrant. Normally, a First Class Magistrate can only hear civil cases where the value of the claim does not exceed $1,000/-. However, where a First Class Magistrate has been declared a Stipendiary Magistrate, the Chief Justice may confer on him special powers so that he can deal with civil claims up to $3,000/-. Second and Third Class Magistrates deal mostly with minor cases. They are all administrative officers. Although either of the two States is bigger than any State in Peninsular Malaysia, the two States are not so developed. The problems of communication and sparseness of population make life difficult for the professional Magistrates who have to go on circuit. It is, therefore, necessary to confer magisterial power on some administrative officers, as in many cases documents have to be attested and arrested persons have to be dealt with urgently when a professional Magistrate is not on the spot.

It is the policy of the Judiciary to take over all court work from administrative officers in the two States but this will take time, due mostly to the reluctance of qualified personnel to join the service and the absence of proper court facilities and, most important, the difficulty of obtaining finance. Steps will have to be taken as soon as possible to speed up the implementation of the policy.

At present, compared with Subordinate Courts in Peninsular Malaysia, Subordinate Courts in Sabah and Sarawak have generally much lower jurisdiction in dealing with civil and criminal matters, so that the bulk of the work ordinarily shouldered by Presidents of Sessions Courts in Peninsular Malaysia has, in Sabah and Sarawak, still to be dealt with by High Court judges. Quite a number of experienced Magistrates are capable of performing functions which in Peninsular Malaysia are dealt with by Presidents of Sessions Courts. While there has been a gradual and systematic enhancement of jurisdiction of the Subordinate Courts in Peninsular Malaysia since Malaysia Day, no such development has taken place in the two States. The volume of work in the Subordinate Courts in the two States has increased since Malaysia Day. The professional Magistrates hold similar legal qualifications as their counterparts in

Peninsular Malaysia. Something has to be done to bring about uniformity in the Subordinate Courts in the whole country in respect of practice and procedure. Active steps have, therefore, been taken to bring this into reality. A proposal has been made to extend the Subordinate Courts Act, 1948, and the Subordinate Courts Rules, 1950, of Peninsular Malaysia, with necessary modifications, to Sabah and Sarawak. To accelerate the process of taking over from administrative officers, the number of Magistrates will have to be increased considerably, not forgetting their supporting staff and other court facilities. The practical effect of the extension will be uniformity of hierarchy in the Subordinate Courts in the whole country and those cases now dealt with by the High Court will be taken over by Presidents of Sessions Courts in the two States.

1. [1953] 2 Q.B. 482.

2. By Act 31/1965, s.15, in force from 16 September 1965.

3. Article 135(3).

4. Added by Act 26/1963, s.16, in force from 16 September 1963.

5. Ibid.

6. In force from 26 August 1976.

7. The following were Ministers of Justice: the late Datuk Suleiman bin Datuk Abdul Rahman, September 1957–September 1959 (he was also Minister of the Interior); the late Tun Leong Yew Koh, September 1959–January 1963; the late Tun Dr. Ismail bin Datuk Abdul Rahman, May 1964–June 1967 (he was also Minister of Home Affairs); Datuk Patinggi Haji A. Rahman Ya'akob, June 1967–March 1968 (he was also Minister of Lands and Mines); Encik Bahaman Samsuddin, March 1968–June 1969; and Datuk Haji Ghani Gilong, June 1969–September 1970.

8. Consisting of three members: (a) the Chief Justice or a judge appointed by him, as chairman; a member appointed by the High Commissioner; and another by the Rulers. Appointments were made 'as and when occasion shall arise'. The Tribunal met only once, see *In re Land Acquisition by the State of Selangor* [1950] M.L.J. 152.

9. Before Independence the courts had power only to declare subsidiary legislation void.

10. Article 4(1).

11. Article 74(1) and (2).

12. Article 75.

13. See *Stephen Kalong Ningkan* v. *Tun Abang Haji Openg and Tawi Sli (No. 2)* [1967] 1 M.L.J. 46.

14. *Ah Thian* v. *Government of Malaysia* [1976] 2 M.L.J. 112; and *Syarikat Banita Sdn. Bhd.* v. *Government of State of Sabah* [1977] 2 M.L.J. 217.

15. 8 January 1977.

16. 8 January 1977.

17. P.U.(A) 521/69.

18. By an amendment to s.74 of the Courts of Judicature Act 7 of 1964 effected by s.13(3) of Act A328/76.

19. Gazette Notification No. 1254.

20. P.U.(A) 320/75.

21. The Government's first attempt to curtail appeals to the Privy Council was made in 1965 when they introduced a Bill to abolish appeals in criminal matters, and in any case in which the Federation or any State is a party and the validity of any law made by Parliament or the legislature of a State is questioned; but the attempt was allowed to lapse in the face of opposition from the Bar. See [1965] 1 M.L.J. xxxv.

The bench has refrained from expressing any view on whether Privy Council appeals should be abolished or retained, as the decision to do so is a political one.

Many think that twenty years after Independence final judgment should come not from judges in a distant land but from judges who have to live with the consequences of their judgment.

After Privy Council appeals have been abolished altogether, my view is that the Federal Court, which will then be the final court of appeal, should be renamed the Supreme Court, and that there should be interposed between the High Courts and the new Supreme Court, a Court of Appeal manned by Judges of Appeal. The law cannot develop consistently unless administered by a small body of permanent and full-time appellate judges. The Lord President and the two Chief Justices should continue to be members of the new Supreme Court, but they should not consider it to be *infra dig* to sit occasionally in the Court of Appeal. For an elaboration of my view, please see August 1976 issue of *Insaf*, published by the Malayan Bar Council, and [1976] 2 M.L.J. cxv.

22. For results of appeals to the Privy Council between 31 August 1957, and 31 December 1977, please see [1977] 2 M.L.J. xciv.

23. By Act 26/1963, s.13, in force from 19 September 1963.

24. [1969] 2 M.L.J. 30.

25. [1963] 1 M.L.J. 129.

26. A president of a sessions court is appointed by the Yang di-Pertuan Agong on the recommendation of the Chief Justice, section 59(3), Subordinate Courts Act 92; and His Majesty may on the advice of the Chief Justice confer upon him special jurisdiction, section 63(3).

A first-class magistrate in a State, however, is appointed by the Ruler or Governor on the recommendation of the Chief Justice, section 78(b); while the appointment of a second-class magistrate by the Ruler or Governor does not require the recommendation of the Chief Justice, section 79(2).

27. By Act 10/1960, s.20, in force from 31 May 1960.

28. By Act 26/63, s.52.

29. Apart from these members from Borneo, the following are currently members of the Commission: the chairman of the Public Services Commission as chairman; Tan Sri H. S. Ong, F.J.; Tan Sri Wan Suleiman, F.J.; Datuk A. Hamid Omar, J.; Datuk Hashim Yeop A. Sani, J.; Datuk Harun M. Hashim, J.; and Tan Sri Datuk M. Salleh Abas, Solicitor-General.

30. By Act 59/66, s.2.

31. [1977] 1 M.L.J. 14.

32. In 1976.

33. See P.U.(B) 83/1969.

34. See P.U.(A) 308/1977.

35. Total with Lord President, the two Chief Justices and four Federal Judges, 28.

This number is disproportionately small. New Zealand with a population of about 3m. has 24 judges, and the city of Auckland alone, with the same population as Penang, has 7. The State of New South Wales, with a population of about 3m, has 36 judges. The number of judges in Malaysia should gradually be increased as more and more courtrooms become available to cope with existing backlog and with the steady increase of new cases.

36. [1971] 1 M.L.J. 1.
37. [1971] 1 M.L.J. 4.
38. [1972] 1 M.L.J. 274.
39. [1972] 2 M.L.J. 129.

✵ V. S. WINSLOW

12. The Public Service and Public Servants in Malaysia

ALTHOUGH much has been written[1] on the public services of the Federation and of the States of Malaysia and on those who belong to them, what has been written is comparatively recent. The 'public service' (if the writer may use this term in this essay as a generic term so as to include the servants who belong to any of the many public services[2] of the Federation and of the States) had generated little interest before 1955, although the uneasy unitary-federal hybrid that was the Malayan Union had been in being since 1948, and the civil service since long before that.

The following reasons may be offered:

First, the public service had been comfortably ensconced on the British colonial bureaucratic civil service model, with its tradition of political impartiality, lengthy, loyal service and a sizeable majority of expatriates (including not only Europeans but also some Indians and Ceylonese) in the top echelon commanding not unattractive salaries. Secondly, it has been only since the Malayan move towards federalism since 1948 with the complete overhaul of 1957 and numerous subsequent modifications to the federal 'engine', the Constitution of Malaysia, that one can claim to have witnessed an increase in its sophistication and vitality rather than a mere 'tinkering' with it, effected by a government not unmindful of the peculiar needs of a developing nation—a nation with a 'mosaic of Heraclitean opposites'[3] seeking to be reconciled with each other.

Thirdly, a large body of case-law has evolved over the last two decades, involving several difficult questions of constitutional interpretation—particularly with regard to the tenure of the public servant—begging for constitutional lawyers to come forward and attempt to reconcile the irreconcilable. Happily, the debate on many of these questions appears to be drawing to a close, and a number of authoritative decisions as well as a few formal constitutional amendments now make the position of the public servant more certain—even if less secure. This may be poor consolation to the public servant but arguably, in the best interests of the country as a whole.[4]

SCOPE OF THE ESSAY

This essay is intended primarily to cover the major developments in the public service from the eve of Independence in 1957 until 1977 under heads most susceptible to convenient treatment, viewing both constitutional amendments[5] as well as case-law casting light on the interpretation of the Constitution as part of one continuous on-going process. Secondly, this essay will focus on the constitutional position of the public servant, particularly the nature of his tenure. Although this part of the essay has received thorough ventilation in excellent previous articles,[6] several recent developments since they were written have made some aspects treated therein rather out-dated. The writer does not propose to go over already well-trodden ground or to labour over now firmly-settled issues. He will instead review the developments and the present state of the law, attempt to evaluate the trends to be seen, if any, and with some diffidence (if the writer may be forgiven for this), offer some comments and criticisms of the existing state of the law.

This essay will *not* cover the public service and the position of public servants under the provisions of the Singapore Constitution; however, reference to the decisions of Singapore courts will be made in so far as they may be relevant to the interpretation of the Malaysian provisions. It will also not cover (i.e. in any detail) the composition and functions of the individual service commissions; the position of other persons employed by the government or remunerated by it but who are not within the jurisdiction of the various service commissions with regard to appointment, promotion or discipline (e.g. the Judiciary, the Attorney-General, the Auditor-General, members of Parliament, and election commissioners); aspects of the public servant's position covered by (a) pure *administrative* law generally, and not specially included in the Constitution, (b) *contract* law only (e.g. the question of damages for dismissal), (c) statutes and rules affecting the *terms of service* (e.g. pensions, provident funds, remuneration) and (d) *public administration*; and finally, details as to the functions and jurisdiction of *branches* of service commissions in the Borneo States, *State* service commissions, and provisions in State constitutions relating to the State public services.

'THE PUBLIC SERVICE'

It is vital at the outset to define for the purposes of this essay, the term 'the public service'.

The term is not used synonymously with 'the civil service'. First, a member of the public service holds 'an office of profit', for Article 160(2) of the Constitution of Malaysia (the interpretation Article) specifies, *inter alia*, that ' "office of profit" means any whole-time office in any of the public services'. However, not all persons who hold an office of profit are public servants, for the definition of 'office of profit' in Article 160(2) goes on to state that it includes certain other offices as well, such as those of judges of the Federal Court or of a High Court, the Auditor-General, and members of Election Commissions. Secondly, Article 132(1) of the Constitution states that, 'for the purposes of this constitution', the public services are: (a) the armed forces; (b) the judicial and legal service; (c) the general public service of the Federation; (d) the police force; (e) the railway service; (f) the joint public services mentioned in Article 133; (g) the public service of each state; and (h) the education service. Clauses (3) and (4) of Article 132 go on to specifically exclude certain offices as not comprising part of the public service and certain categories of persons as not being public servants. The words *'for the purposes of this constitution'* in the opening words of Article 132 are obviously significant. What are these 'purposes'? There appear to be two main purposes: first, each of the 'public services' were intended by the framers of the Constitution to come under the purview of one *service commission*, whose functions were conceived as being primarily to appoint, confirm, emplace on the permanent or pensionable establishment, promote, transfer and exercise disciplinary control over members of the service or services to which its jurisdiction extended.[7] Thus, other persons also remunerated from public funds but who are not 'public servants' for the purposes of the Constitution—such as High Court judges or the Attorney-General—are not subject to the jurisdiction of any service commission.

Secondly, members of the public services specified in Article 132(1) were intended to enjoy a *common degree of tenure* under the Constitution. Accordingly, the same safeguards against dismissal or reduction in rank under Article 135 applied to *all* members of the public services. A further amendment to Article 132 by the addition of clause (2A)[8] made it clear that every member of any of the public services holds office 'during the pleasure' of the Yang di-Pertuan Agong, except that members of the public services of a State held office during the pleasure of the State Ruler or Governor. Other persons paid out of public funds were subject to very special provisions as to tenure.

THE POSITION OF THE PUBLIC SERVANT

What special position does the 'public servant', namely, the member of any of the specified eight public services, hold under the Constitution?

In 1955, a Commission of Enquiry into the Integrity of the Public Services stated in its Report[9] that:

The fundamental principle of employment in the civil establishments is that a man devotes the whole of his working life to the public service in return for emoluments which are proportionate to his status and with a pension to provide for his old age. He can never acquire wealth but he is not exposed to unemployment or to the other risks of commercial life.

A sterling principle indeed, but this ideal before the 1957 Constitution came into being must be somewhat tarnished by the realities of two decades hence. It is submitted that the public servant's position is at present as follows:

(a) He is remunerated out of funds provided by the legislature: a public servant of the Federation is paid out of the Consolidated Fund of the Federation and the public servant of a State is paid out of the Consolidated Fund of the State.

(b) He must be above party politics. He may not engage in political activities of any kind, and cannot canvass for or join a political party except with the permission of the Government, his employer. He must resign from the public service in order to become eligible to stand for election to public office as a potential member of the legislature cannot hold 'an office of profit'. He must be 'officially impartial', by being loyal to any government in power, and must observe complete secrecy on official policy matters. The Malaysian public service follows British tradition in this respect, as it is not based on any kind of 'spoils system' as was once rampant in the United States of America.

(c) He is entitled to equality of treatment with other citizens, in appointment to any office or employment in the public service under Article 8(2) of the Constitution.[10]

(d) He is entitled to impartial treatment *after* appointment, whatever his race, with all other persons in the same grade in the service of the Federation, under Article 136. (State Constitutions generally have an equivalent provision with respect to servants of the State in question.)

(e) He holds office 'during the pleasure' of the Yang di-Pertuan Agong (if a member of a service of the Federation) or of the State Ruler or Governor (if a member of the service of a State): Article 132(2A).

(f) He has no right to hold any kind of post in the public service, whether 'temporary' or 'permanent', non-pensionable or pensionable, whether before he has reached the normal retirement age (55) or after. Neither has he any right not to be dismissed or not to have his employment 'terminated' by any other means.

(g) He has no absolute right to a pension, compensation for loss of office, gratuity or any other allowance. He is only 'eligible' for these. He is only entitled to arrears of salary for the period of his completed service until the time of his valid dismissal or termination of service.

(h) He merely possesses a *degree* of security of tenure under the Constitution, particularly in that dismissal or reduction in rank is subject to Article 135, clauses (1) and (2). However, the meagre protections of Article 135 have been further watered down by subsequent amendments.

(i) Finally, even a public servant may be employed under a contract, in which case his employment is subject to its terms. Unfortunately, his rights and obligations may be amended unilaterally by the government not only by means of rules and regulations having the force of law, but also by means of administrative rulings, such as a requirement that he should pass an examination before he receives any further increments. It appears that a right to alter the terms of service in such a manner will be implied as being in itself another term of service.

Such are the propositions. It will later in this essay be necessary to attempt to show how some of these propositions (namely (e) to (i)) have been established. It may also be instructive to examine how the framework of the public service has developed. However, before either examination, the writer proposes to return to the eve of Independence in 1957 again as it is a convenient point from which to gain a perspective.

PRELUDE TO INDEPENDENCE

The choice of a federal constitutional structure, of course, had already been firmly made by 1948, after the original attempt to impose a unitary system of government on the States of Malaya proved abortive. Federalism, as will be seen, was to have several important implications for the public service in the future. It may here be briefly stated that Malaya was to have, eventually, separate central (federal) and regional (state) services, the concept of 'joint' services and the mechanism of secondment—of federal officers to State services and of State officers to the public service of the Federation.

Secondly, the process of streamlining the public service had begun, in terms of the protection of the 'integrity' of the public service. A commission of enquiry was appointed to enquire into and report on matters affecting the integrity of the public services. In 1955, the commission submitted its Report,[11] which was concerned primarily with how to reduce the opportunities for corrupt practices by improving organization and discipline in the public services. The Commission's findings and criticisms evoked some unhappiness in the Government of the Federation which thought the findings exaggerated or not altogether justified. The fact seems to remain, however, that the Commission did make a profound impression, and in future, beginning in 1956, General Orders on conduct and discipline contained regulations pertaining to the protection of the public services' integrity.

Thirdly, by 1956, the process of 'Malayanization' of the public service was also under way, for the purpose of gradually filling Division One posts with qualified and experienced Malayans. (Two-thirds of Division One posts were at the time filled by expatriates.)[12] A parallel 'Malayanization' process also took place in Singapore. In future, therefore, the public service would carry a decreasingly 'British' stamp, except for certain 'British' principles which any government was unlikely to want to change: political impartiality and integrity.

THE 'REID' COMMISSION: FEDERATION OF MALAYA CONSTITUTIONAL COMMISSION, 1956-1957

A Commonwealth Constitutional Commission under the chairmanship of Lord Reid, appointed to make recommendations for a constitution for the independent Federation of Malaya, accepted the recommendation of the 'principles' put forward by the London Report[13] of 1956 which should be applied in the establishment and control of public services generally. The Reid Commission claimed that it endeavoured to apply these in making its own proposals. They may conveniently be summarized as follows:

(a) political impartiality of the public service should be recognized and safeguarded;
(b) promotions policy should be regulated in accordance with publicly recognized professional principles—i.e. impartially on the basis of qualifications, experience and merit;
(c) a reasonable security of tenure and a freedom from the arbitrary application of disciplinary provisions; and
(d) the establishment of an independent public service commission (to ensure the observance of the foregoing principles).

The second 'principle' was provided for by Article 136, mentioned earlier. The third 'principle' was provided for by Article 135, and the setting up of service commissions. The fourth was provided for by the Reid Commission recommending the setting up of *three* independent commissions: a Public Services Commission, a Judicial and Legal Service Commission, and a Police Service Commission. The draftsmen of the Constitution of 1957 went even further on the last principle by providing for no less than *five* commissions, adding the Armed Forces Council and the Railway Service Commission to the Reid proposals.

Since Independence, it may be added that the Government has accepted yet another 'principle' for the public service: that of adequate remuneration. The Suffian Commission[14] recognized, *inter alia*, the principle of 'fair comparison' to be followed in determining salaries and conditions of service of public servants, by assessment of the comparable net advantages of private employment, taking all factors into account. The result was an upward salary revision for public servants.

It is at this juncture proposed that constitutional developments relating to the public service and public servants be dealt with under convenient heads, rather than purely chronologically. The reason offered is simple: to take the latter approach might result in a hodge-podge, with no clear perspective visible. The amendments to Part X of the Constitution, in particular (dealing with the 'Public Services') have been piecemeal in nature and little understanding of the trends in amendment or interpretation can be gleaned from a purely chronological approach.

THE SERVICE COMMISSIONS

Article 132(1) of the Constitution presently lists eight categories of 'public services' (it originally listed, in 1957, seven categories). These eight services fall within the jurisdiction of a total of six service commissions. One of these commissions, namely, the Public Services Commission, has the lion's share of the services (three) and of the public servants within its jurisdiction. The largest service, the general public service of the Federation, comes within its jurisdiction. (The Public Services Commission ('The PSC') and its jurisdiction will be the subject of the next heading.)

It may be recalled that the Reid Commission recommended the establishment of only three service commissions. These three were in fact established but together with two further commissions— the Armed Forces Council and the Railway Service Commission.

The Armed Forces Council was to be responsible (under the general authority of the Yang di-Pertuan Agong) for the command, discipline and administration of, and all other matters relating to the armed forces, other than matters relating to their operational use.[15]

Members of the railway service (the 'Malayan Railway') would normally have come under the jurisdiction of the Public Services Commission as they would have been part of the general public service of the Federation. However, a White Paper on the Federation of Malaya Constitutional Proposals[16] stated that a separate Railway Service Commission was proposed for three reasons. First, it was of such a size as to require special arrangements. Secondly, it was desirable that a commission responsible for the appointment, promotion and discipline of members of such a 'highly technical service' should have among its members persons experienced in railway service or railway administration. Finally, the possibility was envisaged of the Malayan Railway becoming a statutory public authority in the future, in which case employees of the Malayan Railway would cease to be public servants and it would be much easier to transfer the records of an independent Railway Service Commission to the new statutory authority than it would be to transfer them from the PSC to that authority. In fact, the railway service has not so ceased to be a public service, although there is provision in the Constitution for Parliament to abolish the Railway Service Commission by law if the railway service ceases to be a public service of the Federation.[17]

The Judicial and Legal Service Commission, created in 1957, was abolished in 1960[18] and reappeared in 1963[19] in the new constitution of Malaysia. Since then, its jurisdiction has decreased somewhat.[20]

In 1973, a sixth service commission, the Education Service Commission, was created, together with a new public service, the education service, over which that commission was to have jurisdiction. Article 132(1) was amended to add the education service to the list of the public services and a new Article 141A was added to give jurisdiction over the education service to the Education

Service Commission.[21] The Commission originally consisted of a Chairman and four members. In 1976, the composition was amended to read 'a Chairman and not less than four but not more than eight other members'.[22]

These amendments were designed to give effect to the recommendations of the Royal Commission on the Teaching Services, West Malaysia, under the Chairmanship of Tan Sri Abdul Aziz bin Mohd. Zain and known as the 'Aziz Report'.[23]

The Report pointed out that there were (in 1971) two main groups of teachers, namely Government teachers and various categories of non-Government teachers; and that there were 'clear advantages in having a single teaching service instead of the present profusion of services and categories of teachers'.[24] It recommended that all eligible serving teachers not employed by the Government be given the option of applying for employment by the Government and thus becoming part of a new education service or of applying to be employed by a Central Board which would have control over appointments and discipline. The education service, as it would consist of some 64,000 members in 1973, increasing by 3 per cent yearly, was too large to be conveniently dealt with by the Public Services Commission. Nor was the Public Services Commission considered the most suitable body to deal with the appointment, dismissal, and exercise of disciplinary control in this highly specialized service with its undoubted importance to the nation's future in terms of its educational development.

There is also provision for the powers and functions[25] of the Education Service Commission (other than the power of first appointment to the permanent or pensionable establishment) to be exercised by *boards* appointed by the Yang di-Pertuan Agong.[26] The education service, it may be noted, consists not only of teachers, but also of members of the Education Clerical Service and other school employees who are within the jurisdiction of the Ministry of Education.[27]

The creation of the new education service and corresponding Commission has been welcomed even by opposition members of Parliament, as being clearly in the best interests of education in the country.

THE PUBLIC SERVICES COMMISSION: ITS JURISDICTION AND RELATIONSHIP WITH THE STATES

Before Merdeka, the States already had their own civil services, together with some officers seconded from the Federal public service. The Reid Commission, in determining the functions of the new Public Services Commission for the new Federation, felt that

... the broad principle should be that the Legislature and Government are necessarily responsible for fixing establishments and terms of employment, while the Public Service Commission is charged with the internal administration of the service as a professional body and with the responsibility for public service matters including appointments, promotions, and the application, when necessary, of disciplinary provisions in respect of members of the public service.[28]

The Reid Commission further recommended that in the interests of the proper administration of the States their services should also be subject to the control of an independent body and that for reasons of economy and efficiency, the PSC ought to have the same powers over State employees as they had over Federal. There were to be no separate State commissions in each State.

These recommendations were not, however, fully implemented. A Federal compromise, to protect the interests of the State public services was effected in respect of the above-mentioned second recommendation. An agreement was reached to give the PSC jurisdiction over the members of the public services of only *two* States, Malacca and Penang (former Straits Settlements) on Merdeka Day itself because under the respective constitutions of those two States, their Chief Ministers were to be selected from their Legislative Assemblies to whom the Executive Councils were responsible, and the Governors were to act on the advice of the Executive Councils, presided over by the Chief Ministers. Thus it was felt, apparently, that the Federal PSC had to have jurisdiction over those States' services to ensure that a body truly 'independent' from the Executive controlled them. In the Malay States, the need was less urgent as the Mentri Besar might be an official appointed from outside the Council of State or Legislative Assembly.[29]

Further, the Malay States were given an option: They might either establish their own service commissions as soon as practicable within a certain time-period, or, by laws passed by their legislatures, place responsibility with the PSC over all or any persons in their State public services, such a law to take effect in not less than twelve months from the date of its passing.[30] States have in fact exercised the option, some the first way, and Negri Sembilan and Perlis by the second way. As a provision for any 'gap', it was also provided that if, 'after the relevant date' there was not established and exercising its functions in any State any commission 'corresponding in status and jurisdiction to the Public Services Commission', Federal law could provide for the extension of the jurisdiction of the PSC to members of the State service.[31]

Thus, on Independence, the PSC's jurisdiction was over:

(a) the general public service of the Federation;[32]

(b) 'joint' public services, if established by Federal law; under Article 133;

(c) the public services of the States of Penang and Malacca; and

(d) the public services of other States, if either (i) their State legislatures extended the PSC's jurisdiction to their States or (ii) if the State failed to establish its own commission or extend the PSC's jurisdiction to it 'after the relevant date' and Federal Law therefore extended the PSC's jurisdiction to the State.

In addition the concept of 'joint services' was included in the Constitution. These were shared, common or unified services, common to the two or more States, or to the Federation and one or more of the States.[33] The advantages of a joint service are that the field of recruitment is enlarged, attracting the best men under either the regional or central governments; it might facilitate inter-governmental co-operation, encourage a less parochial outlook and help to avoid an uneconomic duplication in administrative bodies.[34] Two States, Kelantan and Trengganu, had agreed to have a joint service commission. However, it appears that despite the enabling provisions, no joint services have in fact been established, and there has been no enthusiasm for them.

On the other hand, the principle of secondment of officers from one government to another, from a Federal public service or joint service to a State service, or vice versa, provided for under Article 134, has been regularly utilized in practice whenever the services of such officers have been needed.

In 1960, a constitutional amendment[35] to Article 139 extended the jurisdiction of the PSC to the judicial and legal service also. This was in line with the abolition of the Judicial and Legal Service Commission in the same amending Act.

The Malaysia Act, which came into force on Malaysia Day, 16 September 1963, restored the Judicial and Legal Service Commission and returned jurisdiction over that service from the PSC to the Judicial and Legal Service Commission. The Act also made further changes to the PSC's jurisdiction consequent to the inclusion of the Borneo States (and Singapore) in the Federation of Malaysia. For the first time, the establishment of *branches* of the PSC was provided for in the new States of Sabah, Sarawak, and Singapore. The functions of the PSC were now to be discharged by its branch established for the State in question in respect of members of the general public service of the Federation employed in a Federal department in that State.[36] The PSC's jurisdiction would also extend, where there was a branch (except as regards the exercise of disciplinary control), to members of the State public service who were seconded to the general public service of the Federation and who were for this purpose, to be deemed to be members of the general public service of the Federation.[37] For all other purposes they would, under Article 134(2), remain members of the State service to which they belonged, except that the Federation would have to pay their remuneration.

Finally, in 1976, by the Constitution (Amendment) Act, 1976, the PSC's jurisdiction was further extended in that Federal law might provide for a branch of the PSC established in a Borneo State (Sabah or Sarawak) to exercise jurisdiction over any joint service created involving that State as a result of any provision made by Federal law for the joint service.[38] This provision was in line with the further cutting down of the Judicial and Legal Service Commission's jurisdiction.

What conclusions may be drawn from the constitutional amendments with regard to the PSC's jurisdiction? It would seem that since the Reid Commission's Report, the States have retained much of the control over their own services (including their own officers seconded to the Federal government under Article 134), instead of the Reid Commission's stated ideal of centralized control by the PSC over State services ever materializing, even after twenty years.

Also, the PSC has retained control over Federal public service officers seconded to State services (Article 134), over Federal officers employed in a Federal department in a Borneo State (Article 146B(1)), and to a more limited extent, over State public servants seconded to the general Federal public service (Article 146B(7)).

THE CONSTITUTIONAL POSITION OF THE PUBLIC SERVANT: SPECIAL CONSIDERATIONS

The position of the public servant has already been outlined generally in an earlier part of this essay. It is now necessary to examine aspects of his constitutional position more closely. In particular, what is the nature of his tenure under the Constitution?

It may be stated quite shortly that the general rule[39] is that the public servant holds office 'during the pleasure' of the Yang di-

Pertuan Agong, if he is a member of a Federal public service or during the pleasure of the State Ruler or Governor, if he is a member of the public service of a State. Article 132(2A) contains this general rule. However, two major exceptions to this 'rule' are contained in Article 135 clauses (1) and (2) as originally drafted. These are that

(a) no member of any of the services mentioned in Article 132(1) 'shall be dismissed or reduced in rank by an authority subordinate to that which, at the time of the dismissal or reduction, has power to appoint a member of that service or rank'; (Article 135(1)); and that

(b) no member of such a service 'shall be dismissed or reduced in rank without being given a reasonable opportunity of being heard'; (Article 135(2)).

Since clauses (1) and (2) of Article 135 were drafted in 1957, several exceptions (including 'provisos') to both 'exceptions' have been created by subsequent amendments to the Constitution. These will be examined at the appropriate juncture. Suffice it here to say that the public servant's position is infinitely more complicated than any of the three classes of case into one of which any other employee would fall, and which the House of Lords explained in *Ridge* v. *Baldwin*[40] in 1964. The House of Lords was there dealing with the applicability of the rules of natural justice to cases of dismissal. Lord Reid there stated firstly, that in the master and servant type of case, where there was a contract of service, wrongful dismissal was remediable by damages for breach of contract only and there was no right to be heard. Secondly, where one held 'an office at pleasure', there was also no right to be heard before dismissal as the dismissing authority need not give any reason. Only in the third case, where one could only be dismissed for cause, was there a right to be heard as dismissal was the performance of a 'judicial' act. The public servant's position, it may be observed, contains aspects of all three classes of case! Thus, he holds office at pleasure and may also be employed under a contract of service but would nevertheless be entitled to a hearing before any dismissal or reduction in rank can take place.

THE DOCTRINE OF HOLDING OFFICE 'AT PLEASURE'

It has long been established that at common law, the Crown has the right to dismiss its servants at pleasure, and this right is implied as a term in any contract the servant concludes with the Crown. When the Federation of Malaya achieved independence in

1957, there was no express provision in the Constitution to the effect that public servants held office during the pleasure of the King or the State Ruler. However, the Constitution (Amendment) Act, 1960[41] inserted clause (2A) in Article 132 as follows:

> Except as expressly provided by this Constitution, every person who is a member of any of the services mentioned in paragraphs (a), (b), (c), (d), (e) and (f) of clause (1) holds office during the pleasure of the Yang di-Pertuan Agong, and, except as expressly provided by the Constitution of the State, every person who is a member of the public service of a State holds office during the pleasure of the Ruler or Governor.[42]

It appears to be the accepted view, however, that no radical change was brought about by this amendment. Even before Merdeka, it was established in 1927 by *Pillai* v. *State of Kedah*[43] that a servant of the Sultan of Kedah held office at the pleasure of the Sultan, and it was recognized also that in the Federated Malay States (Perak, Selangor, Pahang, and Negri Sembilan) and the Straits Settlements, public servants were already treated as holding office at pleasure.

After Independence, in 1957, the position was unaltered. In *Haji Wan Othman & Ors.* v. *Government of the Federation of Malaya*,[44] Suffian J. (as he then was) said:

> It is undoubted that legally a member of the public service holds office during the pleasure of the Head of State, even before the enactment of clause (2A) of Article 132 of the Constitution, and he may therefore be retired or dismissed without compensation.

Further in *Government of Malaysia* v. *Mahan Singh*[45] Suffian L.P. went on to say that 'the pre-Merdeka law as expounded by *Pillai's* case still applies after Merdeka Day' and that he 'would have expected our constitution-makers to use the clearest of language' if they had intended to make a radical change in the law.

What then was the position after clause (2A) was inserted in Article 132 of the Constitution? Again, it seems that no radical change was made. Clause (2A) was inserted 'to remove any doubt'[46] regarding the tenure of public servants. In *Haji Ariffin* v. *Government of Pahang*,[47] Suffian F.J. (as he then was) had this to say:

> This clause is nothing new—it only reaffirms the previous common law rule that a member of the public service of the State held office during the pleasure of the Ruler. But in so reaffirming the old common law rule, clause (2A) goes further by providing that it is now subject to exceptions expressly provided by the Constitution of the State. In my judgment it is also subject to exceptions provided by the Federal Constitution and by written law.

What does 'the old common law rule' *mean*? First, it appears to mean that the Crown (or Head of State) has the right to dismiss his servants at will and that this right cannot be taken away by any contractual arrangement made by an executive officer or department of State, as such an arrangement would constitute a 'clog' on the right to dismiss at pleasure and such a clog cannot bind the Crown. This seems to be the effect of the English cases culminating in *Terrell* v. *Secretary of State for the Colonies*.[48]

Secondly, it may well be that in respect of clause (2A), all that it says and must mean is that, except as provided by the Constitution (of the Federation or of a State, as the case may be), no public servant has security of tenure. This was the contention of the Attorney-General in the Singapore High Court in *Jacob* v. *Attorney-General*[49] and which was apparently accepted by that Court. In fact, the Federal Constitution does provide for security of tenure to the extent specified in the three clauses of Article 135. These three provisions may be said to constitute 'exceptions' to Article 132(2A). They were so treated by Suffian F.J. (as he then was) in *Haji Ariffin's* case,[50] although MacIntyre F.J. in the same case preferred to say that these three guarantees 'constitute a clog' on the right to dismiss at pleasure.

It is clear from a reading of Article 132(2A) that the right to dismiss at pleasure is subject to the Constitution of the Federation, in respect of public servants of the Federation (including members of joint services) or the Constitution of a State (in respect of members of the public service of that State). The question that arises is whether the right can be curtailed by either statute or contract.

As for statute, Suffian F.J. (as he then was) stated in *Haji Ariffin's* case that the right was subject not only to the Constitution but also to 'written law'. If written law is taken to include statutes or subsidiary legislation, then this seems doubtful as a general proposition. MacIntyre F.J. (dissenting) in the same case disagreed with that proposition in so far as it might embrace written laws inconsistent with the Constitution and chose in fact to limit the proposition to statutes providing for a power to determine service 'for cause'. It is submitted that at least where statute is inconsistent with the Constitution, it cannot curtail the constitutional power to terminate service at pleasure. The common law rule[51] that the power of the Crown to dismiss at pleasure can be curtailed by statute must be read in the light of a written constitution which Malaysia possesses.

As for curtailment of the right by contractual stipulation, there are a number of possibilities. First, at common law although it is not legitimate expressly to exclude the power to dismiss, as it would be a violation of public policy, it seems that it is possible for the contractual terms to be such that it necessarily follows that an implication that the appointment is at pleasure is excluded. Thus, an express provision of a power to determine 'for cause' will necessarily prevent the implication of a power to dismiss at pleasure.[52] However, the position may not be the same where there is an express provision in a written constitution for the right to dismiss at pleasure. This is much more than an 'implication' that may be excluded (although the common law position might still hold had clause (2A) not been inserted in Article 132, as in the years before 1960).

The judgment of MacIntyre F.J. in *Haji Ariffin's* case[53] seems very persuasive in this respect. MacIntyre F.J. extended his argument pertaining to statutes inconsistent with the Constitution to contractual terms inconsistent with the Constitution. He said:

It ... appears to me logical that what the state cannot achieve by legislation it cannot achieve by imposing a contract term in the contract of service of a public servant, contrary to the provisions of the Constitution.[54]

This question has not yet been finally resolved. The question arose in *Haji Ariffin's* case in this manner. Suffian F.J. held that a *Kathi* in the service of Pahang State could be appointed subject to termination of service by notice or payment of salary in lieu of notice and that such a condition was not inconsistent with the Constitution which held that a member of the Pahang public service held office at the pleasure of the State Ruler.

In his view, the Government was not prohibited by law from stipulating that the service of any public servant might be terminated by notice.

Is the Government bound by such a stipulation on its part? MacIntyre J. in *Haji Ariffin's* case thought that such a stipulation would operate as a clog on the exercise of the Crown's pleasure and so became inoperative and void.

On the other hand, Suffian F.J. in the same case felt that although such a stipulation fettered the Crown's right to dismiss at will, this only meant that if, notwithstanding the stipulation, a public servant's service was terminated at will (without notice or payment in lieu of notice), he could not claim damages. In other words both of their Lordships were at least agreed that the Crown was *not* bound by the stipulation. MacIntyre F.J. saying that the stipulation was void, whereas Suffian F.J. would have given the Crown the option of whether to choose to be bound or to avoid keeping to the stipulation altogether. It is still an open question as to whether or not a public servant would be entitled to damages from the Government if the Government were to decide to terminate his services in breach of the contractual stipulation of notice. Of course, this termination may amount to 'dismissal' so that the public servant would have been entitled to a reasonable opportunity of being heard under Article 135(2), and may ask for a declaration that he has not been validly dismissed. However, should he decide not to pursue his constitutional remedy, can he pursue his contractual remedy in damages?

Finally, it may be asked what the rationale is for the right to dismiss at pleasure. The right is said to be based on public policy. The most recent and clear statement of this public policy in Malaysia was in 1975 in *Government of Malaysia* v. *Mahan Singh*[55] where Suffian L.P. said:

> I am of the opinion that the cardinal principle obtaining here during British rule lasting about 125 years that a public servant holds office at the pleasure of the Crown, is an important principle that should not be whittled away in the absence of express statutory words whittling it, for as stated by Sproule J. in *Pillai's* case government employment being for the good of the public, it must not continue when it is no longer for the public good; it is essential for the public good that the Crown should not be hampered in dismissing a servant whose continuance in office it deems detrimental to the best interests of the State and its good government, by any fear of suits in reprisal; indeed such continuance in office may be a danger to the community. The only amendment I would make to the above observation is that in the light of our constitution, these days dismissal must comply with article 135.

It remains for us to consider what the implications of the right to dismiss at pleasure are on the public servant's tenure (apart from Article 135). The cases decided since Independence show that the right to dismiss at pleasure does have some bearing on the security of tenure of the public servant.

The question had arisen as to whether, *inter alia*, a public servant had a right to his post. If he did, then any attempt to terminate his services prematurely would attract the duty to give him a reasonable opportunity to be heard first. Thus, not only dismissal, but also compulsory retirement, abolition of one's post, reverter to one's former post, or termination of services by notice or by payment in lieu of notice under the contract would also attract the right to be heard, which if not granted, would make the 'termination' a nullity.

It was open to the Malaysian courts to hold that at least, as in India,[56] a public servant holding a substantive appointment in a 'permanent' post acquired the right to hold that post. The courts' pronouncements however, have been instructive.

In 1965, Suffian J. in the High Court at Alor Star, held in *Haji Wan Othman & Ors.* v. *Government of the Federation of Malaya*[57] that since a member of the public service held office during the pleasure of the Head of State, 'he may therefore be retired or dismissed without compensation'. This was the forerunner of several cases directly in point.

In *Haji Ariffin* v. *Government of Pahang*[58] the Federal Court of Malaysia decided in 1969 that a *Kathi*, whose service with the Government of the State of Pahang was terminated after seven years by notice according to the contract of service, had had his service lawfully terminated, Suffian F.J. stating that 'I do not think that the plaintiff in our case had a right to remain until the retiring age'. This case therefore established in effect, that a public servant had no right to hold a post *until* the retiring age (55 or as the case may be).

Also in 1969, there was decided by the High Court in West Malaysia in *Thambipillai* v. *The Government of Malaysia*[59] that a public servant, who was compulsorily retired under section 10(a) of the Pensions Ordinance, 1951 at the age of 58½ (when the retirement age had been raised by a Government circular to the age of 60, had no right to hold his post 'once he had passed his 55th birthday' in view of the clear provisions of the Pensions Ordinance, 1951, and that the circular was no more than 'a mere declaration of policy' to raise the retiring age. This case may be taken for the proposition that a public servant has no right to hold his post *after* the normal retiring age (here, 55).

In 1974, in *Government of Malaysia* v. *Lionel*,[60] the Judicial Committee of the Privy Council decided that a public servant who had been appointed to a temporary post and on terms of termination by one month's notice or payment of one month's salary in lieu of notice, had his services validly terminated in accordance with his terms of appointment. Their Lordships were of the view that there was nothing in the Constitution which affected the right of the Government to terminate temporary employment in accordance with the terms of the engagement.

Finally, in 1975, the Federal Court of Malaysia in *Government of Malaysia* v. *Mahan Singh*[61] decided that a public servant on the pensionable establishment, and being a 'permanent' officer, was validly pensioned off in the public interest under section 10(d) of the Pensions Ordinance, 1951, although he was well under the retirement age of 55. Suffian L.P. said that 'with all due respect I do not think that in Malaysia a pensionable officer has a right to his post, unlike the position in India where there are many Supreme Court decisions to the contrary, saying that a pensionable officer has a right, a lien even title to his post equivalent to property'.[62] His Lordship vigorously denied that a public servant, even if pensionable, had any right, lien, or title to his post. He agreed with the proposition that as the public servant held office at pleasure only, he had by the terms of his engagement, no legal right as against the Crown to continuity of employment.

A related question that has arisen is whether the public servant has a right 'not to be dismissed' because Article 132(2A) is limited by Article 135.

In 1965, in *Amalgamated Union of Public Employees* v. *Permanent Secretary (Health)*,[63] Winslow J. in the Singapore High Court said:

It is no doubt true that article 135 of the Federal Constitution confers certain rights on civil servants but these relate to matters such as the manner in which or by whom they may be dismissed. They do not confer any right to office or to pension or any right not to be dismissed.

This passage was approved by Suffian L.P. in the Federal Court in *Mahan Singh's* case.[64]

Thus, if a public servant has any 'right not to be dismissed', it is only in the sense that he may not be dismissed except in accordance with Article 135.

Finally, it may be asked whether the public servant possesses any right to compensation for loss of office, or to pension, gratuity, or other allowances. Here, the courts have consistently held[65] that he has no right to any of these. This is because, in the first place, it follows from the right to dismiss at pleasure; and in the second place, there are express words to this effect in section 5 of the Pensions Ordinance, 1951. Section 5(1) reads:

No officer shall have an absolute right to compensation for past services or to any pension, gratuity or other allowance under this Ordinance, nor shall anything in this Ordinance contained limit the right of the Federal Government or, as the case may be, of the Government of any State or Settlement to dismiss any officer without compensation.

Pensions are, and have been, a privilege which a public servant only becomes 'eligible for' and not 'entitled to'.

Although a public servant holds office at pleasure, he nearly always serves under a contract of service, making his relation between him and the State *contractual*. However, the right to dismiss at pleasure has profound implications for the contractual relationship.

In 1973, Suffian F.J. in *Government of Malaysia* v. *Rosalind Oh Lee Pek Inn*[66] stated that the relationship between a public servant and the Government was contractual, but that the contract was of a special kind, as once appointed, the Government servant acquired a status, and his rights and obligations were no longer determined by consent of both parties but by statute or statutory or administrative rules made by the Government.

In 1976, the Federal Court in *Rajion bin Haji Sulaiman* v. *Government of Kelantan*[67] extended this proposition further. In that case, a workshop clerk in the service of the Government of the State of Kelantan had been appointed at a time when there was no requirement that he should pass an examination when he reached a 'bar' before he could obtain further increments. A 'bar' was later introduced which stopped him from getting further increments. He therefore prayed for a declaration that this stoppage was unlawful and void, and for an account of increments due to him from May 1963 until his retirement in 1973. The Court was unanimous in dismissing the clerk's appeal against the dismissal of his claim by Ibrahim J., and holding the requirement of an examination under the rules of service for clerks in the State Clerical Service, lawful and applicable to him.

Both Wan Suleiman F.J. (with whom Suffian L.P. concurred) and Raja Azlan Shah F.J. concluded that a public servant's conditions of service could be altered unilaterally by *administrative* rules and regulations (and not only by statutory rules), and that this power to alter the terms of service thus followed from the very principle of service at the pleasure of the Rulers. Wan Suleiman F.J. said:[68]

... it would seem that the very principle of service at the pleasure of the Rulers would mean that the rules prevailing at the time of the servant's appointment cannot be expected to be observed for all time to come.

Raja Azlan Shah F.J. added[69] the rationale behind unilateral alteration:

In my view, the rules and regulations relating to the public services under the constitution are directory, liable to be changed to suit the public policy of the State....

PUNISHMENT, TERMINATION OF SERVICE AND THE PROTECTIONS OF ARTICLE 135

The protections afforded to the public servant in Article 135 all concern the 'dismissal' or 'reduction in rank' of the servant. It is therefore important to know when one of these acts is contemplated or is occurring, for any other act does not attract the protections of Article 135, such as the right to be given a reasonable opportunity of being heard. The 'development' of the Constitution here has been by judicial interpretation, for no constitutional amendments have been made here, even to clarify the meaning of the terms that had, for a time, caused difficulty in the courts.

The focus of the debate in the courts has been on the scope of the term 'dismissal'. One question that had arisen was whether 'dismissal' embraced also the term 'removal' which is included in the Indian Constitution's equivalent to Article 135 (namely Article 311).[70] The Indian courts have in fact stated that there is no distinction between the two terms, except that under the service rules in India, dismissal ordinarily disqualified one from future employment whereas removal ordinarily did not.[71] In Malaysia, there appears to be no such difference in the effects of these acts. It seems reasonable therefore to conclude that the two words are synonymous. The Privy Council in *Munusamy*[72] thought they were and the High Court of Malaya in *Thambipillai*[73] also thought the two words 'corresponding in meaning' to the word 'dismissed' in Article 135(2). Although Ong Hock Sim F.J. in *Mahan Singh's* case[74] preferred the view that removal was only a *species* of dismissal, it is with respect, submitted that in Malaysia, the exercise of drawing a distinction is academic, for the only distinction to be drawn is between 'dismissal' and 'termination of services'.[75]

The latter two terms are *not* synonymous. The Malaysian Courts have followed the lead of the Indian Courts by holding that 'dismissal' is a punishment or involves an element of penalty whereas 'termination' does not. 'Reduction in rank' also involves an element of penalty. The Indian Courts had evolved by 1958[76] two 'penalty' tests. A servant was 'punished' if either: (a) he was deprived of a 'right' to hold a post; or (b) he was visited by certain 'evil' consequences, such as a forfeiture of pay or allowances, loss of seniority in his substantive rank, stoppage or postponement of future chances of promotion, loss of any benefits already earned, or even a 'stigma' on his name for misconduct or incompetency.

These tests were applied by the Privy Council in *Munusamy's* case[77] in 1967 so that an immigration officer whose appointment as an assistant passport officer on probation was terminated, he reverting to his substantive post, was held to be not punished and thus not reduced in rank.

Lord Hodson said:

Dismissal is treated as the penal consequence of charges meriting dismissal being established against an officer. Looking at the consequence itself the disciplinary interpretation of dismissal is reinforced by the language of Article 135(3) which immediately follows the relevant Article and contains the significant phrase: 'dismissed or reduced in rank or suffer any *other* disciplinary measure'. This confirms that the punishment element is involved in both cases.[78]

In the Federal Court below,[79] Thomson L.P. had expressed the view that 'dismissal' in Article 135(2) meant nothing less than putting an end to the servant's service by the master, and rejected the 'penalty' test. This view is now mere history. The courts have consistently applied the 'penalty' tests ever since although different results have occasionally been reached by judges according to their view of what is 'penal' in the circumstances.

In *Haji Ariffin's* case,[80] for example, both Suffian F.J. and MacIntyre F.J. accepted the 'penalty' tests and that dismissal was a penalty. However, where the services of the public servant (a *Kathi*) were terminated under a term in his contract of service, Suffian F.J. thought that the termination did not involve a penalty or punishment so as to make it a dismissal within the meaning of Article 135(2). MacIntyre F.J., however, thought that since the premature termination of an appointment for an alleged misconduct involved the loss of a career, future earnings, and prospect of pension, it was also by itself a punishment, and that was the 'penal consequence' which must be implied in the kind of 'dismissal' envisaged by Article 135(2).

It may be instructive to note Suffian F.J.'s 'qualification' in his judgment. He had said there that as there was 'no evidence' that the plaintiff had forfeited any claims to any benefit for which he might otherwise have been eligible, he was therefore of the opinion that the termination of his service was not dismissal. Can we take this to suggest that evidence of forfeiture of any benefit could have turned the termination, *even under contract*, into dismissal?

There is also the case of *Mahan Singh*,[81] decided in 1975 by the Federal Court. In that case, an officer's services were terminated 'in the public interest' and he was pensioned off as a result of a report made by his head of department, under regulation 44 of the General Orders, Chapter D Regulations, 1969, governing conduct and discipline. It was implicit in the judgments that dismissal was a punishment. Sharma J. at first instance, had held that the termination of the plaintiff officer's services amounted to a dismissal within Article 135(2) of the Constitution since the letter of termination would cause doubt about his capacity and character to any future employer and cast a stigma on him.

However, the Federal Court thought that the termination was not dismissal as it was not one of the forms of 'punishment' set out in regulation 36 of the same General Orders, Chapter D.[82]

Further, Suffian L.P. did not think that it could be said that there was any stigma attached to the officer's departure from government service as 'nobody in his right mind would say that such officers, if and when called upon to retire, have left the service under a cloud, and that they have been dismissed though it is true that they have been removed from office'.[83] Thus, applying the penalty tests, this case appears a 'marginal' one.

Nevertheless the courts are firmly of the view that there is a distinction to be drawn between 'dismissal' and mere termination of service of a public officer; and that dismissal, although it results in termination of service, is not any termination of service: it has a special meaning and involves a penalty or punishment.[84]

PUNISHMENT VERSUS TERMINATION OF SERVICES

It is possible to extract from the case-law so far, a number of situations which appear to be terminations of service that do *not* amount to punishments (namely dismissal or reduction in rank).

First, a termination of services which purports to be in accordance with the terms of the engagement, as by means of giving the stipulated period of notice or payment in lieu of notice, is not a punishment.[85] The public servant's remedy lies in damages if the termination is in breach of contract (e.g. if a shorter period of notice is given), but he will not be granted specific performance, or a declaration that he is still in service.[86]

Secondly, reverter to an officer's substantive post (from a probationary or other temporary post) will be held not to be a reduction in rank, and therefore not a punishment.[87]

Thirdly, compulsory or premature retirement will not be considered a punishment, based on the premise that the officer has no 'right' to any post, whether temporary or permanent.[88]

Finally, it seems very likely indeed that the Malaysian courts will consider the abolition of the office which a public officer holds as not being in the nature of a punishment. The issue arose in the case of *Ratnavale* v. *The Government of the Federation of Malaya*[89] but was not expressly resolved as the case was in fact decided on another point. However, as the courts have already decided that a public officer has no right to his post, it seems logically to follow that the abolition of it by the Government is not a punishment, but merely the exercise by the Government of its privilege. It seems at any rate that abolition of a post by *statute* has the effect of discharging the contract so that the Government is under no liability.[90]

IMPLICATIONS OF THE DISTINCTION

The distinction between 'dismissal' and termination under the terms of the engagement has two important implications. First, even where the officer's conduct is in question, it gives the Government the option of terminating his services by notice or payment in lieu of notice, without its having to hold a disciplinary inquiry and grant the officer a full hearing. This is a mechanism that requires the Government to make a small concession, like a month's salary or toleration of the officer's services for yet another month (small solace to the officer), but saves it a great deal of bother. Secondly, even if the Government conducts an inquiry and grants a hearing to the officer with a view to disciplinary action, it may still terminate his services according to the terms of the contract (if any) *whether or not he exculpates himself*, since dismissal was not obligatory. This proposition, remarkable as it may sound, was in fact established by the Privy Council in *Government of Malaysia* v. *Lionel*[91] in 1974. In that case the Government, through the Chief Police Officer (C.P.O.) of Johore Bahru, had terminated his services by payment of one month's salary plus cost of living allowance in lieu of notice after having decided that he had failed to exculpate himself. The tenor of the Privy Council's judgment clearly suggests that even if the officer had exculpated himself, the Government might terminate his services under the contract, for it had always had the right to do so. Ong C.J. in the Federal Court below had regarded the officer as having been dismissed 'as the wording of the C.P.O.'s letter should not be the deciding factor'. The letter really purported to be a dismissal, in his view, and he added that 'calling a spade a pickaxe does not alter the character of that agricultural instrument'.[92] The upshot of the Privy Council's decision is that a spade may indeed be called a pickaxe. Or perhaps it would be more accurate to say that the two implements, dismissal and termination of services under the contract, retain their respective characters, but that the use of either results in the digging of the same hole in the end. One writer[93] has lamented the drawing of 'fine legal distinctions' between 'dismissal' and 'termination of service in accordance with the contract' and the point is well made that this 'unholy emphasis on the sanctity of contract' has the unfortunate effect of depriving the public servant of the valuable protection of the constitutional provisions whose object and purpose must have been to protect the security of tenure of his appointment.[94]

The distinction has another implication: it provides a way of getting round Article 135(1) as well, in that even an 'authority' *subordinate* to that which had the power to appoint a public servant of that rank, may terminate his services in any manner not amounting to the punishments of dismissal or reduction in rank.

On the other hand, if the act purports to be a 'dismissal', a hearing will have to be given to the public servant and the powers of the dismissing authority may well be constrained. There is no doubt that if the allegations of misconduct or incompetence against the public servant are proved to the satisfaction of the disciplinary authority, it may proceed to dismiss him. What, however, if the allegations are *not* proved, or in other words, there is insufficient evidence to substantiate the allegations? The answer to this is not easy. It is submitted that there are three possibilities.

First, if one were to apply Winslow J.'s test in the *A.U.P.E.* case,[95] namely that the rights conferred on public servants by Article 135 relate to matters such as 'the *manner* in which or by whom they may be dismissed', then it is indeed arguable that once a hearing is properly given and if the dismissing authority is of the correct rank, any public servant may be subsequently dismissed except, perhaps, if the authority acted in bad faith.[96]

Secondly, it may be argued that the right to a fair hearing carries with it something more, namely, the right *not* to be dismissed if one succeeds in exculpating oneself. On principle, it seems reasonable to expect that if one is to be dismissed 'for cause', and an inquiry takes place, evidence being led, a finding of the administrative tribunal conducting the inquiry that goes completely against the weight of the evidence will be considered an error of law, which may be quashed should it appear on the face of the record.[97]

There is a third view. This derives from the Singapore High Court case of *Jacob* v. *The Attorney-General*.[98] There, Wee Chong Jin, C.J. expressed the view that 'the High Court in the exercise of its supervisory jurisdiction over inferior tribunals will not interfere merely on the ground of insufficiency of evidence', adding that the law in Singapore was the same as that in England on this point. He cited as authority, however, the House of Lords decision in *Anisminic* v. *Foreign Compensation Commission*.[99] However, it is respectfully submitted that the learned Chief Justice's view was misconceived. *Anisminic* only decided in this context that such an error of law would not be an excess of jurisdiction, not that it was not amenable to any form of review. It is clearly in English law an error within the jurisdiction, which, if it appears on the face of the record, may be quashed by an order of *certiorari*.

The writer humbly submits that the second view stated above is the best one.

OTHER FORMS OF PUNISHMENT

It is to be noted that the rights of Article 135 concern only the imposition of *two* punishments, dismissal or reduction in rank. These are not, however, the only punishments a public servant may be subjected to. Other punishments may take the form of a warning or reprimand at the lowest end of the scale, cover fines, forfeitures of salary, the withholding stoppage or deferment of increments, a reduction in salary, and only at the other extreme, involve reduction in rank or dismissal. These punishments are listed in regulation 36 of the Public Officers (Conduct and Discipline) (General Orders, Chapter 'D') Regulations, 1969, made originally by the Director of Operations under s. 2 of the Emergency (Essential Powers) Ordinance No. 2, 1969. These are still in force and are the applicable regulations on conduct and discipline. The other punishments do not attract the protections of Article 135, but the Chapter 'D' itself provides that some kind of opportunity must be given to a public officer to explain the lapse in his work or conduct before such a punishment is imposed.[100] Regulation 30 provides for the detailed procedure of adjudication in relation to dismissals and reductions in rank, but also allows the disciplinary authority to inflict 'such lesser punishment as it may deem fit' if it is of opinion that the officer does not deserve to be dismissed or reduced in rank.

These regulations of Chapter 'D' have the force of law and should be treated as mandatory,[101] at least in so far as they purport to carry out the objects of Article 135(2) of the Constitution.[102]

THE RIGHT TO BE GIVEN A REASONABLE OPPORTUNITY OF BEING HEARD

Article 135(2) provides that a public servant shall not be dismissed or reduced in rank without being given 'a reasonable opportunity of being heard'. This phrase has raised many questions.

The first question is whether the right embraces both rules of natural justice, namely 'the rule against bias' and 'the right to be heard' (or *audi alteram partem*) or only the latter rule. It has been suggested by Jayakumar[103] that the right embraces both rules. Trindade differs,[104] being of the view that only the right to be heard is included. Strangely enough, both views are based on the same enigmatic passage in the judgment of Lord Denning in *Surinder Singh Kanda* v. *The Government of the Federation of Malaya*. There, he said, after stating generally that there were two rules of natural justice, the rule against bias and the right to be heard:

It follows, of course, that the judge or whoever has to adjudicate must not hear evidence or receive representations from one side behind the back of the other. The Court will not inquire whether the evidence or representations did work to his prejudice. Sufficient that they might do so. The Court will not go into the likelihood of prejudice. The risk of it is enough. No one who has lost a case will believe that he has been fairly treated if the other side has had access to the judge without his knowing.[105]

In its particular context, Lord Denning's words, it is submitted, do not refer to the rule against bias, but the right to be heard, in spite of the use of language suggesting likelihood or risk of bias. The operative word is 'prejudice' and this suggests that His Lordship was referring to the familiar principle[106] that evidence must not be received behind the back of one of the parties, as this would offend the *audi alteram partem* rule. Thus, with respect, Trindade's view is preferable. In any case, a decision to dismiss or reduce in rank may still be open to collateral attack on the basis of bias, as the common law will supply the omission of the legislature, so as to import such a requirement unless expressly excluded.

A second question arises in the context of the actual hearing. Natural justice clearly requires that the public servant should be given notice of the precise charges or allegations against him, adequate notice of the hearing, notice of the likely penalty, and an adequate opportunity to present his case. Thus he must know the evidence against him, and be allowed to adduce evidence or to make any representations. However, it is argued that the public servant may in fact be entitled to, not one, but *two* opportunities to be heard, one on the charges, and one on the penalty to be imposed. The latter is conceived as not merely an opportunity to make a plea in mitigation but the conveyance of information to the servant in advance of the proposed or likely punishment, so that the dismissal, when meted out, will not strike him like a 'bolt from the blue'.

All the cases on the 'two opportunities' doctrine derive from Singapore.[107] First, why has the question not arisen in Malaysia? It would appear that the question may prove academic in Malaysia as under the Chapter 'D' regulations of 1969, governing conduct and discipline, there is no real problem. Regulation 30 therein spells out when an officer should be informed of the proposed dismissal (or reduction in rank) and when he may exercise his right to make representations on the question of his dismissal or reduction in rank.[108]

As for the Singapore cases, it is submitted that they can all be reconciled on the following basis: Natural justice requires that a servant be given (a) notice of the charges, (b) notice of the contemplated (likely) penalty, and (c) a right to make representations as to *both* charges and penalty. If (a) and (b) are given at the same time (as in *Jacob* v. *Attorney-General*),[109] it is only necessary to give the servant a single opportunity during which he may make representations on both charges and penalty. If (b) takes place at a time later than (a) and representations have already been made on (a), then the servant must be given another opportunity to make representations on (b)—as in *Attorney-General* v. *Ling How Doong*.[110] Obviously, then, if neither (a) nor (b) has taken place, the question of failure to allow representations on (b) may not even arise, as the case can be decided simply on the basis of the failure to give the fundamental opportunity to make representations on (a)—as in *Phang Moh Shin's* case.[111]

A third question is whether the hearing needs to be an oral one. On this, *Najar Singh* v. *Government of Malaysia & Anor.*[112] is instructive. The Privy Council had to consider the appellant's argument that regulation 27 of the Chapter 'D' Regulations imposed an obligation to hear him orally, so that 'being heard' meant 'being heard orally', and that his dismissal after an opportunity to make his representations in writing was void. Their Lordships rejected this contention, Viscount Dilhorne saying:[113]

> The word 'heard' does not invariably connote an oral hearing. It can be used and is not infrequently used in relation to something written. The question, 'Have you heard from X' often means, 'Have you had a letter from X?' Its meaning must depend on the context in which it is used and the context in which it is used in these regulations shows that in regulation 27 it cannot have been intended only to mean an oral hearing.

Further, what was important was that the officer concerned should have had a full opportunity of stating his case before he was dismissed. As the Chapter 'D' Regulations did provide this and the appellant had apparently availed himself of the opportunity according to the detailed procedure, there was no denial of natural justice.

Najar Singh concerned regulation 27 in the Chapter 'D' Regulations, rather than Article 135(2) of the Constitution. However, as the wording of regulation 27 'follows' that in Article 135(2) there seems no doubt that all that Article 135(2) requires is a reasonable opportunity to make representations (whether orally or in writing).

In the Federal Court below, Suffian C.J. (as he then was) suggested that if on the evidence, the plaintiff (appellant) had ever demanded an oral hearing and been refused, he might have had a stronger case.[114] However in view of the Privy Council's views, it is unlikely that refusal of an oral hearing to a servant carries the same weight as refusal to allow cross-examination of witnesses against him,[115] as he is still getting his opportunity to make representations and is not really likely to be prejudiced.

One question remains. Does the right to be heard carry with it a right to be represented by counsel? This is a difficult question and the cases are conflicting. The question is framed thus: Where the Constitution is silent on the matter, is there a right to legal representation? (The same considerations apply where statute, or rules are silent on the point.)

On one view, the right to counsel must be accorded to an aggrieved person especially when his reputation or livelihood is at stake, because every man is entitled at common law to appoint an agent to act for him, and that agent may be a lawyer.[116] This right may not be restricted except by express words or necessary implication. The old Singapore case of *Mundell* v. *Mellor*[117] and a Malayan High Court case, *Doresamy* v. *Public Services Commission*[118] would support this view.

On the other hand, on another view, there is no such right in the absence of express requirements in the rules conferring quasi-judicial powers on a domestic tribunal.[119] One Singapore case, *Sithambaram* v. *The Attorney-General*[120] accepted the proposition that where the regulations of a domestic tribunal were silent on legal representation, there was no absolute right to be legally represented. This was a matter for the discretion of the tribunal. It may be added that if a right to cross-examine witnesses is not required by the right to be heard[121] or (even more so) a right to an oral hearing is not required by the right to be heard,[122] then the right to be legally represented seems even less likely to be upheld, for a lawyer's services seem to be not so obviously useful in merely presenting written representations. However, *Doresamy's* case[123] held that the right to legal representation was still to be inferred in a situation where an appeal was to be made in writing.

In one situation, when a Committee of Inquiry invites a public servant to appear before it to exculpate himself on a matter involving dismissal or reduction in rank under the Chapter 'D' Regulations, the Committee is expressly given the discretion to permit representation by an advocate and solicitor.[124]

The Constitution (Amendment) Act, 1976 (Act A 354) inserted a proviso[125] to Article 135(2) so as to create four exceptions to the rule, requiring a right to be heard. In these four cases (the first three drawn substantially from the Indian Constitution's proviso to Article 311(2)). They may be summarized as follows:

(a) The servant has been found guilty on a criminal charge in respect of his conduct for which he is dismissed or reduced in rank;[126]

(b) the proper disciplinary authority is satisfied that for some reason (to be recorded in writing) it is 'not reasonably practicable to carry out the requirements' of clause (2) of Article 135;

(c) The Yang di-Pertuan Agong, or State Ruler (as the case may be) is satisfied that 'in the interests of the security of the Federation or any part thereof it is not expedient to carry out the requirements' of clause (2) of Article 135;

(d) The servant has been made the subject of any order of detention, supervision, restricted residence, banishment or deportation, or he has had imposed on him any form of restriction or supervision under any law relating to security, prevention of crime, preventive detention, restricted residence, banishment, immigration, or protection of women and girls.

The creation of any exceptions to the important right to be heard is no doubt to be regretted, but it is hoped in particular that the very wide discretion given under sub-clauses (b) and (c) is not abused and that those two limbs are not resorted to too often, for they can very easily be employed as 'catch-alls' at the convenience of the Government, and decisions thereunder are not likely to be amenable to judicial review.

DELEGATION AND THE EXERCISE OF THE POWERS OR FUNCTIONS OF A COMMISSION BY OTHER BODIES

Article 144(1) sets out the general duties of a service commission. In particular, a commission shall appoint, promote, or exercise disciplinary control over public servants over whom it has jurisdiction subject to 'any existing law' and the provisions of the Constitution. However, as it is not always convenient for a service commission to exercise every single one of its powers and functions to the exclusion of any other body, the principle of delegation—of one or more functions—finds expression in the Constitution. The 'delegation' may take one of two broad forms. The Constitution may grant directly to a commission the power to delegate certain functions, defining the scope of the delegation and the delegates (as in Articles 140(6)(b)[127] and 144(6)), or may provide for powers and functions to be exercised by other bodies, particularly boards appointed by the Yang di-Pertuan Agong (as in Article 144(5B)).[128] Alternatively, the Constitution may provide for particular laws—federal law, state law or regulations made by the Yang di-Pertuan Agong—to confer certain defined powers and functions to named bodies (as in Articles 144(5A),[129] 135(1), proviso,[130] and 140(1), proviso).[131]

It is not proposed to examine all of these provisions in detail. However, the writer will examine the question of delegation in the context of Article 135(1), which contains another fundamental protection of the public servant (other than a member of the armed forces) namely that 'he may not be dismissed or reduced in rank by an authority subordinate to that which, at the time of the dismissal or reduction, has power to appoint a member of that service of equal rank'.

This provision has not been without its difficulties in interpretation and application. Nor has it been free from being whittled down in that several exceptions—no less than five, in fact—appear to have been created by amendments of the Constitution from Independence until the present day. These aspects will be examined.

ARTICLE 135(1) AND THE PROPER DISMISSING AUTHORITY

It should be noted that Article 135(1) does not say that a public servant must not be dismissed by an authority other than that which did actually appoint him; only that the dismissing authority must *not* be subordinate to that which (at that time of dismissal) had *power* to appoint someone of his rank. The same applies to reduction in rank.

Who has the power to appoint? Since Merdeka Day, the primary power has been vested in the relevant service commission having jurisdiction over the public servant in question.[132] This power may be delegated under the Constitution primarily by virtue of Article 144(6), to any officer in a service to which the commission's jurisdiction extends or to any board of officers appointed by it. Under Article 140(6), the Police Force Commission may delegate to any member of that Commission or the police force or a board of officers of the police force 'its powers or duties'. In the case of *Surinder Singh Kanda* v. *The Government of the Federation of Malaya*, the Privy Council also decided that there could only be, at any one time, *one* authority having the power to appoint.

Lord Denning said:

It appears to their Lordships that there cannot, at one and the same time, be two authorities, each of whom has a concurrent power to appoint members of the police service. One or other must be entrusted with the power to appoint.[133]

He further added that when the Police Service Commission (now renamed the Police Force Commission) delegated any of its functions under Article 144(6), it was 'its own duty and its own power' that it delegated and that it remained throughout the authority which had power to appoint, even when it did so by a delegate.[134] However, it is possible that Lord Denning took this view because of the wording of Article 144(6), whereby the delegate of any of the commission's functions, namely the officer or board in question, 'shall exercise those functions under the direction and the control of the Commission'.

There is no doubt that a commission may delegate its power to *appoint*, to another body under Articles 144(6) or 140(6). This was implicit in the judgments of the Privy Council in *Surinder Singh Kanda*[135] and *Iznan bin Osman*.[136]

Does the delegation of the power to appoint also effect a delegation of the power to dismiss? In the Singapore High Court case of *Jacob* v. *Attorney-General*[137] Wee Chong Jin C.J. expressed the view (obiter) that:

... apart from the Interpretation Act 1965, a power to appoint must necessarily imply a power to dismiss unless the authority of dismissal is expressly vested in some other person or authority.

It is submitted with respect that this view is only applicable where the primary power of appointment is vested in an authority, and nothing is said about who has the power to dismiss. As a service commission is normally invested with the powers not only of appointment but also of disciplinary control (including dismissal), a *delegation* by it of its power of appointment will not be effective to delegate any other powers, which will remain with the commission.

A more difficult question has been whether a commission or 'authority' can delegate its power to dismiss, without also delegating its power to appoint. At first sight, it would seem that it can, since Article 144(6) allows a commission to delegate 'any of its functions under Clause (1)'; and Article 140(6) allows the Police Force Commission to delegate to certain authorities 'its powers or duties'. However, if this is done, the power to dismiss that is delegated may not be validly exercised, for the delegation, which can only be to a subordinate authority, of the power to dismiss, whilst the commission retains the power to appoint, will mean that it will be impossible for the delegate to carry out the power to dismiss without causing a violation of Article 135(1). The question arose in the case of *Government of Malaysia* v. *Iznan bin Osman*.[138] There the Chief Police Officer (C.P.O.) dismissed the respondent (plaintiff), a police constable, purporting to act under powers delegated to him by the Police Force Commission. However, the Police Force Commission had in its instrument of delegation under Article 140(6)(b), delegated in 1962, its functions under Article 140(1) in respect of members of the Police Force to the Commissioner of Police and to such other police officers or boards of police officers 'so as to be exercised as specified in the Police Ordinance, 1952, and in the rules, regulations and standing orders made or purporting to have been made thereunder'. The Ordinance and the rules, regulations and standing orders unfortunately did not give a power of appointment to the C.P.O., as it was vested in the Commissioner, to whom the C.P.O. was subordinate. The respondent claimed a declaration that his purported dismissal was null and void and succeeded before Sharma J. The Federal Court dismissed the Government's appeal, and so did the Privy Council.

The Privy Council held shortly that the C.P.O. was subordinate to the Commissioner (who possessed the power to appoint) and so could not dismiss the respondent.[139]

At first instance, however, Sharma J. noted that there was 'capacity for some conflict' between the provisions of Article 144(6) and Article 135(1) but thought that the conflict could be reconciled if it was held that the Commission had no power to delegate its functions in so far as they related to the dismissal or reduction in rank of the public servant[140] (and he did go on to so hold).

In the Federal Court, the judgment of Lee Hun Hoe C.J. (Borneo) is particularly instructive. He said:[141]

Any delegation of power to dismiss without delegating the power to appoint would result in breach of the Constitution.... The delegation (Exh. D3) states that 'The Police Force Commission delegates its powers under Article 140(1).' At a glance this would seem to be sufficiently wide to include the delegation of the powers of appointment and dismissal. But I do not think the legislature intended to permit the Police Force Commission to delegate its powers under Articles 140(6)(b) or Article 144(6) in such a manner as to conflict with Article 135(1). I say this because the intention of the legislature is clearly reflected by the omission of the words 'notwithstanding the provisions of clause (1) of Article 135' from Articles 140(6)(b) and 144(6). These words, however, appear in clauses (5A) and (5B) of Article 144. The insertion of these words is significant because the person given the power under such a delegation may dismiss a public servant even though he has no power to appoint an officer of equal rank.

Unless the powers of appointment could be delegated or unless those words mentioned earlier were inserted in a particular clause then it would be no use for a delegatee [sic] to be conferred with the power of dismissal.

Matters, however, took a strange turn. Several months before the Privy Council was to hear the appeal in *Iznan's* case, and some months after the Federal Court's decision, the Malaysian Parliament passed the Constitution (Amendment) Act 1976 which came into force on 26 August 1976. S. 30(a) of that Amending Act inserted this additional proviso to Article 135(1):

> And provided further that this Clause shall not apply to a case where a member of any of the services mentioned in this Clause is dismissed or reduced in rank by an authority in pursuance of a power delegated to it by a Commission to which this Part applies, *and this proviso shall be deemed to have been an integral part of this Clause as from Merdeka Day;*

This proviso would have the effect of validating retrospectively as well as prospectively, and purported delegation by a Commission, of a power to dismiss or reduce in rank, whether or not the power of appointment is also delegated to it. The Privy Council in *Iznan* was unwilling to entertain a new argument based on this new amendment as no formal notice had been given to the respondent's advisers or to the officials of the Privy Council that leave to present the argument would be sought, stating further that:

> This attempt to deprive a litigant of a right of property by retrospective legislation passed *pendente lite* is a step of a most unusual character; and that makes it all the more necessary that the respondent should have had an adequate opportunity of meeting the argument before their Lordships could consider it.[142]

However, in *Government of Malaysia* v. *Zainal bin Hashim*,[143] the Federal Court had no qualms about applying the proviso with retrospective effect, thus reversing the trial judge Abdul Hamid J. who had held, following the Federal Court's own decision in *Iznan*, that the Chief Police Officer, Selangor, had no power to dismiss the plaintiff police constable, as he had not been delegated the power to appoint but merely the power to dismiss, by the Police Force Commission.

It seems certain now, therefore, that a 'bare' power to dismiss may be delegated by a Commission and exercised by the delegate, without violating Article 135(1).

It remains only for the writer to outline the exceptions that have been created to the principle in Article 135(1).

The first appeared in 1960,[144] by the addition of a new clause (5A) to Article 144. This provided that Federal law and regulations made by the Yang di-Pertuan Agong might provide for the exercise by any officer or board of officers in a service over which a commission had jurisdiction, 'of any of the functions of the Commission under Clause (1)' except of the powers of first appointment to the permanent or pensionable establishment or promotion notwithstanding the provisions of clause (1) of Article 135.

The second came in 1966,[145] by the addition of clause (5B) to Article 144. By paragraph (i) of this provision as it presently stands, the Yang di-Pertuan Agong may appoint boards to exercise all the powers and functions of the Public Services Commission or the new Educational Service Commission, other than the power of first appointment to the permanent or pensionable establishment, notwithstanding the provisions of Article 135(1), Article 139, and Article 141A. By paragraph (iv), where the Yang di-Pertuan Agong has appointed such a board, the powers or functions delegated shall remain powers or functions to be exercised by the board and cease to be exercisable by the relevant Commission.

The Yang di-Pertuan Agong has in fact appointed boards for the purposes of promotion and discipline, and under paragraph (ii), appeal boards for persons aggrieved by a board's exercise of any functions or powers delegated to it.

In 1968, a proviso was added to Article 135, now a proviso specifically to clause (1) of Article 135.[146] This allows the legislatures of any State (other than Malacca and Penang) to make laws to provide for all powers and functions of a State Public Service Commission (other than the power of first appointment to the permanent or pensionable establishment) to be exercised by a Board appointed by the State Ruler. This provision is in respect only of members of the public services of the States.

The last two exceptions arrived by way of the Constitution (Amendment) Act 1976.[147] This added the second proviso to Article 135(1),[148] and has already been discussed in the context of delegation of the power to dismiss *per se*. The other 'exception' arises by way of an amendment to Article 140(1)[149] by addition of a proviso to it. By this proviso,

... Parliament may by law provide for the exercise of such disciplinary control over all or any of the members of the police force in such manner and by such authority as may be provided in that law, and in that event, if the authority is other than the Commission, the disciplinary control exercisable by such authority shall not be exercised by the Commission; and no provision of such law shall be invalid on the ground of inconsistency with any provision of this Part.

If Parliament should make any such law (thus a 'federal' law) it could be far-reaching indeed in its consequences. It would enable Parliament to grant the powers of dismissal and reduction in rank to any authority, and this would allow Parliament to grant these powers even to senior police officers, like a Chief Police Officer, even to the *exclusion* of the Police Force Commission. If there are any further arguments as to which authority has the power to dismiss, the answer will have to be: *not* the Police Force Commission but the authority granted the disciplinary power by the law. Also, it will allow a validation, in effect, of some existing pre-Merdeka laws that granted powers of appointment and dismissal to various officers like Chief Police Officers and Commissioners, and which could not be modified by the Yang di-Pertuan Agong under Article 162, except so as to accord with the Constitution and would be adjudged, sooner or later, to be void as inconsistent with the Constitution.[150] Now, it is submitted, a Government that wanted to play safe, could gather together and cause the repeal of all such pre-Merdeka laws *en bloc*, and then largely re-enact them as new Federal laws whereupon each old law, taking its breath of life from the proviso to Article 140(1), may yet rise again like a phoenix from the ashes. Alternatively, such pre-Merdeka laws do not even have to be repealed. An enactment of similar provisions will still stand as valid law, and the old provisions can be ignored.

What conclusions may we draw on this part? It seems clear that the protection of Article 135(1) is being whittled down greatly, particularly by the second proviso to Article 135(1) added in 1976, which seems to make nonsense of the protection as stated in Article 135(1). This huge 'exception' is perhaps now rather the rule! On the other hand, the power of first appointment to the permanent or pensionable establishment appears to have remained vested in the service commissions and not vested in other bodies—at any rate, not by means of constitutional amendment. It is here that control by independent service commissions is preserved.

The Lord President of Malaysia, Tun Mohamed Suffian bin Hashim, put it well in a statement in his book—a statement that he was not to know would prove particularly prophetic when the constitutional amendments of 1976 took place shortly thereafter—that:

The trend after independence has, however, been to reduce the powers of the service commissions in regard to discipline and promotion, for experience has shown that delay in disciplinary charges against public servants is not conducive to efficiency and that the executive cannot be efficient unless it has some say in who should and who should not be promoted. No firm in the private sector will for a moment agree that promotions of their staff be entrusted to the decision of a body entirely independent of the board of directors.[151]

1. The major legal or semi-legal contributions touching wholly or in part on the subject of public servants or the public services of Malaysia (including Malaya) include the following: Sheridan, 'A Digest of Dismissal and Reduction in Rank' [1962] *Public Law* 260; S. Jayakumar, 'Protection for Civil Servants: The Scope of Article 135(1) and (2) of the Malaysian Constitution as Developed Through the Cases' [1969] 2 *Malayan Law Journal* liv.; F. A. Trindade, 'The Security of Tenure of Public Servants in Malaysia and Singapore', *Malaya Law Review Legal Essays: In Memoriam Bashir Ahmad Mallal* (1975), 256; and M. Suffian, *An Introduction to The Constitution of Malaysia*, Government Printer, Kuala Lumpur, 2nd edition, 1976, Chapter 10.

There have also been numerous case-notes on the many controversial decisions arising out of this subject.

2. These are enumerated for the purposes of the Constitution, in Article 132(1), paragraphs (a) to (h) (as amended up to August 1976).

3. A phrase employed to describe the Federation of Malaysia by R. L. Watts, *New Federations: Experiments in the Commonwealth*, Oxford, Clarendon Press, 1966.

4. See Suffian L.P. in *Government of Malaysia* v. *Mahan Singh* [1975] 2 M.L.J. 155 at p. 160 (quoted in the text of this essay at p. 279).

5. These have been numerous and will be referred to in their appropriate context in this essay.

6. By S. Jayakumar and F. A. Trindade respectively (*supra*, note 1).

7. See Article 144(1).

8. This was added by the Constitution (Amendment) Act 1960 (No. 10 of 1960), s. 17(b).

9. *Report of a Commission to Enquire into Matters Affecting the Integrity of the Public Services, 1955*, Government Printer, Federation of Malaya, at p. 17.

10. Article 8(2) must be read subject to Article 8(5) as well as Articles 153 and 161A, to take account of the special position of the Malays and natives of the Borneo States.

11. Op. cit. (note 9).

12. This figure is derived from 'A Statement of Policy' on *Malayanisation of the Public Service*, Federation of Malaya, Government Printer, 1956.

13. *The Report of the Federation of Malaya Constitutional Conference, London*, 1956 (paragraphs 40-43).

The Reid Commission itself outlined its recommendations on the Public Services in Chapter VIII of its Report, at pp. 66-9, Government Printer, 1957.

14. *The Royal Commission on the Revision of Salaries and Conditions of Service in the Public Service* (Malaysia), 1967. This Commission was chaired by the Hon. Tan Sri Suffian (as he then was).

15. Article 137(1).

16. *Federation of Malaya: Constitutional Proposals*, Government Printer, 1957.

17. Article 141(5).

18. By the Constitution (Amendment) Act, 1960 (No. 10 of 1960), s.20, effective from 31 May 1960.

19. By virtue of the Malaysia Act 1963 (No. 26 of 1963) effective from 16 September 1963.

20. This is a result of the Constitution (Amendment) Act, 1976 (Act A354). Also see the essay on the Malaysian Judiciary in this volume, by Tun Mohd. Suffian, where the Judicial and Legal Service Commission receives a fuller treatment. This Commission accordingly receives rather scant treatment in this essay, for which the writer trusts he will be forgiven.

21. This was effected by the Constitution (Amendment) Act, 1973 (Act A193), ss. 2 and 4.

22. Constitution (Amendment) Act, 1976 (Act A354), s. 33 (amending Article 141A).

23. *Revised Report of the Royal Commission on the Teaching Services, West Malaysia*, Government Printer, Kuala Lumpur, 1971.

24. Ibid. at p. 94 (Chapter X para 26).

25. See Articles 141A and 144.

26. See Article 144 (5B), paragraph (i)—as substituted in s.5 of the Constitution (Amendment) Act, 1973 (Act A193).

27. See Malaysia, *Parliamentary Debates (Dewan Ra'ayat)* Official Report, Third Parliament, Third Session, April 1973, No. 7, 791-4 (Prime Minister's speech on the second reading of the Constitution (Amendment) Act, 1973, on 26 April 1973).

28. *Report of the Federation of Malaya Constitutional Commission 1957* (op. cit. note 13), para. 155.

29. See R. H. Hickling, *An Introduction to the Federal Constitution*, Federation of Malaya Information Services, 1960, p. 56, and *Federation of Malaya Constitutional Proposals* (op. cit.), para. 48.

30. See Article 139(2) and (3) as originally drafted.

31. Article 139(2).

32. See Article 132(1), para. (c).

33. See Article 133.

34. R. L. Watts, op. cit., p. 229.

35. Constitution (Amendment) Act, 1960 (No. 10 of 1960), s.21(a).

36. Article 146B(1). This provision was added by the Malaysia Act, 1963 (No. 26 of 1963), s.55.

37. See Article 146B(7), which was also added by the same Act.

38. Act A354, s.37, amending Article 146C.

39. S. Jayakumar, op. cit., p. lvi.
It is also the view of Suffian F.J. (as he then was) in *Haji Ariffin* v. *Government of Pahang* [1969] 1 M.L.J. 6, that Article 132(2A) contains the 'rule', and clauses (1) and (2) of Article 135, the two main exceptions in the Federal Constitution. Note, however, the often overlooked third exception also in clause (3) of Article 135.

40. [1964] A.C. 40.

41. No. 10 of 1960, S. 17(b). This came into force on 31 May 1960.

42. The Constitution (Amendment) Act, 1973 (Act A193) added paragraph (h), which listed the new Education Service.

43. 6 F.M.S.L.R. 160.

44. [1965] 2 M.L.J. 31 at p. 32.

45. [1975] 2 M.L.J. 155 at pp. 159–60.

46. Suffian L.P. in *Government of Malaysia* v. *Mahan Singh* [1975] 2 M.L.J. 155 at p. 159.

47. [1969] 1 M.L.J. 6 at p. 14.

48. [1953] 2 Q.B. 482.

49. [1970] 2 M.L.J. 133.

50. [1969] 1 M.L.J. 6.

51. See *Terrell's* Case, *supra*, note 48.

52. *Terrell's* Case, *supra*; *C. B. Reilly* v. *R* [1934] A.C. 176.

53. *Supra*, note 50.

54. Ibid. at p. 18.

55. [1975] 2 M.L.J. 155 at p. 160.

56. *Dhingra* v. *Union of India* [1958] S.C.R. 828.

57. [1965] 2 M.L.J. 31.

58. *Supra*, note 50.

59. [1969] 2 M.L.J. 206.

60. [1974] 1 M.L.J. 3.

61. [1975] 2 M.L.J. 155.

62. Ibid. at p. 158.

63. [1965] 2 M.L.J. 209 at p. 212.

64. *Supra*, note 61.

65. *Haji Wan Othman's* Case, *supra*, note 57 and *Mahan Singh's* Case, *supra*, note 61.

66. [1973] 1 M.L.J. 222.

67. [1976] 1 M.L.J. 118.

68. Ibid. at p. 122.

69. Ibid.

70. Article 311(2) uses the phrase 'No such person ... shall be dismissed or removed or reduced in rank except after an inquiry....'

71. See Seervai, *Constitutional Law of India*, Vol. II, Tripathi, 3rd edition, 1976 at p. 1452.

72. *Munusamy* v. *Public Services Commission* [1967] 1 M.L.J. 199.

73. *Supra*, note 59.

74. *Supra*, note 61.

75. See *Government of Malaysia* v. *Lionel* [1974] 1 M.L.J. 3 at p. 5.

76. The leading case on the 'penalty' tests was *Dhingra* v. *Union of India* (*supra*, note 56).

77. *Supra*, note 72.

78. Ibid. at p. 201. In *Haji Ariffin's* Case (*supra*, note 48) MacIntyre F.J. explained that Lord Hodson was applying the *ejusdem generis* rule.

79. [1964] M.L.J. 239 at p. 244.

80. *Supra*, note 50.

81. *Supra*, note 61.

82. Public Officers (Conduct and Discipline) (General Orders, Chapter 'D') Regulations, 1969.
On the same basis acts like suspension of an officer will also not be 'punishments'.

83. *Supra*, note 61 at p. 161.

84. See *Haji Ariffin's* Case (*supra*, note 50), per Suffian F.J.; and *Lionel's* Case (*supra* note 60) (Privy Council).

85. See *Haji Ariffin's* Case, *supra* note 50; *Gnanasundram* v. *P.S.C.* [1966] 1 M.L.J. 157; *Gnanasundram* v. *Government of Malaysia* [1971] 1 M.L.J. 208; *Lionel's* Case, *supra* note 60 (Privy Council).

86. See *Francis* v. *Municipal Councillors of Kuala Lumpur* [1962] M.L.J. 407.

87. *Munusamy* v. *Public Services Commission* (*supra*, note 72).

88. *Thambipillai's* case (*supra*, note 59); *Mahan Singh* (*supra* note 61).

89. [1963] M.L.J. 393.

90. *C. B. Reilly* v. *R* (*supra*, note 52).

91. *Supra*, note 60.

92. [1971] 2 M.L.J. 172 at p. 173.

93. F. A. Trindade, op. cit. at pp. 282–3.

94. Ibid. at p. 282. See also *Haji Ariffin's* case (*supra*, note 50) per MacIntyre F.J.
Trindade's suggested constitutional amendments to clarify and strengthen the constitutional position of the public servant have unfortunately not materialized.

95. *Amalgamated Union of Public Employees* v. *Permanent Secretary (Health)* [1965] 2 M.L.J. 209 at p. 212.

96. F. A. Trindade, op. cit. at p. 275.

97. S. A. De Smith, *Judicial Review of Administrative Action*, Stevens, 3rd. edition, 1973 at p. 115.

98. [1970] 2 M.L.J. 133.

99. [1969] 2 A. C. 147.

100. See Regulation 29 of the Chapter 'D' Regulations.

101. *Sambasivam* v. *Public Services Commission* [1970] 1 M.L.J. 61 at p. 62.
The Privy Council in *Najar Singh* v. *Government of Malaysia* [1976] 1 M.L.J. 203 also accepted that they have the force of law.

102. *Wong Keng Sam* v. *Pritam Singh Brar* [1968] 2 M.L.J. 158.

103. Op. cit. at p. lxi.

104. Op. cit. at p. 269.

105. [1962] M.L.J. 169 at p. 173.

106. See, e.g. *Errington* v. *Minister of Health* [1935] 1 K.B. 249.

107. These are: *Phang Moh Shin* v. *Commissioner of Police* [1967] 2 M.L.J. 137; *Attorney-General* v. *Ling How Doong* [1969] 1 M.L.J. 154; *Jacob* v. *Attorney-General* [1970] 2 M.L.J. 133; and *Sithambaran* v. *Attorney-General* [1972] 2 M.L.J. 175.

108. See Regulations 30(2) and 30(6).

109. *Supra*, note 107.

110. *Supra*, note 107.

111. *Supra*, note 107.

112. [1976] 1 M.L.J. 203.

113. Ibid. at p. 205.

114. [1974] 1 M.L.J. 138 at p. 141.

115. See *University of Ceylon* v. *Fernando* [1960] 1 All E.R. 631 at p. 641.

116. *Pett* v. *Greyhound Racing Association, Ltd.* [1968] 2 All E.R. 545.

117. [1929] S.S.L.R. 152.

118. [1971] 2 M.L.J. 127.

119. *Pett* v. *Greyhound Racing Association, Ltd.* (No. 2). [1969] 2 All E.R. 221;

Enderby Town Football Club Ltd. v. *The Football Association Ltd.* [1971] 1 All E.R. 215.

120. *Supra*, note 107.

121. See *University of Ceylon* v. *Fernando (supra)*.

122. See *Najar Singh* v. *Government of Malaysia, supra* (Privy Council).

123. *Supra*, note 118.

124. Regulation 30(8).

125. See s.30(b).

126. This would eliminate the need for any inquiry or an action brought for failure to conduct a proper inquiry as occurred in *Kathiravalupillai* v. *Government of Malaysia* [1976] 2 M.L.J. 114.

127. Added by the Constitution (Amendment) Act, 1960 (No. 10 of 1960), s.22.

128. Added by Constitution (Amendment) Act, 1966 (No. 59 of 1966) s.2. Paragraph (i) was substituted by virtue of the Constitution (Amendment) Act, 1973 (Act A193), s.5.

129. Added by the Constitution (Amendment) Act, 1960 (No. 10 of 1960), s. 25(b) and further amended by the Constitution (Amendment) Act, 1966 (No. 59 of 1966), s.2.

130. Added to the end of Article 135 by the Constitution (Amendment) Act, 1968 (No. 27 of 1968), s.2 as the first of the many provisos to the Article. By the Constitution (Amendment) Act, 1971 (Act A31), it was moved up to become the proviso to clause (1) of Article 135.

131. Added by the Constitution (Amendment) Act, 1976 (Act A354), s.32(a).

132. See *Government of Malaysia* v. *Iznan bin Osman* [1977] 2 M.L.J. 1 at p. 3; *Surinder Singh Kanda* v. *Government of the Federation of Malaya* [1962] M.L.J. 169 at p. 171.

133. [1962] M.L.J. 169 at p. 171.

134. Ibid.

135. [1962] M.L.J. 169.

136. [1977] 2 M.L.J. 1.

137. [1970] 2 M.L.J. 133.

138. [1977] 2 M.L.J. 1.

139. Ibid. at p. 3.

140. [1973] 2 M.L.J. 143 at p. 149.

141. [1975] 2 M.L.J. 61 at pp. 64–5. See also Suffian L.P. at p. 61 where he succinctly outlined how delegation might affect a Chief Police Officer's powers.

142. [1977] 2 M.L.J. 1 at p. 4 (Lord Fraser of Tullybelton).

143. [1977] 2 M.L.J. 254.

144. See note 129, *supra*.

145. See note 128, *supra*.

146. See note 130, *supra*.

147. Act A354.

148. Ibid., s.30(a).

149. Ibid., s.32(a).

150. See *Surinder Singh Kanda* v. *Government of the Federation of Malaya* [1962] M.L.J. 169; and *Government of Malaysia* v. *Iznan bin Osman* [1977] 2 M.L.J. 1.

151. Op. cit. (note 1) at pp. 121–2.

13. Financial Provisions of the Malaysian Constitution and their Operation in Practice

THE financial provisions of the Malaysian Constitution are contained in Articles 96 to 112 of the Constitution and they govern the methods by which public funds are to be administered and accounted for at the Federal level as well as the division of revenue between the Federal Government on the one hand and the State Governments on the other. They also define the borrowing powers of the Federation and of the States. These financial provisions and their application have been explained in detail by Tun Mohamed Suffian bin Hashim in Chapter 13 of his book entitled *An Introduction to the Constitution of Malaysia*, and it would therefore be tedious to describe them again in detail in this essay. This essay will therefore only attempt to set out the writer's impressions of the operation of these provisions in practice and their effects during the last twenty years.

In studying the Malaysian Constitution, it should be noted that the financial provisions have undergone very few minor changes during the last twenty years in spite of the tremendous expansion of Malaysia's economy and the growth of its expenditure and revenue during the period. It is also interesting to note that although the financial provisions cover only seventeen Articles in the Constitution, they have nevertheless provided a reasonable basis for the development of the strong and stable economy that Malaysia enjoys today. It is a tribute to the wisdom and farsightedness of Malaysia's legal and financial authors of the Constitution that the basic financial-legal structure that was envisaged twenty years ago is not only still relevant, but is workable and allows sufficient flexibility for effective financial management and steady economic expansion not only today but for the future as well.

The financial provisions of the Constitution are generally those that were in effect during the period of the colonial administration before Independence in 1957. What has really changed, therefore, is not the financial provisions *per se* but 'their operation in practice' as indicated in the title of this essay. It would therefore be useful at this stage to indicate the change in the scope, direction, and magnitude of the Federal Government's Budget so as to be able to appreciate the changing nature of the operation and implementation of the Constitution's financial provisions in practice. The law is important, but what has turned out to be even more important is the administration and management of these laws.

The Federal Expenditure in 1957 amounted to $787 million. In 1977 the Federal Budget Expenditure is estimated at $10,140 million, thus representing a thirteenfold increase over the 1957 level. Federal Government revenue has also increased by about nine times over the level in 1957. Whilst in 1957 the Federal Expenditure constituted only 19 per cent of the Gross National Product (GNP), it constituted about 33 per cent of the GNP in 1977.*

It is clear, therefore, that the Federal Budget has grown significantly and that its role in the economy has also grown substantially. Thus, the Federal Government Budget has become a very potent instrument in influencing the overall growth and longer term potential and prospects of the economy.

The financial provisions in the Constitution relate not only to the Federal Government finances but also to the State Governments and Public Authorities as well. Indeed, the financial provisions directly govern the financial management of the whole public sector of the economy and of course influence the private sector as well. The Federal Government Budget itself constitutes about 70 per cent of the total public sector and this illustrates the strong centralized role of the Federal Government particularly *vis-à-vis* the State Governments and the Public Authorities.

The constitutional provisions underlying the strong centralized financial position of the Federal Government has, of course, an historical basis. In the old Federated Malay States, the colonial government had a similarly strong legal framework which gave strong central financial authority. With the formation of the Federa-

---

* The comparison between 1957 and 1977 is not really on all fours as Sabah and Sarawak joined the Federation in 1963 and hence Federal expenditure on them and revenue derived therefrom have been included thereafter. Nevertheless Federal expenditure and revenue in respect of Sabah and Sarawak constitute only a small percentage of the increase.

tion of Malaya in 1948 and later the independent Federation of Malaya in 1957, these centralized financial provisions were extended to the whole country. However, it should be noted that these legal provisions, because of distance and other special circumstances, were not extended with the same degree of centralization to the East Malaysian States of Sabah and Sarawak. For that matter, the strong centralized financial provisions did not cover Singapore during the period when Singapore was included within Malaysia between 1963 and 1965, as Singapore too enjoyed considerable financial autonomy.

The Constitution's financial provisions have indeed made the Malaysian Federation one of the strongest central governments from the financial point of view. If comparisons are made between Malaysia's financial arrangements with those of other federal systems such as those of the United States, Canada, and Australia, it will be noted that the Malaysian financial system is a very strongly centralized one.

The Federal Government, for instance, is vested with the power and responsibility to obtain and collect all the major revenues. Thus all major taxes such as income tax, customs duties, and licences from motor vehicles, which in most federations are also available to the states, are not available to the State Governments in Malaysia. By the same token, the Malaysian Constitution also provides for all major areas of expenditure to be borne by the Federal Government. Thus expensive subjects such as education and health, which in other federations are paid for by the states, are in Malaysia borne by the Central Government. It will be appreciated that, in theory, whilst the Federal Government has the power to raise all major taxes, it has also the power and capacity either to expand its expenditure or limit it. Thus the Federal Government's centralized position is further strengthened by its independence of action in that it is able to raise revenues or loans and increase its expenditure at any time, as fiscal and monetary policies are within the control of the Federal Government. The Federal Government therefore is in a position to be able to build up surpluses if it wants to, while it is not so with State Governments.

These points are mentioned only to indicate the potential that the Federal Government has in exerting its central authority which is liberally provided for under the Constitution. This does not mean, however, that the Federal Government has indeed been taking advantage of its strong constitutional position for extending central authority. On the contrary, as will be noticed later on in this essay, the Federal Government has in fact over the years taken initiatives to liberalize the allocation of funds to the State Governments, either directly through changes in the law and/or indirectly through undertaking greater Federal expenditure on the projects and programmes of the State Governments even on those subjects which are the responsibility of the State Governments, such as agriculture, veterinary matters, forestry, and local governments.

FEDERAL AND STATE REVENUES

Under the Constitution, all proceeds of revenues from taxation accrue to the Federal Government except those that are assigned to the States under Article 110 of the Constitution and those that are collected by the large local authorities and religious departments. The scope for revenue collection by the States is therefore limited, since the revenue items assigned to the States are not many and they are relatively insignificant. There are fourteen State revenue items as indicated in Appendix A to this essay and the total revenue from all the sources amounted to only about $797 million in 1976, as compared to $6,157 million raised by the Federal Government in the same year. Thus the State Governments' revenue earnings together amounted to only 13 per cent of the total Federal Government revenue in 1976, and this clearly shows up the relative financial strength and relationship between the Federal and State Governments.

The biggest revenue item for the State Governments is from 'lands, mines and forests'. However, not all States have ample land endowments. Neither do all States have tin and other mineral deposits or significant forest reserves. In any case, the revenue from land is generally not large since the land is basically agricultural and underdeveloped and thus unlike the higher land revenues derived from the more developed areas in the urban sectors of the economy. Revenue from entertainments brings a large income to the more developed States but the amounts are small in States where entertainments are, for religious reasons, rigidly controlled.

Similarly, revenue from licences is limited since, here again, all licence fees connected with motor vehicles, electrical installations, and registration of businesses accrue to the Federal Government. Thus the State Governments have limitations from this source as well, and derive their revenue mainly from forest licences and other small and miscellaneous licences which do not amount to much.

Revenue derived from water supplies and drainage and irrigation water rates could be an important source of income to State Governments. However, in practice, it has been found to be extremely difficult to charge higher or more economical rates for water supplies because of the sensitivity connected with this source of revenue. The same applies to irrigation and drainage water rates. It has often, therefore, been difficult to raise water rates both on political as well as on socio-economic grounds.

Local authorities such as Town Boards, Town Councils, Rural Boards, Local Councils, and similar Local Authorities, are the responsibility of the State Governments and where they are not financially viable, the State Governments will have to subsidize them. However, Local Government as an institution has been slow in its development and even where Local Authorities have been established on a more permanent basis, there have been major constraints in terms of their capacity to run these Local Authorities effectively enough to raise reasonable revenues. Consequently, their revenues have also suffered and this has brought a further burden to the State Governments.

The Constitution also provides under Article 110(2) that any of the revenue items in Appendix A could be substituted and if so then another source of revenue of about equal value would be assigned to the States. Thus States have been assured that their revenue which has been allowed under the Constitution would not be reduced. It must be pointed out also that the Constitution does provide for some latitude towards the States in that it allows the State Governments to obtain some proportion of export duties on minerals. It is interesting that Article 110(3A) defines minerals as mineral ores, metal, and mineral oils especially now that Malaysia has become an oil producer at this time of energy problems.

In 1962, the Assignment of Revenue (Export Duty on Iron Ore) Act was introduced to enable State Governments to receive up to a maximum of 10 per cent of the *ad valorem* on the value of exported iron ore. Similarly, an Act entitled Assignment of Export Duty (Mineral Ores), provided State Governments with a portion of export duty collected by the Federal Government in respect of mineral ores other than tin and iron ore. The Act provided for one half of the export duty on bauxite, wolframite, sheelite, columbite-tantalite, copper, ilmenite, zincon, monazite, and manganese, to be assigned to the respective States in Peninsular Malaysia on and after 1 September 1964. These Acts have helped to a certain extent to provide some additional revenue to the States.

Tin-producing States have always benefited from Article 110(3) of the Constitution which allows the States 10 per cent or more, as may be provided, of export duty on tin produced in these States. This source of revenue is not of course available to the non-tin-producing States.

Some States in Peninsular Malaysia, therefore, have gained much more than others in terms of revenue from their mineral sources as a result of these provisions in the Federal Constitution. The States producing iron ore and other mineral ores, as outlined above, stood to gain in 1962 and 1964 due to this new legislation but unfortunately this source of revenue brought only a temporary increase in revenue as production of the minerals declined drastically. Rice-producing States, such as Kedah, have consistently raised the argument that they should also be accorded preference in that although their produce is not exported, they have managed to conserve foreign exchange for the country. Other States like Perak have claimed that the 10 per cent share for export duties on tin is not adequate, considering that Perak is a major producer of tin and tin is a depleting asset.

The discovery of petroleum has provided a strong boost to the revenues of some States but this revenue at present is only available to those States where petroleum is produced as will be elaborated upon later.

EXPENDITURE

As mentioned earlier, the financial commitments of the Federal Government are indeed very large as they relate to subjects coming under the Ninth Schedule to the Constitution, which defines the Federal List of responsibilities. Thus, External Affairs, Defence, Internal Security, Education, Health, and Federal Works and Power, are some of the major areas that are included in the Federal Government's responsibilities for expenditure. All operating and development costs incurred in the provision of these services as well as the expansion of related infrastructural facilities are borne by the Federal Government.

The Federal Government's Operating Expenditure constitutes about 82 per cent of total Federal and State Governments' expenditures together. It will be noted that the State Government's expenditures are minimal compared to the Federal Government's expenditures that are undertaken on Federal projects and programmes which are spread out all over the country and sited in all States.

This significant Federal responsibility for expenditure is understandable as, after all, the Constitution does provide for the bulk of the revenues to accrue to the Federal Government. Nevertheless, because the Federal Government has to incur expenditure in providing and maintaining the Government's infrastructural facilities and services, it does run into budgetary strains from time to time. However, the Constitution provides for the Federal Government to raise new sources of revenue, a power which is not available to State Governments except with the approval of the Federal Government.

Thus, the Federal Government is better disposed towards minimizing the problem of budgetary deficits.

There has been a growing recognition, however, that the State Governments would need to have more funds at their disposal to be able to undertake their own projects and programmes. For this reason, the Federal Government has from time to time provided additional financial sources by way of grants or additional allocations of development funds to the State Governments.

In recent years, therefore, there has been substantial revision in the rates of 'Grants to States' as provided for under Article 109 of the Constitution. The Capitation Grant for instance is payable to each State on an annual basis in accordance with Part I of·the Tenth Schedule as follows:

(a) For the first 50,000 persons at the rate of $15 per person;

(b) For the next 200,000 persons at the rate of $10 per person;

(c) For the remainder at the rate of $4 per person.

However, after consultation with the National Finance Council, these rates were revised with effect from 1 January 1976 on the basis of the last population taken in 1970, with the following new rates:

(a) For the first 100,000 persons at the rate of $20 per person;

(b) For the next 150,000 persons at the rate of $10 per person;

(c) For the next 250,000 persons at the rate of $6 per person;

(d) For the remainder at the rate of $3 per person.

These new rates increased the allocation of the Capitation Grant to the States from $61.2 million to $72 million per year until a new census is undertaken.

Similarly, the State Road Grants were also revised in 1977 after the National Finance Council adopted a Treasury report which recommended the upward revision of the previous rate of $4,600 per mile of State roads per annum. On the advice of the National Finance Council, the Federal Government therefore agreed to increase the rate to $6,200 per mile with retrospective effect from 1974.

Another new feature in the evolution of the financial provisions of the Constitution in recent years was the introduction of 'Revenue Growth Grant' for the State Governments in 1976. This grant is based on the premise that the State Governments should also benefit from the growth of Federal Government revenue. This grant is payable to the States if the Federal Revenue increases by more than 10 per cent in a particular year over the previous year. The amount payable to the States would thus be any sum exceeding 10 per cent of the increase, but subject to a maximum of $50 million per annum and is distributed to State Governments on the following basis:

(a) In the first instance, 50 per cent of the amount available would be distributed equally amongst all the thirteen States.

(b) The remaining 50 per cent of the amount would be divided on the basis of two shares per head for the first 500,000 of a State's population, one share per head for the next 500,000, and a half share per head for the remainder.

It will be noted that the formula has an intrinsic element of preference for distribution of more funds to the smaller States with populations of less than 500,000. Thus the small States such as Perlis, Malacca and Negri Sembilan stand to gain by the new method of distribution of the grant. The new grant was formulated on the premise that States should be able to share the economic prosperity enjoyed by the Federal Government as such prosperity has been achieved through the joint efforts of both the Federal and State Governments.

In order to encourage the State Governments to give greater priority to the basic socio-economic requirements and a higher rate of economic expansion, State Governments are required to utilize these Revenue Growth Grants only for the following specific purposes:

(a) water supply;

(b) public housing;

(c) industrial estate development; and

(d) such other development projects as are approved by the National Finance Council from time to time.

THE FINANCIAL DIFFICULTIES OF THE STATE GOVERNMENTS

Over the years the State Government budgets have been experiencing increasing financial strain. Most State Governments have had budgetary deficits on their current accounts at one time or another, but some States have become inclined to being consistently in deficit year after year. Appendix B to this essay on the State Governments' Consolidated Finance indicates that all the State Government budgets taken together have almost consistently been in current account deficit on the basis of their own sources of revenue and expenditure, before including the Federal Government grants to the States. Since 1975 the gap between the total revenues of the State Governments and their total current expenditures has widened considerably. It is likely that this strain will continue unless further additional grants are made to the States.

There are numerous reasons for this financial strain. However, the major causes are as follows:

(a) State Government revenues are not as elastic as the Federal Government revenues. This is because the rates of State Government taxes, such as land and forest levies, can only be varied after a long lapse of time. Furthermore, State taxes are not the kind that is related to economic growth such as income tax and export and import duties, which are under Federal authority.

(b) The State Governments' Operating Expenditure is to a certain extent dictated by Federal policies, particularly in regard to the revision of salaries in the public sector as it has been the policy to standardize salaries throughout the country. Indeed, some State Governments with very small budgets, such as Perlis and Trengganu, find it exceedingly difficult to finance even the small revisions in salary adopted by the Federal Government and which are extended to State Government employees as well.

(c) Although there have been substantial amounts of State Government development expenditures over the years, which originate from State initiatives or even Federal Government financing, the benefits of these development expenditure or investments have mainly accrued to the Federal Government in the form of income tax and export duties related to the output of these investment projects. Thus the State Government budgets have not been able to derive the revenue benefits from these investments; and as a result State Government revenues have not been able to grow to any significant extent.

(d) Although the costs of goods and services have increased due to inflation, particularly in the last few years, and have raised the budget expenditures of the State Governments, similar increases in revenue due to inflation, such as obtained through the Federal income tax, customs duties, and the sales tax for instance, have not benefited the State Governments.

(e) Although the Federal Government provides the bulk of the financing for development expenditure undertaken by the States, the maintenance of these projects has to be provided by the State Governments. Thus, the State Governments have indirectly to bear additional strain on their operating expenditures, since the staff employed by State Governments for the provision of services and maintenance associated with these development projects, have to be paid by the State Governments.

(f) Finally, the tax collection machinery in the State Governments is not as well developed as the better staffed Federal Government's tax system, so that the growth of State Government revenues has also suffered as a result.

THE IMPLICATION OF
THESE FINANCIAL DIFFICULTIES
FOR THE STATE GOVERNMENTS

Because of the very tight financial position of most State Governments, resulting largely from the present constitutional arrangements in regard to the distribution of financial responsibilities for taxes and expenditure, most State Governments have to be assisted through the State Reserve Fund. Article 109(6) provides for the Federal Government to make grants out of the Reserve Fund to any State for the purpose of development or generally to supplement a State's revenues. Some State Governments, therefore, are inclined to expect the Federal Government to provide supplementary funds to balance any budgetary deficits that may occur on their budget's current account, without being able to do enough to prevent these budgetary deficits in the first place.

Because it is even difficult to balance the current accounts of the State Budgets, most State Governments are unable to provide savings from their operating budgets to finance development projects and programmes. Thus, some State Governments are reluctant to spend money on development and have tended to leave the responsibility for the provision of infrastructural facilities and development programmes to the Federal Government. This has led to the Federal Government increasing its reimbursable grants for development over the years. By this method, the State Governments would undertake development projects and the cost will be reimbursed by the Federal Government. In addition, the Federal Government has been increasing the allocations for directly financed Federal development projects and programmes that are sited in the States.

In 1957, for instance, the Federal Government on its own spent $168 million on development projects and programmes in the States. However, this has increased by 960 per cent to $1,780 million in 1976. Similarly, development projects undertaken by State Governments, for which State Governments were reimbursed by the Federal Government, increased by 340 per cent from $38 million in 1963 to $168 million in 1977. The Federal Government, therefore, has been taking on far greater responsibility and initiatives in the economic development of the States.

In recent years, the implementation of the concept of regional development and the creation of centres of growth has further reduced the responsibility of State Governments in the development field to an even greater extent. The State Governments have also reluctantly accepted the growing influence and responsibility of the Federal Government in initiating and implementing vast development schemes such as that undertaken by the Muda Agricultural Development Authority which manages the rice bowl of the country in Kedah, and the several gigantic land development schemes which have been carved out of virgin jungles, such as the Pahang Tenggara and the Johore Tenggara and the Kemubu Scheme in Kelantan. These projects are financed by the Federal Government from its own resources or from foreign loans such as those from the World Bank and the Asian Development Bank and are thus independent of State control.

THE CREATION OF NEW INSTRUMENTS FOR SOCIO-ECONOMIC DEVELOPMENT

The limited financial resources of the State Governments and their inadequate capacity to implement large socio-economic development projects, have led to greater Federal Government involvement in the development process on behalf of the States. However, the Federal Government itself has become increasingly constrained by its own limitations, not so much in terms of finance, but particularly in terms of the lack of effective implementation capacity and its inadequacy in fulfilling a commercial role to promote a greater involvement and participation of the *Bumiputra* community in the private sector. In the last five years particularly, several statutory bodies have been established to cater for the economic development and involvement of the *Bumiputra* community in the business sector. Some of these new Authorities are the National Trading Company known as Pernas, the Urban Development Authority, the regional development corporations, and the State economic development corporations in respect of the States. These Authorities have been established under separate enactments and are provided with initial launching grants which they operate with considerable autonomy. These statutory authorities, which now number about 55 with about 220 subsidiaries, have been provided with some $2,250 million in the last five years and should therefore be able to play a significant role in economic development that cuts across all State boundaries.

SPECIAL FINANCIAL ARRANGEMENTS: SABAH AND SARAWAK

The East Malaysian States of Sabah and Sarawak have enjoyed a special relationship with the Central Government which is based on the understanding reached at the time these States joined the Federation of Malaysia in 1963. Because of the special circumstances, Sabah and Sarawak obtained under Article 112C additional sources of revenue over and above those which are enjoyed by the States of Peninsular Malaysia. Thus, at the time of joining Malaysia, Sabah and Sarawak were allowed 'Special Grants to the Borneo States' as provided for in Part IV of the Tenth Schedule.

Sarawak was provided with a grant of $5.8 million a year beginning from 1964 and further allocations known as 'Annual Escalating Grants' of $3½ million, $7 million, $11½ million, $16 million, $21 million for each year from 1964 to 1968.

Similarly, in the case of Sabah, a financial formula in the Tenth Schedule provided the State Government with a 'Growth Revenue Grant' which amounted to $67 million from 1964 to 1968.

In accordance with Article 112D, these Special Grants to Sabah and Sarawak were reviewed by the Federal Government and the State Governments concerned in 1968. According to the agreement reached, Sarawak ceased to receive the annual grant of $5.8 million a year with effect from 1 January 1969 but continues to receive the Annual Escalating Grant as follows:

1969	1970	1971	1972	1973
$12.0 mil.	$12.9 mil.	$13.9 mil.	$14.9 mil.	$16.0 mil.

Similarly, according to the agreement reached, Sabah also ceased to receive the 'Growth Revenue Grant' with effect from 1 January 1969 but receives instead another grant as follows:

1969	1970	1971	1972	1973
$20.0 mil.	$21.5 mil.	$23.1 mil.	$24.8 mil.	$26.7 mil.

The financial arrangements should have been further reviewed in 1973 but up to date no such review has been completed.

Furthermore, Part V of the Tenth Schedule also provides 'Additional Sources of Revenue assigned to the Borneo States' of Sabah and Sarawak, *inter alia* as follows:

(a) Import duty and excise duty on petroleum products;

(b) Export duty on timber and other forest products; as well as other financial revenue concessions.

At the same time, Sabah and Sarawak derive the benefits of the Federal Government's development programmes as well as the Federal Government's responsibility for expenditure on defence, security, external relations, education and health and other responsibilities as outlined in the Constitution.

These special concessions for Sabah and Sarawak have sometimes led to claims for more favourable treatment by the State Governments in Peninsular Malaysia. When Sabah and Sarawak joined the

Federation of Malaysia in 1963, both these States were relatively much poorer. Their budgets were small and subject to strain. However, with the additional grants provided by the Central Government to Sabah and Sarawak under the terms of joining Malaysia, Sabah and Sarawak gained substantially. Their budgetary positions on the current account therefore began to gain steady and significant surpluses, as indicated in Appendix C to this essay. It is also noteworthy that these surpluses were accumulated despite the more ambitious expansion programmes that were undertaken by the State Governments.

Federal grants to Sabah increased from $21 million in 1964 to $40 million in 1977, and in the case of Sarawak, these Federal grants increased from $18 million in 1964 to $29 million in 1977. From 1964 to 1977, the Federal Government transferred $585 million to Sabah and $350 million to Sarawak, excluding of course the almost similar amounts provided as development allocations for infrastructure projects in these two States.

Because of these significant transfers of resources from the Federal Government to Sabah and Sarawak, especially for development, the State Governments have been able to generate larger revenues from their own resources. Thus it will be noted from Appendix C Sabah's revenue of $46 million in 1964 has increased by elevenfold to $533 million in 1977. Similarly, Sarawak's revenue from its own resources increased from $35 million to $148 million in 1977.

Sabah and Sarawak therefore are no longer the poor States that they used to be in 1963 when they joined Malaysia. Indeed, given their small populations and vast land, agricultural, timber, and particularly petroleum resources, Sabah and Sarawak have bright prospects for economic growth and financial strength in the years to come.

THE NATIONAL FINANCE COUNCIL

The National Finance Council is established under Article 108 of the Constitution and presently comprises the Prime Minister, such other Ministers as he may designate, and one representative from each of the State Governments, appointed by the Ruler or Governor. The representatives from the State Governments are usually the Mentris Besar or Chief Ministers, and recently the Deputy Prime Minister has acted as Chairman of this Council, with of course the Minister of Finance always present at these financial meetings.

In practice, much of the work of the National Finance Council is concerned with the financial relationships and problems between the State Governments and the Central Government. The State

Governments, either individually or collectively, invariably ask for more financial assistance to be diverted to them. Whereas, in the past, these requests were noted and some adjustments made from time to time, it is, however, evident that in the last few years, the National Finance Council has become more effective in persuading the Federal Government to provide more funds to the States. On the other hand, it is also clear that the Federal Government is giving more attention to the need to transfer more funds and responsibilities to the State Governments. Thus the revision in the Capitation Grants, Road Grants, and the innovation introduced recently in the form of the Revenue Growth Grants, are indications of the more productive and mutually beneficial financial relationships that are emerging between the Federal Government and the State Governments.

THE STATE GOVERNMENTS' BORROWING CAPACITY

One of the major constitutional developments in the relationship between the Central Government and State Governments has been the amendment of Article 111, which now allows the State Governments in Peninsular Malaysia more freedom to borrow. Whereas, under the previous provisions, a State Government could only borrow from the Central Government or from an approved bank for a period not exceeding twelve months, the amended law now allows the State Governments to borrow from the Central Government or from a bank or other financial source, approved for that purpose by the Federal Government, for a period not exceeding five years. Although the amended law would require a State Government to obtain the approval of the Federal Government before a State Government provides a guarantee for such a loan, it is nevertheless a major departure from the previous financial practice, since the State Governments now can borrow up to five years and from any source and particularly from foreign financial centres.

This new amendment, while beneficial to the States, had to be carefully administered in practice, particularly because the State Governments will take some time before they develop their own expertise and capacities to undertake negotiations with the larger and more sophisticated foreign banks. Already there has been some evidence of problems and difficulties that have been encountered by State Governments in dealing with potential lenders. The Central Government, therefore, as final guarantor to these loans, is anxious to ensure that the most favourable financial terms continue to be obtained by the State Governments for the longer term loans that they would want to raise under the new financial provisions. Furthermore, it is essential for the Federal Government to ensure that the State Governments do not borrow more than what they can afford as this would affect their own viability and the credit standing of the Federation. Sabah and Sarawak have their own authority to borrow within the respective States, subject to approval of the Central Bank, and the new amended law will now also apply to them.

PETROLEUM REVENUE FOR THE FEDERAL AND STATE GOVERNMENTS

With the discovery of petroleum off the coasts of Sabah and Sarawak in the early 1970s, the economic and revenue prospects for Malaysia as a whole, and especially the State Governments concerned, have become much more promising. Although Malaysia is a small oil producer with about 200,000 barrels of petroleum per day to its credit, she is nevertheless a net exporter of petroleum. For this reason, the Malaysian economy was not as adversely affected as many other countries by the major increase in oil prices in 1973 and even by the current energy crisis.

Originally, Malaysia had oil agreements that were based on the concept of the Concession System but this was superseded in April 1975 by new agreements that were based on the concept of Production Sharing. Under the old Concession System, the State Governments received a royalty of 12½ per cent of the value of the petroleum produced off the shores of that particular State. Thus, the State Government of Sarawak received about $44 million in 1974 representing the oil royalty that was due from 1971 to 1974.

However, with the incorporation of Petronas, which is the National Petroleum Company and the introduction of the Petroleum Development Act in 1974, all the petroleum agreements made under the Concession System were terminated with effect from 1 April 1975. The new production sharing arrangements provide for the oil companies and Petronas to exploit the petroleum resources of the country on the basis of the following basic formula:

Cash Payment — 10 per cent of production
Cost Oil — Maximum of 20 per cent of production
Profit Oil — 70 per cent or more (depending on cost oil) shared in the ratio of 70 : 30 in favour of Petronas.

For example, if the production of oil for the year is 100,000 barrels, the proceeds from the sale of 5 per cent of production or 5,000 barrels will go to the State concerned, and 5 per cent or 5,000 barrels will go to the Federal Government. 20,000 barrels (or less, depending on the actual cost) will go to the contractor or oil company to meet the cost of production. The balance of 70,000 barrels (or more, depending on the cost of production) will be shared in the proportion of 70 to Petronas and 30 to the oil company, i.e. 49,000 barrels to Petronas and 21,000 barrels to the oil company.

Under the agreements therefore, Petronas pays the Federal Government 5 per cent of the gross sales proceeds as Cash Payment, in return for the petroleum resources vested with Petronas. Similarly, the State Government opposite whose shore the petroleum is produced, is also entitled to 5 per cent of the gross sales proceeds as its Cash Payment.

The Federal Government, in addition, derives petroleum income tax from the private oil companies and Petronas at the rate of 45 per cent on the basis of their relative portions of their incomes earned from petroleum operations as related to the above production-sharing formula.

Since the operation of this agreement, the Federal Government has received about $397 million in 1975 and $312 million in 1976, while the State Governments of Sabah and Sarawak have earned $78 million in 1975 and $77 million in 1976.

With the discovery of oil in the East Coast States of Trengganu and Pahang of Peninsular Malaysia, these relatively poorer States will also stand to benefit considerably, not only in revenue terms but in their overall socio-economic development as well, when the oil starts flowing in the near future.

FINANCIAL ARRANGEMENTS WITH SELANGOR FOR THE FEDERAL TERRITORY OF KUALA LUMPUR

With the decision to establish the City of Kuala Lumpur as Federal Territory, certain new financial arrangements have been made by way of settlement for the transfer of sovereignty of the Territory of Kuala Lumpur from the State Government of Selangor to the Federal Government.

The Federal Territory of Kuala Lumpur was established on 1 February 1974 under the Constitution (Amendment) (No. 2) Act, 1973. The broad criteria for the financial settlement were agreed upon by a Financial Committee that was set up under Article IV of the Kuala Lumpur Agreement, relating to the establishment of the Federal Territory. These financial arrangements can be classified into the following broad categories and the basis for this understanding is given below:

(a) *Capital Payment.* This payment is in respect of the cost of land

and buildings belonging to the State of Selangor within the Federal Territory to be surrendered to the Federal Government. The final settlement of the compensation payable to the State is still in the process of settlement. In the meantime, the Selangor Government has been given an advance amounting to $325 million to date.

(b) *Payment for loss of revenue.* Prior to the establishment of the Federal Territory, the State of Selangor had collected certain types of state revenue within the Territory. These revenues have now ceased to be state revenues on the establishment of the Federal Territory. Therefore it has been agreed that the State of Selangor should be given an annual grant to compensate for this loss of revenue. The amount of this grant which has been agreed to by both parties is $18.3 million annually.

(c) *Sharing of prosperity.* In view of the fact that the State of Selangor is now being deprived of any potential increase in revenue from the Federal Territory in the form of normal revenue increase and capital appreciation, such additional revenue should be shared with the State of Selangor. This arrangement is still being worked out by the Financial Committee.

The State Government also continues to enjoy the Capitation Grant, the Road Grant, and the other grants and privileges that it had enjoyed in the past, although its responsibilities for the management and further development of Kuala Lumpur have now been fully transferred to the Federal Government. So far $325 million has been allocated to the State Government of Selangor and negotiations are still under way to finalize the details of the understanding reached in regard to the full compensation that will finally be paid to the Selangor State Government.

The State Government in the meantime has established its own State Capital at Shah Alam, which is about ten miles outside the Federal Territory of Kuala Lumpur. The State Administration has, however, not yet moved to the new capital and it is still operating from Kuala Lumpur. Although the Selangor Government stands to gain substantially in financial terms due to the transfer of Kuala Lumpur to the Federal Government, which it could use with advantage to develop the other parts of Selangor, there is nevertheless the usual emotional undertone that still pervades which could cause some delay in reaching final details of the financial arrangements for the settlement of this issue.

PARLIAMENTARY FINANCIAL CONTROL AND ACCOUNTABILITY

Many of the Articles governing the financial provisions in the Constitution are related to parliamentary and financial procedural matters. These are basically safeguards to ensure proper financial control and public accountability.

For instance, under Article 97, all revenues raised or received by the Federal Government should be paid into one fund known as the Federal Consolidated Fund. Similarly, Article 99 requires that a statement of the estimated receipts and expenditures of the Federation should be laid before the House of Representatives in the form of an annual statement. Similarly, there are provisions which specify the authority to allocate funds and to request supplementary funds from Parliament.

All these constitutional requirements in financial management could give rise to considerable public debate both within the Houses of Parliament and without, in regard to the quality of Malaysia's budgetary and financial and economic management as well. Indeed, the annual budget in many countries with a parliamentary system of government is subject to severe and critical debate. However, Malaysia's experience is that in practice the budgetary documents are subject to limited and rather casual scrutiny in Parliament. The Budget estimates attract even less critical attention through the mass media or public debate. This is because there has in general been very favourable reception to the Budget and the annual estimates of expenditure and revenue, and consequently there has been very little controversy and limited public interest regarding the levels and directions of public spending. Thus, there has been some complacency within Parliament and amongst the general public in regard to the Government's annual budget expenditure.

This attitude has developed largely because the Government in power at the Federal level has consistently enjoyed an overwhelmingly strong majority in Parliament. The opposition parties have not been able to exert much critical pressure on Government's budgetary policies and practices because of their limited numbers. Mainly for this reason there is a tendency in Parliament for opposition members to take it for granted that the proposed budgetary allocations would be approved in any case, and that it would not be very productive to be too vocal. The same situation is prevalent in the State legislatures as well.

Civil servants also generally have a relatively easier time than their counterparts in other countries, particularly since the presentation of the Government's budget and the parliamentary debates at committee stage on the budgets of individual ministries do not give rise to too much controversy. Whereas the budget debates in other countries have often been the focal point for the discussion of economic policy, over which governments have fought and lost, or risen and fallen, it has been different in Malaysia. This is due to the strong Central Government and the continued political stability, which has also been buttressed by the continuation of basically the same political parties in power. The Malaysian budget has therefore never really provided the anxious moments and strains that have often been experienced by other Governments elsewhere.

The constitutional financial provisions have also consequently been less complicated in their operations not only at the Federal level, but at the level of the relationships between the Central Government and the State Governments, largely because of the fact that during the twenty years of independence, the same political parties have formed the Government at the centre as well as in all the State Governments. When this has not been the case, there can be much more misunderstanding and friction between the State and the Central Government in their financial relationships, as on an occasion when, for a short period, one of the opposition parties at the Federal level formed the Government in one of the thirteen States.

THE AUDITOR-GENERAL

The Constitution provides for the appointment of an Auditor-General by the Yang di-Pertuan Agong on the advice of the Prime Minister under Article 105 of the Constitution, and the Auditor-General is empowered to audit and report on the accounts of the Federal Government. Although the Auditor-General's reports are required by the Constitution to be tabled at the House of Representatives every year, the audit reports are usually submitted after a lapse of more than one year. This is unfortunate since Parliament is, in many cases, faced with a *fait accompli* that may be difficult to rectify in time or even avoid in the following year because of this lapse of time.

However, the problem of timely parliamentary control and public accountability is aggravated further when these annual reports by the Auditor-General are presented to the Public Accounts Committee (PAC) which, in turn, takes some time to report to Parliament. The PAC has to study these reports, call for evidence and then make its recommendations. The Public Accounts Committee Report is then tabled in Parliament, but by the time this is done, there has usually been a lapse of some two to three years between the year reported upon and the submission of the PAC Report to Parliament. Often the issues involved have been overtaken by events or the officials concerned have sometimes been transferred to other duties or may even have left the service. Thus, it becomes difficult for the Public Accounts Committee to play its proper role in making recommendations to improve Parliamentary supervision and public accountability of public funds.

The role of the Auditor-General is becoming more and more important in view of the increasing size of the budget from year to year and the decision of Government to venture into the commercial and industrial sectors in order to achieve the objectives of the New Economic Policy. Hundreds of millions of dollars of public funds have been made available to the statutory corporations in order to achieve these objectives, but whether these funds are properly and economically utilized is a matter of concern to every one and it is, therefore, the duty of the Auditor-General to report on such matters with greater dispatch.

It would, therefore, be useful if the Auditor-General's Reports, which could indeed contribute much towards better financial management and accountability, could be modified to relate to current and *ex ante* auditing, rather than *ex post* auditing. Alternatively, it would also be useful for the Auditor-General's Reports to be undertaken on a current as well as a continuing basis, so that his reports could be presented to Parliament after a much shorter lapse of time, after the completion of a financial year. Similarly, timely and more relevant annual reports from the Auditor-General would also lead to even more effective advice from the Public Accounts Committee, which could also contribute further to the general level of efficiency in financial management.

CONCLUSION

In reviewing the evolution of the financial provisions of the Malaysian Constitution and their operations in practice, it is clear that the original constitutional provisions have served Malaysia well except that the finances of some of the States have not performed as well as might be expected. The management of the Malaysian Budget which covers revenue, the operating expenditures, and the development expenditure have generally been of a high standard. This has enabled the Budget to play a dynamic role in the promotion of economic growth and the attainment of financial stability within the legal framework of these constitutional financial provisions. Furthermore, although the structure of the economy and the socio-economic philosophy has undergone progressive changes, the constitutional financial provisions have been able to cope with these major socio-economic developments with only minimal constitutional changes and amendments.

The Federal Government continues to maintain a strong central position in the Federal/State relationships, while at the same time the State Governments have progressively been given more financial resources and responsibility to improve the harmony in these Federal/State financial relations. At the same time, the establishment of a large number of public authorities, including State economic development corporations, has enabled greater decentralization in the financial authority, control, and administration of public funds.

Public accountability for the significant amount of taxes that has been raised, and the sizeable expenditures incurred, continue to be focused in the parliamentary system. Public interest in the accountability of public funds and the use of these funds for the achievement of Government's policy objectives, however, could be further enhanced through a more sustained cultivation and promotion of a greater interest and awareness in economic and financial management. The financial provisions of the Constitution will no doubt continue to be appraised and amended as and when necessary, to serve the interests of the developing and dynamic economy that Malaysia now possesses. Public involvement, therefore, particularly through Parliament, in the management of the Budget could be further enhanced so as to achieve a more progressive and modern economy. Parliament, for instance, could be more directly and closely involved not only in the approval of public funds as is the case now, but in the formulation of public finance policy especially in the earlier stages, before Supply Bills are tabled in Parliament for its endorsement.

Malaysia has a fine constitutional framework and is blessed with rich potential which could further accelerate the pace of progress and modernization in the financial as well as in the broad socio-economic fields of endeavour. It is, therefore, necessary to ensure that Malaysia continues to maintain high standards of management of her many endowments, within the well-tested constitutional framework of financial provisions that have been discussed in this essay.

APPENDIX A
Part III of the Tenth Schedule of
the Malaysian Constitution

SOURCES OF REVENUE ASSIGNED TO STATES

1. Revenue from toddy shops.
2. Revenue from lands, mines and forests.
3. Revenue from licences other than those connected with mechanically propelled vehicles, electrical installations, and registration of businesses.
4. Entertainments duty.
5. Fees in courts other than federal courts.
6. Fees and receipts in respect of specific services by departments of State Government.
7. Revenue of town boards, town councils, rural boards, local councils, and similar local authorities other than—
   (a) municipalities established under any Municipal Ordinance;
   (b) those town boards, town councils, rural boards, local councils, and similar local authorities which have power under written law to retain their revenues and control the spending thereof.
8. Receipts in respect of water supplies, including water rates.
9. Rents on State property.
10. Interest on State balances.
11. Receipts from land sales and sales of State property.
12. Fines and forfeitures in courts other than federal courts.
13. *Zakat*, *Fitrah*, *Bait-ul-Mal* and similar Muslim revenue.
14. Treasure trove.

APPENDIX B

Estimated Revenue and Expenditure of State Governments—1976 ($ Million)

State	REVENUE				EXPENDITURE					
	Own Sources	Federal Government Grants	Total Revenue	Operating Expenditure	Development				Total Development	Total Expenditure
					State Sources	Reimbursement	Water Supply	Loans		
1. Johore	66.27	18.64	84.91	87.47	24.54	16.17	34.75	—	75.66	162.93
2. Kedah	26.47	17.27	43.74	63.44	7.75	7.48	11.04	30.86	57.13	120.57
3. Kelantan	20.64	9.23	29.87	36.51	19.06	10.91	3.64	28.38	61.99	98.50
4. Melaka	10.53	6.06	16.59	22.33	5.72	2.09	4.54	23.63	35.98	58.31
5. Negri Sembilan	32.41	7.27	39.68	36.00	7.53	2.90	14.13	30.71	55.27	91.27
6. Pahang	66.59	10.28	76.87	76.87	15.39	2.32	16.12	11.13	44.96	121.83
7. Pulau Pinang	23.37	11.86	35.23	36.03	24.52	—	—	56.08	80.60	116.63
8. Perak	85.03	37.35	122.38	122.14	39.86	12.67	35.99	—	88.52	210.66
9. Perlis	2.91	2.48	5.39	7.12	0.55	0.73	3.06	5.45	9.79	16.91
10. Selangor	97.46	251.63	349.09	197.67	104.13	7.11	—	7.92	119.16	316.83
11. Trengganu	18.40	8.44	26.84	38.79	11.12	7.32	—	52.23	70.67	109.46
12. Sabah	213.22	46.78	260.00	256.66	97.99	53.86	7.65	77.40	236.90	493.56
13. Sarawak	133.65	28.51	162.16	177.74	72.76	54.53	—	49.00	176.29	354.03
TOTAL	796.95	455.80	1252.75	1158.77	430.92	178.09	130.92	372.79	1112.72	2271.49

Source: Ministry of Finance.

Note: 1. This table indicates that the State Governments would find it difficult to finance their Operating Expenditure from their 'Own Sources' and even more difficult to finance Development Expenditures. 2. Some States have lesser financial problems.

Revenue and Expenditure of Sabah and Sarawak:1964-1977 ($ million)

Year	State	REVENUE			Operating Expenditure	Current Account Balance	DEVELOPMENT EXPENDITURE					Total Expenditure
		Own Sources	Federal Government Grants	Total Revenue			State Sources	Reimbursement	Water Supply	Loans	Total Development	
1964	Sabah	46	21	67	81	— 14	35	—	2	—	37	118
	Sarawak	35	18	53	70	— 17	14	10	—	—	24	94
1965	Sabah	49	26	75	63	+ 12	42	—	—	—	42	105
	Sarawak	37	23	60	52	+ 8	6	19	—	—	25	77
1966	Sabah	61	30	91	65	+ 26	13	20	—	—	33	98
	Sarawak	44	27	71	53	+ 18	1	24	—	—	25	78
1967	Sabah	97	40	137	83	+ 54	15	16	—	—	31	114
	Sarawak	48	32	80	70	+ 10	2	23	—	—	25	95
1968	Sabah	112	47	159	116	+ 43	30	30	—	—	60	176
	Sarawak	60	36	96	63	+ 33	2	27	—	—	29	92
1969	Sabah	114	66	180	170	+ 10	54	38	—	—	92	262
	Sarawak	56	20	76	59	+ 17	5	20	—	—	25	84
1970	Sabah	128	48	176	174	+ 2	56	38	—	—	94	268
	Sarawak	60	23	83	65	+ 18	13	20	—	—	33	98
1971	Sabah	147	36	183	180	+ 3	45	51	—	—	96	276
	Sarawak	67	23	90	102	— 12	29	19	—	—	48	150
1972	Sabah	131	38	169	124	+ 45	50	68	—	—	118	242
	Sarawak	63	25	88	129	— 41	44	24	—	—	68	197
1973	Sabah	249	51	300	205	+ 95	34	59	—	—	93	298
	Sarawak	69	25	94	119	— 25	42	30	—	—	72	191
1974	Sabah	331	49	380	342	+ 38	46	79	—	—	125	467
	Sarawak	79	11	90	148	— 58	56	43	—	—	99	247
1975	Sabah	220	46	266	271	— 5	100	52	5	42	199	470
	Sarawak	143	30	173	259	— 86	114	39	—	34	187	446
1976 (Estimated Actual)	Sabah	213	47	260	257	+ 3	98	54	8	77	237	494
	Sarawak	134	28	162	178	— 16	73	54	—	49	176	354
1977 (Revised Estimate)	Sabah	533	40	573	412	+ 161	180	12	9	15	216	628
	Sarawak	148	29	177	183	— 6	61	55	—	27	143	326
TOTAL	Sabah	2431	585	3016	2543	+ 473	798	517	24	134	1473	4016
	Sarawak	1043	350	1393	1550	— 157	462	407	—	110	979	2529

➤ S. JAYAKUMAR

14. Emergency Powers in Malaysia

I. INTRODUCTION[1]

EVER since its promulgation on 31 August 1957 the Federal Constitution has contained a Part XI, consisting of three Articles, entitled 'Special Powers Against Subversion and Emergency Powers'. The three Articles are: Article 149 ('Legislation against Subversion') conferring special powers on Parliament to deal with subversion, including a limited power to legislate contrary to provisions of the Constitution; Article 150 ('Proclamation of Emergency') which confers wide ranging special powers to the legislature and executive, upon the issuance of a Proclamation of Emergency, including far wider powers to act inconsistently with the Constitution; and, Article 151 ('Restrictions on Preventive Detention') which sets out certain requirements to be observed in respect of preventive detention.

There is no doubt that the inclusion of these three provisions was influenced by the Report of the Reid Constitutional Commission[2] and, as they originally stood, the three provisions bore a marked similarity to Articles 137, 138 and 139 proposed by the Commission. The Reid Commission, in turn, seems to have been influenced by the emergency which was then existing for it stated that 'We must take note of the existing emergency. We hope that it may have come to an end before the new Constitution comes into force but we must make our recommendations on the footing that it is then still in existence'.[3] The full text of these three Articles, as they presently stand, is set out in the Appendix to this essay. The Appendix also shows the provisions as they originally stood before amendments and also shows the provisions recommended by the Reid Commission.

Since, in many cases, courts were invited to interpret these Articles to limit the powers, it is worthy of note that the Reid Commission was anxious that 'the occasions on which, and so far as possible the extent to which, such powers can be used should be limited and defined'.[4]

The law contained in these three Articles can be said to have evolved and developed in three ways. First, by constitutional amendments; several amendments have significantly altered the scope of the original provisions. Secondly, an impressive body of case-law has emerged (especially on Articles 150 and 151) and these cases have settled many issues of interpretation. The third method of development is the body of legislation and subsidiary legislation enacted pursuant to these Articles representing Government's interpretation of the provisions.

In this essay, the writer will seek to summarize the development of these emergency powers provisions only by the first two ways (by constitutional amendment and by judicial interpretation) and, due to limitations of space, will not attempt to summarize the trends in legislation or subsidiary legislation.

II. THE POWERS UNDER ARTICLE 149
(LEGISLATION AGAINST SUBVERSION)

A. SCOPE OF THE PROVISION

Article 149 (the text of which is set out in the Appendix) provides for limited special powers if an Act of Parliament recites that action has been taken or threatened by any substantial body of persons (whether inside or outside the country):

(a) to cause, or to cause a substantial number of citizens to fear, organized violence against persons or property; or

(b) to excite disaffection against the Yang di-Pertuan Agong or any Government in the Federation; or

(c) to promote feelings of ill-will and hostility between different races or other classes of the population likely to cause violence; or

(d) to procure the alteration, otherwise than by lawful means, of anything by law established; or

(e) which is prejudicial to the security of the Federation or any part thereof.

The speciality of the power is that any provision of that law 'designed to stop or prevent that action' would be valid even if it is inconsistent with Article 5 (liberty of the person), Article 9 (prohibition of banishment and freedom of movement) and Article 10 (freedom of speech, assembly and association). A law enacted under Article 149 would also be valid even if it is outside the legislative power of Federal Parliament and State Governments need not be consulted in the enactment of such law.

When compared with Article 150, the powers here to act inconsistently with the Constitution are limited to only a few Articles. Legislation enacted under Article 149, it seems clear, cannot be inconsistent with other provisions of the Constitution.

A statute enacted under Article 149 can be in force indefinitely since Article 149 does not prescribe a time limit. It ceases to have effect only when it is repealed by Parliament or annulled by resolutions of both Houses of Parliament.

B. DEVELOPMENT OF THE PROVISION BY CONSTITUTIONAL AMENDMENT

Article 149 has been amended once in 1960 by Act 10 of 1960 in force from 31 May 1960. Prior to this, Article 149 had a distinct similarity to the provision recommended by the Reid Constitutional Commission.

The 1960 amendment altered two features of the original Article 149 which were identical with the Reid Constitutional Commission's draft.

First, in the original Article 149 there had to be a link between the recital that certain action had been taken or threatened and the result that it '[caused, or caused] a substantial number of citizens to fear, organized violence against persons or property'. The 1960 amendment provided for four additional alternative descriptions of consequences or results with which the action or threat could be linked. In this way the scope of Article 149 was considerably broadened.

Secondly, the original Article 149 provided that any law enacted thereunder would have validity for only one year although Parliament could make a new law. The 1960 amendment changed this to provide that the law, if not sooner repealed, would cease to have effect if both Houses of Parliament passed resolutions annulling such law. Thus Article 149 legislation can continue indefinitely without the need for Parliament, at fixed periods, addressing itself to the continuing necessity for the law which seems to be the intention of the original provision.

C. DEVELOPMENT THROUGH INTERPRETATION BY THE COURTS

Case law on Article 149 has yet to emerge and the writer has not come across any decision where the courts expressly interpreted this Article. (Interpretation by courts of preventive detention legislation is, of course, relevant, when considering the scope of this Article but those decisions are discussed later in respect of Article 151.)

The writer, however, wishes to raise a few issues that can arise and which the courts may have to decide in the future.

1. *Judicial review over the recital in the Act.* One question that could arise is whether the finding on the existence of circumstances recited in the Act can be reviewed by the courts and whether evidence can be adduced to show that there is no basis for the finding contained in the recital. It is most unlikely that the courts will consider the matters contained in the recital to be justiciable. As will be shown later, the courts have held that the issuance of Proclamations of Emergency and the promulgation of emergency ordinances under Article 150 are not justiciable. This same approach is likely to be followed here and once the court is satisfied that the recital as required by Article 149 exists it would not go behind the recital to decide if it was justifiable.

2. *Judicial review on whether provisions were 'designed to stop or prevent that action'.* However another question, quite distinct from the preceding one, can arise with regard to the provision that 'any provision of that law designed to stop or prevent that action is valid' notwithstanding inconsistency with certain constitutional provisions. Can the courts be asked to decide whether a particular provision in any Article 149 law was indeed designed to stop or prevent the action recited?

If such a question arises in the courts it will be useful to recall that the Reid Constitutional Commission (and this wording of the provision followed its recommendation) specifically felt that this should be a matter for judicial review:

It must be for Parliament to determine whether the situation is such that special provisions are required, but Parliament should not be entitled to authorize infringements of such a character that they cannot properly be regarded as designed to deal with the particular situation. *It would be open for any person aggrieved by the enactment of a particular infringement to maintain that it could not properly be so regarded and submit the question for decision by the court.*[5]

3. *Whether the inconsistency should be express.* A third question is whether a law enacted under Article 149 is deemed inherently to override the constitutional provisions mentioned therein or whether Article 149 only allows for inconsistencies which are express. The Singapore case of *Lee Mau Seng* v. *Minister for Home Affairs, Singapore & Anor.*,[6] interpreting the same Article 149

(which applies in Singapore) made an important qualification when it held that inconsistencies must be express. Thus if provisions of any Article 149 law are not expressly inconsistent with the constitutional provisions concerned, those constitutional provisions will be given effect to.

The Malaysian courts are likely to follow this approach of the Singapore courts which, it is submitted, is the correct interpretation. It should be noted that the *Lee Mau Seng* case has been cited with approval in the Malaysian courts on another aspect, that of the constitutional right to counsel.

III. THE POWERS UNDER ARTICLE 150 (PROCLAMATION OF EMERGENCY)

A. SCOPE OF THE PROVISION

Article 150 enables the Government to exercise a wide range of extraordinary executive and legislative powers. Many of the specific features of this provision will be examined in the discussion below on development of the provision through constitutional amendment and its interpretation by the courts. The main features of the provision, however, are as follows.

First, a Proclamation of Emergency, containing prescribed recitals, is an essential prerequisite before the special powers under the provision can be exercised.[7] The formal issuance of the Proclamation is by the Yang di-Pertuan Agong but, as he acts on advice, it is the Government which proclaims the emergency. Secondly, when there is such a Proclamation in effect, emergency legislation will be valid even if inconsistent with *any* provision of the Constitution[8] (though a few provisions are still inviolable such as provisions relating to religion, citizenship, or language[9] and, further, emergency legislation would also have to comply with Article 151 on preventive detention). This power to legislate contrary to the Constitution is probably the most important aspect of the powers granted under Article 150. Thirdly, the executive is permitted to legislate through emergency ordinances where Parliament is not sitting and pending the sitting of both Houses of Parliament.[10] Such emergency legislation of the executive, like the emergency legislation of Parliament, can be inconsistent with any provision of the Constitution (except provisions relating to religion, citizenship or language). Fourthly, the Federal executive's authority, during an emergency, extends to State matters and it is empowered to give directions to State Governments or officers and authorities thereof.[11] Fifthly, it would appear that while a Proclamation is in effect Parliament can legislate on any matter regardless of whether it is within the Federal List, State List, or Concurrent List, and normal constitutional requirements of consultation with a State Government or the obtaining of the consent or concurrence of any other body are inapplicable.[12] However Parliament is not permitted to extend its normal powers with respect to Muslim Law, Malay custom, or native law or custom in the Borneo States.[13]

These features more than adequately arm the Government with the necessary means to overcome constitutional obstacles when dealing with emergencies.

Of all the powers granted by Article 150 it is submitted that the most significant is the power (of the legislature and the executive) to legislate contrary to the Constitution.

It should be noted that the present scope of clause (6) of Article 150 was brought about by constitutional amendment. The original provision followed the recommendation of the Reid Constitutional Commission, that emergency legislation can be 'repugnant' to fundamental liberties. The Commission did not go beyond recommending that 'Parliament should have power to enact any provision notwithstanding that it infringes fundamental rights or State rights'.[14]

Enormous and awesome though the present power may be, it must be pointed out that the constitutional provisions are not suspended, for Article 150 does not state that *all* laws enacted while a Proclamation is in force can be validly inconsistent with the Constitution. In this regard the writer wishes to offer the following three submissions about laws conflicting with the Constitution.

First, when a Proclamation is issued there would still be in force the body of laws enacted *prior* to the issuance of the Proclamation. These existing pre-proclamation laws (unless they were emergency legislation under previous proclamations) cannot be considered as coming within the scope of Article 150. If they are inconsistent with the Constitution they may be held invalid under the doctrine of supremacy of the Constitution in Article 4.

Secondly, as regards legislation enacted *after* the issuance of the Proclamation, it is only legislation which contains the recital prescribed by Article 150(6)—'which declares that the law appears to Parliament to be required by the reason of the emergency'—that can be inconsistent with the provisions of the Constitution and still be valid. It is not uncommon that during the currency of a Proclamation other legislation, not designed to meet the crisis, may be enacted without such recital. Such laws, it is submitted, fall outside the scope of the doctrine in Article 150(6) of legislating contrary to the Constitution. If such laws conflict with the Constitution, they cannot be saved by Article 150(6) although clause (5) of Article 150 may save the law if the inconsistency relates to Federal-State jurisdiction provisions.

Thirdly, just as it was earlier submitted (on the basis of the Singapore case of *Lee Mau Seng*[15]) that Article 149 authorized only inconsistencies which are express, here too it would seem that Article 150(6) covers inconsistencies which are express. It is therefore submitted that where an emergency statute contains the required recital but is not expressly inconsistent with a specific constitutional provision, then any *implementation* of that legislation without observing that constitutional provision would be unconstitutional.

B. DEVELOPMENT OF THE PROVISION BY CONSTITUTIONAL AMENDMENT

Article 150 has been amended on three occasions, first by Act 10 of 1960 with effect from 31 May 1960; secondly by Act 26 of 1963 with effect from 16 September 1963; and thirdly by Act 68 of 1966 with effect from 20 September 1966.

The first amendment, by Act 10 of 1960, altered the clause (3) of the original Article which, in line with the Reid Commission's proposal, provided that (unless Parliament approved them before the expiration of the period) a Proclamation of Emergency shall have validity only for a duration of two months and that an emergency ordinance (issued by the executive) shall cease to have force fifteen days after the date both Houses are first sitting. The 1960 amendment altered this to provide that both the Proclamation and the emergency ordinance would cease to have effect only when revoked or annulled. This was a significant change. Originally Parliament would have had to address its mind to the continued justification of the Proclamation and the ordinances. The change meant that both Proclamation and Ordinances have indefinite life unless expressly revoked or annulled.

The second amendment, by Act 26 of 1963, broadened the scope of Article 150 in three ways. First, it deleted from clause (1) what could have been construed as restrictive words[16] qualifying the type of emergency envisaged: 'whether by war or external aggression or internal disturbance'; secondly, it widened the scope of clause (5) by strengthening the Federal Parliament's overriding competence over State matters; and thirdly, where the original clause (6) provided that emergency laws could be inconsistent with the provisions of Part II (fundamental liberties) and that Article 79 will not apply in the enactment of such law, the 1963 amendment provided that the inconsistency could be with respect to *any* provision of the Constitution. A new clause (6A) was added to enumerate the few matters which were still entrenched such as provisions on religion, citizenship, or language.

The third amendment, by Act 68 of 1966 was limited to ensuring that the emergency legislation enacted to deal with·the crisis over the dismissal of the Sarawak Chief Minister was within the scope of Article 150. This was achieved by amending both clauses (5) and (6) to provide that emergency legislation would be valid even if there was an inconsistency with the Constitution of the State of Sarawak. As this amending Act was itself emergency legislation (enacted pursuant to a Proclamation of Emergency dated 14 September 1966[17]), this amendment would cease to have effect six months after that Proclamation of Emergency ceases to have effect.

C. DEVELOPMENT THROUGH INTERPRETATION BY THE COURTS

There now exists a significant body of judicial decisions which, through interpretation of the provision, has clarified the substantive as well as procedural law on emergency powers. It is not possible, within the limited length of this essay, to discuss exhaustively all of these cases. Instead what follows is a discussion of the principles, decisions and approach of these cases with respect to the issues and questions arising under Article 150.

1. *Whether the Proclamation of Emergency is issued by the Yang di-Pertuan Agong on advice.* In some cases, when discussing the justiciability of a Proclamation of Emergency or of an emergency ordinance promulgated by the Yang di-Pertuan Agong, some judges have referred to the Yang di-Pertuan Agong as being '*the sole judge*'.[18] This has led some[19] to believe that the judgments concerned are authority for the proposition that the Yang di-Pertuan Agong may issue a Proclamation of Emergency in exercise of his personal discretion.

This writer has elsewhere already fully argued[20] that this is an erroneous interpretation of the cases and that all the available judicial decisions as well as ordinary principles of interpretation, supported by the views of the Reid Constitutional Commission, clearly establish that the Yang di-Pertuan Agong has to act on advice when issuing a Proclamation of Emergency. These arguments will not be repeated here and only the relevant judicial decisions need be referred to.

First, in the case of *Stephen Kalong Ningkan* v. *The Government of Malaysia*[21] where Lord President Barakbah and Azmi C.J.

(Malaya) used the words 'sole judge', their judgments read as a whole show that their choice of those words was with regard to the question whether actions under Article 150 were justiciable. Not only is there no evidence that they meant that the Yang di-Pertuan Agong had a personal discretion but elsewhere in his judgment, the Lord President equated action of the Yang di-Pertuan Agong with action of the *Government*.[22]

Several other cases have clearly shown that the courts consider that the Yang di-Pertuan Agong acts on advice when issuing a Proclamation of Emergency. These cases are:

First, *Stephen Kalong Ningkan* v. *Tun Abang Haji Openg and Tawi Sli (No. 2)*,[23] a High Court decision, where Pike C.J. (Borneo) stated '... since under Article 40 of the Constitution the Yang di-Pertuan Agong is required to act upon the advice of the Cabinet in making a proclamation under Article 150 (and indeed in all other matters except those mentioned in clauses (2) and (3) of Article 40), it cannot, I think, be argued that the power conferred by Article 150 is a prerogative power analogous to certain powers of the British sovereign'.[24]

Secondly, in *Stephen Kalong Ningkan* v. *Government of Malaysia*[25] the Privy Council seemed to equate the Yang di-Pertuan Agong's actions with actions of the Government and when referring to the Proclamation of Emergency of 14 September 1966, the Privy Council referred to '... the Yang di-Pertuan Agong acting, it may be presumed, on the advice of the Federal Cabinet as required by Article 40(1) of the Federal Constitution, proclaimed a state of emergency ...'.[26]

Thirdly, in *N. Madhavan Nair* v. *The Government of Malaysia*,[27] a High Court decision, Chang Min Tat J. also referred expressly to the obligation of the Yang di-Pertuan Agong to act on advice.

To summarize then, the thrust of the judicial decisions is that the Yang di-Pertuan Agong, when issuing a Proclamation of Emergency, must act on advice.[28]

2. *Judicial review of the validity of the Proclamation of Emergency; justiciability.* All efforts have failed to have the courts review the validity of a Proclamation of Emergency by inquiring whether, in the circumstances, a state of emergency did exist. The courts have consistently taken the view that the determination by the Government that an emergency exists, and the issuance of the Proclamation of Emergency, are non-justiciable. The only judicial view expressly asserting the courts' right of judicial review is the dissenting judgment of Ong Hock Thye F.J. in *Stephen Kalong Ningkan* v. *The Government of Malaysia*,[29] but his view has not found

support. Four cases are relevant on this question.

First, in *Stephen Kalong Ningkan* v. *Tun Abang Haji Openg & Tawi Sli (No. 2)*,[30] Pike C.J. (Borneo) relying on the cases of *Bhagat Singh & Ors.* v. *The King Emperor*,[31] *The King Emperor* v. *Benoari Lal Sharma*[32] and *R.* v. *Governor of Brixton Prison*,[33] and *Liversidge* v. *Anderson*[34] concluded that: 'It seems clear from the cases that it is not open to a court to inquire into the sufficiency of the reasons for a declaration of Emergency provided it was made *bona fide.*'[35]

Secondly, in the Federal Court phase of *Stephen Kalong Ningkan* v. *The Government of Malaysia*[36] the majority (Lord President Barakbah and Azmi C.J. (Malaya)) were emphatic in their view that the court could not review the decision of the Government to issue a Proclamation. Both judges relied on the case of *Bhagat Singh* v. *The King Emperor*.[37] Lord President Barakbah felt that '... it is incumbent on the court to assume that the Government is acting in the best interest of the State and to permit no evidence to be adduced otherwise. In short, the circumstances which bring about a Proclamation of Emergency are non-justiciable'. (H. T. Ong F.J. dissented strongly on this point and he felt that the 'inbuilt safeguards' and 'words of limitation' showed that the power of Government was limited and it was open for one to challenge a Proclamation on grounds of *ultra vires.*)

Thirdly, in the Privy Council phase of *Stephen Kalong Ningkan* v. *Government of Malaysia*,[38] their Lordships rather adroitly avoided deciding the question of justiciability and proceeded to discuss the claim of '*in fraudem legis*' on the *assumption* that it was in law justiciable. The Privy Council decision therefore cannot be considered as having decided the issue of justiciability. It should be noted that their Lordships observed that the question 'is a constitutional question of far-reaching importance which, on the present state of the authorities, remains unsettled and debateable'.[39]

Fourthly, in *Public Prosecutor* v. *Ooi Kee Saik & Ors.*,[40] a High Court decision, Raja Azlan Shah J. had occasion to note that counsel had not challenged the validity of the Proclamation and said 'Indeed the proclamation is not justiciable (see *Bhagat Singh* v. *King Emperor* and *King Emperor* v. *Benoari Lal Sharma*)'.[41]

3. *Challenging the validity of the Proclamation on the ground of* mala fides. As shown in the preceding discussion, the courts will not review the justification for the issuance of a Proclamation of Emergency. The immediate question that arises is whether an exception will be made where the Proclamation is challenged on grounds of *mala fides.*

On this point the available judicial pronouncements seem to be at divergence. On the one hand, Pike C.J. in *Stephen Kalong Ning-kan* v. *Tun Abang Haji Openg & Tawi Sli (No. 2)*[42] felt that the cases established that there could be no judicial review 'provided it [the Proclamation] was made *bona fide'*. He thought that the Privy Council 'made it clear' in *The King Emperor* v. *Benoari Lal Sharma*[43] that 'the exclusion of the court's right to inquire into the exercise of such a power depends upon whether or not the act was done *bona fide'*.[44]

However, in the Federal Court phase of *Stephen Kalong Ningkan* v. *The Government of Malaysia,*[45] Azmi C.J. (one of the two judges in the majority) noted that in *King Emperor* v. *Benoari Lal Sharma & Ors.* 'there is something ... in the judgment ... that might suggest that it could still be open to the court to question the *bona fide* of the Yang di-Pertuan Agong',[46] but he dismissed this by saying that the Governor-General in India was 'sole judge' of whether an emergency existed 'and that, therefore, no court may inquire into it'. (Lord President Barakbah did not deal with the question of *mala fides* as being an exception to non-justiciability.)

Azmi C.J.'s distinguishing of *King Emperor* v. *Benoari Lal Sharma & Ors.*, it is respectfully submitted, is not correct and Pike C.J.'s view that there can be review on ground of *mala fides* would appear to be the correct position. It would take future cases to confirm this. However, it should not be forgotten, in the words of Pike C. J. that a plaintiff may be faced with 'grave difficulties of proof' in a challenge based on *mala fides*.[47]

4. *The kind of emergencies envisaged under Article 150.* Since the courts have decided that the decision to issue a Proclamation is not justiciable, it is not surprising that there is very little discussion in the cases of the situations which can be regarded as properly amounting to a 'grave emergency' within the meaning of Article 150. Yet this question may prove to be important if the courts are prepared to assert judicial review where the challenge is on the ground of *mala fides*.

The only available judicial guidance is in the dissenting judgment of Ong Hock Thye F.J. in the Federal Court phase of *Stephen Kalong Ningkan* v. *The Government of Malaysia* (where the learned judge, who felt the Proclamation was reviewable, rejected the contention based on *mala fides*), and the decision of the Privy Council in that case (where their Lordships considered the *mala fides* argument on the assumption that it was justiciable).

It is significant that both these judgments tended to favour a broad interpretation of the concept of emergency. In his dissenting judgment, Ong Hock Thye F.J. avoided giving a narrow meaning to the concept of emergency when he felt that 'it may very well be true that political instability in Sarawak could possibly have serious repercussions on the security of the States ...'.[48]

Their Lordships in the Privy Council were more explicit in their preference of a broad interpretation. Their Lordships felt that the term 'emergency' in Article 150 'cannot be confined to the unlawful use or threat of force in any of its manifestations'[49] and that 'the natural meaning of the word itself is capable of covering a very wide range of situations and occurrences, including such diverse events as wars, famines, earthquakes, floods, epidemics and the collapse of civil government'.[50] This enumeration, it should be noted, was not exhaustive.

As regards the Proclamation to deal with the crisis resulting from the dismissal of the Sarawak Chief Minister, their Lordships, taking this approach, could not 'find any reason for saying that the emergency ... was not grave' and went on to say that

... it was open to the Federal Government, and indeed its duty, to consider the possible consequences of a period of unstable government in a State that, not so long ago, had been facing the tensions of Confrontation and the subversive activities associated with it.[51]

The broad interpretation of the concept of emergency, it is submitted, is significant in that it will make a claim of *mala fides* even more difficult to prove.

5. *The power of the executive to legislate through emergency ordinances.* As pointed out earlier (see A: Scope of the Provision) one of the features of Article 150 is clause (2) which authorizes the Yang di-Pertuan Agong to promulgate ordinances having the force of law 'until both Houses of Parliament are sitting' if satisfied that immediate action is required.

The first observation is that, as is the case with issuance of the Proclamation, here too the Yang di-Pertuan Agong must act on advice. As clarified by Chang Min Tat J. in *N. Madhavan Nair* v. *The Government of Malaysia*,[52]

Emergency rule which passes the legislative power from Parliament to the Yang Dipertuan Agung has not displaced his position as the Constitutional Monarch, bound by the Constitution to act at all times on the advice of the Cabinet.[53]

The second observation is that this is the only instance where the Constitution provides for the executive to exercise primary legislative functions. This legislative power conferred on the executive would ·seem to be as complete as the power of Parliament itself if it had been sitting. Indeed clause (6) of Article 150

provides that provisions of such ordinances could, like emergency
legislation of Parliament, be inconsistent with most provisions of
the Constitution.

In *Public Prosecutor* v. *Ooi Kee Saik & Ors.*,[54] a High Court decision, Raja Azlan Shah J. stated that it was 'clear that the power of
the Yang di-Pertuan Agong to legislate by Ordinance when Parliament is not sitting is co-extensive with the power of Parliament
itself'. The same learned judge in *Johnson Tan Han Seng* v. *Public
Prosecutor*,[55] a Federal Court decision, again had occasion to point
out that the Yang di-Pertuan Agong 'has, and is intended to have,
plenary powers of legislation, as large and of the same nature, as
those of Parliament itself'.[56]

*6. Whether the power to legislate contrary to the Constitution can be dele-
gated; sub-delegated.* Where emergency ordinances or emergency
Acts of Parliament have delegated the power to legislate inconsistently with the Constitution, such delegation in some cases has
been challenged. The main arguments were that such powers
could not be delegated or, alternatively, that such delegation was
so wide as to amount to an abrogation or abdication of legislative
powers. The courts have not upheld these challenges and the clear
doctrine emerging from these cases is that the power to legislate
contrary to the Constitution can indeed be delegated.

The first case which dealt with this issue was *Eng Keock Cheng* v.
Public Prosecutor,[57] a Federal Court decision. The court stated that
Article 150(6), in giving Parliament power to legislate on any subject and to any effect even if contrary to the Constitution 'necessarily includes authority to delegate part of that power to legislate
to some other authority, notwithstanding the existence of a written Constitution'. As regards the argument that the Act was so
wide that it amounted to an abrogation of legislative powers, the
court did not reject the relevance of the doctrine of abrogation.
After examining the Act, it concluded,

However wide this field may be, it is not all embracing and the Act
does set out the policy and scope within which the power is to be exercised. It cannot be said to be an abrogation by Parliament of all its
power to legislate. Parliament still retains its power to legislate, even
within this very field.[58]

In *Osman & Anor.* v. *Public Prosecutor*,[59] a Privy Council decision,
the argument was raised in a different way. One issue was the
validity of emergency regulations conflicting with the Constitution
enacted under emergency legislation declaring that such regulations would be valid notwithstanding anything inconsistent with

any 'written law'. It was argued that 'written law' could not include the Constitution since Article 150(5) itself made a distinction between the Constitution and written law. Their Lordships, however, rejected this argument. They gave effect to the Interpretation and General Clauses Ordinance, 1948, which interpreted 'written law' to include the Constitution and they did not consider the phrase 'any provision of this Constitution or of any written law' in Article 150(5) to indicate that 'written law' in the emergency law had a meaning different from that stated in the 1948 Ordinance. Thus, according to their Lordships, '... If the regulations were inconsistent with the Constitution, nevertheless if "written law" ... in the Act includes the Constitution, the validity of the regulations cannot be impeached'.[60]

In *Government of Malaysia* v. *Mahan Singh*,[61] a Federal Court decision, one argument was that the Yang di-Pertuan Agong may delegate only *part* of his power but could not delegate *all* of his power as that would amount to an abdication of his power. Speaking for the Federal Court, Suffian L.P. stated:

I do not think there is any merit in this argument. If his Majesty may delegate part of his power he may delegate all of it, and there is no question of abdication in the instant case: after promulgating Ordinance No. 2 of 1969 His Majesty remained Yang Dipertuan Agung, still retained such power as he might have wished to exercise, and indeed has since then by P.U. (A) 62/71, section 3, in exercise of his royal power repealed that Ordinance.[62]

The question of delegation and validity of regulations conflicting with the Constitution arose again[63] in the recent case of *Public Prosecutor* v. *Khong Teng Khen & Anor.*,[64] a Federal Court decision where it was argued that only Acts of Parliament and emergency ordinances (but not regulations) are saved by clause (6) of Article 150. Suffian L.P. (with whom Wan Suleiman F.J. concurred) dismissed this claim on the ground that in the Emergency Ordinance the Yang di-Pertuan Agong gave himself wide powers to make essential regulations and one sub-section provided that the regulations shall have effect even if inconsistent with any written law including the Federal Constitution. His Lordship stated that 'because of this subsection, it is lawful in my view for His Majesty to make essential regulations that are inconsistent with the Federal Constitution'. The learned Lord President relying on *Osman & Anor.* v. *Public Prosecutor* also stated that as the Yang di-Pertuan Agong 'has power ... to promulgate an Ordinance ... even though it is inconsistent with the Constitution, he has power to delegate this power to himself'.[65]

Sub-delegation. If, on the basis of all these cases it is permissible to delegate the power to legislate contrary to the Constitution, is it also constitutionally permissible to sub-delegate? The case of *Johnson Tan Han Seng* v. *Public Prosecutor*[66] would suggest an affirmative answer. Here it was argued that the Yang di-Pertuan Agong having delegated to himself power to alter the mode of trial of persons, he could not sub-delegate this power to the Attorney-General. Suffian L.P. (with whom Wan Suleiman F.J. concurred) did not think there had been sub-delegation but even if there was then the regulations [purporting to sub-delegate] were *intra vires* the emergency ordinance and valid on the reasoning of the majority judgments in *Public Prosecutor* v. *Khong Teng Khen & Anor*. Raja Azlan Shah F.J. agreed with the reasoning and conclusion of Suffian L.P. while stating his reasons separately.

7. *Whether delegated power to make emergency regulations continues after Parliament has sat.* It seems clear from clause (2) of Article 150 that the executive's power to legislate by emergency ordinances is a power exercisable 'until both Houses of Parliament are sitting' and once Parliament has sat, this power to issue Ordinances ceases. However, can the executive still continue to make emergency regulations pursuant to power delegated by an emergency ordinance that had not been revoked?

This interesting question arose before the Federal Court in *Public Prosecutor* v. *Khong Teng Khen & Anor*.[67] where it was argued that once Parliament sat, the Yang di-Pertuan Agong could not any longer make such regulations. The majority of the court rejected this argument. Suffian L.P. (Wan Suleiman F.J. concurring) stated that the regulations were made not under Article 150(2) but under the emergency ordinance; that whether Parliament was in existence or sitting, while relevant to the making of ordinances, was irrelevant to the making of regulations.

Ong Hock Sim F.J. dissented; he felt that there was a limitation on the Yang di-Pertuan Agong's power to continue to make subsidiary legislation.

The decision of the majority judgments brings about a most curious legal situation: the executive can no longer make emergency ordinances because Parliament has sat but it can continue to enact emergency subsidiary legislation which (according to other decisions) can also be inconsistent with the Constitution. One way perhaps of reconciling this decision with the spirit of Article 150(2) is that it was open to Parliament to have annulled the emergency ordinances; not having done so, Parliament is deemed to have sanctioned the continued power of making emergency regulations.

8. *Issues turning on Article 150(2): the meaning of summoning Parliament 'as soon as may be practicable' and the meaning of 'when Parliament is not sitting' and 'until both Houses of Parliament are sitting'*. The power of the executive to legislate through emergency ordinances under Article 150(2) is only where the Proclamation is issued 'when Parliament is not sitting' and the power is exercisable only until such time that 'both Houses of Parliament are sitting'. Further the Yang di-Pertuan Agong is to summon Parliament 'as soon as may be practicable'. In some cases the courts were invited to interpret these words restrictively but, as will be shown below, the courts have taken a different approach.

(a) *'as soon as may be practicable'*. In *Public Prosecutor v. Ooi Kee Saik & Ors.*,[68] a High Court decision, it was argued that emergency legislation made when Parliament is not sitting has a temporary existence; that it must receive legislative sanction upon reconvening of Parliament and that this implied that the Yang di-Pertuan Agong must summon Parliament as soon as possible and not wait for one year and nine months after the Proclamation. Raja Azlan Shah J. held that because of this phrase, the Yang di-Pertuan Agong's obligation to summon Parliament was not absolute or unqualified but could be 'what is possible having regard to existing conditions'. The learned judge felt that 'the matter is above judicial review' and that the long delay in summoning Parliament did not affect the validity of the emergency ordinance in that case.[69]

A similar challenge was also made in *Melan bin Abdullah & Anor. v. Public Prosecutor*,[70] a High Court decision, where it was argued that amendments to the Sedition Act by emergency legislation were invalid because Parliament had not been convened for twenty-two months and, thus, Parliament had not been summoned as soon as may be practicable. Ong Hock Thye C.J. (Malaya) first held (incorrectly, it is submitted) that he had no jurisdiction to decide this constitutional question. However he went on to say 'I do not think this or any court is competent to decide when it was practicable for Parliament to be convened during an Emergency'.[71]

(b) *'When Parliament is not sitting'* and *'until both Houses of Parliament are sitting'*. There are several judicial pronouncements which have clarified the meaning of these phrases.

In *Public Prosecutor v. Ooi Kee Saik & Ors.*[72] Raja Azlan Shah J. was of the view that 'when Parliament is not sitting' must mean when Parliament 'is not in session, in other words "when Parliament is prorogued or dissolved"'.[73]

In *Fan Yew Teng v. Public Prosecutor*,[74] a Federal Court decision, the validity of emergency ordinances was challenged on the ground that Article 150(2) envisaged the existence of a Parliament in being and one which had not been dissolved; that as the previous Parliament had been dissolved and elections for a new Parliament had not been completed there was no Parliament in being; that, therefore, there was no power to issue emergency ordinances.

Lee Hun Hoe C.J. (Borneo), delivering the judgment of the court, rejected this interpretation:

> In our opinion the words 'when Parliament is not sitting' in clause (2) mean not only 'when Parliament which is in being is not sitting' but also 'when Parliament has been dissolved and the general election to the new Parliament has not yet been completed'.[75]

In *Public Prosecutor* v. *Khong Teng Khen & Anor.*,[76] a Federal Court decision, Suffian L.P. (with whom Wan Suleiman F.J. concurred) observed that 'sitting' in clause (2) 'means sitting and actually deliberating'.[77] The dissenting judge Ong Hock Sim F.J. disagreed; he referred to Article 55 which states that six months shall not lapse between the last sitting in one session and the date for the first meeting in the next session. Ong F.J. felt that Parliament would still be sitting though a weekend recess is taken. He stated that 'until both Houses of Parliament are sitting' should be given neither an 'absurd nor impossible' meaning and pointed out that Parliament comprises two Houses which 'do not sit at the same time'.[78]

9. *Judicial review of the validity of emergency ordinances.* The courts will not review the decision of the executive to issue emergency ordinances in the same way as they are unwilling to review decisions on issuance of Proclamations of Emergency. In *Public Prosecutor* v. *Ooi Kee Saik & Ors.*,[79] Raja Azlan Shah J. stated that the reasoning for non-justiciability of proclamations 'equally applies to the question of justiciability of Ordinances promulgated under clause (2) of Article 150'. The learned judge attached importance to the words 'if satisfied that immediate action is required' and applied the principles of the Australian case *Australian Communist Party* v. *The Commonwealth*[80] which held that action taken under a power, where the words used in the legislation were 'if he is satisfied' of the existence of a certain state of affairs is not justiciable—so long as the declaration recites the statutory formula.

According to the learned judge the test was whether the Ordinance was issued within the scope of the clause and whether it recited the statutory formulae: 'Once the court has determined that such law lies within the province of a competent authority, the court is not authorized to reweigh what a competent authority has weighed...'.[81]

Reviewing emergency Ordinances on the ground of mala fides. However, in the same case, Raja Azlan Shah J. implied that there could be review where the challenge is on the ground of *mala fides*:

The Ordinance had recited the statutory formula. The recital is conclusive and that closed the door to all review. The onus now shifts to those who wish to challenge its validity by proving *mala fides* or bad faith.[82]

10. *Judicial review of the Proclamation or emergency ordinance for non-compliance with formalities.* We have earlier observed the attitude of the courts to judicial review of the Government's decision to promulgate Proclamations of Emergency and emergency ordinances as well as judicial review on the ground of *mala fides*.

A separate question which has arisen is whether non-compliance with certain formalities in the process of promulgation would justify judicial review of the question whether the instrument has been properly promulgated.

The only case providing guidance here is *N. Madhavan Nair* v. *Government of Malaysia*,[83] a High Court decision. Here it was contended that an emergency ordinance purported to be made by the Yang di-Pertuan Agong was defective as it did not bear the public seal and did not contain the formula and legend usually appended at the end of such ordinances. These defects, it was argued, showed that the Yang di-Pertuan Agong had not assented, that it had not been properly promulgated and therefore was not valid law.

Chang Min Tat J., following several Indian decisions, held that the only legal result of the absence of authentication was that the question whether the Ordinance had been promulgated by the Yang di-Pertuan Agong was open to judicial inquiry; it had to be proved by affidavit or other evidence that the Ordinance was in fact promulgated by him. The learned judge in this case accepted as adequate evidence an affidavit of the Prime Minister that the Yang di-Pertuan Agong had indeed assented.

It is most likely that the same approach would be adopted if non-compliance with similar formalities occurred in respect of a Proclamation of Emergency.

11. *Federal Government's jurisdiction over State matters during an emergency.* Clauses (4) and (5) of Article 150 arm the Federal Government with considerable authority over matters which otherwise

would be considered within the jurisdiction of States. In particular, the Federal Parliament's authority to legislate on State matters is made clear by the terms of clause (5), especially the express provision that Parliament may 'make laws with respect to any matter' notwithstanding anything in the Federal Constitution.

An important question is whether the Federal Parliament, during an emergency, can amend the Constitution of a State. The question arises because clauses (5) and (6) refer only to inconsistencies with the Federal Constitution.

It is probably because of this that (during the *Ningkan* crisis) the Federal Government when enacting emergency legislation in 1966 to modify the provisions of the Sarawak Constitution simultaneously amended Article 150 to add the words 'or in the Constitution of the State of Sarawak' in clauses (5) and (6).

But was this amendment to Article 150 necessary? Do not the wide terms of clauses (5) and (6) enable the Federal Parliament to amend State Constitutions if the emergency so requires? It is submitted that a close reading of the Federal Court and Privy Council decisions in *Stephen Kalong Ningkan* v. *Government of Malaysia* shows that both tribunals are of the view that Article 150 authorizes Parliament to amend State Constitutions (though the Privy Council felt the amendments should not be permanent).

In that case it was argued that emergency legislation could not amend the Sarawak Constitution as this would be contrary to the Sarawak Constitution which, in Article 41, provided that it could be amended by a law enacted by the Sarawak legislature 'but may not be amended by any other means'. (Similar provisions exist in several other State Constitutions.)

In the Federal Court's consideration of the case,[84] Barakbah L.P. felt clause (5) of Article 150 authorized amendments to the Sarawak Constitution and Azmi C.J. (Malaya) also held this should be the position notwithstanding Article 41 of the Sarawak Constitution. Ong Hock Thye F.J. felt that '... the overriding consideration of an emergency which justifies an amendment of the Constitution must no less justify an amendment of the State Constitution, so far as may be strictly necessary'.[85]

The question was more exhaustively discussed in the Privy Council.[86] Their Lordships, on this point, felt first that the agreements and instruments relative to Sarawak's entry into Malaysia showed 'that the parties to that agreement must have realized that the powers of the Federal Parliament conferred by that Article [150] during the currency of a Proclamation of Emergency, might be used to amend, for the time being, the provisions of the Sarawak Constitution of 1963'.[87]

Secondly, their Lordships were impressed by the 'width' of clause (5) which authorized Parliament to make laws 'with respect to any matter' and observed that 'these words could scarcely be more comprehensive'. Their Lordships also noted that clause (1) of Article 150 could apply to a grave emergency affecting any of the States and that 'the powers needed to meet such a situation might include power to modify, at any rate temporarily, the Constitution of the part of the Federation which was principally affected'.[88]

But their Lordships, apparently troubled by Article 41 of the Sarawak Constitution, seemed to confine their decision to temporary amendments only.

The terms of article 41(1) of the Constitution of Sarawak are sufficiently explicit to make it difficult as a matter of implication to amend the Constitution of Sarawak permanently and at its pleasure. But a temporary amendment on exceptional grounds stands on a different footing, and the considerations mentioned lead their Lordships to the conclusion that article 150(5) was intended to arm the Federal Parliament with power to amend or modify the 1963 Constitution of Sarawak temporarily if that Parliament thought such a step was required by reason of the Emergency....[89]

It is submitted, therefore, that where the Federal Parliament resorts to emergency powers to deal with a State crisis, amendments to State Constitutions are unnecessary as Article 150, according to the judicial interpretation, permits temporary modifications of State Constitutions. The Privy Council's qualification of temporariness is somewhat academic since, if a proclamation is not revoked, the emergency legislation would continue to have force unless expressly repealed or revoked. It is interesting that when the Federal Government invoked emergency powers to deal with the 1977 crisis in Kelantan, the emergency legislation, Emergency Powers (Kelantan) Act 1977 (Act 192) was enacted by Parliament to extend to Kelantan the federal executive authority 'in respect of matters which are now within the executive authority of the State of Kelantan, and to confer upon the Ruler of the State of Kelantan, to the exclusion of the Legislative Assembly of the State of Kelantan, the legislative authority of the State of Kelantan in respect of all matters which are now within the legislative authority of the State of Kelantan'.

This was clearly a radical modification of the provisions in the Kelantan Constitution for Government of the State. However, it is significant that the emergency legislation did not amend the State Constitution nor was the Federal Constitution amended expressly to provide for inconsistencies with the Kelantan Constitution.

Instead section 15 of the Emergency Powers (Kelantan) Act 1977 provided:

15. (1) The provisions of this Act and of any subsidiary legislation made thereunder shall prevail notwithstanding anything to the contrary contained in the Constitution of Kelantan or any other written law.

(2) The Constitution of Kelantan and all other written laws shall be read—

(a) *mutatis mutandis* with the provisions of this Act and of any subsidiary legislation made thereunder; and

(b) with all such modifications, adaptations, alterations or changes whatsoever as may be necessary to have the same to accord with the provisions of this Act and of any subsidiary legislation made thereunder.

12. *When do Proclamations of Emergency, and emergency legislation, cease to have effect?* As pointed out *supra* ('Development of the provision by constitutional amendment') Article 150, prior to various amendments, provided that a Proclamation of Emergency and an emergency ordinance would have validity for a limited duration. If Article 150 as it stands now is interpreted literally, both the Proclamation and emergency ordinances by the executive would have validity so long as they are not expressly revoked or annulled. Article 150 provides no time deadline beyond which the Proclamation ceases to have force, and there is no obligation to revoke or annul it. Indeed, during the period between Merdeka Day and the time of writing this essay, four Proclamations of Emergency were issued at various times. None of them have been revoked yet.[90] Where a Proclamation does cease to be in force then, after a period of six months from such cessation, emergency ordinances and Acts of Parliament made under Article 150 will cease to have effect.

Johnson Tan Han Seng v. *Public Prosecutor*,[91] a Federal Court decision, is an important case in so far as it confirms the above literal interpretation of Article 150. In this case one argument was that the 1969 Proclamation of Emergency and the ensuing Emergency Ordinance (under which the impugned 1975 regulations were made) had lapsed by effluxion of time. It was contended that in the seven years after 1969 circumstances had changed and the Ordinance and the Proclamation had 'outlived their purpose and must be considered repealed by effluxion of time'.[92]

This argument had been accepted by trial judge Harun J. who had followed certain U.K. decisions.

The Federal Court however was unanimous in rejecting this argument. Suffian L.P. (with whom Wan Suleiman F.J. concurred) distinguished the decisions relied on by Harun J. and felt that the law in Malaysia, England and India were similar, namely 'it is a matter for the executive to decide whether a Proclamation of Emergency should or should not be terminated, and not for the courts'.[93] After noting that the wording of the provision requires express revocation or annulment, Suffian L.P. stated 'The 1969 Proclamation has not been revoked nor annulled by Parliament. The Ordinance has not been revoked nor annulled. Therefore in my view they are still in force.'[94]

Raja Azlan Shah F.J. agreed with the reasoning and conclusion of Suffian L.P. but in his separate judgment noted that the argument was 'tantamount to saying that the Ordinance and the Proclamation can lose their force without express repeal'. This he thought could only be argued on the premise of repeal by implication which, in turn, required a showing of provisions of a later enactment so inconsistent with an earlier enactment that the two cannot stand together. He pointed out, 'It would be quite inapposite to now say that "a change of circumstances" is a later enactment.'[95]

IV. PREVENTIVE DETENTION (ARTICLE 151)

A. SCOPE OF THE PROVISION

There is no express provision in the Constitution which states that preventive detention is permissible *only* when enacted under Part XI on Emergency Powers. Article 151 purports to apply 'where any law or ordinance made or promulgated in pursuance of this Part provides for preventive detention' but does not state that preventive detention outside Part XI is prohibited. Moreover, item 3(c) of the Federal List (9th Schedule List, I) seems to suggest that there is a general power to legislate on 'Internal Security, including ... preventive detention; restriction of residence'. It could be argued that preventive detention is inherently inconsistent with Article 5 and therefore can only be saved by Article 149 or Article 150 but this is a slender argument because preventive detention can be consistent with some of the rights in Article 5.

The Reid Constitutional Commission felt that 'Preventive detention should be illegal except in so far as it may be allowed by emergency legislation'.[96] In a very rare instance of an official government publication giving an interpretative comment on the Constitution, the *Malayan Constitutional Documents* (2nd ed. Vol. 1),[97] in a footnote to Article 151 quoted this view of the Commission and added

In consequence it would appear (in view of the fact that this Part follows the provisions of the Constitution proposed by the Commission) that preventive detention can only be provided for by virtue of a law or ordinance made under this Part.[98]

Article 151 itself is very brief and its main features are first, that the detained person must be informed of the grounds for his detention; secondly, he must be told of the allegations of fact upon which the detention order is based (but facts need not be disclosed where disclosure would be against national interest); thirdly, he is to have an opportunity to make representations against the detention; fourthly, a specific provision on citizens requires representations from citizens to be considered within three months of receipt of such representations (though this period can be delayed); and, fifthly, the constitution of an advisory board for considering the representations is outlined.

B. DEVELOPMENT OF THE PROVISION BY CONSTITUTIONAL AMENDMENT

Article 151 has been amended on three occasions, first by Act 10 of 1960 with effect from 31 May 1960, secondly by Act 26 of 1963 with effect from 16 September 1963, and thirdly by Act A354 with effect from 27 August 1976.

The first amendment, by Act 10 of 1960, related to clause 1(b) and detention of citizens beyond three months. The original provision provided that the Advisory Board must report that there 'is, in its opinion, sufficient cause for the detention'. This clearly meant that if the Board did not so report no citizen could be detained beyond three months. This was in accord with the recommendation of the Reid Constitutional Commission which felt that 'In no case should a citizen be detained for more than three months unless an Advisory Board appointed by the Chief Justice has reported that there is in its opinion sufficient cause for such detention'.[99]

The 1960 amendment made a significant change when it provided that the Advisory Board was to consider the representations and 'make recommendations to the Yang di-Pertuan Agong'. This reduced the role of the Board for even if it had recommended against detention beyond three months, a citizen could still be detained since a recommendation can only be advisory.

The second amendment, by Act 26 of 1963, made changes of a nomenclature nature in the references to the judges and the courts in clause (3) in line with the changes to the judicial system effected by Act 26 of 1963.

The third amendment, by Act A354 in 1976, was of a fundamental nature and made a radical change to the hitherto cardinal principle that no citizen can be detained beyond three months unless his representations were considered and the Advisory Board had made its recommendations. The 1976 amendment now no longer linked the period of three months with the detention but instead linked it to the time period within which his representations must be considered. Furthermore, this time period could be extended. The effect of the amendment therefore completely changed the scope of clause (1)(b): citizens can now be detained beyond three months (or for that matter beyond any other period) so long as their representations (when made) are considered within three months of receipt thereof. The Malaysian Solicitor-General, writing recently on this amendment, explained it thus:[100]

This is clearly, by its very nature and terms, an amendment of an administrative nature made by the experience gained over the years in the administration of this provision. Obviously, it would be unrealistic to expect the Board to conduct any meaningful enquiry and make suitable recommendations within three months of the detention, if the detainee were to choose to make his representations, say, only two weeks before the expiry of his detention. Hence, the period was altered to one of three months after the receipt of the representations by the Advisory Board, and this would, no doubt, encourage a detainee to make his representations as early as he could.[101]

C. DEVELOPMENT THROUGH INTERPRETATION BY THE COURTS

The law on preventive detention in Malaysia has been also significantly clarified by numerous judicial decisions. The major issues dealt with in these cases will now be discussed.

1. *Judicial review of the subjective satisfaction of the detaining authority.* The Malaysian courts have consistently stated that there can be no judicial review of the subjective 'satisfaction' or decision of the executive to detain a person. The first important case is *Karam Singh* v. *Menteri Hal Ehwal Dalam Negeri, Malaysia*,[102] a Federal Court decision where all the judges felt that the executive's decision was beyond judicial review. As Suffian F.J. (as he then was) stated:

The discretion whether or not the appellant should be detained is placed in the hands of the Yang di-Pertuan Agong acting on Cabinet advice. Whether or not the facts on which the order of detention is to be based are sufficient or relevant, is a matter to be decided by the executive. In making their decision, they have complete discretion and it is not for a court of law to question the sufficiency or relevance of these allegations of fact.[103]

The non-reviewability of the executive's decision to detain was reaffirmed in two other decisions. In *Yeap Hock Seng @ Ah Seng* v. *Minister for Home Affairs, Malaysia & Ors.*,[104] a High Court decision, Eusoffe Abdoolcader J. (referring to *Karam Singh* and Indian decisions) regarded it as 'settled law' that the subjective determination of the executive is non-justiciable. And in *Re P. E. Long @ Jimmy & Ors.*,[105] a High Court decision, Arulanandom J. rejected an argument that the court had a duty to examine whether the grounds of detention are reasonable and if they are not reasonable Article 5(3) would have been violated. He held that Article 5(3) did not impose such a condition. The learned judge also held that where discretion to decide was based on the words 'reason to believe' that there are grounds to justify detention, this discretion must necessarily rest with the arresting officer and 'the courts cannot go behind the decision'.[106] (The learned judge referred, in this regard, to the Singapore decision of *Re Ong Yew Teck*.)[107]

2. *Judicial review on the ground of* mala fides. The preceding discussion must be qualified by the observation that the courts in Malaysia will exercise review where the challenge is based on the ground of *mala fides*. This is the unmistakable impression the writer has from reading *Karam Singh* v. *Menteri Hal Ehwal Dalam Negeri, Malaysia*[108] where all the Federal Court judges considered the merits of the argument of *mala fides* (in the sense of the decision having been made in a cavalier or casual manner). That the learned judges considered and decided on the *mala fides* point shows that that challenge is justiciable. (In this case it was held that the setting out of grounds of detention in the alternative did not show that the detaining authority was cavalier or casual in making the order.)

In *Yeap Hock Seng @ Ah Seng* v. *Minister for Home Affairs, Malaysia & Ors.*, Eusoffe Abdoolcader J. also entertained a claim based on *mala fides*. The learned judge pointed out that what was required to prove *mala fides* was 'proof of improper or bad motive ... and not mere suspicion'[109] and that what has to be made out is not lack of *bona fides* on the part of the police but the want of *bona fides* of the detaining authority 'as well as the non-application of mind on the part of the detaining authority which for this purpose must be taken to be different from the police'.[110]

In any case, as pointed out by Abdoolcader J. in *Yeap Hock Seng*, the onus of proving *mala fides* 'is normally extremely difficult to discharge ...'.[111]

It ought to be observed that the Malaysian judicial approach is different from that in Singapore. In Singapore, the case of *Lee Mau*

Seng v. *Minister for Home Affairs, Singapore & Anor.*[112] held that *mala fides* or bad faith (in the sense of deciding 'without exercising care, caution and sense of responsibility and in a casual and cavalier manner or on vague, irrelevant or incorrect grounds and facts') is *not* justiciable. The learned Chief Justice held it could not be justiciable in the context of the Internal Security Act which vested subjective determination in the executive and he felt that if it was justiciable it would lead to the court substituting the executive's decision with its own decision. The non-justiciability of *mala fides* in Singapore was reiterated in *Wee Toon Lip & Ors.* v. *The Minister for Home Affairs, Singapore & Anor.*[113]

3. *Existence of judicial review whether grounds of detention are within scope of the statute.* Although, as seen, there can be no judicial review of the subjective decision of the executive, it would be incorrect to conclude that judicial review is altogether absent in the area of preventive detention. There are three cases which indicate there can be judicial review to examine whether the grounds of detention as stated in the order are within the scope of the enabling legislation.

In *Yeap Hock Seng @ Ah Seng* v. *Minister for Home Affairs, Malaysia & Ors.,*[114] Abdoolcader J., after stating that the subjective determination of the executive is not justiciable, went on to say that the court 'can examine the grounds disclosed by the Minister to see they are relevant to the object which the Ordinance prescribes'[115] but added the caveat that in doing this the court does not examine the truth or adequacy of these materials.

Abdoolcader J. had occasion to elaborate on this in *Re Application of Tan Boon Liat & Ors.*[116] This case concerned an emergency ordinance, the Emergency (Public Order and Prevention of Crime) Ordinance 1969 which, *inter alia,* provided for preventive detention where the Minister was satisfied such detention was necessary 'to prevent any person from acting in any manner prejudicial to public order ... for the suppression of violence or the prevention of crimes involving violence'. The detainee had been detained under this provision but was informed that the ground of detention was that he was an active member of an international drug distribution syndicate.

Abdoolcader J. felt that

... it is open to the courts, in determining the validity of any order of preventive detention, to consider whether the grounds of detention fall within the scope of the law.... An order of detention based on irrelevant grounds is invalid and if any of the grounds furnished to the detenu are found to be irrelevant while considering the application of the relevant legislation under which the detention is ordered and in that sense foreign thereto, *the satisfaction of the detaining authority on which the order of detention is based is open to challenge and the detention order liable to be quashed.*[117]

After detailed examination, Abdoolcader J. (employing this test) concluded that it was abundantly clear that trafficking in drugs as a member of an international syndicate 'strikes at the very core of public order and any person indulging in such activities must necessarily be acting in a manner prejudicial to public order'.[118]

The identical issue, concerning the same statute, arose in *Re P. E. Long @ Jimmy & Ors.*[119] and Arulanandom J. (like Abdoolcader J.) seems to have considered it permissible to review whether the grounds stated in the detention order are within the scope of the statute.

Both Abdoolcader J.'s and Arulanandom J.'s decisions were upheld by the Federal Court.[120] The Federal Court quoted extensively from Abdoolcader J.'s judgment and agreed with him that the detention 'came within the scope and ambit of the Ordinance'.

It may indeed be a fine line to distinguish between reviewing the 'relevance' of grounds to see if they come within the scope of the Act and, on the other hand, non-justiciability of the relevance of grounds to review the subjective decision of the executive. But the distinction can be made as the above-mentioned cases show.

4. *Existence of judicial review on the ground of failure to comply with fundamental conditions.* The recent Federal Court decision in *Re Tan Boon Liat @ Allen & Anor. et al.*[121] is also important in that it demonstrates that courts will exercise judicial review in preventive detention where certain fundamental conditions (especially those in Article 151 itself) are not met. In this case (different from that of the same name discussed in the immediately preceding section 3), the detention of citizens had extended beyond three months; though they made representations within the three-month period, the Advisory Board made its recommendations only after this period. It was argued that this contravened Article 151(1)(b) [as unamended] and rendered the detention invalid.

The Federal Court (consisting of a full bench of five judges), reversing the judgments of trial judges Abdul Hamid J. and Arulanandom J., held that the detention was unlawful. Suffian L.P. noted that Article 151(1)(b) did not expressly say that the Board must expressly act within the three-month period but felt that the words 'has considered' implied that the Board's intervention was a 'prerequisite'. He held that Article 151(1)(b) was not just procedural but a substantive fundamental condition precedent.[122] Detention was not lawful if this condition precedent was not satisfied.

Likewise Lee Hun Hoe C.J. (Borneo)[123] held that Article 151(1)(b)'s requirements were conditions and that in failing to perform its obligations the Advisory Board had not acted in accordance with law. Ong Hock Sim F.J. (with whom Gill C.J. (Malaya) and Ali F.J. concurred) felt that regardless of whether the provision laid down the law or procedure 'in either case, the provisions are clearly mandatory'. The law as such was violated.[124]

Exclusionary clauses: It should be noted that in this case the Government contended that the detention could not be reviewed because, under the Ordinance, it was provided that the Yang di-Pertuan Agong's decision was 'final and shall not be called into question in any court'. However, Suffian L.P. said this exclusionary provision applied only to 'real decisions and not to *ultra vires* decisions'[125] and cited *Anisminic Ltd.* v. *Foreign Compensation Commission*.[126] Ong Hock Sim F.J. was of a similar view.

Although Article 151(1)(b) has now been amended, it is submitted that the importance of this case is in no way diminished for it can be taken as authority for the proposition that if there has been a breach of fundamental conditions (which, it is submitted, can be conditions in the statute also) the courts can exercise review and the detention may be held unlawful.

5. *Judicial review of the sufficiency of particulars/allegations of fact for the purpose of making representations*. Some Indian cases have held that if the particulars supplied to the detainee are vague, insufficient and irrelevant and therefore prevented him from effectively making representations, this could make the detention unlawful. Such an argument (based on Indian decisions) was made in *Karam Singh* v. *Menteri Hal Ehwal Dalam Negeri, Malaysia*[127] but the Federal Court held that the vagueness, etc. of the allegations of fact did not relate back to the order of detention and could not render the detention (under a valid order) unlawful.

Indeed Suffian F.J. (as he then was), (with whom Azmi L.P. agreed on this point) thought that the sufficiency of the allegations of fact for the purpose of making representations was not justiciable. Following the reasoning of dissenting Sastri J. in the Indian decision of *State of Bombay* v. *Atma Ram*,[128] Suffian F.J. felt that where the subjective nature of preventive detention power excluded judicial inquiry into the sufficiency of the grounds to justify the detention,

... it would be wholly inconsistent to hold that it would be open to the court to examine the sufficiency of the same grounds to enable the person detained to make representations. Indeed the logical result ... would be to invalidate section 8 of the Internal Security Act in so far as it purports to make the satisfaction of the Government the sole condition of a lawful detention.[129]

The learned judge distinguished the Indian cases on two grounds.[130] First, on the ground that in India, preventive detention powers were often exercisable by civil servants who had to be closely scrutinized, and secondly, Article 21 of the Indian Constitution provided that 'no person shall be deprived of his life or personal liberty except according to procedure established by law' whereas the Malaysian Article 5(1) made no mention of procedure.

This writer has elsewhere queried this second ground and asked 'Could not the Malaysian Article 5(1) be regarded as broader (and not narrower) than the Indian Article 21? Is it not a reasonable interpretation of Malaysia's Article 5(1) to view the wording 'in accordance with law' to cover both the procedural and substantive requirements of law?'[131] It is interesting that in the recent case of *Re Tan Boon Liat @ Allen & Anor. et al.*,[132] Lee Hun Hoe C.J. (Borneo) also thought the Malaysian provision 'is wide enough to cover procedure as well.... If the expression "in accordance with law" were to be construed as to exclude procedure then it would make nonsense of Article 5'.[133] He tried to explain Suffian F.J.'s distinction in *Karam Singh* and thought Suffian F.J. 'did not say that procedure was not part of the law'. However, in *Re Tan Boon Liat @ Allen* Suffian L.P. himself recalled that in *Karam Singh* 'I drew a distinction between law and procedure and said in effect that the courts will take a serious view of failure to comply with substantive law but not of failure to comply with procedural law'.[134] He did not modify his position and in that case held Article 151(1)(b) to be 'not just procedural' but substantive.

6. *Whether preventive detention subsequent to criminal proceedings violates Article 7.* The courts have held that the fact that preventive detention was instituted after criminal proceedings does not amount to contravention of Article 7.

In *Public Prosecutor* v. *Musa*,[135] a High Court decision, Syed Othman J. pointed out that Article 7 envisages a trial before a court and that preventive detention based on the subjective satisfaction of the Minister was not a conviction for an offence or crime and the detention order was not punishment for the purpose of Article 7.

Similarly in *Yeap Hock Seng @·Ah Seng* v. *Minister for Home Affairs, Malaysia & Ors.*[136] Abdoolcader J. held that the executive's satisfaction was neither a prosecution nor a trial and noted that 'Indeed the very essence of preventive detention is incarceration without benefit of a prosecution or trial and with no offence proved nor any charge formulated or preferred'.[137]

APPENDIX

DEVELOPMENT OF THE CONSTITUTIONAL PROVISIONS ON EMERGENCY POWERS

Provisions Recommended by 1957 Constitutional Commission.

137.—(1) Subject to the provisions of this Article, if an Act of Parliament recites that action has been taken or threatened by any substantial body of persons, whether inside or outside the Federation, to cause, or to cause any substantial number of citizens to fear, organized violence against persons or property, any provision of such Act designed to stop such action or meet such threat shall be lawful notwithstanding that it is repugnant to any of the provisions of Articles 5, 9, 10, 68 or 73.

(2) Any Act of Parliament to which clause (1) applies shall cease to operate on the expiration of a period of one year from the date of the enactment thereof, without prejudice to the power of Parliament to renew such Act in accordance with the provisions of this Article.

Provisions of the Constitution as they originally stood on Merdeka Day.

149. (1) If an Act of Parliament recites that action has been taken or threatened by any substantial body of persons, whether inside or outside the Federation, to cause, or to cause a substantial number of citizens to fear, organized violence against persons or property, any provision of that law designed to stop or prevent that action is valid notwithstanding that it is inconsistent with any of the provisions of Article 5, 9, or 10, or would apart from this Article be outside the legislative power of Parliament; and Article 79 shall not apply to a Bill for such an Act or any amendment to such a Bill.

(2) A law containing such a recital as is mentioned in Clause (1) shall, if not sooner repealed, cease to have effect on the expiration of a period of one year from the date on which it comes into operation, without prejudice to the power of Parliament to make a new law under this Article.

Provisions of the Constitution as amended and as they stand presently at time of writing (December 1977).

149. (1) If an Act of Parliament recites that action has been taken or threatened by any substantial body of persons, whether inside or outside the Federation—

(a) to cause, or to cause a substantial number of citizens to fear, organized violence against persons or property; or

(b) to excite disaffection against the Yang di-Pertuan Agong or any Government in the Federation; or

(c) to promote feelings of ill-will and hostility between different races or other classes of the population likely to cause violence; or

(d) to procure the alteration, otherwise than by lawful means, of anything by law established; or

(e) which is prejudicial to the security of the Federation or any part thereof,

any provision of that law designed to stop or prevent that action is valid notwithstanding that it is inconsistent with any of the provisions of Article 5, 9 or 10, or would apart from this Article be outside that legislative power of Parliament; and Article 79 shall not apply to a Bill for such an Act or any amendment to such a Bill.

(2) A law containing such a recital as is mentioned in Clause (1) shall, if not sooner repealed, cease to have effect if resolutions are passed by both Houses of Parliament annulling such law, but without prejudice to anything previously done by virtue thereof or to the power of Parliament to make a new law under this Article.

138.—(1) If the Federal Government is satisfied that a grave emergency exists whereby the security or economic life of the Federation or of any part thereof is threatened, whether by war or external aggression or internal disturbance, the Yang di-Pertuan Besar may issue a Proclamation of Emergency, in this Article referred to as a Proclamation.

(2) When a Proclamation is issued in accordance with the provisions of clause (1), if Parliament is not sitting it shall be the duty of the Yang di-Pertuan Besar to summon Parliament as soon as may be practicable.

(3) A Proclamation shall be laid before both Houses of Parliament and, if not sooner revoked, shall cease to operate at the expiration of a period of two months from the date of its issue unless, before the expiration of that period, it has been approved by resolutions in both Houses of Parliament.

150. (1) If the Yang di-Pertuan Agong is satisfied that a grave emergency exists whereby the security or economic life of the Federation or of any part thereof is threatened, whether by war or external aggression or internal disturbance, he may issue a Proclamation of Emergency.

(2) If a Proclamation of Emergency is issued when Parliament is not sitting, the Yang di-Pertuan Agong shall summon Parliament as soon as may be practicable, and may, until both Houses of Parliament are sitting, promulgate ordinances having the force of law, if satisfied that immediate action is required.

(3) A Proclamation of Emergency and any ordinance promulgated under Clause (2) shall be laid before both Houses of Parliament and, if not sooner revoked, shall cease to be in force—

150. (1) If the Yang di-Pertuan Agong is satisfied that a grave emergency exists whereby the security or economic life of the Federation or of any part thereof is threatened, he may issue a Proclamation of Emergency.

(2) If a Proclamation of Emergency is issued when Parliament is not sitting, the Yang di-Pertuan Agong shall summon Parliament as soon as may be practicable, and may, until both Houses of Parliament are sitting, promulgate ordinances having the force of law, if satisfied that immediate action is required.

(3) A Proclamation of Emergency and any ordinance promulgated under Clause (2) shall be laid before both Houses of Parliament and, if not sooner revoked, shall cease to have effect if resolutions are passed by both Houses annulling such Proclamation or ordinance, but without prejudice to anything previously done by virtue thereof or to the power of the Yang di-Pertuan Agong to

Provisions Recommended by 1957 Constitutional Commission.	*Provisions of the Constitution as they originally stood on Merdeka Day.*	*Provisions of the Constitution as amended and as they stand presently at time of writing (December 1977).*
		issue a new Proclamation under Clause (1) or promulgate any ordinance under Clause (2).
	(a) a Proclamation at the expiration of a period of two months beginning with the date on which it was issued; and	
	(b) an ordinance at the expiration of a period of fifteen days beginning with the date on which both Houses are first sitting,	
	unless, before the expiration of that period, it has been approved by a resolution of each House of Parliament.	
(4) While a Proclamation is in operation, notwithstanding anything in this Constitution—	(4) While a Proclamation of Emergency is in force the executive authority of the Federation shall, notwithstanding anything in this Constitution, extend to any matter within the legislative authority of a State and to the giving of directions to the Government of a State or to any officer or authority thereof.	(4) While a Proclamation of Emergency is in force the executive authority of the Federation shall, notwithstanding anything in this Constitution, extend to any matter within the legislative authority of a State and to the giving of directions to the Government of a State or to any officer or authority thereof.
(a) the executive authority of the Federation shall extend to any of the matters within the legislative authority of a State and to the giving of directions to the Government of a State or to any officer or authority thereof;	(5) While a Proclamation of Emergency is in force Parliament may, notwithstanding anything in this Constitution, make laws with respect to any matter enumerated in the State List (other than any matter of Muslim law or the custom of the Malays), extend the duration of Parliament or of a State Legislature, suspend any election, and make any provision consequential upon or incidental to any provision made in pursuance of this clause.	(5) Subject to Clause (6A), while a Proclamation of Emergency is in force, Parliament may, notwithstanding anything in this Constitution *or in the Constitution of the State of Sarawak,* * make laws with respect to any matter, if it appears to Parliament that the law is required by reason of the emergency; and Article 79 shall not apply to a Bill for such a law or an amendment to such a Bill, nor shall any provision of this Constitution or of any written law which requires any consent or concurrence to the passing of a law or any con-
(b) the legislative authority of Parliament shall extend to—		
(i) any matter within the exclusive legislative authority of a State;		
(ii) the extension of the maximum duration of Parliament or of a State Legislature, the suspension of any election required by or under this Constitution or the Constitution of any State, and the making of any provision conse-	(6) No provision of any law or ordinance	

quential upon or incidental thereto; and

(c) if and so long as either House of Parliament is not sitting and the Federal Government is satisfied that existing circumstances require immediate action, the Yang di-Pertuan Besar shall have power to promulgate ordinances having the force of law.

(5) Any provision of an Act of Parliament enacted while a Proclamation is in force shall be valid notwithstanding that it is repugnant to any provision of Part II.

(6) Any provision of an Act of Parliament which would, but for the provisions of this Article, be invalid shall cease to have effect on the expiration of a period of six months after the Proclamation has ceased to operate, except as to things done or omitted to be done before the expiration of the said period.

(7) An ordinance promulgated under this Article shall have the same force and effect as an Act of Parliament, but every such ordinance—

(a) shall be laid before both Houses of Parliament and shall cease to operate at the expiration of fifteen days from the reassembly of both Houses unless before the

made or promulgated in pursuance of this Article shall be invalid on the ground of any inconsistency with the provisions of Part II, and Article 79 shall not apply to any Bill for such a law or any amendment to such a Bill.

(7) At the expiration of a period of six months beginning with the date on which a Proclamation of Emergency ceases to be in force, any ordinance promulgated in pursuance of the Proclamation and, to the extent that it could not have been validly made but for this Article, any law made while the Proclamation was in force, shall cease to have effect, except as to things done or omitted to be done before the expiration of that period.

sultation with respect thereto, or which restricts the coming into force of a law after it is passed or the presentation of a Bill to the Yang di-Pertuan Agong for his assent.

(6) Subject to Clause (6A), no provision of any ordinance promulgated under this Article, and no provision of any Act of Parliament which is passed while a Proclamation of Emergency is in force and which declares that the law appears to Parliament to be required by reason of the emergency, shall be invalid on the ground of inconsistency with any provision of this Constitution *or of the Constitution of the State of Sarawak.**

(6A) Clause (5) shall not extend the powers of Parliament with respect to any matter of Muslim law or the custom of the Malays, or with respect to any matter of native law or custom in a Borneo State; nor shall Clause (6) validate any provision inconsistent with the provisions of this Constitution relating to any such matter or relating to religion, citizenship, or language.

*Temporary amendment vide Act 68/1966 w.e.f. 20.9.1966 which will cease to have effect six months after the date on which the Proclamation of Emergency of 14.9.1966 (P.U. 339A/1966) ceases to have effect.

Provisions Recommended by 1957 Constitutional Commission.	*Provisions of the Constitution as they originally stood on Merdeka Day.*	*Provisions of the Constitution as amended and as they stand presently at time of writing (December 1977).*
expiration of that period it is approved by resolution in both Houses, and (b) may be withdrawn at any time by the Yang di-Pertuan Besar. (8) Where a Proclamation relates to a part only of the Federation, the expression 'State' in this Article means a State wholly or partially within that part.		(7) At the expiration of a period of six months beginning with the date on which a Proclamation of Emergency ceases to be in force, any ordinance promulgated in pursuance of the Proclamation and, to the extent that it could not have been validly made but for this Article, any law made while the Proclamation was in force, shall cease to have effect, except as to things done or omitted to be done before the expiration of that period.
139.—(1) Where any law in force under this Part provides for preventive detention, no citizen of Malaya shall be detained under such law for a period longer than three months unless an advisory board, consisting of three persons who are or have been or are qualified to be judges of the Supreme Court, and are appointed by the Chief Justice, has reported before the expiration of the said period of three months, after considering any representation made in accordance with clause (2), that there is, in its opinion, sufficient cause for such detention. (2) When any person is detained in pursuance of an order made under any law providing for preventive detention, the authority making the order shall, as soon as may be, communicate to such person the grounds		**151.** (1) Where any law or ordinance made or promulgated in pursuance of this Part provides for preventive detention— (a) the authority on whose order any person is detained under that law or ordinance shall, as soon as may be, inform him of the grounds for his detention and, subject to Clause (3), the allegations of fact on which the order is based, and shall give him the opportunity of making representations against the order as soon as may be; (b) no citizen shall continue to be detained under that law or ordinance unless an advisory board constituted as mentioned in Clause (2) has considered any representations made by him under paragraph (a) and has reported, before the expiration of that period, that	**151.** (1) Where any law or ordinance made or promulgated in pursuance of this Part provides for preventive detention— (a) the authority on whose order any person is detained under that law or ordinance shall, as soon as may be, inform him of the grounds for his detention and, subject to Clause (3), the allegations of fact on which the order is based, and shall give him the opportunity of making representations against the order as soon as may be; (b) no citizen shall continue to be detained under that law or ordinance unless an advisory board constituted as mentioned in Clause (2) has considered any representations made by him under paragraph (a) and made recommendations thereon to the Yang di-Pertuan Agong within three months of receiving such

thereof together with the allegations of fact upon which the order is based and shall afford him the earliest opportunity of making a representation against the order:

Provided that the said authority may refuse to disclose facts whose disclosure would be, in the opinion of the authority, against the national interest.

there is in its opinion sufficient cause for the detention.

(2) An advisory board constituted for the purposes of this Article shall consist of a chairman, who shall be appointed by the Yang di-Pertuan Agong from among persons who are or have been judges of the Supreme Court or are qualified to be judges of the Supreme Court, and two other members, who shall be appointed by the Yang di-Pertuan Agong after consultation with the Chief Justice or, if at the time another judge of the Supreme Court is acting for the Chief Justice, after consultation with that judge.

(3) This Article does not require any authority to disclose facts whose disclosure would in its opinion be against the national interest.

representations, or within such longer period as the Yang di-Pertuan Agong may allow.

(2) An advisory board constituted for the purposes of this Article shall consist of a chairman, who shall be appointed by the Yang di-Pertuan Agong and who shall be or have been, or be qualified to be, a judge of the Federal Court or a High Court, or shall before Malaysia Day have been a judge of the Supreme Court, and two other members, who shall be appointed by the Yang di-Pertuan Agong after consultation with the Lord President of the Federal Court.

(3) This Article does not require any authority to disclose facts whose disclosure would in its opinion be against the national interest.

1. In the discussion of judicial decisions in this article, the latest issue of the *Malayan Law Journal* consulted was the issue for December 1977. Cases reported after [1977] 2 M.L.J. 265 are not covered in the discussion.

For a selection of writings wholly or partially dealing with emergency powers in Malaysia, see 1. Low Hop Bing, '*Habeas Corpus* in Malaysia and Singapore' [1977] 2 M.L.J. 1v; 2. M. P. Jain, 'Development of Administrative Law in Malaysia since Merdeka' [1977] 2 M.L.J. ms *ii*; 3. Tan Sri Dato Haji Mohamed Salleh bin Abas, 'Amendment of the Malaysian Constitution' [1977] 2 M.L.J. ms *xxxiv*; 4. Tun Mohamed Suffian, *An Introduction to the Constitution of Malaysia*, 2nd ed. (1976), Chapter 15; 5. S. Jayakumar, *Constitutional Law* (No. 1, *Singapore Law Series*, 1976), Chapter 12; 6. Tan Sri Ong Hock Thye, 'Is the 1969 State of Emergency Still an Existing Fact?' Vol. IX, No. 3 (1976) INSAF 3; 7. R. H. Hickling, 'The Prerogative in Malaysia' (1975) 17 Mal. L.R. 207; 8. S. Jayakumar, 'Emergency Powers in Malaysia: can the Yang di-Pertuan Agong act in his personal discretion and capacity?' (1976) 18 Mal. L.R. 149; 9. Param Cumaraswamy, 'Essential (Security Cases) Regulations 1975—Is the Rule of Law in Jeopardy', paper presented to the Third Malaysian Law Conference, K.L., October 1975; 10. S. Jayakumar, 'Legal Aspects of Emergency Powers in Malaysia' (1969) 2 *Commentary* 17; 11. V. Sinnadurai, 'Proclamation of Emergency—Reviewable?' (1968) 10 Mal. L.R. 130; 12. S. Jayakumar, 'Constitutional Limitations on Legislative Powers in Malaysia' (1967) 9 Mal. L.R. 96; 13. L. W. Athulathmudali, 'Preventive Detention in the Federation of Malaya' (1961) 3 *Journal of the International Commission of Jurists* 100.

2. *Report of the Federation of Malaya Constitutional Commission 1957*, London H.M.S.O. Colonial No. 330.

3. Ibid., para. 173.

4. Ibid., para. 172.

5. Ibid., para. 174, emphasis added.

6. [1971] 2 M.L.J. 137.

7. Article 150(1).

8. Article 150(6).

9. Article 150(6A).

10. Article 150(2).

11. Article 150(4).

12. Article 150(5).

13. Article 150(6A).

14. Para. 175, Commission's Report, see footnote 2.

15. See footnote 6.

16. This wording followed the draft recommended by the Constitutional Commission.

17. P.U. 339A/66.

18. *Stephen Kalong Ningkan* v. *The Government of Malaysia* [1968] 1 M.L.J. 119 (*per* Lord President Barakbah and Azmi C.J. (Malaya)); *Public Prosecutor* v. *Ooi Kee Saik & Ors.* [1971] 2 M.L.J. 108 (*per* Raja Azlan Shah J. at p. 113).

19. (a) Ong Hock Thye F.J. in *Stephen Kalong Ningkan* v. *The Government of Malaysia* [1968] 1 M.L.J. 119 at p. 128; and (b) R. H. Hickling, 'The Prerogative in Malaysia' (1975) 17 Mal. L.R. 207.

20. S. Jayakumar, 'Emergency Powers in Malaysia: can the Yang di-Pertuan Agong act in his personal discretion and capacity?' (1976) 18 Mal. L.R. 149.

21. [1968] 1 M.L.J. 119.

22. Ibid. at p. 122.

23. [1967] 1 M.L.J. 46.

24. Ibid. at p. 46.

25. [1968] 2 M.L.J. 238.

26. Ibid. at p. 240.

27. [1975] 2 M.L.J. 286.

28. For another judicial pronouncement where the judge felt that the Yang di-Pertuan Agong acts on advice see Ong Hock Thye F.J.'s dissenting judgment in *Stephen Kalong Ningkan* v. *The Government of Malaysia* [1968] 1 M.L.J. 119 at p. 128.

29. Ibid.

30. [1967] 1 M.L.J. 46.

31. [1931] L.R. 58 I.A. 169.

32. [1945] A.C. 14.

33. [1962] 2 Q.B. 243.

34. [1942] A.C. 206.

35. [1967] 1 M.L.J. 46 at p. 47.

36. [1968] 1 M.L.J. 119.

37. See footnote 31.

38. [1968] 2 M.L.J. 238.

39. Ibid. at p. 242.

40. [1971] 2 M.L.J. 108. Although the Federal Court, on appeal, held the trial to be a nullity on a technical point, the Federal Court did not disapprove the learned judge's views on emergency powers. This writer, therefore, considers Raja Azlan Shah J.'s views to be still helpful when reviewing the case-law and will, consequently, make references to the case whenever appropriate.

41. Ibid. at p. 113.

42. [1967] 1 M.L.J. 46.

43. [1945] A.C. 14.

44. [1967] 1 M.L.J. 46 at p. 47.

45. [1968] 1 M.L.J. 119.

46. Ibid. at p. 124.

47. [1967] 1 M.L.J. 46 at p. 48.

48. [1968] 1 M.L.J. 119 at p. 128.

49. [1968] 2 M.L.J. 238 at p. 241.

50. Ibid. at p. 242.

51. Ibid.

52. [1975] 2 M.L.J. 286. Also see *Public Prosecutor* v. *Khong Teng Khen & Anor.* [1976] 2 M.L.J. 166 (F.C.) *per* Suffian L.P. at p. 169: '... if Parliament is not sitting, then the executive in the person of His Majesty (acting on responsible advice) may promulgate Ordinances having the force of law....'

53. Ibid. at p. 289.

54. [1971] 2 M.L.J. 108. See footnote 40.

55. [1977] 2 M.L.J. 66.

56. Ibid. at p. 75.

57. [1966] 1 M.L.J. 18. This writer has criticized the decision in his article 'Constitutional Limitations on Legislative Powers in Malaysia' (1967) 9 Mal. L.R. 96.

58. Ibid. at p. 21.

59. [1968] 2 M.L.J. 137.

60. Ibid. at p. 139.

61. [1975] 2 M.L.J. 155.

62. Ibid. at p. 161.

63. See also (a) *Public Prosecutor* v. *Ooi Kee Saik & Ors.* [1971] 2 M.L.J. 108, where Raja Azlan Shah J. rejected the argument that only Parliament could legislate emergency laws and that any legislative power assigned to the executive was an abrogation by Parliament of its power to legislate, and (b) *N. Madhavan Nair* v. *Government of Malaysia* [1975] 2 M.L.J. 286, where Chang Min Tat J. dismissed contentions that the Yang di-Pertuan Agong could not make essential regulations, on the authority of the *Osman* and *Eng Keock Cheng* cases.

64. [1976] 2 M.L.J. 166.

65. Ibid. at p. 170.

66. [1977] 2 M.L.J. 66.

67. [1976] 2 M.L.J. 166.

68. [1971] 2 M.L.J. 108. See footnote 40.

69. Ibid. at p. 133.

70. [1971] 2 M.L.J. 281.

71. Ibid. at p. 283.

72. [1971] 2 M.L.J. 108. See footnote 40.

73. Ibid. at p. 113.

74. [1975] 2 M.L.J. 235.

75. Ibid. at p. 237.

76. [1976] 2 M.L.J. 166.

77. Ibid. at p. 169.

78. Ibid. at p. 172.

79. [1971] 2 M.L.J. 108. See footnote 40.

80. [1951] 83 C.L.R. 1, 178-9.

81. [1971] 2 M.L.J. 108 at p. 114.

82. Ibid.

83. [1975] 2 M.L.J. 287 expressly approved by the Federal Court in *Public Prosecutor* v. *Khong Teng Khen & Anor.* [1976] 2 M.L.J. 166 at pp. 169 and 171.

84. [1968] 1 M.L.J. 119.

85. Ibid. at p. 125.

86. [1968] 2 M.L.J. 238.

87. Ibid. at p. 243.

88. Ibid.

89. Ibid. at p. 244.

90. The four Proclamations are:
     (a) the 1964 Proclamation applicable throughout the Federation (L.N. 271/3.9.1964),
     (b) the 1966 Proclamation applicable only to Sarawak (P.U. 339A/ 14.9.1966),
     (c) the 1969 Proclamation applicable throughout the Federation (P.U. (A) 145/15.5.1969), and,
     (d) the 1977 Proclamation applicable only to Kelantan (P.U. (A) 358/ 8.11.1977).

91. [1977] 2 M.L.J. 66, cited in *Public Prosecutor* v. *Phung Chin Hock* [1977] 2 M.L.J. 261. For a contrary view, see Tan Sri Ong Hock Thye, 'Is the 1969 State of Emergency Still an Existing Fact?' Vol. IX, No. 3 (1976) INSAF 3.

92. This summary of the argument is from the judgment of Raja Azlan Shah F.J.

93. [1977] 2 M.L.J. 66 at p. 69.

94. Ibid. at p. 68.

95. Ibid. at p. 73.

96. *Report of the Constitutional Commission* (see footnote 2), at para. 176.

97. Published by Government Printer, 1962.

98. At page 115.

99. *Report of the Constitutional Commission*, at para. 176.

100. Tan Sri Dato Haji Mohamed Salleh bin Abas, 'Amendment of the Malaysian Constitution' in [1977] 2 M.L.J. Suppl. ms *xxxiv* at p. *xl*.

101. The Solicitor-General added, 'The flexibility of granting discretion to His Majesty to extend this period is desirable from practical considerations. It would, for example, assist in meeting those cases where it would take time for the detainee to compile his representations and have them presented to the Advisory Board, as well as those cases where the Advisory Board may need a somewhat longer time to consider the representations, such as, by seeking further material and particulars to come to a fair decision with regard to the matters raised in the representations.'

102. [1969] 2 M.L.J. 129 at p. 136.

103. Ibid. at p. 151.

104. [1975] 2 M.L.J. 279.

105. [1976] 2 M.L.J. 133.

106. Ibid. at p. 135.

107. [1960] M.L.J. 67.

108. [1969] 2 M.L.J. 129.

109. [1975] 2 M.L.J. 279 at p. 284.

110. Ibid. at p. 108.

111. Ibid. at p. 109.

112. [1971] 2 M.L.J. 137.

113. [1972] 2 M.L.J. 46.

114. [1975] 2 M.L.J. 279.

115. Ibid. at p. 282.

116. [1976] 2 M.L.J. 83, upheld by Federal Court in [1977] 2 M.L.J. 18. This case should not be confused with another case also involving the same party, *Re Tan Boon Liat @ Allen & Anor. et al* [1977] 1 M.L.J. 39 the appeal from which was allowed by Federal Court in [1977] 2 M.L.J. 108. This second case is discussed, *infra*, (4: Existence of judicial review on the ground of failure to comply with fundamental conditions).

117. Ibid. at p. 84 (emphasis added).

118. Ibid. at p. 88.

119. [1976] 2 M.L.J. 133. The learned judge also concluded that it is 'clear that securing public order covers suppression of crimes which endanger the safety of the people and cause harm to society.... Detention of persons found to be trafficking in drugs is therefore well within the scope of the Ordinance as it is a notorious fact that the trafficking in drugs causes serious harm and destroys the body politic not only nationally but also internationally.' (p. 137.)

120. [1977] 2 M.L.J. 18.

121. [1977] 2 M.L.J. 108.

122. Ibid. at p. 109.

123. Ibid. at p. 114.

124. Ibid. at p. 115.

125. Ibid. at p. 109.

126. [1969] A.C. 147. See also Abdoolcader J.'s judgment in *Mak Sik Kwong* v. *Minister of Home Affairs, Malaysia (No. 2)* [1975] 2 M.L.J. 175.

127. [1969] 2 M.L.J. 129.

128. A.I.R. 1951 S.C. 157.

129. [1969] 2 M.L.J. 129 at p. 150.

130. On the relevance of Indian decisions in respect of preventive detention see also the judgment of Ong Hock Thye C.J. (Malaya) in the same case (at p. 141). 'Broadly speaking, Malaysia has more in common with England than with India in so far as problems of preventive detention are concerned. For one thing, like England, Malaysia is compact.... Multiracial though our society is in Malaysia there are no two views regarding subversion ... India on the other hand is a vast subcontinent by itself and people do think differently who are thousands of miles apart having divergent interest.... English courts take a more realistic view of things while Indian judges ... impress me as indefatigable idealists seeking valiantly to reconcile the irreconcilable whenever good conscience is pricked by an abuse of executive powers.' Contra *Yeap Hock Seng @ Ah Seng* v. *Minister for Home Affairs, Malaysia & Ors.* [1975] 2 M.L.J. 279 (*per* Abdoolcader J.). 'Our Constitution and laws providing for preventive detention have been primarily drawn from Indian sources, and accordingly, decisions of ... the Supreme Court of India and indeed also of the High Courts of her several States are of great persuasive authority here upon the borrowed provisions ... where there is a dearth of local authority, the Indian decisions are entitled to the greatest respect and will normally be followed unless the court has cause to disagree with the reasoning of any such decision.'

131. *Constitutional Law Cases from Malaysia and Singapore*, 2nd ed., Malayan Law Journal (1976) at p. 435, 'Notes and Questions'; also in 1st ed. at p. 424.

132. [1977] 2 M.L.J. 108.

133. Ibid. at p. 114.

134. Ibid. at p. 109.

135. [1970] 1 M.L.J. 101.

136. [1975] 2 M.L.J. 279.

137. Ibid. at p. 285.

⇻ H. P. LEE

15. The Process of Constitutional Change in Malaysia

INTRODUCTION

HERMAN FINER[1] once defined 'constitution' in terms of its process of amendment for, in his view, to amend is to 'deconstitute and reconstitute'. The learned author added that the amending clause is so fundamental to a constitution that he was tempted to call it the constitution itself. The importance of the amendment process is particularly highlighted in respect of the Constitution of Malaysia which has often been characterized as a document 'so painstakingly negotiated and agreed upon by the major races in Malaysia'.[2]

The Reid Commission[3] which was entrusted with the task of drawing up the draft constitution on which the new Federation of Malaya in 1957 was to regulate itself, adopted many of the recommendations of the Alliance Party. These recommendations were the product of intensive negotiations and bargaining among the components of the Alliance Party, a coalition of three parties representing the three major races in the country.[4] The Constitution embodies the terms which had been arrived at by three contracting parties to an agreement. It could be asserted that the Constitution is like a 'contract' and therefore the original 'terms' as initially bargained should not be lightly varied through the employment of the amendment process. From this viewpoint, amendments to the Malaysian Constitution assume fundamental significance.

The Constitution of Malaysia is still comparatively 'young' but since 1957 it has been amended on no less than twenty-three occasions.[5] From a conspectus of all the changes which have been effected to the Malaysian Constitution from 1957 to 1977 one would have to arrive inevitably at the conclusion that the Malaysian Constitution has been altered extensively in both major and minor aspects.[6] An analysis of the more fundamental amendments will point indubitably to a truncation of safeguards which had been considered by the Reid Commission as vital for the growth of a viable democratic nation. In subscribing to the adage that a constitution which cannot bend will ultimately be broken, one must also be aware of a constitution which is extremely easy to amend for it may turn out to be worse than having no constitution at all.[7] The frequency of amendments and the deviations from so many of the Reid Commission's recommendations give rise to a query regarding the nature and efficacy of the amendment process under the Malaysian Constitution.

The cornerstone of a constitution lies in its amendment process and a conflict of views will always prevail over how amendable a constitution ought to be and what the model formula for the amendment process should be. It is submitted that the formula should be devised according to the needs and peculiar circumstances of a country. In drawing up the formula embodied in Article 159 of the Federal Constitution, the Reid Commission stated that the method of amending the Malaysian Constitution should not be too difficult as to produce frustration nor too easy as to weaken seriously the safeguards of the Constitution.[8] In Part I of this essay I propose to examine whether these aims of the Reid Commission have been vitiated in the light of various amendments which have been effected to the Malaysian Constitution from 1957 to 1977. Particular emphasis is placed on the Constitution (Amendment) Act, 1971.[9] In Part II, I shall comment briefly on some other aspects arising from the process of constitutional change in Malaysia.

PART I

Metamorphosis of the Amendment Process[10]

ARTICLE 159

Under the Malaysian Constitution, four different modes exist for effecting amendments.[11] They are:

(1) By an Act requiring a simple majority,
(2) By an Act which has been passed by a two-thirds majority in each House of Parliament on the second and third readings,

(3) By an Act which has commanded the support of a two-thirds majority in each House of Parliament on the second and third readings together with the consent of the Conference of Rulers,

(4) By an Act supported by a two-thirds majority in each House of Parliament on the second and third readings together with the concurrence of the Governor of the East Malaysian State concerned.[12] Or if the amendment affects both East Malaysian States, the concurrence of the Governors of both the East Malaysian States.

In respect of amendments requiring the support of a two-thirds majority in each House of Parliament on the second and third readings, this can be said to be the 'general' mode affecting the largest number of provisions in the Constitution. It must be noted that a two-thirds majority refers to a two-thirds support of the total number of members of each House and not two-thirds of the members present and voting.

Certain amendments are excepted from the two-thirds majority vote requirement. These exceptions relate to the following matters:

(i) any amendment to Part III of the Second Schedule or to the Sixth or Seventh Schedule. Part III of the Second Schedule contains mainly supplementary provisions relating to citizenship. The Sixth Schedule provides for the forms of oath and affirmation and the Seventh Schedule provides for the election and retirement of Senators.

(ii) any amendment incidental to or consequential on the exercise of any power to make law conferred on Parliament by any provision of the Constitution other than Articles 74 and 76.

(iii) any amendment made for or in connexion with the admission of any State to the Federation or its association with the States thereof, or any modifications made as to the application of the Constitution to a State, so previously admitted or associated.

(iv) any amendment consequential on an amendment made under paragraph (i).

Any amendment in respect of the above matters can be effected by a simple majority vote. It is to be noted that a simple majority is not a majority of the total members of each House, but a majority of members present and voting.[13]

Amendments which require the consent of the Conference of Rulers in addition to a two-thirds majority support of each House of Parliament are those which relate to the Conference of Rulers itself,[14] the precedence of Rulers and Governors,[15] the federal guarantee of Rulers,[16] and the special position and privileges of Malays and natives of Sabah and Sarawak and the legitimate interests of other communities.[17] The consent of the Conference of Rulers assumes greater importance with the coming into force of Act 30 of 1971 as the Act has now placed within Article 159(5), various other constitutional provisions. The provisions inserted into Article 159(5) are Article 10(4) and any law made under it, Article 63(4), Article 72(4), Article 152 and Article 159(2) as amended.[18]

The fourth mode of amendment under the Malaysian Constitution is by an Act supported by a two-thirds majority in each House of Parliament on the second and third readings together with the concurrence of the Governor of each East Malaysian State concerned or the Governors of the States of Sabah and Sarawak if the amendment affects both East Malaysian States. Such a mode covers matters as listed in Article 161E, namely:

(a) the right of persons born before Malaysia Day to citizenship by reason of a connexion with the State and (except to the extent that different provision is made by the Constitution as in force on Malaysia Day) the equal treatment, as regards their own citizenship and that of others, of persons born or resident in the States of Malaya;

(b) the constitution and jurisdiction of the High Court in Borneo and the appointment, removal and suspension of judges of that court;

(c) the matters with respect to which the legislature of the State may (or Parliament may not) make laws and the executive authority in the State in those matters, and (so far as related thereto) the financial arrangements between the Federation and the State;

(d) religion in the State, the use in the State or in Parliament of any language and the special treatment of natives of the State.

In so far as the operation of the amendment process in Malaysia is concerned, the States of Sabah and Sarawak have placed themselves in a slightly different position in relation to the other States by reserving to themselves these special 'safeguards'.[19]

STATES AND THE AMENDMENT PROCESS

Different organs feature in the Malaysian amendment process. The most important of these organs is the Federal Parliament but an enhanced role in constitutional changes is also reposed in the

Conference of Rulers and the State Governors of Sabah and Sarawak. Malaysia is a federation of thirteen States and, naturally, the question will arise as to the role and power of the States in the amendment process. It will be noted later that the very nature of the original composition of the Senate was conceived by the Reid Commission as a 'block' to amendments which do not find support with the majority of the States, and that subsequent constitutional amendments have rendered meaningless this safeguard of the Malaysian Constitution.[20] The query that will be considered is whether there can be circumstances under which either consultation with or consent of the States is required to effect a proper amendment to the Constitution.[21] The powers of the States (or rather their lack of powers) has been lucidly revealed in the case of *The Government of the State of Kelantan* v. *The Government of the Federation of Malaya and Tunku Abdul Rahman Putra Al-Haj*.[22]

This case arose just prior to the formation of Malaysia. On 9 July 1963, the Government of the Federation of Malaya, United Kingdom, Sabah, Sarawak and Singapore signed the Malaysia Agreement whereby Singapore, Sarawak and Sabah would federate with the existing States of the Federation of Malaya. The new Federation would be called 'Malaysia' and in order to accommodate these changes, constitutional amendments were needed. The Malaysia Act[23] was therefore passed by the Federal Parliament to amend the Federation of Malaya Constitution, 1957, to provide, *inter alia*, for the admission of the three new States and for the alteration of the name of the Federation to that of 'Malaysia'. The Act, after having received the requisite two-thirds majority, was assented to by the Yang di-Pertuan Agong on 26 August, and was to come into operation on 16 September 1963. However on 10 September, the Government of the State of Kelantan commenced proceedings against the Federal Government and the then Prime Minister, Tunku Abdul Rahman, in his capacity as Chief Executive Officer of the Government. The Government of the State of Kelantan asked for declarations that the Malaysia Agreement and the subsequent Malaysia Act were null and void, or alternatively were not binding on the State of Kelantan. The Government of the State of Kelantan based its proceedings on the following grounds:

(a) The Malaysia Act would in effect abolish the Federation of Malaya and therefore was contrary to the 1957 Agreement.

(b) The proposed changes required the consent of each of the constituent States, including Kelantan, and this had not been obtained.

(c) The Ruler of the State of Kelantan should have been a party, which he was not, to the Malaysia Agreement.

(d) It was a constitutional convention that the Rulers of the individual States should be consulted regarding any substantial changes in the Constitution.

(e) The Federal Parliament had no power to legislate for the State of Kelantan in respect of any matter regarding which the State has its own legislation.

On 11 September, the Kelantan State Government applied to the court for an order to restrain the implementation of the provisions of the Malaysia Act pending the disposal of the suit. Thomson C.J. in delivering an historic judgment ignored the procedural technicalities and dismissed the whole case on its merits.[24] Instead of dealing with each of the grounds put forth by the Kelantan State Government, the learned judge said:

... the two things which are attacked in the present proceedings are the action of Parliament in enacting the Malaysia Act and the action of the Government in concluding the Malaysia Agreement.

In each case the gravamen of the charge lies in the admission of the three new States and the change of name without the plaintiff Government having been consulted.... The real question is not whether any such radical change will in fact result from what has been done by Parliament and the Executive Government but whether Parliament or the Executive Government has trespassed in any way the limits placed on their powers by the Constitution. These powers were given by the signatories to the 1957 Agreement and they have not been taken away. If the steps that have been taken are in all respects lawful the nature of the results they have produced cannot of itself make them unlawful. *Fiat justitia, ruat coelum!*[25]

The learned judge then proceeded to examine the relevant powers of Parliament and of the Executive as set out in the Constitution. After noting the various modes of amending the Constitution and emphasizing the non-requirement of a two-thirds majority in respect of constitutional amendments in connexion with the admission of any State, Thomson C.J. referred to the amendments of Article 1(1) and (2) and said:

In doing these things I cannot see that Parliament went in any way beyond its power or that it did anything *so fundamentally revolutionary* as to require fulfilment of a condition which the Constitution itself does not prescribe, that is to say a condition to the effect that the State of Kelantan or any other State should be consulted. It is true in a sense that the new Federation is something different from the old one. It will contain more States. It will have a different name. But if that state of affairs be brought about by means contained in the Constitution itself and which were contained in it at the time of the 1957 Agreement, of which it is an integral part, I cannot see how it can possibly be made out that there has been breach of any foundation pact among the original parties. In bringing about these changes Parliament has done no more than exercise the powers which were given to it in 1957 by the constituent States including the State of Kelantan.[26]

The learned judge also concluded that in respect of the Malaysia Agreement, there was nothing whatsoever in the Constitution requiring consultation with any State Government or the Ruler of any State. Thus the Prime Minister, the Deputy Prime Minister, and four other members of the Cabinet in signing the Malaysia Agreement on behalf of the Federation of Malaya were lawfully exercising a power conferred by the States in 1957.[27]

Thomson C.J.'s judgment serves to highlight the immense powers that have been reposed in the central government and of the totally negligible voice of the States in the amendment process. As has been said:

If the States now ... feel that they have given the centre too much power, it is their own misfortune and their proper course would be to seek amendments to, but not rely on mysterious limitations outside the Constitution.[28]

However it should be noted that not all the States of Malaysia are totally powerless in so far as the amendment process is concerned. Such a description would not hold true in respect of the States of Sabah and Sarawak. In joining the new Federation, these States have reserved certain powers for themselves. Thus certain amendments cannot be effected which affect these two States without their concurrence.[29]

Thomson C.J.'s judgment contains some perplexing dicta in the sense that one is left wondering whether the learned Chief Justice was suggesting that although the Constitution does not prescribe for consultation or consent of the States, yet this is required where the amendment is 'so fundamentally revolutionary'. Sheridan and Groves have written:

Thomson C.J ... opened up two ideas which, it is submitted, should be quickly closed down again. One is that there might be some Act of Parliament so fundamentally revolutionary that, although done in conformity with the Constitution, it would be invalid unless fulfilling some condition, such as State consultation, not prescribed in the Constitution. The second is that an Act of Parliament changing the name of the Federation and admitting new States, or doing anything that makes the new Federation in a sense somewhat different from the old one, though passed in conformity with the Constitution at the time of its passage, might be challenged if contrary to the Constitution as it originally stood.[30]

Jayakumar has pointed out that the 'fundamentally revolutionary' test is too vague and lacks definite criteria for its determination.[31] These dicta of Thomson C.J. have been criticized and it has been further asserted that the learned judge's approach was 'neither correct nor desirable', and that it created rather than solved, problems.[32]

In the light of the *Kelantan* case, the conclusion that can be drawn is that the States, with the exception of Sabah and Sarawak, have no significant role to play in the amendment process.

THE SENATE AND THE AMENDMENT PROCESS

It is pertinent to note that the Legislature in Malaysia is of a bicameral nature, comprising the House of Representatives (*Dewan Ra'ayat*) and the Senate (*Dewan Negara*). It is the latter 'Upper' House which was originally envisaged by the Reid Commission as a major safeguard of the Constitution, in matters concerning amendments to the Constitution. The query which will now be examined is whether this safeguard has any effectiveness at all.

What powers does the Senate wield in the legislative process, *vis-à-vis* money bills, bills other than money bills,[33] and bills amending the Constitution? The mechanics of enacting a law by Parliament are prescribed in Chapter 5 of Part IV of the Constitution. A bill (other than a money bill or a bill making amendments to a money bill) may originate in either House.[34] When a bill has been passed by the House in which it originated it is sent to the other House. Once it has been passed by the other House and agreement has been reached between the two Houses on any amendments made in it, it is presented to the Yang di-Pertuan Agong for his assent. The assent of the Yang di-Pertuan Agong is signified by the affixing of the Public Seal to the bill. Once assent is signified, the bill is published and normally then comes into force.[35]

In respect of a bill other than a bill amending the Constitution the Senate has only 'delaying' powers. If the bill is other than a money bill or a bill amending the Constitution, the Senate has a delaying power of only one year. Thus if the Senate does not approve a bill which has been passed by the House of Representatives, the same bill can be passed by the House of Representatives a year later and if the Senate still withholds its approval the bill can then be presented to the Yang di-Pertuan Agong for his assent. The same applies where the Senate passes a bill with amendments which are not acceptable to the House of Representatives. If the bill is a money bill, it can only originate in the House of Representatives. If such a bill is not passed by the Senate without amendments within a month it may be presented to the Yang di-Pertuan Agong for his assent. In other words, in respect of a money bill, the Senate has a delaying power of only one month.

In regard to the third kind of bill, namely a bill amending the Constitution, the Senate assumes a power greater than a mere delaying power. If the bill is one which seeks to amend the Constitution other than an amendment which is exempted from the provisions of Article 159(3), the power of the Senate assumes the nature of a full-fledged veto. In addition to the requirement of a two-thirds majority in the House of Representatives, such a bill must also obtain the approval of a two-thirds majority in the Senate.[36] As the Reid Commission said:

... Amendments should be made by Act of Parliament provided that an Act to amend the Constitution must be passed in each House by a majority of at least two-thirds of the members voting. In this matter the House of Representatives should not have power to overrule the Senate. We think that this is a sufficient safeguard for the States *because the majority of members of the Senate will represent the States....*[37]

But as one analyses the amendments which have been made to the composition of the Senate, one is drawn to the conclusion that this safeguard is no longer an effective one.

Under the original terms of the Constitution, each State was to elect 2 senators (hereinafter referred to as 'State Senators') whilst the Yang di-Pertuan Agong was empowered to appoint 16 other senators (hereinafter referred to as 'Appointed Senators'). As there were eleven States under the 1957 Federation of Malaya Constitution, the State Senators would outnumber the Appointed Senators by 22 to 16. This proportion would give some semblance of a restraining safeguard against constitutional amendments should the State Senators decide to 'block' any such amendments. This proportion however was altered twice with the ultimate consequence of rendering the vesting of an absolute veto in the Senate virtually meaningless. By Act No. 26 of 1963[38] the number of Appointed Senators was raised to 22. With the formation of Malaysia, the proportion of State Senators to Appointed Senators stood at 28 to 22. By Act No. 19 of 1964[39] the number of Appointed Senators was further increased to 32. The consequence of the second amendment was that for the first time the Appointed Senators outnumbered the State Senators by 32 to 28. This increase of Appointed Senators was further enhanced by the fact that after the 'separation' of Singapore on 9 August 1965, the number of State Senators was reduced to 26. It is obvious therefore that the safeguard as envisaged by the Reid Commission to act as a restraint upon the legislative power of amendment has been deprived of its effectiveness. 'In these circumstances, it is extremely difficult for the State Senators to "block" any amendment. Further, the Appointed Senators need the support of only a handful of State Senators to successfully approve or disallow any amendment.'[40]

It can be queried whether the amendments are contrary to the recommendations of the Reid Commission, which stated:

We think that there should be a substantial majority of elected members even though the powers of the Senate are to be considerably less than the powers of the House of Representatives; and we recommend that Parliament should have power to reduce the number of nominated members [i.e. Appointed Senators] or abolish them if a time should come when that is thought desirable.[41]

It is perhaps possible to find some grounds for justifying the amendment effected by Act No. 26 of 1963. A constitution cannot be expected to remain static forever. It must be adapted to meet inevitable changing circumstances. It could be asserted that in raising the number of Appointed Senators from 16 to 22 the Legislature was trying to bring Article 45(1) to accord with changing circumstances, namely, the formation of Malaysia. As a result of such a momentous event, the number of State Senators was increased by 6.[42] The Legislature in increasing the Appointed Senators by another 6 was trying to maintain the *status quo* as laid down in Article 45(1).

In respect of the amendment effected by Act No. 19 of 1964 which raised the number of Appointed Senators to 32, it is difficult to find any justification. Instead it would be expected that the number of Appointed Senators would be *decreased* by 2, an expectation which would naturally accompany the 'separation' of Singapore from Malaysia.[43] Perhaps the time has come to consider the relevance of the Senate in the legislative process. In 1963, Professor H. E. Groves said: 'During the life of the Federation of Malaya the Senate was not noted for taking legislative initiative nor departing from the legislative programme of the party in control of the House of Representatives.'[44] This indictment of the Senate in 1963 still holds true as Malaysia enters its third decade of independence. Though this 'Upper' House has been frequently looked upon as a 'rubber-stamping' institution, it can be a formidable force to be confronted with should the reins of government pass to a different party. The term of office of a

Senator is six years and it is not to be affected by a dissolution of Parliament.[45] As the Appointed Senators are now in the majority, the Senate can delay and even 'obstruct' the legislative programmes of the different party in power. This can be a sobering thought as Appointed Senators owe no responsibility whatever to the people.

AMENDMENT OF THE AMENDMENT PROCESS

The amendment process as originally embodied in Article 159 was a formula devised by the Reid Commission with the aim of ensuring that the amendment process in Malaysia was neither too difficult as to produce frustration nor too easy as to weaken the constitutional safeguards. We have noted that two successive amendments to the composition of the Senate have resulted in the weakening of a major safeguard of the amendment process. The question now arises as to whether the amendment effected to Article 159 by the Constitution (Amendment) Act, 1971[46] has resulted in the amendment process being rendered too difficult to employ in respect of certain provisions of the Constitution as to produce 'frustration'.

THE CONSTITUTION (AMENDMENT) ACT, 1971

Coming in the wake of the 13 May racial violence,[47] the amending Act or Act A30 of 1971[48] amended Article 10 of the Malaysian Constitution to empower Parliament to pass laws to impose restrictions on the right to freedom of speech. The restrictions aimed at restricting public discussion on four 'sensitive' issues— citizenship, the National Language and the languages of other communities, the special position and privileges of the Malays and the natives of Sabah and Sarawak and the legitimate interests of other communities in Malaysia and the sovereignty of the Rulers. These restrictions extend right up to members of Parliament who are no longer able to seek protection behind the shield of parliamentary privilege.

In relation to the National Language, Article 152 expressly declares the Malay language to be the national language, but this declaration is subject to the proviso that no one can be prohibited or prevented from using any other languages except for 'official purposes'. Originally there was no definition of 'official purposes'. To clear doubts arising from the absence of a definition, a new clause has been added to Article 152 which defines official purposes as meaning 'any purpose of the Government, whether Federal or State, and includes any purpose of a public authority'. The ambit of the usage of the National Language for official purposes can now be visualized as 'public authority' means the Yang di-Pertuan Agong, the Ruler or Governor of a State, the Federal Government, the Government of a State, a local authority, a statutory authority exercising powers vested in it by federal or state law, any court or tribunal other than the Federal Court and High Courts, or any of those persons, courts, tribunals or authorities.[49]

The Constitution (Amendment) Act, 1971 also amended Article 153. Article 153 is the provision which places in the Yang di-Pertuan Agong the responsibility to safeguard the special position of the Malays and the legitimate interests of the other communities. Furthermore, the Yang di-Pertuan Agong is empowered to ensure the reservation for Malays of such proportion 'as he may deem reasonable' of positions in the public service (other than the public service of a State) and of scholarships, exhibitions, and other similar educational or training privileges or special facilities given or accorded by the Federal Government and, when any permit or licence for the operation of any trade or business is required by federal law, then subject to the provisions of that law and Article 153, of such permits and licences.[50]

By virtue of Section 6 of the amending Act, the words 'and natives of any of the Borneo States' were inserted immediately after the words 'Malays' wherever they appear in Article 153. The intention of such an amendment is, according to the Explanatory Statement of the Constitution (Amendment) Bill, 1971, to 'provide for parity of natives of any of the Borneo States with Malays in West Malaysia'.[51] Prior to the amendment the natives of the Borneo States were entitled to reservation of positions in the public service but it was expressly provided that there was to be no reservation of fixed proportion in relation to scholarships, exhibitions, and other educational or training privileges and facilities for the natives. The amendment means that the natives of the Borneo States have been given the same status as the Malays.

In addition to elevating the status of the natives of the Borneo States to parity with the Malays, the Act also empowers the Yang di-Pertuan Agong to direct any University, College, and other educational institutions providing education after the level of Malaysia Certificate of Education or its equivalent where the number of places offered to candidates for any course of study is less than the number of candidates qualified for such places, to reserve such proportion of such places for the Malays and natives of the Borneo States as the Yang di-Pertuan Agong may deem reasonable.

A major impact of the Constitution (Amendment) Act, 1971 is the enhancement of the power and role of the Conference of Rulers in the amendment process. Originally the consent of the Conference was required in respect of any law which sought to amend the following provisions of the Constitution:

(*i*) Article 38   —which deals with the functions and powers of the Conference of Rulers.

(*ii*) Article 70   —which deals with the precedence of Rulers and Governors.

(*iii*) Article 71(1)—which deals with the guarantee by the Federation of the right of a Ruler to succeed and to hold, enjoy and exercise the constitutional rights and privileges of Ruler of a State.

(*iv*) Article 153   —which deals with special rights and privileges of the Malays and the legitimate interests of other communities.

As a result of the Constitution (Amendment) Act, 1971, the consent of the Conference is required for the amendment of various other constitutional provisions, namely, Article 10 as amended and any law made thereunder, Article 63, Article 72, and Article 152 as amended. All these Articles deal with what have been described as 'sensitive' matters. Such a move by Parliament has also been described as an attempt at 'entrenchment' of the amended constitutional provisions.

Is there any justification for describing the Constitution (Amendment) Act, 1971 as an attempt at entrenchment? Prior to this Act, these entrenched provisions could be amended by the general mode of amendment, i.e. they required the support of a two-thirds majority in each House of Parliament on the second and third readings. Now a further element, the consent of the Conference of Rulers, is required. To effect this, Article 159(5) has been amended to incorporate within its ambit the provisions sought to be entrenched. At this stage, the contention of entrenchment is not thoroughly convincing. For instance, if Parliament feels that parliamentary privilege ought to be restored to its original form, it can achieve this by mustering the support of a two-thirds majority and obtaining the consent of the Conference of Rulers. Even if the Conference withholds its consent, Parliament can still achieve the desired objective by simply amending Article 159(5) through a two-thirds majority to remove Article 63 or Article 72 from its ambit. But the Constitution (Amendment) Act, 1971 does not stop at this stage. The suggested solution of circumventing the Conference should it withhold consent has now been blocked by the addition of the words 'or to this Clause' to Article 159(5), thus succeeding in effectively entrenching those provisions. Article 159(5) as amended now reads:

A law making an amendment to Clause (4) of Article 10, any law passed thereunder, the provisions of Part III, 38, 64(4), 70, 71(1), 72(4), 152, or 153 or *to this Clause* shall not be passed without the consent of the Conference of Rulers.[52]

Therefore, the amendment of Article 159(5) to do away with the consent of the Conference of Rulers for the amendment of Article 63 or Article 72 must first of all obtain the consent of the Conference itself. Herein lies the justification for describing the Constitution (Amendment) Act, 1971 as an attempt at entrenchment.

AMENDMENT OF A LAW PASSED UNDER ARTICLE 10

Of all the Acts which have effected amendments to the 'Amendment Process', i.e. to Article 159, the Act which has brought about the most profound changes is the Constitution (Amendment) Act, 1971. One of the declared objectives behind the Act is the removal of certain 'sensitive' issues from the realm of public discussion. To achieve this objective, Article 10 was amended whereby Parliament was empowered to pass laws prohibiting the questioning of the 'sensitive' matters.

The normal legislative procedure is that an ordinary Act of Parliament or an amendment to such an Act need only be passed by a simple majority. In respect of an Act amending the Constitution, the provisions of Article 159 must be complied with. One of the curious implications arising from the amendments to Article 159 effected by the Act is that an exception has been made to the normal legislative procedure for an ordinary Act of Parliament. Since Article 10 has been amended it would mean that a law which prohibits the questioning of the 'sensitive' matters may be passed by a simple majority as it would not amount to infringing or amending the Constitution. It would be expected therefore that if Parliament deems that the proper time has now come to repeal such a law, such a repeal will also be brought about only by a simple majority vote. However this is no longer the case for a law which is passed under the amended Article 10. Section 7 of the Constitution (Amendment) Act, 1971 now provides that 'a Bill for making any amendment to a law passed under Clause (4) of Article 10' cannot be passed in either House of Parliament unless it has been supported on the second and third readings by the votes of not less than two-thirds of the total members of that House. In addition, the consent of the Conference of Rulers is needed.

So far, no law has been passed under the amended Article 10 but effective prohibition on the discussion of 'sensitive' matters has been brought about by the amendment of the Sedition Act, 1948. It is important to note that the amendment to the Sedition Act, 1948 was not effected by a law passed under Article 10 but effected by the emergency Ordinance No. 45 of 1970 promulgated by the Yang di-Pertuan Agong. As such, the curbs on public discussion can be removed if the emergency Ordinance is revoked by the Yang di-Pertuan Agong before Parliament sits or once Parliament is summoned, if it is annulled by resolutions passed by both Houses of Parliament.[53] If the Ordinance is neither revoked nor annulled, the Ordinance promulgated in pursuance of the Proclamation of Emergency automatically ceases to have effect at the expiration of a period of six months from the date the Proclamation of Emergency ceased to be in force.[54] However for the Proclamation to cease to be in force it must again either be revoked by the Yang di-Pertuan Agong or annulled by resolutions passed by both Houses of Parliament, once Parliament is summoned.

Parliament may deem it necessary to prolong the prohibition on the discussion of 'sensitive' matters even after the revocation of the Proclamation of Emergency. In such an event, the amendment to the Sedition Act which was effected by Ordinance No. 45 of 1970 will have to be embodied in an Act of Parliament. Once such an Act is passed under Article 10, the provisions relating to 'sensitive' matters will be firmly entrenched for the repeal of such a law requires a two-thirds majority vote and the consent of the Conference of Rulers. Such a move was initially in the offing as was hinted by the then Attorney-General of Malaysia, Tan Sri Abdul Kadir bin Yusof, when in 1971 he said:

Under the Sedition Act, or *later the new Act under Article 10 of the Constitution*, the power to charge a person for committing an offence relating to sensitive issues is with the Public Prosecutor and with his written consent.[55]

If such a move is translated into action, it will put into true light the magnified role of the Conference of Rulers. When circumstances justify the repeal of the new Act (assuming it is passed), Parliament will find that its ability to legislate on an ordinary law will be subject to the overriding consent of the Conference of Rulers. Such sober considerations may have stayed the hand of the Government for the new Act has yet to be enacted.

MISCELLANEOUS AMENDMENTS TO THE AMENDMENT PROCESS

There have been a few other amendments to Article 159 of the Federal Constitution. For instance, Clause (2) of Article 159 was repealed by Act No. 25 of 1963 with effect from 29 August 1963. This clause reads as follows:

(2) No amendments to this Constitution shall be made before Parliament is constituted in accordance with Part IV, except such as the Legislative Council may deem necessary to remove any difficulties in the transition from the constitutional arrangements in operation immediately before Merdeka Day to those provided for by the Constitution; but any law made in pursuance of this Clause shall, unless sooner repealed, cease to have effect at the expiration of a period of twelve months beginning with the day on which Parliament first meets.

It was under this provision that the first amendment to the Constitution was effected by Ordinance 42 of 1958.[56]

Another amendment consisted of the addition of a new paragraph (bb) to Clause (4) of Article 159. This new paragraph provided another addition to the list of amendments that are excepted from the requirement of a two-thirds majority vote, namely, 'any amendment made for or in connexion with the admission of any State to the Federation or its association with the States thereof, or any modification made as to the application of this Constitution to a State previously so admitted or associated'.[57] This amendment was effected by Act 14 of 1962 and must have been enacted in contemplation of an enlargement of the then existing Federation of Malaya. Under the Constitution as it originally stood before the formation of Malaysia, Article 2 enables new States to be brought into the Federation by an ordinary law, that is, a law passed by a simple majority in Parliament. In connexion with such admission it may be necessary to amend or modify the Constitution 'to meet the requirements of the new member, as was found to be the case when Singapore and the Borneo States joined the Federation'.[58] In 1963, Article 159(4) (bb) was made subject to Article 161E, added by the Malaysia Act. The new Article 161E provides that an amendment to the Constitution made in connexion with the admission to the Federation of a Borneo State must have the approval of a two-thirds majority in each House of Parliament, and that any modification made as to the application of the Constitution to such a State will also require the approval of a two-thirds majority in each House, unless the modification equates or assimilates the position of that State to that of the States of West Malaysia.[59] According to Suffian the words 'a Borneo State' in Article 161E can only refer to Brunei.[60] If the modification equates or assimilates the position of the new member from Borneo to that of the States of West Malaysia, it requires only a simple majority in Parliament. The words 'equates or assimilates' do not cover the situation where the amendment to the Constitution affects the quota of members of the House of Representatives. In such a case, the amendment will require the approval of a two-thirds majority in each House.[61]

CONCLUSION

From the above discussion, it can be observed that: (1) the States have a negligible voice in the amendment process, (2) the Senate in relation to its role as a protector of State interests has been reduced to a 'toothless' organ in the Malaysian Parliament, and (3) the Conference of Rulers has had its power and role in the amendment process highly magnified. The overall viewpoint that can be asserted is that the amendment process under the Malaysian Constitution has metamorphosed through various constitutional amendments to a form which is tangential to the aims of the Reid Commission.

PART II

Other Aspects of Constitutional Change

HASTY AMENDMENTS

One of the main complaints commonly voiced by parliamentarians and members of the public is the speed with which amendments are literally pushed through Parliament. In 1966 a proposal that a provision be inserted into the Constitution laying down a requirement of at least thirty days' notice before any intended amendment was initiated by Dr. Lim Chong Eu in the form of a Private Member's Bill.[62] Dr. Lim referred to the passage of the Constitution and Malaysia (Singapore Amendment) Act, 1965 (Act 53 of 1965) and the Emergency (Federal Constitution and Constitution of Sarawak) Act, 1966 (Act 68 of 1966) which were enacted with a mere few hours' notice to Members of Parliament. The Bill was defeated.[63] In relation to the legislation referred to by Dr. Lim it may be possible to mount an argument that they were 'hot' legislation intended to cope with extremely volatile and highly politically charged situations. However there is no justification for rushing constitutional amendments through Parliament in a less critical context. Indeed such a practice should be frowned upon when the very amendments purport to encroach upon fundamental rights. The latest instance is the Constitution (Amendment) Act 1976 (Act A354 of 1976) which contained many fundamental changes to the Malaysian Constitution. The problem of insufficient time to peruse the amendments was compounded by the vast number of changes, many of which had no bearing upon one another. The Malaysian Bar Council voiced its disapproval in no uncertain terms:

> It was stated in the press that the Government had been working on the amendments contained in the Constitution (Amendment) Act 1976 for the past two (2) years, but the public and the Bar Council had only a few days in which to study the amendments. When fundamental rights are to be changed there should be more time given to the public to study the amendments especially where a minority group's rights are to be affected.... The Founding Fathers when drawing the Constitution took into consideration the views of every community and provided a chapter containing fundamental liberties of which Article 12 is one. In order therefore to amend any of the Articles in the Chapter of fundamental liberties the Government for the time being ought to give wide publicity to the proposed amendment and also give fully the consequences of such amendments and sufficient time for the people to present their views.[64]

RETROSPECTIVE AMENDMENTS

Another point to be made is that retrospective constitutional amendments should as a rule be discouraged. Although Article 7 expressly prohibits retrospective criminal legislation the Government should not resort to retrospective constitutional amendments which will deprive a person of an accrued right. The practice can be more pernicious if the amendments are given a retrospective operation when litigation is under way. This again can be exemplified by the Constitution (Amendment) Act 1976 (Act A354 of 1976) which added *inter alia* a proviso to Article 135(1) to provide that dismissal or reduction in rank by an authority *delegated* by a Commission with power to do so shall be valid notwithstanding that such authority is at the time of the dismissal or reduction in rank subordinate to that which at that time has power to appoint a member of that service of equal rank.[65] Furthermore the new proviso was deemed to have been an integral part of Article 135(1) as from Merdeka Day.[66] An amendment specifically in relation to the Police Force Commission was made to circumvent the requirements of Article 135 in Part X of the Constitution. A proviso was added to Article 140 (which provides for the Police

Force Commission) to enable federal law to be made to provide for disciplinary control over all or any of the members of the police in such manner and by such authority as may be provided in such federal law. The proviso further provides that no provision of such federal law would be invalid even if it is inconsistent with any provision of Part X of the Constitution.[67] At the time of enactment of the amendment Act the case of *Iznan bin Osman* v. *Government of Malaysia*[68] had gone up on appeal to the Privy Council. The case concerned a police constable who had been convicted of the offence of permitting his car to be used as a public service vehicle without a licence. As a result of his conviction he was dismissed by the Chief Police Officer. The dismissal was held by the High Court to be null and void and inoperative on the basis that the Police Service Commission had no power to delegate its functions in so far as they relate to the dismissal or reduction in rank of a public servant.[69] The decision of the late Sharma J. was confirmed by the Federal Court. When the matter came before the Privy Council the Constitution (Amendment) Act 1976 had been passed. On the hearing of the appeal before the Privy Council it was sought to present a new argument based upon the amendment to Article 140. The Privy Council in dismissing the appeal observed:

> Their Lordships are of the opinion that it would not be proper for them to entertain the new argument in this case. No proper notice of it has been given to the respondent, and the respondent's counsel has had no opportunity to consider it and, if necessary, to take instructions upon it. At the very least an adjournment for these purposes would have been required and no Motion for such an adjournment was made on behalf of the appellant. Their Lordships understand that the new argument would have been based upon provisions in the Constitution (Amendment) Act 1976 which purport to take effect retrospectively and thus to deprive the respondent of a vested right which has already been affirmed by the High Court and by the Federal Court in these proceedings. This attempt to deprive a litigant of a right of property by retrospective legislation passed *pendente lite* is a step of a most unusual character; and that makes it all the more necessary that the respondent should have had an adequate opportunity of meeting the argument, before their Lordships could consider it.[70]

The writer detects in the Privy Council's reference to the 'unusual character' of the constitutional amendments some undertones of disquiet. However it is pertinent to note that the Federal Court in the recent case of *Loh Kooi Choon* v. *Government of Malaysia*[71] has given its stamp of approval to retrospective constitutional amendments.[72]

In the case of *Loh Kooi Choon*, the appellant was arrested and detained under a warrant issued under the provisions of the Restricted Residence Enactment.[73] The appellant brought an action claiming damages for wrongful arrest and detention as he was not taken before a magistrate within twenty-four hours of the arrest as prescribed by Article 5(4). The trial judge dismissed his action and he appealed. Before the appeal was heard the Federal Constitution was amended by the Constitution (Amendment) Act 1976 (Act A354 of 1976). The Act provided, *inter alia*, for the exclusion of arrest or detention of any person under the Restricted Residence Enactment from the operation of Article 5(4). This amendment was given retrospective effect to Merdeka Day. On the point whether an amendment of a constitutional provision can operate with retrospective effect, both Raja Azlan Shah F.J. and Wan Suleiman F.J. answered decisively in the affirmative.[74] Raja Azlan Shah F.J. said:

> In so far as an Act of Parliament is concerned, the rule of construction is that in order to determine whether it is retrospective in its operation, the language of the Act itself is not to be construed retrospectively unless it is clear that such was the intention of Parliament. If such was the intention that the Act was to be given retrospective effect even in respect of substantive right or pending proceeding, the courts have no alternative but to give effect to the Act even though the consequences might appear harsh and unjust.[75]

The learned judge added that it was the duty of the appellate court to apply the law prevailing on the date of appeal before it. Raja Azlan Shah F.J. also noted the exception provided in Article 7.

Unless the views expressed by Raja Azlan Shah and Wan Suleiman F.JJ. in *Loh Kooi Choon* are decisively rejected by the Privy Council soon it would appear that challenges to constitutional amendments based on their retrospective effect would not be likely to succeed. Appeals to the Privy Council on constitutional matters will no longer be available for cases decided by the Federal Court after 1 January 1978.

CONSTITUTIONAL CHANGE VIA ARTICLE 150

In considering the process of constitutional change in Malaysia Article 150 must not be overlooked.[76] The powers to act contrary to the Constitution as provided in Article 150 are extensive in scope. Except for certain restrictions in clause (6A) of Article 150, laws passed by Parliament or ordinances promulgated by the

Yang di-Pertuan Agong may contravene any provision of the Constitution. The point to be taken up here is this: when a Proclamation of Emergency is issued by the Yang di-Pertuan Agong and Parliament in exercise of its emergency powers intends to amend the Constitution, is it required to follow the modes prescribed in Article 159? For instance, during the political impasse arising from the *Ningkan* crisis[77] the Emergency (Federal Constitution and Constitution of Sarawak) Act, 1966[78] was passed in pursuance of a Proclamation of Emergency declared by the Yang di-Pertuan Agong over the territories of Sarawak. The amendment Act received a two-thirds majority. It is submitted that, even if the Federal Government does not command a two-thirds majority, the language of Article 150 permits it to pass the amendment Act by a simple majority.[79] Under Article 150(5), Parliament may make laws with respect to 'any matter' *notwithstanding anything in the Constitution.* This power is further underlined by Article 150(6) which provides that no such provision of any Act of Parliament passed during an emergency shall be invalid on the ground of inconsistency with *any* provision of the Constitution.

The extensive emergency powers provided in clauses (5) and (6) of Article 150 are however subject to the limitations imposed by clause (6A) which provide as follows:

Clause (5) shall not extend the powers of Parliament with respect to any matter of Muslim law or the custom of the Malays, or with respect to any matter of native law or custom in a Borneo State; nor shall Clause (6) validate any provision inconsistent with the provisions of this Constitution relating to any such matter or relating to religion, citizenship, or language.

Can the Federal Parliament by simple majority enact emergency legislation to delete clause (6A) and the references to it in clauses (5) and (6) so as to remove these restrictions on the emergency powers? It is submitted that this is not possible for it would deprive clause (6A) of any efficacy. A stronger reason is that the emergency legislation itself would be caught by clause (6A) as it would infringe, albeit indirectly, the matters mentioned in clause (6A). Under Article 150, the emergency ordinance has played a more prominent role in amendments to the Constitution.[80] In summation, Article 150 enables a government to achieve indirectly under the pretext of emergency rule what it may not be able to do directly. This mode of by-passing the amendment process of Article 159 takes on added significance when a party which commands a simple majority comes into power.[81]

IMPLIED LIMITATIONS AND
THE AMENDING POWER

One final aspect of the process of constitutional change in Malaysia turns on the question whether Parliament has an unlimited power of amendment once the modes prescribed by Article 159 are complied with. Is it possible to argue that under certain circumstances, some fetters, even though not expressly provided for in the Constitution, can be implied into the constitutional framework? To assert such a point is to invite the court to adopt a more doctrinaire and creative approach in constitutional interpretation. Such an invitation was issued by counsel for the appellant in *Loh Kooi Choon* v. *Government of Malaysia*.[82]

As mentioned earlier, the case concerned the Constitution (Amendment) Act, 1976 (Act A354) which added a proviso to Article 5(4) to exclude the applicability of clause (4) in respect of arrest and detention under the Restricted Residence Enactment. Counsel for the appellant sought to challenge the validity of the amendment Act along two lines. The first and narrower basis of the challenge relied on the word 'law' in Article 4 which declares the supremacy of the Constitution and states that 'any law passed after Merdeka Day which is inconsistent with this Constitution shall, to the extent of the inconsistency, be void'. It was argued that a law passed to amend the Constitution was a law within the meaning of the term 'law' in Article 4 and since any law passed to amend the Constitution must inevitably be inconsistent with the Constitution, such a law would be void by virtue of Article 4. This argument was rejected by Raja Azlan Shah F.J. and Wan Suleiman F.J.

According to Raja Azlan Shah F.J., once an amendment Act has complied with the process prescribed by Article 159, the Act becomes an integral part of the Constitution. '... It is the supreme law, and accordingly it cannot be said to be at variance with itself.'[83] Wan Suleiman F.J. on the other hand said:

Whilst I would agree that the word 'law' in Article 4 means all laws which Parliament is competent to pass, including federal laws passed to amend the Constitution, I fail to note any ambiguity when Articles 4 and 159 are read together.[84]

Tan Sri Salleh Abas has suggested that what Wan Suleiman F.J. was trying to say was that the framers of the Constitution must have realized that a law passed under Article 159 would inevitably contradict the supremacy clause in Article 4 and that if, despite this, they still included these two Articles in the Constitution, their intention must be that the law passed under Article 159 forms an exception to the operation of Article 4.[85] A further point to be noted is that, although Article 160(2) provides for the definition of 'law' as including written law, etc., such a definition is subject to the phrase 'unless the context otherwise requires'. The word 'law' therefore does not have a constant meaning in every provision of the Constitution.

The second basis of the challenge is far more interesting. It is based on the broader proposition that certain parts of the Constitution, especially the fundamental liberties provisions, cannot be subject to any form of amendment whatsoever. Both lines of argument derived their inspiration from the majority decision in the Indian Supreme Court case of *Golak Nath* v. *State of Punjab*.[86] In that case, the validity of the Constitution (First Amendment) Act 1951, (Fourth Amendment) Act 1955, and the (Seventeenth Amendment) Act 1964 was challenged. These amendment Acts abridged the right to property as guaranteed by Article 31 of the Indian Constitution. The Indian Supreme Court by a six-to-five majority held, *inter alia*, that an amendment to the Constitution is a 'law' within Article 13(2) which declares that any law which takes away or abridges the fundamental rights as embodied in Part III of the Indian Constitution would be void. The Supreme Court also held that fundamental rights were inalienable and inviolable, and that accordingly the Indian Parliament had no power to take away or abridge any of the fundamental rights under the Indian Constitution.[87] Prior to *Golak Nath,* the Supreme Court had been holding that no provision of the Indian Constitution is unamendable as long as the amendment Act has complied with the requirements of Article 368.[88] *Golak Nath* was subsequently overruled in *Kesavananda* v. *Kerala*.[89] However eight of the thirteen Supreme Court judges in *Kesavananda* were not prepared to go so far as to give an unlimited power of amendment to Parliament.[90] These eight judges held that the power to amend does not include the power to alter the 'basic structure or framework of the Constitution' so as to change its identity.[91]

Both Raja Azlan Shah F.J. and Wan Suleiman F.J. rejected the broader argument raised by counsel for the appellant. Wan Suleiman F.J. was of the opinion that if the power to amend fundamental rights was restricted such restrictions would have been expressly provided for in Article 159.[92] Raja Azlan Shah F.J., whilst making a similar observation, also rejected the Indian case-law:

Whatever may be said of other Constitutions, they are ultimately of little assistance to us because our Constitution now stands in its own right and it is in the end the wording of our Constitution itself that is to be interpreted and applied, and this wording 'can never be overridden by the extraneous principles of other Constitutions'.[93]

The Malaysian judiciary has been lauded for its 'pragmatic' approach in its interpretation of Article 159.[94] Whilst agreeing that the courts in interpreting the Constitution must tread the ground 'warily and with great circumspection'[95] one should not ignore the dilemma that can be posed by allowing Parliament an absolute power of amendment. For instance, Raja Azlan Shah F.J., while stating the function of the courts is that of expounding the law, said:

> Those who find fault with the wisdom or expediency of the impugned Act, and with vexatious interference of fundamental rights, normally must address themselves to the legislature, and not the courts; they have their remedy at the ballot box.[96]

What is the position if Parliament amends Article 55(3) to confer upon itself an unlimited life-span?[97] Taking the 'pragmatic' approach to its conclusion the courts would have to uphold such an amendment! Where is the remedy then? It is respectfully submitted that the Indian judicial approach should not be wholly discarded. Indian cases should be regarded as a substratum on which the Malaysian judiciary can develop its own conception of the limits of constitutional government. Undoubtedly, 'what amounts to basic structure can never, in any eventuality, be certain as this will naturally vary from judge to judge and time to time'.[98] But lack of definite criteria should not deter the courts from keeping this avenue open in case a stage of constitutional change is reached whereby constitutional government is eclipsed by absolute dictatorship. In such a context, the judiciary, in order to remain true to its oath to 'preserve, protect and defend' the Constitution, will have to think hard along such conceptual lines; otherwise there will be nothing left to preserve for future generations of Malaysians.

CONCLUSION

The last two decades have witnessed unabated changes to the Malaysian Constitution. A predominant characteristic of the process of constitutional change is the lack of notice given for mature deliberations of intended amendments. A new feature has developed of effecting retrospective amendments which affect accrued rights. The last year in the second decade of the Malaysian Constitution was marked by an unsuccessful attempt to urge the court to adopt a doctrine of implied limitation to curb the parliamentary power of amendment.

APPENDIX A

(This Appendix has been prepared by Mr. S. Sivaswamy, Librarian, Attorney-General's Chambers, Malaysia)

FEDERAL CONSTITUTION

List of amendments from 31st August 1957 to 31st August 1977

Amending legislation	Provision amended	Effective date of amendment	Remarks
1. Constitution (Temporary Amendment) Ordinance, 1958 (*No. 42 of 1958*)	Art. 34 (8)	5.12.1958	Temporary amendment. The Ordinance was repealed by *Act 68 of 1965.*
2. Constitution (Amendment) Act, 1960 (*No. 10 of 1960*)	Arts. 15 (1), (2), 16, 17, 23 (1), (2), 30 (1), 2nd Sch. Part III	1.12.1960 L.N. 309/60	
	Art. 34 (8)	11.9.1960 (See G.N. 3474/59)	
	Arts. 42 (2), (10), 43 (5), 43A, 48 (1) (d), (e), (3), 56 (4), 57 (4), 61 (4), 76 (3), 95A, 119 (1), (4), 122 (3), (4), 125 (4), (5), 132 (1) (d), (2A), (3) (a), 135 (3), 137 (3), 138, 139 (1), 141 (2), 144 (3), (5A), 148 (1), 149 (1), (2), 150 (3), 151 (1) (b), 174 (4).	31.5.1960 L.N. 116/60	
	Arts. 114 (4), 132 (3) (f)	31.8.1957 L.N. 116/60; Act.14/62. s. 33 (1)	
	Arts. 140, 142 (1), 148 (1), (2)	1.4.1961 L.N.103/61	

Amending legislation	Provision amended	Effective date of amendment	Remarks
	Art. 145	16.9.1963 L.N. 263/63	
	Art. 154 (2), (3)	8.8.1960 L.N. 75/61	
3. Constitution (Amendment) Act, 1962 (No. 14 of 1962)	Arts. 14 (1)-(5), 15 (1), (2), 15A, 19 (e), 24 (3), (3A), 25 (1), (1A), (2), (3), 26 (1), (2), (3), 26A, 26B, 155 (2), 160 (2), 1st Sch., 2nd Sch.	1.10.1962 L.N. 164/62	
	Arts. 67 (1), 160(2)	15.7.1962 L.N. 181/62	
	Arts. 17, 18 (1)-(3)	1.7.1963 L.N. 105/63	
	Arts. 18 (4), 35 (1), 46 (1), (2), 62 (3), 65 (4), (5), 76 (4), 99 (1), (3) (c), 108 (4) (g), 110 (3), (3A), (3B), (4), (5), 113 (1)-(4), 114 (5A), 115 (2), 116 (1)-(5), 117, 125 (1), (6A), 132 (3), 148 (2), 8th Sch., 10th Sch. Pt. II.	21.6.1962 L.N. 164/62	
	Arts. 20, 21 (1), (2)	1.2.1964 L.N. 164/62	
	Arts. 23 (1), 39, 159 (4) (bb), (6), 11th Sch.	31.8.1957 s. 33 (1)	
	Art. 160 (2)	16.9.1963 Sch. s. 13 (2) L.N. 263/63.	
	2nd Sch.	1.12.1960 s. 33(2)	
	13th Sch.	21.6.1962 L.N. 277/68	

4. Constitution (Amendment) Act, 1963 (*No. 25 of 1963*)	Arts. 12 (2), 74 (2), 160 (2)	31.8.1957
5. Malaysia Act (*No. 26 of 1963*)	Arts. 16 (d), 18 (4), 50 (3), 71 (4), 109 (6) (a), (b), 118, 131 (1), (2), 139 (2), (3), 144 (6A), 159 (2), 160 (2), 161, 162 (4), 163, 164, 165, 166 (1), (2), (4)-(7), 167 (1)-(5), 168, 170-173, 3rd Sch., 7th Sch., 9th Sch., 10th Sch., 11th Sch., 12th Sch.	29.8.1963
	10th Sch. Pt. II	1.1.1958
	Arts. 1, 3 (2), (3), 4 (3), (4), 5 (2), 8 (5) (c), 9 (2), (3), 10, 14, 15, 16 (a), (b), 16A, 18, 19, 19A, 20 (1) (b), 21, 22, 24, 25, 26A, 28 (3), 28A, 30 (2)-(4), 30A, 30B, 31, 37, 38 (7), 42 (7), (10), 45 (1) (b), 46, 48 (1) (e), 53, 54, 65 (3), 71 (4), (7), (8), 76 (2), 80 (6), 87 (2) (a), (3), (4), 88, 89 (7), 91 (1), 95A (1), 95B, 95C, 95D, 95E, 105 (3), 112A, 112B, 112C, 112D, 112E, 113 (2), (6), (7), 114 (1), (3), 115 (2), 116 (1), (2), 118, 121, 122, 122A, 122B, 122C, 123, 124, 125, 126, 127, 128, 129, 130, 131 (1), 131A, 132 (3), (4), 135 (3), 137 (3) (f), (g), 138, 139 (1), (2), (4), 140 (3) (b), (e), (4), 142 (6), 143 (1) (c), 144 (3), (4), 145, 146A, 146B, 146C, 146D, 148 (1), (2), 150 (1), (5), (6), (6A), 151 (2), 152 (4), 158 (1), (2), 159 (1), (4) (a), (bb), 159A, 160 (2), 161, 161A, 161B, 161C, 161D, 161E, 161F, 161G, 161H, 169 (c), 174, 2nd Sch., 4th Sch., 5th Sch., 6th Sch., 8th Sch., 9th Sch., 10th Sch., 11th Sch., 13th Sch.	16.9.1963 L.N. 214/63
	Art. 76A	31.8.1957 Act 31/65, Sch. 2

Amending legislation	Provision amended	Effective date of amendment	Remarks
6. Constitution (Amendment) Act, 1964 (*No. 19 of 1964*)	Arts. 9 (3), 26 (4), 45 (1) (b), 57 (1), (1A), (2), (2A), 62 (3), 8th Sch.	30.7.1964	
	Art. 35 (2).	1.1.1965 L.N. 352/68	
	Arts. 43B, 43C, 160 (2)	16.9.1963	
7. Constitution and Malaysia Act (Amendment) Act, 1965 (*No. 31 of 1965*)	Arts. 54, 118A, 120 (c), 122 (1), (1A), 146A (4), 160 (2), 7th Sch., 8th Sch., 9th Sch.	1.7.1965	There were a few errors in the amending Act and these were corrected by Legal Notifications *Nos. 289 and 307 of 1965.*
	Art. 95C (1), 11th Sch.	16.9.1963	
	Art. 132 (4) (d)	Malacca— 1.5.1960; Penang— 1.11.1959	
8. Constitution and Malaysia (Singapore Amendment) Act, 1965 (*No. 53 of 1965*)		9.8.1965	This Act made provision for Singapore to cease to be a State of Malaysia. Specific modifications to the Constitution arising therefrom were made by *Act No. 59 of 1966.*
9. Constitution (Amendment) Act, 1966 (*No. 59 of 1966*)	Arts. 1 (2), 3 (3), 14, 15, 16 (a), 16A (a), (b), 18 (2), 19 (1), (4), (6)-(8), 19A, 26A, 28A (1), (4), 30(3), (4), 30A, 30B, 46 (1), (2), 88 (b), 95B (1), 95D, 95E (1), (5), 112A (1), 112B, 112E, 113 (6), 121 (1), 122A (1) (c), 122B (3), (4), 146B (1), (7), (8), 146C (1), 159 (1), 160 (2), (7), 161F, 161G, 161H, 169 (c), 2nd Sch., 8th Sch., 9th Sch.	9.8.1965	

10.	Emergency (Federal Constitution and Constitution of Sarawak) Act, 1966 (No. 68 of 1966)	Arts. 9 (3), 42 (10), 54, 55 (4), 125 (10), 139 (4), 144 (5A) (5B), 146A (1), (3), (5), (6), 146C (3), 148 (2), 159A, 8th Sch.	19.9.1966	
		Art. 71 (7) (b), (8) 10th Sch. Part II	16.9.1963 1.1.1963	
		Art. 150 (5), (6)	20.9.1966	Temporary amendment. Will cease to have effect six months after the date on which the Proclamation of Emergency issued on 14.9.1966 (*P.U. 339A/66*) ceases to be in force.
11.	Constitution (Amendment) Act, 1968 (*No. 27 of 1968*)	Arts. 135, 139 (3), 8th Sch.	9.9.1968	
12.	Constitution (Amendment) Act, 1969 (*Act No. A 1*)	Art. 54 (1), 8th Sch.	18.11.1968	
13.	Resolution of Parliament (*P.U.(B) 83 of 1969*)	Art. 122A (1) (a)	10.4.1969	
14.	Emergency (Essential Powers) Ordinance No. 1,	Art. 55	15.5.1969	Temporary amendment. Ceased to be in force with the passing of the Emergency (Essential Powers) Ordinance

Amending legislation	Provision amended	Effective date of amendment	Remarks
1969 (*P.U.(A) 146 of 1969*), as amended by the Emergency (Essential Powers) Ordinance No. 3, 1969 (*P.U.(A) 170 of 1969*)			No. 32, 1970 (*P.U.(A) 143 of 1970*).
15. Emergency (Essential Powers) Ordinance No. 3, 1969 (*P.U.(A) 170 of 1969*)	Part VII, 8th Sch.	15.5.1969	Temporary amendment. Repealed by the Emergency (Essential Powers) Ordinance No. 79. 1971 (*P.U.(A) 64 of 1971*).
16. Emergency (Essential Powers) Ordinance No. 32, 1970 (*P.U.(A) 143 of 1970*)	Art. 55	12.5.1970	Temporary modification on writs, notices, etc. of Election and retaking of polls. Now spent. See also remarks against item 14.
17. Constitution (Amendment) Act, 1971 (*Act No. A 30*)	Arts. 10 (1), (4), 63 (4), 72 (4), 152 (6), 153 (1), (2), (3), (6), (8), (8A), (9A), 159 (3), (5), 161A (1), (2), (3), (4)	10.3.1971	
18. Constitution (Amendment) (No. 2) Act 1971 (*Act No. A 31*)	Arts. 40 (2) (c), 43A, 43B, 54 (1), 61, 135 (1), (3), 137 (3) (b), 144 (5A), 159 (4) (c), (6), 160 (2), 162 (3), 3rd Sch., 5th Sch., 8th Sch.	24.3.1971	

No. / Act	Provisions	Date	Remarks
19. Constitution (Amendment) Act, 1973 (*Act No. A 193*)	Art. 125 (10) 8th Sch.	19.9.1966 5.5.1973	
20. Constitution (Amendment) (No. 2) Act, 1973 (*Act No. A 206*)	Arts. 132 (1), (2A), 135 (1), 141A, 144 (5B) Arts. 46 (1), (2), 113 (8), 116 (2), 13th Sch.	1.1.1974 P.U.(B) 566/73 23.8.1973	
21. Constitution (Amendment) (No. 2) (Amendment) Act, 1976 (*Act No. A 335*)	Arts. 1 (3), (4), 3 (5), 11 (4), 42 (1), (2), (3), (10), (11), 97 (3), 9th Sch.	1.2.1974 1.2.1974	Amends the transitional provisions on existing State Laws in the Constitution (Amendment) (No. 2) Act, 1973 (*Act No. A 206*).
22. Constitution (Amendment) Act, 1976 (*Act No. A 354*)	Arts. 5 (4), 65 (2) Art. 125A 9th Sch. Arts. 1 (2), 3 (3), 6 (4), 12 (2), 24 (2), (3), (3A), 25 (1A), (2), 32 (2), 33 (1), (2), (3), (4), (5), 34 (2), (6), (7), 35 (2), 37 (2), 38 (2) (a), (6) (a), (7), 42 (10), 48	31.8.1957 16.9.1963 1.1.1976 27.8.1976	

Amending legislation	Provision amended	Effective date of amendment	Remarks
	(1) (f), 54 (1), (2), 99 (2), (4), 100, 101, 106 (2), 108 (1), 111 (2), 112 (2) (a), (b), 114 (7), 122 (1), 122A (1), (5), 128, 135 (1), (2), 138 (2), 140 (1), (3), 141A (2), 144 (3), 146A, 146B (2), (3), (7), (8), 146C (1), (2), (3), marginal note, 146D (1), (2), (3), 148, 151 (1), 160 (2), 161C, 161D, 8th Sch.	27.8.1976	
	Throughout the Constitution in relation to the use of the expressions 'Governor', 'the Borneo States', 'Muslim', 'Muslim religion', 'Muslim Law', 'Muslim Court', 'Muslim revenue', and 'Muslim Wakafs'.		
23. Capitation Grant Act 1977 (*Act No. A 392*)	Part I of 10th Sch.	1.1.1976	

APPENDIX B

LIST OF AMENDMENTS TO ARTICLES FROM 31 AUGUST 1957
TO 31 AUGUST 1977

Article	Amending authority	Effective date	Article	Amending authority	Effective date
1	Act 26/63	16. 9.63		Act 26/63	16. 9.63
	Act 59/66	9. 8.65		Act 59/66	9. 8.65
	Act A 206	1. 2.74	19	Act 14/62	1.10.62
	Act A 354	27. 8.76		Act 26/63	16. 9.63
3	Act 26/63	16. 9.63		Act 59/66	9. 8.65
	Act 59/66	9. 8.65	19A	Act 26/63	16. 9.63
	Act A 206	1. 2.74		Act 59/66	9. 8.65
	Act A 354	27. 8.76	20	Act 14/62	1. 2.64
4	Act 26/63	16. 9.63		Act 26/63	16. 9.63
5	Act 26/63	16. 9.63	21	Act 14/62	1. 2.64
	Act A 354	31. 8.57		Act 26/63	16. 9.63
6	Act A 354	27 .8.76	22	Act 26/63	16. 9.63
8	Act 26/63	16. 9.63	23	Act 10/60	1.12.60
9	Act 26/63	16. 9.63		Act 14/62	31. 8.57
	Act 19/64	30. 7.64	24	Act 14/62	1.10.62
	Act 59/66	19. 9.66		Act 26/63	16. 9.63
10	Act 26/63	16. 9.63		Act A 354	27. 8.76
	Act A 30	10. 3.71	25	Act 14/62	1.10.62
11	Act A 206	1. 2.74		Act 26/63	16. 9.63
12	Act 25/63	31. 8.57		Act A 354	27. 8.76
	Act A 354	27. 8.76	26	Act 14/62	1.10.62
14	Act 14/62	1.10.62		Act 19/64	30. 7.64
	Act 26/63	16. 9.63	26A	Act 14/62	1.10.62
	Act 59/66	9. 8.65		Act 26/63	16. 9.63
15	Act 10/60	1.12.60		Act 59/66	9. 8.65
	Act 14/62	1.10.62	26B	Act 14/62	1.10.62
	Act 26/63	16. 9.63	28	Act 26/63	16. 9.63
	Act 59/66	9. 8.65	28A	Act 26/63	16. 9.63
15A	Act 14/62	1.10.62		Act 59/66	9. 8.65
16	Act 10/60	1.12.60	30	Act 10/60	1.12.60
	Act 25/63	29. 8.63		Act 26/63	16. 9.63
	Act 26/63	16. 9.63		Act 59/66	9. 8.65
	Act 59/66	9. 8.65	30A	Act 26/63	16. 9.63
16A	Act 26/63	16. 9.63		Act 59/66	9. 8.65
	Act 59/66	9. 8.65	30B	Act 26/63	16. 9.63
17	Act 10/60	1.12.60		Act 59/66	9. 8.65
	Act 14/62	1. 7.63	31	Act 26/63	16. 9.63
18	Act 14/62	*(21. 6.62	32	Act A 354	27. 8.76
		(1. 7.63	33	Act A 354	27. 8.76
	Act 25/63	29. 8.63	34	†Ord. 42/58	5.12.58

* Different dates for different provisions of the amendment.
† Temporary amendment. Ceased to have effect.

Article	Amending authority	Effective date	Article	Amending authority	Effective date
	Act 10/60	11. 9.60	57	Act 10/60	31. 5.60
	Act A 354	27. 8.76		Act 19/64	30. 7.64
35	Act 14/62	21. 6.62	61	Act 10/60	31. 5.60
	Act 19/64	1. 1.65		Act A 31	24. 3.71
	Act A 354	27. 8.76	62	Act 14/62	21. 6.62
37	Act 26/63	16. 9.63		Act 19/64	30. 7.64
	Act A 354	27. 8.76	63	Act A 30	10. 3.71
38	Act 26/63	16. 9.63	65	Act 14/62	21. 6.62
	Act A 354	27. 8.76		Act 26/63	16. 9.63
39	Act 14/62	31. 8.57		Act A 354	31. 8.57
40	Act A 31	24. 3.71	67	Act 14/62	15. 7.62
42	Act 10/60	31. 5.60	71	Act 25/63	29. 8.63
	Act 26/63	16. 9.63		Act 26/63	16. 9.63
	Act 59/66	19. 9.66		Act 59/66	16. 9.63
	Act A 206	1. 2.74	72	Act A 30	10. 3.71
	Act A 354	27. 8.76	74	Act 25/63	31 8.57
43	Act 10/60	31. 5.60	76	Act 10/60	31. 5.60
43A	Act 10/60	31. 5.60		Act 14/62	21. 6.62
	Act A 31	24. 3.71		Act 26/63	16. 9.63
43B	Act 19/64	16. 9.63	76A	Act 26/63	31. 8.57
	Act A 31	24. 3.71	80	Act 26/63	16. 9.63
43C	Act 19/64	16. 9.63	87	Act 26/63	16. 9.63
45	Act 26/63	16. 9.63	88	Act 26/62	16. 9.63
	Act 19/64	30. 7.64		Act 59/66	9. 8.65
46	Act 14/62	21. 6.62	89	Act 26/63	16. 9.63
	Act 26/63	16. 9.63	91	Act 26/63	16. 9.63
	Act 59/66	9. 8.65	95A	Act 10/60	31. 5.60
	Act A 206	23. 8.73		Act 26/63	16. 9.63
48	Act 10/60	31. 5.60	95B	Act 26/63	16. 9.63
	Act 26/63	16. 9.63		Act 59/66	9. 8.65
	Act A 354	27. 8.76	95C	Act 26/63	16. 9.63
50	Act 25/63	29. 8.63		Act 31/65	16. 9.63
53	Act 26/63	16. 9.63	95D	Act 26/63	16. 9.63
54	Act 26/63	16. 9.63		Act 59/66	9. 8.65
	Act 31/65	1. 7.65	95E	Act 26/63	16. 9.63
	Act 59/66	19. 9.66		Act 59/66	9. 8.65
	Act A 1	18.11.68	97	Act A 206	1. 2.74
	Act A 31	24. 3.71	99	Act 14/62	21. 6.62
	Act A 354	27. 8.76		Act A 354	27. 8.76
55	Act 59/66	19. 9.66	100	Act A 354	27. 8.76
	Emergency Ord. 1/69	15. 5.69	101	Act A 354	27. 8.76
	Emergency Ord. 32/70	12. 5.70	105	Act 26/63	16. 9.63
			106	Act A 354	27. 8.76
56	Act 10/60	31. 5.60	108	Act 14/62	21. 6.62

Article	Amending authority	Effective date	Article	Amending authority	Effective date
	Act A 354	27. 8.76		Act 59/66	9. 8.65
109	Act 25/63	29. 8.63	122C	Act 26/63	16. 9.63
110	Act 14/62	21. 6.62	123	Act 26/63	16. 9.63
111	Act A 354	27. 8.76	124	Act 26/63	16. 9.63
112	Act A 354	27. 8.76	125	Act 10/60	31. 5.60
112A	Act 26/63	16. 9.63		Act 14/62	21. 6.62
	Act 59/66	9. 8.65		Act 26/63	16. 9.63
112B	Act 26/63	16. 9.63		Act 59/66	19. 9.66
	Act 59/66	9. 8.65		Act A 31	19. 9.66
112C	Act 26/63	16. 9.63	125A	Act A 354	16. 9.63
112D	Act 26/63	16. 9.63	126	Act 26/63	16. 9.63
112E	Act 26/63	16. 9.63	127	Act 26/63	16. 9.63
	Act 59/66	9. 8.65	128	Act 26/63	16. 9.63
113	Act 14/62	21. 6.62		Act A 354	27. 8.76
	Act 26/63	16. 9.63	129	Act 26/63	16. 9.63
	Act 59/66	9. 8.65	130	Act 26/63	16. 9.63
	Act A 206	23. 8.73	131	Act 25/63	29. 8.63
114	Act 10/60	31. 8.57		Act 26/63	16. 9.63
	Act 14/62	21. 6.62	131A	Act 26/63	16. 9.63
	Act 26/63	16. 9.63	132	Act 10/60	*(31. 8.57
	Act A 354	27. 8.76			(31. 5.60
115	Act 14/62	21. 6.62		Act 14/62	21. 6.62
	Act 26/63	16. 9.63		Act 26/63	16. 9.63
116	Act 14/62	21. 6.62		Act 31/65	§(1.11.59
	Act 26/63	16. 9.63			(1. 5.60
	Act A 206	23. 8.73		Act A 193	1. 1.74
117	Act 14/62	21. 6.62	135	Act 10/60	31. 5.60
118	Act 25/63	29. 8.63		Act 26/63	16. 9.63
	Act 26/63	16. 9.63		Act 27/68	9. 9.68
118A	Act 31/65	1. 7.65		Act A 31	24. 3.71
119	Act 10/60	31. 5.60		Act A 193	1. 1.74
120	Act 31/65	1. 7.65		Act A 354	27. 8.76
121	Act 26/63	16. 9.63	137	Act 10/60	31. 5.60
	Act 59/66	9. 8.65		Act 26/63	16. 9.63
122	Act 10/60	31. 5.60		Act A 31	24. 3.71
	Act 26/63	16. 9.63	138	Act 10/60	31. 5.60
	Act 31/65	1. 7.65		Act 26/63	16. 9.63
	Act A 354	27. 8.76		Act A 354	27. 8.76
122A	Act 26/63	16. 9.63	139	Act 10/60	31. 5.60
	Act 59/66	9. 8.65		Act 25/63	29. 8.63
	PU(B) 83/69	10. 4.69		Act 26/63	16. 9.63
	Act A 354	27. 8.76		Act 59/66	19. 9.66
122B	Act 26/63	16. 9.63		Act 27/68	9. 9.68
			140	Act 10/60	1. 4.61

* Different dates for different provisions of the amendment.
§ 1.11.59 in respect of Penang and 1.5.60 in respect of Malacca.

Article	Amending authority	Effective date	Article	Amending authority	Effective date
	Act 26/63	16. 9.63	153	Act A 30	10. 3.71
	Act A 354	27. 8.76	154	Act 10/60	8. 8.60
141	Act 10/60	31. 5.60	155	Act 14/62	1.10.62
141A	Act A 193	1. 1.74	158	Act 26/63	16. 9.63
	Act A 354	27. 8.76	159	Act 14/62	31. 8.57
142	Act 10/60	1. 4.61		Act 25/63	29. 8.63
	Act 26/63	16. 9.63		Act 26/63	16. 9.63
143	Act 26/63	16. 9.63		Act 59/66	9. 8.65
144	Act 10/60	31. 5.60		Act A 30	10. 3.71
	Act 25/63	29. 8.63		Act A 31	24. 3.71
	Act 26/63	16. 9.63	159A	Act 26/63	16. 9.63
	Act 59/66	19. 9.66		Act 59/66	19. 9.66
	Act A 31	24. 3.71	160	Act 14/62	*(15. 7.62
	Act A 193	1. 1.74			(1.10.62
	Act A 354	27. 8.76			(16. 9.63
145	Act 10/60	16. 9.63		Act 25/63	*(31. 8.57
	Act 26/63	16. 9.63			(29. 8.63
146A	Act 26/63	16. 9.63		Act 26/63	16. 9.63
	Act 31/65	1. 7.65		Act 19/64	16. 9.63
	Act 59/66	19. 9.66		Act 31/65	1. 7.65
	Act A 354	27. 8.76		Act 59/66	9. 8.65
146B	Act 26/63	16. 9.63		Act A 31	24. 3.71
	Act 59/66	9. 8.65		Act A 354	27. 8.76
	Act A 354	27. 8.76	161	Act 25/63	29. 8.63
146C	Act 26/63	16. 9.63		Act 26/63	16. 9.63
	Act 59/66	*(9. 8.65	161A	Act 26/63	16. 9.63
		(19. 9.66		Act A 30	10. 3.71
	Act A 354	27. 8.76	161B	Act 26/63	16. 9.63
146D	Act 26/63	16. 9.63	161C	Act 26/63	16. 9.63
	Act A 354	27. 8.76		Act A 354	27. 8.76
148	Act 10/60	*(31. 5.60	161D	Act 26/63	16. 9.63
		(1. 4.61		Act A 354	27. 8.76
	Act 14/62	21. 6.62	161E	Act 26/63	16. 9.63
	Act 26/63	16. 9.63	161F	Act 26/63	16. 9.63
	Act 59/66	19. 9.66		Act 59/66	19. 8.65
	Act A 354	27. 8.76	161G	Act 26/63	16. 9.63
149	Act 10/60	31. 5.60		Act 59/66	9. 8.65
150	Act 10/60	31. 5.60	161H	Act 26/63	16. 9.63
	Act 26/63	16. 9.63		Act 59/66	9. 8.65
	Act 68/66	20. 9.66	162	Act 25/63	29. 8.63
151	Act 10/60	31. 5.60		Act A 31	24. 3.71
	Act 26/63	16. 9.63	163	Act 25/63	29. 8.63
	Act A 354	27. 8.76	164	Act 25/63	29. 8.63
152	Act 26/63	16. 9.63	165	Act 25/63	29. 8.63
	Act A 30	10. 3.71			

* Different dates for different provisions of the amendment.

Article	Amending authority	Effective date		Article	Amending authority	Effective date
166	Act 25/63	29. 8.63		9th Sch.	Act 25/63	29. 8.63
167	Act 25/63	29. 8.63			Act 26/63	16. 9.63
168	Act 25/63	29. 8.63			Act 31/65	1. 7.65
169	Act 26/63	16. 9.63			Act 59/66	9. 8.65
	Act 59/66	9. 8.65			Act A 206	1. 2.74
170	Act 25/63	29. 8.63			Act A 354	1. 1.76
171	Act 25/63	29. 8.63		10th Sch.	Act 14/62	21. 6.62
172	Act 25/63	29. 8.63			Act 25/63	*(1. 1.58
173	Act 25/63	29. 8.63				(29. 8.63
174	Act 10/60	31. 5.60			Act 26/63	19. 9.63
	Act 26/63	16. 9.63			Act 59/66	1. 1.63
1st Sch.	Act 14/62	1.10.62			Act A 392	1. 1.76
2nd Sch.	Act 10/60	1.12.60		11th Sch.	Act 14/62	31. 8.57
	Act 14/62	*(1.12.60			Act 25/63	29. 8.63
		(1.10.62			Act 26/63	16. 9.63
	Act 26/63	16. 9.63			Act 31/65	16. 9.63
	Act 59/66	9. 8.65		12th Sch.	Act 25/63	29. 8.63
3rd Sch.	Act 26/63	29. 8.63		13th Sch.	Act 14/62	21. 6.62
	Act A 31	24. 3.71			Act 26/63	16. 9.63
4th Sch.	Act 26/63	16. 9.63			Act A 206	23. 8.73
5th Sch.	Act 26/63	16. 9.63				
	Act A 31	24. 3.71				
6th Sch.	Act 26/63	16. 9.63				
7th Sch.	Act 25/63	29. 8.63				
	Act 31/65	1. 7.65				
8th Sch.	Act 14/62	21. 6.62				
	Act 26/63	16. 9.63				
	Act 19/64	30. 7.64				
	Act 31/65	1. 7.65				
	Act 59/66	*(9. 8.65				
		(19. 9.66				
	Act 27/68	9. 9.68				
	Act A 1	18.11.68				
	Emergency Ord. 3/69	15. 5.69				
	Act A 31	24. 3.71				
	Act A 193	5. 5.73				
	Act A 354	27. 8.76				

General Modification

Throughout the Constitution for the expressions under column A the expressions under column B were substituted by Act No. A354:

A	B
Governor	Yang di Pertua Negeri
the Borneo States	the States of Sabah and Sarawak
Muslim	Islamic
Muslim religion	religion of Islam
Muslim law	Islamic law
Muslim court	Syariah court
Muslim revenue	Islamic religious revenue
Muslim Wakafs	Wakafs.

* Different dates for different provisions of the amendment.

1. Herman Finer, *The Theory and Practice of Modern Government*, Methuen, London, 4th ed., 1962, p. 127.

2. As stated by the late Prime Minister of Malaysia, Tun Abdul Razak—*Parliamentary Debates on the Constitution Amendment Bill, 1971*, Government Printer, Kuala Lumpur, 1972, p. 3.

3. The Commission was headed by the Rt. Hon. Lord Reid (U.K.). See *Report of the Federation of Malaya Constitutional Commission 1957*, London H.M.S.O. Colonial No. 330, hereinafter referred to as the 'Reid Commission Report'.

4. The three components of the Alliance Party are: (1) the United Malays National Organisation or UMNO, (2) the Malaysian Chinese Association or MCA, and (3) the Malaysian Indian Congress or MIC. The Alliance Party has now expanded into the *Barisan Nasional* (or National Front) which embraces a greater number of parties and controls most of the 154 seats in the House of Representatives.

5. See the Appendix for a complete compilation of all the amendments. The Appendix has been prepared by Mr. S. Sivaswamy, Librarian, Attorney-General's Chambers and is reproduced here with the kind permission of Mr. Sivaswamy and M.L.J. (Pte) Ltd.

6. See my article 'Constitutional Amendments in Malaysia' (1976) Mal. L.R. 59. Subsequent to the publication of this article, Act No. A354 of 1976 and Act No. A392 of 1977 were passed. The former Act has effected extensive and far-reaching changes to the Malaysian Constitution. See Ahmad Ibrahim, 'Legislative Digest' in [1976] M.L.J. xvii-xciv.

7. The desirability of a certain degree of flexibility and a certain degree of rigidity was stressed by the Singapore Constitutional Commission of 1966 when it was asked to consider how certain provisions could be entrenched in the Singapore Constitution. See *Report of the Constitutional Commission 1966*, Republic of Singapore, p. 23.

8. Reid Commission Report, para. 80, p. 31.

9. Act A30 of 1971.

10. This part of the essay incorporates in the main the text of an article published in (1974) *Journal of Malaysian and Comparative Law* 188.

11. See L. A. Sheridan and H. E. Groves, *The Constitution of Malaysia*, Oceana Publications, New York, 1967, pp. 14-15; Suffian, *An Introduction to the Constitution of Malaysia*, Government Printer, Kuala Lumpur, 2nd ed., 1976, pp. 337-41. There is in fact another mode of amending the Malaysian Constitution, i.e., by an Ordinance made by the Yang di-Pertuan Agong during an emergency. See Article 150 of the Malaysian Constitution.

At the extreme end of the scale of constitutional flexibility is the amendment process which prescribes amendment by a simple majority of the legislature. The Constitution of Singapore can be amended 'by a law enacted by the legislature' and there does not appear to be anything to protect the Constitution from amendment by implication. The Constitution (Amendment) (Protection of the Sovereignty of the Republic of Singapore) Act, 1972 has introduced an element of rigidity by requiring a vote of two-thirds of the total electorate at a referendum before Singapore can be incorporated into a federation with any other country. Such a process is further required for the repeal of this new constitutional provision. See Jayakumar, *Constitutional Law*, No. 1, Singapore Law Series, 1976, pp. 50-3.

The American Constitution has been described as 'the most rigid constitution in the world'. Like the Australian Constitution (see s. 128, The Commonwealth of Australia Constitution Act), two stages are involved in the amendment process: 'initiation' and 'ratification'. A proposal to amend the Constitution can be initiated by either two-thirds vote in each House of Congress or by Constitutional Convention called by Congress on the application of the Legislatures of two-thirds of the States. After initiation the proposal must be ratified either by a vote of the Legislatures of three-fourths of the States or by Constitutional Conventions in three-fourths of the States.

12. The States of Penang, Malacca, Sabah and Sarawak each do not have a State Ruler. They have a 'Governor'. The word 'Governor' is replaced with the words 'Yang di-Pertua Negeri' wherever the former appears in the Malaysian Constitution. The Yang di-Pertua Negeri is defined in Article 160(2) to mean the Head of a State in a State which does not have a Ruler. Constitution (Amendment) Act, 1976 (Act A354 of 1976), ss. 41, 42.

13. See Article 62(3) which says 'subject to ... Article 159(3) ... each House shall, if not unanimous, take its decision by a simple majority of members voting...'. Furthermore the Senate can only delay these amendments; it cannot veto them. Article 68(5).

14. Article 38.

15. Article 70.

16. Article 71(1).

17. Article 153.

18. See Suffian, op. cit., pp. 47-9.

19. Clause (2) of Article 161E also mentions another category of amendments, i.e. '(e) the allocation to the State, in any Parliament summoned to meet before the end of August 1970, of a quota of members of the House of Representatives not less, in proportion to the total allocated to the other States which are members of the Federation on Malaysia Day, than the quota allocated to the State on that day'. This category can be ignored as it is not applicable after the end of August 1970.

20. See 'THE SENATE AND THE AMENDMENT PROCESS', *infra*.

21. In Article 2, the Malaysian Constitution requires the consent of a State (expressed by a law made by the Legislature of that State) to be obtained in addition to that of the Conference of Rulers before Parliament can legislate to alter the boundaries of that State.

22. [1963] M.L.J. 355.

23. Act 26 of 1963. The Bill form of the Malaysia Act had been annexed to the Malaysian Agreements.

24. Thomson C.J. said: 'Today, however, the Court is sitting in exceptional circumstances. Time is short and the sands are running out. We cannot close our eyes and our ears to the conditions prevailing in the world around us and a clearer expression of opinion than would be customary is clearly required in a matter which relates to the interests of political stability in this part of Asia and the interests of ten million people, about half a million of them being the inhabitants of the State of Kelantan.' [1963] M.L.J. 355 at p. 357.

25. [1963] M.L.J. 355 at pp. 358-9.

26. Ibid. at p. 359. Emphasis added.

27. By Article 39, the executive authority of the Federation is vested in the Yang di-Pertuan Agong and is exercisable, subject to the provisions of any federal law and with certain exceptions, by him or by the Cabinet or any minister authorized by the Cabinet. By Article 80(1) the executive authority of the Federation extends to all matters with respect to which Parliament may make laws, which includes external affairs including treaties and agreements.

28. S. Jayakumar, 'Admission of New States' (1964) Mal. L.R. 181, at p. 188.

29. See Article 161E.

30. Sheridan and Groves, op. cit., n. 9, at p. 4.

31. See S. Jayakumar, 'Admission of New States' (1964) Mal. L.R. 181.

32. Ibid. at p. 187.

33. For definition of 'money bill', see Article 68(6) of the Malaysian Constitution.

34. Article 66(2), Malaysian Constitution.

35. Parliament however has the power to postpone the operation of any law or to make law with retrospective effect. See Article 66(5) and Article 7(1), Federal Constitution. The latter Article provides for protection against retrospective criminal laws.

36. Article 68(5), Malaysian Constitution.

37. Reid Commission Report, para. 80, p. 31. Emphasis added.

38. The Malaysia Act.

39. The Constitution (Amendment) Act, 1964.

40. S. Jayakumar, 'Constitutional Limitations on Legislative Powers in Malaysia' (1967) Mal. L.R. 109.

41. Reid Commission Report, para. 62, p. 23. Sir William McKell and Mr. Justice Abdul Hamid did not agree with the majority's recommendations. Both these members of the Reid Commission were of the opinion that the Senate should consist of members elected directly by the people of the States—pp. 31-3.

42. Two State Senators from each of the new States of Sabah, Sarawak and Singapore.

43. Instead, the then Minister of Home Affairs and Minister of Justice, Dato' Dr. Ismail, as he then was, in commenting on the amendment said: '... In order to get wider representations in the Senate consequent on the formation of Malaysia this will enable His Majesty to appoint more persons of wider experience and ability to take an active part in the government of this country'. *Parliamentary Debates* (Dewan Ra'ayat), 9 July 1964, col. 1109-1110.

44. Professor H. E. Groves, 'The Constitution of Malaysia—The Malaysia Act', (1963) Mal. L.R. 245 at p. 255.

45. Article 45(3), Malaysian Constitution.

46. Act A30 of 1971.

47. The racial riots were precipitated in the midst of the General Election which was being held on 10 May 1969. No independent Commission of Inquiry was held to determine the causes of the racial riots and to trace the sequence of events. The Government's version of what took place is contained in *The May 13 Tragedy*, a Report of the National Operations Council (1969). See also Tunku Abdul Rahman, *May 13, Before and After* (1969); and Goh Cheng Teik, *The May Thirteenth Incident and Democracy in Malaysia*, Oxford University Press, Kuala Lumpur, 1971.

48. For an analysis of this Act, see the Introduction by Professor Ahmad Ibrahim at pp. ix-xvi of *Parliamentary Debates on the Constitution Amendment Bill, 1971* (1972).

49. See Article 160, Malaysian Constitution. Also refer to the National Language—Malaysia Act (Revised 1971), No. 32. This amendment did not in any way affect Sabah and Sarawak as Article 161 provides for the use of English in these two East Malaysian States for a period of ten years after Malaysia Day. For recent developments in these two States see Suffian, op. cit., pp. 328-30.

50. It is however provided in Article 153 that the Yang di-Pertuan Agong in exercising his functions shall not deprive any person of any public office held by him or of the continuance of any scholarship, exhibition or other educational or training privileges or special facilities enjoyed by him. Neither will Article 153 operate to deprive any person of any right, privilege, permit or licence accrued to or enjoyed or held by him or to authorize refusal to renew to any person any such permit or licence or a refusal to grant to the heirs, successors or assigns of a person or any permit or licence when the renewal or grant might reasonably be expected in the ordinary course of events.

51. It is also provided in Section 6(c) of the Constitution (Amendment) Act, 1971 that the expression 'natives' in relation to a Borneo State shall have the meaning assigned to it in Article 161A, i.e. in relation to Sarawak, 'native' means a person who is a citizen and belongs to one of the following ethnic groups: the Bukitans, Bisayaks, Dusuns, Sea Dayaks, Land Dayaks, Kadazans, Kalabits, Kayans, Kenyahs (including Sabups and Sipengs), Kajangs (including Sekapans, Kejamans, Lahanans, Punans, Tanjongs and Kanowits), Lugats, Lisums, Malays, Melanos, Muruts, Penans, Sians, Tagols, Tabuns and Ukits, or is of mixed blood deriving exclusively from these races.

In relation to Sabah the expression refers to a person who is a citizen, is the child or grandchild of a person of a race indigenous to Sabah, and was born (whether on or after Malaysia Day or not) either in Sabah or to a father domiciled in Sabah at the time of the birth. See Article 161A clauses (6) and (7).

52. Emphasis added.

53. Article 150(3), Malaysian Constitution.

54. Article 150(7), Malaysian Constitution.

55. *Parliamentary Debates on the Constitution Amendment Bill, 1971*, Government Printer, Kuala Lumpur, 1972, p. 189. Emphasis added.

56. The Ordinance inserted a new clause, clause (8), into Article 34 of the Malaysian Constitution.

57. Suffian, op. cit., p. 339.

58. Ibid.

59. The new paragraph (bb) comprises two limbs: (a) any amendment made for or in connexion with the admission of any State to the Federation or its association with the States thereof, and (b) any modification made as to the application of the Constitution to a State previously so admitted or associated. Some ambiguities can arise from limb (b). As Sheridan and Groves have queried: 'No court has yet had to consider what can be described as an application of the constitution "to the state" and what is an application of the constitution *not to a state*. What for example would be the status of an Act of Parliament, passed by a simple majority, purporting to amend Article 74 (1) and the Ninth Schedule by conferring upon itself power to legislate on boarding houses in Perlis?' Sheridan and Groves, op. cit., p. 15.

60. Suffian, op. cit., p. 339.

61. Another 'safeguard' of special interest to Sabah and Sarawak is found in Article 161E (4). The ambit of this clause is lucidly explained by Suffian as follows:

> The Immigration Act, 1963 confers on each East Malaysian state the right and power to exclude non-East Malaysians from entering or residing in that state. Clause (4) of Article 161E says that the Act should be treated as if it has been embodied in the constitution and that an amendment to it affecting such rights and powers should be treated as an amendment to the constitution and requires not only the approval of a two-thirds majority in each House of Parliament, but also the concurrence of the Governor of the East Malaysian state concerned.
>
> During the negotiations leading to the formation of Malaysia, the East Malaysian states obtained the agreement of the Federal Government to their having the right and power to exclude non-East Malaysians from East Malaysia; the Federal Government has rights and powers only as regards the admission into, emigration and expulsion from the Federation *as a whole*.
>
> (Suffian, op. cit., p. 340.)

62. The bill was in fact the first Private Member's Bill to be introduced in the Malaysian Parliament.

63. For the reasons for the Government's objection to the Bill, see *Parliamen-*

tary Debates (Dewan Ra'ayat), 25 October 1966, col. 2269-2284.

64. *Insaf,* December 1976, p. 1.

65. Article 135 basically gives a twin protection to the public servant in Malaysia. Clause (1) of Article 135 ensures that an authority will not have the power to dismiss a public servant or to reduce him in rank unless it has the power at the time of such dismissal or reduction, to appoint a member of the same service of equal rank. Clause (2) ensures that the public servant gets a 'reasonable opportunity of being heard' before he can be dismissed or reduced in rank. See Jayakumar, 'Protection for Civil Servants: The Scope of Article 135 (1) and (2) of the Malaysian Constitution as Developed through the Cases' [1969] 2 M.L.J. liv-lxii; F. A. Trindade, 'The Security of Tenure of Public Servants in Malaysia and Singapore' in G. W. Bartholomew, (ed.), *Malaya Law Review Legal Essays,* Faculty of Law, University of Singapore, 1975.

66. Act A354 of 1976, s.30(a).

67. Ibid., s.32.

68. [1973] 2 M.L.J. 143 (High Court); [1975] 2 M.L.J. 61 (Federal Court); [1977] 2 M.L.J. 1 (Privy Council).

69. See Trindade, op. cit. at pp. 260-2.

70. [1977] 2 M.L.J. 1 at p. 4.

71. [1977] 2 M.L.J. 187.

72. This stamp of approval was reiterated by the Federal Court (comprising Suffian L.P., Lee Hun Hoe C.J. (Borneo) and Wan Suleiman F.J.) in *Government of Malaysia* v. *Zainal Bin Hashim* [1977] 2 M.L.J. 254 where it was held that the amendment to Article 135(1) could be made with retrospective effect. In referring to the observation of the Privy Council in *Iznan,* the Federal Court said: 'All that the above observation means is that in view of the very short notice given by the Government (three days) of their desire to rely on new arguments their Lordships did not consider it fair to allow the Government to do so, not that their arguments if presented and considered would not hold water.'

73. F.M.S. Cap. 39: Reprint No. 12/1973.

74. As for the third judge the Editorial Note in [1977] 2 M.L.J. 187 reported as follows: 'In view of the demise of Ali F.J. the court asked both counsel for the parties under section 42 of the Courts of Judicature Act, 1964 whether they consented to accept judgements by the remaining judges of the court, it being understood that if there was no majority opinion the proceedings should be re-heard. Both counsel consented.'

75. [1977] 2 M.L.J. 187 at p. 190.

76. Since 1957, the Malaysian Constitution has found itself continually weathering a 'storm of exigencies'. Article 150 has been invoked on a number of occasions by the Federal Government to meet various crises erupting at various stages in the nation's life. The launching of an intensive 'confrontation' by Indonesia resulted in a state of emergency being declared by the Yang di-Pertuan Agong on 3 December 1964. Again, on 14 September 1966, a constitutional impasse in Sarawak resulted in Article 150 being invoked by the Federal Government. The Proclamation of Emergency in this instance only extended to the territories of Sarawak. Finally, the ugly events of 13 May led to a Proclamation of Emergency on 15 May 1969. The full scope of Article 150 is dealt with by Jayakumar in his essay 'Emergency Powers in Malaysia' where he has taken into account the recent emergency in Kelantan.

77. See S. M. Thio, 'Dismissal of Chief Ministers' (1966) Mal. L.R. 283.

78. Act 68 of 1966.

79. Cf. S. M. Thio, op. cit. at p. 290. Dr. Thio doubted whether such an Act would have been in accord with the 'spirit' of the Constitution.

80. See Emergency (Essential Powers) Ordinance No. 1, 1969 (P.U.(A)146 of 1969), the Emergency (Essential Powers) Ordinance No. 3, 1969 (P.U.(A.) 170 of 1969), Emergency (Essential Powers) Ordinance No. 32, 1970 (P.U.(A)143 of 1970).

81. In the face of such wide powers, the Constitution as it originally stood provided that a Proclamation of Emergency shall cease to be in force at the expiration of two months from the date on which it was issued, and similarly, any ordinance promulgated by the Yang di-Pertuan Agong automatically lapses and ceases to have effect at the expiration of fifteen days from the date on which both Houses of Parliament are first sitting. They will only continue to have force if they have been approved by a resolution of each House of Parliament before the expiration of each of their respective periods of two months and fifteen days. However, the original clause (3) of Article 150 was replaced by a new clause under the Constitution (Amendment) Act, 1960 (Act 10 of 1960). By virtue of the amendment, neither the Proclamation of Emergency nor ordinance automatically lapses. They have a continuity of life until such time resolutions are passed by both Houses annulling such Proclamation or ordinance.

82. This case is discussed in Tan Sri Salleh Abas, 'Amendment of the Malaysian Constitution' [1977] 2 M.L.J. xxxiv, especially at pp. xliii-xlvi.

83. [1977] 2 M.L.J. 187 at p. 190.
Raja Azlan Shah F.J. also said: 'In the context of clause (1) of Article 160, "law" must be taken to mean law made in exercise of ordinary legislative power and not made in exercise of the power of constitutional amendment under clause (3) of Article 159, with the result that clause (1) of Article 4 does not affect amendments made under clause (3) of Article 159.'

84. Ibid. at p. 192.

85. Tan Sri Salleh Abas, op. cit. at p. xliii.
Tan Sri Salleh Abas said: 'The challenge is thus nothing more than merely finding fault with the draftsman of the Constitution for failing to preface Article 4 with such phrase as "Save as provided in Article 159", or some other similar expression.'

86. *I. C. Golak Nath & Ors.* v. *State of Punjab & Ors.* [1967] 2 S.C.R. 762.

87. It is outside the purview of this essay to analyse in depth the judgments in *Golak Nath.* References can be made to Basu, *Commentary on the Constitution of India,* Sarkar & Sons, 5th ed., 1970 at pp. 494-502; Tan Sri Salleh Abas, op. cit. at pp. xliii-xlvi.

88. *Shankari Prasad* v. *Union of India* [1952] S.C.R. 89; *Sajjan Singh* v. *State of Rajasthan* [1965] 1 S.C.R. 933. Article 368 of the Indian Constitution provides for the general mode of amendment. A Bill to amend the Constitution can originate in either House of Parliament and must be passed by a majority of not less than two-thirds of the members of the House present and voting. In addition those members present and voting who favour the amendment Bill must amount to a majority of the total membership of that House. The amendment process becomes more rigid in respect of amendments to certain provisions of the Constitution. These provisions which include the amendment clause itself relate to the manner of election of the President, the extent of the executive power of the Union and the States, the Judiciary and the State High Courts, any of the three Legislative lists or the representation of States in Parliament. For the amendment of these provisions, the amendment must in addition be ratified by the legislatures of not less than one-half of the States.

89. [1973] S.C.R. Supp. 1.

90. Per Sikri, C.J., and Shelat, Hegde, Grover, Khanna, Jaganmohan Reddy, and Mukherjea, JJ. (Ray, Palekar, Mathew, Beg, Dwivedi, and Chandrachud JJ. dissenting).

91. See *Indira Nehru Gandhi* v. *Raj Narain* A.I.R. 1975 S.C. 2299 for a reaffirma-

tion of the doctrine of 'basic structure'; Tan Sri Salleh Abas, op. cit. at p. xlv.

92. [1977] 2 M.L.J. 187 at p. 193.

However Wan Suleiman F.J. observed:

'I do not feel that the issue before this court would call for my view on whether there are indeed inherent or implied limitations to the power of amendment under Article 159, and must perforce confine myself to the issue before us viz. is the amendment to the fundamental right set out in Article 5 by Act A354/76 constitutional? Nor do I feel called upon to answer the broader issue of whether the power to amend includes the power to abrogate a fundamental right.' (p. 193).

93. Ibid. at pp. 188-9.

94. Tan Sri Salleh Abas, op. cit. at p. xlii.

95. Per Lord Guest in *Akar* v. *Attorney-General of Sierra Leone* [1969] 3 All E.R. 384 at p. 394.

96. [1977] 2 M.L.J. 187 at p. 188.

97. Article 55(3) provides: 'Parliament unless sooner dissolved shall continue for five years from the date of its first meeting and shall then stand dissolved.'

98. Tan Sri Salleh Abas, op. cit. at p. xlv.

Index

ABDOOLCADER, EUSOFFE, DATUK, 240;
as J., 89–90, 92, 352–3, 356
Abdul Hamid bin Mustapha, Datuk,
239; as J., 48, 111, 296, 354
Abdul Kadir bin Yusof, Tan Sri,
383
Abdul Rahman, Tunku, 373;
architect of Constitution, 1; bapa
kemerdekaan, 3; concept of
Malaysia, 8; on racial equality,
24; on religion, 55
Abdul Razak, Tun, 7, 11, 21–2, 126
Abubakar, Sultan, 41
Adjournment debates, 127
Afghanistan, 48
Ahl-al-hall wa'l-'aqd: Johore, 42;
Trengganu, 45
Ahmad Ibrahim, 113–14
Alcohol, use of, 54
Ali F.J., 355
Alliance Party, 48–9, 53, 147, 172,
211–13, 216, 222–3, 369
Amendment of the Constitution:
amendment of amendment pro-
cess, 379, 384–5; Conference of
Rulers and, 371–3, 381–3, 385;
Dewan Negara and, 376–9, 385;
haste in, 385–6, 392; implied
limitations, 390–2; modes of
effecting, 370–2; retrospective,
386–8, 392; significance, 369;
States and, 372–6, 385; (tabulated), 393–405; see also Constitution (Amendment) Acts
Argentina, 48
Armed forces, 265; Council, 269–70;
Yang di-Pertuan Agong and, 270
Arms Act, 1960, 244
Articles of the Constitution: 1, 374;
2, 10, 150; 3, 49, 114; 4, 5, 16,
29, 33, 238, 390–1; 5, 16–17, 28,
30–2, 34, 329, 349, 352, 356, 388,
390; 6, 28, 32; 7, 32, 356, 386; 8,
14, 28, 32–3, 51, 152, 266; 9,
29–30, 329; 10, 12, 28, 30, 154,
329, 372, 379, 381–3; 11, 29, 51;
12, 29, 52, 386; 13, 29–31, 34;
14, 76–7, 80, 154; 15, 77, 85–6,
154; 16, 78, 85, 154; 17, 78–9,
85, 154; 18, 77, 154; 19, 79, 84,
154; 20, 79, 154; 21, 154; 22,
154; 23, 154; 24, 84–5, 88–91,
154; 25, 85–8, 154; 26, 86, 88,
154; 27, 86–90, 154; 28, 154; 29,
154; 30, 154; 31, 154; 32, 102,
107–8; 33, 106; 34, 108–9, 117,
174; 35, 103, 108; 38, 106, 150,
154, 381–2; 40, 141, 336; 42,
114; 43, 126, 141, 153–4; 44,
141, 150–2; 45, 111, 137, 140,
154, 158, 378; 46, 154, 216; 48,
143, 145, 154, 222–3; 50, 154,
222–3;
53, 148, 154, 223; 54, 154, 214;

55, 141, 154, 344, 392; **56**, 154; **57**, 148, 154; **58**, 154; **61**, 154; **62**, 148, 154–5; **63**, 154, 174, 372, 381–2; **64**, 154; **65**, 154; **66**, 150; **67**, 154; **68**, 153; **70**, 150, 154, 381–2; **71**, 150, 154, 174, 176, 381–2; **72**, 372, 381–2; **74**, 371; **75**, 10; **76**, 10, 65, 371; **77**, 246; **79**, 334; **96**, 152, 304; **97**, 304, 321; **98**, 304; **99**, 304, 321; **100**, 304;

101, 304; **102**, 304; **103**, 304; **104**, 304; **105**, 304, 322; **106**, 304; **107**, 304; **108**, 304, 316; **109**, 304, 310, 313; **110**, 174, 304, 307–8; **111**, 304, 317; **112**, 186, 304, 315; **113**, 13, 208, 211; **114**, 13, 208, 211; **115**, 13, 208, 211; **116**, 13, 208, 211–12; **117**, 13, 208, 211; **118**, 208, 211; **119**, 208–9, 211; **120**, 208, 211; **121**, 247; **122**, 232–4, 250–2, 254–5; **125**, 113, 232, 251, 253–4; **128**, 237, 239, 248; **130**, 247, 249; **131**, 246; **132**, 18, 112, 265–6, 269–70, 275–8, 281; **133**, 112, 265, 273; **134**, 273–4; **135**, 265, 267, 269, 275, 277, 279, 281–8, 290–9, 386; **136**, 267, 269; **138**, 251; **139**, 252, 273, 297; **140**, 292–5, 297–8, 386–7; **141**, 270, 297; **144**, 17, 292–5, 297; **146**, 253, 274; **149**, 7, 30, 35, 328–32, 334, 349; **150**, 7, 19, 30, 35–6, 93, 115–17, 151–2, 170, 176, 328–36, 338–49, 388–9;

151, 7, 35–7, 328–9, 331–2, 349–50, 354–6; **152**, 154, 220, 372, 379, 381–2; **153**, 2, 11–12, 13–15, 18–19, 21, 23–4, 29, 114, 150, 154, 177, 220, 380–2; **159**, 10, 150, 154, 174, 176–8, 370, 372, 377, 379, 381–2, 384, 389–92; **160**, 10, 84, 265, 391; **161**, 176, 372, 384; **162**, 16–17, 298; **170**, 179; **171**, 212; **181**, 108, 150, 220

Arulanandom, Fred, J., 240, 352, 354
Asian Development Bank, 181, 314
Assignment of Export Duty (Mineral Ores) Act, 308

Assignment of Revenue (Export Duty on Iron Ore) Act, 1962, 308
Athenian democracy, 220–1
Attorney-General, office of, 237, 251–3, 256, 265, 342
Auditor-General, office of, 265, 322–3
Australia, 136–7, 151, 155, 157, 177, 306
A. Aziz, Ungku, 22
A. Aziz bin Mohd. Zain, Tan Sri, 271
Aziz Ishak, 131
Azlan Shah, Raja, F.J., 388, 390–2; *as* J., 92, 282, 337, 340, 342–5, 349
Azmi bin Mohamed, Tun, 355; *as* C.J., 335, 337–8, 346; *as* J., 223, 239

Bahaman bin Shamsuddin, 235
Bait-ul-Mal, 58, 60
Banishment, prohibition, 28, 33, 329
Bar Council, 386
Barakbah L.P., 116, 335, 337–8, 346; *as* J., 239
Barisan Nasional Party, 147
Birch, F.A.H., 124
Black Tuesday, 13 May 1969, 11–12, 21, 201, 216, 227, 379
Bloodworth, Dennis, 25
Borneo States, 11–12, 80, 82–3, 113, 138, 142–3, 202, 215, 250, 252–3, 265, 273–4, 333, 384–5; High Court, 176, 184–5, 233–4, 240, 245, 248–9, 252, 255, 258–60, 372; special rights, 29–30, 35, 175–7, 198, 372, 379–80; *see also* Sabah, Sarawak
Borrowing, States, 317–18
Bostock-Hill, 240
Braddell, Thomas, 44
Briggs, F.A., 240
Britain, 4, 19, 23, 42–3, 70–1, 166–8, 171; British-protected persons, 72; Civil Service, 263; House of Lords, 275, 287; and Islam, early treaties, 55–7; judiciary, 236; ministerial responsibility in, 125–6, 128; monarch, 106, 113, 246, 250; Par-

liament, 137–8, 150, 155, 225; withdrawal, 175

British Military Administration Proclamations, 1945, 199

British Nationality Act, 1948, 72, 74, 180

British Protectorate, Protected States and Protected Persons Order, 1949, 72

Brunei, 82, 257–8, 385

Budget, Federal: debates, 124, 127, 153; management, 323–4; as proportion of GNP, 305; strain on, 309–10; as subject of controversy, 321–2

Bumiputra, 2, 15, 18, 314

CABINET, 103, 109–10, 116, 138, 140, 147, 154, 187, 336, 351; appointment, 123–4, 126; Committee on Salary, 144; responsibility to Parliament, 123; solidarity, 130–2

Caliph, office of, 47

Canada, 151, 306

Case-law and the Constitution, 16–20, 30–5, 263–4, 329

Centralization of financial authority, 305–7

Chang Min Tat, Datuk, 240; as J., 336, 339, 345

China Press, 23

Chinese nationality laws, 8

Chinese people: discrimination against, 24–5; and litigation, 19; and Malayan Union, 166–7; Penang and Singapore, 167–8

Chu Choon Yong, 33

Citizenship, 7–9, 12, 30, 33, 35, 144, 179–80, 332, 335, 372, 379, 389; acquisition, 73–84; courts and, 91–3; Federated Malay States, 69–70, 72; Federation of Malaya, 70–81, 179–80; Federation of Malaysia, 80–91; Malayan Union, 70; Straits Settlements, 69; termination, 71, 75, 79–80, 84–91, 180; Unfederated States, 70

Civil Law Act, 1937, 57–8; 1956, 58, 65, 151

Civil Law (Extension) Ordinance, 1957, 58

Civil List, 103, 108

Civil Procedure Code, Johore, 44

Civil service, 265, 321; see also Public service

Commission to Enquire into Matters Affecting the Integrity of the Public Services, 1955, 266, 268

Commissioner for Law Revision, office of, 193–4, 200–1, 203, 206

Common law, 4–5, 8, 20, 151, 275, 277–8, 289, 291

Communism, 72, 174; Malaysian Communist Party, 226; Marxism, 2

Companies Act, 1965, 186

Concurrent List, 150, 169–70, 175, 178, 201, 333

Conference of Rulers, 9, 49–50, 54, 102–3, 109, 112, 165, 171, 177, 224, 233, 250–2; and Constitutional amendment, 371–3, 381–3, 385; election of Yang di-Pertuan Agong, 103–6, 158; meetings, 110; National Council for Islamic Affairs, 59–60; Standing Committee, 49

Consolidated Fund, 149, 154, 222, 224, 232, 266, 321

Constituency Delineation Commission, 210

Constitution (Amendment) Acts: 1960, 276, 330, 334, 350; 1962, 76–7, 79, 93, 174, 224–6; 1971, 12, 24, 115, 177, 370, 379–82; 1973, 102, 178, 216, 319; 1976, 28–9, 32, 36, 85, 93, 102, 105, 108–9, 111, 178, 232, 274, 291, 296–7, 350, 386–8, 390

Constitution of Malaysia (Singapore Amendment) Act, 1965, 177, 385

Consultation (Shura), principle of, 47–8

Corruption, attitudes to, 132

Court of Appeal, 20, 247–8

Courts (Amendment) Act, 1971, 243–5

Courts of Judicature Act, 1964, 17, 198, 247, 255

Courts Ordinance, 1948, 243–4

Criminal Procedure Codes, 31, 196, 204, 255

Cromwell, Oliver, 193
Crown Colonies, 8
Customs duties, 306, 312
Customs Duties (Penang) Bill, 1949, 168

Dangerous Drugs Ordinance, 1952, 244
Defence expenditure, 309
Democracy: Athenian, 220–1; parliamentary, 1, 5, 124, 126–7, 157; Westminster model, 157
Democratic Action Party, 220
Denning, Lord, 16–17, 20, 288–9, 293–4
Dental Act, 1971, 198
Detention: administrative, 32; preventive, 6–7, 328, 330, 332, 349–57; unlawful, 31, 36
Development expenditure, 312–14
Dewan Negara, 19, 141, 150, 153, 155–6, 176; appointment, 111, 139, 172, 377; composition, 139–40, 155; and Constitutional amendment, 376–9, 385; functions, 138–9; membership qualifications and disqualifications, 143–5, 155; officers, 149, 154, 157; reform, 157–8; Standing Orders, 155; termination of membership, 147–8; women in, 143
Dewan Ra'ayat, 12–14, 19, 110, 138–41, 150, 155–6, 176, 178, 211, 214–16, 220, 376; composition, 141–3, 155; dissolution, 110–11, 137–8, 141; financial powers, 153, 155, 321–2; membership qualifications and disqualifications, 143–5, 155; officers, 148–9, 154, 157; Standing Orders, 154; termination of membership, 147–8; women in, 143
Dilhorne, Viscount, 290
Director of Operations, office of, 11, 22, 288
Dollar, Malaysian, 231
Due process of law, 31, 34

East India Company, 166
Economic growth, 2, 22, 24, 126, 173, 180–2, 305, 311, 314, 323–4

Education: expenditure on, 306, 309; Malays, 115; responsibility for, 183; rights in respect of, 29, 34, 52; service, 265, 270–1; systems, 197–8; Yang di-Pertuan Agong and, 271, 380
Education Act, 1961, 198
Education Service Commission, 270–1, 297
Election Act, 1963, 209
Election Commission, 14, 112, 142, 158–9, 208, 211, 215, 217–20, 222, 265; membership and functions, 224–6; Ordinance, 1957, 209
Election Offences Act, 1954, 201, 209, 215; (Amendment) Act, 1955, 209; (Amendment) Act, 1961, 209; (Amendment) Act, 1964, 210; amendments, 1969, 215
Election Rules, 146
Elections: codes of conduct, 213–14, 220; free, concept of, 220–1; functional representation, 227–8; laws relating to, 208–10; Presiding Officers, 218–19; principles, 13–14, 29, 71, 138, 169, 210; Returning Officers, 215, 217–18, 223; systems, 227; of Yang di-Pertuan Agong, 103–6, 158; see also General Elections
Elections (Amendment) Act, 1965, 210
Elections (Conduct of Elections) Regulations, 1959, 209, 215, 217; (Amendment) Regulations, 1968, 215; amendments, 1974, 217–19
Elections (Control of Motor Vehicles and Vessels) Regulations, 1959, 209
Elections Ordinance, 1958, 209, 218
Elections (Postal Voting) Regulations, 1959, 209, 215; (Amendment) Regulations, 1968, 215–16
Electoral Behaviour Code, 213–14
Emergency, Proclamations of, 328, 331–49, 383; **1966**, 107, 335–6, 389; **1969**, 348–9; **1977**, 347–8
Emergency, state of, 1948–60, 6–7, 194, 242, 328
Emergency (Criminal Trials) Regu-

lations, 1964, 151

Emergency (Essential Powers) Act, 1964, 152; Ordinance, 1969, 152, 243–5, 288

Emergency (Federal Constitution and Constitution of Sarawak) Act, 1966, 385, 389

Emergency powers, 30, 33, 35–7, 93, 115–17, 151–2, 170, 328–57; Constitutional provisions (tabulated), 358–63

Emergency Powers (Kelantan) Act, 1977, 347–8

Emergency (Public Order and Prevention of Crime) Ordinance, 1969, 36, 353

Employment law, 18

Employment (Restriction) Act, 1968, 93

English common law and equity, 4–5, 57–8, 65, 151

Entertainment revenue, 307

Equality, principle of, 8–10, 14, 24, 28–9, 32–3, 266

Essential (Security Cases) Regulations, 1975, 247

Evidence Act, 19, 65, 204, 255

Executive, 35–6, 152–4, 223–4, 374; parliamentary control, 153–4, 158

Expenditure, 309–12; development projects, 312–14; grants to States, 310–11, 313, 317; as proportion of GNP, 305; State (tabulated), 326

External affairs expenditure, 309

Fatwas, 53, 59; Fatwa Committee, 59–60

Federal Constitution Ordinance, 1957, 237

Federal Court, 17, 30–3, 35–6, 65, 112–13, 116, 185, 198, 203–4, 236–9, 245–9, 255, 286, 291, 295–6, 354, 387; composition and functions, 248–9; power of judges, 253–4

Federal Industrial Development Authority, 181

Federal Legislative Council, 19, 54, 137, 199, 210–12, 384

Federal List, 150, 169, 178, 201, 333, 349

Federal Territory, 50, 58, 65, 102, 114, 140, 142, 178, 219; financial arrangements for, 319–20

Federalism: concept, 163–4; expulsion, 177; federal bias, 169–73; federal-state relationship, 169; judicial system, 185; method of government, 185–7; parochialism within, 180–5, 188; secession, 177

Federated Malay States, 69–70, 72, 164–5, 276, 305; laws, 194, 199

Federation of Malaya Agreement, 1948, 2–4, 47, 70–4, 77, 136, 195, 209, 212, 232, 237, 246, 248–50, 373–5; (Amendment) Ordinance, 1952, 72–5

Financial difficulties, States, 311–14; causes, 312; implications, 313–14

Financial provisions of the Constitution, 304–27, 372; Auditor-General, 265, 322–3; centralization, 305–7; expenditure, 309–11; National Finance Council, 310–11, 316–17; Parliamentary control, 152–3, 320–2; revenue, 307–9; Sabah and Sarawak, 314–16

Finer, Herman, 369

Finer, S. E., 125, 128

Firearms (Increased Penalty) Act, 1971, 244

Fitrah, 58, 60

Foreign Correspondents Association of South-East Asia, 8

Fundamental Liberties, 27–37, 151, 329, 333–4, 386; absolute, 28; qualified, 28–30

Fuqaha, 47

GANDHI, INDIRA, 21

General Elections: **1955**, 210–11; **1959**, 211–12; **1964**, 212–13; **1969**, 213–16, 226–7; **1974**, 216–20

Ghani Gilong, Datuk Haji, 235

Gill C.J., 31, 34–5, 355

Government Gazette, 113, 196, 246

Governor, office of, 8, 57, 69, 259, 266, 275, 372

Groves, H. E., 225–6, 378

Guardianship of Infants Act, 1961, 65

Hadd PUNISHMENTS, 59, 66
Hamoodur Rahman C.J., 62–5
Harun J., 348–9
Health, expenditure on, 306, 309
Hickling, R.H., 115–16, 194, 225
High Commissioner, office of, 74, 210, 249–50
High Court, 31–2, 65, 87, 112–13, 184–5, 196, 198, 233, 236, 238, 240, 245, 248–9, 255, 258, 387; Borneo, 176, 184–5, 233–4, 240, 245, 248–9, 252, 255, 258–60, 372; judges, 254–5; Singapore, 258, 287, 352–3
Hill, J.A., 17
Hindu law, 33
Hodson, Lord, 283
Holmes, Justice, 181
Holy Quran, 59, 61–2, 63–4; Reading competitions, 61
House of Representatives, *see* Dewan Ra'ayat
Houses of Parliament (Privileges and Powers) Ordinance, 1952, 155
Housing, 182–3; expenditure, 311
Hukum Shara (Islamic Law), 42, 44–7, 51, 53–4, 60–1, 65–6, 114, 256, 333, 389
Hussein Alatas, Syed, 13
Hybrid laws, 201–2

IBN TIQTAQA, 47–8
Ibrahim J., 282
Ilbert, 153
Immigration, 19, 23–4; Act, 1959/ 1963, 94, 175, 197
Income Tax Act, 1967, 33
Incorporation (State Legislatures Competency) Act, 1962, 181
India: case-law, 391–2; Constitution, 2–3, 10, 18, 21, 144, 177, 292, 356, 391; judiciary, 18, 20–1, 253; Parliament, 136, 138, 147, 155, 391; Penal Code, 4; President, 106; public service, 279, 281, 283; Supreme Court, 18, 391
Indonesia, 24, 213
Industrialization, 181–2, 311
Inflation, 312
Inter-Governmental Committee Report, 1962, 175, 180, 183, 197–8, 203
Internal Security Act, 1960, 6–7, 184, 353, 356
Interpretation Act, 1965, 294
Interpretation and General Clauses Ordinance, 1948, 341
Islam: in Johore Constitution, 42–5; and law, 4, 57–9, 65–6; in Malay States generally, 47–61, 65–6; in Trengganu Constitution, 45–7; Yang di-Pertuan Agong and, 50, 54, 59, 102, 113–14, 178
Islamic Calendars, 60
Islamic Law (Hukum Shara), 42, 44–7, 51, 53–4, 60–1, 65–6, 114, 256, 333, 389
Islamic Party (PAS), 61
Islamic Research Centre, 60
Islamic Secretariat, 61
Ismail Khan (*later* Tan Sri) J., 92, 239

JAIN, 144
Japanese occupation, 3, 194
Jayakumar, S., 101, 104, 106–7, 112, 116, 288, 376
Jennings, Sir Ivor, 125
Johore, 8, 14, 58, 70, 164, 167–8, 183, 210; Agreement with Britain, 1914, 56; Constitution, 1895, 41–5, 66; courts, 43–4; governing councils, 42–3; laws, 194; Sultans, 41–4, 104, 168
Journal of Malaysian and Comparative Law, 14
Judicial and Legal Service Commission, 233, 251–3, 269–70, 273–4; Borneo, 252–3
Judiciary, 14, 184–5, 265; Bar, 256; and Constitution, 15–21, 237–8, 392; criticism of, 15; direct appointment, 240–1; expatriate, 239–40; federal status, 249–51; function, 21; independence, 19, 221–4, 232–3; judicial commissioners, 233–4; legal education, 256; localization, 239–40; Minister of Justice, 235–7; numbers, 255; Parliament and, 232, 237, 250, 255; period of office, 233;

power of Federal Judge, 253–4; removal, 185, 222, 232; remuneration, 232; subordinate courts, 241–5, 258–60; temporary, 233–5; transfer between High Courts, 254–5; unpoliticized, 241; workload, 245–6; Yang di-Pertuan Agong and, 112–13, 233–4, 243, 246–7, 249, 251–2, 254

Juma'ah Majlis di-Raja, 42

Juma'ah Pangkuan Negeri, 42

Jus sanguinis, 5

Jus soli, 8, 72, 76–7, 81, 168, 179

KATHIS, 53, 57, 59–60, 66

Kedah, 14, 51, 58–60, 69, 102, 142, 164, 166, 173, 256, 309; Agreement with Britain, 1923, 56; laws, 194

Keeper of the Rulers' Seal, office of, 104

Kelantan, 8–10, 14, 51, 58, 70, 102, 142, 164, 166–8, 173, 216, 227, 273; Agreement with Britain, 1910, 56; Constitution, 347–8; *Kelantan* case, 19, 171, 249, 373–6; timber, 172–3

Kelsen, 64

Konfrontasi, 23

Kota Bharu, 10, 61

Kuala Lumpur: Black Tuesday, 11–12, 21, 201, 216, 227, 379; and Senate, 140; *see also* Federal Territory

LABOUR PARTY, 211

Labuan, 69

Land, mine and forest revenue, 307

Language, 12, 30, 35, 332, 335, 379, 389; National Language, 183–4, 219, 256–7, 379–80; qualification for citizenship, 78, 83

Lao Tzu, 6

Law and order, 25

Law Commission, 12

Law Revision Committee, 200–1

Laws: categories, 201; electoral, 208–10; harmonization among States, 192–206, 255; hybrid, 201–2; *laissez-faire*, 202–3; multiplicity, 195–9; political change and, 205;

publication, 194–5; reform, 206; revision, method, 192; revision, phases, 205; validity, 238–9

Lee, B.T.H., 253

Lee, H.P., *v*, 6

Lee Hun Hoe, Tan Sri Datuk, 234, 257–8, 295, 344, 355–6

Legal Profession Act, 1976, 184, 198, 256

Legislative Assemblies of the States, 13, 51, 59, 65, 124, 139, 143, 146–7, 157, 159, 170, 178, 181, 185, 199, 201, 211–12, 214–16, 220, 232; composition, 217; life of, 208, 219

Legislative Council, *see* Federal Legislative Council

Leong Yew Koh, Tun, 235

Liberties, *see* Fundamental Liberties

Liberty, preservation of, 2, 7

Licence revenue, 306–7

Lim Chong Eu, 385

Local Federal Authority, 197

Local government, 183; Elections Act, 1960, 209; financial status, 308; National Council (NCLG), 173, 183, 187

London Agreement, 1963, 197–8

Lord President of the Federal Court, office of, 102, 112–13, 200, 233–4, 236, 245, 248–9, 252, 254

MACDERMOTT, LORD, 7

MacIntyre, Tan Sri, J., 233, 240, 277–8, 284

Mackenzie, W.J.M., 221

McElwaine C.J., 66

Mahathir bin Mohamed, 22, 25

Mahmud M. Hashim, 239

Majlis Ugama Islam, 59

Mala fides, 337–9, 345, 352–3

Malacca, 8, 14, 50–1, 54, 59–60, 69–70, 114, 166, 173, 178, 272–3, 297, 311; Ayer Keroh, 182; Constitution, 50; hospital case, 129–30; laws, 194, 196, 199

Malay Reservations Enactment, 19

Malay rights, 9, 11–12, 23, 28–30, 35, 113–14, 168, 171, 372, 379–80

Malay Rulers, 8, 18–19, 23, 48–9, 51,

102, 164–7, 169, 246, 250, 266, 275; precedence among, 103–4; prerogatives, 12; subjects of, defined, 71–2, 73; *see also* Conference of Rulers

Malay States, 3, 8, 138, 169, 177–80, 272; early Constitutions, 47–8; Federated, 69–70, 72, 164–5, 194, 199, 276, 305; Islam in, generally, 47–61, 65–6; laws, 193, 195–6, 198–9, 201–2; Unfederated, 70, 166

Malaya, Federation of, 171, 178, 192, 194, 306, 373, 384; Agreement, 1948, 2–4, 47, 70–4, 77, 136, 195, 209, 212, 232, 237, 246, 248–50, 373–5; Agreement (Amendment) Ordinance, 1952, 72–5; background, to 1957, 164–7; citizenship, 70–81, 179–80; Constitution, 1957, *v*, *ix*, 48–9, 75–80, 102, 168–74, 179, 195, 247, 369, 377; laws, 199; opposition to, 167–8

Malayan Constitutional Documents, 349

Malayan Law Journal, 15, 20

Malayan Union, 166–7, 179, 242, 263; citizenship, 70; laws, 199; opposition to, 166; Order in Council, 1946, 2, 4

Malaysia, Federation of: birth, 1963, *v*, 8–10, 174–6, 193–4; citizenship, 80–91, 93; Constitution, *see* Articles of the Constitution; financial strength, 306; *see also* Federalism

Malaysia Act, 1963, 9–10, 102, 171, 175, 195, 202, 209, 232, 258, 273, 373–4, 384

Malaysia Agreement, 9, 171, 373–5

Malaysia Day, 16 Sept. 1963, 80–3, 143, 176, 184, 195, 199, 204–5, 232, 234, 248, 251–2, 258, 273, 372

Malaysia Plans, 138; Second, 2, 183; Third, 173

Malaysian Communist Party, 226

Mathew, Sir Charles, 239

Medical Act, 1971, 198

Members of the Administration and Members of Parliament (Pensions and Gratuities) Act, 1971, 154–5

Mental Disorders Ordinance, 1952, 144

Mentri Besar, office of, 51, 124, 272, 316

Merdeka Day, 31 Aug. 1957, 8, 16, 32, 49, 51, 65, 75–8, 81–3, 152, 179, 194, 199, 212, 254, 272, 293, 296, 348, 386, 388, 390

Mid-Term Review of the Second Malaysia Plan, 1971–5, 2

Mineral revenue, 308–9

Mining industry, 174

Ministerial responsibility, 123–33; Britain, 125–6; Malacca hospital case, 129–30; opposition and, 127–8; party system and, 124–5, 129; public opinion and, 130; resignations, 130–1; secrecy, 128

Mohd. Suffian bin Hashim, Tun, *ix–x*, 31, 110, 113, 224, 276, 279–82, 285, 341–2, 344, 348–9, 354–6; as F.J., 18, 276–8, 280–1, 284, 351, 355–6; as C.J., 291; as J., 276, 280; *Introduction to the Constitution of Malaysia*, 107–8, 304, 385

Mohd. Zahir, Datuk, 240

Morrison, Lord, 125

Movement, freedom of, 29, 33, 329

Mufti, office of, 47, 53, 59–60

Musa, Raja, 239

Muslim Advisory Board, Penang, 54

Muslim courts, 249–50

Muslim Courts (Criminal Jurisdiction) Act, 1965, 59

Muslim Law, *see* Islamic Law

Muslim rights, 29–30, 35

NCLG, *see* Local government

Nation building, 180–5, 188

National Association of Perak, 211

National Consultative Council, 13

National Council for Islamic Affairs, 59–60

National Finance Council, 310–11, 316–17

National Front, 220; *see also* Alliance Party

National Land Council, 173

National Language, 183–4, 219,

256–7, 379–80
National Mosque, 60
National Operations Council, 13
Nationality, 71–2, 180; State Nationality Enactments, 1952, 73
Naturalisation Act, 1867, Straits Settlements, 69
Naturalisation Enactments, Federated Malay States, 69–70
Negri Sembilan, 14, 51, 55, 69, 102, 164, 272, 311; laws, 194, 199; Yang di-Pertuan Besar, 103
New Economic Policy, 2, 323
New Zealand, 236, 246
Nilam Puri Institute, Kota Bharu, 61
North Borneo, 199, 204, 257; see also Sabah

ODGERS, W. BLAKE, 193
Offences by Mohammedans Enactment, Johore, 44, 66
Ombudsman, office of, 94
Ong Hock Sim F.J., 283, 342, 355; as J., 92
Ong Hock Thye F.J., 336–8, 346; as C.J., 286, 343; as J., 239–40
Onn bin Jaafar, Dato, 146
Orang asli, 139
Syed Othman J., 356

PAS (ISLAMIC PARTY), 61
PEKEMAS, 220
Pahang, 8, 14, 59–60, 69, 142, 164, 183; defence treaty with Britain, 1887, 55; laws, 194, 199; oil, 319; Sultan, 104
Pakistan, 1, 21, 53; Constitution, 61–5; Islam in, 61–4; Objectives Resolution, 1949, 63–5
Pangkor Engagement, 1874, 55
Pan-Malayan Islamic Party, 172, 211
Parliament: adjournment debates, 127; amendatory powers, 154, 370–92; Budget debates, 124, 127, 153; comparison of Houses, 155–6; composition, 136–8, 155, 217; constituencies, 210, 212, 217, 224–5; contempt, 155; control of Executive, 153–4, 158; delegation, 150–2; deliberative function, 153; democracy, 1, 5, 124, 126–7, 157; dissolution, 110–11, 137–8, 141, 154; dual and triple membership, 145–7; emergency powers, 35–7, 151, 328–57; financial function, 152–3, 320–2; and Fundamental Liberties, 28–30, 33, 151; history, 136–7; and Islamic Law, 65; and judiciary, 232, 237, 250, 255; legislative function, 150–2, 196, 201; life of, 141, 208, 219; membership qualifications and disqualifications, 143–5, 155; ministerial responsibility, 123–33; officers, 148–9; opposition, 127–8; party system, 124–5; and police force, 297–8; privilege, 12; Public Accounts Committee, 124, 127–8, 322–3; Question Time, 124, 127, 153; reform, 156–9; remuneration, 154, 156, 159; Royal Address, 127, 153; Standing Orders, 155; supremacy, 4–5, 150, 172; termination of membership, 147–8; Yang di-Pertuan Agong and, 111–12, 137–41, 145, 154, 157, 376–7; see also Dewan Negara, Dewan Ra'ayat
Parliament (Members Remuneration) Act, 1960, 154
Parliamentary Services Act, 1963, 155
Parochialism, State, 180–5
Party Islam, 227
Party Negara, 211
Party system, 124–5, 129, 221, 226
Patronage, 140, 144
Penal Code, 145, 243–4
Penang, 8, 14, 50–1, 54, 59–60, 69–70, 114, 142, 164, 166–8, 178, 210, 216, 272–3, 297; Constitution, 50; laws, 194, 196, 199
Pensions Ordinance, 1951, 280–1
People's Action Party, 226
People's Progressive Party, 146
Perak, 8, 14, 51, 57, 69, 142, 164, 216, 309; laws, 194, 199
Perak Malay League, 211
Perak Progressive Party, 211

Perlis, 8, 14, 58, 70, 102, 137, 159, 164, 166, 173, 256, 272, 311–12; Agreement with Britain, 1930, 56; Raja, 103

Pernas, 314

Person, liberty of, 28, 30–2, 329

Petroleum Development Act, 1974, 173, 318

Petroleum revenue, 309, 316, 318–19

Petronas, 318–19

Philippines, 236

Pike C.J., 107–8, 336–8

Police Act, 33

Police force, 265, 297–8

Police Ordinance, 1952, 295

Police Service Commission (*later* Police Force Commission), 16, 269, 293–6, 298, 386–7

Poyser C.J., 44, 66

Precedent, doctrine of, 4

President of the Dewan Negara, office of, 148–9, 154; President of the Senate (Remuneration) Act, 1960, 154

Preventive Detention, *see under* Detention

Prime Minister, office of, 51, 59–60, 110, 112–13, 123, 138, 140–1, 148, 154, 155–6, 233, 236–7, 250, 252, 316, 322

Principles of the Constitution, 2–5, 13

Privy Council, 16–17, 19, 33–4, 65, 87–9, 151, 246–7, 286, 290–1, 293–6, 336–41, 346–7, 387–8; Judicial Committee, 113, 185, 203, 246–7, 280

Probate and Administration Act, 59

Property, rights of, 28–9, 31, 34–5, 58

Public Accounts Committee, 124, 127–8, 322–3

Public Authorities (Control of Borrowing) Act, 1961, 186

Public corporations, 186

Public Officers (Conduct and Discipline) (General Orders, Chapter 'D') Regulations, 1969, 268, 284, 288–91

Public service, 17–18, 28, 72, 93–4, 263–99; British influence, 263, 266, 268; Constitutional position of officers, 264, 266–7, 274–92; definition, 265–6; federalism and, 268; General Orders, 268, 284, 288–91; joint services, 273; Malayanization, 268; and politics, 144–5; Reid Commission and, 268–9, 272; secondment, 268, 273; services commissions, 265, 269–71, 292–9; State, 266–7, 271–4, 297; Yang di-Pertuan Agong and, 112, 266–7, 271, 274, 292–3, 297–8

Public Services Commission, 110, 251–2, 269–74, 297

Question Time, 124, 127, 153

Quran, *see* Holy Quran

Racial Tension, 11, 24–5, 87, 167; *see also* Black Tuesday

Rahman Talib, 131–2

Railway service, 265; Commission, 110, 269–70

Raja Permaisuri Agong, office of, 102, 109, 117, 148

Ramadan, 50, 60

Registrar-General of Citizens, 87

Registration of Electors: Ordinance, 1954, 209–10; Regulations, 1955, 209–10; Elections (Registration of Electors) Regulations, 1971, 210

Reid Commission, 1956, 3, 5, 9, 23, 48, 77–8, 102, 111, 116, 169–70, 172; and Constitutional amendment, 369–70, 373, 376–9; and emergency powers, 328–31, 333–5, 349–50; and public service, 268–9, 272, 274

Religion, freedom of, 28–30, 33, 35, 43, 46, 48, 51–2, 332, 335, 372, 389

Reprint of Federal Laws Act, 1965, 206

Restricted Residence Enactment, 388, 390; Selangor, 16–17

Retrospective criminal laws and repeated trials, protection against, 28, 32, 386

Revenue, 307–9, 312; Revenue Growth Grant, 310–11, 317; State (tabulated), 325–6

Revision of Laws Act, 1968, 200, 206

Riker, William H., 163

Royal Address to Parliament, 127, 153

Royal Commission on the Teaching Services (Aziz), 1971, 271

Rubber Excises (Penang) Bill, 168

Rubber industry, 23, 180

Rubin, Alfred P., 165

Rudolph, J. Jr., 178

Rukunegara, 12–13, 20–1

Rulers, *see* Malay Rulers

SABAH, 9, 14, 23, 50–2, 59–60, 80, 102, 114, 138, 141, 143, 171, 174–9, 183–4, 187, 213, 216, 219–20, 242, 250–1, 255, 306, 373, 375–6; Constitution, 50, 176; courts, 257–60; laws, 193–9, 201–4; petroleum, 318–19; revenue and expenditure (tabulated), 327; special financial arrangements, 314–16; *see also* Borneo States

Sajjad Ahmad J., 64–5

Salehuddin Ahmad J., 64

Salleh Abas, Tan Sri, 390

Salmon, Lord, 19

Sarawak, 9, 14, 50, 52, 59–60, 80, 102, 114, 138, 141, 143, 159, 171, 174–9, 183–4, 213, 216, 220, 222, 242, 250–1, 255, 306, 373, 375–6, 389; Constitution, 176, 335, 346–7; courts, 257–60; laws, 193–9, 201–4; petroleum, 318–19; revenue and expenditure (tabulated), 327; special financial arrangements, 314–16; *see also* Borneo States

Sarawak, North Borneo and Brunei (Courts) Order in Council, 1951, 257

Sastri J., 355

Saudi Arabia, 48, 61

Scott, James, *Political Ideology in Malaysia*, 127

Seah, George, J., 240

Secret Societies, 214

Security, 6–7, 30, 33, 329, 349; expenditure, 309; *see also* Emergency powers

Sedition Act, 1948, 12, 33, 93, 209, 220, 343, 383

Selangor, 8, 14, 55, 69, 102, 142, 164, 178, 183, 216; financial arrangements for Federal Territory, 319–20; laws, 194, 199

Senate, *see* Dewan Negara

Separation of Singapore Agreement, 1965, 177

Service commissions, in general, 265, 269–71; delegation of powers and functions, 292–9

Shafii school, 59

Shah Alam, 320

Shariah courts, 51, 58–9, 60–1, 114

Sharma J., 240, 295, 387

Shawal, 60

Sheridan, L.A. and Groves, H.E., 375

Shiv Charan Singh, 194

Shura (consultation), principle of, 47–8

Siam, *see* Thailand

Silke, W.J., 239, 258

Singapore, 9, 14, 69–70, 80, 82, 84, 93–4, 141, 143, 164, 167, 171, 174–6, 179–80, 213, 248–9, 264, 268, 273, 306, 373, 384; High Court, 258, 287, 352–3; laws, 201; secession, 1965, 177, 194–5, 226, 248–58, 289–90, 377–8

Sinnadurai, Visu, 116

Slavery and forced labour, freedom from, 28

Small Estates (Distribution) Act, 59

Social development, 2, 126, 182–3, 314

Societies Act, 1966, 226

Solicitor-General, office of, 252

Speaker of the Dewan Ra'ayat, office of, 148–9, 154; Speaker (Remuneration) Act, 1960, 154

Special Powers Against Subversion, 30, 35–7, 328–32

Special rights, *see* Malay rights, Special rights *under* Borneo States

Speech, association and assembly,

freedom of, 29, 33–4, 329, 379

Sproule J., 279

Standing Orders of Parliament, 155

State Constitutions, amendment of, 346–7

State Councils, 57, 124, 165, 211

State Councils of Muslim Religion, 53, 60

State Departments of Religious Affairs, 53

State Economic Development Corporations, 181

State independence, 169–70, 172

State Legal Advisers, 193, 206, 252

State List, 150, 169–70, 175, 183, 201, 333

State Reserve Fund, 313

State Secretary, office of, 51, 193

Statute Law Revision Acts, 1965, 201

Straits Settlements, 3, 55, 69, 72–3, 166–7, 169, 194, 272, 276; laws, 199, 204; see also Malacca, Penang

Subordinate Courts: Act, 1948, 198, 250, 255, 260; Rules, 1950, 260

Subversion, see Special Powers Against Subversion

Suffian Commission, 1967, 269

Suleiman bin Datuk A. Rahman, Datuk, 235

Sultan, office of, 8, 47, 59, 103; Johore, 41–4; Trengganu, 45

Sultanates, Islamic, 41

Sunnah, 59, 61–2, 64

Supremacy of the Constitution, 16–17, 65–6, 150

Supreme Court, 225, 246–8, 250, 252, 255

Sutherland Ag. J., 16–17

Syria, 48, 61

Tanah Melayu, 22

Taoist philosophy, 6

Taxation, 28, 31, 33, 51, 152, 170, 306–7, 312

Terrell Ag. C.J., 57

Thailand, 1, 25, 49, 166

Thomson, Sir James, Tun, 239, 249, 284; as C.J., 9–10, 17, 171, 187, 374–6

Timbalan Yang di-Pertuan Agong,

office of: disabilities, 109; election, 103–5; functions, 105; immunity, 107; removal, 106

Tin industry, 23, 174, 180, 308–9

Translation of the Malayan laws of the Principality of Johore, 44

Treaty of Federation, 1895, 55

Trengganu, 8, 14, 58, 70, 102, 142, 164, 166, 173, 210, 273, 312; Agreement with Britain, 1919, 56; Constitutions, 45–7; governing councils, 45–6; laws, 194; oil, 319; Raja, 45–7; Sultans, 45

Trindade, Francis, v. 288–9

UMNO, 147, 167, 168; Wanita UMNO, 143; Youth Seminar, 1962, 22

United Kingdom, see Britain

United Malay National Organisation, see UMNO

United Nations Charter, 13

United States of America, 136–7, 158, 177, 181, 227, 266, 306

Universiti Kebangsaan Malaysia, 61

University of Malaya, 61, 256

Urban Development Authority, 314

Wakafs, 53, 58, 65

Wan Suleiman F.J., 282, 341–2, 344, 388, 390–1; as J., 17

Water: revenue, 307–8; supply, 311

Wee Chong Jin C.J., 287, 294

West Indian Federation, 177

Wheare, K.C., 5, 163–4

Whitley J., 44

Williams, John, 234

Winslow, V.S. J., 281, 287

Wong, James, Datuk, 184

Wooding, Sir Hugh, 247

Works and power expenditure, 309

World Bank, 181, 314

Wylie C.J., 36, 151

Yahya, Datuk Haji, 54

Yang di-Pertuan Agong, office of, 9, 11, 18, 21, 30, 49, 51, 60, 123, 148, 150, 173, 215, 322, 329; and armed forces, 270; Civil List, 103; constitutional monarch, 106, 109, 117; creation, 102; disabilities,

108–9; and education, 271, 380; election, 103–6, 158; emergency powers, 35–7, 93, 115–17, 151–2, 332, 334–6, 339–43, 345, 350–1, 355, 383, 389; functions, 109–17, 185, 203, 222, 224, 380; immunity, 107–8; and judiciary, 112–13, 233–4, 243, 246–7, 249, 251–2, 254; and Parliament, 111–12, 137–41, 145, 154, 157, 376–7; and public service, 112, 266–7, 271, 274, 292–3, 297–8; religious status, 50, 54, 59, 102,

113–14, 178; removal, 106; symbolism, 101–2

Yang di-Pertuan Agong (Exercise of Functions) Ordinance, 1957, 105–6

Yang di-Pertuan Besar, office of, 8, 102

Yaqub Ali J., 64

Yong, S.M., Tan Sri, J., 240

ZAINAL ABIDIN, SULTAN, 45

Zakat, 58, 60

Zinah, offence of, 59, 66